East India Company Great Britain

List of marine records

Inktank publishing

East India Company Great Britain

List of marine records

Inktank publishing, 2018

www.inktank-publishing.com

ISBN/EAN: 9783747750964

LIST

OF

MARINE RECORDS

OF THE LATE

EAST INDIA COMPANY,

AND OF SUBSEQUENT DATE,

PRESERVED IN THE

RECORD DEPARTMENT

OF THE

INDIA OFFICE, LONDON.

1896.

INTRODUCTION.

In the latter part of the fifteenth century, in consequence of the "grete "mynysshyng and decaye now of late tyme of the navye of this Reame of England, and "ydleness of the mariners within the same, by the whiche this noble Reame wythin short "process of tyme wythout reformacion be had therein shall not be of habilite ne power "to defend it selfe,"* an Act was passed (4° Henry VII. c. X.) in 1488–89 prohibiting the importation and exportation of merchandise in any but English ships. This, it appears, gave offence to foreign Princes, who, thinking that the law was made to the prejudice of their respective countries and navies, made similar laws with regard to the shipping of their own dominions; "by reason whereof," as stated in the preamble to 1° Eliz. c. XIII. (1558–59) "ther hathe not onely growen greate displeasyre "between the forreyne Prynces and the Kinges of this Realme, but also the "Marchauntes have been sore greved and endomaged." Accordingly, by the Statute last quoted, the former law was repealed, and although this repeal was clogged with many restrictions, it afforded considerable relief and encouragement to English merchants. After this date the Russia Company began considerably to extend its transactions, and a stimulus was given to the development of other commercial enterprises in foreign lands.

The principal seat of trade in northern Europe was now in Holland, where commerce had not been restricted in the same manner as in this country, and there, accordingly, were to be found better ships and more experienced sailors than in England.

Before the establishment of the East India Company, the shipping of England appears to have been on a very limited scale, although this country was, next to Spain, accounted the most powerful maritime State in Europe. It has been stated that in the year 1588 Queen Elizabeth had at sea 150 sail of ships, whereof only 40 were her own, and 110 belonged to her subjects; that, in the same year, there were likewise 150 sail of English merchant ships, of about 150 tons average tonnage, employed in trading voyages to all parts and countries. The Queen's 40 ships carried 12,000 men, or 300 in each ship; the 110 hired vessels 12,100, or 110 in each on an average, and the 150 trading ships carried 6,000 seamen or 40 in each.†

The first practical step taken with the view of obtaining for this country a share in the East Indian trade dates from 1579, in which year Queen Elizabeth sent William Harburn, an English merchant, to Turkey, who obtained from Sultan Amurath III. permission for the English merchants to resort and trade to Turkey, in all respects as freely as the French, Venetians, Germans, and Poles then did, by which concession a foundation was laid for the English Turkey Company, which was established two years later.‡ Previously to this date, the Venetians used to send vessels yearly to Southampton with Turkish, Persian, and Indian merchandise, but by entering upon this trade themselves the English procured commodities from the Levant and from the East much cheaper than formerly, and the returns which it yielded at the beginning are stated to have been three for one.§

* Statutes of the Realm, Vol. II., p. 534.

† "Annals of Commerce," D. Macpherson, Vol. II., p. 187.

‡ Ditto, ditto, p. 165.

§ It is stated in "Lex Mercatoria" that the Turkey Company arose out of the Company of Barbary Merchants, which was incorporated in King Henry VII.'s time.

The first direct voyage to India undertaken by the English was in 1591, in which year three vessels, the "Penelope," the "Marchant Royal," and the "Edward Bonaventure," sailed from Plymouth on the 10th April, under the command of George Raymond and James Lancaster. The former died on the journey, and the latter, after a most adventurous voyage, in which several Portuguese ships were captured, returned to England without his vessels, in August 1594.*

In 1596 another expedition, consisting of three ships, the "Bear," the Bear's Whelp," and the "Benjamin," under the command of Captain Benjamin Wood, was fitted out, principally at the charges of Sir Robert Dudley, for a trading voyage to China. This expedition was, however, not heard of again, not one of the company ever returning to give an account of the rest.

In 1600 Queen Elizabeth granted a charter to George Earl of Cumberland and two hundred and fifteen Knights, Aldermen, and Merchants, for the formation of a corporate body to be styled "the Governor and Company of Merchants of London trading into the East Indies."

On the formation of the East India Company, Richard Hakluyt was appointed historiographer, and their historical and geographical documents were subsequently placed in his custody. He thus had charge of the journals of all the East India voyages from 1600 to the date of his death in 1616. In about 1620, four years after Hakluyt's death, these journals came into the hands of the Reverend Samuel Purchas, having probably been made over to him for publication. Instead of printing them *in extenso*, Purchas resolved to epitomize his materials, and, in this form, he published them in four folio volumes, in 1625, under the title "*Hakluytus Posthumus, or Purchas his Pilgrimes*." It seems doubtful whether most of these original journals were ever returned to the East India House, but, if they were, many of them have since been lost, and of others only fragments now exist. This is much to be regretted, as the earliest journals were the most important, and in many cases the only records of the proceedings of the Company's Agents abroad. Later on, much of this information is contained in letters received by the Court from their Captains and Factors in the East.

No proper provision appears to have been subsequently made for the safe custody of these journals, and consequently those that remain of these priceless records of the past are in many cases defective, and a still greater number are damaged by damp and decay.

The earliest document of this nature, extant in the records of this Office, is a fragment of a Journal, from the 31st July to the 4th August 1605, kept by an officer on board the "Ascension," in the second expedition sent out by the East India Company.

It is proposed in the following introductory remarks to show which are the original journals that are now missing, and where the particulars of those that have been published are to be found.

At a meeting of the Company on the 24th September 1599, certain rules were agreed to for the provision of shipping and other matters, of which the following is an extract:—"First that noe ship shalbe receavid to be brought in by any adventuro^{r} "in this viage to be imployed in the same as his stock or portion of adventure at any "rate whatsoever—Also that all shipping to be imploied in this viage shalbe bought "and provided by suche as shalbe therto appointed for ready money onlie."

The first expedition sent out by the East India Company was placed under the command of Captain (afterwards Sir) James Lancaster. For the fleet to be employed upon this voyage the Company purchased vessels in the river Thames. One of these, the

* "Voyages of Sir James Lancaster to the Indies." The Hakluyt Society, No. LVI.

"Mare Scurge" (also alluded to by the name of the "Malyce Scurge"), a vessel of 600 tons, was bought from the Earl of Cumberland* for 3,700*l*.† When the ship was offered to the Company they entertained great doubts as to the expediency of buying her, "her burthen being so great, whereby the Tunage agreed uppon shalbe so greatly exceeded"; but it was afterwards decided to purchase her, "to the ende the preparation of the viage be not hindred by restinge in an uncertentie of o' shipping." The name of this vessel was subsequently changed to the "Red Dragon."‡ The other vessels of the fleet were the "Hector," the "Ascension," and the "Susan." The "Susan," of 240 tons, was purchased from Mr. Alderman Bannyng for 1,600*l*., he agreeing to re-purchase the vessel at the expiration of the voyage for 800*l*. The "Hector," of 300 tons, and the "Ascension," of 260 tons, were also purchased for this voyage, but it does not appear what sum was paid for either of these. A small ship called the "Guift," of 130 tons, was bought of Mr. Fraunce Chery, of Ratclyff, for the sum of 300*l*., and accompanied the fleet as a victualler. The "Discovery" and the "Godspeed" were also purchased about the same time. In this expedition the "Red Dragon" was commanded by Captain James Lancaster, the "Hector" by Captain John Middleton, the "Ascension" by Master William Brand, and the "Susan" by Master John Heyward. The expedition went to Sumatra and Java. There are no original records relative to this voyage now extant in the India Office, but an account of it has been given in "Purchas his Pilgrimes," Vol. I., Book 3, Chapter 3. It is, however, not stated by whom the journal was kept that is there epitomized, neither is there anything to indicate the author, except that he was some one on board the "Red Dragon." This has been reprinted in "Harris's Voyages," and in "Works issued by the Hakluyt Society," No. LVI.

The second expedition sent out by the East India Company was one for the discovery of a North-West Passage to India. This consisted of two vessels, the "Discovery," of 70 tons, and the "Godspeed," of 60 tons, and was under the command of Captain George Waymouth, who sailed in the "Discovery," whilst the "Godspeed" was commanded by Master John Drew. Captain Waymouth's journal is printed in Purchas (Vol. III., p. 809), and a condensed account of it is given in the Hakluyt Society's Publication No. V. The journal itself is now missing.

On the 23rd March 1604 a second voyage was set out for India. The fleet was under the command of Captain (afterwards Sir) Henry Middleton, and consisted of the same vessels as undertook the first voyage, viz., the "Red Dragon," Captain Henry Middleton; the "Hector," Captain Christopher Colthurst; the "Ascension," Captain Roger Stiles; and the "Susan," Captain William Keeling. This expedition went to Bantam and the Molucca Islands. The "Susan" was lost on the way home, but the other vessels returned in safety. The journals of this voyage no longer exist, but there is a fragment of a journal kept on board the "Ascension," which forms No. I. of the Marine Records in the accompanying list. An account of the expedition was published in 1606 by Walter Burre, who is supposed to have married Sir Henry Middleton's daughter; this pamphlet, now very rare, has been republished by the Hakluyt Society, Vol. XIX. Brief accounts of the voyage are also given in "Purchas" and in "Harris's Voyages."

The next expedition was one to the North-West, under Master John Knight, in the "Hopewell," which sailed in May 1606. John Knight's journal, up to the 26th June,

---

* This vessel had been a ship of war, built by the Earl of Cumberland, one of the gallant adventurers of Queen Elizabeth's age, to cruise against the Spaniards.—Marine Records, Miscellaneous, No. 1.

† Court Minutes, 7th October 1600.

‡ Court Minutes, 11th December 1600.

forms No. II. of the Marine Records. On the 19th of that month they made the coast of Labrador. Knight, with several others, went ashore on the 26th to explore a large island which lay about six miles from the "Hopewell," but they never returned, neither were their bodies discovered. With great difficulty the vessel, which was much damaged by having been on the rocks, was got back to England, where the survivors arrived on the 24th December. Knight's journal, with a continuation by "Oliver Browne, one of the Company," is printed in "Purchas," Vol. 3, p. 827; it has since been published by the Hakluyt Society in Vol. LVI. of their series.

For the third voyage to the East Indies, the "Dragon" and "Hector" were prepared, together with the "Consent," a pinnace of 105 tons. They were commanded respectively by Captain William Keeling, Captain William Hawkins, and Captain David Middleton. The journals of Keeling, Hawkins, and Middleton are epitomized in "Purchas," Vol. 1, p. 188, in "Harris's Voyages," and in the Hakluyt Society's Publication, Vol. LVI. Journals kept on board Keeling's and Hawkins' ships (some imperfect) constitute Nos. III., IV., V., VI., and VIII. of the Marine Records.

The fourth voyage was commanded by Captain Alexander Sharpeigh in the "Ascension," and he was accompanied by Captain Richard Rowles in the "Union," an old vessel of 400 tons, but "thought fit by the Governor and Sir James Lancaster to go the voyage, though her repairs will probably be costly." She was bought for 1,250*l*.* The expedition started from Woolwich the 14th March 1608. Two accounts of this voyage, by Thomas Jones and William Nicols respectively, who were both on board the "Ascension," are given in "Purchas," Vol. 1, p. 228. In the Hakluyt Society's Publication, No. LVI., abstracts are given of Sharpeigh's journal, and of another account of the voyage by the same, given at the end of the journal. The journal itself forms No. VII. of the Marine Records.

At the commencement of their proceedings, the Court of Directors requested Mr. Foulke Grevil, Treasurer of the Navy, to move the Lord Admiral for the use of Woolwich and Deptford Docks,† but now they found it necessary to have docks for their own exclusive use, and they accordingly hired Mr. Greet's dock at Deptford at 30*l*. a year.‡ Up to this time the Company had purchased vessels for their voyages, many of them being old and scarcely fit for the purpose; but by Court Minutes of the 21st August 1607 it was decided to build ships for themselves, and arrangements were made for buying timber and building a great ship for the fifth voyage; another ship of 700 or 800 tons was also to be built and to be ready by Christmas 1608.

On the 17th February 1609, the ship "Bonaventure" was purchased for 2,200*l*., and her name was subsequently changed to the "Expedition." She was not a new vessel, and the repairs necessary before starting on a voyage amounted to 329*l*. 18*s*. 0*d*.§ The command of the "Expedition" was given to Captain David Middleton, who sailed in her for Java and Banda on the 24th April 1609. The journal of this voyage does not now exist. An account of it, extracted from a letter addressed by Captain Middleton to the Company, will be found in "Purchas," Vol. 1, p. 238, but the original of this letter is also missing. A reference to this expedition will be found in "Harris's Voyages," Vol. 1, p. 875.

The Company having begun to build their own vessels, two ships were now completed and ready for launching—one of them of no less than 1,100 tons, and the other a pinnace. To inaugurate so important an event the King consented to name the ships,

* Court Minutes, 13th and 23rd August 1607.

† Court Minutes, 25th September 1600.

‡ Court Minutes, 5th September 1607.

§ Court Minutes, 23rd May 1609.

and accordingly he attended at the docks, accompanied by the Queen and Prince, on the 30th December 1609, in order to take part in the ceremony. His Majesty named the big ship the "Trades Increase," and the pinnace the "Peppercorn."* The King was on this occasion entertained by the Company at a great banquet, all served on dishes and plates of chinaware, and His Majesty placed a great chain of gold and a medal about Sir Thomas Smythe's neck with his own hands.

The "Trades Increase" commanded by Sir Henry Middleton, the "Peppercorn" by Captain Nicholas Downton, and the "Darling," sailed for the East on 1st April 1610. The "Trades Increase" proved an unfortunate vessel. Sir Henry Middleton on his way out called at Mocha, where he was taken prisoner. On his release he proceeded to Bantam, where the "Trades Increase" ran upon a rock and sprang a leak. Whilst being repaired she careened over, and was set on fire and totally destroyed by the Javanese†. Journals of the "Trades Increase" and of the "Peppercorn" are now in existence here (Marine Records, Nos. IX., X., XI., and XII.) and particulars of this voyage are also given in the Hakluyt Society's Publications (Vol. LVI.), in "Harris's Voyages," and in "Purchas his Pilgrimes."

By a regulation due to King Henry VIII., a bounty of *5s.* a ton was directed to be paid to the builders of ships of 100 tons and upwards, and owners were forbidden to sell them to any foreign Power.‡ Accordingly it appears from the Court Minutes of 15th March 1614, that the King had "allowed the Company 921*l.* 5*s.* for the "tonnage of six new ships built by them, viz., the 'Trades Increase,' 'Peppercorn,' "'Clove,' 'Thomas,' 'James,' and 'Osiander'"; subsequently the Company received 491*l.* 10*s.* as bounty on tonnage for the "New Year's Gift," "Hope," and "Expectation."§

In 1611 two expeditions were despatched. One consisted of the "Globe," under Captain Anthony Hippon, a journal of which voyage by P. W. Floris, who went out in the ship as Cape merchant, is now amongst the Records (No. XIII.) and an account of the voyage is also given in "Purchas his Pilgrimes." The second comprised the "Clove," "Hector," and "Thomas," commanded by Captain John Saris. Captain Saris's Journal of the "Clove" is still preserved (No. XIV.). This journal, which records events happening in the years 1611 to 1613, was purchased by the War Office in 1857 for 26*l.* from the executors of the late Colonel Jervis. In August 1889 it was presented by the Secretary of State for War (the Right Honourable E. Stanhope, M.P.) to this Office. A brief reference to Captain Saris's expedition is given in "Harris's Voyages."

What are known as the 9th, 10th, and 11th voyages really formed part of one expedition under the command of Captain Thomas Best. It consisted of the "Dragon," "Osiander," "James," and "Solomon." Captain Best's journal and also two journals kept on board the "Osiander" are still in existence (Nos. XV., XVI., and XVIII.). Accounts of these voyages are also given in the Hakluyt Society's Publications (Vol. LVI.), in "Purchas his Pilgrimes," and in "Harris's Voyages."

The twelfth voyage, in 1611, consisted of the "Expedition" alone, which was commanded by Christopher Newport. Of this no journal now exists amongst the India Office Records, but an account by Walter Payton is given in "Purchas his Pilgrimes."

---

* Domestic Correspondence, Vol. I., No. 92, Cal., p. 576.

† O. C., Vol. II., No. 226, and Vol. III., No. 286.

‡ "The Royal and Merchant Navy under Elizabeth" by M. Oppenheim (English Historical Review, July 1891, p. 472). In Rymer's Fœdera, Vol. XVIII., p. 679, it is stated, "And whereas Queen Elizabeth for the "encouragement of ship-building, gave a premium of 5*s.* per ton for every ship built above the burden of one "hundred tons, which was revived by King James, King Charles now allowed 5*s.* per ton for every ship that "should be built of 200 tons and upwards."

§ Court Minutes, 8th June 1614.

The foregoing voyages had all been undertaken with separate capital accounts, but the next four were supported by a joint stock; they consisted of the following:—

1st. "New Year's Gift," "Hector," "Merchants' Hope," and "Solomon," under the command of Nicholas Downton, in 1614.

2nd. "Samaritan," "Thomas," and "Thomasine," under Captain David Middleton, in 1614.

3rd. "Dragon," "Expedition," "Lion," and "Peppercorn," under Captain Keeling in 1615. This fleet took out Sir Thomas Roe to India as Ambassador from King James I. to the Court of the Great Mogul (Jehangir) at Agra.

4th. "Charles," "Unicorn," "James," "Globe," "Swan," and "Rose," under Captain Benjamin Joseph, in 1616.

The first fleet sent out by the second Joint Stock consisted of the "James," "Anne," "New Year's Gift," "Bull," and "Bee," under Captain Martin Pring, in 1617.

Journals of these last-named five voyages are published in "Purchas his Pilgrimes," and journals of the "New Year's Gift," the "Hector," and the "Bull" are preserved amongst the Marine Records at this Office (Nos. XIX., XX., XXI., and XXV.). This concludes the list of journals that have been separately published; and, so far as is at present known, the only journals, in original or copies, for subsequent voyages, are those now included amongst the Marine Records, as shown in the accompanying list. The statement shown on next page, taken from a very old and damaged document, gives an Abstract of the Stock and Trade adventured by the East India Company between the years 1601 and 1619 inclusive, to which have been added, by way of footnotes, the names of the vessels missing from each voyage, and the manner in which they were severally lost.

As early as the year 1629 the question was considered by the Directors whether it would not be better to freight than to build ships,* the chief arguments at that time against building being the large amount of capital that would have to be invested in ships, and the difficulty of apportioning the cost and expenses of the Company's vessels equally amongst the different adventurers. On further inquiry, however, it was found that no persons were willing to let ships on freight to India, although 30*l.*, 40*l.*, and even 45*l.* per ton had been offered. But later on vessels were obtainable on freight, and in 1642 the rate paid for a voyage to Bantam was 25*l.*, and, in 1645, 20*l.* per ton.† By this time the practice of freighting vessels generally prevailed.

Shortly afterwards, owing to the opposition of the Dutch in the East, and the unsettled state of affairs at home, the Company were reduced to great difficulties, and they failed to raise the capital required for a new Joint Stock. The question had, for some time past, been seriously considered whether the Company should continue to build their own ships, and at a Court held on the 25th April 1645 the Directors had under consideration a proposal to sell Blackwall Docks, and to freight ships when wanted. Nothing further seems to have been done in this matter at the time, but it appears from Court Minutes of the 3rd December 1652, that the Docks were then leased to Mr. Henry Johnson for 21 years at 200*l.* per annum.

During the Commonwealth a number of adventurers sent out ships to compete for a share in the Indian trade, and the condition of the English East India Company became most seriously depressed; but having obtained a new exclusive charter, in 1657, they recommenced operations with activity. They bought some vessels and hired others, the freight at this time ranging from 18*l.* to 22*l.* per ton to Surat and back.

---

* Court Minutes, 29th April, 8th May, and 19th June 1629.

† Marine Records, Miscellaneous, No. 1.

An abstract of the Stock and Trade (ad)ventured by the Governour and Company of Merchants of London traidinge to East India begun in a° 1601 and continued to a° 1619 as well in their distinck as joynt voyadges as foll ——— viz.

Year	Receyved of the adventurers	whereof sent out in mony	in goodes	in shiping, victuails &c.	pd. his matie for subsidie	lycence for mony
In a° 1601*	68373*li*	21742*li*	6860*li*	39771	4550*li*	30000*li*
a° 1603	60450	11160	1142	48150	8919	30000
a° 1606	53500	17600	7280	28620	17054	30000
a° 1607	33000	15000	3400	14600	794	30000
a° 1608	13700	6000	1700	6000	4791	30000
a° 1609	82000	28500	21300	32200	[?0]4257	30000
a° 1610	71581	19200	10681	42500	20000	30000
a° 1611	76375	17675	19000	48700	18756	30000
a° 1612	7200	1250	650	5300	2583	30000
a° 1613	106000	18810	12446	} 272514 (a° 1613–1616)	} 65000 (a° 1613–1616)	30000
a° 1614	107000	13942	23000			30000
a° 1615	107000	26660	26065			30000
a° 1616	109000	52067	16506			60000
a° 1617	200000	} 298000 (a° 1617–1619)	} 152000 (a° 1617–1619)	} 300000 (a° 1617–1619)		} 300000 (a° 1617–1619)
a° 1618	200000					
a° 1619	400000					

Some totall of Thadventures am°(?) 1695179*li* whereof sent out in mony 547686 In goodes 292430 in shiping &c. 638335*li* paid his matie for subsidie 146704 lycence for mony 720000*li*

Shipinge	sent out	Retourned	Remaininge	Lost, worn &c.
a° 1601*	4	4	00	00
a° 1603	4	3	00	1([1])
a° 1606	3	3	00	00
a° 1607	2	00	*00*	2([2])
[a° 1608]	*1*	1	00	*00*
a° 1609	3	1	00	2([3])
a° 1610	4	4	00	00
a° 1611	4	3	00	1([4])
a° 1612	1	1	00	00
a° 1613	5	2	00	3([5])
a° 1614	9	4	2	3([6])
a° 1615	8	5	*2*	1([7])
a° 1616	7	3	*4*	00
a° 1617	9	1	7	1([8])
a° 1618	9	1	8	00
a° 1619	8	0	*8*	*00*
Total	81	retourned 36	*31*	14 and taken by ye ffemmy(ngs).

([1]) The "Susan" was lost on her way home (*Purchas*, I. 187).
([2]) The "Ascension" struck on a shoal at the mouth of the Amlicka river and sank (*ib.* 230); and the "Union" ran on the rocks off the coast of Brittany and was lost (*ib.* 234).
([3]) The "Trades Increase" was beached at Bantam and subsequently berned (*O.C.* 236); the "Darling" was laid up at Patani, June 1615, being worn out (*Purchas*, I, 533).
([4]) Possibly the "Osiander."
([5]) The "Hector" was lost off Jakatra, while careening (*Purchas*, I, 527 and 533); the other two have not been identified.
([6]) The "Thomas" was sunk off Jakatra (*Purchas*, I, 620); the "Thomasine" struck on a shoal near Macassar, Sept. 1615 (*ib.* 515 and 533); the third vessel has not been traced.
([7]) Possibly the "Unicorn," which was lost off the coast of China (*Purchas*, I, 622 and 642).
([8]) This may be the "Sun," which was wrecked on Engano Island (*Purchas*, I, 619).

* The dates given in this column are according to the old style.

Note.—The figures in *italics* are missing in the original paper, which is much damaged.

From this time the Company adopted generally the system of hiring what vessels they required for their trade, and for a single voyage. The manner of taking up shipping was not by open tender, but a Committee of Shipping was appointed, consisting of a few Directors, who were left to provide, in such way as they thought fit, the vessels required, and the Committee themselves fixed the rates of freight they would give. A part at least of the Directors were ship-owners, and these openly and avowedly let their ships to the Company, a practice that was tacitly permitted by the Proprietors.*

Upon the renewal of the Company's Charter by Cromwell, in 1657, all their large ships had become either lost or worn out. The Court, therefore, in consequence of an overture made to them by Captain Millet, "inclined much to encourage the building "of good able three-decked ships of 450 or 500 tons which will be fittest for their "employment; and he is told that if he build such a ship, so that she may be fit for "their service, they will then give her employment before any other ship. And for "the terms of freight he shall have as good as they give to any; but they could not, "at present, make conditions, in regard freight riseth and falleth, according as the "prices of provisions and wages governed."* This was the first instance, followed afterwards by many others, of leave to build for the Company, with a promise of preference in employment, without the stipulation of any other conditions; a principle which, whilst it went to provide a more efficient fleet for the Company, went also to fix a double relation between them and one set of ship-owners; because, these ships being fit only for the Company's trade, their owners naturally endeavoured to continue them in the Company's service. This principle laid the foundation of a permanent body of ship-owners, which, in process of time, produced very important effects.

In 1668 the tenders for building ships on promise of employment not coming in fast enough, the Court, in addition to their former encouragement, offered twenty shillings extra freight per ton for the first two voyages, which implied that the ships were to be entertained for a succession of voyages.

During the period of domestic disturbances, shipbuilding in England had ceased to be carried on with the same energy as before, but it received a stimulus in 1670 by the passing of an Act† ordering that (1) no foreign-built ships shall enjoy the privileges of English or Irish built ships, even although navigated as that Act‡ directs, and although the owners likewise be Englishmen, prize ships only excepted. . . . And in order to encourage the building of good and defensible ships, it was further enacted, that for seven years to come, whoever should build ships with three decks, or with two decks, a half deck and a forecastle, with five feet between each deck, mounted with at least 30 cannon, should for the first two voyages, receive one-tenth of all the customs paid on their cargoes exported or imported. By 1682 so many tenders for building ships had been received, that the Directors were unable to accept them all, and they thereupon withdrew their premium of twenty shillings extra freight for the first two voyages.

After this, the shipping of the East India Company began to improve, and about 1689 the Company published an account of the state of their trade, shipping, and forts, in which it was stated "that within seven years past they had built 16 great ships, "from 900 to 1,300 tons each. . . . That they had now at sea, in India, and "coming home, eleven ships and four permission ships. . . . They had seven "great ships and six permission ones, all for Coast and Bay. . . . They had seven

* Marine Records, Miscellaneous, No. 1.

† 22 & 23 Car. II, cap. 11.

‡ Previous Navigation Act of 1660.

"ships for China and the South Seas, besides about 30 other small armed vessels "constantly remaining in India."*

A little later on, in 1695, the Company again experienced a difficulty in supplying themselves with shipping, owing, it has been suggested, to two causes: 1st, heavy losses by accidents and captures; and, 2ndly, the falling credit of the Company, which made ship-owners less desirous of building for them than formerly.† Accordingly an extra payment of 20*s*. per ton was offered‡ for each voyage for three-decked vessels of 500 tons and upwards, and under these conditions several offers were received. As another mode of overcoming the difficulty the Company became part owners of vessels they desired to employ in their service.§

Upon the formation of the English East India Company the competition for vessels and Commanders was keen between the two Companies, and owners of vessels took advantage of this circumstance to raise their rates.†

Shortly after the union of the two Companies, bye-laws were passed|| to the effect that after Michaelmas 1710, no ship or vessel should be hired or freighted wherein any Director was concerned as an owner; that the Court of Directors should not invest any of the Company's money or effects in shipping, except such small ships as they might have occasion to employ in the East Indies;¶ that all ships to be hired by the Company should be taken up by ballot; and that no tender should be accepted which should not be first made in writing, by the Commander and two of the owners, specifying the names of the owners.

An attempt was made in 1711 to deprive the Committee of Shipping of some of their exclusive authority in the hire of vessels, and a resolution was passed that all tenders of shipping should first be laid before the Court;** but a fortnight later this order was rescinded, and tenders were directed to be again received by the Committee of Shipping.†† At last, however, those who were endeavouring to introduce reforms in connection with the engagement of shipping gained their end, and by a Resolution of the Court of the 13th August 1712, an advertisement was ordered to be issued inviting tenders for shipping, which were to be sent in, sealed, to the Secretary, in order to be laid before the Court. Not the least important effect of this change was that the Court secured all the freight they required at prices considerably below what had been previously paid to owners of vessels.

Very shortly, however, the owners of vessels combined to raise the rate of freight, and in the contest that followed the owners gained the day,‡‡ and succeeded in forcing the Company to pay higher rates than they had at first offered; and as is remarked in a memorandum on the subject, "Here ended, and in this way, the efforts of that period for a reform in the business of freighting ships."† In the following year (1717) the Court, to avoid fresh contests, themselves proposed, in the annual advertisement for tenders, to give the same terms as last year. The rates continued on this footing until raised by the rupture with Spain in 1720, but in 1722 they were again lowered.§§

* Macpherson's "Annals of Commerce," Vol. II., p. 645.
† Marine Records, Miscellaneous, No. 1.
‡ Court Minutes, 9th November 1694.
§ Court Minutes, 5th December 1694.
|| *Vide* "Charters," India Office Records and Court Minutes, 25th May 1710.
¶ This appears to strike immediately at the Company's joining with individuals in the purchase of ships.
** Court Minutes, 27th June 1711.
†† Court Minutes, 13th July 1711.
‡‡ Court Minutes, 8th and 15th August 1716.
§§ Court Minutes, 11th July 1722.

By a resolution of the Court on the 12th August 1724, it was decided that ships which had already performed a journey to India and back should be re-engaged without ballot, and that "ships which are or have been in this Company's service shall for the "future be employed in order as they return home, provided the Commanders comply "with their Charterparties and Instructions." This practically gave almost a monopoly of employment to those vessels that had once been engaged by the Court.

The building of ships for the purpose of the Company was now carried on to such an extent that the Court found it necessary to adopt measures to discourage the laying down of more vessels* and to this end it was "Resolved that henceforth in case of the "mortality or misbehaviour of the Commanders of the ships in this Company's service "the Court of Directors do recommend such persons as they judge proper to the "command of the said ships whenever they are again taken up for the service, and in "so doing that a particular regard be had to such as have served the Company and "their owners faithfully and well. Resolved also that it be recommended by this "Court to all succeeding Courts of Directors to continue in the same method till the "present inconveniencies are remedied by the shipping being reduced to a proper "number for the service."

The above orders for discouraging the building of new vessels for the Company's service were confirmed by the Court on the 10th April 1730; but on the request of Captain Micklefield of the ship "Marlborough," which had been burnt, he was permitted† to build a new vessel in her place for the Company's service. Similar applications made in 1731 and 1732 were also complied with, and thence arose the practice of owners being permitted to build new vessels on the bottoms of old ships, a custom which tended to keep the supply of ships to the Company in the hands of an exclusive set. These were not long in taking advantage of their position, and brought considerable pressure to bear upon the Court with the view of raising the rates of freight,‡ who, however, met the demand by declaring "that, in case the owners do not agree to accept the "Company's terms, public notice be given that the Court are ready to receive tenders "of such ships that are 300 tons and upwards, and may be made fit for a voyage to the "East Indies this season."§ Upon this resolution being communicated to the ship-owners they reluctantly agreed to accept the same freight as before.‖

It was not, however, long before the owners renewed their application for higher terms,¶ and on this occasion the Court yielded to their demands,** the owners having declared that "on a serious consideration they were unanimously of opinion that they could not abate anything of their proposals." The rates now paid were 30*l.* and 33*l.* per ton for coarse and fine goods respectively.

In 1751 the Court gave directions†† for a vessel to be built for the Company's service, for protecting the trade on the Malabar Coast against the pirates there. This vessel was named the "Guardian," and the first Commander was Captain William James.

By an Act of 1772 (12 Geo. III., cap. liv.), owing to the scarcity of oak timber for the use of the Royal Navy, the East India Company were precluded from building any new ships after the 18th March of that year, and by a Resolution of the latter date,

* Court Minutes, 24th and 29th March 1727.

† Court Minutes, 21st October 1730.

‡ Court Minutes, 5th September 1739.

§ Court Minutes, 14th September 1739.

‖ Court Minutes, 28th September 1739.

¶ Court Minutes, 22nd, 23rd, and 24th September 1742.

** Court Minutes, 29th September 1742.

†† Court Minutes, 12th April 1751.

the Court decided that no new ship should be laid down for them until the tonnage of all the ships employed by them should be reduced to 45,000 tons.

An alleged general mismanagement by the Directors of the East India Company led to the appointment, in 1772, of a Parliamentary Committee of Secrecy, to inquire and report upon their affairs generally. The Third Report refers to freight and demorrage. This Committee found that for ten years previously the sum of 5,018,162*l.* 0*s.* 6*d.* had been paid on this account, from which must, however, be deducted the sum of 240,260*l.*, on account of transporting the Company's troops to their settlements. An examination of the charter-party showed "that the Company generally covenant with "owners that the ship is to carry at least 499 tons at certain rates therein specified, "and carry out and bring home 80 tons of iron kintlage or ballast, as part thereof. "That the master, officers, and ship's company shall also be allowed as a part of the "said 499 tons, to carry the quantity of 25 tons outwards, and of 15 tons from "port to port in the East Indies, &c., and also 15 tons homewards; and it is also "covenanted and agreed between the parties, that, notwithstanding the ship is let "to freight but for 499 tons, yet the Company and their factors, &c., may, if they "think fit, lade what more they please, at certain rates, namely, for double kintlage "the sums specified in the said charter-party, and for all further exceedings half "freight."

This Committee remarked that a larger number of ships were taken up than were required by the Company's trade, and they showed that, during the years 1753 to 1772, inclusively, the Company employed 175,086 tons of shipping, builders' measurement, for the importation of 139,627 tons of merchandise, so that the tons of shipping exceeded the tons of merchandise brought home by the amount of 35,459 tons. It was further shown that at the date of their enquiry the Company had an excess of shipping entertained in their service to the extent of 26,360 tons. At this time the Company had 87 ships in their employ, whereas it appeared that 55 ships would be more than sufficient for their trade, and they possessed therefore an excess of 32 vessels, which entailed a wholly unnecessary charge to the amount of 73,904*l.* per annum.

At the commencement of their Report, the Committee hinted at the possible economy that would ensue were the Company to build their own ships, instead of hiring them, but they refrained from making any definite recommendation to that effect.

About the year 1772, the practice of selling the commands of ships in the Company's service began to attract attention. This practice emanated from the principle of perpetuating bottoms, which preserved his position to a Commander who continued to behave well, as long as he chose to retain it. He was consequently enabled to make terms, privately, for resigning, when he thought fit, in favour of another qualified person agreeable to the owners, some of whom were accused of entering into the same traffic when a bottom was first introduced into the service, or a command lapsed. This practice is said to have begun about the year 1750, for a full consideration.* The Company had severely forbidden it, and it was stipulated, both with owners and commanders, that they should abstain from it. In 1772 the Directors had a case brought before them of a Captain whom it was proposed to supersede in this manner,† and although they interfered in the matter the practice continued, and became at length almost universal; the price of a command being sometimes as high as 10,000*l.*

* Marine Records, Miscellaneous, No. 1.

† Court Minutes, 11th August 1772.

Owing to the difficulty experienced in obtaining ships to carry out troops and stores to the East Indies, the Directors were authorized, by an order of Court of the 15th May 1781, to purchase, during the continuance of the war, such ships as they might require to carry troops and stores to India, which were afterwards to be employed by the Company in India or sold there, but not to be sent home with merchandise.*

Towards the close of the American war, the Directors complained bitterly of the oppressive terms of owners for the hire of their shipping, to which, however, they were forced of necessity to submit.† The freights were in this year at the then unexampled rate of 47*l.* per ton, an increase of no less than 9*l.* per ton on the rate of the year immediately preceding. In 1783, the first year of peace, the owners demanded 37*l.* per ton, which was about the price in 1780, when war still raged. The Directors offered 32*l.*, and after much altercation the owners consented to take 35*l.*‡ The Directors then advertised for other ships, whereupon 28 ships were tendered at rates much below the last-named price. The report of the Company's Inspecting Officer on the ships tendered was, however, generally unfavourable, many of them being of a foreign build, others of a slight and weak structure, and some nearly worn out. In the interim the old owners had tendered their vessels at 33*l.* per ton, and as this rate was not very much in excess of that at which the other ships had been offered, their tender was accepted, but at the same time the Committee of Shipping was directed to prepare an estimate of the expense of building, outfit, and other charges of an East India ship, fit for sea, to be laid before the Court on the 1st of May in each year.§

In October 1784 the number of ships abroad and at home in the Company's service was 66, whereas the Court considered that not less than 70 were required for the proper accommodation of the trade, and they therefore obtained permission to commence the construction forthwith of six ships of about 755 tons burthen each for that service,‖ and six more ships were to be built for the season 1786.¶ In November 1785 it was deemed expedient to have three sets of shipping, comprising about 30 ships in each set, and leave was accordingly given for the construction of eight more new ships.**

Under a bye-law of 1773 the employment of ships for more than four voyages was prohibited, but in May 1790 the Court resolved that, from past experience, ships would run three voyages without stripping off their sheathing; and, if the practice should become general, ships which made the outfit of the fourth voyage the repairing voyage, might with great safety perform six voyages. The bye-law was accordingly suspended, and agreements were entered into with the owners for their ships to perform six, instead of only four, voyages.

Even after this concession, the owners of ships employed by the Company were constantly endeavouring, by their combined action, to keep up the rates of freight, whilst the Directors were ever attempting to bring them down to a reasonable and fair scale. This question came before the General Court on the 3rd April 1793, when an opinion was recorded "that some permanent system may be established, upon principles of fair, well regulated, and open competition." Steps were accordingly taken to this

---

* By this Resolution the Company's 9th bye-law was suspended, which ordained, "That the Court of "Directors shall not invest any of the Company's money or effects whatsoever in shipping, except such small "ships as they may have occasion to employ in the East Indies."

† Court Minutes, 25th April 1781.

‡ Court Minutes, 20th and 29th August 1783.

§ Court Minutes, 4th September 1783.

‖ Court Minutes, 4th October 1784.

¶ Court Minutes, 19th January 1785.

** Court Minutes, 8th November 1785.

effect, and on the 5th February 1796 the Court of Directors agreed upon a report to the General Court, from which it appeared that for the current season the Directors had effected a reduction in freight equal to 183,316*l.** So strong, however, was the influence of the shipping interests in the proprietary of the Company, that the proposals of the Court were negatived, on the 17th February, and it was only after several unsuccessful attempts that the Report of the Directors was approved by the General Court on the 10th March following.

On the 28th June 1799 a Bill was brought into the House of Commons, by Mr. Dundas, for regulating the manner in which the Company should in future take up ships for their regular service, which was duly passed and received the Royal assent on the 12th July.†

The introduction of ships built in India formed matter of discussion shortly after a renewal of the Company's exclusive privileges in 1793; and in 1795 the Court sent out instructions to their Governments in India authorizing them to take up such proper ships as they could procure to bring home goods from within the Company's limits. In June of that year an Act was passed‡ authorizing during the then war, and for eighteen months after its conclusion, ships from India, though not British-built or registered, if built within the territories of the Company, to enter their goods and to export goods to India. This provision was extended by subsequent Acts.

In 1810 an Act§ was passed authorizing the Company to engage ships beyond eight voyages, if on repair they should be found fit for the service; also, to take up, by private contract, ships employed in carrying convicts or stores to New South Wales, to bring home cargoes from China or India.

In 1819 an Act was passed to amend and consolidate into one Act the several laws relating to the manner in which the East India Company were required to hire ships.‖

Previously to 1796, commanders of vessels were required to take "an oath against trading to, in, or from India," but, on the recommendation of a Committee appointed at that date "to take into consideration the present and future situation of the commanders of the Company's ships," that oath was abolished, and one substituted for it to be true and faithful to the Company. Commanders had also to give a penalty bond for 10,000*l.* for good behaviour and strict observance of engagements with the Company. The commanders were now permitted to carry on a limited trade on their own account, and a certain amount of tonnage, out and home, not to exceed 99 tons in all, was allowed them for that purpose, the only trade restrictions being "woollens and warlike stores" on the outward journey, and "musk, camphire, arrack, and China raw silk" on the homeward voyage. Every commander was also required to pay into the Company's treasury, on return from each voyage, the sum of 500*l.*¶

The commercial affairs of the East India Company were again considered by a Select Committee of the House of Commons in 1811, whose observations thereon are contained in their Eleventh Report. Shortly afterwards (1813) an Act was passed by which the East India trade was thrown open to private competition, although the

* From the Court Minutes of the 18th January 1814, it appears that the difference between the peace freights paid in 1791 under the old system, and the peace freights allowed to the regular ships in each year on the new system of open competition, exhibits a saving to the Company in 17 years, viz., 1796–97 to 1812–13, of the very considerable sum of 1,896,546*l.*

† 39 Geo. III., cap. 89.

‡ 35 Geo. III., cap. 115.

§ 50 Geo. III., cap. 86.

‖ 58 Geo. III., cap. 83.

¶ Court Minutes, 27th September 1796.

exclusive trade to China, deemed by far the most lucrative at the time, was still reserved to the Company* until the 10th April 1834.

In consequence of the "new situation" in which the Company was placed by the Act above referred to, Committees were appointed for an "investigation of the "Company's Establishments abroad and at home, with a view to the general improve-"ment of their finances."†

In view of the fact that, under the altered conditions of the East Indian trade, it could not be expected that the commanders and officers would obtain much advantage therefrom, it was decided to grant them a fixed rate of pay in lieu of tonnage, and the claim of 500*l.* from the commanders at the end of each voyage was discontinued.‡

Regulations were also sanctioned for the grant of annuities to present and past commanders of regular ships, and also to their widows and children.§ Further, by Court Minutes of the 8th February 1814, a "General Sea Insurance Fund" was established, which was charged at the rate of 5 per cent. on the ship and all cargoes.

The invention of steam as a power of propulsion, and its applicability to ships, began to attract attention in the early years of the present century, and, in 1822, a public meeting was held in London with the view of forming a Steam Navigation Company to trade with India, the result of which was the despatch of Lieutenant (afterward Captain) J. Johnston to Calcutta to see what could be done to prosecute the object in view.‖ At a meeting held in Calcutta it was announced that the Governor General (Lord Amherst) in Council was prepared to recommend a gift of Rs. 20,000, by way of premium, "to whoever, whether individuals or a Company, "being British subjects, should permanently, before the end of 1826, establish a steam "communication between England and India, either by the Cape of Good Hope or "Red Sea, and make two voyages out and two home, occupying not more than "seventy days on each passage." The "Enterprize" was the first steam vessel that proceeded to India. She sailed on the 16th August 1825, under the command of Captain Johnston, and although she took 113 days on the passage, and so failed to obtain the promised premium, she was purchased, on arrival at Calcutta, by the Indian Government, by whom she was employed in connection with the first Burmese war, and proved of great value in carrying despatches from Calcutta to Rangoon. The success thus far of the "Enterprize" encouraged the introduction of steam vessels into the local trade of India.

On the expiration of the Charter of 1813 the trade to China was also thrown open, and, from the year 1834, the East India Company ceased to be traders, and they sold their merchant vessels to various private firms.¶

These introductory remarks on the late East India Company's Mercantile Marine may be brought to an end by the following historical abstract of some of the more important naval engagements fought by the East India Company's ships.

In 1601 the first fleet, under Lancaster, prospected the Island of St. Helena, entered into a treaty with the King of Achin, settled a factory at Bantam, and captured a valuable Portuguese carravel south of the Cape Verde Islands.**

---

* 53 Geo. III., cap. 155.

† Court Minutes, 22nd September 1813.

‡ Marine Records, Miscellaneous, No. 25.

§ Court Minutes, 29th April 1814.

‖ "History of Merchant Shipping," W. S. Lindsay. Vol. IV., p. 339.

¶ Court Minutes, 12th and 26th March 1834.

** Lancaster's voyages. *See* Hakluyt Society's Publication No. LVI.

In 1611 the Company's fleet, under command of Captain Saris,* proceeded to Japan and settled a Company's factory at Firando. In the same year a Portuguese Frigate was captured by Captain Downton off Surat.†

On the 29th November 1612 the Company's fleet, under the command of Captain Thomas Best, engaged the Portuguese fleet off Surat, consisting of four galleons and twenty-six frigates, in two separate actions, when the Portuguese were defeated with great loss.‡

1616. On the 16th August a fleet under Captain Benjamin Joseph encountered a big Portuguese carrack off the Comoro Islands, which he fought for three days, after which she was run ashore and burnt. In this engagement Captain Joseph was killed.§

1618. On the 23rd December an English fleet, under Sir Thomas Dale, engaged the Dutch off Jakatra, and captured their ship the "Black Lion," which was accidentally burnt on the 28th idem. The fight was renewed on the 1st March following, when the Dutch fleet sought safety in flight.‖

1620. An outward bound fleet, under Captain Andrew Shilling, entered Saldanha Bay, and took possession of the country in the name of King James, by a proclamation of the 3rd July. In November and December following Captain Shilling fought two battles, off Jask, with a Portuguese fleet under Ruy Freere de Andrade; the former of which was indecisive, but in the latter Captain Shilling defeated his opponent, but he died shortly afterwards from the effects of a wound he received in the second engagement.¶

1622. A fleet consisting of five ships and four pinnaces, under the command of Captains Blithe and Weddell, defeated a Portuguese fleet off Ormuz, and captured that island in co-operation with the Persian army. In this engagement the Portuguese Admiral, Ruy Freere de Andrade, was taken prisoner.**

1625. Eight strong Portuguese galleons were well beaten off Ormuz by four English and four Dutch vessels, with the loss of 60 English and Dutch, but upwards of 500 Portuguese.††

1653. On the 24th March two English ships fell in with three Dutch vessels at the entrance to the Gulf of Persia. The next day a hot engagement took place, which lasted for eight hours, after which one of the English ships, the "Blessing," was boarded and captured. The other, the "Supply," meanwhile endeavoured to escape, but, being hard pressed, ran ashore, and struck her colours.‡‡

1670. At Japarra, three Dutch ships endeavoured to capture the Company's vessel "Zant," Captain Parrick, and gave her a broadside; but the "Zant" replied and sank the biggest of them, whereupon the other two sailed away.§§

1673. On the 22nd August a fleet of ten of the Company's ships engaged a superior force of 22 Dutch vessels in Pettapoli Bay, when after a stout fight of several hours, some of the English ships were disabled and obliged to retire, and others were captured by the Dutch.‖‖

---

* Marine Records, No. XIV.

† Purchas his Pilgrims, Vol. I., p. 295.

‡ O. C., Vol. I., No. 102. Journal of the "Oseander," Hakluyt Society's Publications, No. LVI.

§ Purchas his Pilgrims, Vol. I., p. 554.

‖ Purchas his Pilgrims, Vol. I., p. 620; O. C., Vol. VI., Nos. 718 and 784.

¶ Marine Records, No. XXX.

** Marine Records, No. XXXIV. (In this journal, which is defective, several important events are missing.) O. C., Vol. VIII., No. 1032; Vol. IX., No. 1076.

†† O. C., Vol. XI., No. 1217.

‡‡ O. C., Vol. XXIII., No. 2335.

§§ O. C., Vol. XXXIV., No. 3859.

‖‖ O. C., Vol. XXXIV, Nos. 3834, 3835, 3836, 3843, 3846, 3857, 3858.

25005. e

1692. On the 3rd February the Company's ship "Samuel," Captain William Freke, fell in with the French vessel "L'Escueist" off the Cape of Good Hope, when an engagement ensued, but the latter was both larger and a better sailer than the "Samuel." Captain Freke, however, fought until his masts were carried by the board, when he was obliged to yield. The French plundered the ship and then obliged the Captain to give a bond for 200*l.* for her ransom.*

1703. On the 8th December the ship "Canterbury" fell in with two French ships of war in the straits of Malacca. These she fought on that day and the next, but was at last obliged to yield, and was taken by the captors to Pondicherry as a prize.†

1746. Nine French ships, under the command of M. Labourdinaies, Governor of Mauritius, met an East India Company's squadron off Negapatam, about the 25th June, when an engagement ensued, which resulted in the flight of the French fleet.‡

1757. The Company's ships "Suffolk," "Houghton," and "Godolphin" fell in with two French frigates off the Cape on the 9th March, and after a smart action beat them off. The Court of Directors highly commended the conduct of the commanders, officers, and crews upon this occasion, and each ship received a gratuity of 2,000*l.* These ships were commanded by Captain Wilson, who was made commander of all the Company's ships, and appointed to the "William Pitt," in which ship he discovered Pitt's Straits in 1759.§

1757. At the recapture of Fort William many of the Company's ships were employed, and in some instances the crews were engaged on shore.‖

1759. On the 15th and 16th May, the Company's ship "Hardwicke" fought an action with two French vessels off Masulipatam.¶ On the 24th November the Dutch, with four frigates of thirty-six guns each, two frigates of twenty-six guns each, and another ship mounting sixteen guns, with crews of fifteen hundred men on board, attempted to capture the British possessions in Bengal; but they were driven back, and captured by the Company's ships "Calcutta," "Duke of Dorset," and "Hardwicke," the commanders of which vessels were subsequently rewarded by the Court.**

On the 26th November in the same year, the Company's ships "Royal George" and "Oxford" intercepted and captured three Dutch ships and three sloops off Calpee.††

1760. On the 31st January the Company's ship "Shaftesbury" stood into Madras Roads, in defiance of two French ships there blockading the town, who attacked her, but, succeeding in beating them off, she then embarked a detachment of troops, and proceeded to St. Thomas, where she engaged and beat off a French frigate. The captain, officers, and crew of the "Shaftesbury" were warmly commended for their gallant conduct on this occasion, and received a reward from the Court.‡‡

1763. The Company's ship "Winchelsea" fought a French frigate single-handed in January off the Hughli river and beat her off, for which her commander, Captain Thomas Howe received the thanks of the Court.§§

---

* O. C., Vol. XLIX., No. 5801.

† O. C., Vol. LVIII., No. 7960.

‡ St. Helena Records, 4th February 1746–47, Vol. XII.

§ Marine Records, 438 H; 397 C and D; and 594 H. Also Court Minutes, 5th October 1757.

‖ Marine Records, 322 C; East Indies, Vol. 2; Bengal Letters Received, Vol. 3.

¶ Marine Records, 568 F.

** Marine Records, 568 F; 308 A; 612 H. Court Minutes, 19th February 1762.

†† Marine Records, 588 D and 17 E.

‡‡ Marine Records, 610 G. Court Minutes, 19th February 1762.

§§ Marine Records, 4 E. Court Minutes, 28rd December 1763.

1779. The Company's ship "Bridgewater" fought an American privateer of superior force on the 8th March, on her way from St. Helena towards England, and beat her off, for which the crew received a reward of 2,000*l*. from the Court of Directors.*

1793. The Company's ships "Triton," "Royal Charlotte," and "Warley," in company with H.M.S. "Minerva," were employed in the blockade of Pondicherry, in July and August, and assisted at the capture of that place.†

1794. The Company's ship "Pigot" fought a gallant action at Bencoolen on the 7th February, with three French frigates, but had to yield to superior force.‡ During this year the Company's ships "William Pitt," "Britannia," and "Houghton," under Commodore Mitchell (who was knighted for his services on this occasion), cruised in the Indian seas as men-of-war for the protection of commerce. They captured two large privateers, and defeated a French squadron of two frigates, a brig of war, and an armed ship. §

1795. When the great expedition was ordered for the West Indies, application was made to the Company for assistance, and fourteen of the Company's ships were fitted out immediately, and others sold to Government and equipped as line-of-battle ships.‖

An expedition was fitted out at St. Helena, consisting of the Company's ships "Goddard," "Manship," "Hawkesbury," "Airly Castle," "Asia," "Essex," and "Busbridge," which proceeded to cruise to windward of the island, where they intercepted and captured a valuable fleet of nine Dutch Indiamen.¶

In the same year, the Company's ships "Bombay Castle," "Exeter," and "Brunswick," were fitted out as men-of-war at Bombay, and assisted in taking the Cape of Good Hope.**

1797. When, upon the outbreak of the mutiny at the Nore, the Court of Directors called upon their officers to serve on board His Majesty's ships for the defence of the river, the request was promptly and zealously answered by the maritime service at large.††

Commodore Farquharson, of the Company's service, on the "Alfred," with a fleet of their ships, fell in with a powerful French squadron of men-of-war on the 29th January; the Indiamen immediately formed the line of battle, and gave chase to the enemy, who crowded all sail, and was soon out of sight. This bold manœuvre saved a valuable fleet to the Company and to the nation.‡‡

1798. This year the Company's ships "Royal Charlotte," "Cuffnells," "Phœnix," and "Alligator," assisted H.M. ships "La Pomone," "Argo," and "Cormorant" in convoying a large fleet of merchantmen and transports to Lisbon. On the 25th of September they fell in with a French fleet of nine sail, consisting of one eighty-gun ship and eight frigates. The signal was made for the Company's ships to form the line with those of His Majesty's, and the convoy were ordered to push for Lisbon. This manœuvre, and the warlike appearance of the Indiamen, deterred the French admiral from attacking them, so that the whole fleet reached Lisbon in safety.§§

1799. The Company's ships "Earl Howe" and "Princess Charlotte," which had been equipped for offensive service by order of the Governor General, received

---

* Marine Records, 42 G. Court Minutes, 10th June 1779.
† Marine Records, 366 K; 150 L; and 182 B.
‡ Marine Records, 503 I.
§ Marine Records, 184 D; 285 RR.
‖ Court Minutes, 19th and 26th August, 4th and 16th September 1795.
¶ Marine Records, 363 D; 331 C; 229 P; and 24 I.
** Marine Records, 125 G; 138 F; 349 C.
†† Court Minutes, 7th and 21st June 1797.
‡‡ Marine Records, 140 H.
§§ Marine Records, 150 O; 178 B; 175 F.

instructions on the 6th January from H.M.S. "Victorious" to cruise between the Palmyra Rocks and Pigeon Island. The commander and officers having received commissions from Government, they were occupied in this service until the close of the year.*

1800. The French frigate "Médée" was taken by the Company's ships "Exeter" and "Bombay."† In the same year a gallant defence was made by the Company's ship "Kent" against the "Confiance" of twenty-six guns, commanded by the celebrated Surcoufe, and though the "Kent" was captured, it was only after having lost her commander and twenty-two men killed and thirty-four wounded; the action lasted nearly two hours.‡

On the 27th of June the Company's ship "Arniston," Captain Campbell Marjoribanks, having just anchored at Bencoolen, was attacked by an armed vessel flying French colours, supposed to be a privateer. The "Arniston" promptly cut her cable, gave chase, and fired several broadsides into her; but, outsailing the "Arniston," by beating to windward, she escaped after a chase of several hours.§

On the 10th November the Company's ship "Phœnix," Captain Moffat, captured a French privateer, the "General Malartie," carrying sixteen guns and one hundred and twenty men.‖

1804. The Company's homeward bound China fleet (with a number of country ships and whalers under protection), having no men-of-war in company, on the 14th February, fell in with the French Admiral Linois, in the "Marengo," eighty-four gun ship, "Semillante," forty guns, "Belle Poule," forty guns, a corvette of twenty-eight guns, and a brig of eighteen guns. The enemy being to windward, Commodore Dance, at the suggestion of Captain Timins, made the general signal to tack. The Indiamen then stood towards the French fleet, engaged them during the two following days, and eventually defeated, and chased them out of sight.¶ Commodore Dance was knighted, and various rewards were distributed among the captains, officers, and seamen.** In the same year the Company's ships "Lord Castlereagh" and "Lady Castlereagh" were fitted out and cruised in the Bay of Bengal for the protection of trade.††

In that year also the Company's ship "Preston" acted as guardship at Kedgeree.‡‡

In 1805 the Company's ships "Earl Camden" and "Wexford" were fitted out in Bombay Harbour, and cruised in the Indian seas for the protection of trade.§§ On the 7th August the "Cumberland," Captain Farrer, under convoy of Sir Thomas Troubridge, received and returned several broadsides, within pistol shot, from the French line-of-battle ship "Marengo," and from a large frigate, her consort.‖‖

In 1806 the Company's ship "Warren Hastings" fought a most gallant action against the French frigate "Piémontaise," and although at last captured, the enemy hauled off several times during the action, which lasted for four hours.¶¶

In 1810 the Company's ships and seamen were employed at the taking of the Isle of France***; and, on the 4th July, the Company's ship "Astell," in company with the

* Marine Records, 203 B, 245 B.
† Marine Records, 138 I.
‡ Court Minutes, 14th April 1801.
§ Marine Records, 149 C.
‖ Marine Records, 175 G.
¶ Marine Records, 303 A, 17 J.
** Court Minutes, 15th August 1804.
†† Marine Records, 188 A, 197 A.
‡‡ Marine Records, 307 C.
§§ Marine Records, 303 B, 173 B.
‖‖ Marine Records, 202 B.
¶¶ Court Minutes, 22rd December 1806.
*** Court Minutes, 8th March 1811.

"Ceylon" and "Windham," was gallantly defended against a very superior force, of two French frigates and a corvette, and escaped, in consequence of the crippled state of her opponents, but her two consorts were captured by the enemy.*

F. C. Danvers,
Registrar and Superintendent of Records.

India Office,
31st March 1896.

* Marine Records, 12 A.

MARINE RECORDS.

Section I.

JOURNALS, &c., OF VOYAGES, 1605—1701.

Journal begins.	Ship.	Captain.	Journal ends.	Ledger or Receipt Book.	Reference Number.	Remarks.
1605 July 31	Ascension - -	Roger Stiles -	1605 Aug. 4	—	I	Journal kept in the second voyage.
1606 May 12	Hopewell - -	John Knight	1606 June 26	—	II	Journal of an attempt to find the North-West Passage.
1607 Mar. 3	Dragon - - -	William Keeling -	1607 April 17	—	III	Fragment of a journal kept in the third voyage by Captain Keeling.
Mar. 4	Hector - -	William Hawkins -	1608 Mar. 12	—	IV	Journal kept in the third voyage. (Portion from 1st Sept. 1607 to 18th Feb. 1608 is missing.)
Mar. 8	Dragon - -	William Keeling -	June 19	—	V	Another journal kept in the third voyage.
Mar. 12	Dragon - -	William Keeling -	1609 Oct. 5	—	VI	Précis of Captain Keeling's journal kept in the third voyage.
Mar. 14	Ascension - -	Alexander Sharpeigh	Aug. 26	—	VII	Journal kept in the fourth voyage.
1608 July 17	Hector - -	William Hawkins -	1608 Aug. 19	—	VIII	Fragment of a journal kept in the third voyage.
1610 April 1	Peppercorn - -	Nicholas Downton -	1611 Jan. 29	—	IX	Journal kept in the sixth voyage.
April 4	Trades Increase and afterwards Peppercorn - -	Sir Henry Middleton Nicholas Downton.	1613 Nov. 19	—	X	Journal kept by Thomas Love in the sixth voyage.
April 19	Peppercorn -	Nicholas Downton	Nov. 19	—	XI	Journal kept by Nicholas Downton in the sixth voyage.
Nov. 15	Trades Increase -	Sir Henry Middleton	1612 Dec. 22	—	XII	Journal kept in the sixth voyage.
1611 Jan. 5	Globe - -	Peter Williamson Floris.	1615 Feb. 17	—	XIII	Translation of Floris's journal in the seventh voyage.
April 3	Clove - - -	John Saris - -	1613 Nov. 17	—	XIV	Journal kept by Captain Saris in the eighth voyage.
1612 Feb. 1	Dragon - -	Thomas Best -	1614 June 15	—	XV	Journal kept by Captain Best in the tenth voyage.
Feb. 8	Hoseander -	Thomas Aldworth -	1613 Aug. 29	—	XVI	Journal kept by Ralph Crosse in the tenth voyage; with copies of wills, accounts, &c.
Feb. 9	Peppercorn - -	Nicholas Downton -	1612 April 13	—	XVII	Abstract of part of Captain Downton's journal in the sixth voyage.
Aug. 31	Hoseander - -	Thomas Aldworth	1613 April 12	—	XVIII	Extracts from a journal kept in the tenth voyage.*
1614 Feb. 25	New Year's Gift -	Nicholas Downton	1615 Nov. —	—	XIX	Journal kept by Edward Dodsworth in the second joint stock voyage; with various notes at end.
Feb. 28	Hector - - - and afterwards Clove.	William Edwardes -	1617 June 15	—	XX	Journal kept by John Monden in the second joint stock voyage.

* XVIII also contains:—(1.) Directions for a voyage to India, based on the journals of the tenth voyage; (2.) Notes based apparently on the journal of the "Lyon" in the second joint stock voyage; (3.) Extracts from the journal of Alex. Child, Master of the "James," 11th March 1616 to 20th July 1617; (4.) Copy of a "Rutter" or sailing directions [by John Davis, of Limehouse]; (5.) Notes on soundings, &c., in the English Channel.

Journal begins.	Ship.	Captain.	Journal ends.	Ledger or Receipt Book.	Reference Number.	Remarks.
1614 Mar. 9	New Year's Gift	Nicholas Downton	1614 Sept. 14	—	XXI	Another journal of the voyage; with draft of a letter to England, dated 27th February 1615.
1615 April 20	Clove	Jas. Foster (Master)	1617 June 19	—	XXII	Journal of a voyage to Bantam and back, kept by John Borden.
July 10	Hoseander	Ralph Coppingall	1616 April 26	—	XXIII	Journal of a voyage from Patani to Firando and thence to Bantam.
Dec. 7	Sea Adventure	William Adams	Oct. 22	—	XXIV	Journal by Edmund Sayers of a voyage from Firando to Siam and back, &c.
1616 Mar. 11	James	Alex. Child (Master)	1617 July 20	—	XVIII	Journal of a voyage from Swally to Jask and back.
1617 Mar. 5	Bull	Martin Pring	1618 Dec. 29	—	XXV	Journal kept by Robert Adams.
Mar. 20	Captain Adams' junk ("Sea Adventure"?)	William Adams	1619 Jan. 8	—	XXVI	Journals kept by Edmund Sayers of two voyages from Firando to Cochin China and back; with notes of events in Firando from 23rd Aug. 1618 to 8th Jan. 1619.
1618 July 25	Moon	Sir Thomas Dale	1618 Nov. 5	—	XXVII	Journal of Richard Bragge.
Oct. 30	Expedition	John Rowe	1619 Jan. 10	—	XXVIII	Journal of a voyage from Surat to Jask and back.
1619 Mar. 21	Charles	John Bickell	1624 June 16	—	XXIX	Journal of a voyage from England to Surat, Jask, &c., and back to England, kept by Henry Crosby.
1620 Feb. 4	Roebuck	Richard Swan (Master).	1622 June 7	—	XXX	Journal of a voyage to the East Indies and back, kept by Richard Swan.
Mar. 18	Exchange	Richard Swanley	1624 June 24	—	XXXI	Journal kept by Richard Swanley, while his ship was attached to the Fleet of Defence.
Mar. 25	London	Andrew Shillinge	1622 June 13	—	XXXII	Journal of a voyage to Surat and back, kept by Archibald Jennison.
1621 Jan. 14	Lesser James	John Wood (master)	1621 May 27	—	XXXIII	Journal of a voyage from London to the Cape, kept by John Wood.
Mar. 19	Jonas	John Weddell	1623 July 22	—	XXXIV	Journal of a voyage to Surat and back, kept by Richard Swanley.
Nov. 23	Palsgrave	-	1622 Sept. 5	—	XXXV	Journal of a cruise in the Fleet of Defence; and of two subsequent voyages.
1622 Feb. 6	Hart	John Bickley	1626 Oct. 17	—	XXXVI	Journal of a voyage to the East Indies and back, kept by John Bickley.
Feb. 25	Hart	John Bickley	Sept. 17	—	XXXVII	Journal of a voyage to the East Indies and back, kept by Andrew Symms.
Mar. 25	Elizabeth	E. Lennyes	1623 Nov. 7	—	XXXVIII	Journal of a voyage from Jacatra to Acheen and back.
Dec. 24	Bull	-	1624 Jan. 27	—	XXXV	Journal of a voyage from Japan to Batavia.
1624 Feb. 22	Anne Royal	-	April 11	—	XXXV	Journal of a voyage from Batavia homewards (unfinished).
Mar. 27	Royal James	John Weddell	1626 Oct. 17	—	XXXIX	Journal of a voyage from London to the East Indies and back, kept by Robert Fox.

Journal begins.	Ship.	Captain.	Journal ends.	Ledger or Receipt Book.	Reference Number.	Remarks.
1624 Mar. 27	Royal James -	John Weddell -	1626 Oct. 17	—	XL	Journal kept by Richard Monck, of a voyage from London to the East Indies and back; with an account of a fight between Captain Weddell's fleet (together with four Dutch ships) and a Portuguese fleet, in the Persian Gulf. Also, minutes of consultations held on board from 2nd April 1624 to 25th April 1625.
Mar. 27	Eagle - and afterwards Scout -	- Nathl. Best (Master).	April 7	—	XLI	Journal of a voyage from London to Surat and thence to Gombroon and back, kept by William Meyner.
1625 Mar. 5	Falcon - and afterwards Royal James	Richard Blyth - John Weddell.	Oct. 19	—	XLII	Journal kept by Francis Pinder, of a voyage from London to Surat, thence to Persia and back, and then to England.
1626 April 7	Discovery -	John Johnson (Master).	1628 Nov. 14	—	XLIII	Journal kept by John Vian, of a voyage from London to various ports in the East Indies and back.
April 7	Discovery - and afterwards Hart -	John Johnson (Master) and Andw. Evans (Master)	1629 Dec. 18	—	XLIV	Journal of the same voyage, kept by David Davies.
April 16	William -	Chris. Browne -	Feb. 14	—	XLV	Journal kept by Andrew Warden, of a voyage from London to various ports in the East Indies and back.
1627 Feb. 24	Hopewell - and afterwards Star -	R. Malim - Andrew Evans (Master).	July 12	—	XLVI	Journal kept by Abraham Sayers in the "Hopewell" outwards, and homewards in the "Star."
Mar. 2	Hart - - and afterwards Royal Mary.	Barth. Goodall	1628 Oct. 4	—	XLVII	Journal kept by Edward Austin from London to various ports in the East Indies.
Mar. 2	Hart - - and afterwards Hopewell	Barth. Goodall* John Pashley.	1629 July 5	—	XLVIII	Journal kept by John Pashley from London to Surat.
July 20	Royal Mary and afterwards Hart and Hopewell -	- - John Pashley.	1630 Jan. 12	—	XLIX	Journal kept by Peter Andrewes from Table Bay to Surat, and thence, after various cruises, back to England.
1628 Mar. 6	Expedition - - and afterwards Hopewell - -	- - - John Pashley.	1629 Dec. 18	—	L	Journal kept by Daniel Hall, of a voyage from London to Surat, thence to Persia and back, and so to England.
May 22	Refuge and afterwards Falcon and Royal Mary.	- -	Nov. 6	—	LI	Journal kept by John Graunt from Bantam to England.
1629 Mar. 25	Discovery - -	John Bickell (or Bickley).	1631 Dec. 16	—	LII	Journal kept by John Vian, of a voyage from London to Surat, Persia, &c., and back to England.
April 10	Charles -	John Weddell -	1630 Nov. 17	—	LIII	Journal kept by Nicholas Sharpe, of a voyage from London to Surat, thence to Persia and back, and then towards England.
April 10	Charles - -	John Weddell - -	1631 April 7	—	LIV	Journal kept by Nicholas Prin, of a voyage from London to Surat, thence to Persia, &c., and back to England.
1630 Mar. 1	William - -	Mathew Wills -	1633 Aug. 6	—	LV	Journal kept by Geo. Marriatt, of a voyage from London to Surat, Persia, &c., and back to England.

* On 3rd October 1627 Captain Goodall died. He was succeeded by Andrew Evans, Master of the "Star," R. Malim, Captain of the "Hopewell," being transferred to the "Star." John Pashley was then appointed Master of the "Hopewell," and the Journal is continued on the "Hopewell" from 13th October.

Journal begins.	Ship.	Captain.	Journal ends.	Ledger or Receipt Book.	Reference Number.	Remarks.
1630 Mar. 16	Blessing - -	- - -	1633 April 30	—	LVI	Journal kept by Andrew Warden, of a voyage from London to Surat, &c., and back to England.
1631 Mar. 14	Jonah and afterwards Exchange. -	- -	Aug. -	—	LVII	Journal of (1) a voyage from Gravesend to Surat, touching at Madagascar, Mohilla, Johanna, Jask, and Gombroon; and (2) a voyage on the West Coast of Sumatra, and thence towards Bantam.
Aug. 18	Blessing - - -	- -	April 30	—	LVIII	Journal of a voyage from Poullambin Point (west end of Java) to Surat, thence to Persia and back, and on to England.
1633 Mar. 1	Discovery - - and afterwards London.	Richard Allnutt -	1637 July 18	—	LIX	Journal kept by Wm. Speare, of a voyage from London to Persia, thence to Surat, and thence after various cruises to Bantam.
Mar. 7	Palsgrave - - and afterwards Discovery - -	John Hall - Richard Allnutt.	Jan. 31	—	LX	Journal kept by Richard Forder, of a voyage from London to Gombroon and Surat, and after various cruises back to London.
1634 Jan. 24	Coaster - - and afterwards Jewel.	John Barnes - -	Dec. 7	—	LXI	Journal kept by John Mucknell, of a voyage from London to Bantam, in the "Coaster," and back to England in the "Jewel."
1636 Mar. 18	Mary -	James Slade -	1640 Jan. 13	—	LXII	Journal kept by Wm. Bayley, of a voyage from London to Surat, and thence, after various cruises, back to England.
1637 April 6	[Dragon ?] - -	John Weddell - -	1638 Feb. 4	—	LXIII	Portion of journal of the voyage of Capt. Weddell's fleet (belonging to Courten's Association) to Acheen, Macao, and Canton, and as far as Acheen on the return voyage.
1639 Mar. 12	London - -	Mathew Wills	1640 July 17	—	LXIV	Journal kept by James Birkedell, of a voyage from England to Surat, and thence, after a voyage to Persia, back again to England.
1641 Dec. 10	Hopewell -	- - -	1644 June 7	—	LXV	Journal of a voyage from London to the Coromandel Coast, and then, after various cruises, back again to England.
1644 April 26	Hinde -	William Broadbent -	June 22	—	LXV	Journal of a voyage from Surat to Malacca, on the way to Macao.
April 26	Hinde - - -	William Broadbent -	1645 Feb. 8	—	LXVI	Journal kept by Richard Mathew, of a voyage from Surat to Malacca and Macao and back.
1645 Feb. 11	Eagle -	Thomas Stevens -	1646 May 28	—	LXVII	Journal kept by Antony Fenn, of a voyage from London to Surat, and back to England.
Sept. 25	Falcon - -	-	1649 Oct. 26	—	LXV	Notes of goods received on board the "Falcon," in various cruises in the East Indies.
1660 Feb. 25	Concord - -	Roger Kilvert -	1663 Feb. 19	—	LXVIII	Journal kept by Ralph Hodgkines, of a voyage from London to the Coromandel Coast; and from Balasore to Masulipatam and Madras, and thence to England.

Journal begins.	Ship.	Captain.	Journal ends.	Ledger or Receipt Book.	Reference Number.	Remarks.
1661 April 12	London	R. Bowen -	1663 April 23	—	LXIX	Journal kept by Edward Newell of a voyage from England to Bantam, and thence, after a voyage to Polcroon, &c., back to England.
1662 Jan. 29	- -	-	1662 July 10	—	LXX	Journal of a voyage from Bantam to London.
1672 Aug. 24	London -	Wm. Basse -	1674 July 27	—	LXXI	Journal kept by Wm. Basse of a voyage from England to Masulipatam and Madras, thence to Bombay, &c., and back to England.
1674 July 3	Bull -	[John Hallwell ?]	1675 Feb. 7	—	LXXII	Journal kept by John Hallwell of a voyage from Bantam to Manilla and back.
1676 Feb. 7	Triplokaine - -	- - -	1676 Sept. 1	—	LXXIII	Journal kept by John Stead of a voyage from Madras to Bantam and back.
Oct. 11	Bull - -	[John Hallwell ?] -	1677 Dec. 1	—	LXXII	Journal kept by John Hallwell of a voyage from Bantam to Malacca and Madras, and back to Bantam.
1677 Feb. 3	Suratt Merchant -	Francis Johnson -	Sept. 18	—	LXXIII	Journal kept by John Stead of a voyage from Madras to England.
1678 June 21	Flying Eagle	John Shaw - -	1679 Jan. 26	—	LXXIV	Journal of a voyage from Bantam to Amoy and back.
1679 Sept. 11	Flying Eagle -	- - -	1680 Mar. 28	—	LXXIV	Journal of a voyage from Bantam to Siam.
Nov. 14	President -	Jonathan Hide -	1682 Jan. 13	—	LXXV	Journal of a voyage from England to Fort St. George, Masulipatam, &c., and from Madras back to England.
1680 June 21	Formosa -	- -	1680 Dec. 10	—	LXXIV	Journal of a voyage from Bantam to Tonquin and back.
Aug. 30	Barnardiston - -	John Slade - -	1682 Jan. 18	—	LXXVI	Journal kept by Thomas Parramoer, mate, of a voyage from England to Bantam and back.
1681 Jan. 4	Persia Merchant -	John Bowers -	Feb. 10	—	LXXVII	Journal of a voyage from England to Bantam and back.
Jan. 27	Recovery - -	[John Hallwell ?] -	1681 Sept. 30	—	LXXII	Journal kept by John Hallwell of a voyage from Balasore to Gombroon and Muscat, and back.
1682 Jan. 14	Recovery - -	[John Hallwell ?] -	1682 Aug. 13	—	LXXII	Journal kept by John Hallwell of a voyage from Balasore to the Maldive Islands and back.
Oct. 19	Carolina - -	John Harding	1683 Sept. 3	—	LXXVIII	Journal of a voyage from England to Batavia, Macao, and other East Indian ports.
1683 Feb. 6	Susanna - -	[John Hallwell ?]	June 25	—	LXXII	Journal kept by John Hallwell of a voyage from Balasore towards England.
Feb. 9	Herbert - -	Henry Udall -	1684 July 23	—	LXXIX	Journal kept by Edmund Uvedale of a voyage from England to the Bay of Bengal and back.
June 15	Massingberd - -	Jos. Haddock	Dec. 22	—	LXXX	Journal kept by Jos. Haddock of a voyage from England to Surat and back.
1685 July 24	Loyal Adventure -	William Goodlad -	1688 April 27	R. B. only.	LXXXI	This ship was lost off Madras on 8 Oct., 1687. *See Cuddalore Consultations*, 13 Oct. 1687.

Journal begins.	Ship.	Captain.	Journal ends.	Ledger or Receipt Book.	Reference Number.	Remarks.
1685 Nov. 12	Herbert - -	Henry Udall - -	1685 Dec. 8	—	LXXIX	Journal kept by Edmund Uvedale of a voyage from London to Sumatra (commencement only).
1686 June 17	Berkeley Castle -	— Consett -	1690 May 30	—	LXXXII	Journal kept by Philip Leigh of a voyage from England to various ports in India, a voyage to Persia and back, and then to England.
Sept. 11	Bengal Merchant	William Perse -	1688 May 8	--	LXXXIII	Journal kept by Wm. Perse of a voyage from England to Bombay and Madras.
Dec. 10	Charles the Second	-	1690 June 19	R. B. only.	LXXXIV	——
1688 Jan. 11	Persia Merchant	Benj. Brangwin -	May 15	R. B. only.	LXXXV	This ship was blown up at Fort St. George.
May 6	Royal James -	Richd. Cook -	1689 Mar. 20	--	LXXXVI	Journal of a voyage from Madras to Sumatra and thence to England.
June 23	John and Rachel -	Robert Fox -	1688 Oct. 1	—	LXXXVII	Journal kept by Nathaniel Ball of a voyage to look for some of the Company's ships expected home.
Sept. 8	Mary - -	Stephen Barber -	1689 Sept. 16	R. B. only.	LXXXVIII	——
1689 Jan. 26	John and Rachel -	Robert Fox -	April 1	—	LXXXVII	Journal kept by Nathaniel Ball of a voyage in search of some of the Company's ships expected home.
Feb. 4	Chandos	John Bonnell	1691 Jan. 1	—	LXXXIX	Journal of a voyage from England to Madras and back.
Feb. 25	Defence - -	Wm. Heath	Sept. 16	—	XC	Journal of a voyage from England to Madras, thence to Macao and back, then to Indrapur, and from Bencoolen to England.
May 30	Princess of Denmark -	[Jos. Haddock] -	1690 Mar. 4	—	LXXX	Journal kept by Jos. Haddock of a voyage from Madras to China and back.
1692 Nov. 10	Elizabeth - -	Benj. Brangwin -	1694 Mar. 23	R. B. only.	XCI	This ship was taken by the French.
1693 Oct. 11	Hawke	James Caulier	1695 Feb. 26	R. B. only.	XCII	——
Nov. 14	Princess of Denmark	John Blewet -	Mar. 28	R. B. only.	XCIII	——
Dec. 12	Resolution -	Abrm. Roberts	Sept. 10	R. B. only.	XCIV	This ship was taken by the French.
Dec. 23	Samuel - -	John Willson - -	Feb. 9	—	XCV	Journal of a voyage from Vizagapatam and Madras to England.
1694 Feb. 1	Nassau -	John Lloyd - -	1696 Mar. 3	—	XCVI	Journal of a voyage from England to Gombroon, Bombay and Surat, and back towards England.
Oct. 13	Benjamin	John Browne -	1698 Jan. 27	—	XCVII	Journal of a voyage from St. Jago to Bombay and other East Indian ports, and back from Bombay to England.
1695 Mar. 15	America - -	Rich. Laycock	1697 Oct. 27	--	LXXII	Journal of a voyage from England to Bombay and Ceylon and back.
Mar. 28	Russell	Wm. Blundell -	Oct. 27	—	XCVIII	Journal of a voyage from England to several ports in Madras and Bengal, from Bengal to Cadiz, and thence to England under convoy.

Journal begins.	Ship.	Captain.	Journal ends.	Ledger or Receipt Book.	Reference Number.	Remarks.
1695 June 18	Tonqueen Merchant -	Page Keeble -	1695 Sept. 12	R. B. only.	XCIX	——
June 26	Defence - -	Wm. Heath -	July 16	R. B. only.	C	——
Nov. 6	Hawke -	John Clarke -	1697 Nov. 30	R. B. only.	CI	——
Nov. 23	Scepter -	Geo. Phenney -	June 1	—	CII	Journal of a voyage from England to Bombay, and thence to Mocha.
Nov. 23	Chambers -	Thos. South - -	1699 June 7	—	CIII	Journal of a voyage from England to Bombay, Surat, Madras, and Mocha, and back from Bombay to England.
Nov. 21	Charles the Second -	John Dorrill -	1698 July 28	—	CIV	Journal of a voyage from England to Ceylon and along the Malabar Coast to Persia; various voyages between Gombroon, Bombay, Muscat, and Surat, and from Bombay back to England.
1696 Jan. 23	Sidney -	Wm. Gyfford -	July 14	—	CV	Journal of a voyage from London to Madras and Bengal, and thence back to England.
Feb. 9	Madras Merchant -	Benjamin Prickman -	April 27	—	CVI	Journal of a voyage from England to Fort St. George, Vizagapatam, Bencoolen, and other East Indian ports and back towards England.
Feb. 12	Sampson	Wm. Erle	Aug. 6	—	CVII	Journal of a voyage from England to Madras, Vizagapatam, and Calcutta, and back to England.
Sept. 4	Madras Merchant -	Benjamin Prickman -	Sept. 20	—	CVIII	Journal of a voyage from England to Madras, Vizagapatam, Acheen, and Priaman.
1697 Jan. 8	Amity - -		June 5	—	CIX	Journal of a voyage from England to the Cape of Good Hope, thence to Bencoolen, and back to England.
Jan. 28	Madras Merchant -	Benjamin Prickman -	Sept. 16	—	CX	Journal of a voyage from the Cape of Good Hope to Johanna, Fort St. George, Cuddalore, Vizagapatam, Sumatra, and Bencoolen, and back to England.
Feb. 1	Fame - -	Robert Betton -	1699 June 27	—	CXI	Journal of a voyage from England to Madras and Fort St. David, and then from Madras back to England. Kept by John Conaway, 1st Mate.
Mar. 21	Thomas -	- -	Dec. 28	—	CXII	Journal of a voyage from England to Bombay and back.
April —	- and Two Brothers -	- John [Best ?].	Jan. 26	—	CXIII	Journal of a voyage to Boston and back via Newfoundland.
1698 Oct. 1	Thorndon -	Wm. Petre -	Dec. 3	R. B. only.	CXIV	——
Oct. 15	Josiah - - -	Rich. Stratton -	1700 Oct. 16	—	CXV	Journal of a voyage from England to Balasore and Pipli and back. Apparently kept by Charles Hill.
Oct. 20	Fleet - -	John Merry - -	1701 Feb. 3	—	CXVI	Journal kept by John Merry, of a voyage from England to Batavia and Amoy, and back to England.

Journal begins.	Ship.	Captain.	Journal ends.	Ledger or Receipt Book.	Reference Number.	Remarks.
1698 Oct. 26	Benjamin	John Brown	1700 Sept. 30	—	XCVII	Journal of a voyage from England to Fort St. George (touching at Cadiz) and of return voyage to England.
Nov. 19	Sidney	Caleb Grantham	July 22	—	CXVII	Journal of a voyage from England to Balasore and Pipli and back.
Dec. 15	London	George Mathew	1701 Aug. 1	— L.	CXVIII CXVIIIA	Journal of a voyage from England to Masulipatam, Balasore, &c., and back to England.
—	Degrave	Wm. Young	1700 Aug. 22	L. only.	CXIX	——
1699 Jan. 1	Antelope	Henry Hammond	1701 May 12	—	CXX	Journal of a voyage from England to Bengal and back.
Jan. 14	Neptune	John Lesly	1700 April 23	—	CXXI	Journal of a voyage from England to Fort St. George, thence to Masulipatam and back, and then to England.
Feb. 20	Hampshire	Francis Fisher	July 23	—	CXXII	Journal of a voyage to Bombay and back (touching at Cadiz).
Mar. 2	Macclesfield	John Hurle	June 17	—	CXXIII	Journal of a voyage from London to China; with details of transactions at Macao and Canton, kept by Robert Douglas, Supercargo, and his Assistants.
Mar. 6	Bedford	Robt. Hudson	Aug. 6	—	CXXIV	Journal of a voyage from England to Bombay, Surat, Calicut, &c., and from Surat back to England.
Mar. —	Mountague	John Caulier	1703 Jan. 12	L. only.	CXXV	——
April 12	Anna	-	1699 Sept. 1	—	CXXVI	Journal of a voyage from Bengal to England.
April 28	Julia	Chas. Coatsworth	1701 July 10	— L.	CXXVII CXXVIIA	Journal of a voyage from England to Batavia and Banjar, kept by C. Coatsworth.
April —	Norris	J. Allison	1699 Nov. —	L. only.	CXXVIII	——
April —	Norris	J. Allison	1701 April 8	L. and R. B. only.	CXXIX CXXIXA	——
June 1	Gracedieu	James Murvell	1700 Feb. 3	R. B. only.	CXXX	——
July 11	Hurley	Geo. Betteris	1699 Sept. 8	—	CXXXI	Journal of a cruise from Gravesend up and down the English Channel, and back towards London.
July 14	Industry	Nathaniel Grantham	1700 Dec. 26	—	CXIII	Two voyages between England and the Straits of Gibraltar.
Aug. 1	Loyal Merchant	Mathew Lowth	1701 Aug. 13	—	CXXXII	Journal of a voyage from England to Bombay, thence to Surat and back, and from Bombay to England.
Aug. 5	Rooke	George Simmonds	1702 April 11	— L.	CXXXIII CXXXIIIA	Journal of a voyage from England to several ports on the Malabar Coast, from Surat to Amoy and back, to Gombroon and back, and then as far as Ceylon towards England.
Aug. 31	Dorrill	Samuel Hide	1701 Sept. 6	—	CXXXIV	Journal of a voyage from England to Batavia and Amoy and back.
Sept. 1	Scepter	Geo. Phenney	1700 Nov. 30	R. B. only.	CXXXV	——

Journal begins.	Ship.	Captain.	Journal ends.	Ledger or Receipt Book.	Reference Number.	Remarks.
1699 Sept. 1	East India Merchant	John Harris	1700 May 15	R.B. only.	CXXXVI	——
Oct. 7	Trumbal	Henry Duffield	April 29	—	CXXXVII	Journal of a voyage from England to Batavia (towards Banjarmassin), kept by — Landon (?).
Oct. 11	Trumbal	Henry Duffield	1702 July 30	—	CXXXVIII	Journal of a voyage from England to Borneo, several voyages between Borneo, Batavia, and China, and back from Borneo to England, kept by Richard Hooper (?).
Nov. 13	King William	John Braddyll	1701 July 28	—	CXXXIX	Journal of a voyage from England to the Coromandel Coast and back towards England, kept by J. Goodfellow. *See also* CXLIII.
Dec. 15	Tankervell	Charles Newnam	Aug. 15	L. only.	CXL	——
Dec. 26	Sommers	John Douglass	1703 April 6	L. only.	CXLI	Contains also various loose papers, including an account of disposal of dead men's goods.
1700 Jan. 1	China Merchant	Francis Hosier	Feb. 8	L. and R.B. only.	CXLII CXLIIA	——
Jan. 13	King William	John Braddyll	1701 Jan. 22	—	CXLIII	Journal of a voyage from Cadiz to Madras, thence to Masulipatam, &c., and then back towards Madras. *See also* CXXXIX.
Feb. 5	Anna	Francis Nelly	1702 Jan. 31	—	CXLIV	Journal of a voyage from England to Madras and Bengal and back to England. *See also* CXXVI (*infra*).
Mar. 7	Tavistock	Mathew Martin	1701 Nov. 22	—	CXLV	Journal of a voyage from England to Calicut, Bombay, Carwar, and Surat, and from Bombay back to England.
Mar. 14	Anna	Francis Nelly	1700 Aug. 12	—	CXXVI	Journal of a voyage to Madras and Bengal. *See also* CXLIV.
April 20	Martha	Thomas Raynes	1702 May 3	—	CXLVI	Journal of a voyage from England to several ports on the Malabar Coast, from Bombay to Gombroon and back, and then from Bombay to Surat and back. Kept by Samuel Goodman.
June 10	Borneo	Henry Barre	July 31	— L. R.B.	CXLVII CXLVIIA CXLVIIB	Journal of a voyage from England to Batavia and Banjar, with an account of general occurrences whilst in the East Indies.
Sept. 17	Rising Eagle	Benjamin Boucher	July 8	— L. R.B.	CXLVIII CXLVIIIA CXLVIIIB	Journal of a voyage from England to Balasore and other ports, and back to England.
Sept. 21	Seaford	Martin Gardiner	Sept. 17	— R.B.	CXLIX CXLIXA	Journal of a voyage from England to Batavia, Macao, Canton, &c., and back again to England.
Oct. 10	Discovery	John Evans	July 9	— L. R.B.	CL CLA CLB	Journal of a voyage from England to Mocha, Socotra, &c., and back to England.
Oct. 19	Sarah	John Roberts	1700 Nov. 1	R.B. only.	CLI	——
Nov. 3	Rising Sun	Arthur Holford	1703 Mar. 31	— L.	CLII CLIIA	Journal of a voyage from England to Batavia and Canton, and then back to England, touching on the Coromandel Coast.
Nov. 16	Phenix	Thos. Lambert	Dec. 16	—	CLIII	Journal of a voyage from England to Madras, Calcutta, Gombroon, Vizagapatam, &c. and back from Madras to England.
Nov. 18	Dashwood	Marmaduke Rawdon	Jan. 7	L. only.	CLIV	——
Nov. 22	Strettham	Roger Myers	July 17	L. only.	CLV	——
..	Strettham	Roger Myers	July 17	L. and R.B. only.	CLVI CLVIA	——
Dec. 2	Neptune	John Lesly	1702 Sept. 15	— L.	CLVII CLVIIA	Journal of voyage from England to Batavia and Amoy and back.
Dec. 5	Bengal Merchant	H. Trenwith	1700 Dec. 17	R.B. only.	CLVIII	——

25005. C

Journal begins.	Ship.	Captain.	Journal ends.	Ledger or Receipt Book.	Reference Number.	Remarks.
1700 —	Degrave -	William Young	1703 Dec. 8	L. only.	CLIX	——
1701 Jan. 24	Loyall Cook	- - -	June 20	—	CLX	Journal of a voyage from England to Batavia, Amoy, and Madras, and back to England.
April 19	Katherine -	William Holman - and afterwards Samuel Croft.	April 13	— L.	CLXI CLXIA	Journal of a voyage from England to Madapollam, Masulipatam, &c., and back towards England.
May 31	Herne	John Law -	April 9	—	CLXII	Journal of a voyage from England to Calicut, Bombay, &c., and back to England.
June 4	Loyall Bliss -		1704 April 5	—	CLXIII	Journal of a voyage from England to Goa, Bombay and Surat, from Surat to Gombroon and back, and then back to England.
July 29	Upton -	John Camell	1703 Dec. 31	L. only.	CLXIV	——
Aug. 10	Macclesfield	Thos. Roberts* and afterwards John Hurle.	1704 Aug. 25	L. only.	CLXV	——
Oct. 2	Rebow	Thos. Dennett -	1703 April 2	L. only.	CXLVI	——
Oct. 10	Macclesfield	Thos. Roberts - and afterwards John Hurle.	1704 April 5	L. only.	CLXVII	——
Oct. 30	Leghorn -	Jacob Wright -	1705 Sept. 13	L. only.	CLXVIII	With separate list of crew, and rough book of accounts.
Nov. 12	Hallifax -	Henry Hudson	1704 Dec. 8	L. only.	CLXIX	——
Nov. 19	Arabia Factor	Abraham Jackson -	1703 Oct. 23	L. only.	CLXX	——
Dec. 7	Samuel and Anna	F. Reddall	1705 June 26	—	CLXXI	Journal of a voyage from England to Bencoolen and Batavia.

* Died 24th October 1701.

Section II.

SHIPS' LOGS, &c., 1702-1856.

Log begins.	Ship.	Captain.	Log ends.	Ledger or Receipt Book.	Reference Number.	Remarks.
1702 Feb. 28	Colchester	-	1703 April 12	—	113 A (1)	To Madras, Bengal, Gombroon, &c.
Mar. 8	Wentworth	Thomas Sax	Oct. 3	—	114 A (1)	To Bengal.
Mar. 9	Union	-	1704 Nov. 7	—	117 A (1)	To China and Madras.
Mar. 27	Panther	R. Robinson	1703 Mar. 20	—	116 A	To Borneo.
April 16	Edward and Dudley	Wm. Lambert	1705 May 2	—	CXIII.	To Batavia and Borneo.
May 7	Martha	S. Goodman	1703 April 17	—	118 A (1)	From Bombay to England.
June 1	Liampo	Thomas Monck	1704 Nov. 17	—	787 A	From Malacca to Amoy, Chusan, Batavia and England.
June 4	Catharine	J. Jenefer	June 13	—	115 A (1)	To Surat, Bombay, and China.
Aug. 7	Samuel and Anna	F. Reddall	1705 Nov. 18	— L.	119 A 119 B	To Borneo and China.
Aug. 14	Mary		1706 Aug. 17	—	261 A (1)	To Cochin, Surat, Bombay, &c.
Oct. 30	Duchess	Hugh Raymond	Jan. 16	—	714 A (1)	To Calcutta.
Nov. 6	Nathaniel	B. Dennis	1704 April 8	—	136 A (1)	From Gombroon to Bombay, Surat, Carwar, &c.
Dec. 10	Tavistock	Matthew Martin	1706 Jan. 17	—	593 A	To Madras and Bengal.
—	Herne	W. Morris	1705 —	L. only.	112 C	——
—	Norris	James Allison	1703 —	L. only.	760 A	——
—	Northumberland	S. Hide	1706 —	L. only.	141 U	——
—	Rapier	Edward Thompson	1705 —	L. only.	765 A	——
1703 Jan. 9	Josiah	Rand. Pye	1704 Dec. 6	— L.	713 A 713 C	To Bombay and Carwar.
Jan. 11	Sidney	John Cradock	May 9	— L.	715 A 715 C	To Batavia.
Jan. 11	Sidney	John Cradock	1705 Nov. 27	—	715 B	To Batavia and Madras.
Jan. 13	Martha	S. Goodman	Feb. 23	—	118 A (2)	To Bengal and Madras.
Feb. 9	Montagu	John Caulier	1706 Aug. 17	-	552 A	To Batavia, Amoy, Bombay, and Surat.
Feb. 11	Streatham	-	1707 Mar. 7	—	311 A	To Batavia, Madras, Acheen, Malacca, Mocha, Gombroon, Surat, and Calicut.
Feb. 24	Abingdon	John Goodfellow	1704 May 14	— L.	687 A 687 E	To Bombay and Anjengo.
Nov. 22	Eaton	George Philipps.	1705 June 26	— L.	720 A 720 B	To Batavia and Whampoa.
Dec. 27	Loyall Cooke	-	1707 Oct. 12	—	130 A	To Madras, Bengal, and Persia. (Incomplete.)
—	Queen	William Legg	1704 —	R.B.only.	356 M	——

Log begins.	Ship.	Captain.	Log ends.	Ledger or Receipt Book.	Reference Number.	Remarks.
1704 Jan. 7	Westmorland	John Gallon	1707 June 20	— R.B.	711 A 711 B	To Bombay, Goa, Surat, Calcutta, and Madras.
Jan. 10	Fetherston	-	May 26	-	712 A	To Batavia.
Aug. 26	Arabia Merchant	-	April 30	—	752 A	To Mocha, Bombay, and Calicut.
Sept. 18	Catharine	J. Tracy succeeded by J. Milford.	1708 Sept. 10	— Two R.B.	115 A (2) 115 D	To Batavia.
Oct. 16	Hampshire	Zachariah Tovey	Mar. 6	—	468 A	To Bombay, Bencoolen, and Batavia.
Oct. 20	Loyall Bliss	R. Hudson	1705 Sept. 9	—	121 A	To Batavia and Bencoolen.
Nov. 22	Abingdon	-	Mar. 11	—	713 B	Journal of proceedings at Bombay and Surat.
Dec. 2	Wentworth	John Sax	1706 Sept. 9	— L.	114 A (2) 114 B	To Bengal.
Dec. 3	Frederick	-	1707 Feb. 28	—	695 A	To Bombay, Gombroon, Madras, and Bengal.
Dec. 5	Somers	Eustace Peacock	1705 June 10	—	705 A	Towards Fort St. George.
Dec. 15	Phœnix	J. Carswell	1708 Sept. 17	—	135 A	To the Malabar Coast, Batavia, &c.
Dec. 20	Europe	H. Bryant	Sept. 15	— L.	204 A 204 J	To Gombroon, Bombay, Surat, &c.
Dec. 20	Panther	-	Sept. 5	—	116 B	To Borneo.
1705 Jan. 2	Nathaniel	B. Dennis	Oct. 29	—	136 A (2)	To Madras and Bengal.
Jan. 4	Union	-	Mar. 6	—	117 A (2)	To the Cape of Good Hope and Brasil.
Feb 1	Somers	Eustace Peacock	1706 Feb. 13	—	705 B	To Bengal.
Mar. 23	Josiah	Rand. Pye	April 22	— L.	713 B 713 C	From Bombay to Gombroon and back, and then towards England.
Mar. 24	Martha	S. Goodman	Feb. 15	—	118 B	From Madras to England.
Oct. 28	Howland	Jonathan Collett	Mar. 10	—	696 A [687 A]	From Cape of Good Hope to England. (With Journal of Ship "Abingdon" No. 687 A.)
Nov. 12	Oley	John Opie	1708 Oct. 23	— L.	704 A 704 B	To Macao.
Dec. 10	Fleet	Thomas Burgis	1707 April 3	—	693 A	To Madras and Bengal.
Dec. 17	Carlton	Philip Brown	1708 Oct. 28	—	666 A	To Bencoolen and Batavia.
Dec. 18	Duchess	Hugh Raymond	Oct. 22	— L. & R.B.	714 A (2) 714 B	To Fort St. George.
—	Halifax	Henry Hudson	1705 —	L. only.	651 D	——
—	Indian Frigate	Robert Hill	1706 —	R.B. only.	783 A	——
—	Prince Frederick	John Wynn	1707 —	L. only.	663 E	——
—	Tankervell	Charles Newnam	1708 —	L. only.	768 A	——
1706 Mar. 23	Aurangzebe	John Edwards	1706 Nov. 20	— Two L.	702 A 702 C & D	To Colombo.
Mar. 25	Northumberland	-	Aug. 19	—	141 A	From the Cape of Good Hope to England.
June 14	Kent	-	1709 Dec. 3	—	317 A	To Batavia, Macao, Whampoa, Madras, and Bengal.
Sept. 27	Rochester	F. Stanes	Feb. 11	—	137 A	To Bencoolen, Batavia, and Bengal.
Oct. 13	Stringer	Isaac Pyke	May 30	— L.	688 A 688 D	To Batavia and Chusan.
—	Halifax	Henry Hudson	1708 —	L. only.	651 E	——

Log begins.	Ship.	Captain.	Log ends.	Ledger or Receipt Book.	Reference Number.	Remarks.
1707 Feb. 1	St. George	Samuel Goodman	1708 April 13	—	584 A	To Bengal.
Feb. 9	Northumberland	H. Dickinson	1710 Sept. 4	—	141 B	To Bencoolen and Batavia.
Feb. 20	Howland	George Cooke	1708 Aug. 22	— L.	696 B 696 D	To Madras, Calcutta, Muscat, and Gombroon.
June 4	Scipio	George Luke Burrish succeeded by Philip Clifton.	1710 Mar. 11	—	725 A	To Bencoolen and Batavia.
Sept. 16	Tavistock	Matthew Martin	Nov. 18	—	593 B	To Bombay, Surat, and Gombroon.
Oct. 1	Albemarle	-	1708 Aug. 14	—	718 A	From Bombay to England.
Nov. 1	Stretham	Harry Gough	1710 Sept. 8	—	605 A	To Bengal and Madras.
Nov. 3	Herne	J. Lane	Aug. 23	—	112 A	To Madras, Bengal, and Holland.
Nov. 15	Donegall	-	1711 Aug. 9	—	716 A	To Madras and Mocha.
Dec. 10	Toddington	Thomas Blow	1710 Mar. 10	—	689 A	To Bengal.
Dec. 20	Recovery	H. Hunter	1709 Dec. 31	—	106 A	To Borneo.
Dec. 24	Litchfield	James Lee	1710 Mar. 9	— L. & R.B.	691 A 691 C	To Madras.
—	Anna	Francis Nelly	—	Two R.B. only.	292 F	Journal and ledger apparently lost with the ship.
—	Harbert	Richard Chadsley	1707 —	R.B. only.	747 A	——
1708 Jan. 11	Montagu	James Stoacks	1710 Mar. 9	—	552 B	To Madras.
Jan. 24	Abingdon	John Lesly	1711 Feb. 6	—	687 C	To Calicut, Goa, Bombay, Surat, Calcutta, and Madras.
Nov. 13	Heathcote	Joseph Tolson	1710 July 4	—	625 A	To Fort St. George.
Nov. 17	Loyall Bliss	R. Hudson	1711 Aug. 9	—	121 B	To Bengal.
Dec. 1	Halifax	Henry Hudson	1712 Sept. 6	— L.	651 A 651 F	To Madras, Bengal, and Whampoa.
Dec. 19	Abingdon	John Lesly	1709 April 28	—	687 B [705 A]	(With Journal of Somers, 705 A.) Journal of Transactions at Blackwall, Calcutta, and Bombay.
Dec. 24	Loyall Cooke	J. Clarke	1711 Aug. 9	—	130 B	To Batavia and China.
Dec. 27	Godolphin	John Ap Rice	1710 Mar. 24	— L. Ship's Account.	594 A 594 K 594 T	To Bombay, Colombo, Anjengo, and Calicut.
—	New George	George Osborne	1711 —	L. only.	769 A	——
1709 Jan. 27	Frederick	Richard Phrip	Oct. 6	— L.	695 B 695 C	To Bencoolen, Batavia, and Madras.
Mar. 14	Carlton	George Lytton	Aug. 8	—	686 B	To Madras and Bencoolen.
April 7	Nathaniel	J. Negus	1710 Sept. 10	—	136 B	To Bencoolen and Batavia.
Sept. 24	Susanna	Richard Pinnell	1711 Oct. 14	— L.	678 A 678 C	To Madras and Bengal.
Oct. 5	Europa	H. Bryant	Oct. 6	— L. & R.B.	204 B 204 K	To Fort St. George and Calcutta.
Oct. 17	St. George	Samuel Goodman	1712 Sept. 27	— L. & R.B.	584 B 584 H	To Madras and Bengal.

Log begins.	Ship.	Captain.	Log ends.	Ledger or Receipt Book.	Reference Number.	Remarks.
1709 Oct. 20	Bouverie	Hugh Raymond	1712 Oct. 4	— L.	692 A 692 D	To Fort St. George.
Oct. 20	Rochester	F. Stanes	Oct. 2	— L. & R.B.	137 B 137 D	To China.
Oct. 22	Blenheim	Abraham Parrot	1711 Aug. 9	— L. & R.B.	697 A 697 B	To Mocha.
Oct. 26	Stringer	Isaac Pyke	1713 Aug. 8	— L.	688 B & C 688 E	To Batavia, Canton, Mocha, and Bombay.
Nov. 4	King William	Nehemiah Winter	1711 Aug. 9	— L.	635 A 635 H	To Bengal.
Nov. 28	Mead	Daniel Needham	Feb. 10	— L.	710 A 710 B	To Bencoolen.
	Sherburne	-	1709 —	R.B. only.	148 B	This ship was taken by the French.
—	Tankervell	Charles Newnman	1713 —	L. only.	768 B	——
1710 Jan. 5	Catherine	E. Godfrey	1712 Oct. 30	—	115 B	To Bombay and Surat.
Feb. 8	Rochester	F. Stanes	Sept. 24	—	137 C	To China.
July 1	Success	Thomas Clapham	June 4	— L. & R.B.	587 A 587 E	To Calcutta and Madras.
Sept. 1	Windsor	Zachary Tovey	June 27	— L.	29 A 29 I	To Bombay, Mocha, &c.
Oct. 12	Averilla	Robert Hurst	Oct. 27	— L. & R.B.	690 A 690 C	To Madras, Fort St. David, and Bengal.
Oct. 14	Dartmouth	Thomas Beckford	1713 Aug. 17	— L. L. & R.B.	698 A 698 D 698 E	To Madras, Bengal, and Gombroon.
Oct. 25	Derby	Thomas Wotton	Aug. 17	—	653 A	To Madras and Bengal.
Nov. 9	Aurangzebe	Edmond Stacey succeeded by Nicholas Luborne.	1712 Oct. 21	— L.	702 B 702 E	To Fort St. David, Madras, and Bengal.
Dec. 10	Howland	George Cooke	June 21	—	696 C	To Batavia and China.
Dec. 11	Hester	Charles Kesar	Sept. 28	— L. & R.B.	694 A 694 D	To Canton.
—	Duchess	John Blacon	—	L. only.	714 C	——
—	Jane	John Austen	1710 —	R.B. only.	796 A	——
—	London	William Upton	1714 —	L. only.	313 M (A)	——
—	Phœnix or Phenix	Edward Peirson	1710 —	L. only.	135 B	——
—	Sherburne	H. Cornewall	1712 —	L. only.	148 C	——
1711 Feb. 7	Litchfield	James Lee	1714 July 22	— L.	691 B 691 D	To Bombay and Surat.
Feb. 15	Montagu	James Stoacks	1713 Sept. 4	— L. & R.B.	552 C 552 L	To Bombay and Surat.
Feb. 17	Toddington	Thomas Blow	Aug. 16	—	689 B	To Bencoolen, Madras, and Batavia.
Mar. 12	Thistleworth	Daniell Small	1712 Sept. 30	— L.	318 A 318 E	To Bencoolen and Batavia. (Ledger with Duke of Cambridge, 700 C.)
Mar. 29	Heathcote	Joseph Tolson	1713 Sept. 25	—	625 B	To Bombay and Surat.
Aug. 23	Nathaniel	J. Negus	Aug. 5	— L.	136 C 136 E	To Bombay.
Oct. 16	Marlborough	Matthew Martin	1714 Sept. 3	—	602 A	To Fort St. George and Bengal.

Log begins.	Ship.	Captain.	Log ends.	Ledger or Receipt Book.	Reference Number.	Remarks.
1711 Nov. 1	Mary	Richard Holden	1713 Aug. 17	— L.	261 A (2) 261 J	To Fort St. George and Bengal.
Nov. 6	Herne	J. Lane	Sept. 5	—	112 B	To China.
Nov. 30	Somers	Eustace Peacock	1715 Mar. 28	— L. & R.B.	705 C 705 D	To Bombay, Muscat, Gombroon, Madras, and Calcutta.
—	Jane	S. Godfrey	1712 —	R.B. only.	796 B	——
—	Kent	Lawrence Minter	1713 —	L. only.	317 L	——
1712 Jan. 14	Success	Page Keble	May 1	—	587 B	To Bencoolen.
Jan. 14	Success	Page Keble	Sept. 12	— Two L.	587 C 587 F	To Bencoolen and Batavia.
Feb. 21	Recovery	J. Beale	1714 Sept. 16	— L. & R.B.	106 B 106 E	To Bengal, Gombroon, Madras, &c.
Mar. 21	Grantham	John Collet	1715 April 4	—	617 A	To Bombay, Batavia, and Madras.
May ? 6	Abingdon	John Lesly succeeded by William Stephens.	1714 June 16	—	687 D	To Bencoolen and Batavia.
Oct. 7	Hanover	James Osborne	1715 Nov. 1	—	677 A	To Madras, Bengal, and Bombay.
Oct. 22	Loyall Bliss	R. Hudson	1714 Aug. 8	— L. & R.B.	121 C 121 E	To China.
Nov. 8	Cardigan	Richard Grainger	1716 April 26	—	668 A	To Bengal, Gombroon, and Madras.
Dec. 12	King William	Nehemiah Winter	1714 Sept. 11	— L.	635 B 635 I	To Madras and Bengal.
—	Blenheim	Abraham Parrot	1719 —	L. & R.B. only.	697 C	——
—	Frederick	Richard Phrip	1715 —	L. only.	695 D	——
1713 Sept. 26	Borneo	Thomas Lewis	1716 June 9	—	674 A	To Bencoolen and Batavia.
Nov. 9	Averilla	Robert Hurst	1715 Oct. 28	—	690 B	To Madras, Bencoolen, and Batavia.
Nov. 26	Bouverie	Thomas Wotton	1716 Aug. 22	—	692 B	To Madras and Calcutta.
Dec. 19	Hester	Charles Kesar	1715 May 24	— L. & R.B.	694 B 694 E	To Canton.
Dec. 19	St. George	Samuel Goodman	1716 April 11	— L.	584 C 584 I	To Madras and Bengal.
—	Arrabella	Alexander Reid	1713 —	L. only.	767 A	——
—	Catharine	E. Godfrey	1717 —	L. & two R.B. only.	115 E	——
—	Howland	George Cooke succeeded by Samuel Lewis.	1714 —	L. & two R.B. only.	696 E	——
1714 Jan. 10	Stretham	Harry Gough	Aug. 3	— L. & R.B.	605 B & C 605 K	To China.
Feb. 16	Thistleworth	Daniell Small	1716 May 15	—	318 B	To Bombay, Surat, and Gombroon.
Sept. 24	Nathaniel	J. Negus	Aug. 20	— L. & R.B.	136 D 136 E (A)	To Bombay, Calicut, &c. Also list of ship's company, 136 F.
Sept. 28	Kent	Lawrence Minter	April 19	—	317 B	To Fort St. David and Madras.
Sept. 29	Heathcote	Joseph Tolson	Aug. 20	—	625 C	To Madras, Balasore, and Calcutta.
Nov. 19	Derby	William Fitzhugh	Sept. 27	—	653 B	To Batavia and Bengal.

Log begins.	Ship.	Captain.	Log ends.	Ledger or Receipt Book.	Reference Number.	Remarks.
1714 Dec. 18	Cardonnell	William Mawson	1717 May 5	— L. & R.B.	708 A 708 C	To Bencoolen, Batavia, and Madras.
Dec. 22	Dartmouth	Thomas Blow	July 30	— L. & R.B.	698 B & C 698 F	To Batavia, Canton, Madras, Acheen, and Fort St. David.
Dec. 27	Stanhope	Wentworth George Pitt.	Sept. 15	—	664 A	To Bombay, Gombroon, and Calcutta.
—	Aurangzebe	Nicholas Luhorne	1715 —	L. & R.B. only.	702 F	—
—	Catherine	E. Godfrey	1717 —	Two L. only.	115 F & G	—
—	Litchfield	James Lee	1715 —	L. & R.B. only.	691 E	—
—	London	William Upton	—	L. & R.B. only.	313 N	—
—	Mary	Richard Holden	1717 —	L. & R.B. only.	261 K	—
1715 Mar. 26	Queen	John Martin	1716 Nov. 5	—	366 A	To Cochin, Carwar, Bombay, Bhatkal, Tellicherry, and Calicut.
Sept. 14	Grantham	Thomas Collet	1717 Aug. 15	—	617 B	To Fort St. George and Bengal.
Nov. 28	Prince Frederick	Edward Martin	1718 June 15	—	663 A	To Madras, Balasore, Calcutta, and Fort St. David.
—	Frederick	Richard Phrip	1715 —	L. & R.B. only.	695 E	—
—	Stringer	John Clarke	1717 —	L. only.	668 F	—
—	Susanna	Richard Pinnell	1715 —	L. only.	678 D	—
1716 Jan. 26	King George	Samuel Lewis	1717 July 8	—	402 A	To Madras, Balasore, and Fort St. David.
Jan. 30	Hester	John Gordon	1718 Aug. 10	— L. & R.B.	694 C 694 F	To Bencoolen.
Mar. 22	Catharine	J. Hunter	1717 Jan. 26	—	115 C	To Bencoolen.
April 2	Princess Amelia	J. Misenor	June 21	— L.	36 A 36 Y	To Bombay, Calicut, &c.
April 12	Sarum	G. Newton	1718 July 20	—	667 A	To Mocha and Bombay.
Sept. 20	Princess Anne	Nicholas Luhorne	1719 Mar. 4	— L. L. & R.B.	707 A 707 C 707 D	To Mocha, Calicut, Tellicherry, Bombay, and Madras.
Nov. 26	Cardigan	Henry Glegg	1718 Oct. 10	— L. & R.B.	668 B 668 E	To Madras and Bengal.
Dec. 29	Townshend	Charles Kesar	Aug. 2	—	660 A	To Canton.
—	Kent	Lawrence Minter	1717 —	L. only.	317 M	—
1717 Jan. 4	Morice	Eustace Peacock	1718 Mar. 22	— L. & R.B.	679 A 679 F	To Bombay only.
Jan. 11	Thistleworth	Charles Small	Aug. 23	— L. & R.B.	318 C 318 F	To Batavia and Borneo.
Mar. 29	Duke of York	A. Dawes	1719 July 23	— L.	94 F 94 N	To Bombay, Gombroon, &c.
Aug. 28	Heathcote	Joseph Tolson	July 3	—	625 D	To Balasore and Calcutta.
Sept. 1	Hartford	Thomas Newsham	Aug. 14	— L.	656 A 656 G	To Whampoa and Batavia.
Sept. 21	Derby	William Fitzhugh	July 12	—	653 C	To Madras and Fort St. David.
Oct. 28	Caernarvon	Josiah Thwaites	July 3	— L. & R.B.	589 A 589 I	To Whampoa, Macao, and Batavia.
Nov. 1	Mary	Richard Holden	July 28	— L. & R.B.	261 B 261 L	To Fort St. George and Vizagapatam.

Log begins.	Ship.	Captain.	Log ends.	Ledger or Receipt Book.	Reference Number.	Remarks.
1717 Nov. 8	King George	Samuel Lewis	1720 Mar. 24	— L.	402 B 402 L	To Madras and Bengal.
Dec. 23	Stanhope	Wentworth George Pitt.	1719 Aug. 17	— L.& R.B.	664 B & C 664 E	To Bombay and Surat.
—	British Merchant	Thomas Gilbert	1721 —	L. & R.B. only.	766 A	——
—	Duke of Cambridge	Daniel Small	1719 —	L. only.	700 C	(Including also Ledger of ship "Thistleworth," 1711–12, No. 318 E.)
—	St. George	Anthony Ryan	—	L. only.	584 J	——
—	Success	Thomas Clapham	1718 —	L. & R.B. only.	587 G	——
—	Susanna	Richard Pinnell	—	L. & R.B. only.	678 E	——
1718 Jan. 2	Addison	Zachary Hickes succeeded by Richard Gosfrith.	1720 Mar. 24	— L. & R.B.	703 A 703 B	To Bombay.
Jan. 22	Dawsonne	John Raymond succeeded by Richard Benfeild.	Sept. 29	—	671 A	To Madras.
Jan. 28	Queen	John Martin	April 1	— L. & R.B.	356 B 356 N	To Bencoolen, Acheen, Madras, and Fort St. David.
Mar. 27	Morice	Eustace Peacock	1719 Aug. 17	— L. & R.B.	679 B 679 F	From Bombay to Mocha and England.
Sept. 30	Prince Frederick	Edward Martin	1720 Oct. 18	— L.	663 B 663 F	To Calcutta.
Oct. 12	Susanna	John Edwards	July 8	— L. & R.B.	678 B 678 F	To Mocha, Calicut, and Cochin.
Oct. 14	Cadogan	John Hill	Aug. 21	—	682 A	To Fort St. David and Bengal.
Oct. 17	King William	James Winter	Aug. 21	— Two L. and R.B.	635 C 635 J & K	To Fort St. David and Madras.
Oct. 17	Marlborough	Richard Mickelfield	June 4	—	602 B	To Fort St. David and Madras.
Oct. 25	Thistleworth	Charles Small	Sept. 10	— L. & R.B.	318 D 318 G	To Java and other islands in the East Indies.
Dec. 13	Hanover	James Osborne	1721 April 16	—	677 B	To Bombay, Tellicherry, and Madras.
—	Essex	John Pinnell	1723 —	L. only.	290 Y	——
—	Princess Amelia	John Misenor	1720 —	L. & R.B. only.	36 W	——
—	Rochester	William Browne	1719 —	L. & R.B. only.	137 E	——
1719 Jan. 3	Godfrey	Samuel Payne	1721 April 3	— L. & R.B.	464 A 464 E	To Madras, Bencoolen, and Batavia.
Feb. 21	Townshend	Philip Worth	1720 Sept. 13	— L. & R.B.	660 B 660 E	To Madras, Bombay, and Tellicherry.
Mar. 21	Craggs	John Wynn	1719 Oct. 14	— L. & R.B.	681 A 681 D	To Batavia.
June 29	Bouverie	Thomas Wotton	1720 Aug. 17	—	692 C	From Gombroon to England.
Sept. 28	Cardigan	Henry Glegg	1721 June 21	— L.	668 C 668 F	To Bengal.
Oct. 6	Greenwich	Richard Kyrby succeeded by John Barnes.	1722 July 13	—	488 A	To Bombay and Gombroon.
Oct. 8	Montagu	John Gordon	1721 July 19	—	552 D	To Whampoa.
Oct. 15	Cardonnell	William Mawson	July 24	— L. L. & R.B.	708 B 708 D 708 E	To Madras and Fort St. David.
Nov. 27	Derby	William Fitzhugh	July 19	—	653 D	To Madras and Bengal.
Dec. 17	Sarum	G. Newton	July 17	—	467 B	To China.
Dec. 18	Bridgewater	Edward Williamson	Aug. 29	— L. & R.B.	42 A 42 Z	To Batavia, China, and Madras.

Log begins.	Ship.	Captain.	Log ends.	Ledger or Receipt Book.	Reference Number.	Remarks.
1719 Dec. 21	Duke of Cambridge	Daniel Small	1721 July 15	—	700 A	To Madras and Bengal.
—	Mary	Richard Holden	1722 —	L. & R.B. only.	261 M	——
1720 Jan. 12	Duke of York	Robert Hyde	1721 Aug. 30	— L. & R.B.	94 B 94 O	To Bengal.
Jan. 24	Hartford	Francis Nelly	Feb. 20	— L. & R.B.	656 B 656 H	To Madras.
Feb. 29	Caernarvon	Josiah Thwaites	Aug. 28	—	529 B	To Whampoa.
April 4	London	William Upton	1722 July 15	— L. & R.B.	313 A 313 O	To Bombay, Surat, and Mocha.
May 18	Borneo	John Shepheard	1720 Oct. 15	—	574 B	From the Cape of Good Hope to England.
Sept. 23	Stretham	George Westcott	1722 Aug. 21	— L. & R.B.	605 D 605 L	To Bengal and Madras.
Nov. 4	Cadogan	John Hill	July 28	— L.	682 B 682 E	To Canton.
Nov. 7	Cæsar	William Mabbot	Mar. 3	— L.	235 A 235 K	To Mocha and Bombay.
Nov. 9	Sunderland	William Hutchinson	1722 April 10	—	675 A	To Mocha, Goa, and Cochin.
Nov. 18	Middlesex	John Pelly	1723 June 12	—	450 A	To Batavia, Madras, and Fort St. David.
Dec. 3	Grantham	Timothy Field	1722 Aug. 22	—	617 C	To Bombay and Surat.
Dec. 15	James and Mary	Thomas Aubone	Sept. 7	—	676 A	To Batavia.
Dec. 21	Macclesfield	Robert Hudson	May 19	— L. & R.B.	669 A 669 D	To Canton.
—	Addison	Leonard Hickes	1721 —	Two R.B. only.	703 C	——
—	Aislabie	Henry Wilson	1722 —	L. & R.B. only.	688 C	——
—	Chandos	Thomas Gilbert	—	R. B. only.	729 A	——
—	Dartmouth	Roger Carter	1720 —	L. & three R.B. only.	698 G	——
—	Fordwich	John Bernard	1721 —	L. & R.B. only.	684 C	——
—	King George	Samuel Lewis	—	L. & R.B. only.	402 M	——
—	Morice	Eustace Peacock	1722 —	L. & R.B. only.	679 G	——
—	Prince Frederick	Edward Martin	1721 —	L. only.	663 G	——
1721 Mar. 11	Drake	William Whitaker	1723 June 8	—	578 A	To Bencoolen and Madras.
May 22	King George	John Houghton	1724 May 27	— L. & R.B.	402 C 402 N	To Bombay, Madras, and Canton.
Oct. 3	Lyell	Charles Small	1723 June 2	— L. L. & R.B.	645 A 645 F 646 G	To Batavia and Whampoa.
Oct. 9	Townshend	Philip Worth	July 23	— L. & R.B.	660 C 660 F	To Mocha and Calicut.
Oct. 13	Fordwich	Richard Gosfright	June 8	— L.	684 A 684 D	To Bengal, Madras, and Fort St. David.
Oct. 16	Desbouverie	[?] Chamboe	June 23	—	699 A	To Calcutta.
Dec. 5	Eyles	James Winter	June 6	— L. & R.B.	661 A 661 E	To Whampoa and Madras.
Dec. 31	Enfield	Charles Rigby	June 13	— L. & R.B.	670 A 670 E	To Fort St. George.
—	Bengal Galley	William Jordan	1725 —	Two R.B. only.	785 A	——
—	Cardigan	[Henry Glegg]	—	L. only.	668 F	——
—	Frances	Thomas Newsham	1723 —	L. & R.B. only.	672 E	——

Log begins.	Ship.	Captain.	Log ends.	Ledger or Receipt Book.	Reference Number.	Remarks.
1721 —	Godfrey	Benjamin Braund	1723 —	L. & R.B. only.	464 F	——
—	Goodfellow -	Daniell Fox	1722 —	R. B. only.	779 A	——
—	Monmouth -	Reginald Kemeys -	—	L. & R.B. only.	682 D	——
—	Nightingale -	William Maskott	—	Two R.B. only.	795 A	——
—	Stanhope -	Wentworth George Pitt.	1724 —	L. & R.B. only.	664 F	——
—	Walpole	Charles Boddam	1725 —	L. only.	293 Y	——
—	[Name unknown]	Edward Bontwell	1723 —	L. only.	795 A	——
1722 Jan. 1	Princess Amelia	John Misenor -	June 3	— L. & R.B.	36 B 36 X	To China.
Jan. 8	Hanover -	John Rond	1724 Nov. 7	—	677 C	To Bombay, Fort St. George, Mocha, and Surat.
Feb. 28	Devonshire -	Lawrence Prince	1723 June 23	—	272 A	To Fort St. George and Bengal.
April 3	Prince Frederick	Edward Martin	1722 Dec. 5	— L. & R.B.	663 C 663 H	To Bombay and Gombroon.
May 30	Greenwich -	John Barnes -	Aug. 20	—	488 B	From St. Helena to England.
Aug. 1	Prince Augustus	Thomas Ryves	1725 May 18	—	665 A	To Mocha and Bombay.
Aug. 24	Barrington	John Hunter -	1724 Mar. 12	— L. & R.B.	685 A 685 C	To Mocha.
Oct. 1	Hartford	Francis Kelly	Nov. 2	— L. & R.B.	656 C & D 656 I	To Whampoa.
Oct. 2	Essex	Jonathan Sommers	1723 July 19	— L.	229 A 229 Z	To Madras and Bengal.
Oct. 2	Sarum -	George Newton	May 30	—	667 C	Towards Madras.
Oct. 13	Montagu	John Gordon	1724 Aug. 23	— L. & R.B.	552 E 552 M	To Whampoa.
Oct. 30	Cærnarvon	Josiah Thwaites -	April 21	— L. & R.B.	589 C 589 J	To Madras and Fort St. David.
Oct. 30	Duke of Cambridge	Daniel Small - -	1725 Nov. 11	— L. & R.B.	700 B 700 D	To Mocha and Bombay.
Nov. 6	Mary	Richard Holden	1724 July 18	— L. & R.B.	261 C 261 N	To Fort St. George and Bengal.
Dec. 10	Derby - -	William Fitzhugh -	July 16	—	653 E	To Bengal, Madras, and Fort St. David.
Dec. 11	Compton	William Mawson -	1726 April 9	— L. & R.B.	666 A 666 D	To Bombay and Gombroon.
Dec. 28	Cardigan -	William Hambly -	1724 May 5	—	668 D	To Madras.
—	Bombay Galley	Benjamin Capp	1729 —	Two R.B. only.	773 A	——
—	Craggs	Caleb Grantham	1724 —	L. & R.B. only.	681 E	——
—	Fort St. George -	Thomas Smith	1722 —	R. B. only.	632 D	——
—	Fort St. George -	Thomas Smith	1723 —	R. B. only.	632 E	——
—	Princess Anne -	Nicholas Luhorne -	1725 —	L. & R.B. only.	707 E	——
1723 Feb. 1	Dausonne - -	Richard Benfeild -	1723 Oct. 31	—	671 B	From Bombay to England.
Feb. 19	Bridgewater -	Edward Williamson -	1724 July 17	— L. & R.B.	42 B 42 AA	To Madras and Bengal.
Mar. 21	Duke of York -	Robert Hyde	1726 May 24	— L. & R.B.	94 C 94 P	To Bombay, Gombroon, &c.

Log begins.	Ship.	Captain.	Log ends.	Ledger or Receipt Book.	Reference Number.	Remarks.
1723 April 1	Swallowfield	George Pitt	1725 Mar. 6	— L. & R.B.	673 A 673 B	To Bencoolen.
July 30	Lethieullier	(?John) Shepheard	1724 July 9	—	667 C	From Bengal to England.
Aug. 20	Greenwich	Richard Lasinby	1726 June 30	—	488 C	To Mocha and Bombay.
Sept. 7	Frances	Thomas Newsham	1725 July 3	— L. & R.B.	672 A 672 F	To Madras, Calcutta, and Balasore.
Sept. 7	Frances	Thomas Newsham	Jan. 29	— L. & R.B.	672 H 672 F	To Madras, Calcutta, and Balasore.
Sept. 17	Monmouth	Reginald Kemeys	1726 July 16	— L. & R.B.	662 A 662 E	To Madras, Viragapatam, Calcutta, Balasore, Bombay, and Surat.
Oct. 3	London	Robert Bootle	1725 April 15	— L. & R.B.	313 B 313 O	To Mocha and Bombay.
Oct. 19	Sunderland	William Hutchinson	June 12	— L. & R.B.	675 B 675 D	To Fort St. George.
Nov. 7	Streatham	[George Westcott]	Aug. 30	—	311 B	To Fort St. George and Calcutta.
Nov. 19	James and Mary	Thomas Aubone succeeded by John Balchen.	1726 April 13	— Two L. & R.B.	676 B 676 D & E	To Bencoolen, Batavia, and Madras.
Dec. 1	Heathcote	Joseph Tolson	1725 June 23	— R.B.	625 D (A) 625 M	To Madras and Calcutta.
Dec. 16	Macclesfield	Robert Hudson	Aug. 9	— L. & R.B.	669 D 669 E	To Canton.
Dec. 21	Aislabie	Henry Wilson	July 5	— L. & R.B.	683 A 683 D	To Calcutta, Madras, and Fort St. David.
—	Drake	William Whitaker	1724 —	L. only	578 I	——
1724 Jan. 17.	Cadogan	John Hill succeeded by William Pricklove.	1726 April 7	— L. & R.B.	682 C 682 F	To Bombay and Gombroon.
Mar. 20	Morice	Eustace Peacock	1725 Mar. 17	— L. & R.B.	679 C 679 H	To Bombay.
Sept. 9	Drake	William Westerbane	1726 Jan. 9	— L. & R.B.	578 B 578 J	To Mocha, Bombay, Tellicherry, Cochin, Goa, and Surat.
Sept. 9	Lyell	Charles Small	1727 Sept. 30	—	646 B	To Madras, Calcutta, Balasore, and Surat.
Sept. 15	Princess Amelia	John Missaer	July 2	— L. & R.B.	36 C 36 Y	To Bombay, Mocha, Batavia, &c.
Oct. 14	Fordwich	Richard Gosfright	1726 Aug. 10	—	684 B	To Madras and Bengal.
Nov. 5	Enfield	Charles Rigby	July 25	— L. & R.B.	670 B 670 F	To Madras and Bengal.
Nov. 6	Lynn	Edward Elliston	Aug. 16	— L. & R.B.	627 A 627 H	To Calcutta, Vizagapatam, and Fort St. George.
Dec. 21	Grantham	Timothy Field	1727 May 21	—	617 D	To Bencoolen, Madras, and Batavia.
Dec. 29	Caesar	William Mabbot	1725 May 18	— L. & R.B.	235 B 235 L	To Whampoa.
—	Houghton	Edward Gibson	1726 —	L. & R.B. only.	438 T	——
—	Lethieullier	John Edwards	1725 —	L. & R.B. only.	657 D	——
1725 Jan. 6	Windham	Robert Lyell	1726 Sept. 5	— L. & R.B.	230 A 230 J	To Bombay and Cochin.
Jan. 22	Eyles	James Winter	Aug. 14	Two J. L. & R.B.	661 B & C 661 F	To Calcutta and Balasore.
April 12	Devonshire	Lawrence Prince	1727 Sept. 4	— L. & R.B.	272 B 272 M	To Bombay, Anjengo, Tellicherry, Madras, and Calcutta.
May 6	Morice	Eustace Peacock	1726 Aug. 3	— L. & R.B.	679 D 679 H	From Surat to Calcutta and England.
Sept. 29	Townshend	Philip Worth	1727 June 2	— L. & R.B.	660 D 660 G	To Batavia and Whampoa.
Oct. 25	Barrington	John Hunter	Sept. 5	— L. & R.B.	685 B 685 D	To Mocha and Bengal.

Log begins.	Ship.	Captain.	Log ends.	Ledger or Receipt Book.	Reference Number.	Remarks.
1725 Oct. 26	Carnarvon -	Josiah Thwaites -	1727 July 9	— L.	589 D 589 K	To Bencoolen and Batavia.
Oct. 31	Craggs -	Caleb Grantham	Sept. 5	— L. & R.B.	681 B 681 F	To Madras.
Nov. 9	Dausonne -	Francis Steward	Oct. 27	—	671 C	To Madras.
Nov. 15	Mary	Thomas Holden	Aug. 27	— L. & R.B.	261 D 261 O	To Fort St. George and Bengal.
Nov. 18	Essex - -	Jonathan Sommers -	Aug. 28	— L. & R.B.	229 B 229 AA	To Madras and Bengal.
Dec. 11	Middlesex -	John Pelly	Aug. 27	—	450 B	To Madras and Calcutta.
—	Stretham -	George Westcott -	1726 —	R.B. only.	605 M	———
1726 Jan. 5	King George -	John Houghton -	1727 Aug. 22	— L. & R.B.	402 D 402 O	To Madras and Balasore.
Jan. 11	Sarum - - -	George Newton	Dec. 19	— L. & R.B.	667 D 667 E	To Fort St. George and Bengal.
Jan. 24	Stanhope -	Wentworth George Pitt.	1728 Mar. 24	— L. & R.B.	664 D 664 G	To Bombay and Fort St. David.
Oct. 30	London -	Robert Bootle	July 25	— L. & R.B.	313 C 313 O	To Madras, Vizagapatam, and Calcutta.
Nov. 16	Montagu - -	John Gordon -	Aug. 31	— L. & R.B.	552 F 552 N	To Madras and Calcutta.
Nov. 17	Derby - -	William Fitzhugh	1727 Aug. 26		653 F	To Madras, Balasore, and Calcutta.
Nov. 28	Princess Anne	Charles Gough -	1729 July 25	— L. & R.B.	707 B 707 F	To Bencoolen.
Dec. 5	Prince Augustus -	Francis Gostlin -	1728 July 25	— L. & R.B.	665 B 665 E	To Canton.
Dec. 11	Prince William -	Thomas Gilbert	July 19	—	324 A	To Madras, Calcutta, and Vizagapatam.
Dec. 6	Lethicullier -	John Shepheard -	1727 Sept. 17	— R.B.	657 A 657 E	To Madras and Bengal.
Dec. 31	Bridgewater -	Edward Williamson	1728 Aug. 5	— L. & R.B.	42 C 42 BB	To Madras and Bengal.
—	Hertford -	Francis Nelly	1729 —	L. only.	656 J	———
1727 Mar. 10	Walpole - -	Charles Boddam	Sept. 11	— L. & R.B.	293 A 293 Z	To Calcutta, Anjengo, Tellicherry, and Mocha.
April 7	Duke of Cumberland -	Benjamin Braund	May 29	— L. & R.B.	562 A 562 I	To Bombay and Mocha.
Aug. 23	Frances - -	John Lawson - -	Aug. 30	— L. & R.B.	672 C 672 G	To Madras and Calcutta.
Oct. 11	Harrison -	Samuel Martin	1728 July 29	— L. & R.B.	644 A 644 D	To Whampoa.
Oct. 21	Heathcote - -	Joseph Tolson	1730 April 21	— R.B.	625 E 625 N	To Madras, Balasore, and Calcutta.
Oct. 21	Prince Frederick -	W. Haynes - succeeded by S. Rodham.	Mar. 25	— L. & R.B.	663 D 663 I	To Mocha.
Dec. 9	Stretham -	George Westcott -	1729 Sept. 8	— L. & R.B.	605 E 605 N	To Fort St. George and Calcutta.
Dec. 12	Sunderland - -	William Hutchinson	Sept. 8	— L. & R.B.	675 C 675 E	To Batavia and Canton.
Dec. 19	George -	George Pitt -	Aug. 8	— L. & R.B.	779 A–A 779 A–F	To Madras and Bengal.
Dec. 19	George -	George Pitt	July 21	—	779 A–B	To Madras and Bengal.
—	Aislabie -	William Birch -	—	L. & R.B. only.	683 E	———
—	Cæsar -	William Mabbot	—	L. & R.B. only.	235 M	———
—	James and Mary -	John Balchen	—	L. & R.B. only.	676 F	———
1728 Feb. 13	Compton - -	John Misenor	1730 Aug. 6	— L. & R.B.	666 B 666 E	To Mocha and Calcutta.
Aug. 24	Moriee - -	Christopher Wilson -	Jan. 22	— L. & R.B.	679 E 679 I	To Mocha and back to St. Helena.
Sept. 24	Houghton -	Philip Worth	June 26	— L. & R.B.	438 A 438 U	To Batavia and Whampoa.
Sept. 25	Monmouth - -	Reginald Kemeys -	Aug. 17	— L. & R.B.	662 B 662 F	To Whampoa.

25005. F

Log begins.	Ship.	Captain.	Log ends.	Ledger or Receipt Book.	Reference Number.	Remarks.
1728 Sept. 27	Enfield	Charles Rigby	1730 July 5	— L. & R.B.	670 C 670 G	To Batavia and Whampoa.
Oct. 9	Cadogan	James Sanders	1731 Nov. 25	— L. & R.B.	682 D 682 G	To Bencoolen and Madras.
Oct. 19	Duke of York	J. Sommers	Sept. 8	— L. & R.B.	94 D 94 Q	To Bengal.
Oct. 29	Greenwich	Richard Lasinby	1730 Sept. 8	— L. & R.B.	488 D 488 J	To Madras and Calcutta.
Dec. 12	Bridgewater	Edward Williamson	1731 Aug. 20	— L. & R.B.	42 D 42 CC	To Madras and Bengal.
—	Fordwich	Richard Gosfright	—	L. & R.B. only.	684 E	—
—	Lynn	Edward Elliston	1730 —	L. & R.B. only.	627 I	—
—	Marlborough	Richard Mickelfield	1729 —	Two R.B. only.	602 K	—
—	Ockham	William Jobson	—	L. only.	706 B	—
—	Princess Carolina	John Flower	1728 —	R. B only.	724 A	—
—	Princess Caroline	Samuel Brasier	1733 —	R.B. only.	723 A	—
1729 Jan. 9	Grantham	Timothy Field	1730 Sept. 10	— L. & R.B.	617 E 617 M	To Fort St. David and Calcutta.
Feb. 14	Drake	John Houghton	1732 Aug. 15	— L. & R.B.	578 C 578 K	To Madras, Calcutta, Gombroon, Bombay, and Surat.
Aug. 14	Lyell	Charles Small	1731 July 3	— L. & R.B.	646 C 646 H	To Batavia and Whampoa.
Sept. 27	Middlesex	John Pelly	1732 Aug. 27	— L.	450 C 450 J	To Fort St. George, Calcutta, Bombay, and Surat.
Sept. 29	London	Robert Bootle	Aug. 18	— L. & R.B.	318 D 318 R	To Calcutta, Bombay, Goa, Madras, and Batavia.
Oct. 15	Mary	Thomas Holden	1731 Aug. 20	— L. & R.B.	261 E 261 P	To Fort St. George and Bengal.
Dec. 6	Lethieullier	John Shepheard	Sept. 2	— L. & R.B.	657 B 657 F	To Bombay, Tellicherry, Cochin, and Goa.
Dec. 13	Prince Augustus	Francis Gostlin	July 1	— L. & R.B.	665 C 665 F	To Canton.
Dec. 13	Prince of Wales	[John] Flower	Mar. 22	—	404 A	To Balasore and Bombay.
Dec. 14	Montagu	Samuel Keate	July 18	— L. & R.B.	552 G 552 O	To Bencoolen.
Dec. 14	Princess of Wales	Thomas Gilbert	June 29	— L. & R.B.	510 A 510 K	To Canton.
Dec. 15	Devonshire	Lawrence Prince	June 29	— L. & R.B.	272 C 272 N	To Whampoa.
Dec. 18	Eyles	Ralph Farr Winter	1730 Sept. 5	— L. & R.B.	661 D 661 G	To Madras and Bengal.
Dec. 22	Prince William	William Beresford	1731 Aug. 17	— L. & R.B.	324 B 324 H	To Bombay and Surat.
Dec. 28	Craggs	Caleb Grantham	July 22	— L. & R.B.	681 C 681 G	To Madras and Vizagapatam.
—	Barrington	John Hunter	1730 —	Two R.B. only.	685 E	—
—	King George	Richard Boulton	1733 —	R.B. only.	402 P	—
—	Windham	Robert Lyell	1730 —	L. & R.B. only.	230 K	—
1730 Oct. 1	Harrison	Samuel Martin	1732 July 12	— L. & R.B.	644 B 644 E	To Batavia, Macao, and Whampoa.
Oct. 2	Heathcote	David Wilkie	Mar. 19	— L. & R.B.	625 F 625 O	To Mocha and Bombay.
Oct. 2	James and Mary	John Balchen	May 29	— L. & R.B.	676 C 676 G	To Bencoolen and Batavia.
Oct. 3	Walpole	Charles Boddam	1733 Aug. 22	— L.&R.B.	293 B 293 AA	To Madras, Calcutta, Vizagapatam, and Mocha.

Log begins.	Ship.	Captain.	Log ends.	Ledger or Receipt Book.	Reference Number.	Remarks.
1730 Oct. 4	Hartford	Francis Nelly succeeded by George Bagwell.	1732 July 24	— L. & R.B.	656 E 656 K	To Batavia and Whampoa.
Oct. 6	Frances	John Lawson	1733 Aug. 5	— L. & R.B.	672 D 672 H	To Calcutta and Madras.
Nov. 17	Derby	William Fitzhugh	April 23	— L. & R.B.	653 G 653 H	To Madras, Fort St. David, and Bengal.
Nov. 30	Cæsar	William Mabbot	1732 June 2	— L. & R.B.	235 C 235 N	To Whampoa.
Dec. 1	Macclesfield	Robert Hudson	June 2	— L. & R.B.	669 C 669 F	To Canton.
Dec. 3	Aislabie	William Birch	1733 Aug. 4	— L. & R.B.	683 B 683 F	To Calcutta, Balasore, and Madras.
—	Dausonne	Francis Steward	1731 —	L. only.	671 D	——
1731 Jan. 6	Duke of Cumberland	Benjamin Braund	1733 May 22	— L. & R.B.	562 B 562 J	To Bengal and Madras.
Jan. 12	Stretham	George Westcott	1732 Aug. 25	— L. & R.B.	605 F 605 O	To Bombay, Goa, Mangalore, Tellicherry, and Cochin.
Jan. 18	George	George Pitt	Aug. 16	— L. & R.B.	799 A–C 799 A–G	To Bengal and Madras.
Mar. 3	Ockham	William Jobson	Aug. 15	— L.	706 A 706 C	To Bengal and Bombay.
Sept. 7	Grantham	Timothy Field	1733 Aug. 9	— L.	617 F 617 N	To Calcutta.
Sept. 21	Houghton	Philip Worth	May 26	— L. & R.B.	438 B 438 V	To Mocha and Bombay.
Sept. 22	Richmond	Charles Gough	July 27	— L. & R.B.	329 A 329 E	To Java and Whampoa.
Sept. 24	Lynn	Edward Elliston	June 24	— L. & R.B.	627 B 627 J	To Whampoa.
Sept. 30	Monmouth	James Montgomery	Nov. 7	— L. & R.B.	662 C 662 G	To Mocha, Bombay, Goa, Calicut, Tellicherry, and Gombroon.
Oct. 5	Windham	Robert Lyell	1734 June 5	— L. & R.B.	230 B 230 L	To Madras, Batavia, and Whampoa.
Dec. 1	Enfield	Thomas Manley	1733 June 14	— L. & R.B.	670 D 670 H	To Bencoolen and Batavia.
Dec. 6	Compton	John Misenor	1734 June 14	— L. & R.B.	666 C 666 F	To China.
Dec. 15	Nassau	William Hutchinson	1733 Aug. 1	— L. & R.B.	544 A 544 N	To Madras and Bengal.
Dec. 18	Bedford	William Wells	1734 May 22	— L. & R.B.	638 A 638 E	To Madras, Calcutta, Mocha, and Jeddah.
Dec. 18	Duke of Lorraine	Christopher Wilson	Aug. 15	— L. & R.B.	650 A 650 F	To Madras, Goa, Surat, Calcutta, and Vizagapatam.
—	Eyles	Ralph Farr Winter	1732 —	Two R.B. only.	661 H	——
1732 Jan. 7	Prince of Orange	Charles Hudson	1733 July 16	— L. & R.B.	636 A 636 F	To Madras and Bengal.
Jan. 17	Marlborough	Thomas Hunt	Aug. 2	— L. & R.B.	602 C 602 L	To Bombay, Goa, Tellicherry, and Cochin.
Jan. 18	Greenwich	Mathew Bookey	Sept. 12	— L.	488 E 488 K	To Bombay and Surat.
June 17	Mary	Ebenezer Thomson	1735 April 14	— L. & R.B.	261 F 261 Q	To Bombay and Bengal.
Sept. 7	Lethieullier	John Shepheard	1734 Mar. 9	— L. & R.B.	657 C 657 G	To Madras.
Sept. 23	Prince William	William Beresford	Feb. 17	— L. & R.B.	324 C 324 I	To Mocha and Bombay.
Sept. 25	Harrington	Robert Jenkins	May 30	— L. & R.B.	654 A 654 E	To Batavia and Bencoolen.
Nov. 12	Devonshire	Lawrence Prince	June 6	— L. & R.B.	272 D 272 O	To Madras and Bengal.
Nov. 24	Prince Augustus	Francis Gostlin	1735 April 15	— L. & R.B.	665 D 665 G	To China.
Dec. 10	Royal Guardian	Henry Hoadly	April 17	— L. & R.B.	641 A 641 F	To Bengal, Bombay, Tellicherry, and Madras.
Dec. 18	Normanton	Charles Rigby	1734 Sept. 4	— L. & R.B.	652 A 652 C	To Madras, Bengal, and Fort St. David.

Log begins.	Ship.	Captain.	Log ends.	Ledger or Receipt Book.	Reference Number.	Remarks.
1732 Dec. 20	Britannia	Caleb Grantham	1734 Aug. 14	— L. & R.B.	285 AA 285 A	To Madras and Bengal.
Dec. 22	Decker	Edward Williamson	1735 Mar. 28	— L. & R.B.	701 A 701 B	To Madras and Bengal.
1733 Jan. 20	Heathcote	Joseph Tolson	Aug. 16	— L. & R.B.	625 G 625 P	To Bombay, Surat, Goa, and Bengal.
Feb. 2	Walpole	[Charles Boddam]	1733 Aug. 6	L. —	625 Q 293 C	From Fort St. George to England.
Mar. 10	Princess of Wales	Robert Mead	1734 Aug. 29	— L. & R.B.	510 B 510 L	To Bombay and Anjengo.
Aug. 29	Princess Louisa	Richard Pinnell	1735 April 26	— L. & R.B.	639 A 639 D	To Mocha and Bombay.
Sept. 12	Montagu	Richard Gosfright	Aug. 19	— L. & R.B.	552 H 552 P	To Balasore, Ingelee, and Madras.
Sept. 14	Lyell	Charles Small	June 9	— L. & R.B.	646 D 646 I	To Bencoolen and Batavia.
Oct. 12	Harrison	Samuel Martin	1733 Aug. 5	— L. & R.B.	644 B 644 F	To Whampoa.
Oct. 27	Hartford	George Bagwell	1735 Oct. 17	— L. & R.B.	656 F 656 L	To Madras and Bengal.
Dec. 2	Grafton	Robert Hudson	June 26	— L. & R.B.	658 A 658 B	To Amoy and Whampoa.
Dec. 12	George	George Pitt	Aug. 24	— L. & R.B.	799 A–D 799 A–H	To Madras, Bengal, and Fort St. David.
Dec. 28	Duke of Dorset	Thomas Gilbert	Aug. 18	— L. & R.B.	612 A 612 I	To Bengal and Fort St. George.
—	Ockham	William Jobson	1734 —	Two R.B. only.	706 D	——
1734 Jan. 1	Marlborough	Thomas Hunt	1736 Oct. 1	— L. & R.B.	602 D 602 M	To Madras and Bengal.
Jan. 4	Drake	John Pelly	1735 July 5	— L. & R.B.	578 D 578 L	To Madras and Calcutta.
Jan. 10	Wilmington	Charles Massey	Aug. 22	— L. & R.B.	640 A 640 R	To Bombay, Surat, and Gombroon.
Jan. 15	Scarborough	George Westcott	1736 Sept. 12	— L. & R.B.	355 A 355 J	To Bombay, Calicut, Cochin, Tellicherry, and Goa.
Jan. 22	King William	James Sanders	April 10	— L. & R.B.	635 D 635 L	To Bombay, Surat, and Mocha.
Jan. 23	Princess Royal	Duncomb Backwell	1735 Oct. 18	— L. & R.B.	405 A 405 O	To Madras and Bengal.
Jan. 24	Middlesex	William Studholm	Sept. 17	— L. & R.B.	450 D 450 K	To Johanna and Bombay.
Sept. 30	Godolphin	Francis Steward	1736 July 17	— L. & R.B.	594 B 594 L	To Madras and Bengal.
Oct. 6	Houghton	Philip Worth	Aug. 10	— L. & R.B.	438 C 438 W	To Batavia, Amoy, and Whampoa.
Oct. 17	Onslow	J. Balchen	Sept. 6	— L. & R.B.	164 A 164 J	To Madras and Bengal.
Oct. 21	Beaufort	Richard Boulton	July 12	— L. & R.B.	637 A 637 E	To Madras and Bengal.
Nov. 7	London	Robert Bootle	Aug. 10	— L. & R.B.	313 E 313 S	To Java, Canton, Macao, and Sumatra.
Nov. 9	Newcastle	Josiah Lewis	1735 Mar. 30	— L. & R.B.	659 A 659 H	From Bourbon to England.
Dec. 10	Duke of Cumberland	Benjamin Braund	1736 Aug. 11	— L. & R.B.	562 C 562 K	To Bencoolen.
Dec. 16	Richmond	Charles Gough	1737 Sept. 1	— L. & R.B.	329 B 329 F	To Whampoa, Bombay, Tellicherry, &c.
Dec. 24	Nassau	William Hutchinson	1736 Aug. 15	— L. & R.B.	544 B 544 O	To Bencoolen and Fort St. David.
—	Derby	Abraham Anselme	1735 —	R.B. only.	653 I	——
—	Queen Caroline	David Wilkie	1736 —	L. & R.B. only.	631 D	——
1735 Feb. 6	Prince of Orange	Charles Hudson	1736 April 24	— L. & R.B.	636 B 636 G	To Madras.
Feb. 11	Wager	Charles Raymond	July 17	— L. & R.B.	592 A 592 G	To Madras and Bengal.

Log begins.	Ship.	Captain.	Log ends.	Ledger or Receipt Book.	Reference Number.	Remarks.
1735 May 13	Haselingfield	William Birch	1737 Aug. 29	— L. & R.B.	642 A 642 R	To Madras and Calcutta.
Sept. 22	Halifax	Thomas Manley succeeded by John Aston and John Blake.	1739 May 17	— L. & R.B.	651 B 651 G	To Madras, Calcutta, Surat, Tellicherry, and Goa.
Sept. 24	Walpole	Charles Boddam	1737 July 29	— L. & R.B.	293 D 293 BB	To Batavia and Canton.
Oct. 5	Britannia	Phineas Frognall	May 19	— L.	285 BB 285 B	To Mocha and Bombay.
Oct. 6	Harrington	Robert Jenkins	Sept. 12	— L. & R.B.	654 B 654 F	To Bombay and Bengal.
Oct. 7	Duke of Lorraine	William Crompton	Aug. 15	— L. & R.B.	650 B 650 G	To Bencoolen and Batavia.
Dec. 2	Prince William	Thomas Langworth	May 20	— L. & R.B.	324 D 324 J	To Madras.
Dec. 3	Princess of Wales	Robert Mead succeeded by Thomas Harry.	July 3	— L. & R.B.	510 C 510 M	To Batavia and Whampoa.
Dec. 4	Shaftesbury	Matthew Bookey	Oct. 1	— L. & R.B.	610 A 610 H	To Madras and Calcutta.
Dec. 10	Defence	James Montgomery	Sept. 20	— L. & R.B.	647 A 647 D	To Madras, Bengal, Bombay, and Tellicherry.
—	Compton	Robert Holmes	1736 —	Two R.B. only.	666 G	—
—	Pelham	Mead Woodford	1737 —	Two R.B. only.	607 E	—
1736 Jan. 5	Lynn	Charles Gilbert	June 29	— L. & R.B.	627 C 627 K	To Bombay and Tellicherry.
Jan. 5	Windham	Richard Shuter	Aug. 10	— L. & R.B.	230 C 230 M	To Bombay, Surat, Tellicherry, and Gombroon.
Feb. 21	Grantham	Roger Hair	July 26	— L. & R.B.	617 G 617 O	To Calcutta and Madras.
May 29	Normanton	Charles Rigby	1736 Sept. 6	— L. & R.B.	652 B 652 D	Towards Canton.
Aug. 27	Princess Louisa	Richard Pinnell	1738 Sept. 26	— L. & R.B.	639 B 639 E	To Calcutta.
Sept. 7	Royal Guardian	Henry Houdly	Aug. 31	— L. & R.B.	641 B 641 G	To Madras and Whampoa.
Sept. 7	Royal Guardian	Henry Houdly	Aug. 26	—	641 C	To Madras and Whampoa.
Sept. 12	Bedford	William Wells	May 24	— L. & R.B.	638 B 638 F	To Madras and Bengal.
Sept. 20	George	Nathaniel White	Aug. 9	— L. & R.B.	799 A-E 799 A-I	To Bencoolen and Batavia.
Sept. 21	Montagu	Daniel Seale	May 15	— L. & R.B.	552 I 552 Q	To Aden and Bombay.
Sept. 23	Wilmington	Charles Massey	1739 April 18	— L. & R.B.	640 B 640 F	To Mocha, Bombay, Gombroon, Tellicherry, and Madras.
Oct. 23	Harrison	Samuel Martin	1738 May 19	— L. & R.B.	644 C 644 G	To Limpoa and Whampoa.
Oct. 25	Lyell	John Acton	1739 June 29	— L. & R.B.	646 E 646 J	To Madras, Bengal, and Bombay.
Dec. 11	Winchester	Richard Sheppard succeeded by John Dove.	1738 Aug. 9	— L. & R.B.	643 A 643 D	To Whampoa.
—	Decker	Edward Williamson	1737 —	Two R.B. only.	701 C	—
—	Devonshire	Lawrence Prince	—	R.B. only.	272 P	—
—	Grafton	Lawrence Prince	—	Two R.B. only.	658 C	—
—	Newcastle	Richard Crabb	—	Two R.B. only.	659 C	—
—	Sussex	Francis Gostlin	—	Two R.B. only.	746 A	—
1737 Jan. 5	Duke of Dorset	Thomas Gilbert	1738 June 21	— L. & R.B.	612 B 612 J	To Fort St. George and Bengal.
Jan. 7	Heathcote	Jonathan Cape	Aug. 15	— L. & R.B.	625 H 625 B	To Bombay and Anjengo.
Feb. 23	Nottingham	Ralph Farr Winter	May 24	— L. & R.B.	287 A 287 O	To Fort St. George.
Aug. 1	King William	James Sanders	1739 July 11	— L. & R.B	635 E 635 M	To Mocha, Bombay, and Tellicherry.

Log begins.	Ship.	Captain.	Log ends.	Ledger or Receipt Book.	Reference Number.	Remarks.
1737 Aug. 1	Queen Caroline	Charles Birkhead	1739 July 3	— L. & R.B.	681 A 631 E	To Bencoolen.
Aug. 2	Godolphin	Francis Steward	Aug. 8	— L. & R.B.	594 C 594 M	To Madras and Whampoa.
Aug. 16	Prince of Wales	John Pelly	Aug. 16	— L. & R.B.	404 B 404 T	To Borneo and Whampoa.
Sept. 28	Scarborough	George Westcott	Aug. 24	— L. & R.B.	355 B 355 K	To Madras, Balasore, Bengal, and Bencoolen.
Oct. 5	Royal George	William Jobson	June 4	— L. & R.B.	17 A 17 S	To Bengal and Batavia.
Oct. 10	Princess Mary	George Martin	Nov. 27	— L. & R.B.	381 A 381 G	To Madras, Calcutta, Ingelee, Fort St. David, and Pondicherry.
Oct. 29	Princess Royal	Duncomb Backwell	July 16	— L. & R.B.	405 B 405 P	To Batavia and Whampoa.
Oct. 31	Duke of Cumberland	Benjamin Braund	Sept. 6	— L. & R.B.	562 D 562 L	To Madras and Bengal.
Nov. 20	Prince of Orange	Charles Hudson	July 13	— L. & R.B.	636 C 636 H	To Batavia and China.
Nov. 22	London	Robert Bootle	July 16	— L. & R.B.	318 F 318 T	To Java, Macao, and Whampoa.
Dec. 18	Beaufort	Thomas Stevens	June 13	— L. & R.B.	637 B 637 F	To Madras.
—	Anglesey	William Studholm	1738 —	Two R.B. only.	785 A	—
—	Resolution	George Bagwell	1739 —	Two R.B. only.	466 G	—
1738 Jan. 5	Nassau	William Hutchinson	Sept. 6	— L. & R.B.	544 C 544 P	To Bombay, Goa, and Tellicherry.
Feb. 6	Wager	Charles Raymond	Sept. 5	— L. & R.B.	592 B 592 H	To Madras and Bengal.
Feb. 8	Onslow	J. Balchen	June 26	— L. & R.B.	164 B 164 K	To Bombay.
Feb. 15	Princess Royal	Duncomb Backwell	1738 Aug. 3	— L. & R.B.	405 C 405 P	Towards China. (With Princess Mary, 381 B).
Mar. 25	Marlborough	Thomas Smith	1740 Oct. 7	— L. & R.B.	602 E 602 N	To Bencoolen and Batavia.
June 11	Harrington	Robert Jenkins	Oct. 9	— L. & R.B.	654 C 654 G	To Bombay, Tellicherry, and Whampoa.
Aug. 23	Walpole	Charles Boddam	Sept. 20	— L. & R.B.	293 E 293 CC	To Borneo and China.
Sept. 11	Duke of Lorraine	William Crompton	Sept. 14	— L. & R.B.	650 C & D 650 H	To Madras and Whampoa.
Sept. 19	Britannia	John Somner	Oct. 25	— L. & R.B.	285 CC 285 C	To Bencoolen.
Oct. 16	Richmond	William Weston	Oct. 28	— L. & R.B.	329 C 329 G	To Calcutta.
Oct. 17	Shaftesbury	Matthew Bookey	Nov. 12	— L. & R.B.	610 B 610 I	To Madras and Bengal.
Oct. —	Prince William	Thomas Langworth	1741 Nov. 24	— L. & R.B.	324 E 324 K	To Bombay, Surat, Goa, Tellicherry, Madras, and Bengal.
Nov. 3	Lynn	Charles Gilbert	1740 Sept. 20	— L. & R.B.	627 D 627 L	To Madras and Bengal.
Nov. 4	Defence	Thomas Coates	Oct. 11	— L. & R.B.	647 B 647 E	To Mocha, Bombay, Cochin, and Anjengo.
Dec. 19	Haselingfield	John Cooke	1741 July 29	— L. & R.B.	642 B 642 F	To Bombay, Surat, and Tellicherry.
Dec. 20	Somerset	Robert Holmes	Feb. 20	— L. & R.B.	626 A 626 E	To Bengal, Bencoolen, and Batavia.
Dec. 25	Houghton	Philip Worth	1740 Sept. 20	— L. & R.B.	438 D 438 X	To Whampoa.
Dec. 29	Warwick	Richard Shuter	Aug. 30	— —	585 A 585 I	To Madras, Calcutta, Bombay, and Tellicherry.
—	Normanton	Reginald Kemeys	1741 —	Two R.B. only.	652 E	—
1739 Jan. 21	Augusta	Augustus Townshend	1740 Sept. 20	— L. & R.B.	629 A 629 E	To Whampoa.
Feb. 15	Grantham	Roger Hale	Sept. 18	— L. & R.B.	617 H 617 P	To Fort St. George and Bengal.
May 14	Royal Guardian	Henry Hoadly	1741 Oct. 7	— L. & R.B.	641 D 641 H	To Madras, Bombay, and Tellicherry.
May 23	Duke	Thomas Hindman	Sept. 29	— L. & R.B.	648 A 648 C	To Bencoolen and Batavia.
Oct. 8	Bedford	William Wells	1742 Sept. 11	— L. & R.B.	638 C, D(1) & D 2 638 G	To Batavia and Bengal.

Log begins.	Ship.	Captain.	Log ends.	Ledger or Receipt Book.	Reference Number.	Remarks.
1739 Oct. 19	East India Yacht	- - -	1740 July 9	—	645 A	To St. Helena.
Nov. 3	Montagu	Fielder Freeman	1741 Nov. 21	— L. & R.B.	652 I (A) 552 R	To Bombay, Surat, and Tellicherry.
Nov. 3	Winchester -	Richard Pinnell	Oct. 9	— L. & R.B.	643 B 643 E	To Batavia and Whampoa.
Nov. 8	Princess of Wales -	Walter Hoxton succeeded by Thomas Harry.	Oct. 2	— L. & R.B.	510 D 510 N	To Calcutta.
Nov. 14	Wilmington -	Leonard Maddox	1740 Nov. 26	— L. & R.B.	640 C 640 G	To Madras.
Dec. 6	Heathcote -	Jonathan Cape -	1741 Oct. 6	— L. & R.B.	625 I 625 S	To Madras and Bengal.
Dec. 19	Haselingfield -	John Cooke	1740 Nov. 18	— L. & R.B.	642 C 642 F	To Bombay, Surat, and Tellicherry.
Dec. 20	Durrington -	Richard Crabb	1741 Oct. 3	— L. & R.B.	613 A & B 613 F & G	To Madras and Bengal.
Dec. 20	Edgbaston -	Stephen Cobham	1742 Aug. 7	— L. & R.B.	622 A 622 F	To Bencoolen and Batavia.
Dec. 20	Edgbaston	Stephen Cobham -	Aug. 21	—	622 B	To Bencoolen and Batavia.
Dec. 21	Colchester -	R. Mickelfield	1741 July 27	— L. & R.B.	113 A (2) 113 D	To Bengal.
Dec. 22	Princess Louisa -	John Pinson - -	Nov. 8	— L. & R.B.	639 C 639 F	To Madras, Calcutta, Bombay, and Tellicherry.
1740 Feb. 8	Halifax -	John Blake -	1742 Dec. 3	— L. & R.B.	651 G 651 H	To Bombay, Madras, Calcutta, and Tellicherry.
Mar. 8	Nottingham -	Thomas Brown -	July 31	— L. & two R.B.	287 B 287 P	To Bombay, Tellicherry, and Madras.
Mar. 15	Duke of Dorset -	Thomas Gilbert -	July 27	— L. & R.B.	612 C 612 K	To Batavia and Whampoa.
Mar. 29	Hardwicke - -	John Hallett	1741 Oct. 3	— L. & R.B.	568 A 568 I	To Calcutta, Madras, and Fort St. David.
April 11	Cæsar - -	Robert Cummings -	1742 Aug. 28	— L. & R.B.	235 D 235 O	To Madras.
June 15	Godolphin	Francis Steward -	Oct. 2	— L. & R.B.	594 D 594 N	To Bombay, Tellicherry, and Whampoa.
Oct. 10	East India Yacht -	Gabriel Steward -	1741 Oct. 2	—	645 B	To St Helena.
Oct. 26	Royal George -	Thomas Field	1742 Nov. 5	— L. & R.B.	17 B 17 T	To Batavia and Bencoolen.
Nov. 9	Prince of Wales	John Pelly -	July 9	— L. & R.B.	404 C 404 U	To Mocha and Madras.
Nov. 19	Prince of Orange	Charles Hudson -	Sept. 16	— L. & R.B.	636 D 636 I	To Madras and Bengal.
Nov. 22	London	Mathew Bootle -	Sept. 17	— L. & R.B.	313 G 313 U	To Madras, Balasore, Fort William, and Bencoolen.
Nov. 23	Nassau -	George Jackson	Nov. 4	— L. & R.B.	544 D 544 Q	To Balasore and Calcutta.
Nov. 23	Onslow - -	J. Balchen - -	1743 Oct. 21	Two J. L. & R.B.	164 C & D 164 L	To Bombay and China.
Nov. 24	Beaufort - -	Thomas Stevens -	1742 Aug. 28	— L. & R.B.	637 C 637 G	To Bengal.
Nov. 24	King William -	James Sanders - succeeded by Joseph Phillips.	Nov. 12	— L. & R.B.	635 F 635 N	To Madras and Bengal.
Nov. 25	Fort St. George -	John Acton -	Aug. 21	— L. & R.B.	632 A 632 F	To Bombay, Tellicherry, and Anjengo.
Dec. 8	Princess Amelia	Samuel Martin -	1741 Aug. 3	— L. & R.B.	36 D 36 Z	To Canton.
—	Princess Mary -	George Martin -	1743 —	L. & R.B. only.	381 H	——
1741 Jan. 20	Queen Caroline -	Charles Birkhead	1742 Nov. 16	— L. & R.B.	631 B 631 F	To Bombay and Surat.
Jan. 21	Northampton - -	Duncomb Backwell -	Oct. 3	— L. & R.B.	198 A 198 L	To China.
Jan. 21	York - -	Henry Lascelles -	Sept. 17	— L. & R.B.	237 A 237 R	To Whampoa.

Log begins.	Ship.	Captain.	Log ends.	Ledger or Receipt Book.	Reference Number.	Remarks.
1741 Feb. 7	Kent - -	William Robson -	1742 Sept. 24	— L. & R.B.	317 C 317 N	To Bengal.
Feb. 23	Admiral Vernon	Benjamin Webster	1743 Aug. 8	— L. & R.B.	623 A 623 E	To Madras.
Feb. 26	Scarborough -	George Westcott	1742 Oct. 1	— L. & R.B.	355 C 355 L	To Acheen, Vizagapatam, and Rogues River.
Mar. 26	Porto Bello - -	Benjamin Fisher	1743 Aug. 26	— L. & R.B.	615 A 615 E	To Bombay, Surat, and Tellicherry.
April 2	Wager -	Charles Raymond	1742 Dec. 2	— L. & R.B.	592 C 592 I	To Madras and Bengal.
May 7	Neptune -	F. D'Abbadie -	1743 May 20	— L. & R.B.	98 A 98 T	To Bencoolen and Batavia.
May 20	Tigris - - -	J. Petre - -	Aug. 31	— L. & R.B.	219 A 219 H	To Bengal.
Sept. 16	Harrington - -	Robert Jenkins succeeded by Charles Foulis.	1744 Nov. 8	— L. & R.B.	654 D 654 H	To Bombay, Tellicherry, and Whampoa.
Sept. 30	Shaftesbury - -	Matthew Bookey	1743 Nov. 17	— L. & R.B.	610 C 610 J	To Madras and Bengal.
Oct. 17	Swift	Henry Watts	1742 Sept. 30	—	616 A	To Madagascar.
Oct. 27	Defence - -	Thomas Coates	1743 Sept. 15	— L. & R.B.	647 C 647 F	To Whampoa.
Oct. 30	Duke of Lorraine -	Jonathan Wilson succeeded by Nathaniel Hancock.	1744 April 11	— L. & R.B.	650 E 650 I	To Bencoolen and Batavia.
Nov. 1	Walpole -	Benjamin Lowe	1743 Sept. 12	— L. & R.B.	293 F 293 DD	To Madras, Vizagapatam, and Calcutta.
Nov. 3	Lynn - - -	Charles Gilbert -	July 10	— L. & R.B.	627 E 627 M	To Fort St. George and Bengal.
Nov. 5	Benjamin - -	B. Way - -	Aug. 9	— L. & R.B.	122 A 122 E	To Bombay and Madras.
Nov. 12	Marlborough -	Thomas Smith	Sept. 8	— L. & R.B.	602 F 602 O	To Madras and Bengal.
Dec. 10	Somerset - -	Christopher Howes - succeeded by Henry Kent.	Sept. 7	— L. & R.B.	626 B 626 F	To Bombay and Surat.
1742 Jan. 5	Augusta -	Augustus Townshend	Sept. 12	— L. & R.B.	629 B 629 F	To Batavia and Whampoa.
Jan. 9	Severn -	J. Collier -	1744 Mar. 29	— L. & R.B.	139 A 139 F	To Borneo.
Jan. 12	Salisbury -	Christopher Burrows	Nov. 9	— L. & R.B.	478 A 478 J	To Bombay, Tellicherry, Gombroon, and Madras.
Jan. 18	Grantham - -	Roger Hale -	Feb. 28	— Two R.B.	617 I 617 Q	To Fort St. George, Bengal, and Bencoolen.
Jan. 20	Houghton -	Isaac Worth	1743 Sept. 11	— L. & R.B.	438 E 438 Y	To Madras and Calcutta.
Feb. 12	Wilmington - -	John Todd - -	Sept. 20	— L. & R.B.	640 D 640 H	To Bengal and Madras.
Feb. 28	Britannia - -	John Somner	Sept. 6	— L. & R.B.	285 DD 285 D	To Gombroon, Bombay, and Tellicherry.
Oct. 14	Duke - -	Thomas Hindman	1744 Dec. 17	— L. & R.B.	648 B 648 D	To Madras and Calcutta.
Oct. 5	Montagu -	Fielder Freeman succeeded by George Cuming.	1745 Mar. 14	— L. & R.B.	552 J 552 S	To Mocha, Bombay, Tellicherry, Goa, Pondicherry, Madras, and Calcutta.
Nov. 2	Exeter -	William Weston -	1744 Oct. 28	— L. & R.B.	138 A 138 O	To Madras and Calcutta.
Nov. 30	Montfort - -	Robert Hauslapp -	Sept. 21	— L. & R.B.	608 A 608 E	To Madras and Bengal.
Dec. 1	Winchester -	Gabriel Steward succeeded by John Samson.	1746 Mar. 18	— L. & R.B.	643 C 643 F	To Madras, Calcutta, and Tellicherry.
Dec. 2	Princess Amelia	Samuel Martin -	1744 Sept. 1	— L. & R.B.	36 E 36 AA	To Madras and Bengal.
Dec. 2	Winchelsea - -	Alexander Adair -	1746 Mar. 15	— L. & R.B.	4 A 4 Q	To Bombay and Calcutta.

Log begins.	Ship.	Captain.	Log ends.	Ledger or Receipt Book.	Reference Number.	Remarks.
1742 Dec. 4	Haselingfield - -	Robert Haldane	1744 Nov. 10	— L. & R.B.	642 D 642 G	To Whampoa.
Dec. 10	Swift - - -	Henry Watts -	1743 Mar. 31	—	616 B	To Table Bay (contains also log of ships "Princess Mary" and "Liverpool").
Dec. 22	Princess Mary	Robert Osborne	Sept. 12	— L. & R.B.	381 B 381 H	From Canton to England (contains also log of "Princess Royal" of 1738).
Dec. 28	Royal Guardian -	William Earl Benson	1744 Oct. 12	— L. & R.B.	641 E 641 I	To Bencoolen.
—	Princess Louisa -	John Pinson -	1742 —	Two R.B. only.	639 G	——
1743 Jan. 2	Princess of Wales -	Thomas Harry -	1744 Oct. 20	— L. & R.B.	510 F 510 O	To Bombay, Tellicherry, and Anjengo.
Jan. 19	Heathcote -	Jonathan Cape -	Sept. 12	— L. & R.B.	625 J 625 T	To Madras and Bengal.
Feb. 15	St. George . -	Robert Robinson	1745 Mar. 15	— L. & R.B.	584 D 584 K	To Calcutta, Bombay, and Surat.
Feb. 28	Colchester -	R. Mickelfield -	Sept. 18	— L. & R.B.	113 B 113 E	To Borneo. (This Ledger contains also two Supplementary Ledgers).
Mar. 30	Hardwicke -	John Hallett -	1746 Aug. 22	— L. and two R.B.	568 B 568 J	To Bombay, Batavia, and Whampoa.
April 20	Princess Mary - -	Robert Osborne	1743 May 7	—	616 B	From the Cape of Good Hope to St. Helena (contains also logs of the "Swift" and the "Liverpool").
May 15	Liverpool - -	Thomas Swanton -	Aug. 1	—	616 B	From St. Helena to England (contains also logs of the "Swift" and the "Princess Mary").
Aug. 26	Edgbaston - -	Stephen Cobham succeeded by John Hereford.	1746 Oct. 10	— L. and two R.B.	622 C 622 G	To Mocha, Bombay, Surat, Calcutta, and Madras.
Sept. 10	Lapwing - -	Henry Watts -	Jan. 4	— L. & R.B.	475 A 475 H	To Madras, Bengal, and Bencoolen.
Sept. 23	Prince of Wales -	John Pelly - -	1745 Oct. 9	— L. & R.B.	404 D 404 V	To Madras.
Sept. 24	Prince William -	Thomas Langworth -	1746 Mar. 17	— L. & R.B.	324 F 324 L	To Madras and Bengal.
Oct. 7	Cæsar -	Matthew Court -	Feb. 20	— L. & R.B.	235E, F, & G 235 P	To Batavia and Bencoolen.
Oct. 22	Durrington - -	Richard Crabb -	1745 Dec. 30	— L. & R.B.	613 C 613 H	To Madras and Bengal.
Nov. 1	Duke of Dorset -	Thomas Frognall -	1746 Mar. 24	— L. & R.B.	612 D 612 L	To Madras and Bengal.
Nov. 8	Beaufort - -	Thomas Stevens	1745 Mar. 10	— L. & R.B.	637 D 637 H	To Madras, Vizagapatam, and Calcutta.
Nov. 22	York - -	Henry Lascelles	Feb. 27	— L. & R.B.	237 B 237 S	To Fort St. George and Whampoa.
Dec. 19	Godolphin - -	John Stevens -	1746 Mar. 25	— L. & R.B.	594 E 594 O	To Bengal.
Dec. 20	Fort St. George, -	John Acton - -	Aug. 25	— L. & R.B.	632 B 632 G	To Gombroon and Bombay.
Dec. 21	Stafford - -	Felix Baker	Feb. 26	— L. & R.B.	560 A 560 H	To Whampoa.
Dec. 31	Warwick - -	Robert Misenor -	1744 Nov. 20	— L. & R.B.	585 B 585 J	To Bombay and Surat.
1744 Jan. 20	Elizabeth - -	R. Pinnell - -	1746 Aug. 26	— L. & R.B.	102 A 102 H	To Bombay and Tellicherry.
Jan. 20	King William	Joseph Phillips -	Feb. 17	— L. & R.B.	635 G 635 O	To Bombay.
Feb. 10	Wager - -	Charles Raymond	Oct. 14	— L. and two R.B.	592 D 592 J	To Batavia and Bengal.
Mar. 3	Benjamin - -	B. Way - -	Aug. 19	— L. & R.B.	122 B 122 F	To Madras.
Mar. 4	Porto Bello - -	Benjamin Fisher	July 20	— L. & R.B.	615 B 615 F	To Batavia.
April 11	Swift - - -	William Stevens	1745 May 20	— L. & R.B.	616 C 616 E	To Madras and Calcutta.
May 2	Orford - -	Edmund Smyth	1747 Feb. 19	— L. & R.B.	630 A 630 C	To Bencoolen and Batavia.

Log begins.	Ship.	Captain.	Log ends.	Ledger or Receipt Book.	Reference Number.	Remarks.
1744 June 26	Winchelsea	Christopher Baron	1746 Jan. 31	—	4 B	To Calcutta.
Sept. 27	Royal George	Thomas Field	1747 June 2	— L. & R.B.	17 C 17 U	To Madras and Bengal.
Oct. 10	Kent	William Robson	1748 June 21	— L. & R.B.	317 D 317 O	To Madras, Calcutta, and Vizagapatam.
Oct. 11	Essex	George Jackson	1747 July 31	— L. & R.B.	229 C 229 BB	To Bombay, Surat, and Mocha.
Oct. 12	Lincoln	John Blake	1746 Oct. 13	— L. & Two R.B.	618 A 618 C	To Madras and Fort St. David.
Oct. 12	London	Mathew Bootle	1747 Dec. 3	— L. & R.B.	313 H & I 313 V	To Madras and Whampoa.
Oct. 13	Queen Caroline	Benjamin Mason	1746 Oct. 8	— L. & R.B.	631 C 631 G	To Bencoolen.
Oct. 13	Scarborough	George Westcott	1747 Feb. 28	— L. & R.B.	355 D 355 M	To Madeira, Madras, Balasore, and Rogues River.
Oct. 27	Admiral Vernon	Benjamin Webster succeeded by Edmund Cooke.	1746 Oct. 8	— L. & two R. B.	623 B 623 F	To Madras and Fort St. David.
Dec. 11	Dolphin	Charles Pigot	Aug. 11	— L. & R.B.	633 A 633 B	To Madras.
Dec. 25	Walpole	Benjamin Lowe	1747 Nov. 24	— L. & R.B.	293 G 293 EE	To Bombay, Tellicherry, and Whampoa.
Dec. 26	Augusta	Augustus Townshend	1748 Jan. 16	— L. & R.B.	629 C 629 G	To Whampoa.
Dec. 26	Pelham	William Wells succeeded by George Lindsay.	1747 Aug. 20	— L. & R.B.	607 A 607 F	To Bombay and Tellicherry.
—	Princess Mary	Robert Osborne	1756 —	L. & two R. B. only.	381 I	———
—	Northampton	[D. Backwell]	1746 —	Two R.B. only.	198 M & N	———
1745 April 22	Onslow	R. Congreve	1748 Aug. 16	— L. & R.B.	164 E 164 M	To Borneo and China.
Oct. 15	Severn	J. Collier	June 23	— L. & R.B.	139 B 139 G	To Bombay, Tellicherry, &c.
Oct. 17	Somerset	Thomas Tolson	1747 Dec. 24	— L. & R.B.	626 C 626 G	To Bencoolen.
Nov. 4	Dragon	Henry Kent	1748 Aug. 4	— L. & R.B.	598 A 598 G	To Batavia and Whampoa.
Dec. 29	Shaftesbury	Matthew Bookey succeeded by William Bookey.	Jan. 12	— L. & R.B.	610 D 610 K	To Whampoa.
Dec. 30	Tavistock	Thomas Coates succeeded by Nathaniel Cush.	Feb. 19	— L. & R.B.	593 C 593 G	To Whampoa.
Dec. 31	Salisbury	Christopher Burrows	April 18	— L. & R.B.	478 B 478 K	To Calcutta.
—	Lapwing	Francis Cheyne	1746 —	L. & R.B. only.	475 I	———
1746 Jan. 11	Montfort	Robert Hanslapp	1748 Jan. 20	— L. & R.B.	608 B 608 F	To Madras and Bengal.
Jan. 12	Sandwich	John Petre	Feb. 13	— L. & R.B.	606 A 606 F	To Whampoa.
Jan. 27	Houghton	Isaac Worth	1749 Mar. 14	— L. & R.B.	438 F 438 Z	To Bencoolen, Fort St. David, Culpee, Jugelee, and Vizagapatam.
Jan. 27	Warwick	Robert Misenor succeeded by Edward Ward.	Jan. 28	— L. & R.B.	585 C & D 585 K	To Bombay, Fort St. David, and Calcutta.
Jan. 31	Marlborough	Thomas Smith	1748 May 5	— L. & R.B.	602 G 602 P	To Madras and Bencoolen.
Feb. 25	Ilchester	John Tedd	Sept. 21	— L. & R.B.	601 A 601 E	To Bombay, Tellicherry, and Fort St. David.
Feb. 27	Lynn	Charles Gilbert	July 20	— L. & R.B.	627 F 627 N	To Bombay.
Feb. 28	Princess of Wales	Thomas Harry	1749 Feb. 8	— L. & R.B.	510 G 510 P	To Calcutta, Vizagapatam, and Fort St. David.

Log begins.	Ship.	Captain.	Log ends.	Ledger or Receipt Book.	Reference Number.	Remarks.
1746 Mar. 26	Exeter	William Weston	1749 Oct. 13	— L. & R.B.	136 B 136 P	To Bombay, Calcutta, &c.
April 9	Princess Amelia	Thomas Best	1747 Feb. 17	— R.B.	36 F 36 BB	To Madras. (This ship was taken by the French on 17th February 1747).
April 24	Bombay Castle	T. Browne	1749 Nov. 19	— L. & R.B.	125 A & B 125 L	To Fort St. David, Pondicherry, &c.
April 28	Portfield	Francis D'Abbadie	1748 Sept. 9	— L. & R.B.	609 A 609 E	To Mocha, Bombay, and Surat.
May 17	Britannia	John Somner	April 28	— L. & R.B.	285 EE 285 E	To Fort St. David.
May 25	Prince Edward	Robert Haldane	Sept. 5	— L. & R.B.	573 A 573 F	To Batavia and Whampoa.
June 10	Norfolk	Nathaniel Hancock	Aug. 25	— L. & R.B.	541 A 541 M	To Bencoolen and Whampoa.
Oct. 17	Cæsar	Matthew Court	Dec. 2	— L. & R.B.	235 H 235 Q	To Batavia and Bengal.
Oct. 18	Eastcourt	William Earl Benson	1749 Aug. 30	— L. & R.B.	586 A 586 E	To Batavia, Balasore, and Calcutta.
Oct. 18	Stafford	Felix Baker	1748 Aug. 29	— L. & R.B.	560 B 560 I	To Batavia and Whampoa.
Oct. 18	York	Henry Lascelles	Aug. 30	— L. & R.B.	237 C 237 T	To Whampoa.
Oct. 19	Prince of Wales	John Pelly	1749 Oct. 8	— L. & R.B.	404 E 404 W	To Batavia and Whampoa.
Oct. 20	St. George	Robert Robinson	1748 Oct. 14	— L. & R.B.	584 E 584 L	To Whampoa.
Oct. 21	Grantham	Walter Wilson	Aug. 16	— L. & R.B.	617 J 617 R	To Batavia and Bencoolen.
Oct. 22	Porto Bello (sloop)	Walter Hooke (master).	1747 June 2	— L. & R.B.	615 C 615 G	From Negapatam to England.
Nov. 2	Anson	Charles Foulis	Sept. 1	— Two R.B.	549 A 549 O	To Ormus, &c.
Nov. 20	Heathcote	Jonathan Cape	June 7	Two R.B. —	625 K 625 U	Towards Mocha.
Nov. 20	Oxford	Thomas Stevens	1749 Aug. 18	— L. & R.B.	588 A 588 E	To Fort St. David, Bencoolen, and Batavia.
Dec. 23	Swift	John Bell	Mar. 6	— L. & R.B.	616 D 616 F	To Fort St. David and Trincomalee.
—	Lapwing	Francis Cheyne	1747 —	L. & R.B. only.	475 J	—
—	Trial	Richard Thelwall	—	L. & R.B. only.	580 H	—
1747 Jan. 6	Lapwing	Francis Cheyne	1749 June 12	— L. & R.B.	475 B 475 K	To Fort St. George and Bengal.
Jan. 30	Benjamin	G. Mead	June 23	— L. & R.B.	122 C 122 G	To Bencoolen, Fort St. David, Pondicherry, &c.
Jan. 30	Durrington	Richard Crabb	1750 July 9	— L. & R.B.	613 D 613 I	To Bombay, Surat, and Mocha.
Jan. 30	Stretham	William Pinnell	1749 Sept. 25	— L. & R.B.	605 G 311 C	To Bombay and Tellicherry.
Jan. 31	Porto Bello	Benjamin Fisher	Nov. 15	— L. and two R.B.	615 D 615 H & I	To Fort St. David and Bengal.
Jan. 31	Prince William	William Webber	1750 Sept. 22	— L. & R.B.	324 G 324 M	To Fort St. David, Calcutta, Colombo, Calicut, Tellicherry, Goa, and Bombay.
Jan. 31	True Briton	Henry Broadley	1749 Sept. 16	— L. & R.B.	297 A 297 Q	To Fort St. David, Vizagapatam, Calcutta, and Tellicherry.
July 11	Admiral Vernon	Edmund Cooke	1750 June 23	— L. & R.B.	623 C 623 G	To Bencoolen, Batavia, and Whampoa.
July 12	Lincoln	John Nanfan	1749 May 14	— Two R.B.	618 B 618 D	To Fort St. David and Trincomalee.
July 13	Fort St. George	William Bressey succeeded by Robert Brown.	1748 Oct. 27	— L. & R.B.	632 C 632 H	To Fort St. David.
July 14	Royal Duke	George Cuming	1750 July 21	— L. & R.B.	614 A 614 E	To Fort St. David, Bombay, Whampoa, and Batavia.
July 18	Swallow	Norton Hutchinson	1749 April 16	— L. & R.B.	634 A 385 J	To Batavia, Fort St. David, and Bengal.

Log begins.	Ship.	Captain.	Log ends.	Ledger or Receipt Book.	Reference Number.	Remarks.
1747 July 28	Rhoda	John McNemara	1750 July 17	— L. &R.B.	596 A 596 F	To Fort St. David, Bengal, and China.
July 29	Delawar	William Steevens	July 2	— L. & R.B.	322 A 322 E	To Fort St. David, Tellicherry, Pondicherry, Borneo, and China.
July 29	Elizabeth	A. Lawrence	1751 May 30	— L.& R.B.	102 B & C 102 I	To Bombay, Bengal, and Madras.
Aug. 11	Edgecote	John Pearse	1750 July 14	— L. & R.B.	599 A 599 E	To Fort St. David, Batavia, and China.
Aug. 13	Edgbaston	John Hereford succeeded by Edward Tiddeman.	Oct. 11	— L. & R.B.	622 D 622 H	To Fort St. David, Pondicherry, and Calcutta.
Aug. 21	Severn	J. Collier	1748 April 19	—	139 C	From Fort St. David to England. (See "Princess Amelia," No. 36 F).
Aug. 26	Royal George	Thomas Field	1750 June 15	— L. & R.B.	17 D 17 V	To Bengal and Batavia.
Sept. 24	Hardwicke	John Samson	1749 July 21	— L. & R.B.	568 C 568 K	To Fort St. David and Whampoa.
Sept. 26	Chesterfield	Edwin Carter	1750 July 6	— L. & R.B.	507 A 507 L	To Fort St. David and Pondicherry.
Oct. 9	Duke of Dorset	Thomas Frognall	1749 Aug. 12	— L. & R.B.	612 E 612 M	To Fort St. David and Whampoa.
Oct. 23	Essex	George Jackson	May 22	— L. & R.B.	229 D 229 CC	To Mocha and Bombay.
Oct. 24	Wager	Josiah Hindman	July 27	— L. & R.B.	592 E 592 K	To Fort St. David and Whampoa.
Nov. 28	Godolphin	John Stevens	Nov. 25	— L. & R.B.	594 F 594 P	To Bencoolen and Batavia.
Dec. 22	Orford	Philip Jodrell	Aug. 26	— L. & R.B.	630 B 630 D	To Gombroon, Bombay, Tellicherry, and Anjengo.
—	Colchester	Richard Wood	1751 —	L. & R.B. only.	113 F	——
—	Dolphin	George Newton	1749 —	Two R.B. only.	633 C	——
—	Winchelsea	Christopher Baron	1750 —	R. B. only.	4 R	——
1748 Jan. 3	Scarborough	Philip D'Auvergne	1749 June 27	— L. & R.B.	355 E 355 N	To Fort St. David, Malacca, and Whampoa.
Feb. 4	Pelham	George Lindsay	1750 June 11	— L. & R.B.	607 B 607 G	To Fort St. David and Whampoa.
Feb. 20	Somerset	Thomas Tolson	June 11	— L. & R.B.	626 D 626 H	To Fort St. David and Whampoa.
Mar. 19	Doddington	Benjamin Mason	June 14	— L. & R.B.	619 A 619 C	To Bombay, Tellicherry, and Whampoa.
May 20	Duke of Newcastle	Francis Fowler	Sept. 15	— L. & R.B.	655 A 655 B	To Batavia, Bencoolen, Fort St. David, Madras, Anjengo, and Tellicherry.
Aug. 28	Boscawen	Benjamin Braund	1751 July 3	— L. & R.B.	572 A 572 E	To Bombay, Surat, Gombroon, and Mocha.
Aug. 30	Salisbury	Christopher Burrows	1750 Sept. 22	— L. & R.B.	478 C & D 478 L	To Bombay, Surat, and Anjengo.
Sept. 27	Dragon	Henry Kent	Sept. 13	— L. & R.B.	598 B 598 H	To Madras, Vizagapatam, and Calcutta.
Oct. 27	Montfort	Robert Hanslapp	July 25	— L. & R.B.	602 C 602 G	To Fort St. David and Whampoa.
Oct. 27	Sandwich	John Petre	Aug. 11	— L. & R.B.	606 B 606 G	To Fort St. David and Whampoa.
Nov. 4	Britannia	John Somner	1752 May 17	— L. & R.B.	285 FF 285 F	To Fort St. David, Bombay, Surat, Bengal, and Madras.
Nov. 7	Tavistock	Nathaniel Cush	1750 Oct. 9	— L. & R.B.	593 D 593 H	To Fort St. David, Vizagapatam, and Bengal.
Nov. 8	Augusta	Thomas Parker	1751 July 2	— L. & R.B.	629 D 629 H	To Fort St. David and Whampoa.

Log begins.	Ship.	Captain.	Log ends.	Ledger or Receipt Book.	Reference Number.	Remarks.
1748 Nov. 11	Griffin	Thomas Dethick	1750 July 21	— L. & R.B.	603 A 603 E	To Fort St. David and Whampoa.
Nov. 12	Walpole	Benjamin Lowe	1751 Aug. 28	— L. & R.B.	293 H 293 FF	To Calcutta, Mocha, and Bombay.
Dec. 26	Marlborough	William Parks	April 2	— L. & R.B.	602 H 602 Q	To Bencoolen and Batavia.
1749 Jan. 11	Warren	Alphonsus Glover	Oct. 5	— L. & R.B.	571 A 571 E	To Bombay, Vizagapatam, Culpee, and Kedgeree.
Jan. 25	Severn	R. Dorrill	Aug. 13	— L. & R.B.	139 D 139 H	To Fort St. David, Calcutta, Bombay, Surat, and Madras.
Feb. 5	Stafford	Felix Baker	Aug. 13	— L. & R.B.	560 C 560 J	To Bombay, Surat, Anjengo, Tellicherry, Cochin, and Whampoa.
Aug. 8	Lapwing	Francis Cheyne	Mar. 26	— L. & R.B.	475 C 475 L	To Fort St. David, Madras, and Calcutta.
Sept. 5	Swallow	John Bell	1752 Feb. 28	Two J. L. & two R.B.	385 A & B 385 K	To Fort St. David, Fort St. George, Bencoolen, and Calcutta.
Sept. 16	Portfield	Carteret Le Geyt	1751 June 26	— L. & R.B.	609 B 609 F	To Fort St. David and Whampoa.
Oct. 16	York	Edward Ward	Sept. 10	— L. & R.B.	237 D 237 U	To Fort St. David and Canton.
Oct. 17	Grantham	Walter Wilson succeeded by John Oliver.	Oct. 8	— L. & R.B.	617 K 617 S	To Fort St. David, Whampoa, and Batavia.
Oct. 17	Prince Edward	Robert Haldane	Aug. 19	— L. & R.B.	573 B 573 G	To Fort St. David, Madras, and Whampoa.
Oct. 17	Suffolk	William Wilson	July 2	— L. & R.B.	397 A 397 H	To Batavia.
Nov. 13	Lynn	William Egerton	1750 Aug. 5	— Two R.B.	627 G 627 O	To Fort St. David and Bengal.
Nov. 14	Kent	William Robson	1752 July 12	— L. & R.B.	317 E 317 P	To Fort St. David, Bombay, and Bengal.
Nov. 14	Norfolk	Nathaniel Hancock	1751 Sept. 21	— L. & R.B.	541 B 541 N	To Fort St. David and Bengal.
Nov. 16	London	William Sedgwick	1752 June 12	— L. & R.B.	313 J & K 313 W	To Fort St. David, Madras, Culpee, Bombay, Mocha, and Calcutta.
Dec. 30	Ilchester	John Tedd	1751 Oct. 7	— L. & R.B.	601 B 601 F	To Gombroon, Bombay, and Tellicherry.
—	Duke of Cumberland	Robert Osborne	1749 —	Two R.B. only.	562 M	This ship was lost on the 16th January 1750, in the Bay of Ayoffe, Cape de Verde. (For list of crew see log of "Expedition" for 1750, 621 A).
1750 Jan. 12	Anson	Charles Foulis	1752 June 25	— L. & R.B.	549 B 549 P	To Bombay, Surat, Tellicherry, and Whampoa.
Jan. 12	Shaftesbury	William Bookey	Sept. 22	— L. & R.B.	610 E 610 L	To Bombay and Surat.
[Jan. ?]	Expedition	- - -	1750 Aug. 10	—	621 A	Imperfect. (Contains a list of the crew of the "Duke of Cumberland" lost in the bay of Ayoffe.)
Feb. 1	Hector	Stephen Kirwan	1754 May 14	— L. & R.B.	486 A 486 J	To Gombroon, Bombay, Surat, Culpee, and Tellicherry.
Mar. 1	Benjamin	G. Meard	1751 Sept. 9	— L. & R.B.	122 D 122 H	To Bengal and Fort St. David.
June 4	India Pilot Boat	George Bere	1750 Nov. 6	—	611 A	To Africa.
June 5	Strickland	Nevell Norway	Nov. 5	—	583 A	To Goree.
Oct. 6	Cæsar	Matthew Court	1752 June 1	— L. & R.B.	235 I 235 R	To Fort St. David and Whampoa.
Oct. 6	Essex	George Jackson	June 24	— L. & R.B.	229 E 229 DD	To Fort St. David, Madras, the Nicobar Islands, and Canton.
Oct. 7	Onslow	T. Hinde	June 19	— L.	164 F 164 N	To Batavia and Bencoolen.
Oct. 10	Warwick	Nicholas Webb	Sept. 30	— L. & R.B.	585 E 585 L	To Madras and Whampoa.
Oct. 23	St. George	Robert Robinson	July 17	— L. & R.B.	584 F 584 M	To Madras and Whampoa.
Nov. 3	Triton	Gilbert Slater	Aug. 10	— L. & R.B.	366 A 366 P	To Fort St. David, Madras, and Whampoa.
Nov. 20	Dragon	Henry Kent	April 6	— L. & R.B.	598 C 598 I	To Madras, Vizagapatam, and Calcutta.

Log begins.	Ship.	Captain.	Log ends.	Ledger or Receipt Book.	Reference Number.	Remarks.
1750 Nov. 20	Duke of Dorset	Thomas Frognall	1752 Sept. 21	— L. & R.B.	612 F 612 N	To Madras, Vizagapatam, Culpee, and Kedgeree.
Nov. 20	Hardwicke	John Samson	Aug. 22	— L. & R.B.	568 D 568 L	To Fort St. David, Vizagapatam, and Culpee.
Nov. 20	Prince Henry	Thomas Best	Dec. 9	— L. & R.B.	325 A 325 H	To Gombroon and Bombay.
Nov. 20	Scarborough	Philip D'Auvergne	1753 Mar. 10	— L. & R.B.	355 F 355 O	To Fort St. David and Culpee.
Nov. 20	Wager	Josiah Hindman	June 18	— L. & R.B.	592 F 592 L	To Fort St. George, Bengal, Bombay, and Surat.
Nov. 26	Anson	John Ramsay	1752 June 21	— L. & R.B.	549 C 549 Q	To Whampoa.
Dec. 17	Prince George	Philip Jodrell	1753 July 8	— L. & R.B.	575 A 575 F	To Bombay, Surat, Tellicherry, Cochin, Goa, and Whampoa.
—	True Briton	Henry Broadley	1753 —	L. & R.B. only.	297 R	——
1751 Jan. 1	Prince George	Philip Jodrell	July 7	— L. & R.B.	575 B 575 F	To Bombay, Surat, Tellicherry, Cochin, Goa, and Whampoa.
Jan. 30	Eastcourt	William Earl Benson	1752 Sept. 19	— L. & R.B.	586 B 586 F	To Bombay and Surat.
Mar. 21	Strethum	Charles Mason	1753 July 12	— L. & R.B.	605 H 605 P	To Mocha and Bombay.
July 12	Durrington	Richard Drake	1754 Nov. 3	— L. & R.B.	613 E 613 J	To Fort St. David, Madras, Culpee, Ingelee, Bombay, and Surat.
Oct. 7	Exeter	William Fernell	1753 July 4	— L. & R.B.	138 C 138 Q	To Batavia, &c.
Oct. 8	Edgecote	John Pearse	Aug. 18	— L. & R.B.	599 B 599 F	To Madras and Whampoa.
Oct. 8	Rhoda	John McNemara	Aug. 4	— L. & R.B.	596 C 596 G	To Madras and China.
Oct. 9	Delawar	Abraham Dominicus	1754 May 28	— L. & R.B.	322 B 322 F	To Madras, Fort St. David, and Batavia.
Oct. 9	Oxford	Thomas Stevens	Mar. 19	— L. & R.B.	388 B 388 F	To Fort St. David, Fort St. George, and Culpee.
Oct. 10	Prince of Wales	William Peck	1753 July 19	— L. & R.B.	404 F 404 X	To Fort St. David, Madras, and Whampoa.
Oct. 11	Houghton	Richard Walpole	June 21	— L. & R.B.	438 G 438 AA	To Whampoa.
Oct. 13	Drake	Benjamin Fisher	Aug. 6	— L. & R.B.	578 E 578 M	To Madras and Whampoa.
Nov. 10	Admiral Vernon	Edmund Cooke	Sept. 13	— L. & R.B.	623 D 623 H	To Calcutta and Madras.
Nov. 10	Chesterfield	Edwin Carter	Dec. 3	— L. & R.B.	507 C 507 M	To Madras and Bengal.
Nov. 22	Godolphin	William Hutchinson	1754 May 20	— L. & R.B.	594 G 594 Q	To Madras, Calcutta, Bencoolen, and Batavia.
Nov. 23	Protector	F. Cheyne	1753 Sept. 28	— Five R.B.	110 A 110 C	To Madras and Bombay.
1752 Jan. 8	Doddington	Norton Hutchinson	1754 June 9	— L. & R.B.	619 B 619 D	To Bombay, Surat, and Mocha.
Jan. 8	Pelham	George Lindsay	1753 Nov. 7	— L. & R.B.	607 C 607 H	To Bombay and Tellicherry.
Jan. 19	Bombay Castle	T. Browne	Nov. 29	— L. & R.B.	125 C 125 M	To Madras and Bengal.
April 13	Delawar	Abraham Dominicus	1752 Aug. 31	—	322 B (2)	From St. Augustin's Bay (Madagascar) towards Madras.
July 8	Royal Duke	George Cuming	1754 July 17	— L. & R.B.	614 B 614 F	To Bombay and Whampoa.
Sept. 26	Dragon	Henry Kent	1755 Mar. 25	Two J. L. & R.B.	598 D & E 598 J	To Madras, Calcutta, and Bencoolen.
Oct. 7	Walpole	Francis Fowler	1754 June 15	— L. & R.B.	293 I 293 GG	To Batavia and Bencoolen.
Oct. 8	Boscawen	Benjamin Braund	Aug. 15	— L. & R.B.	572 B 572 F	To Madras and Whampoa.
Oct. 9	Griffin	Thomas Dethick	July 19	— L. & R.B.	603 B 603 F	To Whampoa.
Oct. 9	Marlborough	William Parks	July 25	— L. & R.B.	602 I 602 R	To Madras and China.
Oct. 9	Suffolk	William Wilson	May 24	— L. & R.B.	397 B 397 I	To Madras and Whampoa.

Log begins.	Ship.	Captain.	Log ends.	Ledger or Receipt Book.	Reference Number.	Remarks.
1752 Oct. 22	Winchelsea	Christopher Baron	1755 Oct. 21	— L. & R.B.	4 C 4 S	To Bombay, Surat, Madras, Calcutta, &c.
Oct. 23	Edgbaston	Edward Tiddeman	1754 July 16	— L. & R.B.	622 E 622 I	To Madras and Whampoa.
Oct. 24	Clinton	John Nanfan	July 11	— L. & R.B.	800 A 800 E	To Madras and Whampoa.
Oct. 25	Harcourt	William Webber	July 15	— L. & R.B.	558 A 558 T	To Madras and Whampoa.
Nov. 9	Colchester	R. Mainwaring	1755 Sept. 30	— L. & R.B.	113 C 113 G	To Madras, Batavia, and Bengal.
Nov. 17	Portfield	Carteret Le Geyt	1754 July 29	— L. & R.B.	609 C 609 G	To Fort St. David, Madras, and Culpee.
Nov. 20	Egmont	Thomas Tolson	1755 Nov. 13	— L. & R.B.	535 A 535 I	To Madras and Culpee.
Nov. 21	Montfort	Frederick Vincent	May 18	— L. & R.B.	608 D 608 H	To Bombay, Madras, and Calcutta.
Nov. 26	Falmouth	Thomas Field	1754 Nov. 16	— L. & R.B.	582 A 582 E	To Madras and Calcutta.
Dec. 5	Elizabeth	E. Wills	1755 Oct. 2	— L. & R.B.	102 D 102 J	To Madras, Bengal, Bombay, &c.
Dec. 22	Salisbury	John Foot	1754 Aug. 3	— L. & R.B.	478 E 478 M	To Gombroon, Bombay, Surat, Tellicherry, and Anjengo.
—	Guardian	William James	1758 —	Two R.B. only.	797 A	——
1753 Jan. 5	Stafford	Felix Baker	1755 Aug. 25	— L. & R.B.	560 D 560 K	To Bombay, Culpee, Ingelee, and Whampoa.
Jan. 6	Sandwich	John Purling	July 2	— L. & R.B.	606 C 606 H	To Bombay, Surat, and Mocha.
Jan. 6	Tavistock	Nathaniel Cush	1754 Nov. 23	— L. & R.B.	593 E 593 I	To Bombay, Goa, Tellicherry, Cochin, and Anjengo.
Mar. 2	Prince Edward	Robert Haldane	1755 July 6	— L. & R.B.	573 C 573 H	To Bombay, Goa, Tellicherry, Cochin, Surat, and Batavia.
Sept. 27	Grantham	John Oliver	Aug. 6	— L. & R.B.	617 L 617 T	To Batavia and Bencoolen.
Sept. 30	Saint George	Robert Robinson	1757 Mar. 4	— L. & R.B.	584 G 584 N	To Madras, Vizagapatam, Calcutta, Tellicherry, Surat, and Whampoa.
Oct. 10	Princess Augusta	Thomas Parker succeeded by Thomas Baddison.	1755 Aug. 14	— L. & R.B.	590 A 590 E	To Batavia and Whampoa.
Oct. 12	Anson	Charles Foulis	Oct. 6	— L. & R.B.	549 D 549 R	To Batavia and Whampoa.
Oct. 13	Triton	Gilbert Slater	Aug. 16	— L. & R.B.	366 B 366 Q	To Madras and Whampoa.
Oct. 26	Ilchester	John Tedd	July 22	— L. & R.B.	601 C 601 G	To Madras and Whampoa.
Oct. 26	True Briton	Henry Broadley	Oct. 3	— L. & R.B.	297 B 297 S	To Fort St. George and Whampoa.
Oct. 27	Onslow	T. Hinde	Aug. 14	— L. & R.B.	164 G 164 O	To Madras and China.
Oct. 29	Essex	George Jackson	Aug. 15	— L. & R.B.	229 F 229 EE	To Madras, Canton, and Whampoa.
Nov. 24	Denham	George Meard	1757 May 2	— L. & R.B.	628 A 628 B	To Madras and Calcutta.
Nov. 27	Norfolk	Pinson Bonham	1755 July 30	— L. & R.B.	541 C 541 O	To Madras.
Dec. 10	Anson	Robert Veitch	1756 Oct. 8	— L. & R.B.	549 E & F 549 S	To Madras, Vizagapatam, Calcutta, Bombay, and Bencoolen.
Dec. 10	York	Edward Ward	1755 Oct. 7	— L. & R.B.	237 E 237 V	To Madras, Vizagapatam, Calcutta, &c.
1754 Jan. 17	Britannia	Nevell Norway	1756 Nov. 29	— L. & R.B.	285 GG 285 G	To Fort St. David, Bengal, Madras, Bencoolen, Batavia, and Whampoa.
Jan. 21	Kent	George Wilson	Aug. 18	—	317 F	To Madras, Bengal, and Whampoa.
Jan. 21	Kent	George Wilson	Aug. 16	— L. & R.B.	317 G 317 Q	To Madras, Bengal, and Whampoa.
Jan. 23	Warren	Alphonsus Glover	Oct. 15	— L. & R.B.	571 B 571 F	To Madras, Bombay, Surat, Tellicherry, and Whampoa.
Jan. 24	London	Richard Ailwright	Dec. 9	— L. & R.B.	313 M 313 X	To Fort St. David, Madras, Bombay, and Culpee.

Log begins.	Ship.	Captain.	Log ends.	Ledger or Receipt Book.	Reference Number.	Remarks.
1754 Feb. 21	Prince Henry	Thomas Best	1755 Nov. 18	— L. & R.B.	325 B 325 I	To Bombay and Anjengo.
Feb. 22	Shaftesbury	William Bookey	Dec. 22	— L. & R.B.	610 F 610 M	To Bombay and Tellicherry.
Feb. 23	Warwick	Nicholas Webb	Aug. 7	— L. & R.B.	585 F 585 M	To Bombay, Tellicherry, and Anjengo.
Oct. 1	Bombay Castle	J. Bristoll	1757 Jan. 7	— L. & R.B.	125 D 125 N	To Madras and China.
Oct. 1	Earl of Holderness	Matthew Court	May 7	— L. & R.B.	604 A 604 D	To Batavia and China.
Oct. 2	Hardwicke	John Samson	1756 Oct. 9	— L. & R.B.	568 E 568 M	To Madras, Vizagapatam, and Culpee.
—	Hardwicke	Samuel Hough	1754 —	Two R.B. only.	568 Q	——
Oct. 2	Prince of Wales	William Peck	1756 July 18	— L. & R.B.	404 G 404 Y	To Madras and Whampoa.
Oct. 3	Prince George	Philip Jodrell	Aug. 25	— L. & R.B.	575 C 575 G	To Bencoolen, Batavia, and Whampoa.
Oct. 3	Rhoda	John McNemara	Dec. 2	— L. & R.B.	596 D 596 H	To Madras and Whampoa.
Oct. 16	Exeter	William Fernell	1757 Mar. 7	— L. & R.B.	138 D 138 R	To Bencoolen and Batavia.
Oct. 17	Drake	Benjamin Fisher	1756 Dec. 2	— L. & R.B.	578 F 578 N	To Whampoa.
Nov. 29	Duke of Dorset	Bernard Forrester	1757 Mar. 19	— L. & R.B.	612 G 612 O	To Madras, Culpee, and Tellicherry.
Dec. 3	Eastcourt	Arthur Evans	1756 Dec. 24	— L. & R.B.	586 C 586 G	To Madras and Bengal.
1755 Jan. 13	Edgecote	John Pearse	1757 Aug. 3	— L. & R.B.	599 C 599 G	To Bombay, Surat, and Mocha.
Jan. 14	Houghton	Richard Walpole	Sept. 13	— L. & R.B.	438 H 438 BB	To Bombay, Gombroon, Surat Malacca, and China.
Jan. 18	Stretham	Charles Mason	Mar. 15	— L. & R.B.	605 I 605 Q	To Bombay.
Feb. 13	Pelham	George Lindsay	Mar. 18	— L. & R.B.	607 D 607 I	To Bombay, Surat, and Tellicherry.
April 16	Dragon	Michael Morgan	1755 Sept. 30	— Two R.B.	598 F 598 K	To Bombay.
Aug. 22	Griffin	Thomas Dethick	1758 Feb. 6	— L. & R.B.	603 C 603 G	To China.
Sept. 7	Delawar	Thomas Winter	Jan. 5	— L. & R.B.	322 C 322 G	To Madras and Calcutta.
Oct. 20	Harcourt	William Webber	Feb. 9	— L. & R.B.	558 B 558 J	To Whampoa.
Oct. 21	Oxford	Thomas Stevens	1757 Dec. 22	— L. & R.B.	588 C 588 G	To Bencoolen and Batavia.
Oct. 22	Marlborough	Alexander MacLeod	1759 Mar. 28	— L. & R.B.	602 J 602 S	To Madras, Vizagapatam, and Calcutta.
Oct. 23	Suffolk	William Wilson	1757 Sept. 13	Two J. L. & R.B.	397 C & D 397 J	To Madras and Whampoa.
Nov. 4	Caernarvon	Norton Hutchinson	1758 Oct. 2	— L. & two R.B.	589 E 589 L	To Madras, Batavia, and Whampoa.
Nov. 5	Godolphin	William Hutchinson	1757 Aug. 13	— L. & R.B.	594 H 594 R	To Madras and Whampoa.
Dec. 24	Stormont	Josiah Hindman	1758 Feb. 10	— L. & R.B.	458 A 458 K	To Madras, Malacca, and Whampoa.
—	Doddington	James Samson	1756 —	Two R.B. only.	619 E	——
1756 Jan. 1	Chesterfield	Edwin Carter	1757 Aug. 6	— L. & R.B.	507 D 507 N	To Madras.
Jan. 1	Hector	John Williams	Nov. 8	— L. & R.B.	486 B 486 K	To Gombroon, Bombay, Tellicherry, and Anjengo.
Jan. 30	Royal Duke	George Cuming	1759 April 13	— L. & R.B.	614 C 614 G	To Bombay, Tellicherry, and Whampoa.
Jan. 31	Clinton	John Nanfan	1757 Nov. 10	— L. & R.B.	600 B 600 F	To Bombay.

Log begins.	Ship.	Captain.	Log ends.	Ledger or Receipt Book.	Reference Number.	Remarks.
1756 Feb. 3	Portfield	Benjamin Godfrey	1757 Aug. 1	— L. & R.B.	609 D 609 H	To Bombay.
July 20	Prince Henry	John Mumford succeeded by Benjamin Reynolds.	1758 Aug. 2	— L. & R.B.	325 C 325 J	To Madras.
Sept. 24	Onslow	T. Hinde	1759 April 12	— L. & R.B.	164 H 164 P	To Batavia and China.
Oct. 23	Norfolk	Pinson Bonham	Mar. 10	— L. & R.B.	541 D 541 P	To Madras and Bencoolen.
Oct. 24	Boscawen	Benjamin Braund	1760 May 1	— L. & R.B.	572 C 572 G	To Madras, Bengal, and Whampoa.
Oct. 24	Princess Augusta	Thomas Baddison	1759 Mar. 14	— L. & R.B.	590 B 590 F	To Fort St. George.
Oct. 24	Sandwich	John Purling	April 12	— L. & R.B.	606 D 606 I	To Whampoa.
Oct. 25	Falmouth	James Dale	May 15	— L. & R.B.	582 B 582 F	To Batavia.
Oct. 25	Warwick	Nicholas Warwick	Mar. 24	— L. & R.B.	585 G 585 N	To Madras and Calcutta.
Oct. 26	Tavistock	Benjamin Jenkins	1760 June 21	— L. & R.B.	593 F 593 J	To Bombay, Madras, and Whampoa.
Nov. 9	Triton	Francis Harris	1759 April 13	— L. & R.B.	366 C 366 R	To Whampoa.
Dec. 20	Walpole	Francis Fowler	1758 May 2	— L. & R.B.	298 J 298 HH	To Madras and Calcutta.
1757 Jan. 8	Worcester	Edward Tiddeman	1760 April 1	— L. & R.B.	278 A 278 R	To Madras, Calcutta, and Vizagapatam.
Jan. 17	Prince Edward	James Haldane	1759 April 27	— L. & R.B.	573 D 573 I	To Acheen and Bombay.
Jan. 21	Fox	Alexander Hume	1760 April 28	— L. & R.B.	456 A 456 M	To San Salvador, Nicobar Islands, Culpee, Kedgeree, Ingelee, Madras and Whampoa.
Jan. 21	Ilchester	John Tedd succeeded by James Ward.	1759 Nov. 30	— L. & R.B.	601 D 601 H	To Bengal.
Jan. 23	Elizabeth	R. Burdell	Mar. 27	— L. & R.B.	102 E 102 K	To Bengal.
Feb. 20	Hawke	Richard Drake	1760 May 3	— L. & R.B.	390 A 390 P	To Bombay, Surat, Tellicherry, and China.
Feb. 20	York	Peter Lascelles	1758 Nov. 22	— Two R.B.	287 F 237 W	To Bombay.
Feb. 21	Anson	Edward Lord Chick	1759 May 1	— L. & R.B.	549 G 549 T	To Bombay.
Feb. 21	Latham	John Foot	Aug. 22	— L. & R.B.	482 A 482 K	To Bombay, Surat, and Mocha.
Aug. 1	Hardwicke	John Sansom succeeded by Brook Samson.	1760 Nov. 14	— L. & R.B.	568 F 568 N	To Madras, Culpee, Vizagapatam, and Masulipatam.
Aug. 8	Diligent	Peter Macleshin	1758 June 28	Two J. L.	320 A & B 320 F	From Bengal to England.
Sept. 27	Britannia	John Blewitt	1760 Dec. 18	— L. & R.B.	285 HH 285 H	To Goa, Bombay, Madras, and Whampoa.
Sept. 28	Prince Henry	Thomas Best	Mar. 28	— L. & R.B.	325 D 325 K	To Batavia, Macao, Whampoa, Madura, &c.
Sept. 28	Prince of Wales	William Roberts	Dec. 9	— L. & R.B.	404 H 404 Z	To Goa, Bombay, Madras, and Whampoa.
Oct. 11	Rhoda	John McNemara	Dec. 23	— L. & R.B.	596 E 596 I	To Bombay, Madras, and Whampoa.
Oct. 13	Osterley	Frederick Vincent	Mar. 26	— L. & R.B.	400 A 400 P	To Whampoa.
Oct. 15	Shaftesbury	Cornelius Inglis	1761 July 4	— L. & R.B.	610 G 610 N	To Madras, Batavia, Bombay, and Goa.
Oct. 15	Winchelsea	Thomas Howe	Jan. 24	— L. & R.B.	4 D 4 U	To Bombay, Madras, and China.
Oct. 16	Tilbury	Roger Mainwaring	1760 Dec. 20	— L. & R.B.	551 A 551 E	To Bombay, Madras, and Whampoa.

Log begins.	Ship.	Captain.	Log ends.	Ledger or Receipt Book.	Reference Number.	Remarks.
1757 Nov. 27	Egmont	John Venner - succeeded by William Robinson.	1759 Dec. 1	— L. & R.B.	535 B 535 J	To Bencoolen.
Nov. 27	Pitt	William Wilson	1760 Apr. 28	— L. & R.B.	525 A 525 I	To Fort St. George, Macao, and Whampoa.
Dec. 12	London	Richd. Allright	1759 June 23	— L. & R.B.	1 A 1 BB	To St. Helena.
—	Grantham	John Oliver	1758 —	R.B. only.	617 U	——
—	Syren	Evan Jones	1757 —	L. & R.B. only.	757 A	——
1758 Jan. 10	Warren	Alphonsus Glover succeeded by Robert Baker and William Scott.	1760 May 21	L. & R.B. only.	571 C 571 G	To Calcutta, Vizagapatam, and Madras.
Jan. 11	Admiral Watson	William Cooke	1759 Nov. 6	— L. & R.B.	624 A 624 D	To Gombroon and Bombay.
Jan. 12	Bombay Castle	R. Doveton	1760 Mar. 28	— L. & R.B.	125 E 125 O	To Bengal.
Jan. 25	Drake	Benjamin Fisher	Dec. 23	— L. & R.B.	578 G 578 O	To Colombo, Bombay, Surat, and Whampoa.
Jan. 25	True Briton	Thomas Crichton	Mar. 24	— L. & R.B.	297 C 297 T	To Bombay.
Feb. 9	Prince George	Lorenzo Collins	Mar. 19	— L. & R.B.	575 D 575 H	To Culpee and Kedgeree.
Mar. 25	Eastcourt	Arthur Evans	April 1	— L. & R.B.	586 D 586 H	To Bombay.
April 7	Stretham	Charles Mason	1759 Nov. 10	— Two R.B.	605 J 605 R	To Bombay, Surat, Madras, and Calcutta.
Aug. 4	Earl of Holderness	Robert Brooke	1760 Aug. 12	— L. & R.B.	604 B 604 E	To Bencoolen.
Aug. 19	Duke of Dorset	Bernard Forrester succeeded by John Allen.	Nov. 10	— L. & R.B.	612 H 612 P	To Bengal.
Sept. 14	Diligent	Peter Macleshin	Aug. 12	—	320 C & D	To Bombay, Madras, Negapatam, &c.
Oct. 2	Essex	George Jackson	Dec. 13	— L. & R.B.	229 G 229 FF	To Madras, Canton, and Whampoa.
Oct. 3	Suffolk	Richard Lewin	1761 Nov. 19	— L. & R.B.	397 E & F 397 K	To Madras, Batavia, and Whampoa.
Oct. 4	Oxford	William Webber	Nov. 20	— L. & R.B.	588 D 588 H	To Madras, Trincomalee, Fort St. David, Pondicherry, Culpee, and Whampoa.
Oct. 4	Valentine	William Fernell	Nov. 19	— L. & R.B.	452 A 452 M	To Trincomalee, Negapatam, Madras, Batavia, and Whampoa.
Oct. 16	Calcutta	George Willson	1760 Nov. 1	— L. & R.B.	308 A 308 O	To Madras and Calcutta.
Oct. 17	Royal George	George Beamish	Aug. 7	— L. & R.B.	17 E 17 W	To Madras and Bengal.
Oct. 18	Admiral Pocock	Thomas Debuke	1761 Nov. 21	— L. & R.B.	498 A 498 I	To Madras, Bombay, Surat, and Whampoa.
Oct. 18	Edgecote	John Pearse	1760 Dec. 19	— L. & R.B.	599 D 599 H	To Batavia and Whampoa.
Oct. 19	Chesterfield	Edwin Carter	Dec. 8	— L. & R.B.	507 K 507 O	To Batavia and Whampoa.
Nov. 2	Hector	John Williams	Dec. 2	— L. & R.B.	486 C 486 L	To Whampoa.
Dec. 30	Stormont	Henry Fletcher	1761 July 8	— L. & R.B.	458 B 458 I	To Madras, Balasore, Culpee, Ingelee, Anjengo, and Bombay.
—	Denham	William Tryon	1759 —	Two R.B. only.	625 C	——
1759 Jan. 5	Walpole	Parson Fenner	1760 Dec. 24	— L. & R.B.	293 K 293 II	To Whampoa.
Jan. 13	Ajax	George Lindsay	1761 Feb. 19	— Two R.B.	620 A 620 B	To Culpee and Ingelee.
Jan. 29	Houghton	Charles Newton	Sept. 19	— L. & R.B.	438 I 438 CC	To Madras, Culpee, Ingelee, Anjengo, and Bombay. [The will of Joseph Colleyson is in this Journal.]

Log begins.	Ship.	Captain.	Log ends.	Ledger or Receipt Book.	Reference Number.	Remarks.
1759 Jan. 30	Prince Henry	Benjamin Reynolds	1760 Oct. 8	— L. & R.B.	325 E 325 L	To Trincomalee, Madras, and Masulipatam.
Feb. 27	Clinton	Nathaniel Smith	Dec. 4	— L. & R.B.	800 C 800 G	To Bombay.
Feb. 27	Godolphin	Collingwood Roddam	1763 July 23	— L. & R.B.	594 I & J 594 S	To Bombay, Muscat, Gombroon, Madras, Bengal, and Mocha.
Feb. 27	Griffin	Thomas Dethick	1761 Jan. 20	— Two R.B.	603 D 603 H	To Bombay, Surat, and China.
Feb. 27	Harcourt	William Webber	July 7	— L. & R.B.	558 C 558 K	To Bombay, Surat, and Mocha.
Mar. 19	Delawar	William Larkins	1760 Nov. 13	— L. & R.B.	322 D 322 H	To Bencoolen.
May 3	London	Richard Allwright	1759 Nov. 9	—	1 B	From Bencoolen to England.
June 25	Syren	Thomas Warner	1760 Sept. 29	—	536 A	To Anjengo and Bombay.
July 6	Expedition	George Best	1759 Oct. 7	—	621 B	From Bahia to Belfast.
Sept. 22	Onslow	T. Hinde	1761 Nov. 2	— L. & R.B.	164 I 164 Q	To Madras and Bengal.
Sept. 23	Triton	Francis Harris succeeded by Charles Barkley.	1762 Nov. 6	— L. & R.B.	366 D 366 S	To Madras, Calcutta, Bombay, Tellicherry, and Whampoa.
Nov. 3	Caernarvon	Norton Hutchinson	Sept. 17	— L. & R.B.	589 F & G 589 M	To Fort St. George, Batavia, Macao, and Whampoa.
Nov. 5	Warwick	James Dewar	July 7	— L. & R.B.	585 H 585 O	To Madras and Whampoa.
Nov. 6	Royal Duke	Peter Pigou	1761 Sept. 12	— L. & R.B.	614 D 614 H	To Culpee and Ingelee.
Nov. 21	Norfolk	Pinson Bonham	1762 Sept. 21	— L. & R.B.	541 E 541 Q (1)	To Whampoa.
Nov. 21	Princess Augusta	Thomas Baddison	Sept. 21	— L. & R.B.	590 C 590 G	To Fort St. George, Whampoa, and Macao.
Nov. 22	Duke of Richmond	Benjamin Godfrey	Aug. 29	— L. & R.B.	492 A 492 E	To Bencoolen, Malacca, and Whampoa.
Nov. 22	Lord Mansfield	Alexander Macleod	Feb. 5	— L. & R.B.	463 A 463 F	To Madras, Balasore, Culpee, Masulipatam, Pondicherry, Tellicherry, and Anjengo.
Nov. 23	Falmouth	James Dale	May 21	— L. & R.B.	582 C 582 G	To Madras and Pondicherry.
1760 Jan. 3	Prince Edward	James Haldane	May 20	— L. & R.B.	578 E 578 J	To Madras, Culpee, and Ingelee.
Jan. 4	Anson	Edward Lord Chick	Feb. 4	— L. & R.B.	549 H 549 U	To Madras and Calcutta.
Jan. 6	Latham	James Moffatt	1761 Oct. 26	— L. & R.B.	482 B 482 L	To Madras, Balasore, Culpee, and Ingelee.
Jan. 19	Mercury	William Harrold succeeded by John Meryweather.	1765 July 20	— L. and three R.B.	554 A & B 554 E	To St Helena, Cape of Good Hope, and Madagascar.
Feb. 17	Sandwich	Andrew Quicke	1762 Jan. 28	— L. & R.B.	606 E 606 J	To Culpee, Ingelee, Madras, Pondicherry, and Bombay.
Feb. 18	Neptune	J. Purling	Sept. 7	— L. & R.B.	98 B 98 U	To Bombay and China.
Feb. 22	York	Peter Lascelles	1763 Feb. 4	— L. & R.B.	237 G 237 X	To Bombay, Surat, Bengal, and Mocha.
Mar. 5	Egmont	Charles Mears	1762 Jan. 28	— L. & R.B.	535 C 535 K	To Bombay and Tellicherry.
Mar. 16	London	John Webb	Feb. 5	— L. & R.B.	1 C 1 CC	To Bombay.
May 15	London	George Baker	1761 July 23	—	600 A	From Madras to Malacca and England.
Oct. 24	Hawke	George Kent	1763 July 24	— L. & R.B.	390 B 390 Q	To Madras, Ingelee, Kedgeree, and Culpee.
Oct. 24	Pitt	Joseph Jackson	1762 Sept. 14	— L. & R.B.	525 B 525 J	To Madras and Whampoa.
Oct. 26	Prince Henry	Charles Haggis	Nov. 5	— L. & R.B.	325 F 325 M	To Whampoa.

Log begins.	Ship.	Captain.	Log ends.	Ledger or Receipt Book.	Reference Number.	Remarks.
1760 Nov. 11	Plassey	James Ward	1762 July 24	— L. & R.B.	567 A 567 E	To Vizagapatam, Culpee, and Ingelee.
Nov. 11	Royal George	N. Skottowe	1763 Mar. 1	— L. & two R.B.	17 F 17 X	To China, Madras, Calcutta, &c.
Nov. 22	Prince George	Andrew Ross	1762 Nov. 3	— L. & R.B.	575 E 575 I	To Bencoolen and Whampoa.
Nov. 23	Osterley	Frederick Vincent	1764 July 2	— L. & R.B.	400 B & C 400 Q	To Bencoolen, Madras, Manilla, Malacca, Cuddalore, and Ingelee.
Dec. 4	Diligent	Peter Macleshin	1762 Mar. 10	— L. & R.B. Two R.B.	320 E (a) 320 G 320 H	To Morundava and Bencoolen.
Dec. 4	Diligent	Peter Macleshin	Feb. 28	— Two R.B.	320 E 595 C	To Bencoolen.
Dec. 4	Fly	Peter Fea	1765 April 30	— L. & R.B.	597 A & B 597 C	To St. Helena and Madagascar.
Dec. 4	Prince Henry	Benjamin Reynolds	1762 Aug. 26	—	325 G	To Madras and Bencoolen.
Dec. 21	Fox	Alexander Hume	1763 July 29	— L. & R.B.	456 B & C 456 N	To Johanna, Madras, Balasore, Ingelee, Bencoolen, and Batavia.
Dec. 22	Earl of Holderness	Robert Brooke	1762 Oct. 19	— L. & R.B.	604 C 604 F	To Madras, Culpee, and Ingelee.
Dec. 22	Warren	Alphonsus Glover	1763 Mar. 4	— L. & R.B.	571 D 571 H	To Madras, Culpee, and Ingelee.
—	Admiral Watson	Francis Fowler	—	L. & R.B. only.	624 E	—
—	Earl Temple	William Foster	1761 —	Two R.B. only.	789 A	—
1761 Jan. 11	London	George Baker	1762 June 12	— R.B.	600 C 600 D	From Madras and Pondicherry to England.
Feb. 6	Boscawen	Benjamin Braund succeeded by Arthur Morris.	1765 June 21	— L. & R.B.	572 D 572 H	To Bombay, Mocha, Surat, and Calcutta.
Feb. 7	London	George Baker	1761 Aug. 21	—	600 B	From Pondicherry to England.
Feb. 17	Royal Captain	Nathaniel Tanner	1763 Aug. 19	— L. & R.B.	556 A 556 F	To Bombay, Gombroon, Trincomalee, and Whampoa.
Feb. 20	Earl of Elgin	Arthur Evans	May 21	— L. & R.B.	559 A 559 E	To Bombay, Surat, and Mocha.
Feb. 24	True Briton	Thomas Crichton	Sept. 7	— L. & R.B.	297 D 297 U	To Bombay, Cochin, Tellicherry, Surat, Madras, and Whampoa.
Mar. 16	Calcutta	George Thomson	April 2	— L. & R.B.	308 B 308 P	To Bombay, Tellicherry, &c.
April 7	General Lawrence	William Scott	1762 June 4	— R.B.	576 A 576 B	To Bombay.
Oct. 8	Tilbury	Roger Mainwaring	1763 Aug. 8	— L. & R.B.	551 B 551 F	To Madras, Culpee, and Ingelee.
Nov. 11	Clinton	Nathaniel Smith	1764 Jan. 14	— L. & R.B.	800 D 800 H	To Bengal.
Nov. 12	Essex	George Jackson	1763 Nov. 17	— L. & R.B.	229 H 229 GG	To Madras and Canton.
Nov. 14	Horsendon	William Marter	Aug. 31	— L. & R.B.	473 A 473 E	To Whampoa.
Nov. 15	Grosvenor	Watkin Partington succeeded by David Saunders.	1764 Mar. 21	— L. & R.B.	495 A 495 G	To Madras and Whampoa.
Nov. 15	Royal Charlotte	J. Clements	1763 Sept. 3	— L. & R.B.	150 A 150 V	To China.
Nov. 23	Worcester	Richard Hall	1762 Nov. 4	— L. & R.B.	278 B 278 S	To Bencoolen and Whampoa.
Nov. 27	Harcourt	Richard Morrison	1763 Sept. 2	— L. & R.B.	558 D 558 L	To Whampoa.
Nov. 28	Walpole	Parson Fenner	1762 Sept. 20	— R.B.	293 L 293 H (a)	To Madras.

Log begins.	Ship.	Captain.	Log ends.	Ledger or Receipt Book.	Reference Number.	Remarks.
1761 Dec. 14	Hardwicke	Brook Samson	1763 Sept. 23	— L. & R.B.	568 G 568 O	To Madras, Masulipatam, and Kedgeree.
Dec. 15	Houghton	Charles Newton succeeded by William Rogers, and William Smith.	1764 Sept. 5	— L. & R.B.	438 J 438 DD	To Acheen, Balasore, Kedgeree, Ingelee, Malacca, Manilla, Whampoa, and Bencoolen.
Dec. 28	Drake	John Smith	1763 Sept. 22	— L.&R.B.	578 H 578 P	To Madras and Bengal.
Dec. 31	Winchelsea	Thomas Howe	1764 Mar. 20	— Two R.B.	4 E 4 T	To Bombay, Madras, &c.
—	Chesterfield	Willoughby Marchant	1761 —	Two R.B. only.	507 P	——
—	Elizabeth	-	1762 —	R.B. only.	102 L	——
—	Norfolk	James McConohie	1761 —	Two R.B. only.	541 Q (?)	——
1762 Jan. 5	Hector	John Williams	1764 Aug. 18	— L. & R.B.	486 D 486 M	To Bombay, Tellicherry, Anjengo, Calicut, Madras, Masulipatam, and Whampoa.
Jan. 29	Britannia	Thomas Bates Rous	Aug. 4	— L. & R.B.	285 I I 285 I	To Bombay, Anjengo, Madras, Masulipatam, and Whampoa.
Feb. 8	Admiral Pocock	Thomas Riddell	1766 July 20	— L.& R.B.	498 B & C 498 J	To Bombay, Surat, Madras, Batavia, Macao, and Whampoa.
Feb. 9	Earl of Ashburnham	Thomas Pearce	1764 June 1	— L. & R.B.	542 A 542 G	To Balasore, Kedgeree, and Ingelee.
Feb. 9	Prince of Wales	Jonathan Court	Jan. 20	— L. & R.B.	404 I 404 AA	To Johanna, Bombay, and Gombroon.
Feb. 11	Clive	John Allen	Jan. 25	— L. & R.B.	533 A 533 E	To Bombay, Surat, and Tellicherry.
Mar. 31	Albion	William Larkins	1763 Oct. 27	— L. & R.B.	81 A 81 L	To China.
April 9	Valentine	William Fernell	1765 Dec. 9	— L. & R.B.	452 B 452 N	To Batavia, Bencoolen, Whampoa, and Macao.
Sept. 25	Plassey	James Ward	1764 June 2	— L. & R.B.	567 B 567 F	To Madras and Cuddalore.
Oct. 4	Falmouth	Geffrie O'Hara	Sept. 18	— L. & R.B.	582 D 582 H	To Madras and China.
Oct. 5	Deptford	William Tryon	1765 April 1	— L. & R.B.	426 A 426 K	To Madras, Culpee, Kedgeree, and Ingelee.
Oct. 6	Egmont	Charles Mears	1764 Sept. 4	— L. &R.B.	535 D 535 L	To Whampoa.
Oct. 18	Hawke	John Cotton	Sept. 11	— L. & R.B.	390 C 390 R	To Madras and Whampoa.
Oct. 18	Neptune	G. Steward	Sept. 9	— L. & R.B.	98 C 98 V	To Madras and China.
Nov. 1	Cruttenden	John Bowland	Sept. 29	— L.& R.B.	531 A 531 E	To China, Manilla, and Bencoolen.
Nov. 4	Admiral Pocock	Benjamin Hooke	1765 Sept. 7	— L. & R.B.	498 D & E 498 K	To Bencoolen, Batavia, and Whampoa.
Nov. 11	Havannah	Thomas Madge	1764 Nov. 14	— L. & R.B.	776 A 776 E	To Whampoa, Macao, and Bencoolen.
Dec. 2	Lord Clive	William Webber	1765 June 11	— L. & R.B.	577 A 577 C	To Madras, Kedgeree, Culpee, Bencoolen, Batavia, Macao, and Whampoa.
Dec. 3	Admiral Watson	Francis Fowler	1763 May 15	—	624 B	From Bengal to England.
Dec. 16	Lord Mansfield	Alexander Mcleod	1765 Aug. 9	— L. & R.B.	463 B 463 G	To Bombay, Surat, Kedgeree, Acheen, Marmagon, Tellicherry, and Anjengo.
—	Elizabeth	- - -	1763 —	R.B. only	102 M	——
1763 Feb. 2	Earl of Middlesex	Henry Fletcher	1766 July 4	— L. & R.B.	579 A 579 D	To Bombay, Tellicherry, Balasore, Ingelee, Batavia, Bencoolen, and Madras.

Log begins.	Ship.	Captain.	Log ends.	Ledger or Receipt Book.	Reference Number.	Remarks.
1763 Feb. 3	Bute	Patrick Maitland	1766 Mar. 25	— L. & R.B.	481 A 481 E	To Bombay, Kedgeree, Madras, Bencoolen, and Batavia.
Feb. 3	Pigot	George Richardson	1764 Nov. 17	— L. & R.B.	503 A 503 J	To Madras, Culpee, and Ingelee.
Feb. 14	Talbot	Thomas Dethick	1766 Aug. 23	— L. & R.B.	474 A 474 E	To Bombay, Tellicherry, Calicut, Surat, Mocha, and Whampoa.
Feb. 15	Latham	James Moffatt	1765 Aug. 19	— L. & R.B.	482 C 482 M	To Bombay, Surat, Tellicherry, Cochin, Goa, Macao, and Whampoa.
Feb. 16	British King	Peter Pigon	Nov. 8	— L. & R.B.	557 A 557 E	To Madras, Kedgeree, and Whampoa.
Feb. 28	Lapwing	John Griffin	1764 Feb. 18	— L. and three R.B.	475 D 475 M	To Fort St. George.
Mar. 2	Royal George	N. Skottowe	April 30	—	17 G	To Calcutta.
Mar. 15	Pitt	Joseph Jackson	1765 Dec. 11	— L. & R.B.	525 C 525 K	To Madras, Whampoa, and Bencoolen.
Mar. 28	Speaker	James Dewar	1764 Dec. 14	— L. & R.B.	548 A 548 E	To Bombay, Tellicherry, and Anjengo.
Sept. 22	Princess Augusta	Thomas Baddison	1766 Mar. 29	— L. & R.B.	590 D 590 H	To Bencoolen, Batavia, and Whampoa.
Sept. 23	Duke of Richmond	Benjamin Godfrey succeeded by Philip Le Geyt, and Thomas Hindman.	June 24	— L. & R.B.	492 B 492 F	To Bencoolen, Batavia, and Whampoa.
Oct. 1	Mercury	William Harrold	1765 July 20	—	554 C	From the Cape of Good Hope to St. Helena, Madagascar, and England. (This is the second part of a journal kept by John Meryweather, the first part of which is missing.)
Nov. 4	Norfolk	John Sandys	Aug. 31	— L. & R.B.	541 F 541 R	To Whampoa.
Nov. 5	Admiral Watson	John Blewitt	1767 Jan. 30	— L. & R.B.	624 C 624 F	To Bencoolen, Batavia, Madras, and Calcutta.
Nov. 6	Worcester	Richard Hall	1765 Sept. 17	— L. & R.B.	278 C 278 T	To Madras and Canton.
Nov. 7	Caernarvon	Norton Hutchinson	Oct. 24	— L. & R.B.	589 H 589 N	To Fort St. George, Kedgeree, Culpee, and Ingelee.
Nov. 8	Devonshire	Andrew Quicke	July 14	— L. & R.B.	272 E 272 Q	To Madras and Bengal.
Nov. 18	Glatton	R. Doveton	Jan. 2	— L. & R.B.	172 A 172 U	To Bencoolen and China.
Nov. 26	Duke of Gloucester	Robert Burdett	Sept. 24	— L. & R.B.	547 A 547 D	To Madras, Batavia, and Whampoa.
Dec. 5	Northumberland	J. Mitford	Aug. 29	— L. & R.B.	141 C 141 V	To Madras and China.
Dec. 7	Duke of Albany	James Haldane	April 30	— L. & R.B.	553 A 553 E	To Madras.
Dec. 8	Lord Holland	Fasham Nairn	Oct. 8	— L. & R.B.	469 A 469 H	To Madras and Whampoa.
Dec. 20	London	John Webb	Dec. 20	— L. & R.B.	1 D 1 DD	To Bombay, Surat, Muscat, Bushire, &c.
Dec. 23	Earl of Lincoln	Peter Hardwicke	Dec. 17	— L. & R.B.	501 A 501 E	To Madras and Canton.
Dec. 23	Vansittart	R. Lewin	Sept. 13	— L. & R.B.	46 A 46 T	To Madras and Bengal.
—	Earl of Holderness	Robert Brooke	1763 —	R.B. only.	604 G	———
1764 Jan. 16	Calcutta	George Thomson	1766 Jan. 2	— L. & R.B.	308 C 308 Q	To Bombay, Bengal, and Madras.
Jan. 19	York	Peter Lascelles	Aug. 20	— L. & R.B.	287 H 287 V	To Bombay, Tellicherry, and Whampoa.
Jan. 20	Anson	Edward Lord Chick	1765 June 22	— L. and two R.B.	549 J 549 V	To Bombay.
Feb. 8	Earl of Elgin	Thomas Cooke	1766 July 24	— L. & R.B.	559 B 559 F	To Bencoolen, Batavia, and Whampoa.
Feb. 9	Success	Henry Gardiner	1764 Nov. 22	— Two R.B.	587 D 587 H	To Calcutta.
Feb. 17	Fort William	E. Roch	1765 Jan. 24	— Two R.B.	91 A 91 L	To Bengal.

Log begins.	Ship.	Captain.	Log ends.	Ledger or Receipt Book.	Reference Number.	Remarks.
1764 Feb. 28	Lapwing	John Griffin	1765 Nov. 30	—	475 E	To Bengal.
Mar. 17	Anson	George Calbreath	Mar. 16	— R.B.	549 I 549 AA	To Acheen and Bengal.
Mar. 17	Beckenham	Newman Mallack	June 15	— Two R.B.	561 A 561 B	To Bencoolen and Batavia.
Mar. 20	Kent	John Milles	1766 Oct. 20	— L. & R.B.	317 H 317 R	To Bengal.
Mar. 29	Prince of Wales	Burnet Abercromby	1765 June 13	— Two R.B.	404 J 404 FF	To Calcutta.
April 3	Solebay	William Richardson	June 20	Two J. Two R.B.	591 A & B 591 C	To Batavia and Bencoolen.
April 22	Asia	C. Inglis succeeded by J. Moffatt.	1767 June 13	— L.	24 A 24 FF	To Bombay and Bengal.
Sept. 26	Tilbury	Roger Mainwaring	1766 Dec. 1	— L. & R.B.	551 C 551 G	To Madras and China.
Sept. 28	Dutton	David Rice	1764 July 19	— L. & R.B.	505 A 505 L	To Whampoa.
Oct. 10	Essex	Francis Reed	1766 Aug. 18	— L. & R.B.	229 I 229 HH	To Whampoa.
Oct. 11	Royal George	N. Skottowe	1767 July 1	— R.B.	17 H 17 Y	To Bencoolen, Banjar, Batavia, Bombay, &c.
Oct. 12	Salisbury	John Wycke	1766 July 25	— L. & R.B.	478 F 478 N	To Whampoa.
Oct. 27	Horsendon	William Marter	Oct. 9	— L. & R.B.	473 B 473 F	To Madras, Malacca, and Whampoa.
Oct. 27	Royal Captain	Nathaniel Tanner	Oct. 4	— L. & R.B.	556 B 556 G	To Madras and China.
Nov. 11	Ankerwyke	A. Ross	Sept. 13	— L. & R.B.	126 A 126 E	To China.
Nov. 11	Grosvenor	David Saunders	Oct. 18	— L. & R.B.	495 B 495 H	To Bencoolen and Whampoa.
Nov. 11	Thames	Charles Haggis	July 20	— L. & R.B.	8 A 8 V	To China.
Dec. 10	Pacific	Charles Barkley	Dec. 18	— L. & R.B.	497 A 497 E	To Madras.
Dec. 10	Ponsborne	John Payne	1767 Mar. 9	— L.& R.B.	462 A 462 K	To Madras, Bengal, and Malacca.
Dec. 11	Grenville	Parson Fenner	1766 Sept. 23	— L. & R.B.	467 A 467 F	To Madras and Bengal.
Dec. 11	Speke	Robert Brooke	1767 Aug. 10	— L. & R.B.	471 A 471 E	To Madras, Bengal, Bencoolen, and Whampoa.
Dec. 23	Hector	Edmund Massey	1766 Aug. 5	— Two R.B.	486 E 486 N	To Madras.
—	Albion	William Larkins	1765 —	R.B. only.	81 M	With 81 L.
—	Princess Royal	- - - -	1768 —	R.B. only.	405 Q	Missing.
1765 Jan. 6	True Briton	Thomas Crichton	1766 Oct. 27	— L. & R.B.	297 E 297 V	To Madras and Bombay.
Jan. 7	Fox	Alexander Hume	1767 Sept. 3	— L. & R.B.	456 D 456 O	To Johanna, Madras, Tellicherry, Bombay, and Canton.
Jan. 7	Hardwicke	Brook Samson	1766 Nov. 28	— L. & R.B.	568 H 568 P	To Madras, Anjengo, Cochin, Tellicherry, and Bombay.
Jan. 8	Clive	John Allen	Dec. 5	— L. & R.B.	533 B 533 F	To Madras and Bombay.
Jan. 8	Royal Charlotte	J. Clements	1767 Aug. 3	— L. & R.B.	150 B 150 W	To Bombay, Surat, and Mocha.
Feb. 21	Harcourt	Collingwood Roddam	Feb. 7	— L. & R.B.	558 E 558 M	To Anjengo, Tellicherry, and Bombay.
June 22	Admiral Pocock	Thomas Riddell	1766 July 23	—	498 F	From Whampoa to England.
July 8	Admiral Stevens	John Griffin	May 29	Two J. L. & R.B.	566 A & B 566 C	From Bengal to England.

Log begins.	Ship.	Captain.	Log ends.	Ledger or Receipt Book.	Reference Number.	Remarks.
1765 Sept. 16	Plassey	William Peters succeeded by John Waddell.	1767 Sept. 7	— L. & R.B.	567 C 567 G	To Whampoa.
Sept. 18	Prince of Wales	Jonathan Court	May 28	— L. & R.B.	404 K 404 BB	To Whampoa.
Oct. 3	Britannia	Thomas Bates Rous	Sept. 1	— L. & R.B.	285 JJ 285 J	To Madras and Bengal.
Oct. 14	Earl of Ashburnham	Thomas Pearce	Sept. 11	— L. & R.B.	542 B 542 H	To Madras and Whampoa.
Oct. 14	Neptune	G. Steward	1768 Jan. 26	— L. & R.B.	98 D 98 W	To Madras and China.
Oct. 15	Glatton	R. Doveton	1767 Sept. 10	— L. & R.B.	172 B 172 V	To Madras and China.
Oct. 16	Duke of Kingston	Richard Morrison	Sept. 21	— L.	545 A 545 E	To Madras and Whampoa.
Oct. 28	Deptford	William Tryon	Aug. 27	— L. & R.B.	426 B 426 L	To Whampoa.
Oct. 29	Duke of Cumberland	Alphonsus Glover succeeded by Augustus Savage.	Aug. 21	— L. & R.B.	562 E 562 N	To Whampoa.
Nov. 1	Hampshire	John Smith	Aug. 25	— L. & R.B.	468 B 468 G	To Madras and Canton.
Nov. 2	Lioness	William Larkins	Aug. 22	— L. & R.B.	502 A 502 E	To Madras and China.
Nov. 13	Havannah	Thomas Madge	July 21	— L. & R.B.	776 B 776 F	To Bencoolen and Whampoa.
Nov. 14	Cruttenden	John Rowland	Aug. 3	— L. & R.B.	531 B 531 F	To Bengal.
Nov. 14	Hawke	John Cotton	Oct. 16	— L. & R.B.	390 D 390 S	To Bencoolen and Whampoa.
Nov. 29	Nottingham	Thomas Howe	1768 Feb. 8	— L. & R.B.	287 C 287 R	To Bombay and Bengal.
Nov. 30	Pigot	George Richardson	1767 Dec. 13	—	502 B	To Madras, Musulipatam, and Kedgeree.
Dec. 11	Duke of Albany	James Haldane	Oct. 3	— L. & R.B.	553 B 553 F	To Bombay, Kedgeree, and Ingelee.
Dec. 12	Speaker	James Dewar	Sept. 26	— L. & R.B.	548 B 548 F	To Madras, Bombay, Tellicherry, and Anjengo.
Dec. 15	Lord Camden	Nathaniel Smith	Aug. 25	— L. & R.B.	419 A 419 K	To Johanna, Madras, Kedgeree, Ingelee, Acheen, and the Nicobar Islands.
—	Falmouth	George Hepburn	—	Two R.B. only.	522 I	—
1766 Feb. 10	Anson	John Lennox	Nov. 27	— L. & R.B.	549 K 549 W	To Madras, Kedgeree, and Ingelee.
Feb. 10	Devonshire	William Mercer	1768 Jan. 31	— L. & R.B.	272 F 272 R	To Madras, Anjengo, Tellicherry, and Bombay.
Jan. 10	Osterley	Frederick Vincent	May 31	— L. & R.B.	400 D 400 R	To Bombay, Surat, and Whampoa.
May 5	Mercury	Henry Gardiner	1767 Sept. 29	— L. and two R.B.	554 D 554 F	To Bengal.
Sept. 6	Hector	John Williams	1768 June 1	— L. & R.B.	486 F 486 O	To Bengal and Madras.
Oct. 4	Earl of Middlesex	John Hasell	Aug. 20	— L. & R.B.	579 B 579 E	To Bencoolen and Batavia.
Oct. 6	Latham	James Moffatt	Aug. 26	— L. & R.B.	482 D 482 N	To Madras and Whampoa.
Oct. 6	Lord Holland	Fasham Nairn	May 28	— L. & R.B.	469 B 469 I	To Madras, Kedgeree, and Ingelee.
Oct. 6	Northumberland	J. Mitford	July 11	— L. & R.B.	141 D 141 W	To China.
Oct. 7	Triton	William Elphinstone	July 25	— L. & R.B.	366 E 366 T	To Madras and Whampoa.
Oct. 18	British King	Richard Williamson succeeded by Daniel Griffiths Hoare	Sept. 21	— L. & R.B.	557 B 557 F	To Bencoolen and Whampoa.
Oct. 18	Earl of Lincoln	Peter Hardwicke	July 12	— L. & R.B.	501 B 501 F	To Madras and Whampoa.
Oct. 20	Houghton	William Smith	Aug. 29	— L. & R.B.	438 K 438 EE	To Madras and Whampoa.
Oct. 31	Calcutta	George Thomson	1769 Sept. 21	— L. & R.B.	308 D 308 R	To Bengal, Bombay, Madras, and Batavia.
Nov. 4	London	Thomas Motley	Aug. 30	— L & R.B.	1 E 1 EE	To Madras and China.
Nov. 15	Lord Clive	Bartlett	1767 April 24	—	577 B	To Boulogne.

Log begins.	Ship.	Captain.	Log ends.	Ledger or Receipt Book.	Reference Number.	Remarks.
1766 Nov. 17	Norfolk	John Sandys	1768 July 14	— L. & R.B.	541 G 541 S	To Kedgeree and Ingelee.
Nov. 19	Vansittart	Robert Fish Palmer	Oct. 8	— L. & R.B.	46 B 46 U	To China.
Dec. 3	Egmont	Charles Mears	1767 Jan. 9	— L. & R.B.	535 E 535 M	To Madras and Kedgeree.
Dec. 16	Earl of Elgin	Thomas Cooke	1768 Sept. 24	— L. & R.B.	559 C 559 G	To Kedgeree, Ingelee, and Vizagapatam.
Dec. 18	Bute	Patrick Maitland	1769 July 7	— L. & R.B.	481 B 481 F	To Bombay, Tellicherry, Calicut, Surat, and Mocha.
Dec. 18	Europa	Henry Hinde Pelly	1768 Aug. 3	— L. & R.B.	425 A 425 K	To Johanna, Madras, Culpee, and Ingelee.
Dec. 18	Northington	John Sealy	Oct. 7	— L. & R.B.	483 A 483 E	To Kedgeree, Ingelee, and Vizagapatam.
Dec. 19	Worcester	Richard Hall	Sept. 9	— L. & R.B.	278 D 278 U	To Bombay, Tellicherry, Cochin, and Anjengo.
—	Prince of Wales	-	—	R.B. only	404 FF	———
1767 Jan. 2	Admiral Pocock	Thomas Biddell	Nov. 25	— L. & R.B.	498 G 498 L	To Bengal.
Jan. 30	Greenwich	Benjamin Hooke	1769 Jan. 13	— L. & R.B.	488 F 488 L	To Bombay and Tellicherry.
Oct. 5	Clive	John Allen	Aug. 4	— L. & R.B.	533 C 533 G	To Batavia and Whampoa.
Oct. 7	Kent	John Milles	June 25	— L. & R.B.	317 I 317 S	To Madras and Culpee.
Oct. 11	Verelst	Thomas Baddison	July 1	— L. & R.B.	550 A 550 C	To Culpee and Ingelee.
Oct. 21	Grosvenor	David Saunders	July 11	— L. & R.B.	495 C 495 I	To Madras, Whampoa, and Macao.
Oct. 22	True Briton	John Johnston	July 28	— L. & R.B.	297 F 297 W	To Madras and Whampoa.
Oct. 23	Pacific	Charles Barkley	June 8	— L. & R.B.	497 B 497 F	To Madras.
Oct. 23	Sea Horse	Edward Dampier	Nov. 9	— L. & R.B.	479 A 479 E	To Madras and Whampoa.
Oct. 25	Duke of Richmond	Thomas Hindman	July 28	— L.	492 C 492 G	To Bencoolen.
Oct. 26	Granby	Joseph Jackson	1770 Aug. 4	— L. & R.B.	499 A 499 E	To Madras, Batavia, and Whampoa.
Nov. 2	Tilbury	William Hunt	1769 Aug. 10	— L. & R.B.	551 D 551 H	To China.
Nov. 5	Dutton	David Rice	Nov. 2	— L. & R.B.	505 R 505 M	To Madras, Ingelee, and Culpee.
Nov. 5	Horsendon	Alexander Jamison	Sept. 27	— L. & R.B.	473 C 473 G	To Madras and Whampoa.
Nov. 7	Queen	George Stainforth	Aug. 4	— L. & R.B.	356 C 356 O	To Madras and Culpee.
Nov. 11	Duke of Gloucester	John Lauder	July 6	— L. & R.B.	547 B 547 E	To Whampoa.
Dec. 5	Ankerwyke	Andrew Ross	1770 May 29	— L. & R.B.	126 B 126 F	To Bombay and Bengal.
Dec. 6	Shrewsbury	Benjamin Jones	Jan. 27	— L. & R.B.	472 A 472 E	To Bombay, Cochin, Anjengo, and Kedgeree.
Dec. 7	Salisbury	John Wyche	1769 Sept. 7	— L.	478 G 478 O	To Culpee and Ingelee.
Dec. 8	Harcourt	Collingwood Roddam	July 26	— L. & R.B.	558 F 558 N	To Whampoa.
Dec. 16	Lord Mansfield	Alexander Macleod	July 20	— L. & R.B.	463 C 463 H	To Madras, Bombay, Cochin, and Whampoa.
Dec. 17	Valentine	Charles Purvis	June 10	— L. & R.B.	452 C 452 O	To Culpee and Ingelee.
Dec. 23	Royal Captain	Nathaniel Tanner	June 23	— L. & R.B.	556 C 556 H	To Bombay, Tellicherry, and Anjengo.
—	Admiral Watson	John Griffin	1774 —	R.B. only	624 G	———
1768 Jan. 5	Essex	Francis Reed	1770 Jan. 18	— L. & R.B.	229 J 229 II	To Madras and Bombay.
Jan. 20	Ponsborne	John Payne	May 26	— L. & R.B.	462 B 462 L	To Madras, Batavia, and China.
Jan. 21	Grenville	Burnet Abercromby	1769 Dec. 1	— L. & R.B.	467 B 467 G	To Madras and Bombay.

Log begins.	Ship.	Captain.	Log ends.	Ledger or Receipt Book.	Reference Number.	Remarks.
1768 Jan. 21	York	George Hayter	1769 Oct. 10	— L. & R.B.	237 I 237 Z	To Madras and Bombay.
Feb. 19	Asia	Robert Preston	Aug. 4	—	24 B	To China.
Aug. 28	Lioness	William Larkins	1770 Aug. 22	— L. & R.B.	502 B 502 F	To Madras, Culpee, and Ingelee.
Sept. 28	Britannia	Robert Rous	Aug. 30	— L. & R.B.	285 KK 285 K	To Madras and Bengal.
Oct. 9	Duke of Albany	John Stewart	Oct. 31	— L. & R.B.	553 C 553 G	To Batavie and Bencoolen.
Oct. 10	Hector	Stephen Williams	July 27	— L. & Two R.B.	486 G 486 P & S	To Madras and Whampoa.
Oct. 11	Neptune	Arthur Gore	Sept. 19	— L. & R.B.	98 E 98 X	To Madras and Whampoa.
Oct. 11	Pigot	George Richardson	July 17	— L. & R.B.	503 C 503 K	To Madras and Whampoa.
Oct. 12	Royal Charlotte	John Clements	Aug. 16	— L. & R.B.	150 C 150 X	To Madras and Bengal.
Oct. 24	Havannah	John White	July 28	— L. & R.B.	776 C 776 G	To Madras and China.
Oct. 25	Cruttenden	William Baker	June 12	— L. & R.B.	531 C 531 G	To China.
Oct. 25	Glatton	Richard Doveton	June 4	— L. & R.B.	172 C 172 W	To China.
Oct. 25	Nottingham	Peter Stoakes	June 17	— L. & R.B.	287 D 287 S	To Madras and Whampoa.
Oct. 25	Plassey	John Waddell	June 2	— L. & R.B.	567 D 567 H	To Madras and Whampoa.
Oct. 26	Earl of Ashburnham	Richard Peirce	Sept. 4	— L. & R.B.	542 C 542 I	To Madras and Whampoa.
Oct. 26	Earl of Lincoln	Peter Hardwicke	Aug. 4	— L. & R.B.	501 C 501 G	To Fort St. George and China.
Oct. 26	Triton	William Elphinstone	July 26	— L. & R.B.	366 F 366 U	To Madras and China.
Nov. 8	Speke	Jeffery Jackson	July 9	— L. & R.B.	471 B 471 F	To Whampoa.
Nov. 9	Devonshire	Matthew Hore	Oct. 6	— L. & R.B.	272 G 272 S	To Madras and Whampoa.
Nov. 11	Hampshire	John Smith	May 22	— L. & Two R.B.	468 C 468 D & H	To Bombay and Bengal.
Nov. 11	Lord Holland	Fasham Nairn	1769 Sept. 18	—	469 C	To Culpee and Ingelee. (This ship was lost on 17th September 1769.)
Nov. 11	Norfolk	James Buggin	1770 Sept. 18	— L. & R.B.	541 H 541 T	To Madras and China.
Nov. 12	Osterley	David Welsh succeeded by Francis Fortescue.	Sept. 4	— L. & R.B.	400 E 400 S	To Madras and Whampoa.
Nov. 27	Earl of Middlesex	John Rogers	1771 July 8	— L. & R.B.	579 C 579 F	To Bencoolen, Bombay, and Whampoa.
Dec. 6	Thames	Charles Haggis	1770 Feb. 1	— L. & R.B.	8 B 8 W	To Bombay, Bengal, and Madras.
Dec. 8	Talbot	Sir Charles Hudson	Mar. 8	— L. & R.B.	474 B 474 F	To Culpee and Ingelee.
Dec. 9	Duke of Grafton	Brook Samson	Sept. 9	— L. & R.B.	508 A 508 F	To Madras and Bengal.
Dec. 9	Duke of Kingston	Richard Morrison	1774 Aug. 21	— L. & R.B.	545 B 545 F	To Madras and Ingelee.
Dec. 10	Deptford	William Tryon	1770 July 10	— L. & R.B.	426 C 426 M	To Johanna, Bombay, Cochin, and Anjengo.
Dec. 13	Prince of Wales	Jonathan Court	1771 June 15	— L. & R.B.	404 L 404 CC	To Madras and Calcutta.
Dec. 24	Anson	John Lennox	1770 Nov. 26	— L. & R.B.	549 L 549 X	To Madras and Bengal.
Dec. 29	Marquis of Rockingham	Alexander Hamilton	Jan. 7	— Two R.B.	493 A 493 D	To Bombay.
1769 Jan. 7	Lord Camden	Nathaniel Smith	1771 Aug. 23	— L. & R.B.	419 B 419 L	To Bombay, Tellicherry, Whampoa, and Macao.
Jan. 7	Speaker	Robert Scott	1770 July 24	— L. & R.B.	548 C 548 G	To Bombay and Anjengo.
Jan. 9	Fox	Alexander Hume succeeded by David Mitchell.	Nov. 28	— L. & R.B.	456 E 456 P	To Bombay and Tellicherry.

Log begins.	Ship.	Captain.	Log ends.	Ledger or Receipt Book.	Reference Number.	Remarks.
1769 Jan. 12	Duke of Cumberland	Augustus Savage	1771 June 28	— L. & R.B.	562 F 562 O	To Bombay, Surat, and Mocha.
Sept. 1	Houghton	William Smith	Aug. 16	— L. & R.B.	438 L 438 FF	To Bengal and Madras.
Sept. 30	Europa	Henry Hinde Pelly	Aug. 10	— L. & R.B.	425 B 425 L	To Madras and Culpee.
Oct. 16	British King	Daniel Griffiths Hoare	1772 June 29	— L. & R.B.	557 C 557 G	To Bencoolen and Whampoa.
Oct. 17	Bridgewater	Nicholas Skottowe	1771 Oct. 5	— L. & R.B.	42 E 42 DD	To Madras and China.
Oct. 17	Earl of Elgin	Thomas Cooke succeeded by Matthew Wilkinson.	1772 Oct. 1	— L. & R.B.	559 D 559 H	To Madras, Batavia, and China.
Oct. 17	Harcourt	Nathaniel Paul	1771 Nov. 19	— L. & R.B.	558 G 558 O	To Bencoolen.
Oct. 17	Valentine	Charles Purvis	Aug. 24	— L. & R.B.	452 D 452 P	To Madras, Macao, and Whampoa.
Oct. 30	Duke of Gloucester	John Lauder	Aug. 22	— L. & R.B.	547 C 547 F	To Madras, Macao, and Whampoa.
Oct. 30	Hawke	John Cotton	Aug. 27	— L. & R.B.	390 E 390 T	To Madras, Malacca, and Whampoa.
Oct. 31	Prime	Anthony Eglinton	1772 Jan. 22	— L. & R.B.	509 A 509 F	To Madras and China.
Nov. 13	Bute	Patrick Maitland	July 18	— L. & R.B.	481 C 481 G	To Madras, Malacca, and Whampoa.
Nov. 13	Egmont	Charles Mears	1771 Oct. 15	— L. & R.B.	535 F 535 N	To Madras, Ingelee, and Culpee.
Nov. 13	Vansittart	Richard Lewin	Sept. 3	— L. & R.B.	46 C 46 V	To Madras and Bengal.
Nov. 14	Resolution	Thomas Atkyns succeeded by Thomas Poynting.	Sept. 16	— L. & R.B.	466 A 466 H	To Whampoa.
Nov. 15	Verelst	Thomas Compton	April 23	—	550 B	To Madras, Culpee, and Ingelee.
Nov. 17	Stafford	Thomas Liell	1772 Aug. 15	— L. & R.B.	560 E 560 L	To Madras and Whampoa.
Nov. 20	Princess Royal	Robert Ker	1771 Sept. 4	— L. & R.B.	405 D 405 R	To Madras, Malacca, and Whampoa.
Nov. 27	Northington	John Sealy	Oct. 1	— L. & R.B.	483 B 483 F	To Bombay, Surat, and Tellicherry.
Nov. 29	Greenwich	Robert Carr	June 27	— L. & R.B.	488 G 488 M	To Bombay.
Dec. 12	Morse	John Horne	1772 July 7	— L. & R.B.	480 A 480 G	To Madras, Culpee, Kedgeree, and Ingelee.
Dec. 13	Admiral Pocock	Thomas Riddell	1771 Aug. 19	— L. & R.B.	498 H 498 M	To Bombay, Tellicherry, and Anjengo.
Dec. 13	Kent	John Milles	Aug. 24	— L. & R.B.	317 J 317 T	To Whampoa.
Dec. 13	Worcester	Richard Hall	Sept. 23	— L. & R.B.	278 E 278 V	To Bombay and Bengal.
Dec. 14	Lord Mansfield	James Angus succeeded by Edward Wilson.	Dec. 14	— L. & R.B.	463 D 463 I	To Madras, Masulipatam, Culpee, and Ingelee.
Dec. 16	Latham	John Prince	Aug. 28	— L. & R.B.	482 E 482 O	To Bencoolen and Whampoa.
1770 Jan. 8	Huntingdon	Peter Pigou	1771 Aug. 20	— L. & R.B.	546 A 546 C	To Madras and Whampoa.
Jan. 18	Northumberland	John Mitford	1772 July 21	— L. & R.B.	141 E 141 X	To Bombay and China.
Jan. 26	True Briton	John Broadley	Jan. 7	— L. & R.B.	297 G 297 X	To Bombay, Cochin, and Tellicherry.
Feb. 10	Duke of Portland	John Hasell	Mar. 19	— L. & R.B.	504 A 504 F	To Bombay, Tellicherry, Surat, and Madras.
Aug. 17	Lapwing	Daniel Owens	1771 April 27	— L. & R.B.	475 F 475 N	From Calcutta to England.

Log begins.	Ship.	Captain.	Log ends.	Ledger or Receipt Book.	Reference Number.	Remarks.
1770 Aug. 30	Duke of Richmond	Thomas Hindman	1772 Oct. 23	— L. & R.B.	492 D 492 H	To Bencoolen, Acheen, and China.
Sept. 7	Queen	George Stainforth	Oct. 26	— L. & R.B.	356 D 356 P	To Madras and Whampoa.
Oct. 5	Ponsborne	Samuel Hough	June 20	— L. & R.B.	462 C 462 M	To Madras and Culpee.
Oct. 6	Asia	Robert Preston	Aug. 11	— L. & R.B.	24 C 24 GG	To Madras and Bengal.
Oct. 6	Salisbury	Philip Bromfield	Oct. 21	— L. & R.B.	478 H 478 P	To Madras and China.
Oct. 6	Sea Horse	Edward Dampier	Aug. 29	— L. & R.B.	479 B 479 F	To Bencoolen and Whampoa.
Oct. 8	Calcutta	William Thomson	Sept. 1	— L. & R.B.	308 E 308 S	To China.
Oct. 18	York	George Hayter	Sept. 2	— L. & R.B.	237 J 237 AA	To Madras and Whampoa.
Oct. 20	Thames	Daniel Clarke	Sept. 2	— L. & R.B.	8 C 8 X	To China.
Oct. 21	Pacific	Charles Barkley	Aug. 29	— L. & R.B.	497 C 497 G	To Madras and Macao.
Oct. 22	Grosvenor	David Saunders	Oct. 28	— L. & R.B.	495 D 495 J	To Madras and Whampoa.
Oct. 22	Horsendon	Alexander Jamison	Sept. 14	— L. & R.B.	473 D 473 H	To Madras and China.
Oct. 23	Glatton	Richard Doveton	Aug. 5	— L. & R.B.	172 D 172 X	To China.
Nov. 4	Grenville	Burnet Abercromby	Sept. 28	— L. & R.B.	467 C 467 H	To Batavia and China.
Nov. 4	Talbot	Sir Charles Hudson	Oct. 21	— L. & R.B.	474 C 474 G	To Madras, Whampoa, and Macao.
Nov. 5	Ankerwyke	James Barwell	Nov. 17	— L. & R.B.	126 C 126 G	To Madras and China.
Nov. 11	Royal Captain	Edward Berrow	1771 Aug. 17	— L. & R.B.	556 D 556 I	To Bencoolen and Whampoa.
Nov. 17	Lord North	William Hambly	1772 Oct. 24	— L. & R.B.	494 A 494 F	To Madras, Balasore, Culpee, and Ingelee.
Nov. 18	Rochford	William Hunt	Dec. 16	— L. & R.B.	470 A 470 E	To Madras and Bengal.
Nov. 20	Cruttenden	William Baker	Aug. 1	— L. & R.B.	531 D 531 H	To China.
Dec. 1	Clive	John Allen	Dec. 18	— L. & R.B.	533 D 533 H	To Bombay, Surat, Kedgeree, and Ingelee.
Dec. 4	Deptford	William Tryon	Dec. 26	— L. & R.B.	426 D 426 N	To Johanna, Bombay, Surat, and Madras.
Dec. 4	Speke	Jeffery Jackson	Aug. 17	— L. & R.B.	471 C 471 G	To Madras and Bengal.
1771 Jan. 1	Shrewsbury	Benjamin Jones	1773 July 22	— L. & R.B.	472 B 472 F	To Bombay, Surat, and Mocha.
Jan. 4	Dutton	Henry Rice	1772 July 24	— L. & R.B.	505 C 505 N	To Bombay, Tellicherry, and Anjengo.
Jan. 30	Pigot	George Richardson	1773 Aug. 10	— L. & R.B.	503 D 503 L	To Bencoolen and Batavia.
Feb. 1	Hampshire	Thomas Taylor	1772 Nov. 28	— L. & R.B.	468 E 468 I	To Bombay.
Feb. 2	Godfrey	Francis Reed	1773 Feb. 2	— L. & R.B.	464 B 464 G	To Bombay and Tellicherry.
Feb. 2	London	John Webb	July 18	— L. & R.B.	1 F 1 FF	To Bombay and China.
Feb. 19	Lord Holland	Fasham Nairn	1771 Nov. 3	— L. & R.B.	469 D 469 J	To Balasore, Kedgeree, Ingelee, and Madras.
May 1	Colebrooke	Arthur Morris	1773 Feb. 15	— L. & R.B.	532 A 532 D	To Kedgeree and Ingelee.
July 13	Lapwing	Henry Gardiner	May 10	— L. & R.B.	475 G 475 O	To Madras and Calcutta.
Oct. 10	Havannah	John White	July 9	— L. & R.B.	776 D 776 H	To Bencoolen and Whampoa.
Oct. 10	Lioness	William Larkins	1771 July 29	— L. & R.B.	502 C 502 G	To Madras and Whampoa.
Oct. 10	Nottingham	Peter Stoakes	1773 June 1	— L. & R.B.	287 E 287 T	To Bengal and Madras.
Oct. 14	Osterley	Francis Fortescue	May 24	— L. & R.B.	400 F 400 T	To Bencoolen and Whampoa.
Oct. 23	Earl of Lincoln	Alexander Tod	Sept. 14	— L. & R.B.	501 D 501 H	To Madras and Whampoa.
Oct. 23	Greenwich	Robert Carr	June 27	— L. & R.B.	488 H 488 N	To Madras, Culpee, and Ingelee.

Log begins.	Ship.	Captain.	Log ends.	Ledger or Receipt Book.	Reference Number.	Remarks.
1771 Oct. 24	Earl of Ashburnham -	Richard Peirce	1773 Sept. 14	— L. & R.B.	542 D 542 J	To Madras and Whampoa.
Oct. 24	Royal Henry -	Robert Rous - -	Oct. 28	— L. & R.B.	476 A 476 E	To Madras, Malacca, and Whampoa.
Oct. 26	Triton - -	William Elphinstone	Nov. 22	— L. & R.B.	366 G 366 V	To Madras and Bengal.
Oct. 27	Duke of Grafton -	Samuel Bull -	Sept. 14	— L. & R.B.	508 B 508 G	To Madras, Culpee, and Ingelee.
Oct. 29	Granby - -	John Johnston	July 6	— L. & R.B.	499 B 499 F	To China.
Nov. 6	Norfolk	James Buggin -	Sept. 8	— L. & R.B.	541 I 541 U	To Madras, Acheen, and China.
Nov. 14	Nassau - -	Arthur Gore	Sept. 17	— L. & R.B.	544 E 544 R	To Madras and Bengal.
Nov. 21	Duke of Albany -	John Stewart	1772 July 27	—	553 D	To Madras and Bengal. (This ship was wrecked on 26th July 1772).
Nov. 23	Lord Camden -	John Reddall -	1773 Aug. 5	— L. & R.B.	419 C 419 M	To Whampoa.
Nov. 26	Fox -	David Mitchell	Sept. 8	— L. & R.B.	456 F 456 Q	To Madras and China.
Dec. 6	Anson - -	John Lennox -	Sept. 17	— L. & R.B.	549 M 549 Y	To Madras and Whampoa.
Dec. 7	Royal Charlette	John Clements	1774 Mar. 21	— L. & R.B.	150 D 150 Y	To Bombay, Surat, and China.
Dec. 8	Duke of Cumberland -	Augustus Savage	1773 July 23	— L. & R.B.	562 G 562 P	To Bombay and Tellicherry.
Dec. 8	Hector - -	Stephen Williams -	Oct. 12	— L. & R.B.	486 H 486 Q	To Bombay and Kedgeree.
Dec. 10	Gatton - -	William Money -	July 3	— L. & R.B.	569 A (1) 569 B	To Whampoa.
Dec. 25	Earl of Sandwich -	Charles Deane -	1774 Feb. 8	— L. & R.B.	490 A 490 E	To Bencoolen.
1772 Jan. 6	Speaker - -	Robert Scott -	1773 Oct. 25	— L. & R.B.	548 D 548 H	To Bombay and Surat.
Jan. 8	Devonshire - -	Robert Morgan -	1774 Jan. 1	— L. & R.B.	272 H 272 T	To Bombay, Surat, Tellicherry, &c.
Feb. 4	Marquis of Rockingham	Alexander Hamilton	1773 Nov. 11	— L. & R.B.	493 B 493 E	To Bombay and Kedgeree.
Mar. 3	Prince of Wales -	Jonathan Court	Aug. 19	— L. & R.B.	404 M 404 DD	To Madras, Culpee, and Ingelee.
Oct. 11	Kent - -	David Thomson -	1774 Aug. 23	— L. & R.B.	317 K 317 U	To Madras and Whampoa.
Oct. 11	Prime - -	James Dundas -	Aug. 23	— L. & R.B.	509 B 509 G	To Bencoolen and Whampoa.
Oct. 12	Ponsborne - -	Samuel Hough	Oct. 17	— L. & R.B.	462 D 462 N	To Madras, Malacca, and Whampoa.
Oct. 12	Royal Captain -	Edward Berrow	1773 Dec. 26	—	556 E	To Whampoa. (The ship was wrecked on the coast of Palowa on 17th December 1773, when the Captain and 30 others were transferred to the Snow "Syren.")
Oct. 12	Worcester -	John Cook - -	1774 July 12	— L. & R.B.	278 F 278 W	To Madras and Whampoa.
Oct. 13	Latham - -	John Prince -	May 25	— L. & R.B.	482 F 482 P	To Madras, Culpee, and Ingelee.
Oct. 14	Princess Royal -	Robert Ker - -	July 6	— L. & R.B.	405 E 405 S	To Bencoolen, Macao, and Whampoa.
Oct. 15	Lord Mansfield -	William Fraser	1773 Sept. 7	—	463 E	To Madras, Kedgeree, and Ingelee. (This vessel was lost on 7th September 1773).
Oct. 20	Mercury - -	John Sharp - -	1774 April 21	— L. & two R. B.	454 A 454 I	To Johanna, Madras, and Calcutta.
Oct. 25	Northington - -	John Sealy -	July 26	— L. & R.B.	483 C 483 G	To Madras, Culpee, and Ingelee.
Oct. 25	Stormont - -	John Rogers -	Sept. 26	— L. & R.B.	458 C 458 J	To Johanna, Madras, and Whampoa.
Oct. 26	Huntingdon - -	Peter Pigou -	April 16	—	546 B	To Madras and Kedgeree. (This ship was lost off Johanna on 16th April 1774.)
Nov. 9	Houghton - -	William Smith -	July 8	— L. & R.B.	438 M 438 GG	To Madras and Bengal.

Log begins.	Ship.	Captain.	Log ends.	Ledger or Receipt Book.	Reference Number.	Remarks.
1772 Nov. 11	Alfred	John Lauder	1775 Mar. 25	— L. & R.B.	140 A 140 O	To Bencoolen and Batavia.
Nov. 12	Duke of Kingston	Raymond Snow	1774 July 2	— L. & R.B.	545 C 545 G	To Whampoa.
Nov. 25	Harcourt	Nathaniel Paul	Oct. 25	— L. & R.B.	558 H 558 P	To Kedgeree and Madras.
Nov. 24	Egmont	Charles Mears	Aug. 24	— L. & R.B.	585 G 635 O	To Kedgeree.
Nov. 25	Bridgewater	Nicholas Skottowe	Sept. 21	— L. & R.B.	42 F 42 EE	To Madras and Bengal.
Dec. 11	Hawke	John Cotton	Sept. 19	— L. & R.B.	390 F 390 U	To Bombay, Onore, Tellicherry, Anjengo, and Cochin.
Dec. 11	Resolution	Thomas Poynting	1775 Jan. 13	— L. & R.B.	466 B 466 I	To Bombay and Kedgeree.
Dec. 14	Duke of Portland	John Sutton	1774 Aug. 17	— L. & R.B.	504 B 504 G	To Bencoolen and Batavia.
Dec. 24	Europa	Henry Hinde Pelly	1775 June 2	— L. & R.B.	425 C 425 M	To Johanna, Bombay, Calicut, Surat, and Mocha.
Dec. 24	Vansittart	Robert Young	Jan. 7	— L. & R.B.	46 D 46 W	To Bombay.
Dec. 25	British King	Daniel Griffiths Hoare.	Aug. 5	— L. & R.B.	557 D 557 H	To Bombay and Calcutta.
Dec. 25	Earl of Bessborough	Thomas Riddell	July 12	— L. & R.B.	574 A 259 E	To Bombay, Bengal, and Whampoa.
1773 Feb. 3	Valentine	James Ogilvie	1774 Aug. 2	— L. & R.B.	452 E 452 Q	To Whampoa.
Mar. 26	Eagle	Edward Wilson succeeded by Matthew Wroe, and Chas. Martin Lefort.	1776 April 20	— L. & R.B.	537 A 537 E	To Madras and Borneo.
Oct. 16	York	George Hayter	1775 Nov. 25	— L. & R.B.	237 K 237 BB	To Bencoolen and Batavia.
Oct. 17	Bute	Richard Bendy	Nov. 17	— L. & R.B.	481 D 481 H	To Madras and Calcutta.
Oct. 18	Asia	Wm. Dick Gamage	1774 Oct. 13	— R.B.	24 D 24 HH	To Madras and Bengal.
Oct. 18	Ceres	Thomas Newte	1775 Aug. 5	— L. & R.B.	215 A 215 S	To Madras and China.
Nov. 1	Morse	George Kent	1776 Sept. 2	— L. & R.B.	480 B 480 H	To Madras, Malacca, and Whampoa.
Nov. 1	Sea Horse	David Arthur	1775 Oct. 3	— L. & R.B.	479 C 479 G	To Balasore, Kedgeree, Ingelee, and Madras.
Nov. 1	True Briton	John Broadley	Aug. 15	— L. & R.B.	297 H 297 Y	To Madras and Whampoa.
Nov. 14	Speke	Jeffery Jackson	Aug. 17	— L. & R.B.	471 D 471 H	To Madras and Bengal.
Nov. 15	Dutton	Henry Rice	Aug. 24	— L.& R.B.	505 D 505 O	To Madras, Vizagapatam, and Kedgeree.
Nov. 29	Pacific	Charles Barkley succeeded by James Williamson.	Oct. 18	— L. & R.B.	497 D 497 H	To Madras and Culpee.
Dec. 14	Northumberland	James Rees	1776 July 4	— L. & R.B.	141 F 141 Y	To Bombay, Surat, and Bengal.
Dec. 14	Thames	Daniel Clarke	1775 Aug. 10	— L. & R.B.	8 D 8 Y	To Bombay, &c.
Dec. 31	Syren	Edward Berrow	1774 Aug. 22	— L. & R.B.	556 E 536 C	From Balambangan to England. (In same book as Journal of "Royal Captain," 1772–3.)
1774 Jan. 29	Stafford	Thomas Liell	1777 Oct. 3	— L. & R.B.	560 F 560 M	To Bombay, Surat, Anjengo, Tellicherry, and Whampoa.
Feb. 10	Calcutta	William Thomson	1776 Aug. 13	— L.& R.B.	308 F 308 T	To Madras, Bombay, Surat, and Tellicherry.
Mar. 22	Royal Charlotte	John Clements	1775 Sept. 19	—	150 E	From Batavia to Bombay and China.

Log begins.	Ship.	Captain.	Log ends.	Ledger or Receipt Book.	Reference Number.	Remarks.
1774 Oct. 1	Syren	Joseph Smith	1777 May 15	— L. & R.B.	536 B 536 D	To Bencoolen and Calcutta.
Oct. 19	Lord North	William Hambly	1776 July 10	— L. & R.B.	494 B 494 G	To Bencoolen and Whampoa.
Oct. 19	Osterley	Francis Fortescue succeeded by Samuel Rogers.	Oct. 8	— L. & R.B.	400 G 400 U	To St. Helena and Bencoolen.
Oct. 19	Queen	George Stainforth	Oct. 14	— L. & R.B.	356 E 356 Q	To Madras and Whampoa.
Oct. 19	Salisbury	Philip Bromfield	Aug. 2	— L. & R.B.	478 I 478 Q	To Madras, Masulipatam, Vizagapatam, and Culpee.
Oct. 20	Colebrooke	Arthur Morris	June 12	— L. & R.B.	532 B 532 E	To Kedgeree, Ingelee, and Madras.
Nov.	Ankerwyke	James Barwell	Oct. 4	— L. & R.B.	126 D 126 H	To Madras and Bengal.
Nov.	Rochford	John Baird	July 15	— L. & R.B.	470 B 470 F	To Bencoolen and Canton.
Nov. 17	Hillsborough	Robert Preston	Oct. 1	— L. & R.B.	437 A 437 K	To Madras, Kedgeree, and Ingelee.
Nov. 19	Grosvenor	David Saunders	Aug. 23	— L. & R.B.	495 E 495 K	To Madras and Whampoa.
Dec. 17	Godfrey	Francis Reed	Sept. 25	— L.	464 C 464 H	To Madras and Bengal.
Dec. 17	Hampshire	Thomas Timbrill	1777 May 15	— L. & R.B.	468 F 468 J	To Bencoolen and Batavia.
Dec. 19	Anson	William Tryon	1776 Jan. 20	— L. & R.B.	549 N 549 Z	From Bengal to England.
Dec. 19	Nottingham	Peter Stoakes	May 31	— L. & R.B.	287 F 287 U	To Madras.
1775 Feb. 2	Grenville	Burnet Abercromby	1777 April 28	— L. & R.B.	467 D 467 I	To Madras, Masulipatam, and Bombay.
Feb. 12	Royal Charlotte	[John Clements]	1775 Aug. 19	—	150 F	From Bombay (?) to England.
Mar. 14	Talbot	Raymond Snow	1776 Dec. 24	— L. & R.B.	474 D 474 H	To Bombay, Madras, and Kedgeree.
Mar. 25	Gatton	William Money	Feb. 14	— L. & R.B.	467 E 569 C	To Bombay. (This book also contains the log of the "Grenville," 1776–7.)
Oct. 2	Royal Henry	Robert Rous	1777 Aug. 25	— L. & R.B.	476 B 476 F	To Madras, Malacca, and Canton.
Oct. 9	Greenwich	Robert Carr	Aug. 20	— L. & R.B.	488 I 488 O	To Madras, Culpee, and Ingelee.
Oct. 9	Lord Holland	Patrick Lawson	Aug. 7	— L. & R.B.	469 E 469 K	To Bencoolen and Whampoa.
Oct. 24	Earl of Sandwich	Charles Deane	1778 Oct. 14	— L. & R.B.	490 B 490 F	To Madras and Whampoa.
Oct. 24	Nassau	Arthur Gore	1777 Aug. 25	— L. & R.B.	544 F 544 S	To Madras and Bengal.
Oct. 24	Norfolk	James Buggin	Dec. 8	— L. & R.B.	541 J 541 V	To Madras and Whampoa.
Oct. 25	Granby	John Johnston	Dec. 6	— L. & R.B.	499 C 499 G	To Madras and Whampoa.
Nov. 6	Prince of Wales	Jonathan Court	Oct. 6	— L. & R.B.	404 N 404 EE	To Madras.
Nov. 7	Fox	David Mitchell	Oct. 12	— L. & R.B.	456 G 456 R	To Madras and China.
Nov. 7	Lord Camden	John Reddall	Nov. 20	— L. & R.B.	419 D 419 N	To Madras, Malacca, and Whampoa.
Nov. 22	Duke of Grafton	Samuel Bull	1778 May 14	— L. & R.B.	508 C 508 H	To Batavia and Bencoolen.
Nov. 23	Lioness	Thomas Larkins	1777 Aug. 23	— L. & R.B.	502 D 502 H	To Madras, Culpee, and Ingelee.
Nov. 24	London	Daniel Webb	Oct. 12	— L. & R.B.	1 G 1 GG	To Madras.
Nov. 24	Shrewsbury	Benjamin Jones	Sept. 15	— L. & R.B.	472 C 472 G	To Culpee and Ingelee.
Dec. 24	Duke of Cumberland	Augustus Savage	Nov. 15	— L. & R.B.	562 H 562 Q	To Madras, Culpee, and Ingelee.
Dec. 24	Triton	William Elphinstone	Sept. 1	— L. & R.B.	366 H 366 W	To Madras and Culpee.
1776 Jan. 13	Mercury	George Forbes	1776 Nov. 26	— L. & R.B.	454 B 454 J	To Cape Coast Castle, St. Thomas, St. Helena, and Table Bay.
Feb. 6	Latham	John Prince	1777 Sept. 14	— L. & R.B.	482 G 482 Q	To Bombay and Surat.

Log begins.	Ship.	Captain.	Log ends.	Ledger or Receipt Book.	Reference Number.	Remarks.
1776 Feb. 7	Marquis of Rockingham.	Alexander Hamilton	1777 May 30	—	493 C	To Bombay, Surat, and Madras.
Feb. 8	Hector	Stephen Williams	1778 Mar. 28	— L. & R.B.	486 I 486 R	To Madras, Bombay, and Tellicherry.
May 30	Grenville	Burnet Abercromby	1777 April 28	—	487 E	From Bombay to Madras and England. (Containing also log of ship "Gatton," 1775–6.)
Sept. 27	Alfred	James Williamson	1778 Oct. 1	— L. & R.B.	140 B 140 P	To Bencoolen and China.
Oct. 13	Egmont	Charles Mears	June 11	— L. & R.B.	535 H 535 P	To Madras and Bengal.
Oct. 13	Stormont	John Rogers	1779 Jan. 2	— L. & R.B.	458 D 458 K	To Madras and Whampoa.
Oct. 15	Valentine	[James Ogilvie]	Nov. 13	—	452 F	To Madras, Vizagapatam, Tranquebar, and Bombay.
Oct. 26	Royal Charlotte	Joseph Cotton	1778 Jan. 2	— L. & R.B.	150 G 150 Z	To Madras and China.
Oct. 26	Worcester	John Cook	Aug. 26	— L. & R.B.	278 G 278 X	To Madras and Whampoa.
Oct. 27	Prince	James Dundas	Aug. 25	— L. & R.B.	509 C 509 H	To Madras and Whampoa.
Oct. 27	Resolution	Thomas Poynting	Oct. 5	— L. & R.B.	466 C 466 J	To Madras and China.
Oct. 27	True Briton	John Broadley	Oct. 20	— L. & R.B.	297 I 297 Z	To Madras and Whampoa.
Oct. 28	Princess Royal	Robert Ker	Oct. 7	— L. & R.B.	405 F 405 T	To Madras and Whampoa.
Nov. 11	Houghton	William Smith	Oct. 2	— L. & R.B.	438 N 438 HH	To Madras, Vizagapatam, and Culpee.
Nov. 12	Bridgewater	William Parker	1779 Mar. 26	— L. & R.B.	42 G 42 FF	To Batavia and Bencoolen.
Nov. 12	Ceres	Thomas Newte	1778 Sept. 22	— L. & R.B.	215 B 215 T	To Madras and Bengal.
Nov. 14	Europa	William Applegath	June 19	— L. & R.B.	425 D 425 N	To Madras, Calcutta, Culpee, and Ingelee.
Nov. 25	Northington	John Durand	1780 Jan. 12	— L. & R.B.	483 D 483 H	To Bombay, Surat, and Kedgeree.
Dec. 10	Earl of Ashburnham	Martin Waghorn	1778 Jan. 20	Two J. L. & R.B.	542 E & F 542 K	From Calcutta to England.
Dec. 12	Hawke	John Cotton	Oct. 3	— L. & R.B.	390 G 390 V	To Bombay and Surat.
Dec. 13	Rochford	John Baird	1779 Dec. 12	— L. & R.B.	470 C 470 G	To Bombay, Surat, Tellicherry, Madras, Kedgeree, and Culpee.
Dec. 25	Sea Horse	David Arthur	1778 Dec. 2	— L. & R.B.	479 D 479 H	To Culpee and Ingelee.
Dec. 25	York	John Atkinson Blanshard.	1779 Mar. 16	— R.B.	237 L 237 CC	To Bombay, Tellicherry, Anjengo, &c.
Dec. 26	Bessborough	Alexander Montgomerie.	1781 Oct. 31	— L. & R.B.	259 A & B 259 F	To Madras, Bombay, Pondicherry, Calcutta, &c.
1777 Jan. 13	Duke of Portland	John Sutton	1778 Dec. 24	— L. & R.B.	504 C 504 H	To Kedgeree and Ingelee.
Mar. 26	Eagle	Arthur Maxwell	1779 May 26	— L. & R.B.	537 D 537 F	To Madras and Calcutta.
April 26	Lord North	William Hambly	Aug. 7	— L. & R.B.	494 C 494 H	To Madras, Bencoolen, and Whampoa.
Oct. 5	Queen	Peter Douglas	1780 Mar. 15	— L. and two R.B.	356 F 356 R	To Batavia and Bencoolen.
Oct. 6	Earl of Mansfield	William Fraser	1779 Nov. 30	— L. & R.B.	530 A 530 F	To China.
Oct. 31	Godfrey	Francis Reed	1780 Mar. 3	— L. & R.B.	464 D 464 I	To Madras and Kedgeree.
Oct. 31	Grosvenor	John Coxon	1779 Nov. 16	— L. & R.B.	495 F 495 L	To Madras, Culpee, and Ingelee.

Log begins.	Ship.	Captain.	Log ends.	Ledger or Receipt Book.	Reference Number.	Remarks.
1777 Nov. 1	Mount Stuart	John Stewart	1780 Mar. 21	— L. & R.B.	555 A 555 B	To Madras and Kedgeree.
Nov. 2	Hillsborough	Pitt Collet	Feb. 23	— L. & R.B.	437 B 437 L	To Madras, Malacca, and Whampoa.
Nov. 14	Royal George	Thomas Foxall	1779 Dec. 21	— L. & R.B.	17 I 17 Z	To Madras and China.
Nov. 17	Glatton	Richard Doveton	1780 Feb. 23	— L. & R.B.	172 F 172 Y	To Madras and China.
Nov. 18	Latham	John Prince	1779 Nov. 25	— L. & R.B.	482 H 482 B	To Madras and China.
Dec. 1	Southampton	John Lennox	1780 Oct. 21	— L. & three R.B.	538 A 538 D	To Kedgeree, Madras, and Trincomalee.
Dec. 2	Shrewsbury	John Coggan	Mar. 18	— L. & R.B.	472 D 472 H	To Calcutta and Madras.
Dec. 8	Eagle	Arthur Maxwell	1779 April 7	— L. & R.B.	537 B & C 537 F	To Madras and Calcutta. (The portion of Journal from 25th June 1778 to 23rd October 1778 is missing).
Dec. 12	Duke of Kingston	Robert Maw	1778 Nov. 4	— L. & R.B.	545 D (1) 545 H	To Madras, Culpee, and Ingelee.
Dec. 14	Royal Henry	Ralph Dundas	1780 Nov. 5	— L. & R.B.	476 C 476 G	To Bombay, Madras, Kedgeree, and Whampoa.
Dec. 15	Gatton	Charles Chisholme succeeded by Job Strong.	Mar. 4	— L. & R.B.	569 A (2) 569 D	To Bengal and Madras.
Dec. 15	Morse	George Kent succeeded by Joseph Elliott.	1781 April 21	— L. & three R.B.	480 C & D 480 I	To Bombay, Tellicherry, Madras, and China.
Dec. 16	Calcutta	William Thomson	Feb. 28	— L. & R.B.	308 G 308 U	To Madras, Bengal, and Calcutta.
Dec. 16	Nassau	Arthur Gore	1780 Oct. 21	— L. & three R.B.	544 G & H 544 T	To Madras, Pondicherry, and Kedgeree.
Dec. 31	Colebrooke	[Arthur Morris]	1778 Aug. 31	—	532 C	Towards Bombay. (This vessel struck on a rock near False Bay, Cape of Good Hope, and was lost.)
1778 Jan. 1	Royal Admiral	Joseph Huddart	1780 Feb. 21	— L. & R.B.	338 A 338 J	To Bombay.
Jan. 30	Stafford	George Hutchinson	1779 Aug. 30	—	560 G	To Madras and Kedgeree. (This ship was wrecked on the 29th August 1779.)
Aug. 10	Granby	John Johnston	1782 Jan. 28	— L. & three R.B.	499 D 499 H	To Madras and Whampoa.
Aug. 10	Norfolk	Samuel Charles Bonham.	1781 April 11	— L. & three R.B.	541 K 541 W	To Madras.
Aug. 23	Fox	John Blackburn	Dec. 28	— L. & three R.B.	456 H 456 S	To Madras, Kedgeree, and Barrabulla.
Aug. 24	Halsewell	Richard Peirce	1782 Feb. 1	— L. & three R.B.	465 A & B 465 D	To Madras, Malacca, and Whampoa.
Aug. 25	Atlas	Allen Cooper	Jan. 30	— L. & two R.B.	27 A 27 P	To Madras, Bombay, and China.
Sept. 9	Earl of Oxford	John White	Jan. 26	— L. & three R.B.	489 A 489 G	To Madras and Whampoa.
Sept. 21	Duke of Grafton	Samuel Bull	Jan. 9	— L. & R.B.	508 D & E 508 I	To Madras, Pondicherry, Surat, Bombay, and Kedgeree.

Log begins.	Ship.	Captain.	Log ends.	Ledger or Receipt Book.	Reference Number.	Remarks.
1778 Oct. 5	Earl Talbot	Thomas Hindman	1781 Mar. 10	— L. & R.B. Two R.B.	410 A 410 J 410 I	To Kedgeree and Madras.
Oct. 26	Ganges	G. Richardson	April 5	— L. & R.B.	86 A 86 Q	To Madras and Bengal.
Nov. 15	Lord Holland	Patrick Lawson	1780 Jan. 14	— L. & R.B.	469 F 469 L	To Madras and Whampoa.
Nov. 18	Alfred	James Brown	1781 April 14	— L. & R.B.	140 C 140 Q	To China.
Nov. 19	Resolution	Thomas Poynting	1780 Dec. 31	— L. & R.B.	466 D 466 K	To Bombay, Mangalore, Onore, and Madras.
Nov. 21	Mercury	George Forbes succeeded by Augustus Joseph Applegath.	1784 June 19	— L. & two R.B.	454 C, D, & E 454 K	To Bombay, Madras, Calcutta, Bussora, Muscat, Bushire, and Mangalore.
Dec. 4	Worcester	John Cook	1781 April 7	— L. & two R.B.	278 H 278 Y	To Whampoa and Macao.
Dec. 5	Ceres	Raymond Snow	Mar. 29	— L. & three R.B.	215 C 215 U	To Bengal and Acheen.
1779 Jan. 1	Earl of Sandwich	Charles Deane	1782 Jan. 25	— L. & three R.B.	490 C 490 G	To Madras and Whampoa.
Jan. 1	Prime	James Dundas	May 22	— L. & three R.B.	509 D 509 I	To Bombay and Madras.
Jan. 3	Hawke	John Cotton	1781 Feb. 23	— L. & R.B.	390 H 390 W	To Bombay.
Jan. 4	Princess Royal	Robert Ker	Oct. 31	— L. & three R.B.	405 G & H 405 U	To Batavia, Bencoolen, and Pulo Penang.
Jan. 22	Walpole	Burnet Abercromby	Dec. 31	— L. & R.B.	293 M 293 JJ	To Madras and Calcutta.
Feb. 2	True Briton	Thomas Timbrill	1782 Jan. 16	— L. & R.B.	297 J 297 AA	To Madras, Masulipatam, Vizagapatam, &c.
Mar. 19	Duke of Kingston	Justinian Nutt	1781 Dec. 27	— L. & three R.B.	545 D (2) 545 I	To Madras and Calcutta.
Sept. 1	Britannia	George Hutchinson	Dec. 15	— L. & R.B.	285 LL 285 L	To Bombay, Madras, and Whampoa.
Sept. 25	Stormont	John Rogers	1782 Feb. 1	— L. & three R.B.	458 E 458 L	To Bally, Macao, and Whampoa.
Sept. 29	Royal Charlotte	Joseph Cotton	May 9	— L. & two R.B.	150 H 150 AA	To Bombay, Madras, and China.
Oct. 10	Bridgewater	William Parker	Jan. 5	— L. & two R.B.	42 H 42 GG	To Madras and China.
Oct. 10	London	Daniel Webb	Jan. 31	— L. & R.B.	1 H 1 HH	To Madras and China.
Oct. 11	Contractor	James Baldwin	1783 Jan. 4	— L. & R.B.	319 A 319 I	To Madras, Tellicherry, Bombay, and Whampoa.
Oct. 11	York	John Atkinson Blanchard.	1782 Jan. 30	— Two R.B. L. & R.B.	237 M 237 DD 237 EE	To Madras and Whampoa.
Oct. 12	Duke of Portland	John Sutton	1783 Jan. 2	— L. & three R.B.	504 D & E 504 I	To Madras, Kedgeree, Tellicherry, Bombay, and Whampoa.
Oct. 14	Lascelles	Thomas Wakefield	1782 Jan. 21	— L. & two R.B.	408 A 408 I	To Madras and China.

Log begins.	Ship.	Captain.	Log ends.	Ledger or Receipt Book.	Reference Number.	Remarks.
1779 Nov. 23	Ponsborne	Frederick Le Mesurier	1782 Dec. 16	— L. & three R.B.	462 E 462 O	To Madras, Goa, Bombay, &c.
—	Eagle	Arthur Maxwell	1780 —	R.B. only.	537 G	——
—	Hinde	Richard Bendy	—	Two R.B. only.	395 C	——
1780 Feb. 5	Pigot	Robert Morgan	1782 Apr. 5	— L. & three R.B.	503 I 503 M	To Whampoa.
Feb. 5	Rochford	James Tod	1783 Aug. 28	— L. & three R.B.	470 D 470 H	To Madras, Visagapatam, and Calcutta.
Feb. 8	Earl of Mansfield	William Fraser	1782 May 23	— L. & three R.B.	530 B 530 G	To Whampoa.
Feb. 15	Neptune	Robert Scott	July 23	— L. & two R.B.	98 F 98 Y	To Madras and Bengal.
Feb. 24	Bellmont	William Dick Gamage	May 10	— L. & two R.B.	444 A 444 H	To Madras and Kedgeree.
Mar. 8	Glatton	John Clements	May 27	— L. & two R.B.	172 G 172 Z	To China, Bencoolen, &c.
Mar. 8	Royal Admiral	Joseph Huddart	1783 Aug. 31	— R.B. L. & R.B.	338 B 338 K 338 L	To Bombay, Madras, and Negapatam.
Mar. 23	Vansittart	Robert Young succeeded by William Agnew.	1782 April 7 —	— L. & R.B.	46 E 46 X	To China.
June 4	Lord Holland	Stephen Williams	June 22	— L. & two R.B.	469 C 469 M	To Macao and Whampoa.
July 29	Lively	Thomas Forrest [From 1783, Jan. 1, William Mackintosh.]	1783 July 8	— L. & two R.B.	534 A 534 B	To Madras and Calcutta.
Aug. 7	Rodney	John Corner	June 12	— L. & three R.B.	442 A & B 442 I	To Madras, China, &c.
Sept. 15	Queen	Peter Douglas	1784 Feb. 11	— L. & R.B.	356 G 356 S	To Madras, Bencoolen, and Whampoa.
Sept. 16	Lord North	William Hambly	1783 Mar. 29	— L. & three R.B.	494 D 494 I	To Bencoolen and Whampoa.
Sept. 30	Latham	John Prince succeeded by Edward Robertson.	1785 Oct. 4	— L. & R.B.	482 I & J 462 S	To Bombay, Madras, Kedgeree, Culpee, and Whampoa.
Oct. 1	Osterley	Samuel Rogers	1783 Nov. 5	— L. & three R.B.	400 H & I 400 V	To Bombay and Whampoa.
Oct. 14	Essex	Arthur Morris	Nov. 22	— L. & R.B.	229 K 229 JJ	To Madras, Trincomalee, Bombay, and Whampoa.
Oct. 23	Valentine	John Lewis	April 4	— L. & three R.B.	452 G 452 R	To Madras, Negapatam, &c.
Nov. 14	Asia	Robert Maw	April 25	— L. & two R.B.	24 E 24 I I	To Bombay and China.
Nov. 14	Hastings	Hugh Fraser succeeded by John Thompson.	Feb. 7	— L. & three R.B.	459 A 459 C	To Macao and Whampoa.
Nov. 14	Locko	Patrick Lawson	Nov. 14	— L. & three R.B.	457 A & B 457 F	To Bombay and Whampoa.
Dec. 26	Southampton	John Lennox	1785 July 16	— L. & R.B.	538 B 538 A	To Bombay, Madras, and Calcutta.

Log begins.	Ship.	Captain.	Log ends.	Ledger or Receipt Book.	Reference Number.	Remarks.
1780 —	Grosvenor	John Coxon	1783 —	Two R.B. only.	495 M	—
—	Hinchinbrooke	Arthur Maxwell	1784 —	Two R.B. only.	722 A	—
—	Resolution	[Thomas Poynting]	—	L. only.	466 L	This ledger only contains accounts of Lascars.
1781 Jan. 25	Nassau	Arthur Gore	1785 Sept. 30	— L. & R.B.	544 I 544 U	To Bombay, Tellicherry, Kedgeree, Macao, and Whampoa.
Jan. 27	Tartar	Edward Fiott	1783 Aug. 7	— L. & three R.B.	539 A 539 B	To Madras and Calcutta.
Feb. 5	Northumberland	James Ross	1784 May 30	— L. & R.B.	141 G & H 141 Z	To Bencoolen and China.
Feb. 10	Lord Mulgrave	James Urmston	1783 Sept. 25	— L. & three R.B.	581 A 581 B	To Madras, Balasore, and Kedgeree.
Mar. 14	Chapman	Thomas Walker	Mar. 18	— L. & R.B.	218a, A 218a, D	To Madras and Bengal.
Mar. 14	Fortitude	Charles Gregorie	1782 June 23	— Two R.B.	540 A 540 B	To Madras and Bengal.
Mar. 31	Chesterfield	Bruce Boswell	1786 Aug. 10	— L. & three R.B.	507 F & G 507 Q	To Madras, Calcutta, Bombay, Batavia, and Whampoa.
April 5	Deptford	James Elkington	1783 Aug. 28	— L. & two R.B.	425 E 425 O	To Madras and Kedgeree.
July 23	Ceres	Thomas Price	1784 Oct. 6	— L. & R.B.	215 D 215 V	To Madras, Bengal, and Bombay.
July 24	Dutton	James West	July 5	— L. & R.B.	505 E 505 P	To Bombay, Madras, Kedgeree, and Whampoa.
July 25	Fox	Jonathan Court	1782 Aug. 12	— L. & R.B.	456 I & J 456 T	To Macao, Sooloo, and Barrabulla.
July 27	Alfred	James Brown	1786 July 28	— L. & R.B. L.	140 D & E 140 R 140 S	To Madras, Bengal, Bombay, and China.
July 27	Ganges	John H. Dempster	1785 April 6	— L. & R.B.	86 B 86 R	To Bengal, Bombay, and China.
Aug. 4	Royal Henry	Ralph Dundas	1784 May 28	— L. & three R.B.	476 D 476 H	To Madras, Bombay, and China.
Aug. 6	Calcutta	William Thomson	1785 Sept. 13	— L. & R.B.	308 H & I 308 V	To Madras, Bengal, Batavia, and China. (Containing also some extracts from a log dating from 30th April 1782 to 3rd February 1785.)
Aug. 6	Earl Talbot	Robert Taylor	1784 Aug. 29	— L. & R.B.	410 B 410 K	To Rio Janeiro, Bombay, Madras, Masulipatam, and Kedgeree.
Aug. 6	Morse	Joseph Elliott	Sept. 6	— L. & R.B.	480 E 480 J	To Bombay, Madras, and China.
Aug. 6	Norfolk	Samuel Charles Bonham.	Sept. 9	— L. & R.B.	541 L 541 X	To Bengal.
Aug. 6	Royal Bishop	William Meare	1785 July 8	— L. & R.B.	485 A & B 485 D	To Bombay, Tellicherry, Bencoolen, Madras, and Pulo Penang.
Aug. 23	Warren Hastings	Thomas Larkins	1784 Oct. 27	— L. & R.B.	9 A & B 9 Z	To Bengal and Bombay.
Aug. 24	Kent	Peter Stoakes	Feb. 14	— L. & R.B.	41 A 41 J	To Madras and Bengal.
Aug. 27	Hawke	Peter Rivington	1785 June 20	— L. & R.B.	390 I 390 X	To Rio Janeiro, Bombay, Whampoa, &c.
Aug. 27	Worcester	John Cook succeeded by John Hall.	1784 July 14	— L. & R.B.	278 I 278 Z	To Madras and Bengal.

Log begins.	Ship.	Captain.	Log ends.	Ledger or Receipt Book.	Reference Number.	Remarks.
1781 Dec. 13	Spy	John Sherwood	1783 Dec. 16	— L. & two R.B.	548 A 548 B	To St. Helena and various cruises round that island.
Dec. 31	Antelope	Henry Wilson	June 5	— L. & R.B.	570 A 570 C	To Macao.
—	Blandford	Peter Pigon	1792 —	Two R.B. only.	782 A	——
—	Earl of Hertford	Daniel Clarke	1783 —	Two R.B. only.	791 A	——
—	Major	David Arthur	1784 —	Two R.B. only.	780 A	——
—	Nottingham	George Curtis	1782 —	Two R.B. only.	287 V	——
1782 Feb. 14	General Coote		1784 Sept. 5	—	441 A	To Madras, Malacca, Macao, and Whampoa.
Feb. 15	Britannia	Edward Cumming	1783 Sept. 27	— L. & two R.B.	285 MM 285 M	To Bencoolen.
Feb. 27	Winterton	Raymond Snow	1784 July 20	— L. & two R.B.	451 A 451 D	To Madras and Kedgeree.
Feb. 28	Europa	William Applegath succeeded by Charles Gardyn.	1785 Aug. 6	— L. & two R.B.	425 E 425 O	To Madras, Bombay, and Bushire.
Feb. 28	Rodney	Henry Wakeman	1784 July 2	— L. & two R.B.	442 C 442 J	To Madras and Kedgeree.
Mar. 2	Francis	Henry Grueber	Aug. 7	— L. & R.B.	443 A 443 G	To Madras and Whampoa.
Mar. 2	General Goddard	Thomas Foxall	Nov. 30	— L. & R.B.	440 A & B 440 H	To Madras, Anjengo, and Bombay.
Mar. 2	Montagu	Thomas Brettell	July 27	— L. & R.B. Two R.B.	552 K 552 T 552 W	To Madras and Whampoa.
May 30	Mercury	Augustus Joseph Applegath.	June 29	—	454 F	From Bombay to Madras, Mangalore, and England. (This is evidently a part of the same voyage as that recorded in 454 C, D, and E, Robert Peck the writer being second and afterwards first mate.)
June 10	Resolution	Thomas Poynting succeeded by David Tolme.	1785 July 21	— L. & R.B.	466 E 466 K	From Balasore and Calcutta to Bombay and England.
July 24	Neptune	R. Scott	1783 Sept. 13	—	98 G	From Bombay to England.
Sept. 21	York	John Atkinson Blanshard.	1784 Aug. 31	— L. & R.B.	237 N 237 FF	To Madras and China.
Sept. 23	Barwell	Robert Carr	Sept. 11	— L. & R.B.	420 A 420 H	To Madras, Balasore, and Kedgeree.
Sept. 24	Houghton	James Monro	Aug. 5	— L. & R.B.	438 O 438 I I	To Madras, Macao, and Whampoa.
Oct. 6	Lord Macartney	William Hall	Oct. 27	— L. & R.B.	415 A 415 G	To Madras and Kedgeree.
Oct. 7	Stormont	Robert Fairfull	Sept. 11	— L. & R.B.	458 F 458 M	To Madras, Macao, and Whampoa.
Oct. 8	Atlas	Allen Cooper	Sept. 9	— L. & two R.B.	27 B 27 Q	To Madras and Bengal.
Oct. 8	Bellmont	William Dick Gamage	Oct. 6	— L. & R.B.	444 B 444 I	To Madras and Kedgeree.
Oct. 8	Halsewell	Richard Peirce	Oct. 16	— L. & R.B.	465 C 465 E	To Madras and Bengal (incomplete.)
Oct. 8	London	John Eastabrooke	1785 May 12	— L. & R.B.	1 I 1 I I	To Madras and China.
Oct. 8	True Briton	Henry Farrer	Dec. 10	— L. & R.B.	287 K 287 BB	To Madras, Bombay, and Whampoa.
Oct. 9	Earl of Oxford	John White	1784 Dec. 18	— L. & R.B.	489 B 489 H	To Madras and Bengal.

Log begins.	Ship.	Captain.	Log ends.	Ledger or Receipt Book.	Reference Number.	Remarks.
1782 Oct. 9	Vansittart	W. Agnew	1785 Aug. 23	— L. & R.B.	46 F 46 Y	To Madras, Bengal, and Batavia.
Oct. 10	Walpole	Henry Churchill	1782 Oct. 28	— L. & R.B.	293 N 293 KK	To Bencoolen and Whampoa.
Oct. 21	Pigot	Robert Morgan	1785 July 30	— L. & three R.B.	503 F 503 N	To Madras and Kedgeree.
Oct. 28	Earl of Sandwich	John Wordsworth	May 19	— L. & three R.B.	490 D 490 H	To Madras, Batavia, and China.
Dec. 5	Bessborough	Alexander Momtgomerie.	Aug. 24	— L. & R.B.	259 C 259 G	To Bombay, Cochin, Anjengo, and Bengal.
Dec. 5	Sulivan	Stephen Williams	July 20	— L. & R.B.	257 A 257 H	To Bombay, Tellicherry, Cochin, and Whampoa.
Dec. 13	Glatton	C. Drummond	1786 May 17	— L. & R.B.	172 H & I 172 AA	To Bombay, Surat, Bengal, Madras, and Bencoolen.
Dec. 16	General Elliott	Robert Drummond	1784 Sept. 7	— L. & R.B.	269 A 269 G	To Bombay, Cochin, Tellicherry, and Goa.
Dec. 22	Raymond	Richard Pennell	July 17	— L. & R.B.	458 A 453 F	To Bombay.
—	Busbridge	Alexander Tod	1803 —	L. only	413 H	——
—	Duke of Atholl	James Rattray	1784 —	Two R.B. only.	790 A	——
—	Duke of Kingston	Justinian Nutt	1785 —	Two R.B. only.	545 J	——
—	Fairford	John Haldane	1784 —	Two R.B. only	788 A	——
—	Greyhound	Robert Anderson	1786 —	L. & two R.B. only.	771 A	——
—	Lascelles	Thomas Wakefield	—	L. & R.B.	408 J	——
—	Swallow	Sober Hall	1783 —	L. only	385 L	——
1783 Jan. 10	Trial	James Methurst Poynter.	1784 April 21	— L. & R.B.	580 A 580 C	From Calcutta to Bencoolen and England.
Feb. 9	Fox	Jonathan Court	1783 July 20	—	456 J	From Calcutta to England.
Mar. 12	Swallow	Richard Bendy	—	R.B. only	385 M	——
April 22	Surprise	David Asquith	Nov. 20	—	447 A	From Bengal to England.
Sept. 16	Nerbudda	James Rattray	1784 May 10	— L. & R.B.	252 A 252 B	From Calcutta to England.
Sept. 26	Ponsborne	William Hammett	1785 July 6	— L. & R.B.	462 F 462 P	To Madras and Whampoa.
Sept. 27	Middlesex	John Rogers	Aug. 17	— L. & R.B.	450 E 450 L	To Madras and Whampoa.
Oct. 11	Foulis	George Blachford	Aug. 18	— L. L. & R.B.	455 A 455 C 455 D	To Madras, Malacca, and Whampoa.
Oct. 12	Contractor	William Mackintosh	Oct. 14	— L. & R.B.	319 B 319 J	To Madras and Whampoa.
Oct. 23	Fox	John Blackburn	1784 Oct. 29	— L. & R.B.	456 K 456 U	To Madras, Culpee, and Kedgeree.
Oct. 27	Fox	John Corner	1786 Aug. 31	— L. and three R.B.	456 L 456 V	To Johanna, Madras, and Calcutta.
Oct. 28	Royal Charlotte	J Pryce	1785 Oct. 7	— L. & R.B.	150 I 150 BB	To Madras and Bencoolen.
Oct. 28	Valentine	John Lewis	Sept. 15	— L. & R.B.	452 H 452 S	To Madras and Kedgeree.
Nov. 10	Berrington	John Johnston	July 16	— L. & R.B.	392 A 392 G	To Madras and Kedgeree.

Log begins.	Ship.	Captain.	Log ends.	Ledger or Receipt Book.	Reference Number.	Remarks.
1783 Nov. 10	Hillsborough - -	William Hardcastle -	1785 Sept. 26	— L. & R.B.	437 C 437 M	To Madras, Kedgeree, and Calcutta.
Nov. 25	Earl of Mansfield	William Fraser -	1784 Oct. 10	— L. & R.B.	530 C 530 H	To Madras and Bengal.
Nov. 27	Earl Cornwallis	Burnet Abercromby -	1785 Oct. 25	— L. & R.B.	348 A 348 H	To Madras and Kedgeree.
Dec. 26	Lord Camden -	Thomas Walker -	1786 June 22	— L. & R.B.	419 E 419 O	To Johanna, Bombay, Madras, Kedgeree, and Mocha.
Dec. 26	Neptune - - -	R. Scott	1785 Oct. 6	— L. & R.B.	98 H 98 Z	To Bombay and Tellicherry.
Dec. 26	Royal Admiral	Joseph Huddart -	1786 June 3	— L. & R.B.	338 C 338 M	To Bombay, Anjengo, and Whampoa.
—	Fortitude - -	Lawrence Bowden	1784 —	L. & R.B. only.	540 C	——
—	Prime -	Philip Sharpe	1783 —	Two R.B. only.	509 J	——
1784 Feb. 15	Kent - -	- -	1785 June 22	—	11 B	From China to England.
April 10	Sampson - -	Edward Ledger -	1787 Aug. 10	—	736 A	To Surat, Bombay, Persia, and Arabia (containing also journals of the "Alexander," "Prince of Orange," and "Ossory."
May 22	Nassau -	Arthur Gore	1785 Sept. 30	—	544 J & M	Portion of Journal of voyage to Bombay, Tellicherry, Kedgeree, Macao, and Whampoa. [*See* 544 I.]
Oct. 4	Nassau - -	Arthur Gore - -	1785 June 17	—	544 K & L	Portion of Journal of voyage to Bombay, Tellicherry, Kedgeree, Macao, and Whampoa. [*See* 544 I.]
Oct. 14	Houghton -	James Monro -	1786 June 15	— L. & R.B.	438 P 438 JJ	To Madras and Whampoa.
Oct. 14	Raymond -	Henry Smedley -	Oct. 10	— L. & R.B.	453 B 453 G	To Batavia, Bencoolen, Pulo Penang, and Croc.
Oct. 15	Britannia - - -	Edward Cumming	June 24	— L. & R.B.	285 NN 285 N	To Madras and China.
Oct. 15	Osterley -	Samuel Rogers -	Aug. 14	— L. & R.B.	400 J 400 W	To Madras, Malacca, and China.
Oct. 28	Winterton -	Raymond Snow	Nov. 13	— L. & R.B.	451 B 451 E	To Madras, Calcutta, and Kedgeree.
Oct. 29	Essex -	John Strover -	Sept. 10	— L. & R.B.	229 L 229 KK	To Madras, Whampoa, and Macao.
Oct. 31	General Coote -	James Baldwin -	Sept. 21	— L. & R.B.	441 B 441 G	To China.
Nov. 8	Francis -	James Urmston -	July 28	— L. & R.B.	443 B 443 H	To Madras and Calcutta.
Nov. 27	Asia	J. D. Foulkes -	Oct. 18	— L. & R.B.	24 F 24 JJ	To Bencoolen and China.
Nov. 29	Locko	John Baird	Aug. 8	— L. & R.B.	457 C 457 G	To Whampoa.
Dec. 13	Rodney - -	Henry Wakeman	June 26	— L. & R.B.	442 D 142 K	To Johanna, Madras, and Culpee.
—	Montagu	Thomas Brettell -	—	Two R.B. only.	552 V	This ship was blown up on the 6th December 1785, and one of the books contains a list of 33 people lost.
1785 Jan. 4	Dutton -	James West -	1785 Aug. 9	— L. & R.B.	505 F 505 Q	To Madras and Bengal.
Jan. 11	Deptford	John Gerrard -	1786 Sept. 21	— L. & R.B.	426 F 426 P	To Johanna, Madras, Calcutta, and Kedgeree.
Jan. 11	Northumberland -	J. Rees	1787 June 21	— L. & R.B.	141 I 141 AA	To Bombay, Surat, and China.
Jan. 12	Barwell - -	Robert Carr -	1786 Sept. 7	— L. & R.B.	420 B 420 I	To Whampoa.
Jan. 12	Duke of Montrose -	Alexander Gray -	1787 June 16	— L. & R.B.	775 A 775 H	To Bombay, Tellicherry, Anjengo, and Whampoa.
Jan. 13	Lascelles -	Thomas Wakefield	1786 June 1	— L. & R.B.	408 B 408 K	To Whampoa.

Log begins.	Ship.	Captain.	Log ends.	Ledger or Receipt Book.	Reference Number.	Remarks.
1785 Jan. 24	Bushbridge	Thomas Robertson	1786 Aug. 19	— L. & R.B.	413 A 413 I	To Whampoa.
Jan. 27	General Elliot	Robert Drummond	July 3	— L. & R.B.	269 B 269 H	To Whampoa.
Jan. 29	Atlas	Allen Cooper	July 3	— L. & R.B.	27 C 27 R	To China.
Jan. 30	King George	Jonathan Court	June 24	— L. & R.B.	402 E 402 Q	To Bombay and Calcutta.
Feb. 10	Warren Hastings	Thomas Larkins	June 17	— L. & R.B.	9 C 9 AA	To China.
Feb. 25	Lord Macartney	James Hay	Oct. 10	— L. & two R.B.	415 B 415 H	To Whampoa.
Feb. 26	Belmont	Charles Stewart	Sept. 27	— L. & R.B.	444 C 444 J	To Macao and Whampoa.
Mar. 8	Resolution	David Tolme	1785 July 21	—	465 F	From St. Helena to England. (Continuation of a log which is missing.)
April 26	Earl Talbot	Robert Taylor	1787 July 21	— L. & R.B.	410 C 410 L	To Madras and Bengal.
July 18	Minerva	Charles Clapp	1785 July 18	With 14 A		At Pulo Penang.
July 20	Swallow	Robert Anderson	1786 Jan. 19	— L. & R.B.	385 C 385 N	From Bengal to England.
Oct. 18	General Goddard	Thomas Foxall	1787 Sept. 22	L. & R.B.	440 O 440 I	To Johanna, Madras, Malacca, and Whampoa.
Oct. 18	Kent	Richard Hardinge	July 20	— L. & R.B.	41 C 41 K	To Batavia, &c.
Oct. 21	Sulivan	Robert Pouncy	Sept. 5	— L. & R.B.	257 B 257 I	To Madras, Macao, and Whampoa.
Nov. 1	Ganges	J. Williamson	Sept. 1	— L. & R.B.	86 C 86 S	To Madras and Bengal.
Nov. 2	Manship	Charles Gregorie	May 23	— L. & R.B.	363 A 363 H	To Madras and Calcutta.
Nov. 16	Earl of Mansfield	Brodie Hepworth	Oct. 14	— L. & R.B.	530 D 530 I	To Bencoolen and Whampoa.
Nov. 16	London	John Eastabrooke	Dec. 17	— L. & R.B.	1 J 1 JJ	To Madras and China.
Nov. 16	Queen	Peter Douglas	1788 Oct. 1	— L. & R.B.	356 H 356 T	To Bombay and Whampoa.
Nov. 16	Valentine	Thomas Wale	1787 Aug. 23	— L. & R.B.	452 I 452 T	To Madras and Whampoa.
Nov. 17	Fort William	George Simson	Sept. 19	— L. & R.B.	91 B 91 M	To Madras and China.
Nov. 17	Ponsborne	James Thomas	Oct. 24	— L. & R.B.	462 G 462 Q	To Madras and Whampoa.
Nov. 19	Foulis	George Blachford	1788 Nov. 27	— L. & R.B.	455 B 455 E	To Madras, Bengal, Bombay, and Whampoa. (The ledger contains a list of the ship's Company for 1790.)
Nov. 25	Dublin	William Smith	1786 Oct. 3	— L. & R.B.	399 A 399 G	To Madras and Calcutta.
Nov. 25	Vansittart	R. Lewin	1787 Aug. 18	L. & two R.B.	46 G 46 Z	To Madras and China.
Dec. 1	Middlesex	John Rogers	Oct. 25	— L. & R.B.	450 F 450 M	To Madras and Whampoa.
Dec. 2	Worcester	John Hall	1788 Aug. 5	— L. & R.B.	278 J 278 AA	To Madras and Whampoa.
Dec. 3	York	William Huddart	1787 Dec. 7	— L. & R.B.	237 O 237 GG	To Whampoa.
Dec. 3	York	William Huddart	Mar. 29	—	237 P	To China.
Dec. 4	Walpole	Henry Churchill	1788 Aug. 2	— L. & R.B.	293 O 293 LL	To Madras, Bengal, and Whampoa.
Dec. 15	Europa	Augustus Joseph Applegath.	1787 Oct. 24	— L. & R.B.	425 F 425 P	To Madras and Whampoa.
Dec. 16	Earl Cornwallis	Thomas Hodgson	Jan. 19	— L. & R.B.	348 B 348 I	To Whampoa.
Dec. 17	Berrington	Thomas Ley	Sept. 15	— L. & R.B.	392 B 392 H	To Calcutta and Madras.

Log begins.	Ship.	Captain.	Log ends.	Ledger or Receipt Book.	Reference Number.	Remarks.
1785 Dec. 17	Hillsborough	William Hardcastle	1789 Mar. 19	— L. & R.B.	487 D & E 487 N	To Calcutta, Batavia, Bombay, Malacca, and China.
Dec. 19	Earl of Oxford	John White	1787 Oct. 26	— L. & R.B.	489 C 489 I	To Madras and Kedgeree.
—	Intelligence	William Clifton	1786 —	L. and three R. B. only.	772 A	——
—	Trial	James Methurst Poynter.	1787 —	Two R.B. only.	580 D	——
1786 Jan. 4	Stormont	George Curtis	1783 July 23	— L. & R.B.	458 G 458 N	To China.
Jan. 9	Rockingham	John A. Blanshard	1787 Sept. 19	— L. & R.B.	124 A 124 I	To Bombay, Surat, and Tellicherry.
Jan. 12	Contractor	William Mackintosh	July 25	— L. & R.B.	319 C 319 K	To Whampoa.
Jan. 14	Neptune	George Scott	Aug. 9	— L. & R.B.	98 I 98 A A	To China.
Jan. 15	Pitt	George Cowper succeeded by Frederick Thesiger.	Sept. 8	— L. & R.B.	525 D 525 L	To Whampoa.
Jan. 15	William Pitt	Charles Mitchell	June 11	— L. & R.B.	184 A 184 R	To Bengal.
Jan. 16	Bessborough	Alexander Montgomerie.	1788 Aug. 23	— L. & R.B.	259 D 259 H	To Bombay and Canton.
Jan. 16	Royal Charlotte	Josiah Pryce	1787 July 28	— L. & R.B.	150 J 150 CC	To Java and China.
Jan. 16	Southampton	William Hall	July 18	— L. & R.B.	538 C 538 F	To Whampoa.
Jan. 17	Phœnix	James Rattray	June 21	— L. & R.B.	175 A 175 O	To Madras and Bengal.
Jan. 31	Pigot	George Ballantyne	Sept. 20	— L. & R.B.	503 G 503 O	To Whampoa.
Feb. 7	Royal Bishop	William Mears	Oct. 29	— L. and three R.B.	485 C 485 E	To Whampoa.
Feb. 15	Lord North	John Bartlet	Sept. 1	— L. & R.B.	494 E 494 J	To China.
Mar. 2	Carnatic	Lestock Wilson	Sept. 6	— L. & R.B.	165 A 165 N	To China.
Mar. 2	Ravensworth	Collingwood Roddam	1788 April 21	— L. & R.B.	565 A 565 B	To Madras, Calcutta, and Bencoolen.
Mar. 8	Ranger	Edmund Elliston	1787 July 14	— L. & R.B.	421 A (1) 421 E	To Whampoa and Manilla.
Mar. 10	Bridgewater	William Parker	July 27	— L. & R.B.	42 I 42 HH	To China.
Mar. 14	Chapman	John Fox	July 19	— L. & R.B.	218 A–B 218 A–E	To China.
Mar. 16	Lansdown	William Story	1790 Sept. 9	— L. and three R.B.	564 A & B 564 C	To Madras, Calcutta, and Whampoa.
Mar. 30	Mars	William Farington	1787 Dec. 9	—	563 A	To Whampoa.
April 3	Swallow	Robert Anderson	April 6	— L. and two R.B.	385 D 385 O	To Calcutta and Madras.
Aug. 7	Bombay	-	1786 Oct. 29	—	48 A	From Bombay to Diego Garcia.
Aug. 21	Ranger	John Buchanan	1787 Mar. 23	— L. and three R.B.	421 A (2) 421 F	From Bengal to Madras and England.
Sept. 22	King George	George Millett	1788 July 22	— L. & R.B.	402 F 402 R	To Bombay and Whampoa.
Oct. 10	Lord Camden	Nathaniel Dance	1789 Aug. 6	— L. & R.B.	419 F 419 P	To Calcutta, Madras, Bombay, and Whampoa.
Oct. 22	Thetis	Justinian Nutt	1788 July 29	— L. & R.B.	387 A 387 H	To Calcutta.

25005. Q

Log begins.	Ship.	Captain.	Log ends.	Ledger or Receipt Book.	Reference Number.	Remarks.
1786 Nov. 6	Locko	John Baird	1787 Feb. 14	— L. and three R.B.	457 D 457 H	To Lisbon.
Nov. 6	Locko	John Baird succeeded by Charles Saraways.	1789 Jan. 11	— L. and three R.B.	457 E 457 H	To Bombay and Whampoa.
Nov. 6	Princess Royal	James Horncastle	1788 Sept. 19	— L. and three R.B.	405 I 405 V	To Madras, Bengal, and Bombay
Nov. 6	Royal Admiral	Joseph Huddart	Aug. 8	— L. & R.B.	338 D 338 N	To Madras and Whampoa.
Nov. 8	Britannia	Edward Cumming	Aug. 11	— L. and two R.B.	285 OO 285 O	To Bengal.
Nov. 8	Lascelles	Richard Atherton Farington.	June 21	— L. & R.B.	408 C 408 L	To Madras and China.
Nov. 16	Chesterfield	John Cranstoun succeeded by Charles Chambers.	June 24	(Two J.) L. & R.B.	507 H & I 507 R	To Bencoolen and Pulo Penang
Nov. 18	Admiral Barrington	Charles Lindegren	Aug. 19	— L. & R.B.	512 A 512 B	To Whampoa.
Nov. 19	Rodney	Allen Chatfield	Sept. 12	— L. and two R.B.	442 E 442 L	To Calcutta.
Nov. 20	Atlas	Allen Cooper	Aug. 25	— L. and two R.B.	27 D 27 S	To Bengal.
Nov. 20	Henry Dundas	Angus McNab	Aug. 18	— L. & R.B.	331 A 331 G	To Madras and Bengal.
Nov. 20	Osterley	Joseph Clarkson	Oct. 27	— L. & R.B.	400 K 400 X	To Madras and China.
Dec. 2	Melville Castle	Philip Dundas	Aug. 2	— L. & R.B.	268 A 268 H	To Bombay and Whampoa.
Dec. 4	Bushbridge	Thomas Robertson	May 27	— L. & R.B.	413 B 413 J	To Madras and Calcutta.
Dec. 5	Earl Fitzwilliam	James Dundas	Aug. 23	— L. & R.B.	491 A 491 E	To Madras and Whampoa.
Dec. 5	Glatton	Charles Drummond	Dec. 9	— L. & R.B.	172 J 172 BB	To Madras and China.
Dec. 5	Houghton	James Monro	July 29	— L. & R.B.	438 Q 438 KK	To Madras, Pulo Penang, Macao, and Whampoa.
Dec. 5	Minerva	Robert Fairfull	1789 June 3	— L. & R.B.	14 A 14 V	To Madras, Calcutta, Bombay, and China.
Dec. 6	Francis	Robert Burrowes	1788 Sept. 26	— L. & R.B.	443 C 443 I	To Batavia and Bencoolen.
Dec. 6	Princess Amelia	Stephen Williams	Oct. 4	— L. & R.B.	36 G 36 CC	To Madras and Calcutta.
Dec. 8	Hawke	Richard Pennell	Aug. 28	— L. & R.B.	390 J 390 Y	To Madras, Macao, and Whampoa
Dec. 11	Rose	John H. Dempster	July 29	— L. and two R.B.	59 A 59 S	To Madras and China.
—	Prince of Wales	-	1789 —	— L. & R.B.	404 O	Missing.
1787 Jan. 1	Woodcot	Ninian Lowis	Jan. 24	— L. & R.B.	445 A 445 F	To Madras and China.
Jan. 8	General Elliot	Robert Drummond	1788 June 18	— L. & R.B.	296 C 296 I	To Bombay.
Jan. 20	Dover	John Douis	Aug. 20	— L. & R.B.	506 A 506 B	To Whampoa.
Jan. 22	Warren Hastings	John P. Larkins	Oct. 23	— L. & R.B.	9 D 9 BB	To Bombay and China.
Jan. 23	Marquis of Lansdown	David Tolmé	Aug. 20	— L. & R.B.	373 A 373 G	To Whampoa.
Jan. 31	Earl of Wycombe	John William Wood	May 26	— L. & R.B.	409 A 409 H	To Whampoa.
Feb. 5	Hartwell	Edward Fiott	1787 May 24	—	461 A	Towards China.
Feb. 17	Lord Walsingham	John Paiba	1788 Dec. 16	— L. & R.B.	346 A 346 G	To Whampoa.
Mar. 7	Nottingham	Archibald Anderson	Aug. 16	— L. & R.B.	287 G 287 W	To China.
April 2	Belvedere	William Greer	Nov. 3	— L. & R.B.	332 A 332 G	To Macao and Whampoa.

Log begins.	Ship.	Captain.	Log ends.	Ledger or Receipt Book.	Reference Number.	Remarks.
1787 May 18	Ranger - -	John Buchanan -	1788 Nov. 30	— L. & three R.B.	421 B 421 F	To Madras and Bengal.
Sept. 27	Barwell -	Thomas Welladvice -	1789 April 30	— L. & R.B.	420 C 420 J	To Madras, Bencoolen, and Whampoa.
Sept. 28	Deptford -	John Gerrard -	Sept. 29	— L. & R.B.	426 G 426 Q	To Bombay, Whampoa, and Macao.
Oct. 26	Bellmont -	William Dick Gamage	June 5	— L. & R.B.	444 D 444 K	To Bombay and Whampoa.
Oct. 26	Dutton -	James Hunt - succeeded by Andrew Aitchison.	Aug. 4	[Two J.] L. & R.B.	505 G & H 505 R	To Bombay and Whampoa.
Oct. 28	Asia - - -	John Davy Foulkes -	Sept. 28	— L. & R.B.	24 G 24 KK	To Bombay and China.
Oct. 28	Raymond	Henry Smedley -	Sept. 21	— L. & R.B.	453 C 453 H	To Bombay, Batavia, Macao, and Whampoa.
Nov. 2	Lord Hawkesbury -	John Barkley	Aug. 6	— L. & R.B.	323 A 323 I	To Bencoolen and Whampoa.
Nov. 9	Essex -	John Strover	Aug. 5	— L. & R.B.	229 M 229 LL	To Batavia and Whampoa.
Nov. 10	Earl Cornwallis -	Thomas Hodgson	Aug. 6	— L. & R.B.	348 C 348 J	To Madras and Whampoa.
Nov. 13	Duke of Montrose -	Joseph Dorin	Sept. 23	— L. & R.B.	775 B 775 I	To Bombay and Whampoa.
Nov. 19	Carnatic	John Corner -	Sept. 5	— L. & R.B.	165 B 165 O	To Madras and China.
Nov. 25	Albion	Thomas Allen -	July 22	— L. & R.B.	81 B 81 N	To Madras and China.
Nov. 26	Ceres - -	Thomas Price - -	May 30	—	215 E	To Madras and China.
Nov. 26	Ceres -	Thomas Price -	June 30	— L. & R.B.	215 F 215 W	To Madras and China.
Nov. 26	Contractor - -	John Bartlet -	Dec. 26	— L. & R.B.	319 D 319 L	To Madras, Batavia, and Whampoa.
Dec. 10	General Coote - -	James Baldwin -	Aug. 19	— L. & three R.B.	441 C 441 H	To Madras and Whampoa.
Dec. 10	Phœnix -	Alexander Gray -	Aug. 29	— L. & R.B.	175 B 175 P	To Bengal and Madras.
Dec. 13	Bridgewater - -	William Parker -	Sept. 25	— L. & R.B.	42 J 42 H	To Madras, Whampoa, and Macao.
Dec. 22	Kent -	Richard Hardinge -	June 26	— L. & R.B.	41 D 41 L	To Bengal.
Dec. 22	Manship - -	Charles Gregorie -	July 14	— L. & R.B.	363 B 363 I	To Madras and Calcutta.
Dec. 24	Dublin - -	William Smith -	Sept. 23	— L. & R.B.	399 B 399 H	To Bombay, Madras, and Calcutta.
Dec. 24	Northumberland -	James Rees - -	Aug. 26	— L. & two R.B.	141 J 141 BB	To Bombay, Madras, and Bengal.
Dec. 31	Boddam - -	Joseph Elliott	July 11	— L. & R.B.	351 A 351 G	To Madras, Malacca, and Macao.
1788 Jan. 8	Lord Macartney -	James Hay -	1790 June 25	— L. & two R.B.	415 C 415 I	To Madras, Bencoolen, Bombay, and Macao.
Jan. 8	William Pitt - -	Charles Mitchell	1789 April 16	— L. & R.B.	184 B 184 S	To Bengal.
Jan. 10	Triton - -	William Agnew	June 5	— L. & two R.B.	366 I 366 X	To Madras and Bengal.
Jan. 20	Queen Charlotte	George Dixon -	1788 Oct. 1	—	477 A	From Canton to England.
Jan. 21	Earl Talbot - -	John Woolmore -	1789 May 16	— L. & R.B.	410 D 410 M	To Whampoa.
Jan. 24	Winterton - -	George Dundas -	1790 July 9	— L. & three R.B.	451 C 451 F	To Johanna, Bombay, and Mocha.
Jan. 28	Prince William Henry	Ralph Dundas -	1789 June 12	— L. & R.B.	389 A 369 G	To Bombay, Tellicherry, and Cochin.
Feb. 1	Neptune -	George Scott - -	Aug. 11	— L. & R.B.	98 J 98 BB	To China.
Feb. 6	King George - -	Nathaniel Portlock	1788 Sept. 12	—	402 G	From Whampoa to England.
April 15	Airly Castle	Charles Stewart	1789 Sept. 1	— L. & R.B.	321 I 321 K	To Calcutta, Madras, and Bencoolen.

Log begins.	Ship.	Captain.	Log ends.	Ledger or Receipt Book.	Reference Number.	Remarks.
1788 May 22	Swallow	Robert Anderson	1790 Jan. 25	— L. & R.B.	385 E 385 P	To Calcutta, Madras, and Negapatam.
July 22	Admiral Sir Edward Hughes.	Joseph Smith	1789 June 12	— L. & R.B.	511 A 511 B	From Bombay to Whampoa and England.
Oct. 1	Thetis	Justinian Nutt	1790 July 26	— L. & R.B.	387 B 387 I	To Bombay and Whampoa.
Oct. 15	Fort William	George Simson	Sept. 20	— L. & R.B.	91 C 91 N	To Bombay and China.
Oct. 15	Valentine	John Lewis	May 26	— L.	452 J 452 U	To Madras and Whampoa.
Oct. 16	Pitt	Edward Manning	Sept. 7	— L. & R.B.	525 E 525 M	To Bencoolen and Whampoa.
Oct. 17	General Elliott	Robert Drummond	June 21	— L. & R.B.	269 D 269 J	To Bombay and Whampoa.
Oct. 22	Scarborough	John Marshall	1789 June 17	—	355 G	From Whampoa to England.
Oct. 28	Rockingham	John A. Blanshard	1790 June 19	— L. & R.B.	124 B 124 J	To Madras and China.
Oct. 31	Britannia	Edward Cumming	Sept. 9	— L. & R.B.	285 PP 285 P	To Whampoa.
Oct. 31	Warley	Henry Wilson	Aug. 7	— L. & R.B.	182 A 182 L	To Madras and China.
Nov. 13	Ocean	James Tod	July 30	— L. & R.B.	222 A 222 S	To Madras and China.
Nov. 13	Sulivan	Robert Pouncy	June 19	— L. & R.B.	257 C 257 J	To Madras and Whampoa.
Nov. 14	Europa	Augustus Joseph Applegath.	July 8	— L. & R.B.	425 G 425 Q	To Madras, Pulo Penang, and Whampoa.
Nov. 27	Duke of Buccleugh	Thomas Wall	Aug. 7	— L. & R.B.	132 A 132 H	To Madras and China.
Nov. 27	Nottingham	Archibald Anderson succeeded by George Max.	July 12	[Two J.] L. & R.B.	287 H & I 287 X	To Madras and Whampoa.
Nov. 30	General Goddard	Thomas Foxall	June 25	— L. & R.B.	440 D 440 J	To Bengal and Madras.
Dec. 9	Lady Penrhyn	William Cropton Sever.	1789 Aug. 24	—	496 A	From Whampoa to England.
Dec. 10	Melville Castle	Philip Dundas	1790 June 22	— L. & two R.B.	268 B 268 I	To Bengal.
Dec. 24	Bushridge	Thomas Robertson	June 1	— L. & R.B.	413 C 413 K	To Madras and Calcutta.
Dec. 24	Pigot	George Ballantyne	July 6	— L. & R.B.	503 H 503 P	To Madras and Calcutta.
Dec. 27	Rose	John H. Dempster	May 20	— L. & R.B.	59 B 59 T	To Madras and Bengal.
1789 Jan. 16	Berrington	Thomas Ley	Aug. 21	— L. & R.B.	392 C 392 I	To Madras and Calcutta.
Jan. 26	Chesterfield	Henry Burges	Oct. 6	— L. & R.B.	507 J 507 S	To Madras, Bencoolen, and Calcutta.
Jan. 26	Houghton	James Monro	1791 Feb. 22	— L. & R.B.	438 B 438 LL	To Madras, Calcutta, and Masulipatam.
Jan. 26	Ponsborne	James Thomas	1789 June 24	— L. & R.B.	462 H 462 K	To Bombay, Tellicherry, and Anjengo.
Jan. 26	Vansittart*	Lestock Wilson	Aug. 25	— R.B.	46 H 46 AA	Towards China.
Jan. 27	Earl of Oxford	William White	1790 Aug. 20	— L. & R.B.	489 D 489 J	To Calcutta, Madras, and Bencoolen.
Jan. 27	Lascelles	Richard Atherton Farington.	June 5	— L. & R.B.	408 D 408 M	To Whampoa.
Jan. 28	Walpole	Henry Churchill	July 17	— L. & R.B.	293 P 293 MM	To Batavia and Whampoa.
Jan. 31	Earl of Mansfield	Brodie Hepworth	Aug. 2	— L. & R.B.	530 E 530 J	To Whampoa.
Feb. 10	Ganges	Joseph Garnault	May 21	— L. & R.B.	86 D 86 T	To China.
Feb. 12	Middlesex	John Rogers	May 22	— L. & R.B.	450 G 450 N	To Whampoa.
Feb. 25	King George	John Sherwood	May 25	— L. & R.B.	402 H 402 S	To China.
Mar. —	Alexander	(?) Richards	1789 Sept. 4	—	174 A	To Whidah (Guinea). (With Sampson, 786 A.)

* This ship was wrecked and the crew left her in the boats on the 25th August. The "Nonsuch" and the "General Elliott" returned with the ship's crew and secured part of the treasure. As all the crew could not be accommodated in the "Nonsuch" and the "General Elliott," some of them were embarked in the long boats for Prince of Wales's Island. This book also contains Journals of the "Nonsuch" and the "Europa."

Log begins.	Ship.	Captain.	Log ends.	Ledger or Receipt Book.	Reference Number.	Remarks.
1789 April 19	Earl of Wycombe	John William Wood	1790 June 19	— L. & R.B.	409 B 409 I	To China.
Sept. 16	Nonsuch - -	J. Lloyd -	1789 Oct. 14	—	46 H	To China. (With Vansittart.)
Oct. 19	Minerva -	Robert Fairfull -	1791 Aug. 3	— L. & R.B.	14 B 14 W	To China.
Nov. 2	Royal Charlotte -	Josiah Pryce -	Aug. 22	— L. & R.B.	150 K 150 DD	To Bencoolen and China.
Nov. 17	Francis - -	Robert Burrowes -	Aug. 8	— L. & R.B.	443 D 443 J	To Bombay and Whampoa.
Nov. 17	Triton - - -	William Agnew -	Aug. 10	— L. & R.B.	366 J 366 Y	To Madras and Whampoa.
Nov. 20	Hindostan -	William Mackintosh	Aug. 19	— L. & R.B.	267 A 267 F	To Madras and China.
Nov. 30	Barwell -	Thomas Welladvice -	July 29	— L. & R.B.	420 D 420 K	To Bombay and Whampoa.
Dec. 1	Earl of Abergavenny	John Wordsworth	Sept. 23	— L. & R.B.	341 A 341 G	To Bombay and Whampoa.
Dec. 2	Osterley - -	Joseph Clarkson	Aug. 8	— L. & R.B.	400 L 400 Y	To Bombay and Whampoa.
Dec. 14	Lord Thurlow -	William Thomson -	Sept. 29	— L. & R.B.	330 A 330 G	To Madras, Penang, and Whampoa.
Dec. 18	Belvedere - -	William Greer -	Oct. 25	— L. & R.B.	332 B 332 H	To Madras, Malacca, and Macao.
—	London	John Eastabrooke	1790 Dec. 15	— L. & R.B.	1 K 1 KK	To Bombay.
1790 Jan. 1	Ceres -	George Stevens	1791 Oct. 11	— L. & R.B.	215 G 215 X	To Madras and China.
Jan. 1	Marquis of Lansdown	David Tolmé -	Aug. 4	— L. & R.B.	373 B 373 H	To Whampoa.
Jan. 1	Woodcot - -	Ninian Lewis	Sept. 24	— L. & R.B.	445 B 445 G	To Madras and Whampoa.
Jan. 4	Europa - -	Augustus Joseph Applegath.	1790 July 8	—	46 H	From China to England. (With Vansittart.)
Jan. 11	Earl Fitzwilliam -	James Dundas	1791 Nov. 4	— L. & R.B.	491 B 491 F	To Madras and Calcutta.
Jan. 25	Prince William Henry	Ralph Dundas	Aug. 5	— L. & R.B.	389 B 389 H	To Cadiz, Calcutta and Madras.
Jan. 25	Princess Amelia	George Millett -	May 23	— L. & R.B.	36 H 36 DD	To Calcutta.
Jan. 31	Queen -	Peter Douglas -	1792 June 21	— L. & R.B.	356 I 356 U	To Madras, Bombay, and Calcutta.
Feb. 5	Sir Edward Hughes -	Robert Anderson	1791 Aug. 5	— L. & R.B.	354 A 354 H	To Madras and Whampoa.
Feb. 8	Henry Dundas	Angus McNab	Sept. 5	— L. & R.B.	331 B 331 H	To Bombay and Whampoa.
Feb. 8	Rodney - -	Allen Chatfield	June 15	— L. & R.B.	442 F 442 M	To Calcutta and Madras.
Feb. 14	William Pitt -	Charles Mitchell -	Aug. 9	— L. & R.B.	184 C 184 T	To Bengal.
Feb. 22	Hillsborough	Edward Coxwell	Aug. 4	— L. & R.B.	437 F 437 O	To Whampoa.
Feb. 24	Princess Royal - -	James Horncastle -	June 14	— L. & R.B.	405 J 405 W	To Bombay and Anjengo.
Feb. 26	Bellmont	William Dick Gamage	Aug. 4	— L. & R.B.	444 E 444 L	To Whampoa.
Mar. 1	Royal Admiral - -	Essex Henry Bond -	Aug. 12	— L. & R.B.	338 E 338 O	To China.
Mar. 1	Warren Hastings -	John P. Larkins	Oct. 14	— L. & R.B.	9 E 9 CC	To Calcutta and Madras.
Mar. 1	Worcester - -	John Hall - -	Sept. 29	— L. & R.B.	278 K 278 BB	To Bombay and Goa.
Mar. 2	Hawke - -	Richard Pennell -	1794 Oct. 6	— L. & R.B.	390 K 390 Z	To Calcutta and Madras.
Mar. 29	Earl Talbot - -	John Woolmore	1791 Sept. 27	— L. & R.B.	410 E 410 N	To China.
Mar. 30	Lord Walsingham -	James Young -	Sept. 29	— L. & R.B.	346 B 346 H	To Whampoa.
April 26	Prince of Orange -	[?] Daniell - -	1790 June 27	—	636 E	From Barbadoes to England. (With Sampson, 1784-87, 736A.)
May 15	Swallow - -	George Curtis - -	1792 Feb. 17	— L. & R.B.	385 F 385 Q	To Madras, Calcutta, Negapatam, &c.
Oct. 23	Albion -	William Parker	June 14	— L. & R.B.	81 C 81 O	To Madras and China.

Log begins.	Ship.	Captain.	Log ends.	Ledger or Receipt Book.	Reference Number.	Remarks.
1790 Oct. 25	Taunton Castle	James Urmston	1792 Aug. 13	— L. & R.B.	107 A 107 J	To Bombay and China.
Nov. 10	Alfred	James Farquharson	May 25	— L. & R.B.	140 F 140 T	To Madras and China.
Nov. 15	Canton	Thomas Brettell	June 5	— L. & R.B.	288 A 288 J	To Bombay and Whampoa.
Nov. 22	Britannia	Edward Cumming	May 21	— L. & R.B.	285 QQ 285 Q	To Bombay and Whampoa.
Nov. 22	General Coote	James Baldwin	May 29	— L. & R.B.	441 D 441 I	To Madras and Whampoa.
Dec. 5	Surprise	N. Anstis	1791 Sept. 27	[Two J]	447 B & C	From Whampoa to England.
Dec. 6	True Briton	Henry Farrer	1792 May 18	— L. & R.B.	297 L 297 CC	To Madras and Whampoa.
Dec. 7	Woodford	Charles Lennox	July 21	— L. & R.B.	265 A 265 K	To Bencoolen and Whampoa.
Dec. 21	Earl Cornwallis	Thomas Hodgson	May 9	— L. & R.B.	348 D 348 K	To Madras, Macao, and Whampoa.
1791 Jan. 5	Raymond	Henry Smedley	Sept. 10	— L. & R.B.	453 D 453 I	To Bombay and Tellicherry.
Jan. 6	Lord Hawkesbury	John Barkley	Sept. 13	— L. & R.B.	323 B 323 J	To Calcutta.
Jan. 20	Dutton	James Hamilton succeeded by Peter Sampson.	Nov. 10	— L. & R.B.	505 I 505 S	To Madras and Calcutta.
Jan. 20	Dutton	James Hamilton succeeded by Peter Sampson.	1793 Jan. 14	—	505 J	To Madras and Calcutta.
Jan. 25	Kent	Richard Hardinge	1792 Aug. 11	— L. & R.B.	41 E 41 M	To Madras and Bengal.
Feb. 2	Northumberland	James Rees	Aug. 24	— L. & R.B.	141 K 141 CC	To Bengal and Madras.
Feb. 3	Lord Camden	Nathaniel Dance	Aug. 18	— L. & R.B.	419 G 419 Q	To Calcutta and Madras.
Feb. 8	Phœnix	Alexander Gray	June 30	— L. & R.B.	175 C 175 Q	To Madras and Bengal.
Feb. 18	Asia	John D. Foulkes	Dec. 3	— L. & R.B.	24 H 24 LL	To Bengal, Madras, and Bencoolen.
Feb. 21	Manship	John Lloyd	Dec. 1	— L. & R.B.	363 C 363 J	To Madras and Bengal.
Mar. 7	Essex	John Strover	Sept. 29	— L. & R.B.	229 N 229 MM	To Bombay, Calicut, &c.
Mar. 12	Airly Castle	Charles Stewart	1793 Feb. 8	— L. & R.B.	321 B 321 L	To Madras, Calcutta, and China.
Mar. 12	Dublin	William Smith	July 25	— L. & R.B.	399 C 399 I	To Madras, Calcutta, and Whampoa.
Mar. 21	Bridgewater	Gregory M. Lewin	April 23	— L. & R.B.	42 K & L 42 J J	To Bengal, Madras, Bombay, and China.
April 19	Deptford	John Gerrard	1792 June 13	— L. & R.B.	426 H 426 R	To Madras, Bencoolen, and Calcutta.
Oct. 24	Rockingham	John A. Blanshard	1793 July 9	— L. & R.B.	124 C 124 J	To Bombay and China.
Oct. 25	Ocean	Andrew Patton	June 11	— L. & R.B.	222 R 222 T	To Madras and China.
Oct. 27	Nottingham	John Barfoot	July 30	— L. & R.B.	287 J 287 Y	To China.
Nov. 7	Middlesex	John Rogers	July 23	— L. & R.B.	450 H 450 O	To Bombay and Whampoa.
Nov. 7	Sulivan	Robert Pouncy	Sept. 25	[Two J] L. & R.B.	257 D & E 257 K	To Bombay and China.
Nov. 21	Sir Edward Hughes	Robert Anderson	July 19	— L. & R.B.	354 B 354 I	To Madras, Whampoa, and Batavia.
Nov. 22	Carnatic	John Corner	1792 July 26	— L. & R.B.	165 C 165 P	To Madras and China.
Nov. 24	Lord Macartney	James Hay	1793 July 24	— L. & R.B.	415 D 415 J	To Madras and Whampoa.
Dec. 9	Europa	Augustus Joseph Applegath.	May 18	— L. & R.B.	425 H 425 R	To Madras, Kedgeree, and Calcutta.
Dec. 10	Duke of Buccleugh	Thomas Wall	Sept. 14	— L. & R.B.	132 B 132 I	To Bombay and China.
Dec. 17	Boddam	John Jones	1792 June 4	— L. & R.B.	351 B 351 H	To Madras and Whampoa.

Log begins.	Ship.	Captain.	Log ends.	Ledger or Receipt Book.	Reference Number.	Remarks.
1791 Dec. 23	General Goddard	Thomas Wakefield	1793 June 1	— L. & R.B.	440 E 440 K	To Calcutta.
1792 Jan. 2	Melville Castle	Philip Dundas	Aug. 6	— L. & R.B.	268 C 268 J	To Madras, Masulipatam, and Calcutta.
Jan. 5	Duke of Montrose	Joseph Dorin	July 16	— L. & R.B.	775 C 775 J	To Bombay and Calicut.
Jan. 17	Contractor	John Bartlet	Aug. 10	[Two J] L. & R.B.	319 E & F 319 M	To Madras and Calcutta.
Jan. 23	Valentine	Iver McMillan	Sept. 20	— L. & R.B.	452 K 452 V	To Calcutta, Madras, and Bencoolen.
Jan. 26	General Elliot	Robert Drummond	Sept. 30	— L. & R.B.	269 E 269 K	To Bombay, Surat, and Tellicherry.
Jan. 31	Lascelles	Richard Atherton Farington.	June 5	— L. & R.B.	408 E 408 N	To Whampoa.
Jan. 31	Lascelles	Richard Atherton Farington.	May 6	—	408 F	To Whampoa.
Feb. 4	Earl of Wycombe	John William Wood	Aug. 2	— L. & R.B.	409 C 409 J	To Bencoolen and China.
Feb. 8	Pousborne	James Thomas	Aug. 1	— L. & R.B.	462 I 462 S	To Madras, Calcutta, and Vizagapatam.
Feb. 21	Busbridge	Thomas Robertson	Sept. 27	— L. & R.B.	413 D 413 L	To Madras and Calcutta.
Feb. 22	Rose	John H. Dempster	Sept. 23	— L. & R.B.	59 C 59 U	To Bengal and Madras.
Mar. 5	Thetis	Justinian Nutt	July 23	— L. & R.B.	387 C 387 J	To Whampoa.
Mar. 8	King George	Richard Colnett	Oct. 26	— L. & R.B.	402 I 402 T	To Madras and Calcutta.
Mar. 9	Walpole	Henry Churchill	July 27	— L. & R.B.	293 Q 293 NN	To Whampoa.
April 3	Bellmont	William Dick Gamage	Jan. 15	— L. & R.B.	444 F 444 M	To Calcutta.
April 3	Bellmont	William Dick Gamage succeeded by James Stewart.	Oct. 4	—	444 G	To Calcutta.
April 6	Earl Talbot	Jeremiah Dawkins	Nov. 2	— L. & R.B.	410 F 410 O	To Bengal.
April 8	Royal Admiral	Essex Henry Bond	Sept. 25	— L. & R.B.	338 F 338 P	To Port Jackson and Whampoa.
May 16	Ossory	John Tyrrell	1792 May 20	—	723 A	(With Sampson. 736 A.)
July 24	Bellona	-	1794 Sept. 29	—	353 A	To Port Jackson and Whampoa.
Sept. 21	Swallow	George Curtis	Feb. 25	— L. & R.B.	385 G 385 R	To Calcutta, Madras, and Bombay.
Oct. 26	Chesterfield	Henry Burges	Oct. 15	— L. & R.B.	507 K 507 T	To Bombay, Whampoa, and Macao.
Oct. 30	Triton	Philip Burnyeat	Sept. 21	— L. & R.B.	366 K 366 Z	To Madras, and Whampoa.
Nov. 10	Brunswick	Allen Cooper	Nov. 5	— L. & R.B.	349 A 349 G	To Bombay, Macao, and Whampoa.
Nov. 10	Pitt	Edward Manning	1793 Sept. 10	—	525 F	From Calcutta to England.
Nov. 12	Royal Charlotte	Josiah Pryce	1795 Feb. 19	— L. & R.B.	150 L 150 EE	To Madras and China.
Nov. 12	Warley	Henry Wilson	Jan. 12	— L. & R.B.	182 B 182 M	To Madras, Pondicherry, and China.
Nov. 14	Woodcot	Ninian Lowis	1794 Oct. 8	— L. & R.B.	445 C 445 H	To Madras and Calcutta.
Nov. 25	Ganges	Joseph Garnault	1793 April 16	— L. & R.B.	86 E 86 U	To Madras and Bengal.
Dec. 10	Berrington	Thomas Ley	1794 May 29	— L. & R.B.	392 D 392 J	To Madras, Balasore, and Calcutta.
Dec. 10	Exeter	Lestock Wilson	Dec. 12	— L. & R.B.	138 E 138 S	To Bombay and China.
Dec. 13	Rodney	Allen Chatfield	Oct. 10	— L. & R.B.	442 G 442 N	To Madras and Calcutta.
Dec. 28	Worcester	John Hall	May 24	— L. & R.B.	278 L 278 CC	To Bencoolen.
—	Hindostan	William Mackintosh	—	L. & R.B. only.	267 G	——
—	Winterton	George Dundas	1795 —	Two R.B. only.	451 G	——
1793 Jan. 14	Princess Royal	James Horncastle	1793 Sept. 27	— Two R.B.	405 K 405 X	To Java. (Towards China.)
Jan. 25	Britannia	Thomas Cheap succeeded by Thomas Barrow.	1795 July 26	— L. & R.B.	285 RR 285 R	To Madras, Calcutta, &c.

Log begins.	Ship.	Captain.	Log ends.	Ledger or Receipt Book.	Reference Number.	Remarks.
1793 Jan. 25	Minerva - -	Kennard Smith -	1794 Oct. 2	— L. & R.B.	14 C 14 X	To China.
Jan. 29	Francis - -	Robert Burrowes -	May 14	— L. & R.B.	443 E 443 K	To Madras and Calcutta.
Jan. 29	Lord Thurlow - -	William Thomson	Dec. 13	— L. & R.B.	330 B 330 H	To Manilla and Macao.
Feb. 7	Barwell	Thomas Welladvice	Oct. 6	— L. & R.B.	420 E 420 L	To Bombay, Tellicherry, &c.
Feb. 7	Earl of Oxford	William White -	Oct. 17	— L. & R.B.	489 E 489 K	To Madras and Calcutta.
Feb. 11	Osterley -	James Foy	Nov. 26	— L. & R.B.	400 M 400 Z	To Manilla and Whampoa.
Feb. 11	William Pitt -	Charles Mitchell	1795 Sept. 13	— L. & R.B.	184 D 184 U	To Bengal, and thence on a cruise, touching at Batavia, Bencoolen, &c.
Feb. 18	Glatton -	Charles Drummond -	Jan. 5	— L. & R.B.	172 K 172 CC	To China.
Feb. 22	London - -	James L. Grant -	1794 Sept. 1	— L. & R.B.	1 L 1 LL	To Bombay.
Feb. 25	Fort William	George Simson -	Dec. 15	— L. & R.B.	91 D 91 O	To Madras and Bengal.
Mar. 7	Marquis of Lansdown	Joseph Boulderson -	Oct. 20	— L. & R.B.	373 C 373 I	To Madras and Calcutta.
Mar. 8	Hillsborough - -	Edward Brown -	Oct. 8	— L. & R.B.	437 G 437 P	To Calcutta and Madras.
Mar. 13	Ceres	George Stevens	Dec. 18	— L. & R.B.	215 H 215 Y	To China.
Mar. 14	Pigot -	George Ballantyne	Feb. 7	— Two R.B.	503 I 503 Q	To Bencoolen. (This ship was taken by the French on 7th February 1794).
Mar. 16	Earl of Abergavenny -	John Wordsworth -	1795 Feb. 13	— L. & R.B.	341 B 341 H	To Manilla and Whampoa.
Mar. 26	Henry Dundas - -	Walter Carruthers	1794 Dec. 18	— L. & R.B.	331 C 331 I	To Batavia and Whampoa.
Mar. 30	Hawke	Richard Pennell -	Dec. 2	— L. & R.B.	390 L 390 AA	To Whampoa.
April 1	Lord Walsingham -	James Young -	Nov. 27	— L. & R.B.	346 C 346 I	To Whampoa.
April 8	Warren Hastings	Francis W. Leigh	Oct. 21	— L. & R.B.	9 F 9 DD	To Bengal.
April 10	Northumberland	Charles Jones -	Oct. 17	— L. & R.B.	141 L 141 DD	To Calcutta.
April 15	Deptford	John Gerrard -	Oct. 18	— L. & R.B.	426 I 426 S	To Calcutta.
April 24	General Coote -	Robert Williams -	Dec. 10	— L. & R.B.	441 E 441 J	To Madras and Calcutta.
April 26	Earl Cornwallis -	Thomas Hodgson -	Oct. 30	— L. & R.B.	348 E 348 L	To Calcutta.
May 1	Belvedere -	Charles Christie -	Dec. 27	— L. & R.B.	332 C 332 I	To Bombay, Tellicherry, Calicut, and Quilon.
May 2	Earl Fitzwilliam	James Tweedale -	Dec. 17	— L. & R.B.	491 C 491 G	To Bombay, Surat, and Tellichery.
May 23	Prince William Henry	Ralph Dundas -	Oct. 8	— L. & R.B.	389 C 389 I	To Madras and Calcutta.
May 29	Queen Charlotte -	William Fairfax -	Mar. 30	—	477 B	To Madras and Calcutta.
Aug. 16	Kent -	Richard Hardinge -	Oct. 11	— L. & R.B.	41 F 41 N	To Bengal.
Oct. 18	Manship - -	John Lloyd - -	1795 Dec. 8	— L. & R.B.	363 D 363 K	To Madras and Bengal.
Oct. 19	Carnatic - -	James Jackson -	1796 Feb. 19	— L. & R.B.	165 D 165 Q	To Madras and China.
Oct. 19	Melville Castle -	John Lambe - -	Jan. 13	— L. & R.B.	268 D 268 K	To Madras and Calcutta.
Oct. 19	Rockingham -	Hugh Lindsay -	1795 Nov. 24	— L. & R.B.	124 D 124 L	To Madras and Calcutta.
Oct. 21	Lord Camden - -	Nathaniel Dance -	Sept. 14	— L. & R.B.	419 H 419 R	To Madras.
Oct. 23	Dutton - -	Peter Sampson -	Aug. 28	— L. & R.B.	505 K 505 T	To Madras.
Oct. 30	Essex - -	John Strover	Nov. 25	— L. & R.B.	229 P 229 NN	To Madras, Balasore, and Calcutta.
Nov. 1	Asia - -	John D. Foulkes	Nov. 24	— L. & R.B.	24 I 24 MM	To Bengal and Madras.
Nov. 5	General Goddard	William Taylor Money	Nov. 30	— L. & R.B.	440 F 440 L	To Madras and Bengal. (In reference to capture of Dutch ships off St. Helena, see R. & L. 714/1894.)
Nov. 6	Dublin - -	William Smith -	1796 Jan. 2	— L. & R.B.	399 D 399 J	To Madras and Whampoa.

Log begins.	Ship.	Captain.	Log ends.	Ledger or Receipt Book.	Reference Number.	Remarks.
1793 Nov. 7	Airly Castle	John Gale succeeded by Samuel Barnard.	1795 Nov. 30	— L. & R.B.	321 C 321 M	To Madras and Calcutta.
Nov. 7	Airly Castle	John Gale	1794 May 8	—	321 D	Towards Madras.
Nov. 11	Phœnix	Wemyss Orrok	1795 Aug. 22	— L. & R.B.	175 D 175 R	To Madras.
Nov. 12	Bombay Castle	Alex. Montgomerie	1794 Oct. 13	— L. & R.B.	125 F 125 P	To Bombay and China.
Nov. 14	Albion	William Wills	1796 Feb. 16	— L. & R.B.	81 D 81 P	To China.
Nov. 14	General Elliot	Adam Drummond	1795 Sept. 1	— L. & R.B.	269 F 269 L	To Bengal.
Nov. 16	Busbridge	Samuel Maitland	Dec. 10	— L. & R.B.	413 E 413 M	To Madras and Calcutta.
Nov. 18	Bridgewater	William Parker	Dec. 26	— L. & R.B.	42 M 42 KK	To Bombay and China.
Nov. 19	Boddam	John Jones	1796 Jan. 5	— L. & R.B.	351 C 351 I	To Madras and Whampoa.
Nov. 20	Duke of Buccleugh	Thomas Wall	Jan. 25	— L. & R.B.	132 C 132 J	To China.
Nov. 25	Queen	Milliken Craig	Jan. 11	—	412 A	To Madras and Calcutta.
Nov. 29	True Briton	Henry Farrer	Feb. 26	— L. & R.B.	297 M 297 DD	To Bombay and China.
Dec. 9	Lord Macartney	James Hay	Jan. 7	— L. & R.B.	415 E 415 K	To Madras and Whampoa.
Dec. 10	Earl of Wycombe	John William Wood	1795 Nov. 25	— L. & R.B.	409 E 409 K	To Bencoolen.
Dec. 11	Lord Hawkesbury	John Price	Dec. 8	— L. & R.B.	323 C 323 K	To Madras and Calcutta.
Dec. 14	Woodford	Charles Lennox	1796 Jan. 28	— L. & R.B.	265 B 265 L	To Bombay, Batavia, &c.
Dec. 19	Harriot	John Luard	1795 Sept. 17	— L. & R.B.	275 A 275 N	To Madras, Balasore, and Calcutta.
Dec. 24	Duke of Montrose	Patrick Burt	Sept. 3	— L. & R.B.	775 D 775 K	To Bombay and Tellicherry.
Dec. 24	Princess Amelia	George Millett	1794 May 29	— L. & R.B.	36 I 36 EE	To Madras and Bengal.
Dec. 29	Nancy	Alexander Paterson	1795 Feb. 26	—	439 I	To Calcutta and Madras.
—	Houghton	Robert Hudson	1796 —	L. & R.B. only.	438 MM	———
1794 Jan. 17	Europa	Augustus Joseph Applegath.	1795 Dec. 31	— L. & R.B.	425 I 425 S	To Calcutta, Madras, and Bencoolen.
Jan. 17	Ponsborne	James Thomas	Aug. 26	— L. & R.B.	462 J 462 T	To Whampoa.
Jan. 22	Rose	Alexander Gray	Sept. 4	— L. & R.B.	59 D 59 V	To Bengal.
Jan. 27	Valentine	Iver McMillan	Aug. 27	— L. & R.B.	452 L 452 W	To Calcutta.
Jan. 30	Sulivan	Sampson Hall	Aug. 28	— L. & R.B.	257 F 257 L	To Whampoa.
Feb. 31	King George	Richard Colnett	Aug. 29	— L. & R.B.	402 J 402 U	To Whampoa.
Feb. 1	Contractor	John Bartlet	Sept. 2	— L. & R.B.	319 G 319 N	To Calcutta.
Feb. 1	Middlesex	John Rogers	Sept. 4	— L. & R.B.	450 I 450 P	To China.
Feb. 1	Nottingham	John Barfoot	Oct. 6	— L. & R.B.	287 K 267 Z	To Whampoa.
Feb. 1	Ocean	Andrew Patton	Sept. 10	— L. & R.B.	222 C 222 U	To China.
Feb. 15	Canton	Thomas Brettell succeeded by Abel Vyvyan.	Oct. 14	— L & R.B.	288 B 288 K	To Whampoa.
Feb. 15	Raymond	Henry Smedley	Aug. 31	— L. & R.B.	453 E 453 J	To Bombay, Cannanore, and Anjengo.
Feb. 15	Taunton Castle	Edward Studd	Sept. 30	— L. & R.B.	107 B 107 K	To China.
Feb. 17	Alfred	James Farquharson	Oct. 10	— L. & R.B.	140 G 140 U	To China.
Feb. 17	Sir Edward Hughes	James Urmston	Aug. 31	— Two L. & R.B.	354 C 354 J & K	To Bombay and Tellicherry.

Log begins.	Ship.	Captain.	Log ends.	Ledger or Receipt Book.	Reference Number.	Remarks.
1794 Mar. 1	Ganges	Joseph Garnault	1795 Aug. 28	— L. & R.B.	86 F 86 V	To China.
Mar. 3	Pitt	Edward Manning	Dec. 8	— L. & R.B.	525 G 525 N	To Calcutta.
Mar. 3	Walpole	Thomas Butler	Jan. 18	— L. & R.B.	298 R 298 OO	To China.
Mar. 4	Thetis	Henry Bullock	1796 Jan. 15	— L. & R.B.	387 D 387 K	To Bengal and Madras.
Mar. 12	Sugar Cane	Thomas Musgrave	1795 April 2	—	435 A	From Calcutta to Madras and England.
May 1	Orpheus	George Bowen	Dec. 25	—	364 A	To Calcutta.
May 1	Royal Admiral	Essex Henry Bond	1796 April 11	— L. & R.B.	338 G 338 Q	To Calcutta, Madras, and Trincomalee.
May 2	Lascelles	Francis Kempt	Mar. 21	— L. & R.B.	408 G 408 O	To Calcutta.
May 3	Holderness	George Wright	1795 Nov. 17	—	484 A	To Calcutta.
May 3	Mercury	John Cristal	Nov. 10	—	454 G	To Calcutta.
May 8	Indian Trader	David Dunlop	1796 Jan. 2	—	449 A	To Calcutta.
May 13	Comet	Sampson Baker	1795 Nov. 9	—	302 A	To Bengal and Madras.
May 13	Echo	William Catline	Sept. 14	—	516 A	To Calcutta.
May 14	Lady Shore	John Christopher (?)	Nov. 14	—	429 A	To Calcutta.
May 14	Latona	H. Christopher (?)	Dec. 28	—	500 A	To Calcutta.
July 25	Dart	Robert Grey	Aug. 24	—	529 A	To Balasore and Calcutta.
Sept. 11	Young William	James Mortlock	1796 Aug. 4	—	427 A	To Port Jackson and Whampoa.
Nov. 11	Boddington	-	1795 Aug. 7	—	414 A	From Pulo Penang to England.
Nov. 18	Indispensable	William Wilkinson	Sept. 4	[Two J.]	434 A & B	From Whampoa to England.
Nov. 26	Arniston	Camp. Majoribanks	1797 Mar. 27	— L. & R.B.	149 A 149 I	To Madras and China.
Nov. 29	Brunswick	Thomas Palmer Ackland.	Sept. 11	— L. & R.B.	349 C 349 H	To Bombay and Whampoa.
Dec. 1	Bombay Castle	John Hamilton	Sept. 8	— L. & R.B.	125 G 125 Q	To Bombay and China.
Dec. 24	Earl Howe	James Steward	Aug. 29	— L. & R.B.	203 A 203 I	To Bengal, Bombay, and China.
Dec. 26	Kent	George Saltwell	Mar. 17	— L. & R.B.	41 G 41 O	To China.
Dec. 29	Exeter	Lestock Wilson	1796 Dec. 31	— L. & R.B.	138 F 138 T	To Bombay and China.
Dec. 31	Earl Cornwallis	Thomas Hodgson succeeded by James Douglas.	Oct. 18	— L. & R.B.	348 F 348 M	To China.
—	Queen	Milliken Craig	—	L. & R.B. only.	356 V	——
—	Swallow	William Clifton	1798 —	L. & R.B. only.	385 S	——
1795 Jan. 16	Warren Hastings	F. W. Leigh	1797 Mar. 24	— L. & R.B.	9 G 9 EE	To China.
Feb. 18	Prince William Henry	Ralph Dundas	1796 Dec. 15	— L. & R.B.	389 D 389 J	To Calcutta.
Feb. 20	Northumberland	James Rees	1797 Mar. 25	— L. & R.B.	141 M 141 EE	To China.
Feb. 21	Worcester	John Hall	Feb. 24	— L. & R.B.	278 M 278 DD	To Calcutta and Bencoolen.
Feb. 22	General Coote	Charles Dundas	Mar. 30	— L. & R.B.	441 F 441 K	To Whampoa and Macao.
Feb. 23	London	James Ludovic Grant	1796 Sept. 16	— L. & R.B.	1 M 1 MM	To Bombay.
Feb. 23	Lord Thurlow	William Thomson	Sept. 13	— L. & R.B.	330 C 330 I	To Madras and Calcutta.

Log begins.	Ship.	Captain.	Log ends.	Ledger or Receipt Book.	Reference Number.	Remarks.
1795 Feb. 23	Osterley	James Foy	1797 Mar. 27	— L. & R.B.	400 N 400 AA	To San Salvador and Whampoa.
Feb. 23	Princess Amelia	George Millett	1796 Sept. 10	— L. & R.B.	36 J 36 FF	To Bombay.
Feb. 25	Barwell	Thomas Welladvice	Sept. 10	— L. & R.B.	420 F 420 M	To Bombay, Calicut, Anjengo, and Quilon.
Feb. 25	Francis	Robert Burrowes	Sept. 17	— L. & R.B.	443 F 443 L	To Madras and Calcutta.
Feb. 26	Deptford	William McNamara	1797 Mar. 24	— L. & R.B.	426 J 426 T	To China.
Feb. 26	Hillsborough	Richard Hutt	1796 Sept. 14	— L. & R.B.	437 H 437 Q	To Madras and Bengal.
Feb. 27	Earl of Oxford	Harry Kendall	Sept. 16	— L. & R.B.	489 F 489 L	To Madras and Calcutta.
Feb. 28	Minerva	Kennard Smith	Sept. 13	— L. & R.B.	14 D 14 Y	To Madras.
Mar. 9	Liberty	Richard Carey	1795 Oct. 4	—	433 A	To Christopher's Island, West Indies.
Mar. 11	Woodcot	William Haig - succeeded by Andrew Hannay.	Oct. 20	— L. and two R.B.	445 D 445 I	To Madras and Calcutta.
Mar. 11	Woodcot	William Haig - succeeded by Andrew Hannay.	1797 Jan. 21	—	445 E	To Madras and Calcutta.
Mar. 24	Prince of Wales	William Charlton	Aug. 15	—	404 P & Q	To Madras, Trincomalee, Colombo, and Whampoa.
Mar. 25	Berrington	George Robertson	1798 Jan. 22	— L. & R.B.	392 E 392 K	To Madras and Colombo.
Mar. 25	Lord Walsingham	James Young	1796 Aug. 29	— L. & R.B.	346 D 346 J	To Madras and Calcutta.
Mar. 30	Hawke	Richard Edwards	1797 Jan. 23	— L. & R.B.	390 M 390 BB	To Calcutta and Madras.
Mar. 30	Henry Dundas	John Campbell	Mar. 21	— L. & R.B.	331 D 331 J	To Madras and Bengal.
April 9	Marquis of Lansdown	Joseph Boulderson	1796 Sept. 8	— L. & R.B.	373 D 373 J	To Calcutta.
April 10	Cirencester	Martin Lindsay	1797 Jan. 30	— L. & R.B.	179 A 179 I	To China.
April 23	Earl Fitzwilliam	James Tweedale	Mar. 23	— L. and two R.B.	491 D 491 H	To Madras and Kedgeree.
April 27	Rodney	Walter Carruthers	1796 Sept. 15	— L. & R.B.	442 H 442 O	To Rio Janeiro and Madras.
May 1	General Medows	- - -	1795 Aug. 2	—	290 A	From China to Calcutta. (With the "Eliza Ann.")
May 7	Belvedere	Charles Christie	1797 Mar. 30	— L. & R.B.	332 D 332 J	To Macao and Whampoa.
May 11	Sovereign	- - -	Feb. 24	—	195 A & B	To Port Jackson and Calcutta.
May 13	Boyd	Robert Young	Jan. 8	—	446 A	To Rio Janeiro and Calcutta.
May 21	Fort William	George Simson	1798 Jan. 27	— L. & R.B.	91 E 91 P	To Madras and Whampoa.
June 2	Princess of Wales	Robert Abbon Mash	1796 Aug. 29	—	510 H	To Calcutta.
June 6	Bellona	William Ward Farrer	Aug. 30	—	353 B	To Calcutta.
July 9	Isabella	George Wilkinson	Aug. 27	—	60 A	To Bengal.
July 13	Mary	Thomas Stephenson	Sept. 28	—	261 G	From Bengal to England.
July 22	Ceres	T. Hedley	1797 Mar. 20	—	215 I	To New South Wales and China.
Aug. 14	Brunswick	Charles Ryland	April 8	—	349 B	To Calcutta.
Aug. 21	Surprise	Patrick Campbell	1796 June 2	—	447 D	From Calcutta to England.
Aug. 22	Britannia	Thomas Nixon	Oct. 10	— L. & R.B.	285 S 285 TT	To Calcutta.

Log begins.	Ship.	Captain.	Log ends.	Ledger or Receipt Book.	Reference Number.	Remarks.
1795 Aug. 24	Achilles	Robert Hogg	1797 Jan. 19	—	514 A	From Liverpool to Calcutta.
Aug. 26	John and James	James Johnson	1796 Aug. 31	—	418 A	To Calcutta.
Aug. 31	Iris	John B. Salisbury	Nov. 11	—	431 A	To Balasore and Calcutta.
Aug. 31	Sally	Robert Brown	1797 Jan. 16	—	411 A	To Calcutta.
Sept. 2	Pursuit	John Barker	Jan. 26	—	406 A	To Calcutta.
Sept. 3	Britannia	Thomas Barrow	1796 Aug. 25	—	285 SS	To Barbadoes and Martinique.
Sept. 4	Eliza Ann	John Lloyd	Aug. 9	—	290 A	From Calcutta and Madras to England. (Containing also part of Journal of ship "General Medows" 1795.)
Sept. 7	Sally	Robert Brown	1797 Jan. 16	—	411 B	To Calcutta.
Sept. 21	Earl Spencer	Thomas Denton	Jan. 10	—	227 A	To Bengal.
Sept. 25	Chichester	Benjamin Blake	1796 July 16	—	526 A	From Calcutta to Madras and England.
Sept. 26	Dart	Robert Grey	1797 Jan. 25	—	529 B	To Calcutta.
Oct. 26	Harriet	Matthew Sparrom	1796 July 4	[Two J.]	275 B 275 C	From Calcutta to England.
Oct. 31	Georgiana	J. Luard	1797 June 10	— L. & R.B.	156 A 156 K	To Bengal.
Nov. 23	Berwick	John McTaggart	1796 Aug. 4	—	61 A	From Calcutta to England.
Nov. 24	Britannia	William Layman	1797 Mar. 24	—	285 VV	To Whampoa from Bombay.
Nov. 24	Carron	F. Simpson	1796 Sept. 16	—	513 A	From Whampoa to England.
Nov. 25	Eliza Ann	John Lloyd	July 10	—	290 B	From Calcutta to England.
Nov. 28	Britannia	Thomas Dennett	June 28	—	285 UU	From Calcutta to England.
Dec. 21	Nonsuch	Robert Duffin	May 10	—	436 A	From Calcutta to England.
Dec. 23	Anna	Mungo Gilmore	Sept. 12	—	292 A	From Calcutta to England.
Dec. 30	Royal Charlotte	W. Greenway	Sept. 19	—	150 M	From Calcutta to England.
—	John	David Merrylees	1797 —	L. & R.B. only.	756 A	——
1796 Jan. 2	Chichester	Benjamin Blake	1796 July 16	—	526 B	From Bengal to Madras and England.
Jan. 3	Surat Castle	H. Laurie	Sept. 9	—	205 A	From China to England.
Jan. 4	Earl of Wycombe	John William Wood	1797 Mar. 13	— L. & R.B.	409 E 409 L	To Madras.
Jan. 8	General Medows	William Macdonald	1796 June 21	—	428 A	From Calcutta to England.
Jan. 8	Ocean	John Bowen	1797 Aug. 26	—	222 E	To Bengal.
Jan. 11	Friendship	[?] Black	1798 Oct. 28	—	358 C [433 A]	To Cape of Good Hope. This vessel was taken by the French Privateer "L'Aventure" on 27th October 1796. The crew were placed on the American ship "Henry," and the journal was continued on that vessel till 1st November (with 433 A).
Jan. 14	Nottingham	John Barfoot	Jan. 19	— L. & R.B.	287 L 287 AA	To Bombay, Macao, and Whampoa.
Jan. 14	Taunton Castle	Edward Studd	Mar. 29	— L. & R.B.	107 C 107 L	To Bombay and China.
Jan. 15	Canton	Abel Vyvyan succeeded by Ethelbert Lyne.	1799 Jan. 30	— L. & R.B.	288 C & D 288 L	To Madras, Trincomalee, Colombo, and Whampoa.

Log begins.	Ship.	Captain.	Log ends.	Ledger or Receipt Book.	Reference Number.	Remarks.
1796 Jan. 16	Gabriel	John Caise	1797 Feb. 6	—	370 A	From Calcutta to England.
Jan. 19	Essex	John Strover	1798 Mar. 10	— L. & R.B.	229 Q 229 OO	To Madras, Bengal, Bombay, &c.
Jan. 19	Lord Camden	Nathaniel Dance	1799 Aug. 17	— L. & R.B.	419 I & J 419 S	To Madras, Calcutta, &c.
Jan. 21	William Pitt	Sir Charles Mitchell	1798 Mar. 13	— L. & R.B.	184 E 184 V	To Madras, Bengal, and Bombay.
Jan. 25	Harriot	Charles Patterson	1797 Mar. 30	—	275 E	To Cape of Good Hope and St. Helena.
Jan. 25	Manship	John Cumberlege	1798 Mar. 12	— L. & R.B.	368 E 368 L	To Madras and Bombay.
Jan. 27	Exeter	Richard Whitford	Mar. 17	—	138 G	To Bengal, Bombay, &c.
Jan. 30	Asia	John D. Foulkes	Dec. 18	— L. & R.B.	24 J 24 NN	To Bengal, Madras, Bombay, and China.
Jan. 30	General Goddard	Thomas Graham	June 2	— L. & R.B.	440 G 440 M	To Madras, Calcutta, and Prince of Wales's Island.
Jan. 31	Abercromby	John Gilmore	1796 Aug. 4	—	527 A	From Kedgeree to England.
Feb. 1	Berwick	John McTaggart	Aug. 4	—	61 B	From Calcutta to England.
Feb. 1	Ganges	T. Patrickson	July 2	—	86 G	From Bengal to England.
Feb. 2	Queen	C. M. Venner	Jan. 19	—	356 J	To Table Bay.
—	Queen	Milliken Craig	1805 —	L. & R.B. only.	356 W	——
Feb. 8	Alfred	James Farquharson	1798 May 16	— L. & R.B.	140 H 140 V	To Madras and China.
Feb. 8	Dublin	William Smith	Jan. 22	— L. & R.B.	599 E 399 K	To Bombay, Calcutta, and Colombo.
Feb. 8	Europa	Charles Jones	Feb. 4	— L. & R.B.	425 J 425 T	To Calcutta, Madras, and Bencoolen.
Feb. 8	Ocean	Andrew Patton	1797 Mar. 3	— Two R.B.	222 D 222 V	To Madras and Java.
Feb. 8	Thetis	Henry Bullock	1798 Jan. 29	— L. & R.B.	387 E 387 L	To Bengal, Colombo, and Trincomalee.
Feb. 10	Trojan	Edward Redman	1797 Feb. 22	—	422 A	From England to Table Bay and back.
Feb. 13	Woodford	Charles Lennox	1798 May 3	[Two J] L. & R.B.	265 C & D 265 M	To Bombay, Colombo, and China.
Feb. 15	Bangalore	James Trayer	1797 Jan. 16	—	424 A	From Calcutta to England.
Feb. 18	Cecilia	E. H. Palmer	Jan. 23	—	372 A	From Calcutta to England.
Feb. 22	Melville Castle	John Lambe	1798 Jan. 19	— L. & R.B.	268 E 268 L	To Madras and Trincomalee.
Feb. 24	Boddam	George Palmer	Aug. 28	— L. & R.B.	351 D 351 J	To Madras and Whampoa.
Feb. 26	Lord Macartney	James Hay	Sept. 7	— L. & R.B.	415 F 415 L	To Madras, Calcutta, and Prince of Wales's Island.
Mar. 1	Bridgewater	John Skottowe	Jan. 29	— L. & R.B.	42 N 42 LL	To Bengal.
Mar. 2	Princess Charlotte	Charles Elton Prescott.	1797 Nov. 16	— L. & R.B.	245 A 245 E	To Madras.
Mar. 3	Rockingham	Hugh Lindsay	1798 Jan. 19	— L. & R.B.	124 E 124 M	To Madras.
Mar. 9	Castor	- -	Feb. 8	—	528 A	To Calcutta.
Mar. 11	Airly Castle	John Esplin	Jan. 24	— L. & R.B.	321 E 321 N	To Madras.
Mar. 15	Malabar	William Edmeades	1797 Nov. 11	— L. & R.B.	398 A 398 C	To Bombay, Tellicherry, and Mahé.

25005. T

Log begins.	Ship.	Captain.	Log ends.	Ledger or Receipt Book.	Reference Number.	Remarks.
1796 Mar. 18	Henry Addington -	Richard A. Farrington	1798 May 17	— L. & R.B.	170 A 170 H	To China.
Mar. 25	Coverdale - -	Benjamin Gowland -	Mar. 8	—	347 A	To Calcutta.
Mar. 26	Varuna - -	Henry Mathias Elmore.	1797 April 17	—	357 A & B	From Calcutta to England.
Mar. 28	Lord Hawkesbury -	John Price -	1798 Sept. 4	— L. & R.B.	323 D 328 L	To Madras and Calcutta.
Mar. 30	Good Hope - -	John Woodbridge Hilton.	1797 Dec. 11	— L. & R.B.	396 A 396 C	To Bombay and Mahé.
April 1	True Briton - -	William Stanley Clarke.	1798 Mar. 22	— L. & R.B.	297 N 297 EE	To Whampoa and Macao.
April 9	Pitt -	John Gerrard	Aug. 3	— L.	525 H 525 O	To Madras and Calcutta.
April 11	Union -	R. Owen - -	1797 Jan. 15	—	117 B	To Calcutta.
April 15	Minerva - -	Thomas Blany -	1798 Mar. 16	— L. & R.B.	14 E 14 Z	To Bengal.
April 25	Walter Boyd - -	J. M. McCulloch -	Aug. 21	—	416 A	To Kedgeree and Calcutta.
April 26	Lascelles - -	Francis Kempt	Dec. 18	— L. & R.B.	408 H 408 P	To Madras, Kedgeree, and Calcutta.
April 28	Thames - -	Robert Williams -	Mar. 1	— L. & R.B.	8 E 8 Z	To China.
April 30	Royal Admiral -	William Dorset Fellowes.	1799 Jan. 16	— L. & R.B.	338 H 338 R	To Calcutta and Madras.
May 11	Albion - -	Andrew Timbrell -	1798 Dec. 24	— L. & R.B.	81 E 81 Q	To Bombay and China.
May 12	Cuffnells - -	Charles Bowland Cotton.	May 11	— L. & R.B.	178 A 178 H	To China.
May 13	Duke of Buccleugh -	Thomas Wall -	Aug. 22	— L. & R.B.	132 D 132 K	To China.
May 16	Tellicherry - -	Sampson Baker -	Mar. 16	—	352 A	To Calcutta.
May 21	Busbridge -	John Dobree - -	1799 Aug. 14	— L. & R.B.	418 F & G 418 N	To Madras, Kedgeree, and Calcutta.
May 25	Caledonia -	AlexanderBannatyne	1797 April 9	—	359 A	From Calcutta to England.
May 30	Carnatic -	James Jackson -	1798 Mar. 16	— L. & R.B.	165 E 165 R	To China.
June 1	Glatton - -	Charles Drummond -	Aug. 23	— L. & R.B.	172 L 172 DD	To China.
June 2	Walmer Castle -	Essex Henry Bond -	May 19	— L. & R.B.	181 A 181 J	To China.
June 9	Phœnix -	Wemyss Orrok -	1799 Mar. 29	— L. & R.B.	175 E 175 S	To Bengal and Madras.
June 10	Prince of Wales -	William Milner -	1797 July 18	—	404 R	To Port Jackson, Macao, and Whampoa.
June 11	Queen - -	Milliken Craig -	1798 Jan. 20	—	412 B	To Madras, Bencoolen, and Calcutta.
June 11	Sir Stephen Lushington	George Gooch -	Aug. 3	— L. & R.B.	274 A 274 H	To Madras and Calcutta.
June 15	Royal Charlotte -	William Roper -	May 9	— L. & R.B.	150 N 150 FF	To China.
June 16	Prince of Wales -	William Charlton -	1797 Aug. 16	—	404 S	From Pulo Penang to England.
June 28	Loyalist - -	Francis Walton -	1798 Jan. 26	—	417 A	To Balasore and Calcutta.
July 5	Harriet - - -	Henry Archer -	1797 April 23	—	275 D	To Madras. (*See also* 275 F.)
July 7	Ranger - -	Patrick Campbell -	April 5	—	421 C	To Vizagapatam and Calcutta.
July 19	Lady Shore -	John Willcocks -	1796 Nov. 17	—	429 B	From Cape of Good Hope to England.

Log begins.	Ship.	Captain.	Log ends.	Ledger or Receipt Book.	Reference Number.	Remarks.
1796 July 21	Duff	James Wilson	1798 July 31	—	407 A	To Rio Janeiro, Otaheite (Society Islands), and Whampoa.
July 22	Fame	Henry Liddell	Jan. 17	—	242 A	To Vizagapatam and Calcutta.
Aug. 2	Three Sisters	Graham Steel	1797 Feb. 19	—	433 A	From Bengal to England.
Aug. 12	Alexander	W. Wallace	1798 Jan. 15	—	174 B	To Bengal.
Aug. 13	Princess Mary	James Nash	1799 Mar. 21	— L. & R.B.	381 C 381 J	To Calcutta, Madras, and Colombo.
Aug. 16	Maria	James Thomas Bishop	1798 April 12	—	291 aA	To Calcutta and Penang.
Sept. 1	Eliza Ann	Robert Hughes	1799 Mar. 23	—	290 C	To Madras, Trincomalee, and Colombo.
Sept. 1	Harriet	Henry Archer	1798 Nov. 15	—	275 F	To Madras, Calcutta, and Colombo.
Sept. 6	Bellona	William Ward Farrer	July 15	—	353 C	To Madras, Pondicherry, and Amboyna.
Sept. 10	Princess of Wales	Robert Abbon Mash'	Jan. 12	—	510 I	To Madras.
Sept. 18	Isabella	G. Wilkinson	Aug. 12	—	60 B & C	To Madras, Bombay, and Bengal.
Sept. 21	Berwick	William Wauchope	1797 Oct. 31	—	41 C	To Madras.
Sept. 21	Sir Edward Hughes	James Urmston	1798 Sept. 6	— L. & R.B.	354 D 354 L	To Bombay, Cochin, and Cannanore.
Sept. 26	Swallow	William Clifton	1797 May 23	—	385 H	From Bengal to Penang, Madras and England.
Oct. 11	Ellegood	Francis Holman	1798 Jan. 4	—	430 A	To Madras, Colombo, and Bombay.
Oct. 22	Britannia	Thomas Barrow	Dec. 21	— L. & R.B.	285 WW 285 T	To Madras and Calcutta.
Oct. 29	Marquis Cornwallis	John Roberts	1797 Aug. 24	—	336 A	From Calcutta to England.
Dec. 5	Indispensable	William Wilkinson	July 27	—	434 C	From Whampoa to England.
Dec. 13	Duckenfield Hall	James Moring	1798 Oct. 29	—	403 A	To Madras, Macao, and Whampoa.
Dec. 15	Crown	James Stranack	1799 Mar. 23	—	522 A & B	To Madras, Pulo Penang, and Calcutta.
Dec. 15	Hillsborough	Richard Hutt	1798 Aug. 10	— L. & R.B.	437 I 437 R	To Madras.
Dec. 15	Hindostan	William Mackintosh	1799 Jan. 15	— L. & R.B.	267 B 267 H	To Bombay and Whampoa.
Dec. 15	Neptune	Nathaniel Spens	Feb. 25	— L. & R.B.	98 K 98 CC	To Bombay and China.
Dec. 15	Warley	Henry Wilson	Jan. 22	— L. & R.B.	182 C 182 N	To Bombay and China.
Dec. 22	Lord Thurlow	William Thomson	1798 Aug. 14	— L. & R.B.	330 D 330 J	To Madras and Calcutta.
Dec. 31	Amazon	William Waring succeeded by Charles Hooper.	July 11	—	523 A	To Whampoa.
—	Martha	T. Barnard	1797 —	R.B. only	118 C	To Calcutta.
1797 Jan. 1	Earl Talbot	Jeremiah Dawkins succeeded by John Dale.	1798 Oct. 21	— L. & R.B.	410 G & H 410 P	To Madras, Malacca, and Whampoa.
Jan. 1	Princess Royal	Peter Foulister	Nov. 28	—	405 N	To Madras and Calcutta.
Jan. 6	Earl of Abergavenny	John Wordsworth	1799 Feb. 6	— L. & R.B.	341 C 341 I	To Bombay and Whampoa.
Jan. 13	Ariadne	John Walker succeeded by Alexander Stirling.	1798 Aug. 7	—	515 A & B	To Madras and Calcutta.

Log begins.	Ship.	Captain.	Log ends.	Ledger or Receipt Book.	Reference Number.	Remarks.
1797 Jan. 26	King George -	Richard Colnett	1798 Aug. 14	—	402 K	To Madras.
Jan. 28	Lord Walsingham	Thomas Smales	1799 Mar. 21	— L.& R.B.	346 E 346 K	To Madras and Bengal.
Jan. 28	Marquis of Lansdown	Joseph Bouldarson	1798 Aug. 10	— L. & R.B.	373 E 373 K	To Madras and Pondicherry.
Jan. 30	Houghton	Robert Hudson	Aug. 9	— L. & R.B.	438 S 438 NN	To Madras and Calcutta.
Jan. 30	Sulivan	Sampson Hall	Sept. 8	— L. & R.B.	257 G 257 M	To Bombay, Calicut, and Mahé.
Feb. 2	Ceres	George Stevens	1799 Feb. 15	— L. & R.B.	215 J 215 Z	To Madras and China.
Feb. 3	Duke of Montrose	Patrick Burt	Aug. 21	— L. & R.B.	775 E 775 L	To Calcutta.
Feb. 5	Atlantic	Richard Howard	July 17	—	524 A & B	To Madras and Calcutta.
Feb. 8	Malabar	William Edmeades	1800 Aug. 1	—	398 B	To Rio Janeiro, Madras, and Calcutta.
Feb. 22	Ganges	Joseph Garnault	1799 May 13	— L. & R.B.	86 H 86 W	To China.
Feb. 25	Earl Spencer	Charles Raitt	Mar. 25	— L. & R.B.	227 B 227 I	To Madras and Bengal.
Feb. 27	Prince William Henry	Roger Baskett -	Mar. 30	— L. & R.B.	389 E 389 K	To Madras and Kedgeree.
Feb. 28	Coutts	Robert Torin	1798 Oct. 9	— L. & R.B.	171 A 171 I	To China.
Mar. 3	Cirencester	Thomas Robertson	Oct. 28	— L. & R.B.	179 B 179 J	To China.
Mar. 3	Hawke	David Bristow Baker	1799 Mar. 28	— L. & R.B.	390 N 390 CC	To Madras and Kedgeree.
Mar. 10	Princess Royal	John Wedgborough -	1798 Mar. 26	—	405 L	From Bombay to England.
Mar. 29	Albion	John Parson	July 3	—	81 F	To Bengal.
Mar. 31	Hope	James Horncastle	Oct. 20	— L. & R.B.	168 A 168 N	To China.
April 1	Arniston	William McNamara -	Feb. 20	— L. & R.B.	149 B 149 J	To China.
April 1	Pursuit -	John Barker	Aug. 6	—	406 B	To Calcutta.
April 1	Queen	John Timins	1799 Jan. 20	—	356 K	To Calcutta and Kedgeree.
April 3	Friendship	John Newham	1798 Sept. 10	—	358 A	To Calcutta, Kedgeree, and Madras.
April 4	Earl of Wycombe	Dixon Meadows	1800 Feb. 6	— L. & R.B.	409 F & G 409 M	To Madras, Bombay, and Calcutta.
April 5	Ranger	John Ilingston Bythewood.	1798 Feb. 5	—	421 D	From Calcutta to England.
April 21	Admiral Gardner	Edward C. Bradford	1799 Sept. 2	— L. & R.B.	284 A 248 F	To Calcutta and Bencoolen.
May 5	Henry Dundas	Walter Carruthers	Aug. 28	— L. & R.B.	331 E 331 K	To Madras and Bengal.
May 6	Mildred	Michael Jordan	Mar. 19	—	448 A	To Calcutta.
May 8	Belvedere -	Charles Christie	1800 Feb. 3	— L. & R.B.	332 E 332 J	To Bombay, Colombo, Cannanore, &c.
May 8	Varuna	Henry Mathias Elmore	1799 Aug. 13	—	357 CD&E	To Calcutta, Kedgeree, and Madras.
May 18	Calcutta	- -	April 30	—	308 J	From Calcutta to England.
May 29	Northumberland	A. Aickman	Jan. 25	—	141 N	To Bengal.
July 1	Eurydice	Alexander Muirhead	May 4	—	423 A	To Calcutta and Culpee.
July 2	Barwell	John Cameron	Oct. 17	—	420 G	To Port Jackson and China.

Log begins.	Ship.	Captain.	Log ends.	Ledger or Receipt Book.	Reference Number.	Remarks.
1797 Aug. 27	Ocean	John Bowen	1798 Jan. 20	—	222 F	From Cape of Good Hope to England.
Aug. 31	Surat Castle	D. Isbister	1799 Aug. 1	—	205 B	To Bombay and China.
Oct. 16	Britannia	Thomas Dennett	Mar. 13	—	285 XX	From Whampoa to England.
Nov. 20	Bombay Castle	John Hamilton	Oct. 8	— L. & R.B.	125 H 125 K	To Bombay and China.
Nov. 20	Brunswick	James Ludk. Grant	Oct. 5	— L. & R.B.	349 D 349 I	To Bombay and Whampoa.
Nov. 20	Worcester	John Hall	1800 Mar. 10	— L. & R.B.	278 N 278 EE	To Calcutta, Colombo, and Madras.
Nov. 21	Duff	James Wilson	1798 July 31	—	407 B	From Macao to England.
Nov. 24	Earl Howe	Robert Burrowes	1800 Oct. 16	— L. & R.B.	203 B 203 J	To Bombay, Madras, and Bengal.
Dec. 7	Princess Royal	Peter Foubister	1798 Oct. 21	—	406 M	From Prince of Wales's Island to Madras, Calcutta, and England. (The Journal is in two parts, of which the first is missing.)
Dec. 17	Rose	Alexander Gray	Aug. 17	— L. & R.B.	59 E 59 W	To Madras and Bengal.
—	Earl Fitzwilliam	James Tweedale	1800 —	R.B. only.	491 I	——
—	Princess Amelia	John Ramsden	1797 —	R.B. only.	36 GG	——
—	Raymond	Henry Smedley	1800 —	Two R.B. only.	453 K	——
—	Woodcot	Andrew Hannay	1799 —	R.B. only.	445 J	——
1798 Jan. 1	Walpole	Thomas Butler	July 31	— L. & R.B.	293 S 293 PP	To Bombay, Madras, and Calcutta.
Jan. 3	London	James Thomas	Sept. 28	—	1 N	To Bombay and Madras.
Jan. 6	Princess Charlotte	Charles Elton Prescott.	1800 Nov. 5	— L. & R.B.	245 B 245 F	To Madras, Calcutta, Bombay, and Mocha.
Jan. 8	Good Hope	John Woodbridge Hilton.	1799 Aug. 22	— L. & R.B.	396 B 396 D	To Madras.
Jan. 11	Dover Castle	Peter Sampson	Aug. 27	— L. & R.B.	232 A 232 G	To Madras.
Feb. 5	Caledonian	Stephen Hawes	1800 Sept. 11	—	380 A	To Rio Janeiro, Whampoa, Calcutta, and Madras.
Feb. 13	Contractor	Henry Hughes	June 27	—	319 H	To Macao and Calcutta.
Feb. 17	Dublin	Robert Reay	June 28	— L. & R.B.	399 F 399 L	To Whampoa, Madras, and Calcutta.
Feb. 19	Airly Castle	John Esplin succeeded by Alexander Nash.	1799 Sept. 19	— L. & R.B.	321 F & G 321 O	To Whampoa.
Feb. 24	Bridgewater	John Skottowe	Sept. 26	— L. & R.B.	42 O 42 MM	To China.
Feb. 24	Lord Duncan	George Saltwell	1800 July 6	— L. & R.B.	210 A 210 H	To Bencoolen, Bengal, and Madras.
Feb. 28	Fort William	George Simson	1799 Sept. 23	— L. & R.B.	91 F 91 Q	To China.
Mar. 2	Melville Castle	John Lambe	Aug. 27	— L. & R.B.	268 F 268 M	To Bombay and Cannanore.
Mar. 6	Walpole	Corbyn Morris Venner	1800 Mar. 21	—	293 T	To Rio Janeiro, China, and Madras.
Mar. 9	Rockingham	Edward Harriman	1799 Aug. 24	— L. & R.B.	124 F 124 N	To Bombay.
Mar. 12	Osterley	John Wintersgill Piercy.	1800 June 27	—	400 O	To Madras, Trincomalee, and Calcutta.
Mar. 14	Thetis	Henry Bullock	Mar. 13	— L. & R.B.	387 F 387 M	To Trincomalee, Madras, and Calcutta.

Log begins.	Ship.	Captain.	Log ends.	Ledger or Receipt Book.	Reference Number.	Remarks.
1798 Mar. 15	Berrington	George Robertson	1799 Sept. 13	— L. & R.B.	392 F 392 L	To Madras and Calcutta.
Mar. 29	Tellicherry	Sampson Baker	Oct. 22	—	352 B	To Calcutta.
April 5	Calcutta	William Maxwell	1800 June 28	— L. & Two R.B.	308 K 308 W	To Calcutta, Bombay, and Madras.
April 28	Ardaseer	-	1799 Aug. 1	—	518 A	From Bombay to England.
June 19	Georgiana	Henry Leigh	1800 June 9	— L. & R.B.	156 B & C 156 L	To St. Helena and Cape of Good Hope.
June 23	Thames	Robert Williams	1801 April 19	— L. & R.B.	8 G 8 AA	To Bombay and China.
June 25	Coverdale	Benjamin Gowland	1800 June 27	—	347 B	To Madras and Calcutta.
June 28	Earl Cornwallis	James Tennent	July 1	—	348 G	To Madras, Ceylon, and Calcutta.
June 30	Cuffnells	Charles B. Cotton	Oct. 29	— L. & R.B.	178 B 178 I	To Bombay and China.
June 30	Royal Charlotte	William Roper	1801 May 28	— L. & R.B.	150 O 150 GG	To Madras, Bombay, and China.
July 2	Alligator	John Gibson	1800 May 3	—	519 A	To Madras and Calcutta.
July 7	Ocean	Robert Abbon Mash	June 24	—	222 G	To Madras and Bengal.
July 7	Phœnix	J. Tyrie	June 25	—	175 F	To Madras and Calcutta.
July 13	Orpheus	John Cristall	June 21	—	364 B	To Madras and Calcutta.
July 13	Thames (Extra Ship.)	Henry Passmore	Oct. 16	—	8 F	To Madras and Calcutta.
July 15	Sarah Christiana	Stephen Collins	1799 Dec. 4	—	362 A	To Madras.
Aug. 6	Minerva	Joseph Salkeld	1801 Mar. 16	—	14 F	To New South Wales and Bengal.
Sept. 13	Scaleby Castle	Patrick Gardner	1799 July 18	—	34 A, B & C	From Bombay to England.
Sept. 18	Carnatic	James Jackson	1800 July 25	— L. & R.B.	165 F 165 S	To Bombay and China.
Sept. 20	Taunton Castle	Essex Henry Bond	Aug. 2	— L. & R.B.	107 D 107 L	To Bombay and China.
Oct. 10	Highland Chief	-	1799 July 13	—	350 A	From Calcutta to England.
Nov. 19	Cuvera	-	July 25	—	369 A	From Calcutta to England.
Nov. 20	Anna	James Horsburgh	Aug. 30	—	292 B	From China to England.
Dec. 7	Manship	John Cumberlege	1800 Aug. 6	— L. & R.B.	363 F 363 M	To Madras and Calcutta.
Dec. 8	Sir Edward Hughes	James Urmston	June 25	— L. & R.B.	354 E 354 M	To Bombay, Calicut, and Madras.
Dec. 14	Lord Thurlow	William Thomson	1799 Nov. 24	— L. & R.B.	330 E 330 K	To Madras and Calcutta.
Dec. 20	Alfred	James Farquharson	1800 Dec. 6	— L. & R.B.	140 I 140 W	To Madras and China.
Dec. 20	Glatton	Charles Drummond	1801 June 5	— L. & R.B. and RiverPay R.B.	172 M 172 FF 172 EE (With FF)	To Bencoolen and China.
Dec. 22	Walmer Castle	George Bonham	June 2	— L. & R.B.	181 B 181 K	To Bombay and China.
Dec. 25	William Pitt	Sir Charles Mitchell	1800 Aug. 2	— L. & R.B.	184 F 184 W	To Bengal and Madras.
—	Exeter	Lestock Wilson	1799 —	L. only.	138 U	——
—	Henry Addington	Thomas Wakefield	1798 —	R.B. only	170 I	——

Log begins.	Ship.	Captain.	Log ends.	Ledger or Receipt Book.	Reference Number.	Remarks.
1799 Jan. 2	Preston - -	Thomas Garland Murray.	1800 Aug. 9	— L. & R.B.	307 A 307 G	To Madras and Calcutta.
Jan. 8	Boddam - -	George Palmer -	July 29	— L. & R.B.	351 E 351 K	To Madras and Whampoa.
Jan. 14	Marquis of Lansdown	William Tryon White	July 31	— L. & R.B.	373 F 373 L	To Madras and Calcutta.
Jan. 22	Britannia - -	Thomas Barrow	1802 Jan. 11	— L. & R.B.	285 YY 285 U	To Madras, Calcutta, Bombay, and China.
Jan. 22	Rose - - -	Wemyss Orrok	1800 Nov. 28	— L. & R.B.	59 F 59 X	To Madras and Bengal.
Jan. 24	Sir Stephen Lushington	George Gooch -	Nov. 17	— L. & R.B.	274 B 274 I	To Calcutta and Bencoolen.
Jan. 25	Lord Hawkesbury -	William Donaldson -	Nov. 19	— L. & R.B.	323 E 323 M	To Bengal.
Jan. 25	Minerva -	Kennard Smith -	Sept. 28	— L. & R.B.	14 G 14 AA	To Madras and Calcutta.
Feb. 7	Cornwallis - -	George Romaine	1799 Sept. 28	— L. & R.B.	270 A 270 D	From Madras to England. A diary. [Containing also copy of correspondence.]
Feb. 8	Carron - -	- - -	July 25	—	513 B & C	From China to England.
Feb. 9	Gabriel - -	- -	July 17	—	370 B	From Bengal to England.
Feb. 18	Woodford -	James Martin	1800 Sept. 7	— L. & R.B.	265 E 265 N	To Rio Janeiro and Bombay.
Feb. 23	Duke of Buccleugh -	Thomas Wall - -	Nov. 21	— L. & R.B.	132 E 132 L	To China.
Feb. 24	Hope -	James Horncastle	Nov. 26	— L. & R.B.	168 B 168 O	To China.
Feb. 25	Hindostan -	George Millett -	Nov. 20	— L. & R.B.	267 C 267 I	To Whampoa.
Feb. 27	Albion - -	Andrew Timbrell	Aug. 6	— L. & R.B.	81 G 81 R	To Bombay.
Mar. 1	Princess of Wales	Gilbert Michell -	1799 July 26	—	510 J	From Madras to England.
Mar. 4	Warley -	Henry Wilson	1800 Dec. 6	— L. & R.B.	182 D 182 O	To China.
Mar. 6	Asia -	Robert Wardlaw -	Nov. 19	— L. & R.B.	24 L 24 OO	To Bengal and Madras.
Mar. 8	Charlton	Thomas Welladvice -	Nov. 19	— L. & R.B.	301 A 301 F	To Madras and Calcutta.
Mar. 11	Earl of Abergavenny -	John Wordsworth	Dec. 10	— L. & R.B.	341 D 341 J	To Pulo Penang and Whampoa.
Aug. 3	Princess Mary - -	James Nash -	1801 May 5	— L. & R.B.	381 D 381 K	To Calcutta, Culpee, and Kedgeree.
Aug. 30	Earl Mornington	George Simpson succeeded by William Patten.	1802 Aug. 19	— L. & R.B.	375 A 375 C	To Calcutta and Kedgeree.
Oct. 28	Cirencester -	Thomas Robertson -	1801 June 17	— L. & R.B.	179 C 179 K	To Bombay and China.
Oct. 29	Ganges - -	Alexander Gray -	1802 Nov. 16	— L. & R.B.	86 I 86 X	To Bombay and China.
Oct. 30	Canton - - -	Thomas Lushington	1801 July 25	— L. & R.B.	288 E 288 M	To Bombay and Whampoa.
Oct. 31	Arniston	Campbell Marjoribanks.	July 29	— L. & R.B.	149 C 149 K	To Bencoolen and China.
Dec. 1	Asia - - -	G. McInnes - -	1800 June 3	—	24 K	From Bombay to London.
Dec. 24	Lady Burges - -	Archibald F. W. Swinton.	1801 Sept. 4	— L. & R.B.	310 A 310 D	To Madras and Bengal.
Dec. 26	Brunswick	James Ludk. Grant -	July 30	— L. & R.B.	349 E 349 J	To Madras and Whampoa.
Dec. 26	Walthamstow - -	William Taylor Money.	July 23	— L. & R.B.	196 A 196 G	To Madras and China.
Dec. 27	Ceres -	George Stevens	July 30	— L. & R.B.	215 K 215 AA	To Madras and China.

Log begins.	Ship.	Captain.	Log ends.	Ledger or Receipt Book.	Reference Number.	Remarks.
1799 Dec. 27	Porcher	Benjamin Blake	1800 Nov. 24	—	398 A	From Calcutta to England.
Dec. 28	Admiral Rainier	William Lay	Oct. 28	—	342 A	From Calcutta to England.
Dec. 30	Mornington	James Carnegy	Oct. 9	—	374 A	From Calcutta to England.
—	Earl Talbot	John H. Dempster	1799 —	R.B. only	410 Q	——
—	Swallow	John Laard	1801 —	L. & R.B. only.	385 T	——
—	True Briton	Henry Farrer	1802 —	L. & R.B. only.	297 FF	——
1800 Jan. 2	Caledonia	George Thomas	1800 July 7	—	359 B	From Bengal to England.
Jan. 4	Earl St. Vincent	John Brook Samson	1801 July 15	— L. & R.B.	209 A 209 I	To Madras and China.
Jan. 6	Lord Nelson	Robert Spottiswoode	July 16	— L. & R.B.	294 A 294 D	To Madras and Whampoa.
Jan. 6	Marquis Wellesley	Bruce Mitchell	July 18	— L. & R.B.	212 A 212 G	To Madras and China.
Jan. 10	Hugh Inglis	William Fairfax	1802 Jan. 26	— L. & R.B.	231 A 231 H	To Whampoa.
Jan. 17	Cartier	James Nash	1800 Oct. 28	[Two J.]	394 A & B	From Amboyna to England.
Jan. 28	Arran	John Barker	Sept. 30	—	520 A	From Calcutta to England.
Jan. 29	Eliza Ann	G. G. Richardson	Sept. 30	—	290 D	From Calcutta to England.
Feb. 1	Exeter	A. Dunlop	Sept. 26	— L. & R.B.	138 H 138 V	To Bengal.
Feb. 11	Castle Eden	Alexander Cuming	1801 Dec. 12	— L. & R.B.	296 A 296 G	To Bengal, Madras, and Vizagapatam.
Feb. 22	Bengal	Adam Cumine	Sept. 4	— L. & R.B.	177 A 177 F	To Bengal.
Feb. 24	City of London	Abraham Green	Dec. 31	— L. & R.B.	151 A 151 G	To Bengal and Madras.
Feb. 24	Phœnix	William Moffat	1802 July 24	— L. & R.B.	175 G 175 T	To Bengal, Bombay, Tellicherry, &c.
Mar. 8	Coutts	Robert Torin	Feb. 16	— L. & R.B.	171 B 171 J	To China.
Mar. 10	Bombay Castle	John Hamilton	Jan. 29	— L. & R.B.	125 I 125 S	To China.
Mar. 11	Dorsetshire	John Ramsden	Feb. 9	— L. & R.B.	13 A 13 K	To China.
Mar. 11	Exeter	Henry Meriton	Feb. 3	—	138 I	To China.
Mar. 11	Neptune	Nathaniel Spens	1801 Dec. 17	— L. & R.B.	98 L 98 DD	To China.
Mar. 13	Lady Jane Dundas	Hon. Hugh Lindsay	Sept. 3	— L. & R.B.	309 A 309 E	To Bengal.
Mar. 17	Britannia	R. H. Palmer	1800 Nov. 7	—	285 ZZ	From Madras to England.
Mar. 20	Tellicherry	Sampson Baker	1801 Dec. 1	—	352 C	To Calcutta, Madras, and Colombo.
Mar. 25	Rockingham	Thomas Butler	1802 July 20	—	124 G	To Bombay, Madras, and Bengal.
Mar. 28	Earl Spencer	Charles Raitt	1801 Nov. 7	— L. & R.B.	227 C 227 J	To Bengal.
Mar. 28	Lord Walsingham	Thomas Smales	Dec. 17	— L. & R.B.	346 F 346 L	To Kedgeree.
April 8	Royal Admiral	William Wilson	1802 Aug. 4	—	338 I	To Port Jackson, Otaheite (Society Islands), Whampoa, and Macao.
April 12	Melville Castle	John Lambe	Mar. 13	—	268 G	To Calcutta and Bombay.
April 17	Travers	Thomas Sanders	Mar. 3	—	279 A	To Calcutta, Anjengo, and Bombay.
April 18	Herculean	John R. Franchlin	1801 Nov. 8	—	339 A	To Calcutta and Bencoolen.
April 21	Indian Chief	-	Oct. 3	—	377 A	From New York to Hamburg, Yarmouth, and Calcutta, and thence to England.

Log begins.	Ship.	Captain.	Log ends.	Ledger or Receipt Book.	Reference Number.	Remarks.
1800 April 28	Skelton Castle	Mathew Isacke	1802 Mar. 8	—	304 A	To Calcutta, Anjengo, and Bombay.
May 10	Friendship	Hugh Reid	1801 June 17	—	358 B	From Port Jackson to Bengal and England.
June 27	Georgiana	Henry Leigh	1802 April 6	— L. & R.B.	158 D 158 M	To Bengal.
July 1	Anna	Patrick Clark	1801 May 6	—	292 C	From Bengal to England.
July 14	Hawke	David Bristow Baker	Dec. 5	— L. & R.B.	390 O 390 DD	To Madras and Colombo.
July 22	Prince William Henry	Roger Baskett	Dec. 5	— L. & R.B.	389 F 389 L	To Madras and Vizagapatam.
July 24	Sir Edward Hughes	James Urmston	Nov. 5	— L. & R.B.	354 F 354 U	To Madras, Vizagapatam, &c.
Aug. 22	Apollo	R. Brown	Jan. 28	Two J. only.	159 A & B	From Madras to England.
Aug. 28	Queen	John Timins	May 6	—	356 L	From Madras to England.
Sept. 1	Varuna	William Ward Farrer	June 19	—	357 F	From Calcutta and Kedgeree to England.
Oct. 3	Highland Chief	William Greenway ?	June 11	—	350 B & C	From Calcutta to England.
Oct. 10	Triton	David Dunlop	Mar. 30	—	366 L	From Madras to England.
Oct. 17	Suffolk	John Robinson	1802 Mar. 10	—	397 G	To Calcutta.
Oct. 21	Nottingham	John Barfoot	Aug. 16	— L. & R.B.	287 M 287 BB	To Bombay.
Oct. 22	Henry Addington	Thomas Wakefield	July 27	— L. & R.B.	170 B 170 J	To Bombay and China.
Oct. 24	Ocean	Andrew Patton	July 29	— L. & R.B.	222 H 222 W	To Bombay and Whampoa.
Oct. 26	Whim	John H. Fellers succeeded by Andrew Barclay.	1801 Dec. 4	—	378 A	To Madras.
Oct. 27	Carnatic	Horatio Beevor	1802 July 26	— L. & R.B.	165 G 165 T	To Bencoolen and China.
Nov. 17	Bridgewater	George Lukin	1801 Nov. 8	—	42 P	To Madras.
Nov. 19	Nutwell	John Cristall succeeded by John Caise.	1802 April 13	—	383 A	To Madras and Calcutta.
Nov. 20	Sir Edward Hamilton	Andrew Robertson	April 28	—	384 A	To Calcutta and Kedgeree.
Nov. 21	Earl St. Vincent	R. Williams	Feb. 10	—	209 B	To Calcutta.
Nov. 22	Ceres	Thomas Todd	Mar. 19	—	215 L	To Bengal.
Nov. 25	Thames	B. Eilbeck	Mar. 27	—	8 H	To Calcutta.
Nov. 28	Experiment	John Nelson Whyte	May 4	—	127 A	To Bengal.
Nov. 28	Rose	Christopher Kymer	April 23	—	59 G	To Bengal.
Dec. 1	Airly Castle	Alexander Nash	July 21	— L. & R.B.	321 H 321 P	To Bombay, Tellicherry, and Cochin.
Dec. 1	Perseverance	-	Feb. 21	— L. & R.B.	255 A 255 J	To Calcutta. (The Journal is in two parts.)
Dec. 6	Dover Castle	Peter Sampson	1803 Sept. 3	— L. & R.B. Ship's Account.	232 B 232 H 232 M	To Madras, Calcutta, and Macao.
Dec. 8	Hindostan	George Millett	1802 Aug. 2	— L. & R.B.	267 D 267 J	To Madras and Whampoa.
Dec. 10	Grant	-	Jan. 18	—	376 A	To Calcutta.
Dec. 11	Betsy	Charles Hooper ?	Mar. 24	—	368 A	To Calcutta.
Dec. 12	Admiral Gardner	Edward C. Bradford	July 28	— L. & R.B.	284 E 284 G	To Madras, Malacca, and China.
Dec. 13	Hind	William Catlin succeeded by William Gibson.	Feb. 23	—	395 A & B	To Calcutta.
Dec. 15	Harmony	James Wickham	Mar. 1[illegible]	—	362 A	To Madras and Calcutta.

Log begins.	Ship.	Captain.	Log ends.	Ledger or Receipt Book.	Reference Number.	Remarks.
1800 Dec. 16	True Briton	William Stanley Clarke.	1803 Feb. 21	— L. & R.B.	297 O 297 GG	To Madras, Amboyna, and Whampoa.
Dec. 17	Calcutta	William Maxwell	1802 Aug. 17	— L. & R.B.	308 L 308 X	To Madras and Calcutta.
Dec. 18	Charlton	John A. Cumberlege	Aug. 11	— L. & R.B.	301 B 301 G	To Calcutta, Vizagapatam, and Madras.
Dec. 16	Duke of Montrose	Patrick Burt	Sept. 16	— L. & R.B.	775 F 775 M	To Madras and Calcutta.
Dec. 19	Minerva	G. Richardson	Feb. 24	—	14 H	To Calcutta.
Dec. 20	Scarborough	John Scott	April 22	[Two J.]	355 H & I	To Calcutta.
Dec. 24	Ganges	F. Brown	Mar. 3	—	86 J & K	To Calcutta.
Dec. 27	Asia	Robert Wardlaw	1803 Sept. 1	— L. & R.B.	24 M 24 PP	To Madras, Calcutta, and China.
Dec. 27	Bellona	Edward Lamb	1802 Mar. 7	—	353 D	To Bengal.
Dec. 27	Lord Duncan	George Saltwell	July 10	— L. & R.B.	210 B 210 I	To China.
Dec. 28	Automatic	Anthony Curtis	Mar. 13	—	517 A	To Calcutta.
Dec. 31	Hope	James Horncastle	July 29	— L. & R.B.	168 E 168 P	To Madras and China.
Dec. 31	Walpole	James Sandilands	Oct. 6	— L. & R.B.	293 U 293 QQ	To Madras, Calcutta, and Bencoolen.
Dec. 31	Windham	Thomas Graham	July 11	— L. & R.B.	230 D 230 N	To Whampoa.
Dec. 31	Worcester	Searles Wood	July 15	— L. & R.B.	278 O 278 FF	To Bombay, Tellicherry, and Quilon.
—	Cornwallis	George Romaine	1800 —	R.B. only.	270 E	——
—	Earl Talbot	John H. Dempster	1804 —	R.B. only.	410 R	"Ship supposed to have been lost in the China Seas, 22nd October 1800."
—	Kent	Robert Rivington	1801 —	Two R.B. only.	41 F	——
—	Queen	Milliken Craig	1800 —	Two R.B. only.	356 X	This ship was burnt at San Salvador on 9th July 1800.
1801 Jan. 1	Countess of Sutherland.	Charles Eggleston	1802 Feb. 15	[Two J.]	401 A & B	From Calcutta to England.
Jan. 1	Fort William	Joseph Boulderson	July 21	— L. & R.B.	91 G 91 R	To Bombay and Surat.
Jan. 2	Sir Stephen Lushington	George Gooch	Aug. 7	— L. & R.B.	274 C 274 J	To Madras and Calcutta.
Jan. 5	Earl Howe	Robert Burrowes	Aug. 27	— L. & R.B.	203 C 203 K	To Bengal.
Jan. 10	Marian	- - -	1801 Nov. 1	—	388 A	From Calcutta to England.
Jan. 14	Belvedere	James Peter Pearson	1802 Oct. 29	— L. & R.B.	332 F 332 L	To Rio Janeiro and Whampoa.
Jan. 14	Woodford	James Martin	Oct. 28	— L. & R.B.	265 F 265 O	To Whampoa and Macao.
Jan. 15	Duke of Buccleugh	Thomas Wall	Sept. 30	— L. & R.B.	132 F 132 M	To China.
Jan. 15	Lucy Maria	Walter Dawes	Jan. 11	—	391 A & B	From Calcutta to England.
Jan. 16	Albion	Andrew Timbrell	Oct. 18	— L. & R.B.	81 H 81 S	To China.
Jan. 17	Taunton Castle	Thomas B. Peirce	Oct. 14	— L. & R.B.	107 E 107 N	To China.
Jan. 19	Alfred	James Farquharson	Oct. 26	— L. & R.B.	140 J 140 X	To China.
Jan. 19	Lord Thurlow	John Dale	April 13	— L. & R.B.	330 F 330 L	To Madras.

Log begins.	Ship.	Captain.	Log ends.	Ledger or Receipt Book.	Reference Number.	Remarks.
1801 Jan. 20	Surat Castle	-	1801 Oct. 31	—	205 C	From Bombay to England.
Jan. 23	Princess Charlotte	Benjamin Richardson	1803 Feb. 10	— L. & R.B.	245 C 245 G	To Madras and Amboyna.
Jan. 23	Warley	Henry Wilson	1802 Oct. 29	— L. & R.B.	182 E 182 P	To China.
Jan. 24	Sir John Borlase Warren.	William James Davis	May 5	—	360 A	To Calcutta.
Feb. 3	Earl of Abergavenny	John Wordsworth	Nov. 3	— L. & R.B.	341 E 341 K	To Malacca and China.
Feb. 11	Henry Dundas	Walter Carruthers	Aug. 27	— L. & R.B.	331 F 331 L	To Bengal.
Feb. 17	Boddam	John Jones	July 24	— L. & R.B.	351 F 351 L	To Madras, Penang, and Whampoa.
Feb. 17	Preston	Thomas Garland Murray.	Oct. 4	— L. & R.B.	307 B 307 H	To Bengal and Bencoolen.
Mar. 6	Triton	David Dunlop	1801 Mar. 31	—	366 M	At Long Reach and Deptford. [Incomplete].
Mar. 8	Lord Hawkesbury	William Donaldson	1802 July 24	— L. & R.B.	323 F 323 N	To Bombay, Tellicherry, Anjengo, and Quilon.
Mar. 16	Harriet	Alexander Sinclair	1801 Dec. 7	—	275 G	From Calcutta to England.
Mar. 17	Thetis	John Power	Nov. 10	—	337 G	From Madras to England.
Mar. 30	Minorca	John Leith	1803 Feb. 28	—	335 A & B	To Port Jackson and Whampoa.
Mar. 30	Nile	James Simter	Mar. 5	—	334 A	To Port Jackson and Canton.
April 2	Hope	R. Dennison	1801 Nov. 7	—	168 C & D	From Bombay to England.
April 5	Aurora	Mungo Gilmore	1802 Jan. 27	—	228 A	From Bengal to England.
April 10	Comet	Thomas Larkins	1803 Feb. 10	— L. & R.B.	302 B 302 D	To Calcutta.
April 14	Sarah Christiana	Charles Graham	1802 Sept. 25	— L. & R.B.	283 B 283 E	To Calcutta.
May 2	Hope	W. H. Dunbar	Mar. 25	—	168 F	From Calcutta to England.
May 6	Anna	James Horsburgh ?	1801 Dec. 26	—	292 D	From Bombay to England.
May 12	Elizabeth	Stephen Hawes	1802 Sept. 24	— L. & R.B.	102 F 102 N	To China.
May 13	Sovereign	Gilbert Michell	1803 Mar. 7	— L. & R.B.	195 C 195 J	To Bombay, Bengal, and Madras.
May 16	Canada	William Wilkinson	Mar. 25	—	314 A	To Rio Janeiro, Port Jackson, Macao, and Whampoa.
May 19	Manship	John Logan	1803 July 11	— L. & R.B.	363 G 363 N	To Colombo and Calcutta.
May 19	Mornington	George Kelso	1802 Mar. 13	—	374 B	From Kedgeree to England.
June 1	Surat Castle		1801 Nov. 7	—	205 D	From Bombay to England.
June 18	Caledonia	George Thomas	1802 May 18	—	359 C	From Calcutta to England.
June 22	Ann	Alexander Sinclair	Dec. 17	— L. & R.B.	211 A 211 J	To Madras and Calcutta.
June 23	Union	J. Luke	April 2	—	117 C	From Calcutta to London.
June 26	Princess Mary	Andrew Grieve	Dec. 15	— L. & R.B.	381 E 381 L	To Calcutta, Culpee, and Kedgeree.
June 27	Gilwell	C. H. Sheen	April 17	—	361 A	To Madras.
July 1	Exeter	John Macintosh	Mar. 22	(Two J.)	138 J & K	To Bengal.

Log begins.	Ship.	Captain.	Log ends.	Ledger or Receipt Book.	Reference Number.	Remarks.
1801 July 1	Star	Robert Scott	1802 Jan. 6	— L. & R.B.	371 A 371 B	From Amboyna to England.
July 2	General Stuart	Robert Abbon Mash	1803 April 13	— L. & R.B.	218 A 218 H	To Madras and Bengal.
July 2	Hercules	L. Bells	July 5	—	77 A	To New South Wales and China.
July 6	Monarch	Thomas Mortimer	1802 Sept. 14	— L. & R.B.	300 A 300 F	To Madras.
July 11	Caledonian	John Craig	1803 April 18	— L. & R.B.	380 B 380 C	To Madras, Calcutta, and Kedgeree.
July 12	Northampton	Robert Barker	April 18	— L. & R.B.	198 B 198 O	To Bombay and Bengal.
July 16	Atlas	Richard Brooks	June 7	—	27 E	To Rio Janeiro, Port Jackson, and China.
July 16	Eliza Ann	John Parson	1802 Mar. 5	[Three J.]	290 E, F, & G	From Calcutta to England.
Aug. 4	Medway	William Babazon	April 7	[Two J.]	382 A & B	From Calcutta to England. [382 B contains a small Cargo Book.]
Aug. 24	Experiment	J. Palmer	April 25	—	127 B	From Bengal to England.
Sept. 27	Swallow	Arthur Muter	1803 Aug. 9	—	385 I	From Calcutta to Mocha, Madras, and England.
Oct. 19	Wellesley	Peter Gordon	1804 Feb. 30	—	276 A & B	From Calcutta to England.
Oct. 20	Thames	Robert Williams	1803 June 30	— L. & R.B.	8 I 8 BB	To Bombay and China.
Oct. 22	Arniston	Campbell Marjoribanks	May 15	— L. & R.B.	149 D 149 L	To Bencoolen and China.
Oct. 22	Walmer Castle	Essex Henry Bond	June 25	— L. & R.B.	181 C 181 L	To Bombay and China.
Oct. 22	Canton	Thomas Lushington	July 11	—	288 F 288 N	To Bombay and Whampoa.
Oct. 28	Britannia	Benjamin Stout	1802 June 6	[Two J.]	285 AAA and 285 BBB	From Calcutta to England.
Nov. 1	Perseus	John Davison	Aug. 22	—	365 A	To Rio Janeiro and Port Jackson.
Nov. 3	Coromandel	A. Sterling	1803 July 4	—	206 A	To New South Wales and China.
Nov. 19	Ann	J. Stewart	1802 June 25	—	211 B	From Calcutta to England.
Nov. 21	Alnwick Castle	Charles Elton Prescott	1803 June 17	— L. & R.B.	189 A 189 H	To Madras and China.
Nov. 21	Marquis of Ely	Andrew Hannay	July 19	— L. & R.B.	193 A 193 I	To China.
Nov. 23	Stirling Castle	[?] Hongman	1802 July 22	—	367 A	From Calcutta to England.
Dec. 4	Lady Burges	Archibald F. W. Swinton.	1803 Sept. 24	— L. & R.B.	310 B 310 E	To Madras and Calcutta.
Dec. 5	Lady Jane Dundas	Hon. Hugh Lindsay	June 7	— L. & R.B.	309 B 309 F	To Madras and Calcutta.
Dec. 5	Marchioness of Exeter	John Locke	Sept. 21	— L. & R.B.	166 A 166 H	To Madras, Amboyna, and Batavia.
Dec. 7	Marquis Wellesley	Bruce Mitchell	Sept. 7	— L. & R.B.	212 B 212 H	To Madras and Calcutta.
Dec. 8	Cirencester	Thomas Robertson	June 27	— L. & R.B.	179 D 179 L	To Madras and China.
Dec. 9	Perseverance	James Tweedale	June 22	— L. & R.B.	255 C 255 J	To Madras and Whampoa.
Dec. 11	Eliza	Francis Holman	1801 June 20	—	68 A	From Calcutta to England.
Dec. 15	Atlas	Thomas Musgrave	1804 Jan. 12	—	27 F	To Rio Janeiro, New South Wales, and China.
1802 Jan. 4	Bengal	Adam Currie	1803 May 26	— L. & R.B.	177 B 177 G	To Madras and Bengal.

Log begins.	Ship.	Captain.	Log ends.	Ledger or Receipt Book.	Reference Number.	Remarks.
1802 Jan. 4	Clyde	George McCall	1802 July 22	—	345 B	From Calcutta to England.
Jan. 4	United Kingdom	A. Campbell (Chief Mate) succeeded by George Richardson.	1804 Jan. 21	— L. & R.B.	277 A & B 277 G	To Madras and Calcutta. On 11th October 1802 A. Campbell gave over command of the ship to G. Richardson.
Jan. 4	Walthamstow	William Agnew	1803 May 26	— L. & R.B.	196 B 196 H	To Bengal.
Jan. 7	Cuffnells	Charles B. Cotton	Sept. 16	— L. & R.B.	178 C 178 J	To China.
Jan. 7	David Scott	Charles Jones	June 9	— L. & R.B.	188 C 188 N	To China.
Jan. 19	Ceres	W. Dunsford	June 25	— L. & R.B.	215 M 215 BB	To China.
Jan. 19	Royal Charlotte	Robert Patterson	June 22	— L. & R.B.	150 P 150 HH	To China.
Jan. 24	Althea	Arundel Roberts	1802 Dec. 2	—	521 A	From Bengal to England.
Jan. 25	Glatton	William Macnamara	1803 June 20	— L. & R.B.	172 N 172 GG	To China.
Jan. 28	Brunswick	Philip Hughes	1805 June 17	— L. & R.B.	349 F 349 K	To San Salvador and Whampoa.
Feb. 1	David Scott	C. Gib	1802 Aug. 18	[Two J.]	183 A & B	From Bombay to England.
Feb. 1	Triton	Nicholas Anstis	Oct. 19	—	366 O	From Kedgeree and Calcutta to England.
Feb. 8	Alexander	J. Normand	1803 Dec. 18	—	174 C	To Rio Janeiro, Port Jackson, and Bombay.
Feb. 9	Sir Edward Hughes	James Urmston	June 20	— L. & R.B.	354 G 354 O	To Bombay, Surat, &c.
Feb. 14	Clyde	George McCall	1802 July 22	—	345 A	From Calcutta to England.
Feb. 14	Earl St. Vincent	John Brook Samson	1803 July 7	— L. & R.B.	209 C 209 J	To Bombay and Anjengo.
Feb. 26	Tellicherry	George Welstead	May 23	— L. & R.B.	352 D 352 E	To Calcutta.
Mar. 9	Neptune	John Reddie	Sept. 2	— L. & R.B.	98 M 98 EE	To China.
Mar. 11	Britannia	Thomas Barrow	April 16	— L. & two R.B.	285 CCC 285 V	To Madras.
Mar. 13	Betsy	W. W. Bampton	1802 Oct. 9	—	368 B	From Calcutta to England.
Mar. 13	Herculean	Samuel Butler	1804 May 24	— L. & R.B.	339 B & C 339 D	To Bombay, Surat, Calcutta, &c.
Mar. 16	Asia	G. McInnes	1802 Aug. 11	—	24 N	St. Helena to London.
Mar. 17	Triton	Nicholas Anstis	Oct. 19	—	366 N	From Calcutta to England.
Mar. 19	Fame	John Valentine Baker	1803 Sept. 30	— L. & R.B.	242 B 242 E	To Calcutta and Bencoolen.
April 6	Admiral Aplin	John Rogers	April 13	— L. & R.B.	337 A 337 B	To Madras.
April 8	Scaleby Castle	Patrick Gardner	1802 Nov. 25	—	34 E	From Bombay to England.
April 19	Minerva	George Weltden	1804 Jan. 18	— L. & R.B.	14 I 14 BB	To Calcutta.
April 24	Lord Eldon	Jasper Swete	Jan. 17	— L. & R.B.	148 A 148 I	To Bengal.
April 24	Sir William Bensley	Robert Rhode	1803 Sept. 21	— L. & R.B.	247 A 247 G	To Calcutta.
May 1	Travers	Thomas Sanders	Nov. 8	L. & R.B.	279 B 279 I	To Bombay, Calicut, &c.

Log begins.	Ship.	Captain.	Log ends.	Ledger or Receipt Book.	Reference Number.	Remarks.
1802 May 18	Skelton Castle	Frederick Pitman	1803 Nov. 8	— L. & R.B.	304 B & C 304 E	To Madras.
May 27	Tottenham	Thomas Jones	1804 June 23	— L. & R.B.	199 A 199 G	To Bengal.
July 3	Scaleby Castle	Patrick Gardner	1802 Dec. 3	—	34 D	From Bombay to England.
July 5	Devaynes	William Adderley	1804 May 26	— L. & R.B.	223 A 223 G	To Madras and Bengal.
Aug. 27	Lord Duncan	Anthony Murray	June 7	— L. & R.B.	210 C 210 J	To Madras and Bengal.
Sept. 1	Henry Addington	John Kirkpatrick	Sept. 20	— L. & R.B.	170 C 170 K	To Bombay and China.
Sept. 2	Castle Eden	Alexander Cuming	April 14	— L. & R.B.	296 B 296 H	To Madras.
Oct. 14	Ocean	Andrew Patton succeeded by John C. Lochner.	1803 May 7	— L. & R.B.	222 I 222 X	To Bombay.
Oct. 25	Royal George	John F. Timins	1804 Sept. 22	— L. & R.B.	17 J 17 AA	To China.
Oct. 29	Earl Camden	Nathaniel Dance	Sept. 25	— L. & R.B.	303 A 303 D	To Bombay and Whampoa.
Oct. 31	Bombay Castle	Archibald Hamilton	Sept. 6	— L. & R.B.	125 J 125 T	To Bombay and China.
Nov. 4	Rolla	Robert Cumming	Nov. 8	—	312 A	To New South Wales, Macao, and Whampoa.
Nov. 15	Cumberland	William Ward Farrer	1814 Sept. 28	— L. & R.B.	202 A 202 G	To Madras and China.
Nov. 22	Admiral Gardner	Edward C. Bradford	1804 June 26	— L. & R.B.	284 C 284 H	To Madras and Calcutta.
Nov. 25	City of London	Samuel Landon	Nov. 9	— L. & R.B.	151 B 151 H	To Madras and Bengal.
Nov. 28	Cecilia	Thomas Thomas	1803 June 27	—	372 B & C	From Calcutta to England.
Nov. 28	Varuna	John Lowe	Sept. 24	—	357 G, H, & I.	From Calcutta and Kedgeree to England.
Nov. 29	Sir Stephen Lushington.	George Gooch	1804 June 21	— L. & R.B.	274 D 274 K	To Madras and Calcutta.
Dec. 1	Shaw Byramgore	[?] Bowen	1803 Aug. 14	—	340 A	From Calcutta to England.
Dec. 7	Harriet	William Lynch	1804 May 26	— L. & R.B.	275 H 275 O	To Madras and Calcutta.
Dec. 8	Baring	Dixon Meadows	Jan. 21	— L. & R.B.	246 A 246 H	To Madras and Calcutta.
Dec. 9	Carmarthen	John Dobree	Sept. 8	— L. & R.B.	142 A 142 I	To Bengal and Bencoolen.
Dec. 9	Experiment	James Carnegie	Mar. 5	— L. & R.B.	127 C 127 F	To Bombay.
Dec. 9	Windham	Thomas Graham	Oct. 28	— L. & R.B.	230 E 230 O	To Madras, Calcutta, &c.
Dec. 10	Walpole	James Sandilands	Mar. 26	— L. & R.B.	293 V 293 RR	To Madras.
—	Cullands Grove	Archibald Anderson	1814 —	Two R.B.	748 A	——
—	Lord Nelson	Robert Spottiswoode	—	L. & R.B.	284 E	——
1803 Jan. 1	Admiral Rainier	William Lay	1803 Sept. 27	—	342 B & C	From Calcutta to England.
Jan. 3	Charlton	Thomas Welladvice	1804 June 25	— L. & R.B.	301 C 301 H	To Calcutta.
Jan. 6	Calcutta	William Maxwell	Nov. 8	— L. & R.B.	308 M 308 Y	To Madras and Calcutta.
Jan. 6	Earl Howe	Robert Burrowes	June 27	— L. & R.B.	203 D 203 L	To Madras and Bengal.

Log begins.	Ship.	Captain.	Log ends.	Ledger or Receipt Book.	Reference Number.	Remarks.
1803 Jan. 6	Hugh Inglis	William Fairfax	1805 Mar. 19	— L. & R.B.	231 B 231 I	To Madras and Bengal.
Jan. 7	Ruby	John Hitchings	1803 Aug. 17	[Three J.]	379 A, B, & C.	From Calcutta to England.
Jan. 8	Lord Castlereagh	George Robertson	1805 Mar. 23	— L. & R.B.	188 A 188 I	To Madras, Bengal, and Bencoolen, &c.
Jan. 19	Lady Castlereagh	William Edmeades	1804 Dec. 11	— L. & R.B.	197 A 197 I	To Bengal.
Jan. 24	Earl Mornington	B. Fergusson	1803 July 5	—	375 B	From Madras to England.
Jan. 24	Warren Hastings	Thomas Larkins	1804 Sept. 24	— L. and two R.B.	9 H 9 FF	To China.
Jan. 24	Wexford	John Henry Pelly succeeded by William Stanley Clarke.	Sept. 20	— L. & R.B.	173 A 173 H	To Madras and China.
Jan. 26	Huddart	Thomas Gabriel Bayliff.	June 5	— L. & R.B.	217 A 217 I	To Bombay.
Jan. 29	Ann and Amelia	— Galloway	1803 Oct. 10	—	80 A	From Calcutta and Madras to England.
Feb. 2	Union	John Macintosh	1804 April 30	— L. & R.B.	117 D 117 R	To Madras.
Feb. 5	Mangles	H. Reid	1803 Oct. 10	—	89 A	From Calcutta to England.
Feb. 7	Coutts	Robert Torin	1804 Sept. 26	— L. & R.B.	171 C 171 K	To China.
Feb. 7	Dorsetshire	Robert Hunter Brown	Sept. 27	— L. & R.B.	13 B 13 L	To China.
Feb. 7	Europe	William Gelston	Dec. 23	— L. & R.B.	204 C 204 L	To Madras and Bengal.
Feb. 7	Exeter	Henry Meriton	Sept. 17	— L. & R.B.	138 L 138 W	To China.
Feb. 7	Marquis Cornwallis	Isaac Godsalve Richardson.	1803 Sept. 12	— L. and two R.B.	336 B & C 336 D	From Bombay to England.
Feb. 12	Ceylon	Thomas Hudson	1804 Nov. 13	— L. & R.B.	291 A 291 H	To Bombay, Calcutta, and Madras.
Feb. 15	Ocean	John Mertho	1803 Oct. 27	—	232 J	To Port Philip (Australia).
Feb. 18	Essex	George Bonham	1805 April 9	— L. & R.B.	229 R 229 PP	To Ceylon and Bombay.
Feb. 19	Cumbrian	- -	1803 Oct. 3	—	83 A	From Bombay to England.
Feb. 21	Warley	Henry Wilson	1804 Sept. 20	— L. & R.B.	182 F 182 Q	To China.
Feb. 21	Preston	Henry Sturrock	Dec. 8	— L. & R.B.	307 C 307 I	To Calcutta, Madras, and Bencoolen.
Feb. 22	Earl of Abergavenny	John Wordsworth	Sept. 28	— L. and two R.B.	341 F 341 L	To Whampoa.
Feb. 22	Woodford	James Martin	1805 Mar. 29	— L. & R.B.	265 G 265 P	To Whampoa.
Feb. 25	Hope	James Pendergrass	1804 Sept. 26	— L. & R.B.	168 G 168 Q	To China.
Mar. 5	Princess Mary	Andrew Grieve	1805 Feb. 18	— L. & R.B.	381 F 381 M	To Calcutta.
Mar. 8	Ganges	William Moffatt	1804 Oct. 4	— L. & R.B.	86 L 86 Y	To China.
Mar. 24	Alfred	James Farquharson	Sept. 24	— L. & R.B.	140 K 140 Y	To China.
Mar. 30	Lord Melville	Charles Lennox	1805 April 17	— L. & R.B.	144 A 144 H	To Bengal and Madras.
Mar. 26	Auspicious	John Barker	1804 Jan. 17	—	344 A & B	From Calcutta to England.

Log begins.	Ship.	Captain.	Log ends.	Ledger or Receipt Book.	Reference Number.	Remarks.
1803 April 25	Earl Spencer - -	Charles Raitt -	1805 April 16	— L. & R.B.	227 D 227 K	To Bengal and Madras.
April 25	Glory - -	Thomas Rumbold Taylor, succeeded by John Perry and Robert James Douglas.	Mar. 15	— L. & R.B.	295 A 295 C	To Madras and Colombo.
April 28	Tigris -	Charles Graham -	1804 Dec. 31	— L. & R.B.	219 B 219 I	To Bengal.
May 8	General Stuart - -	Thomas Mortimer -	Nov. 23	— L. & R.B.	218 B 218 I	To Madras.
May 12	Northampton -	Robert Barker -	1805 Feb. 9	— L. & R.B.	198 C 198 P	To Bengal.
May 13	Ann -	Thomas Price	Mar. 6	— L. & R.B.	211 C 211 K	To Bombay and Madras.
July 7	Georgiana -	Henry Leigh - -	1807 April 25	— L. & R.B.	156 E & F 156 N	To St. Helena and Cape of Good Hope.
July 7	Lowjee Family -	Thomas Kidd -	1803 Dec. 13	—	343 A	From Bombay to England.
Aug. 5	Euphrates -	George Welstead -	1805 April 12	— L. & R.B.	262 A 262 F	To Madras and Calcutta.
Aug. 22	Britannia -	Jonathan Birch -	April 15	— L. & R.B.	285 DDD 285 W	To Madras.
Sept. 11	United Kingdom -	George Richardson -	1804 Jan. 21	—	277 B (2)	From Madras to England.
Oct. 24	Winchelsea	Walter Campbell -	1805 Oct. 28	— L. & R.B.	4 F 4 V	To Bombay and China.
Oct. 26	Cirencester - -	Thomas Robertson	Nov. 20	— L. & R.B.	179 E 179 M	To Bombay, Madras, and China.
Oct. 28	Walmer Castle - -	Essex Henry Bond	Nov. 5	— L. & R.B.	181 D 181 M	To Bencoolen and China.
Nov. 28	Thames - -	John Skottowe -	Nov. 25	— L. & R.B.	8 J 8 CC	To China.
Nov. 30	David Scott - -	Charles Jones - -	April 30	— L. & R.B.	183 D 183 O	To Bombay and Madras.
Dec. 5	Marchioness of Exeter	Alexander Nash	Oct. 23	— L. & R.B.	166 B 166 I	To Madras and Bengal.
Dec. 7	Elphinstone - -	Milliken Craig -	Mar. 29	— L. & R.B.	201 A 201 G	To Bombay and Bengal.
Dec. 7	Marquis Wellesley -	Charles Le Blanc -	Oct. 31	— L. & R.B.	212 C 212 I	To Madras and Bengal.
Dec. 14	Fame - -	John Valentine Baker.	Sept. 9	— L. & R.B.	242 C 242 F	To Madras and Calcutta.
Dec. 15	Marquis of Ely - -	Andrew Hannay succeeded by Arthur Augustus Brocas.	Nov. 7	— L. & R.B.	193 B 193 J	To Madras and China.
Dec. 15	Sir William Bensley	Robert Rhode -	Sept. 7	— L. & R.B.	247 B 247 H	To Madras and Calcutta.
Dec. 17	Canton -	Thomas Lushington -	Nov. 14	— L. & R.B.	288 G 288 O	To Madras and Whampoa.
Dec. 19	Lady Jane Dundas -	Hon. Hugh Lindsay	Oct. 26	— L. & R.B.	309 C 309 G	To Madras and Calcutta.
Dec. 22	Lord Nelson - -	Wemyss Orrok - succeeded by Frederick Gaillard.	Oct. 10	— L. & R.B.	294 B 294 F	To Madras and Calcutta.
Dec. 24	Sir William Pulteney	J. Marshall - -	1804 Oct. 6	—	190 A	From Bengal to England.
Dec. 30	Union - -	William Stokoe -	Sept. 1	—	177 E (1)	From Bengal to England.
Dec. 31	Eliza Ann - -	Mungo Gilmore -	Sept. 27	—	290 H	From Calcutta to England.
—	Prince of Wales -	John Price - -	1823 —	Two R.B. only.	404 FF 404 GG	The Journal and Ledger were apparently lost with the ship.
—	Princess Royal	- - -	1803 —	R.B. only	405 Y	(Missing.)
—	Sir Edward Hughes -	Thomas Barrow -	1807	L. and two R.B. only.	354 P	—
1804 Jan. 9	Waller - - -	Lieutenant Alexander Davidson, R.N.	1804 April 27	— L. & R.B.	298 A 298 B	From Calcutta to England.
Jan. 14	Lady Burges - -	Archibald F. W. Swinton.	1805 Oct. 26	— L. & R.B.	310 C 310 F	To Bengal.
Jan. 14	Royal Charlotte -	Richard Francklin -	Nov. 29	— L. & R.B.	150 Q 150 H	To China.

Log begins.	Ship.	Captain.	Log ends.	Ledger or Receipt Book.	Reference Number.	Remarks.
1804 Jan. 15	Perseverance	James Tweedale	1805 Oct. 25	— L. & R.B.	255 D 255 K	To Whampoa.
Jan. 18	Dover Castle	George Richardson	Oct. 19	— L. & R.B.	232 C 232 I	To Calcutta.
Jan. 18	Neptune	William Donaldson	1803 Nov. 9	— L. & R.B.	98 N 98 FF	To China.
Jan. 18	True Briton	Henry Hughes	1805 Nov. 20	— L. & R.B.	297 P 297 HH	To Whampoa.
Jan. 27	Asia	Henry P. Tremenheere.	Oct. 18	— L. & R.B.	24 O 24 QQ	To Bengal and Madras.
Jan. 27	Bengal	Adam Cumine	Oct. 23	— L. & R.B.	177 C 177 H	To Madras and Bengal.
Feb. 11	Earl St. Vincent	John Brook Samson	Oct. 25	— L. & R.B.	209 D 209 K	To Bombay, Tellicherry, &c.
Feb. 11	Walthamstow	Donald McLeod	Oct. 23	— L. & R.B.	196 C 196 I	To Colombo and Bombay.
Feb. 25	Arniston	James Jameson	Nov. 18	— L. & R.B.	149 E 149 M	To China.
Feb. 25	Ceres	William Dunsford	Oct. 28	— L. & R.B.	215 N 215 CC	To China.
Feb. 25	Cuffnells	Henry Halkett	Nov. 4	— L. & two R.B.	178 D 178 K	To China.
Feb. 25	Taunton Castle	Thomas Burston Peirce.	Nov. 21	— L. & R.B.	107 F 107 O	To China.
Feb. 27	Alnwick Castle	Albert Gledstanes	Oct. 28	— L. & R.B.	189 B 189 I	To China.
Feb. 28	Anna	Thomas Scott	Jan. 11	—	292 E	From Bengal to England.
Mar. 1	Maria	William Brown Greenway.	Mar. 30	—	291 (A) B	From Calcutta to England.
Mar. 12	Tottenham	James Dalrymple	1806 Jan. 22	— L. & R.B.	199 B 199 H	To Bengal and Bencoolen.
Mar. 15	Lord Eldon	Jasper Swete succeeded by J. W. Young.	Jan. 15	— L. & R.B.	143 B 143 J	To Madras, Bengal, and Bencoolen.
April 4	Worcester	Searles Wood	Feb. 8	— L. & R.B.	278 P 278 GG	To Madras and Bombay.
April 5	Experiment	Peter Campbell	1805 Oct. 18	— L. & R.B.	127 D 127 G	To Bombay.
April 16	Airly Castle	John Mackintosh succeeded by William Burgess.	1806 July 9	— L. & R.B.	321 I 321 Q	To Bengal and Madras.
April 16	Lord Hawkesbury	James Timbrell	Mar. 29	— L. & R.B.	323 G 323 O	To Madras and Bengal.
April 30	Alexander	John R. Francklin	1805 Oct. 28	— L. & R.B.	174 D 174 K	To Bengal and Madras.
April 30	Monarch	Stephen Hawes	Oct. 22	— L. & R.B.	300 B 300 G	To Calcutta and Madras.
May 3	Sovereign	Richard Meriton succeeded by Henry Vaughan.	Aug. 1	— L. & R.B.	195 D 195 K	To Bengal and Madras.
May 31	Indus	George Weltden	Dec. 21	— L. & R.B.	225 A 225 G	To Madras.
May 31	Union	William Stokoe	1804 Oct. 6	—	117 E (2)	Portion of Journal of voyage from Bengal to England.
June 1	Travers	Thomas Sanders	1806 July 12	— L. & R.B.	279 C 279 G	To Calcutta and Bencoolen.
June 6	Lord Keith	Patrick Ramage	Feb. 6	— L. & R.B.	187 A 187 I	To Madras and Bengal.
June 7	Union	John Mackintosh	May 20	— L. & R.B.	117 F 117 S	To Bengal.
June 23	Harriet	William Lynch	Feb. 3	— L. & R.B.	275 I 275 P	To Madras and Calcutta.
June 25	Ocean	Thomas McTaggart	Jan. 23	— L. & R.B.	222 L 222 Y	To Madras and Calcutta.
June 30	United Kingdom	John Henry Pelly	Feb. 10	— L. & R.B.	277 C 277 H	To Madras and Calcutta.
July 7	Haddart	William John Eastfield.	Feb. 3	— L. & R.B.	217 B 217 J	To Madras and Bengal.
July 10	Devaynes	William Adderley	July 4	— L. & R.B.	228 B 228 H	To Bombay, Madras, &c.
July 12	Skelton Castle	James Normand	Feb. 1	— L. & R.B.	304 D 304 F	To Bombay.
Aug. 26	Ocean	John Mertho	1805 Oct. 15	—	222 K	From Port Jackson, New South Wales, to China.
Oct. 19	Royal George	Charles B. Gribble	1806 Oct. 28	— L. & R.B.	17 K 17 BB	To Bombay and China.

Log begins.	Ship.	Captain.	Log ends.	Ledger or Receipt Book.	Reference Number.	Remarks.
1804 Oct. 22	Wexford - -	William Stanley Clarke.	1806 Oct. 22	— L. & R.B.	173 B 173 I	To Bombay and China.
Oct. 24	Bombay Castle -	Archibald Hamilton	Nov. : 7	— L. & R.B.	125 K 125 U	To Bombay and China.
Oct. 25	Henry Addington	John Kirkpatrick -	Oct. 11	— L. & R.B.	170 D 170 L	To Bombay and China.
Nov. 16	Earl Howe	Anthony Murray	Oct. 9	— L. & R.B.	203 E 203 M	To Madras and China.
Nov. 17	Lord Duncan -	Edward C. Bradford	Sept. 23	— L. & R.B.	210 D 210 K	To Madras and Calcutta.
Nov. 19	Charlton	George Wood -	Sept. 18	— L. & R.B.	301 D 301 I	To Madras and Calcutta.
Nov. 21	Surrey -	John A. Cumberlege	Sept. 8	— L. & R.B.	191 A 191 H	To Madras and Bengal.
Nov. 22	Ocean	James John Williamson.	Nov. 14	— L. & R.B.	222 M 222 Z	To Madras and China.
Nov. 24	Walpole - -	James Sandilands	July 22	— L. & R.B.	293 W 293 SS	To Madras and Calcutta.
Nov. 25	Ceylon -	Thomas Hudson -	Sept. 12	— L. & R.B.	291 B 291 I	To Madras, Calcutta, &c.
Nov. 29	Belle	Alexander Foggs -	1805 Sept. 7	—	306 A	From Calcutta to England.
Dec. 7	Windham -	John Stewart -	1806 Oct. 14	— L. & R.B.	230 F 230 P	To Madras and China.
Dec. 8	Phœnix	John Ramsden -	1807 June 20	— L. & R.B.	175 H 175 T	To Bengal, Bombay, &c.
Dec. 13	Carmarthen -	John C. Lochner -	1806 July 8	— L. & R.B.	142 B 142 J	To Madras and Calcutta.
Dec. 20	Calcutta - -	John Reddie -	1807 June 8	— L. & R.B.	308 N 308 Z	To Calcutta, Madras, &c.
Dec. 31	Admiral Gardner -	George Saltwell	1806 Aug. 30	— L. & R.B.	284 D 284 I	To Madras and Colombo.
—	Baring -	Dixon Meadows	—	L. & R.B. only	246 I	——
—	Duke of Montrose -	John Paterson	—	L. & R.B. only	775 N	——
—	Glatton -	Charles Drummond -	1805 —	L. & R.B. only	172 HH	——
—	Princess Charlotte -	John Logan - -	1808 —	R.B. only	245 H	——
1805 Jan. 1	Metcalfe	Matthew Isacke -	1806 Sept. 18	— L. & R.B.	167 A 167 G	To Bombay, Bengal, and Madras.
Jan. 8	Earl Camden -	Henry Morse Samson	Sept. 6	— L. & R.B.	303 B 303 D	To Bombay, Pulo Penang, and Colombo.
Jan. 9	City of London -	Samuel Landon -	Aug. 26	— L. & R.B.	151 C 151 I	To Bombay.
Jan. 11	Devonshire - -	James Murray	Sept. 23	— L. & R.B.	272 I 272 U	To Madras, Calcutta, Colombo, &c.
Jan. 14	Cumberland -	William Ward Farrer	Oct. 25	— L. & R.B.	202 B 202 H	To Madras and China.
Jan. 14	Dorsetshire	Robert Hunter Brown	Dec. 19	— L. & R.B.	13 C 13 M	To Madras, Calcutta, and China.
Jan. 14	Ganges -	Thomas Talbot Harrington.	1807 May 29	— Three R.B.	86 M 86 Z 86 AA & 86 BB	To Madras, Bengal, and China.
Jan. 14	Warley -	Henry Wilson -	1806 Nov. 18	— L. & R.B.	182 G 182 R	To Madras and China.
Jan. 17	Lady Castlereagh -	Thomas Garland Murray.	Sept. 9	— L. & R.B.	197 B 197 J	To Bengal.
Jan. 18	Castle Eden - -	Richard Colnett -	July 12	— L. & R.B.	296 C 296 I	To Madras, Calcutta, and Bencoolen.
Jan. 18	Coutts - -	James Hay -	Nov. 3	— L. & R.B.	171 D 171 L	To Madras and China.
Jan. 18	Hope - - -	James Pendergrass -	Oct. 30	— L. & R.B.	168 H 168 R	To Madras and China.
Jan. 22	Preston - -	Henry Sturrock -	1807 May 13	— L. & R.B.	307 D 307 J	To Madras, Calcutta, and Bombay.
Jan. 24	General Stuart	John Rogers -	1806 June 13	— L. & R.B.	218 C 218 J	To Madras and Bengal.
Jan. 24	Jane, Duchess of Gordon.	John Cameron	1807 June 22	— L. & R.B.	299 A 299 B	To Madras and Calcutta.
Feb. 12	Comet - -	James Moring -	June 4	— L. & R.B.	302 C 302 E	To Madras, Calcutta, &c.

Log begins.	Ship.	Captain.	Log ends.	Ledger or Receipt Book.	Reference Number.	Remarks.
1805 Feb. 27	Tigris	Charles Graham	1807 May 20	— L. & R.B.	219 C 219 J	To Bengal and Madras.
Mar. 1	Retreat	William Hay	1806 May 16	— L. & R.B.	192 A 192 F	To Bombay.
April 1	Europe	William Gelston	1807 April 17	— L. & R.B.	203 D 203 M	To Madras and Bengal.
April 4	Ann	James Masson	May 10	— L. & R.B.	211 D 211 L	To Madras and Calcutta.
April 5	William Pitt	William Edmedes	June 22	— L. & R.B.	184 H 184 X	To Madras and Bengal.
April 17	Streatham	John Dale	June 19	— L. & R.B.	185 A 185 H	To Madras and Bengal.
April 19	Glory	Horatio Beevor	April 12	— L. & R.B.	295 B 295 D	To Madras, Calcutta, and Trincomalee.
April 19	Northampton	Robert Barker	May 15	— L. & R.B.	198 D 198 Q	To Madras and Bengal.
April 19	Sarah Christiana	Thomas Mackeson	May 8	— L. & R.B.	282 C 282 F	To Madras and Calcutta.
April 29	Union	Arthur Muter succeeded by James Fairfax.	1805 Nov. 28	— L. & R.B.	117 G 117 T	To Madras and Bengal.
May 2	Diana	John Eckford	1807 May 23	— L. & R.B.	239 A 239 E	To Madras and Calcutta.
May 2	Sir William Pulteney	Henry Christopher	May 28	— L. & R.B.	190 B 190 H	To Bombay and Bengal.
May 4	William Pitt	J. Boyce	Aug. 7	—	184 G	To New South Wales and China.
May 30	Euphrates	Philip Herbert	Aug. 4	— L. & R.B.	262 B 262 G	To Calcutta.
June 14	Northumberland	George Raincock	Nov. 5	— L. & R.B.	141 O 141 FF	To Bengal, Madras, and Bombay.
June 15	Britannia	Jonathan Birch	1805 Oct. 31	— L. & R.B.	285 EEE 285 X	To Madras.
July 10	Hope	-	1806 June 2	—	168 I	From Calcutta to England.
July 20	Albion	Benjamin Richardson	1808 Feb. 23	— L. & R.B.	81 I 81 T	To Madras, Bengal, and China.
Aug. 26	Milford	George Douglas	1806 May 16	—	281 A	From Bombay to England.
Nov. 1	Scaleby Castle	John Guise	Oct. 11	— L. & R.B.	34 F 34 V	From China to England.
Nov. 7	Elphinstone	Milliken Craig	1807 Aug. 22	— L. & R.B.	201 B 201 H	To Bombay and China.
Nov. 11	Winchelsea	William Moffatt	Aug. 18	— L. & R.B.	4 G 4 W	To Bombay and China.
Nov. 13	Perseverance	James Tweedale	1808 Mar. 19	— L. & R.B.	255 E 255 L	To Bencoolen, Penang, and Whampoa.
Nov. 21	Hugh Inglis	William Fairfax	1807 Oct. 19	— L. & R.B.	231 C 231 J	To Madras and Calcutta.
Nov. 27	Ceres	William Dunsford	Aug. 27	— L. & R.B.	215 O 215 DD	To Bombay and China.
Dec. 3	Margaret	Benjamin Fergusson	1806 July 2	—	280 A	From Calcutta to England.
Dec. 5	Lady Jane Dundas	Hon. Hugh Lindsay	1807 Sept. 9	— L. & R.B.	309 D 309 H	To Madras, Calcutta, and Penang.
Dec. 6	Sir William Bensley	George Hooper	July 30	— L. & R.B.	247 C 247 I	To Madras and Calcutta.
Dec. 9	Alexander	John R. Francklin	Oct. 12	— L. & R.B.	174 E 174 L	To Madras and Bengal.
Dec. 9	Alnwick Castle	Charles Elton Prescott.	Aug. 25	— L. & R.B.	189 C 189 J	To Madras and China.
Dec. 9	David Scott	John Locke	Aug. 19	— L. & R.B.	183 E 183 P	To Madras and China.
Dec. 9	Essex	George Bonham	Aug. 29	— L. & R.B.	229 S 229 QQ	To Madras and China.
Dec. 9	Lord Castlereagh	Christopher Kymer	Oct. 20	— L. & R.B.	188 B 188 J	To Bengal and Madras.
Dec. 9	Lord Nelson	William Charles Hutton.	Oct. 29	— L. & R.B.	294 C 294 G	To Calcutta, Madras, and Bombay.
Dec. 10	Walmer Castle	Luke Dodds	Aug. 22	— L. & R.B.	181 E 181 N	To Bombay and China.
Dec. 12	Bengal	Adam Cumine	Oct. 21	— L. & two R.B.	177 D 177 I	To Madras and Bengal.

Log begins.	Ship.	Captain.	Log ends.	Ledger or Receipt Book.	Reference Number.	Remarks.
1805 Dec. 30	Asia	Robert Wardlaw	1807 Oct. 30	— L. & R.B.	24 P 24 RR	To Madras and Bengal.
—	Carnatic		1818 —	Petty Cash Book No. 1	165 AA	——
—	Exeter	Henry Meriton	1806 —	L. only	138 X	——
1806 Jan. 8	Lord Melville	Charles Lennox	1808 May 24	— L. & R.B.	144 H 144 I	To Madras, Bengal, &c.
Jan. 18	Sovereign	Alexander Campbell	1807 Sept. 8	— L. & R.B.	195 E 195 L	To Madras and Calcutta.
Jan. 23	Dover Castle	George Richardson	1808 May 27	— L. & R.B.	232 D 232 J	To Calcutta and Madras.
Feb. 3	Cirencester	Henry Halkett	Mar. 26	— L. & R.B.	179 F 179 N	To China.
Feb. 3	Marquis of Ely	James Dalrymple	Mar. 31	— L. & R.B.	193 C 193 K	To China.
Feb. 3	Marquis Wellesley	Charles Le Blanc	Sept. 29	— L. & R.B.	212 D 212 J	To Bengal and Madras.
Feb. 4	Arniston	Peter Wedderburn	Jan. 6	— L. & R.B.	149 F 149 N	To China.
Feb. 5	Marchioness of Exeter	Alexander Nash	Feb. 24	— L. & R.B.	166 C 166 J	To Madras and Bengal.
Feb. 5	Neptune	Thomas Buchanan	April 21	— L. & R.B.	98 O 98 GG	To China.
Feb. 13	Surat Castle	D. Isbister	1806 Dec. 11	— Cargo Book.	205 E 205 F	From China to England.
Feb. 20	Monarch	Stephen Hawes	1807 Oct. 28	— L. & R.B.	300 C 300 H	To Madras and Calcutta.
Feb. 20	Royal Charlotte	Robert Patterson	1808 Mar. 23	— L. & R.B.	150 R 150 JJ	To China.
Feb. 24	Glatton	James Halliburton	Mar. 31	— L. & R.B.	172 O 172 I I	To China.
Mar. 1	Thames	Matthew Riches	Mar. 9	— L. & R.B.	8 K 8 DD	To China.
Mar. 4	Experiment	James Normand	1807 May 29	— L. & R.B.	127 E 127 H	To Bombay.
Mar. 8	Tottenham	Thomas Jones	1808 May 13	— L. & R.B.	199 C 199 I	To Madras and Bengal.
Mar. 10	Huddart	Thomas Gabriel Bayliff.	1807 Oct. 6	— L. & R.B.	217 C 217 K	To Bombay.
Mar. 12	Indus	George Weltden	1808 Jan. 6	— L. & R.B.	225 B 225 H	To Madras and Calcutta.
Mar. 19	Lord Eldon	John William Young	1807 Dec. 15	— L. & R.B.	143 C 143 K	To Madras and Bengal.
Mar. 20	Lord Keith	Patrick Ramage succeeded by John Mayne.	Dec. 31	— L. & R.B.	187 B 187 J	To Bengal and Bencoolen.
Mar. 21	Baring	Dixon Meadows	1806 July 9	—	246 B	From St. Helena to England.
Mar. 24	Ocean	Thomas McTaggart	1807 Nov. 15	— L. & R.B.	222 N 222 AA	To Bengal and Bencoolen.
Mar. 27	Harriet	William Lynch	Oct. 16	— L. & R.B.	275 J 275 Q	To Calcutta.
April 1	Earl St. Vincent	Charles Jones	Sept. 7	—	209 E	To Bombay and Goa.
May 8	Sir Stephen Lushington.	George Gray	1808 Mar. 1	— L. & R.B.	274 E 274 L	To Colombo and Bombay.
June 6	Earl Spencer	George Heming	Feb. 11	— L. & R.B.	227 E 227 L	To Colombo and Bombay.
June 28	Union	John Macintosh	May 11	— L. & R.B.	117 H 117 U	To Madras and Calcutta.
Aug. 4	Dorsetshire	Robert Hunter Brown.	1806 Nov. 2	—	13 D	[Journal of a part of the same voyage as that recorded in 13 C. To Madras, Calcutta, and China.]
Sept. 4	Carmarthen	James Ross	1808 Jan. 11	— L. & R.B.	142 C 142 K	To Bombay.

Log begins.	Ship.	Captain.	Log ends.	Ledger or Receipt Book.	Reference Number.	Remarks.
1806 Sept. 4	General Stuart	John Rogers	1808 May 11	— L. & R.B.	218 D 218 K	To Madras and Bengal.
Sept. 4	Travers	John Collins	Feb. 29	— L. & R.B.	279 D 279 H	To Bombay.
Sept. 29	Devaynes	William Adderley	April 9	— L. & R.B.	223 C 223 I	To Madras and Calcutta.
Oct. 12	Mercury	- -	1807 April 17	—	454 H	From Calcutta to England.
Oct. 27	Alfred	George Welstead	1809 Feb. 10	— L. & R.B.	140 L 140 Z	To Bencoolen and China.
Nov. 3	Retreat	William Hay	1808 July 28	— L. & R.B.	192 B 192 G	To China.
Nov. 10	Castle Eden	Richard Colnett	Oct. 5	— L.	296 D 296 J	To Madras and Calcutta.
Nov. 12	Duke of Montrose	John Paterson	1809 Feb. 10	— L. & R.B.	775 G 775 O	To Calcutta.
Nov. 15	Admiral Gardner	William Eastfield	1808 May 31	— L. & two R.B.	284 F 284 J	To Madras and Calcutta.
Nov. 28	William Pitt	J. Boyce	1807 July 24	—	184 I	From China to England.
Dec. 8	Lord Duncan	Edward C. Bradford	1808 Oct. 4	— L. & R.B.	210 E 210 L	To Madras and Bengal.
Dec. 9	City of London	Joseph Yates	Sept. 28	— L. & R.B.	151 D 151 J	To Calcutta.
Dec. 9	Metcalfe	Matthew Isacke	Oct. 1	— L. & R.B.	167 B 167 H	To Bombay, Madras, and Bengal.
Dec. 9	United Kingdom	William Parker D'Esterre.	May 31	— L. & R.B.	277 D 277 I	To Madras.
Dec. 9	Worcester	Searles Wood	1809 Feb. 14	— L. & R.B.	277 Q 277 HH	To Madras, Malacca, and Bombay.
Dec. 12	Walthamstow	Donald McLeod	1807 Oct. 28	— L. & R.B.	196 D 196 J	To Bengal.
Dec. 16	Sinclair	J. H. Jackson	Aug. 5	(Two J.)	283 A 283 B	From Whampoa to England.
—	Britannia	Jonathan Birch	1808 —	L. & two R.B. only.	285 Y	——
—	Fame	James Jameson	1809 —	R. B. only.	242 G	——
—	Lady Burges	Archibald F. W. Swinton.	1806 —	R. B. only.	310 G	——
—	Nottingham	Walter Campbell	1808 —	L. & R.B. only.	287 CC	——
—	True Briton	William Stanley Clarke.	1812 —	L. & R.B. only.	297 I I	——
1807 Jan. 8	Airly Castle	William Burgess	1808 Oct. 13	— L. & R.B.	321 J 321 R	To Calcutta, Madras, &c.
Jan. 8	Ceylon	Thomas Hudson succeeded by W. H. Harris.	1809 May 23	— L. & R.B.	291 C 291 J	To Madras, Penang, and Bengal.
Jan. 8	Charlton	George Wood	1808 Oct. 17	— L. & R.B.	301 E 301 J	To Bombay, Calcutta, &c.
Jan. 8	Lord Hawkesbury	Samuel Smith succeeded by Edward Lynch Harmsworth.	Sept. 20	— L. & R.B.	323 H 323 P	To Calcutta.
Jan. 8	Surrey	John Altham Cumberlege.	Sept. 20	— L. & R.B.	191 B 191 I	To Madras and Bengal.
Jan. 8	Walpole	James Sandilands	Dec. 31	— R.B.	293 X 293 TT	To Madras, Calcutta, and Penang.
Jan. 23	Devonshire	James Murray	Oct. 13	— L. & R.B.	272 J 272 V	To Bombay, Goa, &c.
Jan. 23	Taunton Castle	James Timbrell	Oct. 31	— L. & R.B.	107 G 107 P	To China.
Jan. 26	Earl Camden	Henry Morse Samson	Oct. 25	— L. & R.B.	303 C 303 F	To Penang and Whampoa.
Jan. 28	Hope	James Pendergrass	Nov. 1	— L. & R.B.	168 J 168 S	To China.
Jan. 29	Coutts	James Hay	Nov. 2	— L. & R.B.	171 E 171 M	To China.

25005. A a

Log begins.	Ship.	Captain.	Log ends.	Ledger or Receipt Book.	Reference Number.	Remarks.
1807 Jan. 29	Woodford	James Martin	1808 Oct. 31	— L. & R.B.	265 H 265 Q	To China.
Jan. 31	Lady Castlereagh	Thomas Garland Murray.	Sept. 25	— L. & R.B.	197 C 197 K	To Madras and Bengal.
Jan. 31	Surat Castle	Alexander Robertson	1809 July 12	— L. & R.B.	205 F 205 K	To China.
April 3	Royal George	Charles B. Gribble	June 28	— L. & R.B.	17 L 17 CC	To Bombay, Madras, Persia, and China.
April 11	Warley	William Augustus Montagu.	Oct. 29	— L. & R.B.	182 H 182 S	To Madras, Bombay, and China.
April 13	Earl Howe	Anthony Murray	1808 Sept. 26	— L. & R.B.	203 F 203 N	To Bengal and Madras.
April 13	Wexford	Charles Barnard	1809 July 10	— L. & R.B.	173 C 173 J	To Madras, Bombay, and Persia.
April 14	Windham	John Stewart	1808 Aug. 19	— L. & R.B.	230 G 230 Q	To Bengal and Bencoolen.
June 20	Georgiana	Henry Leigh	1809 May 15	— L. & R.B.	156 G 156 O	To Calcutta.
July 3	Tigris	Dugald MacDougall	June 27	— L. & R.B.	219 D 219 K	To Madras and Bengal.
July 4	Northampton	Thomas Sanders	Feb. 2	— L. & R.B.	198 E 198 R	To Bengal.
July 4	Union	Frederick Gaillard	Jan. 13	—	117 I	To Bombay.
July 6	Sarah Christiana	Thomas Mackeson	Jan. 16	— L. & R.B.	305 A 282 G	To Calcutta.
July 10	Ann	James Masson	June 17	— L. & R.B.	211 E 211 M	To Madras and Calcutta.
July 10	Diana	John Marshall	June 21	— L. & R.B.	239 B 239 F	To Madras and Calcutta.
July 15	Sir William Pulteney	Henry Christopher	Feb. 10	— L. & R.B.	190 C 190 I	To Bombay and Surat.
Oct. 15	Elphinstone	Milliken Craig	Oct. 20	— L. & R.B.	201 C 201 I	To Bombay and China.
Oct. 15	Essex	Richard Nisbet	Oct. 27	— L. & R.B.	229 T 229 RR	To Bombay and Whampoa.
Oct. 15	Phœnix	John Ramsden	July 6	— L. & R.B.	175 I 175 V	To Madras.
Oct. 15	Walmer Castle	Luke Dodds	Nov. 28	— L. & R.B.	181 F 181 O	To Bencoolen and China.
Nov. 30	Alnwick Castle	Charles Elton Prescott	Nov. 21	— L. & R.B.	189 D 189 K	To Madras and China.
Nov. 30	Canton	John Christopher Lochner.	Nov. 25	— L. & R.B.	288 H 288 P	To Madras and China.
Nov. 30	Ceres	William Dunsford	Sept. 14	— L. & R.B.	215 P 215 EE	To Madras and China.
Nov. 30	David Scott	John Locke	Nov. 20	— L. & R.B.	183 F 183 Q	To Madras and China.
Nov. 30	Dorsetshire	Robert Hunter Brown	Dec. 18	— L. & R.B.	13 E 13 N	To Madras and China.
Nov. 30	Ocean	James John Williamson.	Oct. 21	— L. & R.B.	222 O 222 BB	To Madras and Whampoa.
Dec. 3	Exeter	Henry Meriton	April 24	— L. & R.B.	138 M 138 Y	To Madras and China.
Dec. 9	Baring	James Carnegie	1808 May 30	— L. & R.B.	246 C 246 J	To Madras.
Dec. 14	Hugh Inglis	William Fairfax	1809 Aug. 24	— L. & R.B.	231 D 231 K	To Madras and Bengal.
Dec. 14	Preston	Henry Sturrock	June 19	— L. & R.B.	307 E 307 K	To Madras and Calcutta.
—	Calcutta	William Maxwell	1808 —	Three R.B. only.	308 AA & 308 BB	——
—	Cuffnells	Robert Welbank	1809 —	L. & R.B. only.	178 L	——
—	Cumberland	William Ward Farrer	1808 —	L. & R.B. only.	202 I	——
—	Experiment	John Logan	—	R.B. only.	127 I	——
—	Ganges	Thomas Talbot Harrington.	—	—	86 BB	Containing a List of Ship's Company taken on board the "Earl St. Vincent" from "Ganges," which was lost off Cape of Good Hope.
—	Henry Addington	John Kirkpatrick	—	L.&R.B. only.	170 M	——

Log begins.	Ship.	Captain.	Log ends.	Ledger or Receipt Book.	Reference Number.	Remarks.
1807 —	Winchelsea	William Moffatt	1812 —	L. & R.B.	4 X	——
1808 Jan. 13	William Pitt	Charles Graham	1809 Aug. 24	— L. & R.B.	184 J 184 Y	To Madras and Bengal.
Jan. 14	Lord Castlereagh	Christopher Kymer	1810 May 12	— L. & R.B.	188 C 188 K	To Bengal and Bencoolen.
Jan. 27	Euphrates	Philip Herbert	1809 Aug. 19	— L. & R.B.	262 C 262 H	To Madras and Calcutta.
Jan. 27	Sir William Bensley	George Hooper	Aug. 9	— L. & R.B.	247 D 247 J	To Madras and Calcutta.
Jan. 27	Sovereign	Alexander Campbell	Aug. 8	— L. & R.B.	195 F 195 M	To Madras and Bengal.
Jan. 27	Streatham	John Dale	1810 Aug. 6	— L. & R.B.	185 B 185 I	To Madras and Bengal.
Jan. 28	Alexander	Thomas Price	1809 June 17	— L. & R.B.	174 F 174 M	To Bombay.
Jan. 28	Earl St. Vincent	John Brook Samson	Aug. 13	— L. & R.B.	209 F 209 L	To Bombay and Goa.
Jan. 28	Northumberland	John R. Francklin	Aug. 23	— L. & R.B.	141 P 141 GG	To Madras and Bengal.
Jan. 29	Lord Keith	Peter Campbell	1810 Jan. 20	— L. & R.B.	187 C 187 K	To Ceylon and Bengal.
Feb. 11	Harriet	William Lynch	1809 Aug. 12	— L. & R.B.	275 K 275 R	To Madras and Calcutta.
Feb. 11	Huddart	William Nesbitt	July 17	— L. & R.B.	217 D 217 L	To Bombay.
Mar. 7	Indus	George Weltden	Aug. 11	— L. & R.B.	225 C 225 I	To Madras and Calcutta.
Mar. 29	Lord Eldon	John William Young	Aug. 23	[Two J.] L. & R.B.	143 D & E 143 L	To Bombay.
Mar. 29	Monarch	Stephen Hawes	1810 Feb. 27	— L. & R.B.	300 D 300 I	To Madras and Calcutta.
Mar. 29	Travers	John Collins	1808 Nov. 7	— R.B.	279 E 279 I	This ship was wrecked on 7th November 1808.
April 4	Carmarthen	James Ross	1809 Oct. 20	— L. & R.B.	142 D 142 L	To Bombay.
April 9	Earl Spencer	George Homing	1810 Feb. 23	— L. & R.B.	227 F 227 M	To Calcutta and Penang.
June 24	Walthamstow	Thomas Jones	Sept. 1	— L. & R.B.	196 E 196 X	To Madras and Bengal.
July 6	General Stuart	James Jameson	May 19	— L. & R.B.	218 E 218 L	To Madras and Bengal.
July 7	Ocean	Thomas McTaggart	July 31	— L. & R.B. Two R.B	222 P 222 CC 222 DD	To Madras and Calcutta.
July 7	Sir Stephen Lushington.	James Hay	1809 Aug. 10	— L. & R.B.	274 F 274 M	To Madras.
July 8	Union	George Simpson	1810 Oct. 23	— L. & R.B.	117 J 117 V	To Madras and Bengal.
July 11	Tottenham	Henry Hughes	Aug. 6	— L. & R.B.	199 D 199 J	To Madras and Bengal.
July 12	Devaynes	James Normand	Aug. 8	— L. & R.B.	223 D 223 J	To Bombay, Madras, and Bengal.
Aug. 1	Thomas Grenville	William Patterson	1809 Oct. 30	— L. & R.B. L.	10 A 10 O (A) 10 O (B)	From China to England.
Sept. 3	Ceylon	John Stewart	1808 Oct. 6	—	291 D	The end of a missing Journal.
Oct. 17	Cuffnells	Robert Welbank	1811 Feb. 8	— L. & R.B.	178 L 178 M	To Bencoolen and China.
Oct. 17	Neptune	William Donaldson	1810 Oct. 26	— L. & R.B.	98 P 98 HH	To Bombay and China.
Oct. 17	Warren Hastings	Thomas Larkins	Sept. 25	—	9 I	To Calcutta and China.
Oct. 18	Scaleby Castle	John Loch	Oct. 1	— L. & R.B.	34 G 34 W	To Bombay and China.

Log begins.	Ship.	Captain.	Log ends.	Ledger or Receipt Book.	Reference Number.	Remarks.
1808 Oct. 20	Lord Melville	John Nelson Whyte	1810 Sept. 5	— L. & R.B.	144 C 144 J	To Madras and Bengal.
Oct. 24	Cumberland	Peter Wedderburn	Oct. 8	— L. & R.B.	202 C 202 J	To Bombay and China.
Nov. 16	Perseverance	James Tweedale	Oct. 2	— L. & R.B.	255 F 255 M	To Madras, Penang, and China.
Nov. 18	Carnatic	A. F. W. Swinton	Aug. 25	— L. & R.B.	165 H 165 U	To Madras and Bengal.
Nov. 18	Nottingham	Walter Campbell	Oct. 6	— L. & R.B.	287 N 287 DD	To Madras and China.
Dec. 3	Baring	James Carnegie	Aug. 29	— L. & R.B.	246 D 246 K	To Madras and Bengal.
Dec. 8	Lady Castlereagh	William Hamilton	Sept. 14	— L. & R.B.	197 D 197 L	To Bengal and Madras.
Dec. 8	Lord Duncan	Edward C. Bradford	Aug. 25	— L. & R.B.	210 F 210 M	To Madras and Bengal.
Dec. 8	United Kingdom	William Parker D'Esterre.	1811 Mar. 1	— R.B.	277 E & F 277 J	To Calcutta. Taken by the French, 18th November 1809.
—	Asia	Henry P. Tremenheere.	1808 —	R.B. only	24 SS	——
—	Calcutta	- - -	—	R.B. only	308 AA	——
—	Europe	-	1808 —	Two R.B. only.	204 M (a)	——
—	Jane, Duchess of Gordon.	John Cameron	1813 —	Two R.B. only.	259 C	Journal and ledger apparently lost with the ship.
—	Lady Jane Dundas	John Eckford	1815 —	Two R.B. only.	309 I	——
—	Lord Nelson	William Charles Hutton.	1808 —	Two R.B. only.	294 H	——
—	True Briton	George Bonham	1809 —	Two R.B. only.	297 JJ	——
1809 Jan. 2	Castle Eden	Richard Colnett	1810 Aug. 15	— L. & R.B.	296 E 296 K	To Madras, Calcutta, &c.
Jan. 2	City of London	Joseph Yates	1811 Jan. 28	— L. & R.B.	151 E 151 K	To Madras, Bengal, and Bencoolen.
Jan. 2	Glatton	James Halliburton	1810 Aug. 1	— L. & R.B.	172 P 172 JJ	To China.
Jan. 2	Princess Amelia	Edward Balston	Oct. 13	— L. & R.B.	36 K 36 HH	To China.
Jan. 2	Royal Charlotte	Henry Rush	Nov. 8	— L. & R.B.	150 S 150 KK	To China.
Jan. 5	Devonshire	James Murray	Sept. 1	— L. & R.B.	272 K 272 W	To Calcutta and Madras.
Jan. 14	Albion	Benjamin Richardson	Sept. 28	— L. & R.B.	81 J 81 U	To China.
Jan. 14	Metcalfe	Matthew Isacke	Aug. 23	— L. & R.B.	167 C 167 I	To Madras and Bengal.
Jan. 16	Coutts	John Boyce	Nov. 18	— L. & R.B.	171 F 171 N	To China.
Jan. 16	Dover Castle	George Richardson	July 7	— L. & R.B.	232 E 232 K	To Bombay.
Jan. 16	Marchioness of Exeter	Alexander Nash	Sept. 14	— L. & R.B.	166 D 166 K	To Bombay.
Jan. 16	Marquis of Ely	Brook Kay	Oct. 8	— L. & R.B.	193 D 193 L	To China.
Jan. 16	Marquis Wellesley	Charles Le Blanc	Sept. 10	— L. & R.B.	212 E 212 K	To Ceylon and Bengal.
Jan. 16	Surrey	John A. Cumberlege	Sept. 5	— L. & R.B.	191 C 191 J	To Madras and Bengal.
Feb. 9	Taunton Castle	James Timbrell	April 23	— L. & R.B.	107 H 107 Q	To Bombay.
Feb. 16	Thames	Matthew Riches	Nov. 2	— L. & R.B.	8 L 8 EE	To China.
Feb. 22	Retreat	Thomas Herbert Harris.	Aug. 7	— L. & R.B.	192 C 192 H	To Madras and Calcutta.
Mar. 2	Earl Howe	William John Eastfield	Nov. 15	— L. & R.B.	203 G 203 O	To Madras and Bengal.
Mar. 18	Providence	H. Reid	May 22	—	176 A	From Calcutta to England.
April 14	Henry Addington	John Kirkpatrick	Sept. 14	— L. & R.B.	170 E 170 N	To Bengal and Madras.
April 15	William	Rodney Kampt	Feb. 19	—	226 A	To Bombay.

Log begins.	Ship.	Captain.	Log ends.	Ledger or Receipt Book.	Reference Number.	Remarks.
1809 April 17	Boyne	J. Nichol	1810 May 30	—	45 A	From Calcutta to England.
May 1	Northampton	Thomas Sanders	Aug. 9	— L. & R.B.	198 F 198 S	To Bombay and Ceylon.
May 1	Sarah Christiana	Thomas Mackeson	Nov. 14	— L. & R.B.	282 D 282 H	To Calcutta and Madras.
May 1	Sir William Pulteney	Henry Christopher	Oct. 31	— L. & R.B.	190 D 190 J	To Bengal.
May 1	Union	Frederick Gaillard	Aug. 18	— L. & R.B.	117 K 117 W	To Bombay.
May 1	William Pitt	William Crowder	Nov. 23	— L. & R.B.	184 K 184 Z	To Bengal and Madras.
May 5	Lady Lushington	George Nicholls	Nov. 2	— L. & R.B.	221 A 221 E	To Bengal.
June 1	David Scott	- -	Feb. 2	—	183 G	From Bombay to England.
June 1	Warren Hastings	C. P. Macfarlane	June 12	— L. & R.B.	9 J 9 GG	To Madras.
June 21	Georgiana	Henry Leigh	1811 Sept. 10	— L. & R.B.	156 H 156 P	To Madras and Bengal.
July 1	Upton Castle	Hugh Adams	1809 Dec. 25	[Two J.]	333 A & B	From Bombay to England.
July 27	Larkins	A. Barclay	1810 Mar. 18	—	104 A	From Bengal to London.
July 30	Lord Castlereagh	R. Cooper	1809 Dec. 10	—	188 D	From Bombay (?) to England.
Oct. 12	Fort William	[?] Parsons	1810 June 29	—	91 H	From the East Indies to England.
Oct. 28	Wexford	William Stanley Clarke.	1811 Sept. 19	— L. & R.B.	173 D 173 K	To Bombay and China.
Nov. 3	Arniston	Samuel Landon	Sept. 19	— L. & R.B.	149 G 149 O	To Bombay and China.
Nov. 11	Winchelsea	Hon. Hugh Lindsay	Aug. 14	— L. & R.B.	4 H 4 Y	To Bombay and China.
Nov. 22	Woodford	James Martin	Oct. 1	— L. & R.B.	265 I 265 R	To Madras and China.
Nov. 23	Alfred	George Welstead	Oct. 9	— L. & R.B.	140 M 140 AA	To Madras and China.
Nov. 28	Cumbrian	John Tate	1810 Aug. 25	—	83 B	From Bombay to London.
Dec. 7	William Pitt	Charles Graham	1812 Mar. 25	— L. & R.B.	184 L 184 AA	To Madras, Bengal, and Borneo.
Dec. 13	Astell	Robert Hay	1811 Oct. 28	— L. & R.B.	12 A 12 L	To Madras and Calcutta.
Dec. 13	Elphinstone	Milliken Craig	Aug. 20	— L. & R.B.	201 D 201 J	To Bombay and China.
Dec. 15	Hugh Inglis	John Wood	1812 April 4	— L. & R.B.	231 E 231 L	To Madras, Calcutta, and Bourbon.
Dec. 19	Ceylon	Henry Meriton	Jan. 8	—	291 E	To the Cape of Good Hope.
Dec. 21	Alexander	William Younghusband.	1811 Dec. 27	— L. & R.B.	174 G 174 N	To Bombay and Madras.
Dec. 21	Euphrates	Philip Herbert	1812 May 7	— L. & R.B.	262 D 262 I	To Madras and Calcutta.
Dec. 22	Europe	W. Gelston	1810 Aug. 29	[Two J.] L. & R.B.	204 E & F 204 N	From Bombay to England.
Dec. 23	Tigris	Dugald MacDougall	1811 May 13	— L. & R.B.	219 E 219 L	To Madras and Bengal.
Dec. 27	Sir Stephen Lushington	James Hay	Oct. 16	— L. & R.B.	274 G 274 N	To Bombay and Madras.
Dec. 28	Northumberland	John R. Francklin	1812 Aug. 24	— L. & R.B. L.	141 Q 141 HH 141 II	To Madras, Calcutta, and Batavia.
—	Asia	Henry P. Tremenheere.	1820 —	R.B. only	34 SS (A)	—
—	Charlton	Charles Mortlock	1810 —	Two R.B. only.	301 K	—

Log begins.	Ship.	Captain.	Log ends.	Ledger or Receipt Book.	Reference Number.	Remarks.
1809 —	Earl Camden	Henry Morse Samson	1810 —	Two R.B. only.	303 G	—
—	Penang	Henry P. Tremenheere.	1823 —	L. & R.B. only.	755 A	—
1810 Jan. 1	Cirencester	Henry Halkett	1811 Nov. 20	— L. & R.B.	179 G 179 O	To China.
Jan. 5	Phœnix	John Ramsden	1812 Sept. 7	— L. & R.B.	175 J 175 W	To Madras, Bengal, and Batavia.
Jan. 6	David Scott	John Locke	1811 Oct. 23	— L. & R.B.	183 H 183 R	To Madras and China.
Jan. 6	Preston	Henry Sturrock	1812 Aug. 25	— L. & R.B.	307 F 307 L	To Madras, Bengal, and Java.
Jan. 11	Surat Castle	Alexander Robertson	1811 Oct. 22	— L. & R.B.	205 G 205 L	To China.
Jan. 17	Lady Carrington	W. Atkins	1810 Dec. 13	—	180 A	To Calcutta.
Jan. 22	Alnwick Castle	Peter Rolland	1811 Nov. 18	— L. & R.B.	189 E 189 L	To China.
Jan. 24	Canton	George Gray	Nov. 23	— L. & R.B.	288 I 288 Q	To China.
Feb. 3	Sovereign	Alexander Campbell	June 12	— L. & R.B.	195 G 195 N	To Madras and Bengal.
Feb. 5	Ann	Peter Cameron	Nov. 4	— L. & R.B.	211 F 211 N	To Madras and Bengal.
Feb. 5	Diana	John Marshall	Oct. 14	— L. & R.B.	239 C 239 G	To Madras and Calcutta.
Feb. 5	Indus	George Weltden	Oct. 29	— L. & R.B.	225 D 225 J	To Madras and Calcutta.
Feb. 5	Sir William Bensley	George Hooper	Oct. 14	— L. & R.B.	247 E 247 K	To Madras and Calcutta.
Feb. 7	Charles Grant	T. T. Harington	1810 Nov. 29	— L. & R.B.	38 A 38 L	From Bombay to England.
Feb. 19	Earl St. Vincent	John Brook Samson	1811 Sept. 10	— L. & R.B.	209 G 209 N	To Bengal and Madras.
Feb. 19	Exeter	James Timbrell	Oct. 5	— L. & R.B.	138 N 138 Z	To Bombay.
Feb. 19	Thomas Grenville	William Patterson	Sept. 16	— L. & R.B.	10 B 10 P	To Colombo and Calcutta.
Feb. 27	Royal George	Albert Gledstanes	Oct. 19	— L. & R.B.	17 M 17 DD	To China.
Mar. 5	Harriet	William Lynch	Oct. 5	— L. & R.B.	275 L 275 S	To Madras, Calcutta, and Vizagapatam.
Mar. 6	Carmarthen	James Ross	1812 Mar. 2	— L. & R.B.	142 E 142 M	To Bombay.
Mar. 6	Midas	Charles Otway Mayne	1810 June 5	— L. & R.B.	271 A 271 B	To Calcutta.
Mar. 8	Lord Eldon	John William Young	1812 Nov. 20	— L. & R.B.	143 F 143 M	To Bombay, Bengal, and Batavia.
Mar. 12	Juliana	J. R. J. Toussaint	1811 Aug. 9	— L. & R.B.	75 A 75 D	To Madras and Bengal.
April 6	Batavia	John Mayne	1812 Dec. 4	— L. & R.B.	213 A 213 D	To Ceylon, Bengal, and Batavia.
April 7	Lord Keith	Peter Campbell	1811 Oct. 28	— L. & R.B.	187 D 187 L	To Bengal.
April 9	Earl Spencer	George Heming	Oct. 22	— L. & R.B.	227 G 227 N	To Bengal and Madras.
April 9	Tyne	Robert Brooks	Oct. 14	— L. & R.B.	326 A 326 B	To Bengal and Madras.
April 10	Larkins	Thomas Dambleton	Aug. 19	— L. & R.B.	104 B 104 J	To Calcutta.
April 13	Monarch	Thomas Havard	1812 May 7	— L. & R.B.	300 E 300 J	To Madras and Calcutta.
April 21	Hebe	Robert Johnson	1811 Aug. 8	— L. & R.B.	266 A 266 B	To Calcutta.
April 29	Bombay	Archibald Hamilton	Nov. 28	— Two L. & R.B.	48 B 48 M & N	To China.
May 18	Cornwallis	- -	1810 Nov. 19	—	270 B	From Bombay to England.

Log begins.	Ship.	Captain.	Log ends.	Ledger or Receipt Book.	Reference Number.	Remarks.
1810 June 7	Providence	A. Barclay	1812 Oct. 17	—	176 B	To New South Wales and China.
June 18	James Sibbald	G. Harrower	1810 Dec. 17	—	64 A	From Bombay to England.
July 4	Bheemoolah	F. Patrick, David Chauvet and Charles Brodie successively.	1812 Mar. 9	—	273 A	From Calcutta to England.
Sept. 21	Ann	C. Clarke	1811 May 14	—	311 G	From Bengal to England.
Oct. 29	Dorsetshire	Robert Hunter Brown	1812 Dec. 10	— L. & R.B.	13 F 13 O	To Bombay and China.
Oct. 29	Essex	Richard Nisbet	Aug. 5	— L. & R.B.	229 U 229 SS	To Bombay and Whampoa.
Oct. 29	Walmer Castle	Luke Dodds	Sept. 8	— L. & R.B.	181 G 181 P	To Bencoolen and China.
Nov. 1	Cumberland	T. H. Wilkinson	July 11	— L. & R.B.	202 D 202 K	To Bombay and China.
Nov. 17	Henry Addington	John Kirkpatrick	July 3	— L. & R.B.	170 F 170 O	To Bombay and China.
Nov. 22	Windham	Joseph Lautour	1811 Oct. 19	— L. & R.B.	230 H 230 R	From Bourbon to England.
Nov. 26	Hope	James Pendergrass	1812 Oct. 7	— L. & R.B.	168 K 168 T	To Madras, Singapore, and China.
Nov. 26	Princess Amelia	Edward Balston	Oct. 1	— L. & R.B.	36 L 36 I I	To Madras and China.
Nov. 27	Taunton Castle	Benjamin Richardson	Sept. 10	— L. & R.B.	107 I 107 R	To Madras and China.
Dec. 7	Rose	James Sandilands	June 29	— L. & R.B.	59 H 59 Y	To Madras and Bengal.
Dec. 10	Carnatic	A. F. W. Swinton	June 23	— L. & R.B.	165 I 165 V	To Madras and Calcutta.
Dec. 10	Castle Eden	Richard Colnett	May 14	— L. & R.B.	296 F 296 L	To Madras and Calcutta.
Dec. 10	Metcalfe	Matthew Isacke	July 1	— L. & R.B.	167 D 167 J	To Madras and Bengal.
Dec. 10	Northampton	Thomas Barker	April 29	— L. & R.B.	198 G 198 T	To Bombay and Madras.
Dec. 10	Union	James Fairfax	May 16	— L. & R.B.	117 L 117 X	To Bengal.
Dec. 11	Union	George Simpson succeeded by Robert Rankine.	Sept. 22	— Two L. & R.B.	117 M 117 Y & Z	To Bombay and Bengal.
Dec. 21	Huddart	William Nesbitt	Aug. 28	— L. & R.B.	217 E 217 M	To Madras, Bengal, and Java.
Dec. 21	John Palmer	H. A. Reid	1811 Oct. 1	—	258 A	From Bengal to England.
Dec. 27	Ceylon	John Stewart	Aug. 9	[Two J.] L. & R.B.	291 F & G 291 K	From Bourbon to England.
Dec. 28	Marchioness of Exeter	William Baynes	1812 June 23	— L. & R.B.	166 E 166 L	To Bengal.
1811 Jan. 9	Ceres	Hugh Scott	July 25	— L. & R.B.	215 Q 215 FF	To China.
Jan. 9	Warley	John Collins	Aug. 1	— L. & R.B.	182 I 182 T	To China.
Jan. 10	Baring	James Carnegie	Sept. 18	— L. & R.B.	246 F 246 M	To Calcutta and Madras.
Jan. 10	Streatham	John Dale	Sept. 11	— L. & R.B.	185 C 185 J	To Madras and Bengal.
Jan. 11	Europe	William Gelston	Sept. 26	— L. & R.B.	204 G 204 O	To Madras and Calcutta.
Jan. 12	Devonshire	James Murray	Sept. 3	— L. & R.B.	272 L 272 X	To Calcutta and Madras.
Jan. 21	General Stuart	James Jameson	Oct. 1	— L. & R.B.	218 F 218 M	To Madras and Bengal.
Jan. 24	Marquis of Ely	James Dalrymple	July 4	— L. & R.B.	193 E 193 M	To China.
Jan. 24	Ocean	Thomas McTaggart	Sept. 5	— L. & R.B.	222 Q 222 KK	To Madras and Calcutta.
Jan. 24	Warren Hastings	Guntor Lyde Brown	July 25	— L. & R.B.	9 K 9 HH	To China.
Jan. 25	Cambridge	Charles Mortlock	Sept. 29	— L. & R.B.	66 A 66 F	To Bengal.
Jan. 25	Devaynes	Octavus Brooks	Aug. 31	— L. & R.B.	223 E 223 K	To Madras and Calcutta.
Jan. 25	Sir William Pulteney	Henry Christopher	Sept. 1	— L. & R.B.	190 E 190 K	To Madras and Bengal.
Jan. 26	Charles Grant	John Loch	July 30	— L. & R.B.	38 B 38 M	To China.

Log begins.	Ship.	Captain.	Log ends.	Ledger or Receipt Book.	Reference Number.	Remarks.
1811 Jan. 31	Lord Melville	James George Crabb	1812 Sept. 25	— L. & R.B.	144 D 144 K	To Bengal and Madras.
Feb. 4	Lowther Castle	William Crowder	July 16	— L. & R.B.	50 A 50 O	To China.
Feb. 8	James Sibbald	John Blanshard	Sept. 3	— L. & R.B.	64 H 64 J	To Madras and Calcutta.
Feb. 10	Perseverance	James Tweedale	June 28	— L. & R.B.	255 G 255 N	To Whampoa.
Feb. 22	Dover Castle	George Richardson	1813 Mar. 17	— L. & R.B.	232 F 232 L	To Calcutta, Madras, &c.
Feb. 22	Lord Castlereagh	Christopher Kymer	Dec. 28	— L. & R.B.	188 E 188 L	To Bengal and China.
Feb. 23	Surrey	Samuel Beadle	July 9	— L. & R.B.	191 D 191 K	To Bengal and Madras.
Feb. 23	Walthamstow	Thomas Jones	June 28	— L. L. & R.B.	196 F 196 L 196 M	To Bengal and Acheen.
Feb. 25	Canada		1811 Nov. 18	—	314 B	From Macao to England.
Feb. 26	Scaleby Castle	Thomas Talbot Harrington.	1812 Dec. 15	— L. & R.B.	34 H 34 X	To Bombay and China.
Mar. 5	Antelope		1811 May 27	—	570 B	From China to Palawan.
Mar. 7	Warren Hastings	Charles Jones	1813 Oct. 6	— L. & R.B.	9 L 9 II	To China.
Mar. 9	Moffatt	Benjamin Barber	1812 June 16	— L. & R.B.	43 A 43 H	To Bombay.
Mar. 11	David Scott	George Williamson	Oct. 29	— L. & R.B.	183 I 183 S	To Bengal.
Mar. 11	Lady Castlereagh	George Simpson	1813 June 19	[Two J.] L. & R.B.	197 E & F 197 M	To Bengal, Bencoolen, and Madras.
Mar. 11	Marquis Wellesley	Charles Le Blanc	April 22	— Two R.B.	212 F 212 L & M	To Bengal and Madras.
Mar. 11	Retreat	Thomas Watson Leech.	1812 Oct. 22	— L. & R.B.	192 D 192 I	To Bengal.
Mar. 11	Tottenham	John Barnet Sotheby	Oct. 20	— L. & R.B.	199 E 199 K	To Bengal.
April 8	Lady Lushington	John Hine	Oct. 28	— L. & R.B.	221 B 221 F	To Bengal.
April 8	Lord Forbes	Lewis Owen Edwards	Oct. 15	— L. & R.B.	220 A 220 C	To Bengal.
April 10	Baring	Henry Templer	Dec. 18	— L. & R.B.	246 E 246 L	To Calcutta.
April 13	Harleston	Thomas Walker	Oct. 10	— L. & R.B.	253 A 253 B	To Calcutta and Bencoolen.
April 16	Charles Mills	George Raincock	May 11	[Two J.] L. & R.B.	200 A & B 200 D	To Bombay.
April 24	Minerva	John Anderson	Sept. 5	— L. & R.B.	14 J 14 CC	To Calcutta.
April 27	William Pitt	Charles William Butler.	Oct. 26	— L. & R.B.	184 M 184 BB	To Bengal.
May 14	Providence	A. Barclay	Oct. 17	—	176 C & D	To New South Wales and China.
June 12	General Graham	William Watson succeeded by William Bendal.	1813 May 18	—	254 A	To Port Jackson and Whampoa.
June 14	Guildford	Magnus Johnson	1812 Nov. 21	—	78 A	To Sydney and Calcutta.
June 22	Inglis	William Hay	July 18	— L. & R.B.	30 A 30 M	To China.
Sept. 13	Tigris	Dugald MacDougall	1813 June 11	— L. & R.B.	219 F 219 M	To Bengal.
Sept. 16	Mary		Aug. 12	—	261 H & I	To Port Jackson and Calcutta.
Sept. 19	Portsea	— Burgh	1812 Oct. 29	—	208 A	To Calcutta.
Oct. 1	Caroline	G. Harrower	June 2	[Two J.]	152 A & B	From Bombay to England.
Oct. 15	Neptune	William Donaldson	1813 July 27	— L. & R.B.	98 Q 98 II	To Bombay and China.

Log begins.	Ship.	Captain.	Log ends.	Ledger or Receipt Book.	Reference Number.	Remarks.
1811 Oct. 16	Cabalva	Jonathan Birch	1813 Aug. 2	— L. & R.B.	155 A 155 F	To Bombay and China.
Oct. 17	Arniston	Walter Campbell	1818 July 30	— L. & R.B.	149 H 149 P	To Bombay and China.
Oct. 17	Thames	Matthew Riches	1813 Sept. 9	— L. & R.B.	8 M 8 FF	To China.
Oct. 23	Coutts	John Boyce	Aug. 20	— L. & R.B.	171 G 171 O	To Bombay and China.
Oct. 24	Royal Charlotte	Henry Rush	July 2	— L. & R.B.	150 T 150 LL	To Bombay and China.
Nov. 6	Caroline	G. Harrower	1812 June 2	—	152 A	From Bombay to England. Portion from 16th May to 1st June missing.
Nov. 6	Earl of Balcarras	C. C. McIntosh	July 29	— L. & R.B.	35 A 35 K	From China to England.
Nov. 13	Maitland	John Stevens	Sept. 8	—	67 A	From Bengal to England.
Nov. 15	Royal George	Chas. Besley Gribble	1813 Oct. 8	— L. & R.B.	17 N 17 EE	To Madras and China.
Nov. 16	Winchelsea	William Moffatt	Sept. 8	— L. & R.B.	4 I 4 Z	To Madras and China.
Nov. 19	David Scott	John Locke	Oct. 8	— L. & R.B.	183 J 183 T	To Madras and China.
Nov. 19	Surat Castle	Alexander Robertson	June 9	— L. & R.B.	205 H 205 M	To China.
Nov. 21	Cuffnells	Robert Welbank	Aug. 6	— L. & R.B.	178 F 178 N	To Madras and China.
Nov. 30	Asia	Hy. P. Tremenheere	July 12	— L. & R.B.	24 Q 24 TT	To Bengal.
Nov. 30	Astell	James Hay	June 26	—	12 B	To Madras and Bengal.
Nov. 30	Astell	James Hay	1812 Aug. 1	— L. & R.B.	12 C 12 M	To Madras (containing also a journal of the "Castle Huntley").
Nov. 30	Larkins	Thomas Dumbleton	1813 July 19	— L. & R.B.	104 C 104 K	To Bengal.
Dec. 3	Prince Regent	Thos. Herbert Harris	July 13	— L. & R.B.	25 A 25 K	To Madras and Bengal.
Dec. 5	Earl St. Vincent	Wm. Larkins Pascall	June 17	— L. & R.B.	204 H 204 M	To Madras and Bengal.
Dec. 10	Chapman	John Constable	July 7	— L. & R.B.	218a C 218a F	To Bombay and Bengal.
Dec. 19	Lady Carrington	William Hawkey	Dec. 13	— L. & R.B.	180 B 180 F	To Bombay, Madras, and Bengal.
Dec. 28	Bengal	George Nicholls	June 29	— L. & R.B.	177 E 177 J	To Madras and Bengal.
Dec. 28	Glatton	James Halliburton	Sept. 9	[Two J.] L. & R.B.	172 Q & R 172 KK	To China.
Dec. 28	Marquis of Huntley	Donald McLeod	Aug. 18	— L. & R.B.	7 A 7 L	To China.
Dec. 28	Wexford	Charles Barnard	Aug. 20	— L. & R.B.	173 E 173 L	To China.
Dec. 30	Elphinstone	Milliken Craig	Aug. 23	— L. & R.B.	201 E 201 K	To China.
1812 Jan. 13	Alnwick Castle	Peter Rolland	Aug. 28	— L. & R.B.	189 F 189 M	To China.
Jan. 13	Bombay	Montgomerie Hamilton.	Aug. 24	— L. & R.B.	48 C 48 O	To China.
Jan. 13	Harriet	William Lynch	1812 Oct. 14	— R.B.	275 M 275 T	To Madras and Bengal.
Jan. 13	Indus	George Weltden	1813 Dec. 10	— L. & R.B.	225 E 225 K	To Madras and Bengal.
Jan. 13	Lord Keith	John Freeman	Sept. 27	— L. & R.B.	187 E 187 M	To Madras and Bengal.
Jan. 13	Sovereign	Alexander Campbell	July 17	— L. & R.B.	195 H 195 O	To Madras and Bengal.
Jan. 14	Ann	Peter Cameron	Dec. 13	— L. & R.B.	211 H 211 O	To Madras and Bengal.
Jan. 17	Cirencester	Henry Halkett	Sept. 13	— L. & R.B.	179 H 179 P	To Batavia and China.
Jan. 21	City of London	Thomas Jenkins	Oct. 14	— L. & R.B.	151 F 151 L	To Madras and Bengal.
Jan. 30	Sir William Bensley	Albert Gledstanes	June 11	— L. & R.B.	247 F 247 L	To Madras and Bengal.
Feb. 24	Princess Charlotte of Wales.	John Craig	1814 Oct. 4	— L. & R.B.	53 A 53 J	To Bengal and China.
Feb. 26	Apollo	Charles B. Tarbutt	June 27	— L. & R.B.	159 C 159 F	To Bengal, Batavia, &c.
Feb. 26	Broxbornebury	Thomas Pitcher	1813 Sept. 28	— L. & R.B.	82 A 82 E	To Madras and Bengal.

Log begins.	Ship.	Captain.	Log ends.	Ledger or Receipt Book.	Reference Number.	Remarks.
1812 Feb. 26	Fairlie - -	William P. D'Esterre	1814 June 29	— L. & R.B.	147 A 147 D	To Bengal, Batavia, Madras, &c.
Feb. 26	Lord Duncan - -	Thomas Price -	1813 Oct. 5	— L. & R.B.	210 G 210 N	To Bombay.
Feb. 26	Thomas Grenville -	William Patterson -	Dec. 24	— L. & R.B.	10 C 10 Q	To Bengal.
Mar. 1	Barrosa - - -	B. Fergusson -	1812 Dec. 31	[Two J.]	99 A & B	From Bengal to England.
Mar. 4	Cornwall - -	G. Henderson	Dec. 15	—	90 A	From Bengal to England.
Mar. 12	Diana - -	David Bowman -	1814 June 15	— L. & R.B.	239 D 239 H	To Batavia and Bengal.
Mar. 12	Earl Howe - -	George Hooper	1813 Aug. 14	— Two R.B.	203 H 203 P	To Bengal and Madras.
Mar. 12	Juliana - -	Richard Rawes -	Sept. 15	— L. & R.B.	75 B 75 E	To Batavia.
Mar. 12	Sir Godfrey Webster -	James Pearson -	1814 July 16	— L. & R.B.	256 A 256 B	To Bengal and Bombay.
Mar. 17	Alexander - -	Chas. Hazell Newell	1813 Sept. 17	— L. & R.B.	174 H 174 O	To Bengal and Bencoolen.
Mar. 28	Carmarthen - -	James Ross - -	1814 May 21	— L. & R.B.	142 F 142 N	To Bengal and Bombay.
May 1	Regent -	James Haig	1813 July 22	—	2 A	From Calcutta to England.
May 5	Scaleby Castle - -	- - -	1812 Dec. 7	—	34 I	(Incomplete).
May 24	Regent - -	James Haig - -	1813 May 9	—	2 B	From Calcutta to England.
May 28	Euphrates - -	Philip Herbert	Jan. - 2	—	262 E	To Ceylon.
June 3	Northampton	Thomas Barker succeeded by A. P. Barker.	May 17	— L. & R.B.	198 H 198 U	To Ceylon and Bengal.
June 7	Indefatigable -	John Cross	1814 June 9	—	786 A	To Port Jackson.
June 25	Guildford - -	Magnus Johnston -	1813 June 10	—	78 B	From Calcutta to England.
July 8	Admiral Gambier -	Edward Sindrey -	May 29	[Two J.]	241 A & B	From China to England.
July 8	General Graham	William Watson succeeded by William Bendal.	May 16	—	254 B	From China to England.
July 29	Fort William -	J. R. Parrish	July 15	—	91 I	From China to England.
Aug. 1	Inglis - -	William Hay	1814 Sept. 20	— L. & R.B.	30 B 30 N	To Bengal and China.
Sept. 18	Sir William Burroughs	Thos. Watkin Court	1813 May 28	—	263 A	From Calcutta to England.
Oct. 5	Charles Grant -	John Loch -	1814 Sept. 10	— L. & R.B.	38 O 38 N	To Bombay and China.
Oct. 5	General Harris -	Chas. Elton Prescott	Oct. 7	— L. & R.B.	32 A 32 J	To Bombay and China.
Oct. 5	Marquis of Ely -	James Dalrymple	Oct. 21	— L. & R.B.	193 F 193 N	To Bombay and China.
Oct. 5	Perseverance -	Thomas Buchanan -	Nov. 11	— L. & R.B.	255 H 255 O	To Bombay and China.
Oct. 12	Marquis Camden -	Matthew Isacke -	Sept. 16	— L. & R.B.	58 A 58 J	To Bombay and China.
Oct. 31	Bridgewater - -	Philip Hughes - -	Oct. 10	— L. & R.B.	42 Q 42 NN	To Madras and China.
Nov. 4	Princess Amelia -	Edward Balston -	Sept. 1	— L. & R.B.	36 M 36 JJ	To China.
Nov. 6	Castle Huntley -	John Paterson -	1813 Oct. 6	[Two J.] L. & R.B.	3 A & B 3 L	From Calcutta to England. (*See also* log of "Astell," 12 C.)

Log begins.	Ship.	Captain.	Log ends.	Ledger or Receipt Book.	Reference Number.	Remarks.
1812 Nov. 9	Atlas - -	Charles Otway Mayne	1814 Oct. 6	— L. & R.B.	27 G 27 T	To Madras and China.
Nov. 26	Metcalfe -	Henry Morse Samson	July 2	— L. & R.B.	167 E 167 K	To Madras and Bengal.
Nov. 28	Marquis of Wellington	John Wood - -	Oct. 29	— L. & R.B.	56 A 56 K	To Madras and Bengal.
Nov. 28	Rose - -	James Sandilands -	June 16	— L. & R.B.	59 I 59 Z	To Madras.
Nov. 30	Coldstream -	J. P. Mansell	1813 Sept. 29	— L. L. & R.B.	5 A 5 J 5 K	To Madras and Bengal.
Dec. 8	Lord Melville -	James George Crabb	1816 Nov. 7	— L. & R.B.	144 E 144 L	To Madras and Bengal.
Dec. 18	Cumberland -	Thomas Hutton Wilkinson.	1814 Aug. 23	— L. & R.B.	202 E 202 L	To China.
Dec. 18	Hope - -	James Pendergrass -	Oct. 5	— L. & R.B.	168 L 168 U	To China.
Dec. 16	Hugh Inglis	James Fairfax -	Nov. 9	— L. & R.B.	231 F 231 M	To Madras, Calcutta, and Vizagapatam.
Dec. 18	Walmer Castle -	Luke Dodds -	Oct. 11	— L. & R.B.	181 H 181 Q	To China.
—	Ceres -	Hugh Scott	—	L. & R.B. only.	215 GG	—
—	Marchioness of Ely	Brook Kay -	—	L. & R.B. only.	6 I	—
1813 Jan. 2	Devaynes -	John Short -	July 26	— L. & R.B.	223 F 223 L	To Madras and Bengal.
Jan. 2	General Stuart - -	James Jameson -	July 15	— L. & R.B.	218 G 218 N	To Madras and Bengal.
Jan. 2	Lowther Castle -	William Crowder	1813 Oct. 20	—	50 B	To China.
Jan. 2	Lowther Castle -	William Crowder succeeded by Henry Hill.	1814 Oct. 25	— L. & R.B.	50 C 50 P	To China.
Jan. 2	Ocean -	Thomas McTaggart -	June 3	— L. & R.B.	222 R 392 FF	To Madras and Bengal.
Jan. 2	Sir William Pulteney	Henry Christopher	Sept. 8	— L. & R.B.	190 F 190 L	To Madras and Bengal.
Jan. 2	Union - -	Robert Rankine - succeeded by W. Lock.	Dec. 24	— L. & R.B.	117 N 117 AA	To Bengal.
Jan. 2	Warley - -	John Collins	Nov. 2	— L. & R.B.	182 J 182 U	To China.
Jan. 4	Huddart -	William Nesbitt	July 5	— L. & R.B.	217 F 217 N	To Madras and Bengal.
Jan. 13	Hindostan	[?] Neesh -	1813 Aug. 13	—	267 E	From Calcutta to England.
Jan. 21	Lord Eldon	Jacob Cowles -	1814 June 28	— L. & R.B.	143 G 143 N	To Batavia.
Jan. 27	Batavia -	John Mayne -	Dec. 9	—	213 B	To Bengal and Bombay.
Jan. 30	Moffatt - -	Simon Lee - -	Oct. 13	— L. & R.B.	43 B 43 I	To Madras and Bengal.
Jan. 30	Tottenham - -	John Barnet Sotheby	Sept. 8	— L. & R.B.	199 F 199 L	To Madras and Bengal.
Jan. 30	Union - - -	William Younghusband.	Sept. 23	— L.&R.B.	117 O 117 BB	To Madras and Bengal.
Feb. 4	Hannah - -	William Denniston -	1813 Aug. 20	[Two J.]	240 A & B	From Bombay to England.
Feb. 5	Retreat -	Thomas W. Leech -	1814 Aug. 29	— L. & R.B.	192 E 192 J	To Bengal and Bencoolen.
Feb. 15	Carnatic -	Arch. Fr. Wm. Swinton.	Oct. 1	— L. & R.B.	165 J 165 W	To Bengal.
Feb. 15	Marchioness of Exeter	William Baynes -	1815 Jan. 11	— L. & R.B.	166 F 166 M	To Ceylon and Bengal.
Feb. 15	Streatham - -	Charles Mortlock -	1814 Dec. 31	— L. & R.B.	185 D 185 K	To Bengal, Batavia, and Amboyna.
Feb. 15	William Pitt - -	C. Graham -	Sept. 10	— L. & two R.B.	184 N 184 CC	To Ceylon and Bengal.
Mar. 2	Charles Mills - -	George Raincock -	July 4	— L. & R.B.	200 C 200 E	To Bombay.
Mar. 2	David Scott - -	George Williamson -	July 23	— L. & R.B.	183 K 183 U	To Bombay.
Mar. 2	James Sibbald -	John Blanshard -	July 18	— L. & R.B.	64 C 64 J	To Bombay.

Log begins.	Ship.	Captain.	Log ends.	Ledger or Receipt Book.	Reference Number.	Remarks.
1813 Mar. 2	Lady Lushington -	John Hine -	1815 Jan. 2	— L. & R.B.	221 C 221 G	To Bengal.
Mar. 2	Lord Forbes -	Lewis Owen Edwardes	1814 Oct. 24	— L. & R.B.	220 B 220 D	To Bengal and Bombay.
Mar. 2	Minerva -	John Anderson -	Sept. 17	— L. & R.B.	14 K 14 DD	To Calcutta and Bombay.
Mar. 5	Northumberland	John R. Francklin	Aug. 17	— L. & R.B.	141 R 141 JJ	To Bengal.
May 21	Bengal Merchant	Thomas Ross -	Mar. 31	—	85 A	To Bengal.
July 23	Discovery - -	-	1813 Sept. 5	—	120 A	Journal of the proceedings of the "Discovery" while "on survey."
Oct. 6	Herefordshire -	Charles Le Blanc	1814 Oct. 24	[Two J.] L. & R.B.	49 A & B 49 N	From China to England.
Oct. 7	Neptune	Edward Smith Ellis -	1815 Aug. 15	— L. & R.B.	98 R 98 JJ	To Bombay and China.
Oct. 8	Bombay - -	Archibald Hamilton	1816 Mar. 1	— L. & two R.B.	48 D 48 P	To Bombay and China.
Oct. 8	Cabalva -	Jonathan Birch -	1815 Aug. 31	— L. & R.B.	155 B 155 F	To Bombay and China.
Oct. 11	Elphinstone -	Milliken Craig -	July 26	— L. & R.B.	201 F 201 L	To Bombay and China.
Oct. 11	Lady Melville	John Christopher Lochner.	Sept. 6	— L. & R.B.	22 A 22 K	To Bombay and China.
Oct. 11	Scaleby Castle - -	Thos. T. Harrington	Nov. 14	— L. & R.B.	34 J 34 Y	To China.
Oct. 18	Woodbridge -	G. H. Tweedy -	1814 July 6	—	233 A	From Calcutta to England.
Nov. 1	General Wellesley	J. L. Heathorn -	May 23	—	236 A	From Calcutta to England.
Nov. 4	Essex -	Richard Nisbett	Sept. 16	— L. & R.B.	229 V 229 TT	To Madras and China.
Nov. 8	General Kyd	Alexander Nairne	Nov. 2	—	52 A	To Madras and Point de Galle.
Nov. 8	Glatton -	James Halliburton -	1815 April 8	[Two J.] L. & R.B.	172 S & T 172 LL	To China.
Nov. 8	Marquis of Huntley -	Donald McLeod -	Aug. 30	— L. & R.B.	7 B 7 M	To Madras and China.
Nov. 8	Royal Charlotte -	Henry Rush	Oct. 7	— L. & R.B.	150 U 150 M	To Batavia and China.
Nov. 8	Winchelsea -	William Moffatt	June 25	— L. & R.B.	4 J 4 AA	To Madras and China.
Nov. 9	Vansittart - -	H. Reid - -	1814 Oct. 13	—	46 I	From Bengal to England.
Nov. 10	Castle Huntley	John Paterson -	1815 Aug. 26	— L. & R.B.	3 C 3 M	To Madras and China.
Nov. 14	Surat Castle -	Alexander Robertson	Sept. 20	— L. & R.B.	205 I 205 N	To Batavia and China.
Nov. 23	Asia - -	Hy. P. Tremenheere	Feb. 7	— L. & R.B.	24 R 24 UU	From Madras to England.
Nov. 22	Astell	Wm. Hy. Hardyman	Aug. 14	— L. & R.B.	12 D 12 N	To Madras and Calcutta.
Nov. 22	Europa -	William Gelston -	Aug. 8	— L. & R.B.	204 H 204 P	To Madras and Calcutta.
Nov. 28	Baring - -	James Carnegie -	1814 July 4	— L. & R.B.	246 G 246 N	To Madras and Calcutta.
Dec. 22	Dorsetshire	Nathaniel Turner -	1815 Sept. 6	— L. & R.B.	13 G 13 P	To China.
Dec. 22	Henry Addington	John Kirkpatrick -	Sept. 26	— L. & R.B.	170 G 170 P	To China.
Dec. 22	Thames -	Matthew Riches -	Oct. 3	— L. & R.B.	8 N 8 GG	To China.
Dec. 23	Wexford	Charles Barnard -	Sept. 12	— L. & R.B.	173 F 173 M	To China.
Dec. 27	Coutts - -	John Boyce - -	Oct. 23	— L. & R.B.	171 H 171 P	To China.
—	Devonshire - -	James Murray - -	—	Two R.B. only.	272 Y	——
1814 Jan. 5	Lord Keith -	Peter Campbell -	July 27	— L. & R.B.	187 F 187 N	To Madras and Bengal.
Jan. 6	Prince Regent	Thomas Herbert Harris.	Oct. 14	— L. & R.B.	25 B 25 L	To Madras.

Log begins.	Ship.	Captain.	Log ends.	Ledger or Receipt Book.	Reference Number.	Remarks.
1814 Jan. 12	Surrey	Samuel Beadle -	1815 Aug. 11	— L. & R.B.	191 E 191 L	To Madras and Bengal.
Jan. 14	Marchioness of Ely	Brook Kay -	Oct. 31	— L. & R.B.	6 A 6 J	To Madras and Bengal.
Jan. 24	Archduke Charles	J. P. Jeffreys -	1814 Nov. 21	—	216 A	From China to England.
Jan. 31	Alexander -	Chas. Hazell Newell	Oct. 9	— L. & R.B.	174 1 174 P	To Madras and Bengal.
Feb. 15	Thomas Grenville -	William Patterson -	1815 Aug. 1	— L. & R.B.	10 D 10 R	To China.
Mar. 5	Phœnix - -	John Pyke - -	Oct. 14	— L. & R.B.	175 K 175 X	To Bengal and Madras.
Mar. 7	Discovery - -		1814 Sept. 13	—	120 B	Journal of the proceedings of the "Discovery" while "on survey."
Mar. 10	Warren Hastings -	Thomas Larkins	1815 Oct. 2	— L. & R.B.	9 M 9 JJ	To Bengal.
Mar. 19	Ann - -	Peter Cameron -	Nov. 9	— L. & R.B.	211 H(A) 211 P	To Bengal and Bencoolen.
Mar. 19	Larkins - -	Thomas Dumbleton -	Nov. 7	— L.& R.B.	104 D 104 L	To Bengal.
Mar. 19	Tigris - - -	Dugald Macdougall	July 31	— L. & R.B.	219 G 219 N	To Bombay and Tellicherry.
Mar. 21	Indus - -	George Weltden -	July 27	— L. & R.B.	225 F 225 L	To Bombay and Tellicherry.
Mar. 24	Lady Castlereagh -	George Simpson -	Nov. 7	— L. & R.B.	197 G 197 N	To Bengal.
April 14	Lady Carrington -	Henry Becher -	1816 Feb. 15	— L. & R.B.	180 C 180 G	To Bengal and Bencoolen.
June 9	Coldstream - -	James P. Mansell	1815 Nov. 7	— L. & R.B.	5 B 5 L	To Bengal.
June 20	Cuffnells -	Robert Welbank -	1816 May 31	— L. & R.B.	178 G 178 O	To Bengal, Madras, and China.
June 20	Marquis of Wellington	George Betham	Feb. 3	—	56 B	To Rio de Janeiro, New South Wales, and China.
June 20	Royal George	Chas. Besley Gribble	June 8	— L. & R.B.	17 N (A) 17 FF	To Bengal and China.
Oct. 13	Charles Grant -	John Loch	July 2	— L. & R.B.	38 C (A) 38 O	To Bombay and China.
Oct. 13	David Scott - -	John Locke -	July 1	— L. & R.B.	183 L 183 V	To Bombay and China.
Oct. 17	Marquis Camden -	Henry Morse Samson	1815 June 29	— L. & R.B.	58 B 58 K	To Bombay and China.
Oct. 19	Essex - -	Richard Nisbet	1816 July 18	— L. & R.B.	229 W 229 UU	To Bombay and China.
Oct. 19	Inglis - -	William Hay -	July 3	— L. & R.B.	30 C 30 O	To Bombay and China.
Oct. 23	Earl Spencer - -	William Mitchell	1815 June 20	—	227 H	From China to England.
Oct. 31	Vansittart - -	Robert Stair Dalrymple.	1816 July 10	— L. & R.B.	46 J 46 BB	To Bombay and China.
Nov. 28	Atlas -	Charles Otway Mayne	July 2	— L. & R.B.	27 H 27 U	To Madras and China.
Nov. 28	Bridgewater -	Philip Hughes -	July 9	— L. & R.B.	42 R 42 OO	To Madras and China.
Nov. 28	General Harris -	George Welstead	June 21	— L. & R.B.	32 B 32 K	To Madras and China.
Nov. 29	General Kyd	Alexander Nairne	Aug. 20	— L. & R.B.	52 B 52 J	To China.
Nov. 29	Herefordshire -	Charles Le Blanc	Aug. 22	—	49 C	To China.
Dec. 15	Lowther Castle	Charles Mortlock	June 22	— L. & R.B.	50 D 50 Q	To Madras and China.
Dec. 26	Metcalfe - -	Thomas Sanders	Oct. 21	— L. & R.B.	167 F 167 L	To Madras and Bengal.
Dec. 26	Princess Charlotte of Wales.	John Craig -	Oct. 23	— L. & R.B.	53 B 53 K	To Madras, Bengal, and Bombay.
Dec. 26	Rose - - -	Thomas McTaggart -	Aug. 16	— L. & R.B.	59 J 59 AA	To Madras.
Dec. 28	Ceres - - -	Hugh Scott	Aug. 21	— L. & R.B.	215 R 215 HH	To China.
—	St. Helena - -	John Augustus Atkinson.	1822 —	L. & R.B. only.	327 B	———
1815 Jan. 1	Isaac Todd	F. Smith - - -	1815 Sept. 21	—	186 A	From China to England.

25005. D d

Log begins.	Ship.	Captain.	Log ends.	Ledger or Receipt Book.	Reference Number.	Remarks.
1815 Jan. 2	Lord Melville -	James George Crabb	1816 July 5	— L. L. & R.B.	144 F 144 M 144 N	To Madras and Bengal. (Missing).
Jan. 10	Huddart - -	Charles Weller -	Aug. 26	— L. & R.B.	217 G 217 O	To Calcutta and Bencoolen.
Jan. 11	Lord Eldon - -	Jacob Cowles - -	Aug. 10	— L. & R.B.	143 H 143 O	To Madras, Bengal, and Bencoolen.
Jan. 17	Northumberland -	John R. Francklin -	Sept. 4	— L. & R.B.	141 S 141 KK	To Madras, Bengal, and Bencoolen.
Jan. 24	Alnwick Castle -	Peter Rolland -	July 3	— L. & R.B.	189 G 189 N	To China.
Jan. 24	Walmer Castle -	David Sutton - -	June 10	— L. & R.B.	181 I 181 R	To China.
Jan. 25	Hope - -	James Pendergrass -	June 6	— L. & R.B.	168 M 168 V	To China.
Jan. 25	Princess Amelia -	Edward Balston -	June 8	— L. & R.B.	86 N 86 KK	To China.
Jan. 26	Marquis of Wellington	John Wood - -	Aug. 13	— L. & R.B.	56 C 56 L	To Madras and Bengal.
Jan. 26	William Pitt - -	Charles Graham	Aug. 8	— L. & R.B.	184 O 184 DD	To Madras and Bengal.
Jan. 27	Warley - - -	John Collins - -	June 10	— L. & R.B.	182 K 182 V	To China.
Jan. 30	Cambridge - -	J. Toussaint -	1815 Sept. 16	—	66 B	From China to England.
Feb. 1	Streatham - -	Peter Grant - -	Dec. 2	— L. & R.B.	185 E 185 L	To Madras. (With Precedents, &c., Book No. 1.)
Feb. 9	Sir William Pulteney	Thomas Dawney	1816 Aug. 8	— L. & R.B.	190 G 190 M	To Bengal and Bombay.
Feb. 13	Surrey - -	T. Raine - -	1815 Oct. 19	—	191 F	From China to England.
Feb. 18	Apollo - -	Charles B. Tarbutt -	1816 Aug. 25	— L. & R.B.	159 D 159 G	To Bengal and Bombay.
Mar. 7	Fairlie - -	Thomas E. Ward -	Dec. 17	— L. & R.B.	147 B 147 E	To Bengal and Batavia.
Mar. 9	Minerva - -	Simon Lee - -	Aug. 21	— L. & R.B.	14 L 14 EE	To Bengal.
Mar. 10	Carmarthen	James Ross - -	Sept. 21	— L. & R.B.	142 G 142 O	To Bombay, Tellicherry, &c.
Mar. 10	Carnatic -	John Blanshard	July 24	— L. & R.B.	165 R 165 X	To Bengal.
Mar. 10	James Sibbald - -	James K. Forbes -	1817 Jan. 31	— L. & R.B.	64 D 64 K	To Bengal and China.
Mar. 10	Lord Castlereagh -	Christopher Kymer -	1816 Sept. 20	— L. & R.B.	188 F 188 M	To Bengal.
Mar. 13	Warren Hastings	Richard Rawes -	July 11	— L. & R.B.	9 N 9 KK	To China.
Mar. 17	Union -	John E. Johnson -	1817 Feb. 7	— L. & R.B.	117 P 117 CC	To Bengal and Batavia.
Mar. 21	David Scott - -	George Heming	1816 Sept. 26	— L. & R.B.	183 M 183 W	To Bombay.
Aug. 22	Thomas Grenville -	William Patterson -	1817 Jan. 10	— L. & R.B.	10 E 10 S	To China.
Sept. 15	Surrey - -	Samuel Beadle	Feb. 18	— L. & R.B.	191 G 191 M	To Madras and Batavia.
Sept. 18	Europe -	John Mills	July 2	—	204 I	To Madras, Batavia, and Bengal. The portion of the Journal from 2nd January to 24th May is missing.
Nov. 3	Cabalva - -	John Hine - -	June 3	— L. and two R.B.	155 C 155 G	To Bombay and China.
Nov. 3	Castle Huntley -	John Paterson -	June 16	— L. & R.B.	3 D 3 N	To Bombay and China.
Nov. 3	Lady Melville - -	John C. Lochner -	June 9	— L. & R.B.	22 R 22 L	To Bombay and China.
Nov. 3	Marquis of Huntley -	Donald McLeod -	June 10	— L. & R.B.	7 C 7 N	To Bombay and China.
Nov. 4	Cumberland - -	Thos. H. Wilkinson -	May 19	— L. & R.B.	202 F 202 M	To Bombay and China.
Nov. 7	Marquis of Ely - -	James Dalrymple -	July 16	— L. & R.B.	193 G 193 O	To Bombay and China.
Nov. 22	Cornwall -	Jeremiah R. J. Toussaint.	April 2	— L. & R.B.	90 B 90 E	To China.
Dec. 2	General Hewett	Walter Campbell -	June 10	— L. & R.B.	37 A 37 F	To Batavia and China.
Dec. 2	Lord Lyndock - -	James Crichton -	June 28	— L. & R.B.	224 A 224 B	To Pulo Penang and Whampoa.

Log begins.	Ship.	Captain.	Log ends.	Ledger or Receipt Book.	Reference Number.	Remarks.
1815 Dec. 16	Fort William - -	John Innes - -	1817 July 30	— L. & R.B.	91 J 91 S	To Madras and China.
Dec. 16	Regent - - -	Philip Ripley -	July 29	[Two J.] L. & R.B.	2 C & D 2 G	To Madras and China.
Dec. 19	Lady Flora - -	Thomas Brown -	1816 June 12	—	226 A	From Macao to England.
Dec. 26	Wexford - -	Charles Barnard -	1817 Oct. 10	— L. & R.B.	173 G 173 N	To Madras and China.
—	Batavia - -	John Mayne -	1816 —	R.B. only.	213 E	——
—	Elphinstone - -	Thomas Haviside -	1817 —	Two R.B. only.	201 M	——
1816 Jan. 2	Lady Castlereagh -	George Simpson -	July 12	— L. & R.B.	197 H 197 O	To China.
Jan. 3	Cambridge - -	John Freeman	July 9	— L. & R.B.	66 C 66 G	To China.
Jan. 4	Coldstream -	James Cozwell	June 20	— L. & R.B.	5 C 5 M	To China.
Jan. 14	Northampton	J. A. Tween	1816 Sept. 26	—	198 I	From China to England.
Jan. 15	Asia -	Hy. P. Tremenheere	1817 July 14	— L. & R.B.	24 S 24 VV	To Madras and Calcutta.
Jan. 15	Barkworth -	Thomas Lynn -	Aug. 29	— L. & R.B.	194 A 194 B	To Batavia and China.
Jan. 15	Sovereign - -	John Alex. Telfer -	Sept. 6	— L. & R.B.	195 I 195 P	To China.
Jan. 15	Surat Castle - -	William Hope	July 9	— L. & R.B.	205 J 205 O	To China.
Jan. 19	Marchioness of Ely -	Brook Kay -	July 15	— L. & R.B.	6 B 6 K	To Calcutta and Madras.
Jan. 19	Providence - -	And. Timbrell Mason	Aug. 21	— L. & R.B.	176 E 176 G	To China.
Jan. 20	Warren Hastings -	Thomas Larkins -	June 17	— L. & R.B.	9 O 9 LL	To Madras and Bengal.
Jan. 22	Lord Keith - -	Peter Campbell -	July 23	— L. & R.B.	187 G 187 O	To Madras and Bengal.
Jan. 31	Larkins - -	Thomas Dumbleton -	Mar. 4	— L. & R.B.	104 E 104 M	To Madras.
Feb. 13	Earl of Balcarras	James Jameson	June 17	— L. & R.B.	35 B 35 L	To China.
Feb. 13	Marchioness of Exeter	Thomas Gilpin -	June 25	— L. & R.B.	166 G 166 N	To China.
Feb. 13	Phœnix - -	John Pyke - -	June 5	— L. & R.B.	175 L 175 Y	To Madras and Bengal.
Feb. 13	Prince Regent - -	Thos. Herbert Harris	June 12	— L. & R.B.	25 C 25 M	To Madras and Bengal.
Feb. 15	Hugh Inglis - -	James Fairfax	July 2	— L. & R.B.	231 G 231 N	To China.
Feb. 15	Windham - -	Joseph Andrews	June 25	— L. & R.B.	230 I 230 S	To China.
Feb. 17	Scaleby Castle -	William Moffatt -	July 17	— L. & R.B.	34 K 34 Z	To China.
Mar. 14	Astell - - -	Francis Cresswell	Sept. 2	— L. & R.B.	12 E 12 O	To Bengal.
Mar. 14	Batavia - -	John Mayne -	Aug. 15	— L. & R.B.	213 C 213 F	To Bengal.
Mar. 14	Lady Campbell - -	Thomas Marquis -	Sept. 15	— L. & R.B.	214 A 214 C	To Batavia, Bengal, and Madras.
Mar. 15	Alexander - -	Henry Cobb -	July 10	— L. & R.B.	174 J 174 Q	To Bombay.
Mar. 15	Mangles - -	Benjamin Bunn -	Sept. 17	— L. & R.B.	89 B 89 G	To Bengal and Bencoolen.
Mar. 22	Ann - - -	James Masson -	July 3	— L. & R.B.	211 I 211 Q	To Bombay and Tellicherry.
Mar. 30	Lady Carrington -	Dugald Macdougall	Aug. 28	— L. & R.B.	180 D 180 H	To Calcutta.
April 13	Buckinghamshire -	Frederick Adams -	May 12	— L. & R.B.	18 A 18 K	To Bombay and China.
May 1	Potton - - -	Thomas Wellbank -	1816 Nov. 22	—	26 A	From Calcutta to London.
June 13	Princess Amelia -	Edward Balston -	1817 Aug. 26	— L. & R.B.	36 O 36 LL	To China.
Oct. 24	Bombay - -	Archibald Hamilton	1818 June 22	— L. & R.B.	48 E 48 Q	To Bombay and China.
Oct. 24	Charles Grant -	Hugh Scott -	June 16	— L. & R.B.	38 D 38 P	To Bombay and China.

Log begins.	Ship.	Captain.	Log ends.	Ledger or Receipt Book.	Reference Number.	Remarks.
1816 Oct. 24	General Harris	George Welstead	1818 Oct. 13	— L. & R.B.	32 C 32 L	To Bombay and China.
Oct. 24	Inglis -	William Hay	June 8	— L. & R.B.	30 D 30 P	To Bombay and China.
Oct. 24	Lowther Castle	Charles Mortlock	July 3	— L. & R.B.	50 E 50 R	To Bombay and China.
Oct. 24	Vansittart - -	Robt. Stair Dalrymple	July 8	— L. & R.B.	46 K 46 CC	To Bombay and China.
Dec. 4	Bridgewater	Philip Hughes	July 2	— L. & R.B.	42 S 42 PP	To Madras and China.
Dec. 4	Herefordshire -	John Money	June 4	— L. & R.B.	49 D 49 P	To Madras and China.
Dec. 28	Atlas -	Charles Otway Mayne	July 14	— L. & R.B.	27 I 27 V	To Bengal and China.
Dec. 26	General Kyd -	Alexander Nairne	Aug. 31	— L. & R.B.	52 C 52 K	To Bengal and China.
—	Marquis Camden	Thomas Larkins	—	L. & R.B. only.	58 L	——
1817 Jan. 6	Marquis of Wellington	Robert Johnson	June 12	— L. & R.B.	56 D 56 M	To Madras and Bengal.
Jan. 6	Minerva	George Richardson	July 25	— L. & R.B.	14 M 14 FF	To Madras and Bengal.
Jan. 17	Rose	Thomas McTaggart -	July 1	— L. & R.B.	59 K 59 BB	To Madras.
Jan. 20	Streatham -	John Dale	May 27	— L. & R.B.	185 F 185 M	To Madras and Bengal.
Jan. 23	Princess Charlotte of Wales.	Chas. Besley Gribble	July 8	— L. & R.B.	53 C 53 L	To Madras and Bengal.
Jan. 28	Waterloo -	Jonathan Birch	June 3	— L. & R.B.	39 A 39 K	To China.
Jan. 30	Winchelsea -	William Adamson -	June 15	— L. & R.B.	4 K 4 BB	To Penang and China.
Feb. 1	Prince Blucher	M. T. Weathrall -	1817 July 18	—	248 A	From Calcutta to England.
Feb. 15	Carnatic -	John Blanshard	1818 July 4	— L. & R.B.	165 L 165 Y	To Bengal.
Feb. 15	Dorsetshire	Nathaniel Turner	May 25	— L. & R.B.	13 H 13 Q	To China.
Feb. 15	William Pitt -	Charles Graham	June 1	— L. & R.B.	164 P 184 EE	To Madras and Bengal.
Feb. 18	Royal George	Chas. Sheldon Timins	May 23	— L. & R.B.	17 O 17 GG	To China.
Feb. 21	Aurora -	Thomas Haviside -	1817 Sept. 22	—	228 B	From Whampoa to England.
Mar. 3	Lord Castlereagh -	Wm. Younghusband	1818 Aug. 29	— L. & R.B.	188 G 188 N	To Bengal.
Mar. 5	Thomas Grenville	Richard Alsager	July 4	— L. & R.B.	10 F 10 T	To Bengal.
Mar. 10	Northumberland	William Mitchell	Oct. 6	— L. & R.B.	14 T 14 LL	To Bengal and Bencoolen.
Mar. 19	Huddart -	Charles Weller	July 14	— L. & R.B.	217 H 217 P	To Bombay and Tellicherry.
Mar. 21	Carmarthen	James Ross	July 20	— L. & R.B.	142 H 142 P	To Bombay.
Mar. 21	Union	J. E. Johnson -	Oct. 14	— L. & R.B.	117 Q 117 DD	To Bengal and Madras.
Mar. 25	Cornwallis -	Thomas Brown -	Mar. 9	—	270 C	To Madras.
Oct. 27	Buckinghamshire -	Frederick Adams -	1819 May 19	— L. & R.B.	18 B 18 L	To Bombay and China.
Oct. 27	Canning - -	William Patterson -	May 31	— L. & R.B.	23 A 23 I	To Bombay and China.
Oct. 27	Duke of York - -	Archibald H. Campbell	June 1	— L. & R.B.	94 E 94 R	To Bombay and China
Oct. 27	Earl of Balcarras -	James Jameson -	May 4	— L. & R.B.	35 C 35 M	To Bombay and China.
Oct. 27	Marquis of Huntley -	Donald McLeod -	June 21	— L. & R.B.	7 D 7 O	To Bombay and China.
Oct. 27	Thomas Coutts	Wm. Marjoribanks	June 5	— L. & R.B.	15 A 15 I	To Bombay and Calcutta.
Dec. 6	London - -	Walter Campbell -	May 30	— L. & R.B.	1 O 1 NN	To Madras and China.
Dec. 8	Castle Huntley	H. A. Drummond -	Sept. 1	— L. & R.B.	3 E 3 O	To Bengal and China.
Dec. 8	Dunira	Montgomerie Hamilton	Oct. 7	— L. & R.B.	21 A 21 I	To Bengal and China.
Dec. 9	Princess Amelia	Edward Balston -	June 1	— L. & R.B.	36 P 36 MM	To Madras and China.
1818 Jan. 8	Hastings -	- - -	1818 Nov. 27	—	459 B	From Calcutta and Madras to England.

Log begins.	Ship.	Captain.	Log ends.	Ledger or Receipt Book.	Reference Number.	Remarks.
1818 Jan. 22	Marchioness of Ely	Brook Kay -	1819 Jan. 27	— L. & R.B.	6 C 6 L	To Madras and Bengal.
Jan. 24	Prince Regent -	Thomas H. Harris	June 9	— L. & R.B.	25 D 25 N	To Madras and Bengal.
Feb. 10	Fairlie - -	Thomas E. Ward -	July 9	— L. & R.B.	147 C 147 F	To Calcutta, Bombay, and Tellicherry.
Feb. 11	Mangles - -	Benjamin Bunn - succeeded by R. T. Lardner.	Nov. 17	—	89 C	To Madras and Bengal.
Feb. 20	Scaleby Castle -	John Barnet Sotheby	June 5	— L. & R.B.	34 L 34 AA	To China.
Feb. 21	Henry Porcher	James P. Anstice -	July 6	— L. & R.B.	73 A 73 D	To Bengal and Bombay.
Feb. 21	Lady Melville	John Stewart -	June 24	— L. & R.B.	22 C 22 M	To China.
Feb. 21	Orwell - -	Thomas W. Leech -	June 23	— L. & R.B.	20 A 20 I	To China.
Feb. 25	Cabalva - -	James Dalrymple -	1818 July 1	—	155 D	Towards China. (Lost on 7th July 1818 in Cargados Shoal.)
Feb. 25	Perseverance -	Henry Templer -	1819 June 24	— L. & R.B.	255 I 255 P	To Penang and Whampoa.
Mar. 6	Astell -	Francis Cresswell -	July 6	— L. & R.B.	12 F 12 P	To Madras and Bengal.
Mar. 7	Phœnix - - -	Thomas White -	Sept. 1	— L. & R.B.	175 M 175 Z	To Madras and Bengal.
Mar. 19	Lady Lushington -	T. Dormer -	May 5	— L. & R.B.	221 D 221 H	To Bombay.
Mar. 23	Lord Keith -	John Freeman -	July 22	— L. & R.B.	187 H 187 P	To Madras and Bengal.
Mar. 24	Northampton - -	Charles Tebbut	July 20	— L. & R.B.	198 J 198 V	To Madras and Bengal.
April 6	Asia - - -	Thomas F. Balderston	June 27	— L. & R.B.	24 T 24 WW	To Madras and Bengal.
April 6	General Hewett -	Peter Cameron -	Sept. 30	— L. & R.B.	37 B 37 G	To Bengal.
April 8	Warren Hastings -	Thomas Larkins -	July 29	— L. & R.B.	9 P 9 MM	To Madras.
July 9	Moffatt -	Simon Lee	Oct. 12	— L. & R.B.	43 C 43 J	To China.
July 10	Regent -	Philip Ripley -	Aug. 29	— L. & R.B.	2 E 2 H	To China.
Nov. 10	Northampton - -	Charles Tebbut - succeeded by W. Bains.	July 15	—	198 K	From Calcutta to England.
Nov. 12	Charles Grant -	Hugh Scott - -	1820 June 7	— L. & R.B.	38 F 38 Q	To Bombay and China.
Nov. 12	Essex - - -	Richard Nisbet	June 12	— L. & R.B.	229 X 229 VV	To Bombay and China.
Nov. 12	Inglis - - -	Thomas Borradaile	June 30	— L. & R.B.	30 E 30 Q	To Bombay and China.
Nov. 12	Lowther Castle - -	Charles Mortlock	May 16	— L. & R.B.	50 F 50 S	To Bombay and China.
Nov. 12	Vansittart -	Robt. Stair Dalrymple succeeded by H. Cowan.	July 4	— L. & R.B.	49 L 49 DD	To Bombay and China.
Nov. 12	William Pitt - -	Charles Graham -	Oct. 25	— L. & R.B.	184 Q 184 FF	To Bencoolen and China.
Nov. 13	Marquis Camden -	Thomas Larkins -	June 30	— L. & R.B.	58 C 58 M	To Bombay and China.
Dec. 12	Bombay - -	Archibald Hamilton	Nov. 7	— L. & R.B.	48 F 48 R	To Bombay and China.
Dec. 12	General Kyd - -	Alexander Nairne -	July 23	— L. & R.B.	52 D 52 L	To Madras and China.
Dec. 14	Waterloo - -	Richard Alsager -	June 14	— L. & R.B.	39 B 39 L	To Bengal and China.
Dec. 15	Herefordshire -	William Hope -	Nov. 2	— L. & R.B.	49 E 49 Q	To Bombay and China.
Dec. 15	Windsor -	John R. Francklin -	July 25	— L. & R.B.	29 B 29 J	To Madras and China.
Dec. 18	Atlas -	Chas. Otway Mayne	Aug. 3	— L. & R.B.	27 J 27 W	To Bengal and China.
1819 Jan. 25	General Harris -	George Welstead -	July 31	— L. & R.B.	32 D 32 M	To China.
Jan. 25	Warren Hastings	Richard Rawes -	July 28	— L. & R.B.	9 R 9 HH	To China.
Jan. 26	Rose - - -	Thomas McTaggart -	June 2	— L. & R.B.	59 L 59 CC	To Madras and Bengal.
Jan. 28	Minerva -	John Mills - -	June 5	— L. & R.B.	14 N 14 GG	To Madras and Bengal.
Feb. 23	Lord Castlereagh -	Wm. Younghusband	May 6	— L. & R.B.	168 H 188 O	To China.
Feb. 23	Thomas Grenville -	William Manning -	June 28	— L. & R.B.	10 G 10 U	To Madras.

Log begins.	Ship.	Captain.	Log ends.	Ledger or Receipt Book.	Reference Number.	Remarks.
1819 Feb. 24	Bridgewater	Charles Timins	1820 July 28	— L. & R.B.	42 T 42 QQ	To China.
Feb. 24	Cornwall	John P. Wilson	May 5	— L. & R.B.	90 C 90 F	To China.
Feb. 24	Marquis of Ely	George Richardson	Nov. 1	— L. & R.B.	193 H 193 P	To China.
Feb. 26	Golconda	James T. Edwards	1819 Oct. 22	—	260 A	From Madras to England.
Feb. 27	Carnatic	John Blanshard	1820 July 4	— L. & R.B.	165 M 165 Z	To Bengal.
Mar. 5	Matilda	William Hamilton	April 23	— L. & R.B.	264 A 264 B	To China.
Mar. 9	Kellie Castle	Alexander Lindsay	June 2	— L. & R.B.	92 A 92 H	To China.
Mar. 16	Apollo	George Tennent	April 29	— L. & R.B.	159 E 159 H	To China.
Mar. 18	Catherine	W. Knox	Mar. 15	—	97 A	To Madras.
Mar. 25	Barrosa	H. Hutchinson	Aug. 10	—	99 C	To Bombay.
Mar. 25	Marquis of Hastings	C. Arkcoll	June 1	—	74 A	To Bombay.
Mar. 25	Marquis of Wellington	John Wood	July 4	— L. & R.B.	56 E 56 N	To Bengal and Madras.
Mar. 25	Princess Charlotte of Wales.	Chas. Besley Gribble	June 27	— L. & R.B.	53 D 53 M	To Bengal and Madras.
Mar. 26	Lady Nugent	B. Swanston	1819 Dec. 1	—	154 A	From Madras to England.
April 5	York	James Talbert	1820 April 15	—	237 Q	To Bombay.
April 23	Abberton	Lucas Percival	May 29	—	55 A	To Bengal.
April 23	Almorah	Thomas Winter	June 3	—	243 A	To Bengal and Madras.
April 23	Fame	Samuel Remmington	Aug. 16	—	242 D	To Bengal.
April 28	Hooghly	J. T. Lamb	June 4	—	181 A	To Bengal.
June 5	Kingston	Wm. Atkins Bowen	Aug. 29	—	244 B	To Bengal and Madras.
June 14	Princess Charlotte	William Vaughan	Sept. 2	—	246 D	To Bengal.
June 16	St. Helena	-	1821 Nov. 6	—	327 A	From St. Helena to Cape of Good Hope and Benguela and back, and thence to England.
Aug. 19	Commodore Hayes	J. M. Ardlie	1820 May 8	—	161 A	From Calcutta to England.
Oct. 19	Thomas Coutts	W. Marjoribanks	1821 June 19	— L. & R.B.	15 E 15 J	To Bombay, Madras, and China.
Nov. 2	Earl of Balcarras	James Jameson	May 16	— L. & R.B.	35 D 35 N	To Bombay and China.
Nov. 2	London	Peter Cameron	June 18	— L. & R.B.	1 F 1 OO	To China.
Nov. 2	Thames	Charles Le Blanc	May 16	— L. & R.B.	8 O 8 HH	To Bombay and China.
Nov. 2	Warren Hastings	Thomas Larkins	June 20	— L. & R.B.	9 Q 9 OO	To Bombay and China.
Nov. 19	Castle Huntley	H. A. Drummond	July 14	— L. & R.B.	3 F 3 P	To China.
Nov. 20	Asia	Thos. F. Balderston	July 16	—	24 U	To Bengal and China.
Nov. 20	Astell	Francis Cresswell	July 4	— L. & R.B.	12 G 12 Q	To Bengal and China.
Dec. 17	Canning	William Patterson	July 11	— L. & R.B.	23 B 23 J	To Bombay and China.
Dec. 17	Lady Melville	John Stewart	Oct. 24	— L. & R.B.	22 D 22 N	To Bombay, Bengal, and China.
Dec. 18	Streatham	Thomas Haviside	1820 Sept. 8	— L. & R.B.	185 C 185 N	To Bengal and China.
Dec. 31	Prince Regent	John Innes	1821 July 18	— L. & R.B.	25 E 25 O	To Madras and China.
—	Larkins	Robert Locke	1820 —	L. & R.B. only.	104 N	——
1820 Jan. 1	Duke of York	Arch. H. Campbell	1821 June 27	— L. & R.B.	94 F 94 S	To Madras and China.

Log begins.	Ship.	Captain.	Log ends.	Ledger or Receipt Book.	Reference Number.	Remarks.
1820 Jan. 1	Marquis of Huntley -	Donald McLeod -	1821 Oct. 17	— L. & R.B.	7 E 7 P	To Bombay and China.
Jan. 3	Dunira - - -	MontgomerieHamilton	Oct. 13	— L. & R.B.	21 B 21 J	To Bombay, Bengal, and China.
Jan. 5	Mercury - - -	D. D. Conyers - succeeded by Lieutenant W. S. Collinson, Bo. Mar.	Nov. 14	—	454 H (a)	Journal of various cruises, the ship touching at Muscat, Bombay, Bussora, Bushire, &c.
Jan. 25	Dorsetshire -	Samuel Lyde -	Aug. 27	— L. & R.B.	13 I 13 R	To China.
Jan. 25	Winchelsea - -	William Adamson -	Sept. 10	— L. & R.B.	4 L 4 CC	To China.
Jan. 31	Buckinghamshire -	Frederick Adams -	July 18	— L. & R.B.	18 C 18 M	To China.
Feb. 28	General Hewett -	James Pearson -	July 4	— L. & R.B.	37 C 37 H	To China.
Feb. 28	Moira - -	William Hornblow	Nov. 14	—	96 A	To Madras, Bengal, and Bombay.
Feb. 28	Scaleby Castle -	John Barnet Sotheby	June 25	— L. & R.B.	34 M 34 BB	To China.
Feb. 29	Lady Campbell -	Thomas Marquis -	June 25	— L. & R.B.	214 B 214 D	To China.
Feb. 29	Princess Amelia -	Nathaniel Turner -	June 12	— L. & R.B.	36 Q 36 NN	To China.
Feb. 29	Woodford - -	Alfred Chapman -	Feb. 27	—	265 J	To Madras.
Mar. 1	Marchioness of Ely -	Brook Kay - -	July 5	— L. & R.B.	6 D 6 M	To China.
Mar. 1	Orwell - -	Thomas Sanders -	June 14	— L. & R.B.	20 B 20 J	To China.
Mar. 2	Coromandel -	William Hunter -	April 4	—	206 B	To Madras.
Mar. 20	Lady Carrington	Thomas E. Ward	Nov. 17	—	180 E	To Madras and Bengal.
April 8	Brothers -	Ralph Stamp -	April 12	—	251 A	To Bombay.
April 10	Camden -	James Johnson	April 7	—	250 A	To Bombay.
April 19	Coldstream - -	Thomas Dormer - succeeded by William Heppenstall.	May 29	—	5 D	To Madras and Bengal.
April 27	King George the Fourth.	Henry Peter Auber -	Sept. 5	—	238 A	To Calcutta.
April 28	James Sibbald - -	J. K. Forbes -	Sept. 9	—	64 E	To Bengal.
April 28	Lady Raffles - -	James Coxwell -	Aug. 30	—	160 A	To Bengal.
May 2	Regret -	Thomas Wellbank -	Aug. 3	—	249 A	To Bombay and Tellicherry.
May 6	Phœnix - -	Alexander Gordon -	Aug. 8	—	175 N	To Bengal.
May 11	Hyperion - - -	Robert Wright Norfor	Aug. 14	—	386 A	To Bombay. (Incomplete.)
May 15	Asia - - -	John Patterson -	June 22	—	24 V	To Bombay.
May 27	Clyde - -	Thomas Blair -	Aug. 28	—	345 C	To Calcutta, Madras, and Colombo.
May 31	Providence - -	John Adair - -	Nov. 8	—	176 F	To Bengal and Madras.
June 3	Richmond - -	James Kay - -	Oct. 3	—	329 D	To Calcutta, Madras, and Colombo.
June 8	Brampton - - -	Samuel Moore -	Oct. 31	—	328 A	To Bengal.
June 10	Waterloo - -	H. R. Wilkinson -	Oct. 29	—	32 C	To Bengal and Madras.
June 21	Asia - -	James Lindsay -	Oct. 25	—	24 W	To Bengal.
June 22	Timandra - -	John Price - -	Oct. 4	—	289 A	To Bengal.
Nov. 6	Farquharson - -	William Cruickshank	1822 June 26	— L. & R.B.	40 A 40 H	To Bombay and China.
Nov. 6	Inglis - -	Thomas Borradaile - succeeded by J. Dudman, 14th February 1822.	May 27	— L. & R.B.	30 F 30 R	To Bombay and China.
Nov. 6	Marquis Camden -	Thomas Larkins -	1823 May 22	— L. & R.B.	58 D 58 N	To Bombay and China.
Nov. 6	Repulse - -	John Paterson -	1822 July 31	— L. & R.B.	51 A 51 G	To China.
Nov. 6	Royal George - -	Charles S. Timins -	May 22	— L. & R.B.	17 F 17 HH	To Bombay and China.
Nov. 20	Atlas - - -	Chas. Otway Mayne	Oct. 1	— L. & R.B.	27 K 27 X	To Bengal and China.

Log begins.	Ship.	Captain.	Log ends.	Ledger or Receipt Book.	Reference Number.	Remarks.
1820 Nov. 20	Lowther Castle	Charles Mortlock -	1822 Sept. 20	— L. & R.B.	50 G 50 T	To Bengal and China.
Dec. 19	Waterloo - -	Richard Alsager -	Sept. 11	— L. & R.B.	39 D 39 M	To Bombay and China.
1821 Jan. 3	Charles Grant -	Hugh Scott - -	Sept. 17	— L. & R.B.	38 F 38 R	To Bombay and China.
Jan. 3	Kent - -	Henry Cobb -	Aug. 3	— L. & R.B.	41 H 41 Q	To Bombay and China.
Jan. 4	General Harris -	George Welstead -	1823 May 7	— L. & R.B.	32 E 32 N	To Madras and China.
Jan. 5	Kellie Castle -	Alexander Lindsay -	1822 Sept. 23	— L. & R.B.	92 B 92 I	To Madras and China.
Feb. 21	Vansittart -	W. H. C. Dalrymple	Nov. 29	— L. & R.B.	46 M 46 EE	To Bombay and China.
Feb. 28	Bridgewater - -	William Mitchell -	Sept. 19	— L. & R.B.	142 U 142 RR	To China.
Feb. 28	Hythe - -	John P. Wilson -	June 1	— L. & R.B.	28 A 28 G	To China.
Mar. 1	Herefordshire -	William Hope -	May 15	— L. & R.B.	49 F 49 R	To China.
Mar. 2	Windsor -	Thomas Haviside -	June 10	— L. & R.B.	29 C 29 K	To China.
Mar. 3	Minerva -	John Mills - -	Feb. 22	— L. & R.B.	14 O 14 HH	To China.
Mar. 7	Bombay - -	Charles Graham - succeeded by J. Stanton.	May 29	— L. & R.B.	48 G 48 S	To China.
Mar. 19	Thomas Grenville -	James B. Burnett -	July 3	— L. & R.B.	10 H 10 V	To Madras and Bengal.
Mar. 23	Marquis of Wellington	John Blanshard -	July 3	— L. & R.B.	56 F 56 O	To Madras and Bengal.
April 17	Albion - -	Charles Weller -	Sept. 30	—	81 J (A)	To Madras and Bengal.
May 14	Kingston -	Wm. Atkins Bowen	Sept. 30	—	244 C	To Bengal and Madras.
May 17	Barrosa -	Henry Hutchinson	June 12	—	99 D	To Bengal and Madras
May 17	Florentia - -	Samuel Remmington	Oct. 14	—	54 A	To Bengal and Madras.
May 18	Princess Charlotte of Wales.	Christopher Biden -	Aug. 5	— L. & R.B.	53 E 53 N	To Bengal.
May 19	Rose - - -	Thomas McTaggart -	Aug. 6	— L. & R.B.	59 M 59 DD	To Bengal.
July 20	Scaleby Castle - -	D. R. Newall -	Nov. 12	— L. & R.B.	34 N 34 CC	To China.
Oct. 11	Earl of Balcarras -	Peter Cameron -	1823 July 1	— L. & R.B.	35 E 35 O	To Bengal and China.
Oct. 11	Thomas Coutts -	Alexander Chrystie -	June 10	— L. & R.B.	15 C 15 K	To Madras and China.
Oct. 17	Sir David Scott -	William Hunter -	July 14	— L. & R.B.	33 A 33 G	To Bengal and China.
Oct. 17	William Fairlie -	Kennard Smith -	July 2	— L. & R.B.	57 A 57 G	To Madras and China.
Nov. 9	Berwickshire - -	J. Shepherd - -	April 18	— L. & R.B.	31 A 31 G	To Bombay and China.
Nov. 9	Duke of York - -	Arch. H. Campbell -	April 10	— L.	94 G 94 T	To Bombay and China.
Nov. 9	Dunira - -	Montgomerie Hamilton	June 6	— L. & R.B.	21 C 21 K	To Bombay and China.
Nov. 26	Duchess of Athol -	E. M. Daniell - -	July 7	— L. & R.B.	19 A 19 G	To Madras, Bengal, and China.
Nov. 28	Macqueen - -	James Walker -	June 18	— L. & R.B.	11 A 11 G	To Bombay and China.
Nov. 29	Orwell - -	Thomas Sanders -	July 7	— L. & R.B.	20 C 20 K	To Bombay and China.
Dec. 12	Thames -	William Haviside -	1824 Feb. 17	— L. & R.B.	8 P 8 I I	To Bengal and China.
—	General Kyd -	Alexander Nairne -	1823 —	L. only.	52 M	———
1822 Jan. 7	Buckinghamshire -	Frederick Adams -	May 23	— L. & R.B.	18 D 18 N	To Bombay and China.
Jan. 23	London - -	John Barnet Sotheby	Aug. 9	[Four J.] L. & R.B.	1 Q to T 1 PP	To Madras and China.
Jan. 24	Asia - -	Thos. F. Balderston -	May 28	— L. & R.B.	24 X 24 YY	To Madras.

Log begins.	Ship.	Captain.	Log ends.	Ledger or Receipt Book.	Reference Number.	Remarks.
1822 Feb. 14	Canning	William Patterson	1823 July 12	— L. & R.B.	23 C 23 K	To Bencoolen and China.
Mar. 8	Regent	R. W. Norfor	Oct. 28	— Two R.B.	2 F 2 I & J	To China.
Mar. 15	Marquis of Huntley	J. S. H. Fraser	June 6	— L. & R.B.	7 F 7 Q	To China.
Mar. 16	Princess Amelia	T. Williams	May 26	— L. & R.B.	36 R 36 OO	To China.
Mar. 18	Lady Melville	Richard Clifford	June 6	— L. & R.B.	22 E 22 O	To China.
Mar. 26	Prince Regent	John Innes	June 24	— L. & R.B.	25 F 25 P	To Madras.
April 9	Astell	T. W. Aldham	July 1	— L. & R.B.	12 H 12 R	To Madras and Bengal.
April 12	Layton	David Miller	Feb. 8	—	16 A	To Bencoolen.
April 20	Warren Hastings	George Mason	Aug. 18	— L. & R.B.	9 S 9 PP	To Madras and Bengal.
April 21	Orient	Thomas White	1824 July 22	—	47 A	To Calcutta.
April 22	General Hewett	James Pearson succeeded by T. W. Barrow.	1823 Aug. 28	— L. & R.B.	37 D 37 I	To Bengal.
April 22	Marchioness of Ely	Brook Kay	Aug. 22	— L. & R.B.	6 E 6 N	To Bengal.
April 23	Dorsetshire	Samuel Lyde	May 30	— L. & R.B.	13 J 13 S	To Bengal.
April 24	Winchelsea	William Adamson	June 19	— L. & R.B.	4 M 4 DD	To Bengal.
May 23	Coldstream	George Stephens	July 25	— L. & R.B.	5 E 5 N	To Madras and Bengal.
Oct. 17	Royal George	Christopher Biden	1824 May 5	— L. & R.B.	17 Q 17 II	To Bengal and China.
Nov. 13	Farquharson	William Cruickshank	April 14	— L. & R.B.	40 B 40 J	To Bombay and China.
Nov. 13	General Kyd	Alexander Nairne	April 30	— L. & R.B.	52 E 52 N	To Bengal and China.
Nov. 13	Inglis	Samuel Serle	May 17	— L. & R.B.	30 G 30 S	To Bombay and China.
Nov. 14	Herefordshire	William Hope	May 4	— L. & R.B.	49 G 49 S	To Bombay and China.
Nov. 14	Kent	Henry Cobb	Mar. 29	— L. & R.B.	41 I 41 R	To Bengal and China.
Nov. 14	Repulse	John Paterson	June 16	— L. & R.B.	51 B 51 H	To China.
Dec. 13	Hythe	J. P. Wilson	June 6	— L. & R.B.	28 B 28 H	To Bengal and China.
Dec. 13	Windsor	Thomas Haviside	July 1	— L. & R.B.	29 D 29 L	To Bengal and China.
Dec. 14	Bridgewater	William Mitchell	May 9	— L. & R.B.	42 V 42 SS	To Bombay and China.
Dec. 27	Kellie Castle	E. L. Adams	June 4	— L. & R.B.	92 C 92 J	To Madras and China.
Dec. 27	Waterloo	Richard Alsager	April 26	— L. & R.B.	39 E 39 N	To Bombay and China.
Dec. 30	Scaleby Castle	David Rae Newall	May 11	— L. & R.B.	34 O & P 34 DD	To Bombay and China.
—	Castle Huntley	H. A. Drummond	1823 —	L. & R.B. only.	3 Q	——
—	St. Helena	James Fairfax	1830 —	L. & R.B. only.	327 C	——
1823 Feb. 13	Charles Grant	William Hay	1824 May 18	— L. & R.B.	38 G 38 S	To China.
Feb. 24	Warren Hastings	Richard Rawes	July 13	— L. & R.B.	9 T 9 QQ	To China.
Feb. 26	Bombay	John Hine	April 27	— L. & R.B.	48 H 48 T	To China.
Feb. 27	Lowther Castle	Thomas Baker	June 15	— L. & R.B.	50 H 50 U	To China.
Feb. 27	Vansittart	W. H. C. Dalrymple	July 14	— L. & R.B.	46 N 46 FF	To China.
Mar. 1	Atlas	Chas. Otway Mayne	June 25	— L. & R.B.	27 L 27 Y	To Madras and China.
Mar. 12	Princess Charlotte of Wales.	C. B. Gribble	May 28	— L. & R.B.	53 F 53 O	To Madras and Bengal.
Mar. 13	Marquis of Wellington	John Blanshard	June 16	— L. & R.B.	56 G 56 P	To Madras and Bengal.

Log begins.	Ship.	Captain.	Log ends.	Ledger or Receipt Book.	Reference Number.	Remarks.
1823 April 3	Potton - -	Thomas Wellbank -	1824 Sept. 11	—	26 B	To Bengal.
April 15	Florentia - -	John Wimble -	May 24	—	54 B	To Bengal.
April 18	Abberton - - -	Lucas Percival -	July 5	—	55 B	To Bengal.
April 24	Minerva -	George Probyn -	Aug. 18	— L. & R.B.	14 P 14 II	To Bengal.
April 24	Thomas Grenville -	William Manning -	June 4	— L. & R.B.	10 I 10 W	To Bengal.
May 10	Rockingham -	C. Beach - -	July 7	—	124 H	To Bengal.
May 10	Royal George - -	William Reynolds -	July 14	—	17 R	To Bengal.
June 10	Buckinghamshire -	Richard Glasspoole -	July 27	— L. & R.B.	18 E & F 18 O	To China.
Nov. 17	Duke of York -	A. H. Campbell - succeeded by W. Pitman.	1825 April 6	— L. & R.B.	94 H 94 U	To Bombay, Madras, and China.
Nov. 17	Thos. Coutts - -	Alexander Chrystie -	April 21	— L. & R.B.	15 D 15 L	To Bombay and China.
Nov. 18	Castle Huntley -	H. A. Drummond -	June 7	— L. & R.B.	3 G 3 R	To Bombay and China.
Nov. 18	General Harris -	G. Welstead - -	May 20	— L. & R.B.	32 F 32 O	To Bencoolen and China.
Nov. 20	Macqueen - -	James Walker -	May 17	— L. & R.B.	11 B 11 H	To Bengal and China.
Nov. 28	Duchess of Athol -	E. M. Daniell - -	April 20	— L. & R.B.	19 B 19 H	To Bengal and China.
Dec. 17	Canning - -	James Head - succeeded by Philip Baylis.	Oct. 6	— L. & R.B.	23 D 23 L	To Bengal and China.
Dec. 17	Earl of Balcarras -	P. Cameron - -	May 28	— L. & R.B.	35 F 35 O (a)	To Bengal and China.
Dec. 17	London - -	J. B. Sotheby - -	Oct. 3	[Three J] L. & R.B.	1 U, V, & W 1 QQ	To Bombay and China.
Dec. 31	Dunira - - -	M. Hamilton - -	July 7	— L. & R.B.	21 D 21 L	To Bombay and China.
Dec. 31	Lady Melville -	Richard Clifford -	June 14	— L. & R.B.	22 F 22 P	To Madras and China.
Dec. 31	Marquis Camden -	T. Larkins - -	June 15	— L. & R.B.	58 E 58 O	To Bombay and China.
1824 Jan. 9	William Fairlie -	Kennard Smith -	June 1	— L. & R.B.	57 B 57 H	To Madras and China.
Feb. 28	Princess Amelia -	Thomas Williams -	June 29	[Two J.] L. & R.B.	36 S & T 36 PP	To China.
Mar. 1	Orwell - -	Wm. R. Farrer -	July 16	— L. & R.B.	20 D 20 L	To China.
Mar. 5	Marquis of Huntley -	J. S. H. Fraser -	July 1	— L. & R.B.	7 G 7 R	To China.
Mar. 5	Thames -	William Haviside -	July 20	— L. & R.B.	8 Q 8 JJ	To China.
Mar. 30	Asia - -	T. F. Balderston -	June 23	— L. & R.B.	24 Y 24 ZZ	To Madras and Bengal.
Mar. 31	Marchioness of Ely -	Charles E. Mangles -	May 16	— L. & R.B.	6 F 6 O	To Madras and Bengal.
April 2	Rose - -	Thomas Marquis -	July 29	— L. & R.B.	59 N 59 EE	To Madras and Bengal.
April 29	Astell - -	John Levy - -	June 21	— L. & R.B.	12 I 12 S	To Madras and Bengal.
April 29	Prince Regent -	Henry Hosmer -	July 20	— L. & R.B.	25 G 25 Q	To Calcutta.
May 10	Boyne - -	George Stephens -	Aug. 18	—	45 B	To Bengal and Madras.
May 15	Layton - -	David Miller -	Aug. 12	—	16 B	To Calcutta and Bencoolen.
May 17	Claudine - -	George Nicholls -	June 21	—	44 A	To Bengal and Madras.
May 29	General Hewett -	T. W. Barrow - -	Aug. 18	— L. & R.B.	37 E 37 J	To Bengal.
July 12	Juliana - -	A. Fothringham -	July 28	—	75 C	To China and Quebec.
July 12	Moffatt - -	R. R. Brown - -	Aug. 1	—	48 D	To China.
Nov. 6	Vansittart - -	W. H. C. Dalrymple	1826 June 19	— L. & R.B.	46 O 46 GG	To Bombay and China.
Nov. 6	Windsor - -	Thomas Haviside -	June 6	— L. & R.B.	29 E 29 M	To Bombay, Madras, and China.

Log begins.	Ship.	Captain.	Log ends.	Ledger or Receipt Book.	Reference Number.	Remarks.
1824 Nov. 17	Berwickshire -	John Shepherd -	1825 May 18	— L. & R.B.	31 B 31 H	To Bengal and China.
Nov. 20	General Kyd -	Alexander Nairne -	1826 April 8	— L. & R.B.	52 F 52 O	To Bengal and China.
Nov. 20	Hythe -	John P. Wilson -	May 27	— L. & R.B.	28 C 28 I	To Bengal and China.
Nov. 23	Repulse -	John Paterson -	April 5	— L. & R.B.	51 C 51 I	To China.
Dec. 6	Bridgewater -	John R. Manderson	May 2	— L. & R.B.	42 W 42 TT	To Bengal and China.
Dec. 20	Farquharson -	William Cruickshank	May 29	— L. & R.B.	40 C 40 J	To Bombay and China.
Dec. 20	Inglis -	Samuel Serle -	May 9	— L. & R.B.	30 H 30 T	To Bombay and China.
Dec. 20	Scaleby Castle -	David Rae Newall -	June 16	— L. & R.B.	34 Q 34 EE	To Bengal and China.
Dec. 21	Kellie Castle -	Edw. L. Adams -	Mar. 4	— L. & R.B.	92 D 92 K	To Bombay and China.
Dec. 22	Sir David Scott -	John A. Tween -	1824 May 26	— L. & R.B.	33 B 33 H	To Bengal and China.
—	Kent -	Henry Cobb -	—	R.B. only.	41 S	An article on "The Burning of the Kent," a painting by T. M. Hemy, is attached to this Receipt Book.
1825 Jan. 4	Atlas -	John Hine	1826 June 15	— L. & R.B.	27 M 27 Z	To Madras and China.
Jan. 4	Herefordshire -	William Hope -	May 17	— L. & R.B.	49 H 49 T	To Madras and China.
Feb. 17	Minerva -	George Probyn -	June 5	— L. & R.B.	14 Q 14 JJ	To Calcutta.
Feb. 17	Princess Charlotte of Wales.	Christopher Biden -	July 3	— L. & R.B.	53 G 53 P	To Ceylon and Bengal.
Feb. 17	Warren Hastings -	George Mason -	July 28	— L. & R.B.	9 U 9 SS	To Madras.
Mar. 4	Charles Grant -	William Hay -	Oct. 18	— L. & R.B.	38 H 38 T	To Bengal and China.
Mar. 4	Lowther Castle -	Thomas Baker -	June 1	— L. & R.B.	50 I 50 V	To China.
Mar. 4	Warren Hastings -	Richard Rawes -	July 25	— L. & R.B.	9 V 9 RR	To China.
Mar. 10	Bombay -	John Charretie -	July 11	— L. & R.B.	48 I 48 U	To China.
April 18	Commodore Hayes -	L. W. Moncrief -	Jan. 16	—	161 B	To Madras.
April 18	Guildford -	Magnus Johnson -	June 20	—	78 C	To Madras and Bengal.
April 18	James Sibbald -	James K. Forbes -	1825 Oct. 16	—	64 F	To Bombay.
April 18	Marquis of Wellington	John Blanshard	1826 July 18	— L. & R.B.	56 H 56 Q	To Bengal.
April 18	Thomas Grenville -	William Manning	Aug. 7	— L. & R.B.	10 J 10 X	To Bengal.
April 19	Malcolm -	James Eyles -	1825 Sept. 22	—	70 A	To Madras.
April 21	Duke of York -	Robert Locke -	1826 July 10	— L. & R.B.	94 I 94 V	To China.
April 27	Cambridge -	James Barber -	1825 Oct. 30	—	66 D	To Bombay.
April 28	Coldstream -	William Hall -	1826 June 18	—	5 F	To Madras and Bengal.
May 2	Albion -	Charles Weller -	July 12	—	81 K	To Madras and Bengal.
May 2	Childe Harold -	William W. West -	June 10	—	62 A	To Madras and Bengal.
May 3	Maitland -	John L. Studd -	1825 Nov. 15	—	67 B	To Bombay.
May 10	Berwick -	John M. Ellbeck -	Dec. 5	—	61 D	To Bengal.
May 18	Broxbornebury -	Thomas Fewson -	1826 Oct. 23	—	82 B	To Madras, Bengal and China.
May 18	Orient -	Thomas White -	Sept. 18	—	47 B	To China.
May 18	Roxburgh Castle -	George Denny -	May 27	—	108 A	To China and Quebec.
May 24	Bussorah Merchant -	Francis G. Stewart -	1825 Dec. 22	—	63 A	To Madras and Calcutta.

Log begins.	Ship.	Captain.	Log ends.	Ledger or Receipt Book.	Reference Number.	Remarks.
1825 May 24	Lord Hungerford	James Talbert	1825 Dec. 10	—	69 A	To Bengal.
June 3	Henry Porcher	John Thomson	1826 Oct. 9	—	73 B	To New South Wales and China.
June 6	Countess of Harcourt	Thomas Delafons	June 18	—	146 A	To China and Halifax.
June 8	Java	Thomas Driver	Mar. 11	—	169 A	To Bengal.
Aug. 16	Eliza	William Faith	Feb. 22	—	68 B	To Calcutta.
Aug. 27	Clyde	Daniel Nesbitt Munro	April 15	—	345 D	To Bengal.
Nov. 17	Edinburgh	Henry Bax	1827 May 1	— L. & R.B.	95 A 95 E	To Bombay and China.
Nov. 18	Abercrombie Robinson	John Innes	April 17	— L. & R.B.	71 A 71 E	To Bombay and China.
Nov. 24	Thames	William Haviside	Oct. 12	— L. & R.B.	8 B 8 KK	To Bengal and China.
Dec. 6	Waterloo	Richard Alsager	1826 May 18	— L. & R.B.	39 F 39 O	To Bengal and China.
Dec. 9	Earl of Balcarras	Peter Cameron	1827 May 16	— L. & R.B.	35 G 35 P	To Bengal and China.
Dec. 9	Macqueen	James Walker	May 7	— L. & R.B.	11 C 11 I	To Bengal and China.
Dec. 9	Sir David Scott	William Hunter	July 10	— L. & R.B.	33 C 33 I	To Bengal and China.
Dec. 10	Dunira	M. Hamilton	Aug. 27	— L. & R.B.	21 E 21 M	To Bengal and China.
Dec. 23	Duchess of Athol	E. M. Daniell	April 20	— L. & R.B.	19 C 19 I	To Bombay and China.
Dec. 23	Thomas Coutts	Alex. Chrystie	April 4	— L. & R.B.	15 E 15 M	To Bombay and China.
Dec. 27	George the Fourth	Thomas W. Barrow	May 16	— L. & R.B.	79 A 79 E	To Bengal and China.
—	Buckinghamshire	Richard Glasspoole	1826 —	L. & R.B. only.	18 P	———
—	Royal George	Charles S. Timins	—	L. & R.B. only.	17 JJ	This ship was burnt on the 24th December 1825.
1826 Jan. 9	Castle Huntley	H. A. Drummond	1827 June 13	— L. & R.B.	3 H 3 S	To Madras and China.
Jan. 12	Lady Melville	Richard Clifford	Aug. 28	— L. & R.B.	22 G 22 Q	To Bengal and China.
Jan. 18	Marquis of Huntley	J. S. H. Fraser	July 18	— L. & R.B.	7 H 7 S	To Madras and China.
Feb. 9	Marquis Camden	Gilson E. Fox	June 8	— L. & R.B.	58 F 58 P	To China.
Mar. 7	Canning	B. Broughton	May 8	— L. & R.B.	23 E 23 M	To China.
Mar. 7	General Harris	Joseph Stanton	May 9	— L. & R.B.	32 G 32 P	To China.
Mar. 7	London	J. B. Sotheby	June 23	— L. & R.B.	1 X 1 RR	To China.
Mar. 7	Orwell	W. E. Farrer	June 28	— L. & R.B.	20 E 20 M	To China.
Mar. 7	William Fairlie	Thomas Blair	June 5	— L. & R.B.	57 C 57 I	To China.
Mar. 22	Marchioness of Ely	Charles Edward Mangles.	June 12	— L. & R.B.	6 G 6 P	To Madras and Bengal.
Mar. 22	Rose	Thomas Marquis	July 26	— L. & R.B.	59 O 59 FF	To Madras and Bengal.
Mar. 23	Prince Regent	Henry Hosmer	June 22	— L. & R.B.	25 H 25 R	To Madras and Bengal.
April 13	Marquis of Hastings	William Ostler	Jan. 13	—	74 B	From China to England.
April 17	Abberton	Lucas Percival	June 21	—	55 C	To Madras and Bengal.
April 17	Lady Raffles	James Coxwell	July 4	—	160 B	To Madras and Bengal.
April 25	Asia	T. F. Balderson	Aug. 31	—	24 BB	To Bengal.
May 18	Asia	T. F. Stead	June 2	—	24 AA	To China and Quebec.
May 18	Florentia	T. W. Aldham	June 9	—	54 C	To Bengal.
May 18	Malcolm	James Eyles	June 8	—	70 B	ToMadras and Bengal.
May 26	James Sibbald	J. K. Forbes	April 21	—	64 G	To Madras and Bengal.
May 27	Ann and Amelia	H. W. Ford succeeded by James Trist.	June 23	—	80 B	To China and Quebec.

Log begins.	Ship.	Captain.	Log ends.	Ledger or Receipt Book.	Reference Number.	Remarks.
1826 May 27	Lord Amherst	John Cragie	1827 May 31	—	76 A	To China.
May 31	Hercules	William Vaughan	1826 Dec. 1	—	77 B	To Madras and Bengal.
June 3	Asia	William Adamson	1827 June 5	—	24 Z	To Whampoa.
June 3	Moffatt	R. R. Brown	June 4	—	43 E	To China.
June 8	Cambridge	James Barber	Feb. 1	—	66 E	To Madras.
June 10	Isabella	William Wiseman	July 3	—	60 D	To China.
June 10	Princess Amelia	James Kellaway	July 2	—	36 U	To China.
June 19	Winchelsea	R. B. Everest	July 17	—	4 N	To China.
June 20	Cornwall	W. Younghusband	1826 Dec. 31	—	90 D	To Bengal.
June 21	Lady Kennaway	Thomas Surflen	Dec. 14	—	65 A	To Bengal.
Aug. 10	Coldstream	George Stephens	1827 April 26	—	5 G	To Madras.
Aug. 14	Fort William	James Neish	Jan. 15	—	91 K	To Bengal.
Aug. 16	Cumbrian	Joseph Blyth	Feb. 12	—	83 C	To Madras.
Nov. 14	Atlas	John Hine	1828 July 8	— L. & R.B.	27 N 27 AA	To Bombay and China.
Nov. 17	Lowther Castle	Thomas Baker	April 29	— L. & R.B.	50 J 50 W	To Bombay and China.
Nov. 24	Berwickshire	John Shepherd	1827 April 11	— L. & R.B.	31 C 31 I	To Bengal and China.
Nov. 25	Lord Lowther	Charles Steward	April 19	— L.	72 A 72 E	To Bombay and China.
Nov. 29	Duke of York	Robert Locke	1828 April 25	— L. & R.B.	94 J 94 W	To Bengal and China.
Nov. 29	Herefordshire	J. C. Whiteman	April 15	— L. & R.B.	49 I 49 U	To Bengal and China.
Dec. 1	Mangles	William Carr	1827 May 11	—	89 D	To Bombay.
Dec. 14	Scaleby Castle	David R. Newall	1828 July 15	— L. & R.B.	34 R 34 FF	To Bengal and China.
Dec. 15	Vansittart	W. H. C. Dalrymple	July 11	— L. and two R.B.	46 P 46 HH	To Bengal and China.
Dec. 28	Hythe	John P. Wilson	May 3	— L. & R.B.	28 D 28 J	To Bombay and China.
Dec. 28	Inglis	Samuel Serle	July 8	— L. & R.B.	30 J 30 U	To Madras, Bengal, and China.
Dec. 28	Windsor	A. F. Proctor	July 5	— L. & R.B.	29 F 29 N	To Madras, Bengal, and China.
1827 Jan. 1	England	John Reay	1827 July 6	—	88 A	To New South Wales and China.
Jan. 1	Farquharson	William Cruickshank	1828 May 24	— L. & R.B.	40 D 40 K	To China.
Jan. 3	Charles Grant	William Hay	May 12	— L. & R.B.	38 I 38 U	To Bombay and China.
Jan. 12	General Kyd	Alexander Nairne	May 12	— L.	52 G 52 P	To Madras and China.
Jan. 12	Waterloo	William Manning	May 6	— L. & R.B.	39 G 39 P	To Madras and China.
Jan. 13	Bombay	John Charretie	May 14	— L. & R.B.	48 J 48 V	To Madras and China.
Feb. 26	Duke of Sussex	W. H. Whitehead	July 8	— L. & R.B.	87 A 87 E	To China.
Feb. 26	Kellie Castle	W. H. Ladd	June 2	— L. and three R.B.	92 E 92 L	To China.
Mar. 1	Boyne	W. L. Pope	1827 Sept. 25	—	45 C	From China to England.
Mar. 13	Alfred	J. Pearson	1828 Mar. 3	—	140 N	To China.
Mar. 13	Broxbornebury	Thomas Fewson	Mar. 18	—	82 C	To China.

Log begins.	Ship.	Captain.	Log ends.	Ledger or Receipt Book.	Reference Number.	Remarks.
1827 Mar. 13	Lord Hungerford -	William Heathorn	1828 Mar. 27	—	69 B	To China.
Mar. 20	Barrosa -	H. Hutchinson -	April 15	—	99 R	To China.
Mar. 27	Minerva	George Probyn	June 5	— L. & R.B.	14 R 14 KK	To Madras and Bengal.
Mar. 27	Princess Charlotte of Wales.	Christopher Biden	July 12	— L. & R.B.	53 H 53 Q	To Madras and Bengal.
Mar. 28	Warren Hastings -	George Mason -	Aug. 18	— L. & R.B.	9 W 9 TT	To Bengal.
April 25	Marquis of Wellington	Alfred Chapman -	July 15	— L. & R.B.	56 I 56 R	To Bengal and Madras.
April 25	Thomas Grenville -	Charles Shea -	Sept. 5	— L. & R.B.	10 K 10 Y	To Bengal.
May 11	Astell -	John Levy -	July 3	—	12 J	To China and Halifax.
May 12	Childe Harold	W. W. West -	June 11	—	62 B	ToBengal and Madras.
May 21	Larkins - -	W. Campbell -	July 5	—	104 F	To China.
May 21	Parmelia - - -	J. Wimble - -	July 22	—	145 A	To Bengal, Vizagapatam, and Madras.
May 30	Lord Melville - -	Robert Brown - -	July 9	—	144 G	To Bengal and Madras.
June 17	Neptune -	John Cumberlege -	Aug. 6	—	98 S	To Bombay, Bengal, and Madras.
Nov. 13	Guildford -	Magnus Johnson -	May 7	—	78 D	From China to England.
Nov. 15	Bridgewater	J. R. Manderson -	Mar. 18	— L. & two R.B.	42 X 42 UU	To Bombay and China.
Nov. 15	Marquis of Hastings -	J. J. Drake - -	May 30	—	74 C	From China to England.
Nov. 19	Dunira - - -	M. Hamilton -	1829 April 22	— L. & R.B.	21 F 21 N	To Bombay and China.
Nov. 19	Edinburgh -	Henry Bax -	April 30	— L. & R.B.	95 B 95 F	To Bombay and China.
Nov. 19	General Harris - -	Joseph Stanton	July 17	— L. & R.B.	32 H 32 Q	To Bengal and China.
Nov. 29	Repulse	C. B. Gribble - -	1828 April 18	— L. & R.B.	51 D 51 J	To Bengal and China.
Dec. 3	Sir David Scott - -	J. O. McTaggart -	1829 April 25	— L. & R.B.	33 D 33 J	To Bengal.
Dec. 3	Thomas Coutts -	Alex. Chrystie	July 16	— L. & R.B.	15 F 15 N	To Bengal and China.
Dec. 14	Buckinghamshire	Richard Glasspoole -	1828 May 26	— L. & R.B.	18 G 18 Q	To Bengal and China.
Dec. 18	Berwickshire - -	Frederick Madan -	1829 April 22	— L. & R.B.	31 D 31 J	To Bengal and China.
Dec. 18	Reliance - -	Charles S. Timins	July 8	— L. & R.B.	123 A 123 D	To Bengal and China.
Dec. 19	Marquis of Huntley	J. S. H. Fraser -	June 12	— L.	7 I 7 T	To Bengal and China.
1828 Jan. 1	Duchess of Athol -	E. M. Daniell - -	April 22	— L. & R.B.	19 D 19 J	To Bombay and China.
Jan. 1	George the Fourth -	Thomas W. Barrow -	June 15	— L. & R.B.	79 B 79 F	To Bengal and China.
Jan. 1	Marquis Camden -	T. Larkins -	Aug. 8	— L. & R.B.	58 G 58 Q	To Bombay and China.
Jan. 3	AbercrombieRobinson	John Innes - -	May 19	— L. & R.B.	71 B 71 F	To Bombay and China.
Jan. 16	Macqueen - -	James Walker -	June 15	— L. & R.B.	11 D 11 J	To Madras and China.
Jan. 16	William Fairlie -	Thomas Blair - -	June 3	— L. & R.B.	57 D 57 J	To Madras and China.
Jan. 17	Lord Lowther - -	Charles Steward -	July 3	— L.	72 B 72 F	To Madras and China.
Feb. 1	Castle Huntley - -	Thomas Dunkin -	July 20	— L. & R.B.	3 I 3 T	To China.
Feb. 24	Earl of Balcarras -	B. Broughton - -	July 15	— L. & R.B.	35 H 35 Q	To Bengal and China.
Mar. 1	Orwell - - -	Wm. E. Farrer -	Aug. 13	— L. & R.B.	20 F 20 N	To China.
Mar. 3	Canning -	Philip Baylis -	May 20	— L. & R.B.	23 F 23 N	To China.
Mar. 3	London - -	Timothy Smith -	May 13	— L. & R.B.	1 Y 1 SS	To China.
Mar. 15	Prince Regent - -	Henry Hosmer -	July 21	— L. & R.B.	25 I 25 S	To Madras and Bengal.
Mar. 17	Rose - - -	Thomas Marquis -	Sept. 22	— L. & R.B.	59 F 59 GG	To Madras and Bengal.

Log begins.	Ship.	Captain.	Log ends.	Ledger or Receipt Book.	Reference Number.	Remarks.
1828 April 8	Marchioness of Ely	Chas. Edd. Mangles	1829 July 4	— L. & R.B.	6 H 6 Q	To Madras and Bengal.
April 8	Asia	T. F. Balderston	June 13	— L. & R.B.	24 CC 24 BBB	To Madras and Bengal.
April 29	Hercules	William Vaughan	July 14	—	77 C	To Madras and Bengal.
April 29	Malcolm	James Eyles	July 22	—	70 C	To Madras and Bengal.
May 13	Abberton	Lucas Percival	Sept. 2	—	55 D	To Bengal.
May 14	James Pattison	Joseph Grote	July 7	—	84 A	To Bengal.
May 16	Lady Kennaway	Thomas Delafons	June 12	—	65 B	To China and Nova Scotia.
May 21	Lord William Bentinck	J. Craigie	May 27	—	105 A	To China.
May 29	Moira	R. Thornhill	July 14	—	96 B	To Bengal and Madras.
Mar. 29	Susan	G. Holiday	Feb. 12	—	103 A	To Bengal.
June 2	Coromandel	Thomas Boyes	Feb. 3	—	206 C	To Bengal.
June 12	Barrosa	H. Hutchinson	1828 Dec. 20	—	99 F	To Bengal.
June 12	Coldstream	David Miller	1829 Jan. 10	—	5 H	To Bengal.
June 12	Maitland	Joseph Short	Aug. 24	—	67 C	To Bengal.
June 12	Moffatt	R. R. Brown	1828 Dec. 18	—	43 F	To Bengal.
June 13	James Sibbald	Richard Cole	1829 Jan. 13	—	64 H	To Bengal.
June 18	William Money	W. B. Fulcher	Jan. 27	—	207 A	To Bengal.
Nov. 21	Bridgewater	J. R. Manderson	1830 June 3	— R.B.	42 Y 42 VV	To Bengal and China.
Nov. 21	Buckinghamshire	Richard Glasspoole	Sept. 23	— L. & R.B.	18 H 18 R	To Bombay and China.
Nov. 21	Herefordshire	William Hope	July 31	— L. & R.B.	49 J 49 V	To Bombay and China.
Nov. 21	Lady Melville	Richard Clifford	July 30	— L. & R.B.	22 H 22 R	To Bengal and China.
Dec. 8	Farquharson	John Cruickshank	Oct. 1	— L. & R.B.	40 E 40 L	To Bengal and China.
Dec. 8	General Kyd	Samuel Serle	Sept. 25	— L. & R.B.	52 H 52 Q	To Bombay and China.
Dec. 8	Inglis	J. Dudman	Sept. 27	— L. & R.B.	30 J 30 V	To Bengal and China.
Dec. 22	Duke of York	R. Locke	July 30	— L. & R.B.	94 K 94 X	To Bengal and China.
Dec. 22	Hythe	G. C. Arbuthnot	Aug. 16	— L. & R.B.	28 E 28 L	To Bengal and China.
1829 Jan. 5	Atlas	John Hine	Aug. 6	— L. & R.B.	27 O 27 BB	To Bombay and China.
Jan. 5	Duke of Sussex	W. H. Whitehead	Aug. 2	— L. & R.B.	87 B 87 F	To Bombay and China.
Jan. 5	Kellie Castle	E. L. Adams	Sept. 28	— L. & R.B.	92 F 92 M	To China.
Jan. 19	Thames	J. K. Forbes	Aug. 30	— L. & R.B.	8 S 8 LL	To Madras and China.
Jan. 19	Windsor	Thomas Haviside	Sept. 28	— L. & R.B.	29 G 29 O	To Madras and China.
Jan. 25	Repulse	Henry Gribble	Aug. 5	— L. & R.B.	51 E 51 K	To Madras and China.
Mar. 5	Scaleby Castle	J. B. Burnett	Oct. 18	— L. & R.B.	34 S 34 GG	To China.
Mar. 5	Waterloo	D. R. Newall	Oct. 1	— L. & R.B.	89 H 89 Q	To China.
Mar. 10	Charles Grant	R. B. Everest	Oct. 21	— L. & R.B.	38 J 38 V	To China.
Mar. 10	Lowther Castle	G. K. Bathie	Oct. 18	— L. & R.B.	50 K 50 X	To China.
Mar. 12	Vansittart	Robert Scott	Oct. 15	— L. & R.B.	46 Q 46 II	To China.
Mar. 20	Minerva	George Probyn	May 4	— L. & R.B.	14 S 14 LL	To Madras.
Mar. 20	Thomas Grenville	Charles Shea	July 12	— L. & R.B.	10 L 10 Z	To Madras and Bengal.
April 19	Princess Charlotte of Wales	Christopher Biden	Aug. 31	— L. & R.B.	53 I 53 R	To Bengal.

Log begins.	Ship.	Captain.	Log ends.	Ledger or Receipt Book.	Reference Number.	Remarks.
1829 April 25	Marquis of Wellington	Alfred Chapman	1830 Aug. 10	— L. & R.B.	56 J 56 S	To Bengal and Madras.
May 11	Asia	H. Ager	Sept. 18	—	24 DD	To China.
May 18	Zenobia	J. A. Douglas	June 26	—	157 A	To Bengal and Madras.
May 19	Mangles	William Carr	July 22	—	89 E	To China and Nova Scotia.
May 25	Catherine	B. Fenn	June 9	—	97 B	To Bengal.
June 1	Eliza	David Sutton	Aug. 20	—	68 C	To Bengal.
June 1	Ganges	E. M. Boultbee	Mar. 15	—	86 N 86 O	To Bengal and Madras.
June 1	Lady Nugent	J. Wimble	Oct. 18	—	154 B	To Bengal. (Incomplete.)
Nov. 18	Duchess of Athol	E. M. Daniell	1831 April 12	— L. & R.B.	19 E 19 K	To Bombay and China.
Nov. 18	Thomas Coutts	Alexander Chrystie	April 13	— L. & R.B.	15 G 15 O	To Bombay and China.
Nov. 19	William Fairlie	Thomas Blair	April 19	— L. & R.B.	57 E 57 K	To Bengal and China.
Dec. 3	Abercrombie Robinson.	John Innes	May 10	— L. & R.B.	71 C 71 G	To Bombay and China.
Dec. 3	Macqueen	B. Lindsay	May 10	— L. & R.B.	11 E 11 K	To Bengal and China.
Dec. 18	Dunira	J. P. Wilson	April 20	— L. & R.B.	21 G 21 O	To Bengal and China.
Dec. 18	General Harris	J. Stanton	May 4	— L. & R.B.	32 I 32 R	To Bengal and China.
Dec. 18	Reliance	Charles S. Timins	May 19	— L. & R.B.	123 B 123 E	To Bengal and China.
Dec. 23	Orwell	R. M. Isacke	May 3	— L. & R.B.	20 G 20 O	To Bombay and China.
1830 Jan. 4	Berwickshire	Frederick Madan	May 4	— L. & R.B.	31 E 31 K	To Bombay and China.
Jan. 4	Marquis Camden	T. Larkins	July 14	— L. & R.B.	58 H 58 R	To China.
Jan. 5	Edinburgh	Henry Bax	May 7	— L. & R.B.	95 C 95 G	To Bombay and China.
Jan. 18	London	T. Smith	May 18	— L. & R.B.	1 Z 1 TT	To China.
Jan. 19	Castle Huntley	H. A. Drummond	July 5	— L. & R.B.	3 J 3 U	To Madras and China.
Mar. 3	Astell	J. Laurence	June 27	— L. & R.B.	12 K 12 T	To China.
Mar. 3	Sir David Scott	D. J. Ward	June 22	— L. & R.B.	33 E 33 K	To China.
Mar. 4	Canning	Philip Baylis	June 21	— L. & R.B.	23 G 23 O	To China.
Mar. 4	Earl of Balcarras	B. Broughton	June 10	— L. & R.B.	35 I 35 R	To China.
Mar. 4	George the Fourth	T. W. Barrow	June 8	— L. & R.B.	79 C 79 G	To China.
Mar. 4	Lord Lowther	R. C. Fowler	June 24	— L. & R.B.	72 C 72 G	To China.
Mar. 17	Morley	W. Harrison	1830 Oct. 7	—	162 A	From China to England.
Mar. 20	Larkins	W. Campbell	Oct. 13	—	104 G	From China to England.
April 25	Susan	G. Holiday	1831 June 27	—	103 B	To Madras and Bengal.
April 26	Lady Kennaway	L. W. Moncrief	June 20	—	65 C	To Madras and Bengal.
April 27	Protector	G. Waugh	June 18	—	110 B	To Madras and Bengal.
April 30	Lady East	G. Denny	Aug. 3	—	111 A	To Madras and Bengal.
May 4	Bengal Merchant	G. R. Fox	Aug. 23	—	85 B	To Madras and Bengal.
May 10	Ann and Amelia	William Richards	June 22	—	80 C	To China.
May 11	Marquis of Hastings	Joseph Short	June 29	—	74 D	To Madras and Bengal.
May 13	Recovery	H. C. Chapman	May 27	—	106 C	To Madras and Bengal.
May 15	Malcolm	James Eyles	May 25	—	70 D	To Madras and Bengal.
May 19	Henry Porcher	G. J. Redman	July 11	—	73 C	To Madras and Bengal.
May 27	Roxburgh Castle	T. Buttanshaw	May 20	—	108 B	To Bengal.
May 30	Stakesby	T. Johnson	July 11	—	109 A	To Madras and Bengal.

Log begins.	Ship.	Captain.	Log ends.	Ledger or Receipt Book.	Reference Number.	Remarks.
1830 June 2	Maitland - -	James T. Brown -	1831 Mar. 31	—	67 D	To Bengal.
Dec. 7	Buckinghamshire -	Richard Glasspoole -	1832 Mar. 30	— L. & R.B.	18 I 18 S	To Bombay and China.
Dec. 7	Marquis of Huntley -	John Hine - -	June 20	— L. & R.B.	7 J 7 U	To Bombay and China
Dec. 7	Thames	James Keith Forbes	April 13	— L. & R.B.	8 T 8 MM	To Madras and China.
Dec. 8	Lady Melville - -	Robert Clifford -	April 24	— L. & R.B.	22 I 22 S	To Bengal and China.
Dec. 21	Farquharson - -	John Cruickshank	May 4	— L. & R.B.	40 F 40 M	To Bengal and China.
Dec. 21	General Kyd -	Alexander Nairne -	May 8	— L. & R.B.	52 I 52 R	To Bombay and China.
Dec. 23	Duke of Sussex	W. H. Whitehead -	April 17	— L. & R.B.	87 C 87 G	To Bombay and China.
1831 Jan. 4	Repulse - -	Henry Gribble	April 21	— L. & R.B.	51 F 51 L	To Madras and China.
Jan. 6	Vansittart - -	Robert Scott - -	April 18	— L. & R.B.	46 R 46 JJ	To Bengal and China.
Jan. 19	Hythe -	Thomas Shepherd -	May 19	— L. & R.B.	28 F 28 L	To Bombay and China.
Jan. 20	Herefordshire -	William Hope	May 22	— L. & R.B.	49 K 49 W	To Bombay and China.
Jan. 24	Warren Hastings	H. B. Avarne - -	June 18	— L. & R.B.	9 X 9 UU	To China.
Mar. 5	Duke of York -	R. Locke - -	June 30	— L. and two R.B.	94 L 94 Y	To China.
Mar. 5	Inglis -	J. Dudman -	June 5	— L. & R.B.	30 K 30 W	To China.
Mar. 5	Rose - - -	T. Marquis -	May 23	— L. & R.B.	59 Q 59 HH	To China.
Mar. 5	Waterloo - -	W. R. Blakeley -	Mar. 31	— L. & R.B.	39 I 39 R	To China.
Mar. 19	Bombay -	James Kellaway -	June 19	— L. & R.B.	48 K 48 W	To China.
Mar. 19	Lowther Castle -	Henry Harris	June 25	— L. & R.B.	50 L 50 Y	To China.
Mar. 19	Minerva - -	George Probyn -	May 8	— L. & R.B.	14 T 14 MM	To Madras and Bengal.
Mar. 19	Scaleby Castle	J. Hillman -	June 23	— L. & R.B.	34 T 34 HH	To China.
Mar. 21	Winchelsea -	P. H. Burt -	Sept. 3	— L. & R.B.	4 O & P 4 EE	To China.
April 1	Maitland -	James T. Brown -	1831 Aug. 29	—	67 E	From Calcutta to England.
April 19	Thomas Grenville	Charles Shea	1832 June 27	— L. & R.B.	10 M 10 AA	To Bengal.
May 18	Mangles	William Carr	May 23	—	89 F	To China and Nova Scotia.
May 19	Coldstream - -	William Hall	July 6	—	5 I	To China and Quetta.
May 30	Duke of Buccleugh -	A. Henning - -	May 19	—	132 G	To Madras and Bengal.
June 17	Orient	Thomas White -	July 11	—	47 C	To Bengal.
June 24	Oriental - -	J. Leader -	July 9	—	134 A	To Bengal.
June 27	Duke of Northumberland.	W. L. Pope - -	June 19	—	133 A	To Bengal.
July 15	Ganges - -	E. M. Boultbee -	Sept. 29	—	86 P	To Bengal.
July 16	Moira - -	S. Beadle -	July 27	—	96 C	To Bengal.
Dec. 12	Asia - - -	G. K. Bathie	1833 Mar. 25	— L. & R.B.	24 E 24 CCC	To Bengal and China.
Dec. 12	Duchess of Athol -	E. M. Daniell -	May 4	— L. & R.B.	19 F 19 L	To Bombay and China.
Dec. 12	Orwell -	James Dalrymple -	May 2	— L. & R.B.	20 H 20 P	To Bombay and China.
Dec. 19	Hooghly	P. J. Reeves -	1832 June 15	—	131 B	From China to England.
Dec. 22	Sir David Scott -	D. J. Ward -	1833 Aug. 12	— L. & R.B.	33 F 33 L	To Madras, Bengal, China.
Dec. 26	Dunira - -	M. Hamilton - -	May 28	— L. & R.B.	21 H 21 P	To Madras and China.

Log begins.	Ship.	Captain.	Log ends.	Ledger or Receipt Book.	Reference Number.	Remarks.
1831 Dec. 26	George the Fourth	T. W. Barrow	1833 April 10	— L. & R.B.	79 D 79 H	To Bombay and China.
Dec. 26	Macqueen	R. Lindsay	April 30	— L. & R.B.	11 F 11 U	To Madras and China.
Dec. 26	Marquis Camden	T. Larkins	July 5	— L. & R.B.	58 I 58 S	To Bombay and China.
Dec. 26	Thomas Coutts	Alex. Chrystie	May 1	— L. & R.B.	15 H 15 P	To Bombay and China.
Dec. 26	William Fairlie	Thomas Blair	June 18	— L. & R.B.	57 F 57 L	To Madras and China.
1832 Jan. 25	Abercrombie Robinson	John Innes	May 11	— L. & R.B.	71 D 71 H	To Bombay and China.
Jan. 25	Charles Grant	J. R. Manderson	May 20	— L. & R.B.	38 K 38 W	To Bengal and China.
Jan. 25	Reliance	C. S. Timins	July 16	— L. & R.B.	123 C 123 F	To Madras, Bengal, and China.
Jan. 29	Larkins	W. Campbell	1832 Aug. 16	—	104 H	From China to England.
Feb. 8	London	T. Smith	1833 May 16	— L. & R.B.	1 AA 1 UU	To Madras and China.
Feb. 8	Windsor	A. F. Proctor	July 11	— L. & R.B.	29 H 29 P	To China.
Feb. 26	Lord Amherst		1832 Sept. 5	—	76 B	In China Sea.
Mar. 12	Canning	Philip Baylis	1833 April 11	— L. & R.B.	23 H 23 P	To China.
Mar. 12	Edinburgh	D. Marshall	June 18	— L. & R.B.	95 D 95 H	To China.
Mar. 18	Berwickshire	H. L. Thomas	June 16	— L. & R.B.	31 F 31 L	To China.
May 5	Lord Lowther	R. C. Fowler	June 21	— L.& R.B.	72 D 72 H	To China.
May 18	Barrosa	O. H. Wilson	July 4	—	99 G	To China.
May 21	Bolton	Thomas Wedlock Aldham.	May 25	—	234 A	To Bengal.
May 27	Earl of Balcarras	B. Broughton	July 12	— L. & R.B.	35 J 35 S	To China.
May 30	Moffatt	James Cromarty	June 22	—	43 G	To China.
May 31	Broxbornebury	R. B. Shettler	June 11	—	82 D	To China.
June 9	Layton	Richard Saunders	June 14	—	16 C	To Madras and Bengal.
June 9	Recovery	T. Wellbank	June 19	—	106 D	To Bengal.
June 18	Cæsar	Henry Thompson	May 27	—	235 J	To Madras and Bengal.
July 13	Lord Amherst	John Hicks	May 21	—	76 C	To Bengal
July 14	Ann and Amelia	William Compton	Sept. 15	—	80 D	To Bengal.
July 17	Georgiana	H. Clement	Sept. 17	—	156 I & J	To Bengal.
July 23	Bencoolen	W. Tullis	July 1	—	158 A	To Bengal.
Dec. 3	Bombay	James Kellaway	1834 April 21	— L. & R.B.	48 L 48 X	To Bengal and China.
Dec. 3	Duke of Sussex	W. H. Whitehead	June 14	— L. & R.B.	87 D 87 H	To Bombay and China.
Dec. 8	Marquis of Huntley	John Hine	June 3	— L. & R.B.	7 K 7 V	To Bombay and China.
Dec. 6	Duke of York	R. Locke	1833 May 19	— R.B.	94 M 94 Z	To Madras and Bengal.
Dec. 13	Inglis	J. Dudman	1834 May 5	— L. & R.B.	30 L 30 X	To Madras, Bengal, and China.
Dec. 17	Buckinghamshire	Charles Shea	July 3	— L. & R.B.	18 J 18 T	To Madras, Bengal, and China.
Dec. 18	Herefordshire	Edward Foord	May 14	Two J. L. & R.B.	49 L & M 49 X	To Bombay and China.
Dec. 18	Kellie Castle	R. Pattullo	May 2	— L. & R.B.	92 G 92 N	To Madras, Bengal, and China.
Dec. 18	Warren Hastings	Thomas Sandys	May 23	— L. & R.B.	9 Y 9 VV	To Madras, Bengal, and China.
Dec. 19	Thames	John Rodes Pidding	May 6	— L.	8 U 8 NN	To Bombay and China.
1833 Jan. 2	Lowther Castle	Henry Harris	June 11	[Two J.] L. & R.B.	50 M & N 50 Z	To Bombay and China.

Log begins.	Ship.	Captain.	Log ends.	Ledger or Receipt Book.	Reference Number.	Remarks.
1833 Jan. 11	Larkins - -	W. Campbell -	1834 June 16	—	104 I	To Bengal and China.
Jan. 16	Castle Huntley	C. K. Johnstone -	May 18	—	3 K	To Madras and China.
Jan. 16	Vansittart -	Robert Scott - -	May 31	— L. & R.B.	46 S 44 KK	To Madras, Bengal, and China.
Jan. 18	Farquharson - -	John Cruickshank	April 29	— L. & R.B.	40 G 40 N	To Bombay and China.
Jan. 31	Lady Melville	Thomas Shepherd	May 7	— L. & R.B.	22 J 22 T	To Bombay and China.
Mar. 4	Prince Regent -	Richard Aplin -	June 19	— L. & R.B.	25 J 25 T	To China.
Mar. 18	Scaleby Castle -	J. Hillman -	April 1	— L. & R.B.	34 U 34 II	To China.
Mar. 18	Thomas Grenville -	James Burnett Burnett.	May 31	— L. & R.B.	10 N 10 BB	To China.
Mar. 18	Waterloo -	W. R. Blakely -	April 25	— L. & R.B.	89 J 39 S	To China.
Mar. 21	Minerva -	William Tiechurst -	June 9	— L. & R.B.	14 U 14 NN	To China.
Mar. 28	Rose - -	T. Marquis -	June 6	— L. & R.B.	59 R 59 II	To China.
May 16	William Money -	J. O'Brien -	Oct. 8	—	207 B	To China.
May 20	Moira	T. A. Johnson -	Nov. 12	—	96 D	To China.
May 20	Orient - -	Thomas White -	Aug. 1	—	47 D	To Madras and Bengal.
May 23	Elizabeth -	John Craigie -	Sept. 3	—	102 G	To China.
June 25	Bengal Merchant	John Campbell	June 20	—	85 C	To Bengal.
June 25	Severn -	G. M. Braithwaite	Aug. 28	—	139 E	To Bengal.
June 25	Sherburne -	J. Corbyn -	Aug. 20	—	146 A	To Bengal.
July 15	Catherine - -	R. Fenn - -	June 17	—	[illegible]7 C	To Bengal.
July 15	D'Auvergne -	P. De Huquet -	July 26	—	100 A	To Bengal.
July 15	Duke of Argyll	Henry Bristow	July 25	—	93 A	To Bengal.
July 16	General Palmer -	W. Thomas - -	Mar. 12	—	101 A	To Bengal.
Aug. 19	David Clark -	R. Rayne - -	June 28	—	153 A	From Calcutta to Singapore and China.
1836 Dec. 29	Atalanta -	John P. Campbell -	1837 April 13	[2 J's.] R.B.	807 & B 807 G	To Bombay. [The R.B. is with the "Berenice," 813 D.]
1837 Mar. 16	Berenice -	Capt. George Grant, I.N.	June 14	— R.B.	813 A 813 D	To Bombay. [This R.B. also contains receipts of the "Atlanta," 807 G.]
Oct. 11	Semiramis -	Capt. George Barnes Brucks, I.N.	1838 April 17	— R.B.	812 A, B, & C, 812 G	To Bombay, Mauritius, and Cochin.
1838 July 15	Semiramis - -	Lieut. John Patterson Porter, I.N., succeeded by Lieut. Charles Harrison Berthon, I.N., and Comr. John Park Sanders, I.N.	1844 July 21	—	812 D	Journals of voyages between Bombay, Kurrachee, Bushire, Cochin, and Surat.
Aug. 1	Atalanta - -	Lieut. Frederick Parry Webb, I.N., succeeded by Lieuts. Robert Lowe, I.N., Charles Harrison Berthon, I.N., F. W. Hopkins, I.N., &c.	1850 July 17	—	807 C & D	Journals of several voyages between Bombay, the Persian Gulf, Aden, and Suez.
Sept. 12	Berenice - -	Comr. William Lowe, I.N., succeeded by Lieuts. James Anthony Young, I.N., William Charles Barker, I.N., and John Glen Johnston, I.N.	1845 Jan. 19	—	813 B & C	Journals of voyages between Bombay, Kurrachee, Muscat, Aden, and Suez.

Log begins.	Ship.	Captain.	Log ends.	Ledger or Receipt Book.	Reference Number.	Remarks.
1838 Nov. 1	Hugh Lindsay -	Lieut. Philip Lewis Powell, I.N., succeeded by Lieuts. Frederick Parry Webb, I.N., Chas. Dugald Campbell, I.N., and John James Frushard, I.N.	1839 Nov. 21	—	805 A	Journals of voyages from Bombay— (a) To Aden. (b) To Suez. (c) To Muscat and Bussorah.
1839 Mar. 7	Zenobia - -	G. R. Fox - -	July 14	—	808 A	From Glasgow to Bombay.
Aug. 9	Hugh Lindsay	Lieutenant Charles Dugald Campbell, I.N., succeeded by Lieutenants John James Frushard, I.N., and Harry H. Hewett, I.N.	1841 April 22	—	805 B	Journals of voyages between Bombay, Muscat, Kurrachee, and Bassein.
Aug. 26	Queen - -	Walter Warden -	1840 Mar. 29	— L. & R.B.	800 A–A 800 A–F	To Calcutta.
Oct 7	Zenobia -	Lieut. Henry A. Ormsby, I.N., succeeded by Lieut. Alexander Henry Gordon, I.N., and Alfred Newman.	1842 Nov. 2	—	808 B	Journal of voyage between Bombay and Suez.
—	Cleopatra -	Lieut. John Park Sanders, I.N.	1839 —	R.B.	799 D	———
—	Nemesis -	William Hutcheons Hall.	1843 —	L.	809 C	———
Jan. 15	Sesostris -	Capt. Robt. Moresby, I.N.	1840 Feb. 27	—	804 B	Towards Ceylon.
Jan. 11	Sesostris - -	Capt. Robt. Moresby, I.N.	April 19	— R.B.	804 A & B 804 G	To the Cape of Good Hope.
April 10	Victoria - -	Lieut. George Borlase Kempthorne, I.N., succeeded by Lieuts. John Shaw Grieve, I.N., Andrew Nisbett, I.N., William Charles Barker, I.N., Frederick Erskine Manners, I.N., and George Norris Adams, I.N.	1854 Nov. 13	—	810 A & B	Journals of voyages between Bombay, Aden and Suez.
1840 July 8	Zenobia - -	Alfred Newman	1842 Nov. 27	—	808 C	Journals of two voyages between Bombay and Suez.
July 19	Sesostris - -	Capt. Robt. Moresby, I.N., succeeded by Lieuts. James Anthony Young, I.N., and Benjamin Hamilton, I.N.	1846 Aug. 18	—	804 D	Journals of several voyages from Bombay to Aden.
Aug. 18	Cleopatra - -	Lieut. Frederick Parry Webb, I.N., succeeded by Lieuts. John Bird, I.N., Henry Carne Boulderson, I.N., and Edward Webb Stone Daniell, I.N.	1845 April 21	—	799 A & B	From Bombay to Kurrachee, Suez, and Aden.
Dec. 19	Sesostris - -	Capt. Robt. Moresby, I.N., succeeded by Lieut. James Rennie, I.N.	1844 July 8	—	804 C	Journals of several voyages between Bombay, Muscat, Kurrachee, and Aden.

Log begins.	Ship.	Captain.	Log ends.	Ledger or Receipt Book.	Reference Number.	Remarks.
1841 April 3	Auckland - -	Comr. William Lowe, I.N., succeeded by Lieuts. Harry H. Hewett, I.N., and Richard Ethersey, I.N., Comr. Henry Blops Lynch, I.N., and Lieut. Allen Edward Ball, I.N.	1844 June 4	—	811 A	Journals of several voyages between Bombay, Aden, Mocha, Suez, Kurrachee, Singapore, and Chusan.
Sept. 29	Medusa -	Lieutenant Harry H. Hewett, I.N.	1842 Aug. 30	—	812 A	From Colombo to Singapore, Amoy, and Shanghai.
1842 Mar. 8	Memnon - -	Comr. Frederick Thomas Powell, I.N.	June 22	— R.B.	814 A 814 C	To Mauritius.
May 9	Acbar - -	Capt. John Pepper, I.N., and Comr. Richard Ethersey, I.N.	1844 Aug. 6	— R.B.	803 A & B 803 C	Journals of two voyages:— (1) To Macao. (2) From Bombay to Aden.
July 30	Semiramis - -	Lieut. Charles Harrison Berthon, I.N., succeeded by Commander John Park Sanders, I.N., and Lieutenants Edward Webb Stone Daniell, I.N., Benjamin Hamilton, I.N., and John James Frushard, I.N.	1853 Aug. 3	—	812 E	Journals of voyages between Bombay, Aden, and Suez.
1843 April 1	Memnon - -	Comr. Frederick Thomas Powell, I.N.	1843 April 30	—	814 B	Journal of voyage between Bombay and Kurrachee.
July 1	Acbar -	Capt. John Pepper, I.N.	Sept. 16	—	803 C	From Macao to Suez.
1844 Jan. 3	Nemesis - -	A. William Oliver -	1844 Feb. 16	—	809 A	Between Bombay, Kurrachee, and Bassein.
June 13	Auckland -	Comr. Henry Alexander Ormsby, I.N.	Sept. 25	—	811 B	Also Abstract in 820.
June 20	Acbar - -	Commander Richard Ethersey, I.N., succeeded by Lieutenants John William Young, I.N., and Allen Edward Ball, I.N.	1854 May 14	—	803 D	Journals of a series of voyages between Bombay, Aden, and Suez.
Aug. 27	Acbar - -	Commander Richard Ethersey, I.N., succeeded by Lieutenant John William Young, I.N.	1845 Oct. 9	—	803 E	Also Abstract in 820.
Aug. 30	Sesostris - -	Comr. James Anthony Young, I.N., succeeded by Comr. John James Frushard, I.N.	Nov. 27	—	804 E	Also Abstract in 820.
Sept. 9	Nemesis - - -	R. S. Ross - -	1844 Oct. 18	—	809 B	Also Abstract in 820.
Sept. 23	Cleopatra -	Lieut. Edward Webb Stone Daniell, succeeded by Lieut. Benj. Hamilton, I.N.	1845 Oct. 26	—	799 E	Also Abstract in 820.
Nov. 3	Fame - -	John William Lewis	Mar. 29	—	801 A & B	From Glasgow to Calcutta.
1845 April 21	Atalanta - - -	Lieut. John William Young, I.N.	May 9	—	807 E	Also Abstract in 820.
May 1	Queen - -	Lieut. John Glen Johnston, I.N.	July 13	—	800 A & B	From Bombay to Suez.
May 21	Victoria -	Lieut. William Chas. Barker, I.N.	Nov. 25	—	810 C	Also Abstract in 820.
June 7	Megna - -	J. Digney	Sept. 26	—	808 A	Printed Journal of an experimental voyage up the Ganges.
June 24	Queen - -	Lieut. John Glen, Johnston, I.N.	Sept. 6	—	800 A–C 800 A–D	From Suez to Aden. (Also Abstract in 820.)

Log begins.	Ship.	Captain.	Log ends.	Ledger or Receipt Book.	Reference Number.	Remarks.
1846 Mar. 16	Auckland - -	Comr. Henry Carne Boulderson, I.N., succeeded by Lieutenants Benjamin Brangwin, I.N., and John William Young, I.N.	1847 Oct. 18	—	811 C	Also Abstract in 820.
Mar. 24	Victoria -	Lieutenant William Charles Barker, I.N.	1846 Oct. 8	—	810 D	Also Abstract in 820.
April 8	Sesostris -	Comr. John James Frushard, I.N., succeeded by Lieutenant Benjamin Hamilton, I.N., Comr. Thomas Grere Carless, I.N., and Capt. William Lowe, I.N.	1848 Mar. 24	—	804 F	Also Abstract in 820.
April 25	Acbar -	Lieut. John William Young, I.N., succeeded by Lieutenant Benjamin Hamilton, I.N.	1847 Nov. 8	—	808 F	Also Abstract in 820.
May 24	Semiramis -	Lieut. Edward Webb Stone Daniell, I.N.	Mar. 18	—	812 F	Also Abstract in 820.
June 28	Atalanta -	Lieut. Alexander Henry Gordon, I.N.	1848 Mar. 10	—	807 F	Also Abstract in 826.
Oct. 25	Moozuffer -	Commander Richard Ethersey, I.N., succeeded by Commander Harry H. Hewett, I.N.	1849 Jan. 27	— L. & R.B.	802 A 802 B 802 C	To Bombay, Aden, Kurrachee, Suez, and Madras.
1847 Sept. 25	Ajdaha -	Comr. John Park Sanders, I.N., succeeded by Comr. Alexander Henry Gordon, and Lieutenants Charles Dugald Campbell, I.N., Henry William Grounds, I.N., James Rennie, I.N., and William Chas. Barker, I.N.	1854 June 23	— L. & R.B.	815 A 815 B	Journal of a voyage to Bombay and of several voyages between Bombay, Aden, and Suez.
Oct. 15	Queen - - -	Capt. Thomas Grere Carless, I.N.	1848 April 2	—	800 A-E	Also Abstract in 820.
1848 Oct. 3	Feerooz	Comr. John James Frushard, I.N., succeeded by Lieutenant Alan Hyde Gardner, I.N., Commanders James Rennie, I.N., and Henry Albert Matthew Drought, I.N., and Lieut. William Balfour, I.N.	1851 April 18	—	818 A	Journal of voyages between Bombay, Aden, and Suez.
1855 Feb. 24	Assaye -	Comr. Edward Webb Stone Daniell, I.N.	1855 Mar. 14	—	817 A	From Bombay to Mangalore and Aden.
1856 Aug. 15	Coromandel - -	Commander Charles Dugald Campbell.	1856 Dec. 3	— L.	816 A 816 B	To Madras.

Section III.

MISCELLANEOUS.

No.	Subject.	Data.	Remarks.
1	Historical Sketch of Shipping Concerns of the East India Company, and papers on other Marine subjects.	1600 to 1796	Original lists.
2	East India Company's Ancient Commerce. Papers relating to -	1673, 1781–2, &c.	
3	Abstracts of Ships' Journals - - - -	1610 to 1623.	
4	Miscellaneous Papers :—Bills of Lading, Commissions, &c.	1606 to 1723	Formerly Birdwood Records :— EE & FF.
5	Rough Accounts kept in the Sixth Voyage - - -	1610 to 1611	R, a, 2.
6	Accounts of Richard Cooke in the Eighth Voyage	1611 to 1613	R, b, 1.
7	Index to a missing list of Sailors - - -	1626	R, b, 4.
8	Lists of Boatswain's stores issued aboard the "Expedition" -	1638 to 1640	R, b, 2.
9	List of Stores on the "Jonah" - - - -	1639	R, b, 8.
10	Copies of Wills of Deceased Sailors, Inventories of their Goods, and Accounts of Wages aboard the "Reformation."	1639	R, b, 9.
11	Copies of Wills, and Inventories, of persons deceased on the "Restoration."	1660 to 1661	R, b, 10.
12	The same for ship "London"; also Record of Consultations held on board.	1664 to 1665	R, b, 11.
13	"A Book of Entertainment of Mariners." [Lists of Sailors, &c., engaged, with notes of sums paid as imprest, and with signatures of those thus enrolled.]	1665 to 1668	R, b, 5.
14	Ledger account of payments to sailors and soldiers - - -	1669 to 1674	R, b, 6.
15	Letters written or received by William Bass, Captain of ship "London."	1672 to 1674	JJ, c, 1.
16	Purser's accounts for ship "London" - - - -	1675 to 1676	R, b, 7.
17	Letters written and consultations held on board the "Loyal Adventure" during a voyage to the Philippine Islands and China.	1684 to 1686	R, a, 4.
18	Letters written or received by Captain Finch Reddall, of the "Samuel and Anna" on her voyage to China and Bengal, and back.	1702 to 1705	R, a, 5.
19	Letters written or received by Captain William Lambert, of the "Edward and Dudley," during a voyage to Banjarmassim.	1703 to 1704	R, a, 6.
20	Accounts of Goods, Stores, Crew, &c., on board the "Loyal Cook."	1708	R, b, 3.
21	Abstract of Proceedings of Court of Directors regarding Shipping.	September 1739 to July 1799.	
22	Do. do. do. do. -	January 1780 to March 1792.	
23	Marine and Shipping Committees. Rough Notes relating to subjects dealt with by.	1782 to 1785	With index.
24	Lost Ships. Various papers in Joint Committee of Warehouses and Shipping.	1810	
25	Commercial and Shipping Affairs. Minutes of Special Committee	1813 to 1814	
26	Committee of Shipping. Extracts from Minutes of - -	1802 to 1815	
27	Committee of Shipping. Minutes of - -	23rd November 1803 to 11th April 1804.	
28	Do. do. - -	23rd April 1813 to 13th April 1814.	With index.
29	Do. do. - - -	20th April 1814 to 12th April 1815.	Do.
30	Do. do. - - - -	18th April 1815 to 10th April 1816.	Do.
31	Do. do. - - -	17th April 1816 to 9th April 1817.	Do.

No.	Subject.	Date.	Remarks.
32	Committee of Shipping. Minutes of - - - -	15th April 1818 to 14th April 1819.	With index.
33	Do. do. - - -	20th April 1819 to 12th April 1820.	Do.
34	Do. do. - - - - -	19th April 1820 to 11th April 1821.	Do.
35	Do. do. - - - -	18th April 1821 to 10th April 1822.	Do.
36	Do. do. - - - -	April 1822 to April 1823	Do.
37	Do. do. - - -	April 1823 to April 1824	Do.
38	Do. do. - - - -	April 1824 to April 1825	Do.
39	Do. do. - - - -	April 1825 to April 1826	Do.
40	Do. do. - - -	April 1826 to April 1827	Do.
41	Do. do. - -	April 1827 to April 1828	
42	Do. do. - - -	April 1828 to April 1829	
43	Do. do. - - - -	April 1829 to April 1830	
44	Do. do. - - - -	April 1830 to April 1831	
45	Do. do. - - -	April 1831 to April 1832	
46	Do. do. - - - -	April 1832 to April 1833	
47	Do. do. - - -	April 1833 to April 1834	
48	Alphabetical Index to Minutes of 1832 - - - -	——	
49	Illicit Trade. Printed volume giving the proceedings of the Court of Directors, &c.	1799	
50	Private Trade from India. MS. copies of letters and suggestions.	1800	
51	Committee on Private Trade. Minutes of the - - -	April 1810 to April 1811	
52	Committee of Correspondence. Minutes on Marine matters -	28th April 1824 to 25th September 1827.	With index.
53	Do. do. do. -	3rd October 1827 to 14th April 1830.	Do.
54	Do. do. do. -	5th May 1830 to 30th October 1832.	Do.
55	Do. do. do. -	7th November 1832 to 4th February 1835.	Do.
56	Minutes of Court of Directors or of Committees relating to Marine matters.	11th October 1837 to 27th February 1839.	Do.
57	Do. do. do. do. -	6th March 1839 to 11th February 1840.	Do.
58	Do. do. do. do. -	12th February 1840 to 1st June 1841.	Do.
59	Do. do. do. do. -	2nd June 1841 to 27th July 1842.	Do.
60	Do. do. do. do. -	3rd August 1842 to 29th December 1843.	Do.
61	Do. do. do. do. -	3rd January 1844 to 24th June 1845.	Do.
62	Do. do. do. do. -	2nd July 1845 to 30th September 1846.	Do.
63	Do. do. do. do. -	7th October 1846 to 29th December 1848.	Do.
64	Do. do. do. do. -	3rd January 1849 to 26th March 1851.	Do.
65	Do. do. do. do. -	2nd April 1851 to 30th December 1853.	Do.
66	Do. do. do. do. -	4th January 1854 to 28th December 1855.	Do.

No.	Subject.	Date.	Remarks.
67	Minutes of Court of Directors or of Committees relating to Marine matters.	2nd January 1856 to 30th June 1858.	With index.
68	Minutes of Court of Directors or of Committees relating to Marine matters. Minutes of Council or of Committees relating to Marine matters.	1st July to 31st August 1858. 1st September 1858 to 30th April 1859.	Do.
69	Do. do. do. do. -	3rd May to 29th November 1859.	Do.
70	Do. do. do. do. -	26th November 1859 to 18th February 1867.	Do.
71	Court Minutes and Papers relating to Marine subjects - -	1844 to 1859	
72	Register of "Court Committee Papers" - - -	November 1851 to August 1866.	With index.
73	Minutes of Council on Miscellaneous Marine matters. (2 vols.) -	1864 to 1866	
74 to 81	Original Collections referring to matters considered in Marine Committee.	1838	
82 to 91	Do. do. do. do. -	1839	
92 to 102	Do. do. do. do. -	1840	
103 to 112	Do. do. do. do. -	1841	
113 to 122	Do. do. do. do. -	1842	
123 to 131	Do. do. do. do. -	1843	
132 to 140	Do. do. do. do. -	1844	
141 to 149	Do. do. do. do. -	1845	
150 to 158	Do. do. do. do. -	1846	
159 to 167	Do. do. do. do.	1847	
168 to 173	Do. do. do. do. -	1849	
174 to 180	Do. do. do. do.	1850	
181 to 186	Do. do. do. do. -	1851	
187 to 195	Do. do. do. do. -	1848	
196 to 201	Do. do. do. do. -	1852	
202 to 207	Do. do. do. do. -	1853	
208 to 213	Do. do. do. do. -	1854	
214 to 219	Do. do. do. do. -	1855	
220 to 228	Do. do. do. do.	1856	
229 to 241	Do. do. do. do. -	1857	
242 to 255	Do. do. do. do. -	1858	
256 to 266	Do. do. do. do. -	1859	
267	Original Collections to Marine Minutes. Numbered 1 to 199 -	1859	
268 to 277	Do. do. Numbered 200 to 2,354	1860	
278 to 286	Do. do. Numbered 1 to 1,904 -	1861	
287 to 295	Do. do. Numbered 1 to 1,780	1862	
296 to 304	Do. do. Numbered 1 to 1,999 -	1863	
305 to 311	Do. do. Numbered 1 to 1,559 -	1864	
312 to 317	Do. do. Numbered 1 to 1,361 -	1865	
318 to 322	Do. do. Numbered 1 to 1,517	1866	
323	Do. do. Numbered 1 to 395	1867	
324	Letters to the Company on various Marine subjects - -	1716 to 1814	
325	Do. do. do. - -	1785 to 1814	With list.
326	Register of Home Letters received in the Public, Marine, and Ecclesiastical Department.	7th January 1836 to 1st September 1839.	

No.	Subject.	Date.	Remarks.
327	Register of Home Letters received in the Public, Marine, and Ecclesiastical Department.	September 1839 to December 1846.	
328	Register of Secretarial Marine Correspondence. Letters received.	1855 to 1858	With index.
329	Register of Home Letters received in the Marine and Transport Department, showing their disposal, &c.; with index to names and subjects.	23rd November 1859 to December 1860.	
330	Do. do. do. do. -	1861	
331	Do. do. do. do. -	1862	
332	Do. do. do. do. -	1863	
333	Do. do. do. do. -	1864	
334	Do. do. do. do. -	1865	
335	Do. do. do. do. -	1866	
336	Do. do. do. do. -	1st January to 30th April 1867.	
337	Do. do. do. do. -	30th April 1867 to 31st December 1868.	No index.
338	Home Letters Out Book, Marine Branch - - -	3rd December 1837 to 8th September 1838.	With index.
339	Do. do. - - -	13th September 1838 to 25th April 1839.	Do.
340	Do. do. - -	25th April to 10th December 1839.	Do.
341	Do. do. - - -	13th December 1839 to 31st July 1840.	Do.
342	Do. do. - - -	1st August 1840 to 6th July 1841.	Do.
343	Do. do. -	8th July 1841 to 22nd March 1842.	Do.
344	Do. do. - -	23rd March to 26th October 1842.	Do.
345	Do. do. - -	27th October 1842 to 13th July 1843.	Do.
346	Do. do. - - -	15th July 1843 to 15th March 1844.	Do.
347	Do. do. -	20th March to 21st November 1844.	Do.
348	Do. do. - - -	21st November 1844 to 2nd October 1845.	Do.
349	Do. do. - - -	3rd October 1845 to 6th July 1846.	Do.
350	Do. do. - - -	6th July 1846 to 28th May 1847.	Do.
351	Do. do. - - - -	2nd June 1847 to 28th July 1848.	Do.
352	Do. do. - -	6th August 1848 to 31st October 1849.	Do.
353	Do. do. - - -	1st November 1849 to 30th November 1850.	Do.
354	Do. do. - - -	4th December 1850 to 30th November 1851.	Do.
355	Do. do. - - -	4th December 1851 to 30th November 1852.	Do.
356	Do. do. - - - -	1st December 1852 to 24th August 1854.	Do.
357	Do. do. - - -	24th August 1854 to 29th December 1855.	Do.
358	Do. do. - - - -	2nd January 1856 to 31st March 1857.	Do.

No.	Subject.	Date.	Remarks.
359	Home Letters Out Books, Marine Branch - - -	1st April to 30th September 1857.	With index.
360	Do. do. - -	1st October 1857 to 31st March 1858.	Do.
361	Do. do. -	1st April to 1st September 1858.	Do.
362	Do. do. - - - -	4th September 1858 to 8th March 1859.	Do.
363	Do. do. - -	2nd April to 9th October 1859.	Do.
364	Do. do. - - -	2nd November 1859 to 24th April 1860.	Do.
365	Do. do. - -	25th April to 27th November 1860.	Do.
366	Do. do. - -	27th November 1860 to 11th June 1861.	Do.
367	Do. do. - -	12th June to 31st December 1861.	Do.
368	Do. do. - -	1st January to 8th August 1862.	Do.
369	Do. do. - -	9th August 1862 to 17th February 1863.	Do.
370	Do. do. - -	18th February to 17th September 1863.	Do.
371	Do. do. - - - -	18th September 1863 to 30th May 1864.	Do.
372	Do. do. - - -	1st June 1864 to 5th May 1865.	Do.
373	Marine Department. Demi-Official Home Letters - -	9th April 1838 to 6th August 1866.	
374	Marine Department Home Letters. Guard Book of Original Drafts (Approved Finance Committee).	November 1859 to July 1861.	
375	Do. do. do. do. -	August 1861 to December 1862.	
376	Do. do. do. do. -	January 1863 to December 1864.	
377	Do. do. do. do.	January 1865 to April 1867.	
378	Various Letters, &c., relating to Shipping. Guard Book -	1839 to 1860	
379	Fragmentary Correspondence on Marine Subjects, &c. -	1794 to 1835	
380	Reference Papers in Original. Guard Book - -	1861 to 1867	
381	Register of Marine Letters received from the three Presidencies; showing dates of receipt, replies, &c.	1855 to 1858	
382	Abstracts (printed) of Marine Letters received from the three Presidencies.	1861 to 1866	
383	Rough Abstracts of Letters sent to India, Madras, and Bombay -	1859 to 1867	
384	Secretary's Letters to the three Presidencies - - -	1st May 1835 to 24th November 1845.	
385	Paragraph Book, giving abstract of subjects in despatches to India.	1837 to 1860	
386	"Board's Collections," being Abstracts of Public Letters and Consultations from India on Marine Subjects.	1796 to 1806	
387	Abstracts of India and Bengal Letters received - - -	January 1830 to October 1858.	
388	General and Marine Department Letters from India and Bengal. MS. duplicates.	19 of 1836 to 118 of 1840	
389	Do. do. do. do.	1 of 1841 to 46 of 1842	
390	Do. do. do. do. -	1 of 1843 to 14 of 1844	
391	Do. do. do. do. -	1 of 1845 to 146 of 1846	

25005. L 1

No.	Subject.	Date.	Remarks.
392	General and Marine Department Letters from India and Bengal. MS. duplicates.	1 of 1847 to 48 of 1849	
393	Do. do. do. do. -	1 of 1850 to 26 of 1852	
394	Do. do. do. do. -	5 of 1853 to 21 of 1855	
395	Do. do. do. do. -	1 of 1856 to 42 of 1858	
396	Bengal Letters received in Marine Department - - -	1839 to 1846	
397	Do. do. do. - -	1847 to 1854	
398	India Letters received in Marine Department - -	1855 to 1858	With indexes.
399 to 401	Marine Letters received from the Government of India; with Collections. (3 vols.)	1858	
402	Marine Letters and Enclosures, 1 to 9. New series - -	1858	
403 to 408	Marine Letters and Collections. (6 vols.) - -	1859	
409 to 411	Do. do. (3 vols.) - - -	1860	
412	Marine Letters and Enclosures - - - - -	1861	
413	Do. do. - - - -	1862	
414	Do. do. - - -	1863	
415	Do. do. - - - -	1864	
416	Do. do. -	1865	
417	Do. do. - - -	1866	
418	Do. do. - - -	1867	
419	Letters received from India by other Departments and transferred to Marine Department for disposal.	1858	
420	Do. do. do. do. -	1859	
421	Do. do. do. do. -	1860	
422	Do. do. do. do. -	1861 to 1865	
423	Original (signed) Marine Letters received from the Government of India and Secretaries to the Governments of India and Bengal, with list at commencement and index at end of book.	3rd November 1858 to end of 1859.	(1.)
424	Do. do. do. do. -	1860	(2.)
425	Do. do. do. do. -	1861	(3.)
426	Do. do. do. do. -	1862	(4.)
427	Do. do. do. do. -	1863 to 1864	(5.)
428	Do. do. do. do.	1865 to 1867	(6.)
429	Secretary's Letters received from Bengal -	1860 to 1864	
430	Marine Despatches to India. MS. duplicates of - - -	1 of 1857 to 61 of 1858	
431	Marine Despatches to Government of India. List at commencement and index at end of volume.	15th September 1858 to end of 1859.	(1.)
432	Do. do. do. do. -	1860	(2.)
433	Do. do. do. do. -	1861	(3.)
434	Do. do. do. do. -	1862 to 1863	(4.)
435	Do. do. do. do. -	1864 to April 1867	(5.)
436	Marine Despatches to Bengal. Drafts of - -	1 of 1861 to 60 of 1862	
437	Marine Collections. Duplicates of - - - -	1831 to 1850	
438	Do. do. - - -	1851 to 1859	
439	Madras Letters received. Abstracts of - - -	January 1830 to October 1858.	
440	Marine and Public Letters received from Madras - -	19 of 1837 to 18 of 1845	
441	Do. do. do. - - -	1 of 1846 to 9 of 1849	
442	Do. do. do. - -	1 of 1850 to 21 of 1856	

No.	Subject.	Date.	Remarks.
443	Marine and Public Letters received from Madras - -	1 of 1857 to 38 of 1859	
444	Indexes to Letters received from Madras - - - -	1855 to 1858	
445	Marine Letters received from Madras; with enclosures. Also Marine Letters, Military Branch.	1859	
446	Do. do. do. do. -	1860	
447	Do. do. do. do. -	1861	
448	Do. do. do. do. -	1862	
449	Do. do. do. do.	1863	
450	Do. do. do. do. -	1864	
451	Do. do. do. do. -	1865	
452	Do. do. do. do. -	1866	
453	Letters received from Madras by other Departments and transferred to Marine Department for disposal.	1859 to 1865	
454	Original (signed) Marine Letters received from Madras. List at commencement and index to subjects at end of book.	5th November 1858 to end of 1859.	(1.)
455	Do. do. do. do. -	1860 to 1861	(2.)
456	Do. do. do. do. -	1862 to 1867	(3.)
457	Marine Despatches to Madras. With list and index -	29th September 1858 to end of 1859.	(1.)
458	Do. do. do. -	1860 to 1861	(2.)
459	Do. do. do. -	1862 to April 1867	(3.)
460	Bombay Marine Letters received. Abstracts of - -	January 1830 to October 1858.	
461	Marine and Forest Department Letters from Bombay. Précis of, para. by para.	7th October 1818 to 30th November 1822.	1 Vol.
	Followed by Marine Letters - - - -	7th October 1823 to 15th August 1832 (No. 17).	
462	Bombay Letters received in Marine Department - - -	1838 to 1844	
463	Do. do. do. - -	1845 to 1850	
464	Do. do. do. -	1851 to 1858	
465	Marine or Steam Letters from Bombay -	1 to 83 of 1838	
466	Steam Department Letters from Bombay - - -	1 of 1839 to 134 of 1840	
467	Marine Department Letters from Bombay - -	2 of 1841 to 83 of 1843	
468	Do. do. - - -	1 of 1844 to 91 of 1846	
469	Do. do. - - -	1 of 1847 to 114 of 1849	
470	Do. do. - - -	1 of 1850 to 63 of 1852	
471	Do. do. - - -	1 of 1853 to 66 of 1856	
472	Do. do. - -	1 of 1857 to 59 of 1858	
473	Marine Letters received from Bombay, with enclosures - -	1858	
474	Do. do. do. -	1858	New Series, 1 to 13.
475 & 476	Do. do. do. - -	1859	
477	Do. do. do.	1860	
478	Do. do. do. -	1861	
479	Do. do. do. -	1862	
480	Do. do. do. - -	1863	
481	Do. do. do. - -	1864	
482	Do. do. do. - -	1865	
483	Do. do. do. - -	1866	
484	Bombay Letters (various) transferred to Marine Department for disposal.	1858 to 1866	

No.	Subject.	Date.	Remarks.
485	Five Miscellaneous Collections (Bombay) - - -	1849 to 1857	
486	Original (signed) Marine Letters received from Bombay. List at commencement and index of subjects at end of volume.	9th November 1858 to end of 1859.	(1.)
487	Do. do. do. do. -	1860	(2.)
488	Do. do. do. do. -	1861	(3.)
489	Do. do. do. do. -	1862	(4.)
490	Do. do. do. do. -	1863 to 1864	(5.)
491	Do. do. do. do. -	1865 to March 1867	(6.)
492	Abstracts of Despatches to Bombay - - - -	1769 to 1813	
493	Marine and Forest Department Despatches to Bombay - -	31st October 1827 to 25th May 1836.	
494	Marine Despatches to Bombay. MS. copies - - -	1 of 1855 to 87 of 1856	
495	Do. do. - - -	1 of 1857 to 57 of 1858	
496	Do. do. With list and index of subjects -	15th September 1858 to end of 1859.	(1.)
497	Do. do. do. do. -	1860	(2.)
498	Do. do. do. do. -	1861	(3.)
499	Do. do. do. do. -	1862	(4.)
500	Do. do. do. do. -	1863	(5.)
501	Do. do. do. do. -	1864 to 1867	(6.)
502	Marine Despatches to Bombay. Drafts of - -	1 of 1863 to 18 of 1867	
503	Abstracts of Bombay Letters - - - - - -	1770 to 1817	
504	Abstracts of Bombay Consultations - -	1790 to 1811	
505	List of Company's own ships outward bound, with particulars -	1722 to 1810	
506	List of Times appointed for Ships of the several Seasons - - and Lists of Ships in the Service, with Lists of Directors - -	1773 to 1800; 1775 to 1800	
507	Lists of Times appointed for Ships of the several Seasons - - and Lists of Ships in the Service, with Lists of Directors - -	1792 to 1829; 1805 to 1828	
508	Lists of Times appointed for Ships of the several Seasons - - and Lists of Ships in the Service, with Lists of Directors -	1801 to 1832; 1801 to 1832	
509	Lists of Ships abroad - - - - - -	1807 to 1832	
510	Hardy's List of Ships. Guard Book of printed Lists of Ships sailing to Foreign Ports.	1838 to 1847	
511	Jerusalem Lists. Guard Book of - - - - -	January 1858 to August 1867.	
512	Lloyd's Lists - - - - - - -	1st January to 30th June 1859.	
513	Do. - - - - -	1st July to 31st December 1859.	
514	Do. - - - - - -	1st January to 30th June 1860.	
515	Do. - - - - -	1st July to 31st December 1860.	
516	Do. - - - - -	1st January to 30th June 1861.	
517	Do. - - - - -	1st July to 31st December 1861.	
518	Do. - - - - -	1st January to 30th June 1862.	
519	Do. - - - - - -	1st July to 31st December 1862.	
520	Do - - - -	1st January to 30th June 1863.	

No.	Subject.	Date.	Remarks.
521	Lloyd's Lists - - - - -	1st July to 31st December 1863.	
522	Do. - - - -	1st January to 30th June 1864.	
523	Do. - - - - -	1st July to 31st December 1864.	
524	Do. - - - - - -	1st January to 30th June 1865.	
525	Do. - - - - -	1st July to 31st December 1865.	
526	Do. - - - - -	1st January to 30th June 1866.	
527	Do. - - - - -	1st July to 31st December 1866.	
528	Do. - - - - - - -	1st January to 30th June 1867.	
529	Ships. Alphabetically arranged, with particulars of measurement, tonnage, &c.	——	
530	Ships tendered for the service of the United East India Company. Printed volume of Minutes of Committee and Court with list of Contents.	1st January 1780 to 31st March 1791.	
531	Do. do. do. do. -	31st March 1791 to 24th February 1796.	
532	Do. do. do. do. -	24th February 1796 to 24th September 1800.	
533	Do. do. do. do. -	24th September 1800 to 13th April 1803.	
534	Do. do. do. do. -	20th April 1803 to 27th September 1809.	
535	Terms for freighting Ships for Cargoes from Bengal - -	1797 to 1801	Printed vol.
536	Terms for building and freighting Ships - -	1804	Printed vol. with MSS.
537	Terms for hiring Ships - - - -	1808 to 1812	Do.
538	Extra Ships. Terms and Conditions for Freightage - -	1812 to 1822	With index.
539	Building and Hiring Ships. Terms for - -	1822 to 1830	Printed volume.
540	Reports on Freights and other matters - -	1802 to 1808	
541	Licenses for Ships to trade to India - - -	1814 to 1816	
542	Do. do. - - - -	1817 to 1818	
543	Do. do. - - -	1819 to 1820	
544	Do. do. - - -	1821 to 1823	
545	Arrivals and Departures of Company's Ships at Bombay. Returns, giving particulars, &c.	1816 to 1855	
546	Do. do. do. do.	1838 to 1856	
547	Returns giving Tonnage, &c., of Foreign Ships entering Indian Ports.	1795 to 1800	
548	Foreign Ships. Returns of Arrivals at, and Departures from, Bombay, with other particulars.	1816 to 1855	
549	Merchant Vessels, &c. Returns from Bombay, giving various particulars.	1816 to 1826	
550	East India Docks: Reports of Ships unloading - .	1825	
551	Do. do. - - -	1826	
552	Do. do. - -	1829	
553	Do. do. - - -	1831	
554	Do. do. -	1832	
555	Do. do. -	1833	
556	Miscellaneous Returns regarding various Vessels -	——	

No.	Subject.	Date.	Remarks.
557	Steam Boats, Prevention of Explosions on. Printed Report of Select Committee of House of Commons. With evidence.	1817	
558	Steam Navigation. Prevention, &c., of Calamities by. Report of Select Committee of House of Commons. With evidence.	1831	
559	Steam Navigation to India. Minutes of Evidence before Select Committee of the House of Commons.	1832	
560	Steam Navigation to India. Appendix to Report of Select Committee.	1833	
561	Means of promoting Steam Communication with India. Report of Select Committee of House of Commons. With evidence.	1834	
562	Application of Steam Navigation to Internal and External Communications of India. MS. copies of various letters, &c. With list of contents.	1826 to 1833	(1.)
563	Ditto, ditto. Reports of Committee. Resolutions of Court, &c.	1826 to 1833	(2.)
564	Ditto, ditto. Various information on the subject. - - -	1826 to 1833	(3.)
565	Ditto, ditto. Minutes of Evidence before Sub-Committee, &c. -	1832	(4.)
566	Ditto, ditto. Index to 561 and 562 *supra* - -	—	
567	Ditto, ditto. Copies of Letters, &c. - - - -	1828 to 1834	(5.) With list of contents.
568	Ditto, ditto. Copies of Letters, &c. - - - -	1829 to 1834	(6.) Do.
569	Ditto, ditto. Copies of Letters, &c. - - - -	1825 to 1836	(7.) Do.
570	Ditto, ditto. Copies of Letters, &c. - - -	1825 to 1836	(8.) Do.
571	Ditto, ditto. Copies of various Despatches, &c. -	1834	(9.)
572	Ditto, ditto. Copies of various Despatches, &c. - - -	1835	(10.)
573	Ditto, ditto. Papers regarding the Euphrates Expedition - -	1834 to 1836	(11.)
574	Ditto, ditto. Papers regarding the Euphrates Expedition -	1834 to 1838	(12.)
575	Ditto, ditto. Copies of various Papers - - -	1833 to 1835	(13.)
576	Ditto, ditto. Copies of Correspondence between the Court of Directors and the Indian Governments.	1825 to 1835	(14.)
577	Ditto, ditto. Copies of various Reports of Committees, &c. -	1827 to 1836	(15.)
578	Ditto, ditto. Memorandum and Appendix on the progress of the "Atalanta" and "Berenice."	October 1836	(16.)
579	Ditto, ditto. Papers relating to the construction, &c., of the "Atalanta" and "Berenice."	1835 to 1837	(17.)
580	Ditto, ditto. Copies of various papers relating to the purchase, repairs, &c. of the "Semiramis."	1837 to 1838	(18.)
581	Ditto, ditto. Reports of Committees, &c. - - -	1825 to 1839	(19.)
582	Ditto, ditto. Tenders and Papers relating to a steamer for Calcutta to replace the "Irrawaddy."	1836 to 1837	(20.)
583	Ditto, ditto. Copies of Miscellaneous Papers - - -	1836 to 1840	(21.)
584	Ditto, ditto. Copies of Miscellaneous Papers - -	1822 to 1840	(22.)
585	Drawings of East India Company's Steam Vessels "Cleopatra" and "Sesostris." In folio.	—	
586	Steam Communication with East Coast of Africa. Various Reports, &c.	1810, &c.	
587	Steam Navigation in Asia. Copies of Papers relating to Seas, Rivers, and Countries.	1810 to 1830	
588	Steam Navigation, &c. Various printed pamphlets bound together.	1833 to 1837	
589	Suggestions for a Steam Squadron. Original Minutes of Sir Robert Grant and others. Enclosure to Marine Letter from Bombay.	1836	
590	River Steam Navigation in Bengal. Report by Captain Johnston.	1837	
591	Steam Department at Bombay. Statements of expenses incurred	1st May 1838 to 30th April 1855.	

No.	Subject.	Date.	Remarks.
592	Steam Communication with India and China. Correspondence with Peninsular and Oriental Company, &c.	1839	
593	Steam Vessels. Various papers relating to -	1841	(1.) With index.
594	Ditto. Various papers relating to - - -	1843	(2.) Do.
595	Ditto. Pamphlets, &c. - - - - -	1842 to 1844	(3.) Do.
596	MS. Index to the above three volumes - -	——	
597	Steam Navigation, Regulation of. Act 9 & 10 Vict. cap. 100 -	1846	
598	Miscellaneous Extracts of Steam Logs of several Vessels of Indian Navy referred to in Bombay Marine Letter No. 66 of 1850.	——	
599 to 603	Steamers, tugs, light-vessels, &c. Specifications, plans, and drawings.	1858 to 1859	
604	Coal Resources of India. Printed Reports of Investigating Committee.	1841 to 1845	
605	Bombay Naval Establishments. Financial Statement - -	30th April 1835	
606	Do. do. do. - -	30th April 1836	
607	Do. do. do. - -	30th April 1837	
608	Do. do. do. - -	1st May 1838	
609	Do. do. do. - -	1st May 1839	
610	Do. do. do.	1st May 1840	
611	Do. do. do. - -	1st May 1841	
612	Do. do. do. - -	1st May 1842	
613	Do. do. do. - -	1st May 1843	
614	Do. do. do. -	1st May 1844	
615	Do. do. do. -	1st May 1845	
616	Do. do. do.	1st May 1846	
617	Do. do. do. -	1st May 1847	
618	Do. do. do. - -	1st May 1848	
619	Do. do. do. -	1st May 1849	
620	Do. do. do. -	1st May 1850	
621	Do. do. do. - - -	1st May 1851	
622	Do. do. do. -	1st May 1852	
623	Do. do. do. - -	1st May 1853	
624	Do. do. do. - -	1st May 1854	
625	Do. do. do. - -	1st May 1855	
626	Do. do. do. - -	1st May 1856	
627	Do. do. do. - -	1st May 1857	
628	Do. do. do. -	1st May 1858	
629	Do. do. do. -	1st May 1859	
630	Do. do. do. -	1st May 1867	
631	Do. do. do. -	1st April 1869	
632	Do. do. do. -	1st April 1870	
633	Do. do. do. - -	1st April 1871	
634	Do. do. do.	1st April 1872	
635	Do. do. do. -	1st April 1873	
636	Do. do. do. - -	1st April 1874	
637	Do. do. do. - -	1st April 1875	
638	Do. do. do. - -	1st April 1876	

No.	Subject.	Date.	Remarks.
639	Bombay Naval Establishment. Financial Statement - -	1st April 1877	
640	Do. do. do. - - -	1st April 1878	
641	Rough Estimates of Expenditure on Marine Subjects - -	1838 to 1844	(1.)
642	Do. do. do.	1845 to 1857	(2.)
643	Do. do. do. - -	1858 to 1867	(3.)
644	Company's own ships. Instructions, regulations, &c., regarding Commanders, Mates, and Surgeons. List of Applications from Mates.	1736 to 1810	
645	Company's own ships. Orders and Instructions to Commanders	1819	Printed vol.
646	Do. do. do. do. -	1825	Do.
647	Commanders and Officers of Company's own Ships. Proceedings of Special Committee to consider principles of appointment.	1815	
648	Appointment of Officers and Midshipmen of Company's own ships, &c. Regulations regarding.	1815 to 1833	
649	Company's own ships. Nominal list of Commanders and Mates -	1796 to 1828	
650	Company's own ships. Descriptions of Commanders and Officers, with particulars of service.	1815 to 1832	With index.
651	Commanders in Company's Service. Register with dates of resignation or death.	1737 to 1832	
652	Commanders and Mates. Descriptions, &c. - -	1771 to 1778	With nominal index.
653	Do. do. - -	1778 to 1782	Do.
654	Do. do. - -	1783 to 1787	Do.
655	Do. do. - - -	1788 to 1793	Do.
656	Do. do.	1794 to 1797	Do.
657	Do. do. - - -	1798 to 1801	Do.
658	Do. do. - -	1802 to 1803	Do.
659	Do. do. - -	1804 to 1806	Do.
660	Do. do. -	1807 to 1809	Do.
661	Do. do. -	1814 to 1816	Do.
662	Do. do. - -	1817 to 1820	Do.
663	Do. do. - -	1821 to 1824	Do.
664	Do. do. - -	1821 to 1824	Do.
665	Do. do. -	1825 to 1829	Do.
666	Do. do. -	1830 to 1833	Do.
667	List of Commanders and other ranks down to Carpenters, who have served the Company since 28th August 1828. With age, service, date of discharge, &c.	1828 to 1834	
668	Extra Ships. Nominal List of Masters and Mates - -	1796 to 1825	
669	Certificates of age or baptism of various Marine Officers, &c. Nos. 1 to 800.	1780 to 1820	List enclosed.
670	Ditto, ditto. Nos. 801 to 1720 - -	1780 to 1820	No list.
671	Baptismal Certificates and Certificates of Competence of various midshipmen.	1820 to 1830	
672	Surgeons and Surgeons' Mates. Nominal List, year by year, showing ships, &c.	1801 to 1814	
673	Ditto, ditto. List of Appointments to various Ships in each year -	1809 to 1833	
674	Seafaring Europeans employed in Vessels which arrived at and sailed from Madras. List in alphabetical order.	1830	
675	European Seamen in Merchant Service belonging to Bombay and Surat. Returns from Bombay.	1793 to 1820	
676	Free Mariners. Nominal list -	1791 to 1809	
677	Free Mariners in Indian ships. Register of applications considered by the Court of Directors.	1802 to 1814	

No.	Subject.	Date.	Remarks.
678	Free Mariners. List of applications to Court of Directors -	1810 to 1832	
679	Abstracts of Reports on Bombay Marine - - - -	1798 to 1811	
680	Bombay Marine. List of officers and men in the various Ships. Returns from Bombay.	March 1766 to June 1775	
681	Ditto. Annual Returns giving lists of Establishments -	1784 to 1815	
682	Ditto. Guard Book of Returns from Bombay, giving Statement of the Establishment of the Ships and Vessels of War.	1812 to 1836	
683	Bombay Marine Officers. List of particulars - - -	1795 to 1807	Alphabetical index.
684	Do. do. - -	1807 to 1827	
685	Officers of Bombay Marine Establishment. Alphabetical list showing dates of promotion, &c.	1801 to 1830	
686	Bombay Marine Establishment. List of Europeans, giving age, &c.	1821 to 1827	
687	Midshipmen. Certificates of Birth or Baptism. Also Correspondence. Nominal list enclosed.	1827 to 1840	
688	Lists of Appointments to Bombay Marine and Pilot Service. Baptismal Certificate and Form of Allegiance attached in many instances.	1822 to 1832	
689	Volunteer Cadets. Appointments to Bombay Marine and to Bengal and Bombay Pilot Services.	1794 to 1830	
690	Europeans, including Engineers, Seamen, &c., on Bombay Marine Establishment. Lists for each year in alphabetical order.	1818 to 1833	
691	Officers, Engineers, &c., of Bombay Marine. Guard Book of lists.	1st May 1863 to July 1877.	
692	Bombay Marine Establishments. Returns of Officers and Salaries.	1st April 1876	
693	Do. do. do. do. -	1st April 1877	
694	Lists of Civil Servants (European and East Indian) in Bombay Marine Offices.	1876 to 1879	
695	Bombay Marine Officers Furlough Ledger -	1796 to 1815	With index.
696	Bombay Marine Vessels. Periodical Returns from Bombay, giving number of guns, names of officers, &c.	1870 to 1874	
697	Do. do. do. do. -	1874 to 1882	
698	Bombay Marine. Casualties among Europeans. Annual Returns.	1777 to 1834	
699	Casualties in Bombay Marine Establishment. Returns, with particulars.	January 1824 to January 1826.	
700	Casualties in the Bombay Marine. Monthly Returns - -	July 1824 to December 1834.	
701	Indian Navy. Alphabetical List of Vessels with the Number of Guns and Names of the Officers.	1854 to 1858	
702	Indian Navy Vessels and Employment List, showing complements and Stations.	22nd January 1858 to 23rd December 1859.	
703	Do. do. do. do. -	7th January 1860 to 25th March 1863.	
704	Appointments in Indian Navy and Bengal Pilot Service. Queen's approval. Guard Book.	1858 to 1861	
705	Indian Navy. Alphabetical list of Officers and Pursers - -	1834 to 1860	
706	Officers and Crews of various Steam Vessels - - -	1837 to 1861	
707	Indian Navy. List of Officers. Returns from Bombay -	January 1844 to July 1853.	
708	Do. do. do. - -	October 1853 to January 1860.	
709	Indian Navy. Return of Officers, Engineers, &c. - -	1st April 1860 to January 1863.	
710	Ditto. Volunteers (Cadets) for. Original nominations, baptismal and other certificates.	1838 to 1844	With nominal index.

No.	Subject.	Date.	Remarks.
711	Indian Navy. Volunteers (Cadets) for. Original nominations, baptismal and other certificates.	1844 to 1848	With nominal index.
712	Do. do. do. do. -	1849 to 1856	Do.
713	Do. do. do. do. -	1854 to 1858	Do.
714	Do. do. do. do.	1858 to 1859	Do.
715	Ditto. Volunteers (Officers) for. Date of rank and name of ships with dates of sailing.	1888 to 1862	
716	Indian Navy. "Volunteers" (Cadets). Printed form of oath with signature in each case.	1838 to 1854	
717	Ditto. Including Captain's Clerks - -	1855 to 1858	
718	Captain's Clerks in Indian Navy. Gradation List. Guard Book	1848 to 1860	
719	Seamen in Indian Navy. Nominal list in alphabetical order, showing age, ship, date of discharge, and other particulars.	July 1840 to 1859	
720	Seamen entered in Indian Navy. Returns from India giving names, age, &c.	1860 to 1863	
721	Ditto, ditto. Monthly lists - - - -	July 1840 to August 1855.	
722	Ditto, ditto. Monthly lists - - -	September 1855 to September 1862.	
723	European Seamen in Indian Navy. Returns from Bombay -	1848 to 1855	
724	Do. do. do. -	1855 to 1858	
725	Do. do. do. -	1858 to 1859	
726	Do. do. do. -	1859 to 1860	
727	Do. do. do.	1860 to 1861	
728	Do. do. do. -	1863 to 1864	
729	Seamen in Indian Navy. Fragmentary List, in alphabetical order, giving particulars of entry, discharge, &c.	1846 to 1863	
730	Marine Boys. List from India giving age, date of indenture, and other particulars.	March 1843 to December 1864.	
731	Ditto. List in alphabetical order, giving particulars, &c. -	1842 to 1861	
732	Engineers in Indian Navy. List with dates of promotions	1837 to 1859	
733	Engineers. Guard Book of Lists, giving particulars of family allotments.	1838 to 1860	
734	Engineers and others. Applications for Marine situations -	1837 to 1858	Nominal list enclosed.
735	Do. do. do. -	1840 to 1841	Do.
736	Engineers, Boiler Makers, and Apprentices. Lists from Bombay, giving age, service, &c.	December 1838 to April 1844.	
737	Do. do. do. do. -	July 1844 to June 1847	
738	Do. do. do. do.	July 1847 to May 1849	
739	Do. do. do. do. -	June 1849 to October 1850.	
740	Do. do. do. do. -	November 1850 to March 1852.	
741	Do. do. do. do. -	April 1852 to December 1853.	
742	Do. do. do. do. -	March 1854 to July 1857	
743	Do. do. do. do. -	August 1857 to January 1860.	
744	Engineers' Family Remittances. Returns of sums left for payment in England.	October 1860 to October 1866.	
745	Lists of Europeans in Indian Navy Establishments and particulars of Casualties. In alphabetical order for each year.	1835 to 1845	
746	Casualties among European Seamen of the Indian Navy. MS. Returns from Bombay.	January 1835 to October 1859.	

No.	Subject.	Date.	Remarks.
747	Casualties among European Seamen of the Indian Navy. MS. Returns from Bombay.	November 1859 to September 1863.	
748	Indian Navy. Annual lists of Casualties, &c. - - -	1st May 1834 to 30th April 1840.	
749	European Seamen omitted from General Return of 1837–38, showing what has become of them so far as can be traced.	1851	
750	Deserters from the Indian Navy - - - -	1841 to 1862	
751	Do. do. - - -	1862 to 1863	
752	Indian Navy. Pay and Audit Code - - -	1853	
753	Do. do. - - - -	1862	
754	Bengal Marine Establishments. Letter and enclosure from Fort William giving statement and list of names -	1st May 1831	
755	European Officers, including Engineers and Seamen, in Marine and Steam Department, Bengal. Lists from Fort William.	1848 to 1852	
756	Do. do. do. do. -	1853 to 1860	
757	Bengal Marine Establishments. Annual Reports for each year in MS.	1844–45 to 1851–52	
758	Do. do. do. do. -	1852–53 to 1856–57	
759	Bengal Marine Establishments. Financial Statements - -	1873 to 1874	
760	Bengal Civil and Marine Casualties - - -	May 1824 to January 1843.	
761	Ditto, ditto. Returns of - - - - - -	January 1857 to February 1864.	
762	Bengal Naval Brigades. MS. List of European Officers and Seamen who served on the books of H.M.'s vessel "Calcutta."	1st August 1858 to 31st December 1859.	
763	Ditto. Names of Officers and European Seamen employed, being original printed copy with autograph signatures, and enclosure of Marine Letter from Fort William, No. 28. Also Alphabetical List of European Officers and Seamen of the Indian Navy serving with Bengal Naval Brigades.	15th July 1859 1860	
764	Bengal Pilot Service. List of volunteers in alphabetical order with dates of promotion.	1796 to 1824	
765	Do. do. do. do. -	1796 to 1858	
766	Ditto. Volunteers for. Guard Book of Nominations, Declarations, and Certificates of Birth, &c., in original.	1818 to 1844	(1.) With index.
767	Do. do. do. do. -	1844 to 1858	(2.) Do.
768	Do. do. do. do. -	1859 to 1861	(3.) Do.
769	Bengal Pilot Service. List of Rank of Volunteers -	1838 to 1861	
770	Ditto. List of employés. Returns from Calcutta -	1793 to 1833	
771	Ditto. List of employés. Returns from Calcutta - -	March 1836 to October 1853.	
772	Ditto. List of employés. Returns from Calcutta - - -	November 1853 to October 1862.	
773	Ditto. Printed rules and regulations - - -	1827	
774	Masters and Mates for extra Ships. Records of Service -	1796 to 1802	(1.) With index.
775	Do. do. do. - - -	1802 to 1809	(2.) Do.
776	Do. do. do. -	1810 to 1819	(3.) Do.
777	Do. do. do. - -	1819 to 1832	(4.) Do.
778	Service List of Indian Navy - - - -	Commencing 1838	With index.
779	Petitions for Relief by Mariners and Widows of Mariners. With original certificates, &c.	1795 to 1798	Nominal list enclosed.
780	Do. do. do. do.	1803	Do.
781	Petitions for Relief from Poplar Fund or Compensation -	1815 to 1830	Do.
782	Do. do. do. -	1831 to 1835	Do.
783	Do. do. do. - -	1836 to 1854	Do.

No.	Subject.	Date.	Remarks.
784	Poplar Pensioners. Register of Applications, with particulars, Nos. 1 to 853.	1788 to 1809	(1.)
785	Ditto, ditto. Nos. 1 to 1936a - - - -	1809 to 1821	(2.) With index.
786	Ditto, ditto. Nos. 1937 to 3559, and list of all pensions with particulars.	1821 to 1838	(3.) Do.
787	Register of Applications for Pensions from Poplar Fund, with particulars, &c. Numbered 1937 to 3459.	1822 to 1834	
788	Pensioners on Poplar Fund, &c. List in alphabetical order, with particulars.	4th April 1821	
789 to 840	Petitions with Certificates and other Documents attached for Pensions, Compensations, &c. The cases are numbered from 1 to 3559, and each volume contains a nominal list of the applicants.	1809 to 1838	
841	Ditto, ditto. Unnumbered - - -	1836	
842	Marine Annuitants. List only - - - - -	*circa* 1835	
843	Letters from Officers and others soliciting compensation, A to G. With certificates and particulars in original.	1831 to 1834	
844	Ditto, ditto, H to S. With certificates and particulars in original	1831 to 1836	
845	Commanders and Officers in Company's Service. Claims to Compensation, being précis of replies to Circular of Court of Directors.	1836	With index.
846	Marine Service Compensations, with particulars. List given	1835 to 1836	
847	Marine Compensations. Draft reports - - -	1835 to 1838	
848	Compensations for Marine Services. Details in each case -	1836	With index.
849	Statement of Services in East India ships by Midshipmen and other applicants for annuities, numbered 1 to 100.	1834	Nominal list enclosed.
850	Ditto, ditto. Nos. 101 to 731 - - - -	1834, &c.	
851	Poplar Fund and Maritime Pensions. Order Books authorising Accountant-General to prepare warrants for payment.	1838 to 1840	With index.
852	Do. do. do. do. -	1841 to 1842	Do.
853	Do. do. do. do. -	1843 to 1851	Do.
854	Do. do. do. do. -	1851 to 1858	Do.
855	List of Seamen discharged from the Bengal Marine, who have claims on the Company. Also Statement of Balances due to deceased Men. Letter and enclosure from Fort William.	1821	
856	Account current of Estates of Deceased Mariners. Returns from Bombay with ledger account to each name.	1784 to 1834	
857	Estates of deceased Officers and Seamen of Indian Navy. List in alphabetical order showing amounts due.	1820 to 1862	
858	Accounts Current of Estates of deceased Seamen of Indian Navy.	1st May 1835 to 30th April 1843.	
859	Deceased Officers and Seamen of Indian Navy. Statements of Deposits in the Bombay Treasury.	October 1835 to December 1852.	
860	Ditto, ditto. Statements of Unclaimed Deposits in the Bombay Treasury.	January 1852 to July 1854.	
861	Ditto, ditto. Register of Deposits in Bombay Treasury - -	August 1854 to February 1859.	
862	Do. do. do. - -	March 1859 to February 1863.	
863	Estates of deceased British Merchant Seamen realized in India and remitted to England. Quarterly Statements.	1855 to 1865	
864	Ditto, ditto. Statements of Deposits in the Bombay Treasury -	June 1865 to September 1873.	
865	Embarkation of Troops by various Ships. Guard Book of reports.	1857	
866	Do. do. do. do. -	1858	
867	Do. do. do. do. -	1859 to 1864	
868	Do. do. do. do. -	1865 to 1866	

No.	Subject.	Date.	Remarks.
869	Freight Accounts of Homeward Troopships -	1st August 1860 to 1864	With index.
870	Do. do. -	1865 to 1870	
871	Freight Accounts of Outward Troopships - -	1st August 1860 to 1866	With index.
872	Freight Accounts, Homeward. Register of -	August 1860 to 1871	
873	Surgeons' Bills in original, for Attendance on Officers and Men on various Troopships.	1843 to 1848	(1.) With alphabetical index.
874	Do. do. do. do. -	1849 to 1858	(2.) Do.
875	Ledger of Purchases - - -	1829 to 1830	Incomplete.
876	Stores for Company's own Ships, Sloops, and Hoys. Original invoices.	1832 to 1834	
877	Warrants to Treasury to pay allowances from Buying Office Fee Fund.	September 1811 to September 1814.	
878	Naval Medal Lists - - -	1843 to 1847	
879	Naval Prize Money. Lists of distribution with receipts, re the "Isle of France," "Rosario," and other ships.	1828, 1829, &c.	
880	Miscellaneous Papers on Marine Subjects. Guard Book -	1836 to 1841	(1.) With index.
881	Ditto, ditto. Copies of Forms - - - - -	1835 to 1852	(2.) Do.
882	Ditto, ditto. Copies of Forms - -	1852 to 1866	(3.) Do.
883	Navy Courts-Martial. Papers regarding -	1836 to 1840	
884	Articles of Agreement between Commanders and Crews of 13 Vessels.	1836 to 1851	One bundle.
885	Warden's Journal, being private diary of C. W. Warden, Master Pilot, Bengal.	1837 to 1874	
886	Letter book of ditto - -	1858 to 1874	
887	List of Passengers to and from India in various vessels, Return of	1838 to 1845	
888	Native Servants who have come to England with Passengers. Register of deposits on account of.	July 1838 to March 1858	
889	Marine Contracts and other legal documents, a bundle of	1840 to 1864	
890	"India." Collection of Papers regarding Compensation to the Owners of the.	1844 to 1860	
891	Trade of the Red Sea and Persian Gulf. MS. copies of miscellaneous papers relating to.	1773 to 1778	
892	Lighthouses. Correspondence between the Court of Directors and the Governor General, Bengal, with Proceedings of the Bengal Government.	1807 to 1813	
893	Plan for Naval Defence of India, with Index -	1796	
894	Ship Timber. Report, &c., on the Forests of Canara and Malabar.	1811	
895	Ditto. Abstract of Evidence before Committee of House of Commons.	1814	
896	De Mannevillette's Directions for navigating from the Channel to the East Indies. Translated by Jeffreys.	1769	
897	Improvement of the Navy of Great Britain. Suggestions by Gabriel Snodgrass in a letter to the East India Company.	1797	
898	Merchant Shipping Acts and Circulars - - -	1854 to 1873	
899	Docks and Shipping. Various Acts of George III. - -	1793 to 1811	With MS. indexes.
900	Universal Signals. Suggestions by John McArthur - -	——	Printed pamphlet.

INDEX.

SECTIONS I. AND II.—SHIPS.

(*The reference is to the* page *on which the entry occurs.*)

A.

B.

C.

H.

I.

J.

K.

L.

Y.

Z.

SECTIONS I. AND II.—CAPTAINS, &c.

(The reference is to the page on which the entry occurs.)

A

B.

C.

D.

E.

F.

G.

H.

N.

O.

P.

T.

U.

V.

W.

SECTION III.—MISCELLANEOUS.

[*The reference is to the number of the entry.*]

ERRATA.

p. 43 (ship Salisbury). "Captain John Wycke" should be "Wyche."
p. 54 (ship York). "J. A. Blanchard" should be "Blanshard."
p. 60 (ship Valentine). "Captain Wale" should be "Wall."
p. 70 (ship Arniston). "Majoribanks" should be "Marjoribanks."
pp. 78 and 81 (ship Orpheus). "Cristall" should be "Cristal."
p. 87 (ship Exeter). "Menton" should be "Meriton."
p. 87 (ship Ganges). "Moffatt" should be "Moffat."
pp. 90, 94, 100, 104. "Harrington" should be "Harington."
p. 95 (ship Winchelsea). "Moffatt" should be "Moffat."
p. 99. "Ceyon" should be "Ceylon."
p. 102 (ship Guildford). "Johnston" should be "Johnson."
p. 104 (ship Essex). "Nisbett" should be "Nisbet."
p. 117 (ship Lord Amherst). "Cragie" should be "Craigie."
p. 129 (Nos. 168–195). These entries should run:—168–176; 1848. 177–182; 1849. 183–9; 1850. 190–5; 1851
p. 131 (No. 383). "Sent to" should be "received from."
p. 132 (Nos. 396–8). These are indexes only.
p. 132 (No. 437). "Duplicates" should be "List of duplicates."
p. 133 (Nos. 462–4). These are indexes only.
p. 134. Add, as No. 504A, "List of ships sent to India, 1791 to 1837."
p. 134 (No. 505). "1722" should be "1772."
p. 135 (Nos. 530–1). Add "with index (No. 530A)."
p. 135 (Nos. 532–4). Add "with index (No. 532A)."
p. 135 (No. 546). "1858" should be "1856."
p. 138 (No. 648). Add "and lists of officers."
p. 138. Take out No. 664.
p. 140 (No. 722). "1862" should be "1863."
p. 140 (No. 745). Add "two copies."
p. 142. No. "850" should be "850A–G."
p. 143 (No. 884). Take out "one bundle."

LONDON: Printed by EYRE and SPOTTISWOODE,
Printers to the Queen's most Excellent Majesty.

LIST

OF

FACTORY RECORDS

OF THE LATE

EAST INDIA COMPANY,

PRESERVED IN THE

RECORD DEPARTMENT

OF THE

INDIA OFFICE, LONDON.

1897.

LIST

OF

FACTORY RECORDS

OF THE LATE

EAST INDIA COMPANY,

PRESERVED IN THE

RECORD DEPARTMENT

OF THE

INDIA OFFICE, LONDON.

1897.

TABLE OF CONTENTS.

INTRODUCTION.

Amongst the early records of the East India Company none are of more interest than those which detail the proceedings of their Agents and Factors in the East, in their endeavours to establish factories and promote trade of the English direct with the several Native powers. In effecting this many difficulties had to be overcome, and the opposition of the Native traders, who naturally put every obstacle in the way of the diversion of their trade to other channels, had to be combated, as well as the more serious obstructions on the part of the Portuguese and Dutch to the establishment of trading stations in the East by the English.

The seventeenth century was the time of greatest establishment of factories in the East, and may, on that account, be considered the "Factory Period" of the East India Company, the only territorial acquisitions obtained by them within that century being as follows :—

1639. Madraspatam (" Chineepatam," Fort St. George);
1668. Bombay;
1690. Tegnapatam (Fort St. David); and
1694. Anjengo.

After the union of the two East India Companies, at the beginning of the eighteenth century, the acquisitions of territory in the East became both more frequent and more extensive, and the subsequent years of the Company's existence may, therefore, not inappropriately be designated as the "Territorial Period."

Most of the minor factories did not send home their proceedings to England, neither did they, as a rule, communicate directly with the East India Company, but only through the principal factories to which they were subordinate,—such as Bantam, Surat, Fort St. George, Bombay or Calcutta. In the following observations it is not intended to give details regarding those factories for which no separate records now exist at this Office; whilst, with regard to the others, only some brief particulars will be given relative to their first establishment, and, when abolished, the dates at which they either ceased to be maintained as permanent trading stations, or were classed as Presidencies, from which time their Proceedings are embodied in the series of "Presidency Records."

In the establishment of factories at the various commercial ports visited by their ships, the East India Company did but follow an immemorial custom, handed down from the time of the Phœnicians, if not from still earlier days, and that plan of conducting their business was resolved upon at the very commencement of their organization. At a meeting of the Court on the 10th February 1600-1 the Directors " proceading to establish and enacte certain Decrees and lawes fitt for the " present occasion, and to be vsed as directions for the guiding of the trade and " traffique belonging to ye present voyage, nowe to be sett forth Do at this assemblie " ordeine and Decree thes severall ordinaunces to be holden and kept as standing " ordinaunces to be used in the voyages wthout alteration or chaunging the teno^r whereof " hereafter ensue videlt "—of which ordinances the following is an extract :—

" And furthermore yt is ordered that yf upon the deliu^{r}ies of his ma^{ties} lr̃es to the " prinnces of those places where o^r shipps shall arrive the generall & factors shalbe " peaceablie received & entertayned as m^{r}chaunts to commerce & traffique wth the " people of those Cuntries or places, & be secured & warranted hereafter to frequente

" & visite those partes. Then yt is ordayned & decreed that there shalbe selected " out of the yongest sorte of the factors, or others entertayned or voluntarily " suffred to goe in the voiadge such and soe many of the aptest & towardest of " them as o^r principall m^rchaunt shall thincke meete, & wch shall have best approved " themselfes fitt for the imploym^t of the Companie, to resyde and abide in the saide " places where they shalbe soe peaceablie received yf they may be permitted " therevnto takinge sufficient & carefull order for the defrayinge & supplyinge of " there Chardge, vntyll those places shalbe hereafter visited by another fleete sent " frõ hence. And leaveinge wth them such advyse & direction for ther better " informacõn howe to carrie themselves in those places, as by the good direction of " o^r principall merchaunt wth thadvyse of suche as he shall consulte w^thall thereof " shalbe thought meete and as tyme & experience of those places shall directe " them whilst the shippes Do lye in thes partes."

Instructions to the above effect were embodied in the commission issued to James Lancaster for the Company's first voyage, but no special orders were therein given regarding the place or places at which factors should be left, though he probably received verbal instructions on that point. In the Commissions to the Commanders of subsequent expeditions, they were specifically instructed as to the ports at which they were to call and settle factories.

The first factory established by the Company was at Bantam, and they soon spread their operations over the neighbouring islands. On the third voyage a visit was paid to Amboyna for the purchase of cloves. A little later they took possession of Polaroon and Rosengin, but the animosity of the Dutch raised every possible obstruction to their successful trading. The English and Dutch Companies levied war upon each other in these parts, which state of things culminated in the massacre of the members of the English Factory at Amboyna, on the 27th February 1623. By this time the Company had established factories at Achin, Tiku, and Priaman, in Sumatra; at Bantam and Jakatra, in Java; at Sukadana and Banjarmasin, in Borneo; at Amboyna, Polaroon, Rosengin, and Macassar; also in Siam and at Patania on the Malay Peninsula; at Firando in Japan; whilst in India they had a factory at Surat, with subordinate agencies at Gogo, Ahmedabad, Cambay, and Ajmir, and factories at Calicut, Cranganore, Patna, Agra, and Masulipatam. In a more westerly direction they had established trade at Jask and Gombroon, and at Mocha in the Red Sea. In making these last-named acquisitions the East India Company clearly recognised —what had at an earlier period been discovered by the Portuguese—that if they desired to obtain a monopoly of the Indo-European trade, they must be in a position to dominate, if not to destroy, those branches of it which passed respectively by way of the Red Sea and the Persian Gulf to the Mediterranean ports.

Notwithstanding its exclusive privileges, the East India Company was not permitted to pursue its trade to the East uninterruptedly. In 1635, Courten's Association obtained a charter from Charles I., under which agencies were settled at Goa, Baticola, Carwar, Achin, and Rajapur, and this had the effect of greatly depressing the trade of the former Company, until at last, in 1649, the two Companies were united.

In the early days of trade with India, it seems to have been customary to send home two copies of letters by different routes; the originals appear generally to have been sent by ship, whilst duplicates were transmitted *viâ* the Persian Gulf and Aleppo. Unfortunately, in a great number of cases, the duplicates have been preserved and the originals lost or destroyed. As giving some idea of the curiosities contained in the records of this early period, I may instance that in 1675 the skeleton of a mermaid was sent home, which the Court presented to His Majesty.

Towards the end of the 17th century the Company had been trying hard to get their privileges confirmed by the House of Commons, as a resolution had been passed by that body in 1693 that it was the right of all Englishmen to trade to the East Indies, or any part of the world, unless prohibited by Act of Parliament. The Company therefore proposed to advance 700,000*l*. at 4 per cent. interest for the public service, on condition of their privileges being confirmed by Parliament, but were outbid by a number of merchants who offered 2,000,000*l*. at 8 per cent. provided they might have the exclusive trade to India vested in them, and should not be obliged to trade as a joint stock unless they should afterwards desire to be incorporated for that purpose. The original list of subscribers to the above amount is still in existence.

At a Court of Directors of the new Company, held the 8th November 1698 at Mercers' Hall, two months and three days after its formation, a disposition was expressed to agree to a union with the old Company upon reasonable terms; and it was agreed that, upon ascertaining what proposals the old Company would make, " this Court will then endeavour to gett a full authority to treat with them in order to attain a happy conclusion."

Accordingly, an agreement was come to about the beginning of 1702, the terms of which were embodied in three deeds, all dated the 22nd July of that year. The several charters and deeds by which this union was effected are still in existence.

Very little now remains of the home records of the new or English East India Company. Indeed, as yet I have only been able to find two books, in one of which the following curious statement occurs :—" At a Court of Directors held at Skinners'-" hall on Wednesday, the 19th April 1699, the Court was informed that there are " engines and paddles to move ships when they are becalmed, and it was moved that " one might be sent at the Company's charge by the 'Gosfreight' or the 'Rook.' " Ordered—That one of the said engines be provided by Mr. Shepheard upon the " Company's account."

Until the completion of the union between the two Companies, each Company conducted its own business, besides which a joint committee was formed entitled the " Committee of Managers." There are three volumes of the minutes of proceedings of this joint committee, extending from the 31st July 1702 to the 18th March 1709. The first Court of Directors of the United East India Company was held on the 23rd March 1709, at which date the union may be said to have been completed. With this union a change also came over the character of the Company itself. Up to this time it had established factories and developed trade throughout the East; now it was destined to enter upon a period of conquests. Before this date it had added materially to the wealth of the nation by increasing its commerce; but it was now to add to its political importance by an increase of its territorial possessions.

The "O.C."* collection contains letters and proceedings relating to all the Company's factories, but from some of them there exist elsewhere other documents, not infrequently of striking interest. Particulars relating to several of the minor factories will be found principally in the proceedings of those to which they were subordinate. Thus, in the records from Bantam, Batavia, Surat, Bombay, Fort St. George, and Calcutta, each of which at one time or another became the chief presidency town, will be found particulars of all the minor factories, in addition to which, however, some of the more important of these latter seem to have also corresponded direct with Court of Directors, and to have sent home to them copies of

* The full title of this Collection, which is included amongst the Factory Records, is "Original Correspondence from India, with collateral documents, originating at any places between England and Japan." These documents extend from 1602 to 1709.

their proceedings. These direct communications, are, however, sadly defective. The following is a list of the Company's several settlements and factories at the end of the seventeenth century:—

St. Helena.
Persia—
  Gombroon.
  Shiraz.
  Ispahan.
Amadavad (Ahmedabad).
Broach.
Surat.
Swally.
Bombay.
Karwar.
Anjengo.
Tellicherri.
Calicut.
Porto Novo.
Cuddalore.
Fort St. David.
Chingee.
Fort St. George.
Petapoli.
Metchlepatam (Masulipatam).
Madapollam.
Vizagapatam.
Orissa.
Balasor.
Fort William.
Chuttanuttee (Calcutta).
Hugli.
Dacca.
Kasimbazar.
Maldah.
Rajamaul.
Patna.
Lucknow.
Agra.
Sumatra—
  Fort York (Bencoolen).
  Indrapore.
  Tryamong.
  Sillebar.
Cochin China—Tonquin.

The above were handed over by the London East India Company to the United Company at the union of the former with the English East India Company. At the same time the latter handed over the following factories which they had established, viz.:—

Surat.
Metchlepatam.
Madapollam.
Bay of Bengal.
Pulo Condore.
Borneo.

The following places had by this time, for one reason or another, ceased to be occupied by the London East India Company:—

Mocha.
Jask.
Gogo.
Cambay.
Ajmir.
Cranganor.
Tanjore.
Conimere.
Pulicat.
Armagaon.
Golconda.
Patna.
Malay Peninsula—Patani.
Sumatra—
  Achin.
  Tiku.
  Priaman.
  Jambi.
Java—
  Bantam.
  Batavia.
Borneo—
  Sukadana.
  Banjarmasin.
Macassar.
Amboyna.
Polaroon.
Rosengin.
Siam.
China—
  Amoy.
  Tywan.
  Macao.
  Canton.
Japan—Firando.

At the union of the two Companies the several minor factories were made subordinate to the three Presidencies of Bombay, Madras, and Bencoolen (Sumatra) respectively. By a Commission, dated 30th December 1709, Fort William in Bengal was also constituted a Presidency.

The Factory Records included in the accompanying list formed part of the Old Records on which Sir George Birdwood submitted a Report in 1878. The twenty-seven combined volumes which contained consultations from various factories, dated between the years 1623 and 1708, have been broken up and their contents re-arranged—together with the "Injured" and "Damaged" Papers, the "Factory Diaries and Consultations," and other documents—under the headings of the several factories to which they refer. In the following brief introduction to these old Factory Records, as well as in the annexed list of them, the alphabetical order has been adopted rather than the chronological order of the establishment of the several factories, as affording greater convenience for purpose of reference.

Report on the Old Factories and their Records.

Anjengo.—Anjengo is situated on a strip of sandy soil, on the coast of Travancore, 72 miles north-west of Cape Comorin. Anjengo was formerly an important place of trade; it was frequented at an early date by the Portuguese, and subsequently by the Dutch. Its exports consisted principally of pepper, and calicoes of an excellent quality. It has now declined into a mere fishing town.

In consequence of the obstruction caused by the Dutch to the East India Company's trade at Karwar and Rajapur, the attention of the Chief Factor at Calicut was directed to the desirability of finding other places where they could obtain pepper and cassia lignum (cassia lignea, a kind of coarse cinnamon). The Queen Ashure, of Attinga, had more than once made an offer to the English to permit them to settle a factory in her country. This, after some preliminary investigations, was now accepted, and in March 1688, with the consent of the Queen, two factories were established, the one at Retturah (Vittoor) and the other at Brinjaon (Villenjum). The Dutch offered the most strenuous obstruction to the settlement of the English in Attinga, but, on the 29th July 1694, the Queen signed an Ola under which she granted to the Company the hill of the Tonges, in Anjengo, with permission to erect a fort thereon, together with warehouses and residences for their factors; and she also granted to them all the pepper in the Attinga country that they might contract and pay for at a certain fixed rate.* The English fort at Anjengo was completed some time in 1697.

During the wars of the Karnatic, Anjengo was used as a depôt for military stores, and as the point from which the first news of outward bound ships reached Madras. The trade had, however, almost completely fallen off. These advantages served only a temporary purpose, and in 1792 the town was reported to be in a hopeless state of decline. In 1809, during the disturbances in Travancore, the roadstead of Anjengo was completely blockaded; in the following year the post of Commercial Resident was abolished, and the station was made subordinate to the Political Resident at Trevandrum.† In 1813 the Factory at Anjengo was finally abolished.

Anjengo is celebrated as having been the birthplace of Robert Orme, the historian, who was born there in 1728. His father, Dr. Alexander Orme, was chief of the Factory from 1723 to 1728. Anjengo was also the birthplace of Elizabeth Sclater, daughter of Mr. May Sclater, who was appointed a writer for Bombay in January 1736. She married Mr. Daniel Draper, at Bombay, on the 28th July 1758, and was Sterne's, and the Abbé Raynal's, "Eliza." She died at Bristol in the year 1778, aged 35.

* O.C., Nos. 5915, 5921, 5922, and 6012.
† Imperial Gazetteer of India.

A number of letters to and from Anjengo will be found in the "O. C." Collection of Records.

The Factory at Anjengo was, at first, placed under the President of Surat, but it was subsequently made subordinate to Bombay. By a Despatch of the 28th February 1727, the Court ordered that all proceedings of that Factory were to be entered in a Consultation Book, which was to be sent to Bombay to be brought into their General Books in order to be periodically sent home. This course was continued until 1775, from which date copies of the Diary and Consultations of the Factory were sent home separately. Those now extant are continuous from the 4th January 1775 to the 31st December 1804, with the exception of those for 1799 and 1800, which are missing. Besides these there is a Political Diary extending from 21st August 1796 to the 27th December 1797; an imperfect collection of Miscellaneous Letters, &c., from the 9th September 1704 to 17th December 1769; and a short treatise on Attinga dated in 1727.

Balasor.—The principal port of the district of the same name. It is situated on the Burabalang river about seven miles from the coast in a straight line. Balasor was at one time an important place of trade, and in one of the early records of this Office it is designated as the port town of Bengala.* The principal articles of export were rice, sugar, silk, saltpetre. The East India Company's ships appear to have traded at Balasor as early as 1633. On the 2nd February 1635 the President at Surat received from Agra the King's firman for liberty of trade in the whole of Bengal, but restraining the Company's shipping only to the port of Pipli. Probably upon the strength of this firman most authorities have asserted that the East India Company's first factory in Bengal was at Pipli; but I can find no confirmation of the statement that they ever had a factory there. The Portuguese, however, did have a factory at Pipli.

It is certain that about this time the Company had a connection at Balasor, but trade there was greatly obstructed by the Dutch, insomuch that it was necessary for the English to carry on their business in armed boats.* The right to establish a factory at Balasor was granted to the Company in 1642; and in 1645 and 1646, in return, it is alleged, for medical services rendered to the Great Mogul, Shah Jehan, and to his viceroy Sultan Shuja, the Nawab of Bengal, by Surgeon Gabriel Boughton, of the Company's ship "Hopewell," additional privileges were conceded to the Company in respect of their factories at Hugli and Balasor. In 1657 the Agency at Balasor was made subordinate to the Factory at Hugli.† Balasor was now fortified and the English were thus enabled to maintain their footing there during the long struggles between the Afghans and the Moghuls, and subsequently between the Moghuls and the Mahrattas, for supremacy in Orissa. About the year 1700 the mouth of the Burabalang river began to fill up, and eventually the coast line advanced, leaving Balasor inland. The commerce of Balasor and its importance were eventually transferred to Calcutta.

A number of letters from Balasor are included in the O. C. Collection. There is only one volume of separate Balasor Records, consisting of the Diary and Consultations of that Factory between December 1679 and March 1687.

Bombay.—The first visit of the English to Bombay appears to have been in September 1626, when both Dutch and English fleets repaired thither, landed some

* O. C. 1536.

† Letters from the Court, 31st December 1657, 27th February and 22nd March 1658.

men, and set on fire all that could be burnt in a small fort and town adjoining. Thirty years later the President at Surat realised the importance of the place, and, writing to the Court, observed that at Bombay is no ill air, but a pleasant fruitful soil, and excellent harbour, but, he added, it is impossible for the English alone to fortify there seeing the Portuguese, whose country it is, will with their utmost force prevent it.* In 1659, the President at Surat had an examination made of the west coast of India, with the view of discovering some strong place that could be fortified, and recommended to the Court the following places, viz., Danda Rajapore, Bombay, and Vassava, "hopeing you will please to obtaine a Command from the King of " Portugall to the Govern^{t}. of India for the free residing or possession of the said " places, they being so convenient for your affaires."†

Bombay island was ceded to the English Crown in 1661, as part of the dower of the Infanta Catharine on her marriage with Charles II., and, in 1668, the King handed it over to the East India Company on payment of an annual rent of 10*l.* In 1687 the chief control of all the Company's possessions in India was transferred from Surat to Bombay, which was erected into an independent Presidency in 1708 on the amalgamation of the London with the English East India Company. In 1773 Bombay was placed in a position of qualified subordination to the Governor General at Calcutta.

The Bombay Records, included in the Factory Series, extend from 1669 to 1710, and comprise, besides a few early papers relating to disagreements between Deputy Governor Henry Young and his subordinates (18th February to 14th September 1669), a slightly defective series of Consultations extending from the 18th March 1670 to the 15th May 1704; copies of Letters despatched (also imperfect) from 8th March 1670 to the 4th January 1710; and copies of Letters received from March 1670 to April 1704. In this last series are several important gaps.

Subsequent letters and proceedings relating to Bombay will be found in the Presidency series of Records. With regard to Bombay Consultations, these are continuous from 1704, but in the Letters received from and despatched to Bombay there is a serious gap which is only partially filled by documents in other Collections. Thus the regular series of Letters received from Bombay, subsequently to 1704, commences only with 1760 and of Despatches to Bombay with 1753.

Borneo.—The principal ports of Borneo were at Sambas, Landak, and Sukadana on the west of the Island, and Banjarmassin on the south, all of which places are now included in the Dutch territories. The principal products of the country are described as "fine diamonds, camphor, the best ginger, mirabolans, sugar, soap, bigars, " victualls abundantly, orrenges, lemonds and rice, sinnomon but not good, turtle " shells."‡

The first reference to Borneo, in the Records here, occurs in a letter from John Saris to the Company, dated the 4th December 1608, wherein he states, "I have many " times certified your worships of the trade the Flemings follow to Soocadanna, " which place yieldeth great store of diamonds, and of their manner of dealing for " them for gold principally which comes from Baniermassen." In consequence of this representation a pinnace was ordered to proceed to Sukadana (in 1612), when an investment was made in diamonds§ and a factory settled, which was placed in charge of Augustin Spalding.‖ In April 1614 a factory was established at Sambas,

* O. C. 1241.

† O. C. 2839.

‡ O. C. 638.

§ O. C. 90.

‖ Journal of Peter Floris for the seventh voyage, Purchas his Pilgrimes, Vol. I., p. 320.

and in the following year trade was opened with Banjarmasin.* In the same month a vessel was sent to Landak with the view of establishing a factory there, but the Dyaks, instigated by the Dutch and Chinese, refused to allow it, or, indeed, to trade with the English.† Eight years later (1622) the Matram sent an army and surprised and ransacked Sukadana; Edward Pike, the factor, was killed by an explosion of gunpowder, and the following year the factory was abandoned,‡ and thus appears to have ended for a time the English trade with Borneo.

In 1699 the English East India Company opened up a trade with Banjarmasin and established a factory there. A few years later (1704) permission was obtained from the King for the erection of a fortification for the protection of the Company's establishment there, and after the union of the two East India Companies a strong factory was erected, but on the 27th June 1707 the natives attacked the English settlement and the factory was withdrawn. In 1738 trade was re-opened at Banjarmasin, but owing to the opposition of the Dutch, who in May 1747 blockaded the place, it was again abandoned.

In January 1761 a treaty was concluded with the King of Sulu, under which the Island of Balambangan, off the extreme north coast of Borneo, was granted to the English, and in 1771 an expedition was sent from Bombay to take possession of the place. But on the 26th February 1775 a band of Sulus captured the fort at Balambangan and carried away a large amount of booty, whereupon the factory was removed to Labuan, an island off the north-west coast of Borneo. In 1803 Balambangan was again occupied by the East India Company, but they withdrew their establishment in the following year.

The Records relating to Borneo will be found principally in the O. C. Records and in those relating to Java. The only separate volume of Borneo Records, which includes papers between 1648 and 1814, contains documents dated between 1771 and 1779 relating to Balambangan, and two documents, dated in 1812, referring to a treaty with the Sultan of Banjarmasin, whereby, on the retirement of the Dutch, he handed over to the East India Company all his sovereign rights in a large portion of his dominions.

Broach.—The chief town of the district of the same name in Gujarat, situated on the right bank of the Narbada river, about 30 miles from its mouth. Its principal products were indigo, calicoes, cotton yarn, and sword blades; it was considered the chief place in India for the last-named article and for baftas.§

On the 3rd November 1614, at a Council held at Swally, it was determined to appoint a Factor for Broach and other places, and accordingly John Oxwicke and another were sent there.‖ Under date the 22nd July 1616 Sir Thomas Roe obtained a firman from the Emperor Jehangir for residence and freedom of trade at this town,¶ and a factory was established there. The factory at Broach was made subordinate to Surat, and subsequently to Bombay. On the union of the new English Company with the original London Company, Broach is mentioned as one of the latter Company's factories in the Bombay Presidency.

The only separate Factory Records relating to Broach now extant here comprise the Diary and Consultations from 1st January 1775 to 30th December 1781; Revenue

---

* O. C. 327.

† O. C. 139, 150, 458, 662.

‡ O. C. 1059, 1092.

§ A kind of calico, so called from the Persian "bafta" (woven), O. C. 241–258.

‖ O. C. 168.

¶ O. C. 380–408 I.

Consultations from 1st January 1779 to 30th December 1780; and Proceedings of a Special Committee appointed by the Governor of Bombay in 1777 "for investigating affairs at the settlement of Broach and its Dependencies."

Burdwan.—A division of the Bengal Presidency. Burdwan can hardly be considered a factory, but the few separate records which exist for that district could not conveniently have been included in any other series than that of the Factory Records. In consideration of the English agreeing to assist the Nabob, the latter, by a Treaty dated the 27th September 1760, assigned to the Company the lands of Burdwan, Midnapore, and Chittagong. This was subsequently confirmed by a firman from the King Shah Alam under date the 30th September 1765.* The only Burdwan Records consist of the Proceedings of the Provincial Council of Revenue from the 16th May 1774 to the 30th December 1779.

Calcutta and Sutanati.—During the administration of Shaista Khan the English in Bengal were subjected to much oppression, and their factors had to submit to considerable extortions, until, in 1685, it was resolved to seek redress by force of arms. These hostilities exasperated the Emperor Aurangzeb, who ordered that the English should be expelled from his dominions. The Company's factories were seized and their affairs were brought to the brink of ruin. Job Charnock, the Agent, retired from Hugli, with the English factory there, and established it at Sutanati, about 26 miles lower down the river from Hugli town. The new settlement gradually extended itself to Kalikata (Calcutta) and Govindpur, and in 1689 it was determined to make Calcutta the headquarters of the Company's Bengal factories. In 1696 Fort William was built, and under a grant from Azamu-sh-Shan, grandson of Aurangzeb and Governor of Bengal, dated in 1698, the Company were permitted to purchase the towns of Sutanati, Govindpur, and Calcutta.

The Calcutta Factory Records comprise an imperfect set of Diaries and Consultations from 16th July 1690 to 22nd December 1708; copies of Letters despatched (imperfect) from the 17th July 1690 to the 21st August 1705; and copies of Letters received (also imperfect) from June 1690 to November 1704. The Bengal Presidency Proceedings (*see* Presidency Records) date from 1704.

Cambay.—The town of Cambay, in the Province of Gujarat, is situated at the head of the Gulf of Cambay, on the north of the estuary of the River Mahi. Its principal articles of export were cloth, tapestry, satins, and other goods, quilts, carpets, bloodstones, and other jewels.† In Mr. Foulke Grevil's Report (10th March 1600) on the Memorial of the promoters of the East India Company for permission to trade to the East Indies, it is remarked that the kingdom of Cambaia is the most fruitful of all India.‡ King James gave the Company letters to the King of Cambay, amongst others, but the Court at that time entertained small hope of trade there because of the Portuguese who commanded the waters in those parts.§ The "Ascension" visited Cambay in 1609, but met with opposition from the Portuguese‖; but on the 21st October 1612, Articles were agreed upon between the Governor of Ahmedabad on behalf of the Great Mogul, and Thomas Best on behalf of the King and the East India Company, for settling a trade and factory in Cambay and other parts of the Mogul's dominions.¶

---

* Aitchison's Treaties, Vol. I., pp. 47 and 59.

† O. C. 190, 258, 1264, 1306.

‡ Bruce's Annals, Vol. I., pp. 121–126.

§ Court Minutes, 7th December 1607.

‖ O. C. 12, 65.

¶ E. I. Cal., No. 674 I., and Court Book III., 121–131.

The trade at Cambay does not appear to have come up to the expectations entertained of the place, owing to the opposition of the Portuguese, so that, it was observed, in a letter to the Court, "unless they were quite rooted out there is no hope of any good to be done there for us."*

Cambay does not appear to have risen to any great importance under the East India Company. The factory there was subordinate to Surat and subsequently to Bombay, and the only separate records from thence now existing here are comprised in a single volume which contains the proceedings of the Resident from the 1st January 1804 to the 29th June 1807.

Cape of Good Hope.—Table Bay was much used by the outgoing vessels of both the English and Dutch East India Companies as a place for refreshing on the way to India. In the year 1620, Captains Andrew Shilling and Humphrey Fitzherbert, on their outward voyage, met a Dutch fleet in Table Bay, and hearing that they intended forming a settlement there, resolved to anticipate them by taking immediate and formal possession of the place in the name of King James, which they carried into execution without molestation from the Dutch officers.† No further steps, however, appear to have been taken in the matter, and the Cape continued to be indiscriminately frequented, for the purpose of obtaining refreshments, by mariners of all nations, though without any attempt at colonization or settlement, till the year 1652.

In that year an expedition was sent out from Holland which reached the Cape on the 6th April and took possession of it on behalf of the Dutch Government. Against this the East India Company protested, as the place had already been annexed by the English, but the Dutch continued in possession until 1795, when an English fleet, under Sir G. K. Elphinstone, and land forces under Sir Alured Clarke, took possession of the place in order to secure it against the French for the Prince of Orange. The Cape of Good Hope was now constituted a British possession, and General Craig was appointed the first Governor.

Under the Treaty of Peace that was signed at Amiens in 1801, the Cape was ordered to be restored to the Dutch, and it was handed over to them on the 20th February 1803.

Hostilities having recommenced in Europe, an expedition under Sir David Baird retook the Cape on the 18th January 1806, and the Colony was finally ceded to England at the Congress of Vienna in 1815.

Mr. John Pringle, who left St. Helena in the "Orpheus" which joined Sir G. K. Elphinstone's expedition to the Cape, appears to have remained there as the East India Company's Agent, when the Colony was taken possession of by the English, and he continued in that capacity until his death in June 1815. The earliest records in the Cape of Good Hope series consists of some unimportant letters from Mr. Jochem van Plettenburg, second in command at the Cape, addressed to the East India Company, and dated in 1773 and 1774. Next, there is a description and drawing of Croem or Crontz Riviere Bay in south-east Africa, by Lieutenant Henry Pemberton; and after this follow Mr. Pringle's letters. The collection comprises altogether twenty-four volumes, which contain Miscellaneous Correspondence from 1773 to August 1823; copies of Letters from the Cape to the Court of Directors, from the 4th April 1795 to the 16th March 1831; from the Cape to various parts, 3rd June 1808 to 30th April 1836; and Letters received at the Cape between the 31st May 1808 and the 30th April 1836. In 1835, upon the East Indian trade being

---

* O. C. 261.

† O. C. 897 and 907; also Factory Records (Miscellaneous), Vol. 10.

thrown open, the Company ceased to have any agent of their own at the Cape, but such services as they required were performed by commercial houses already established there.

Celebes.—The principal port of Celebes was Macassar, where the Dutch had, at an early date, established a factory.* Macassar was formerly a mart of considerable importance for spice and other imports, receiving cloves, nutmegs, and mace from the Moluccas; pepper from Banjarmasin; sapanwood from Bima (Soembawa); sandal-wood from Bima and Timore; cotton cloths from India proper; wax, benzoin and elephants' teeth from Camboja; slaves, gumlac, tortoise shells, and cassia lignum from various parts; sugar, green ginger and China-roots from China, &c. Its chief indigenous exports were rice, arrack, native gold, and some tortoise shells.

In October 1612 Peter Floris sent some cloths to Macassar, which was, it is believed, the first instance of the English trading there. The Company's ship "Darling" having failed to settle a factory at Amboyna, Captain Jourdain proceeded to Macassar, where he arrived on the 16th July 1613, and established a factory which he left in charge of George Cokayne. In the following year the King gave permission to Cokayne to erect a house at Macassar.† Cokayne was succeeded by George Chauncey, who, in the absence of the other factors, abandoned the factory, but it was re-established by Captain Ball in 1615 who again placed Cokayne in charge of it.‡

In July 1667 the Dutch, having a quarrel with the King, attacked the forts at Macassar, which they captured, whereupon the King was forced to agree to a peace dictated by the enemy. Under this treaty the Dutch seized the English Company's servants and property and carried them away to Batavia. Although the Court desired to re-settle their factory at Macassar, it appears that, owing to the obstruction of the Dutch, this was never effected.

The records relating to Macassar will be found mostly in the O. C. Collection, and in the Java Records. The one separate volume relating to Celebes contains extracts from these and other documents arranged as materials for a history of the Company's factory at Macassar.

Ceylon.—The first intercourse of the English with Ceylon took place in 1762. The King of Kandy having sent to Madras to solicit the assistance of the English to protect him and his country from the oppression and usurpation of the Dutch, Mr. John Pybus was sent to treat with the King and to make such observations on the country as might tend to promote the future advantage of the Company with regard to the trade on that Island. This embassy, however, led to no practical result. In 1781 Mr. Hugh Boyd was sent on a somewhat similar mission, which also ended as the previous one had done. On the rupture between Great Britain and Holland, in 1795, a force was sent against the Dutch possessions in Ceylon, where the opposition offered was so slight that by the following year the whole of their forts were in the hands of the English Commander. On this occasion, Mr. R. Andrews was accredited to the Court of Kandy by the Madras Government, and joined the forces which captured Trincomali. At first the island was placed under the care of the East India Company, but, in 1802, the whole seaboard of Ceylon became, by the Treaty of Amiens, a possession of the British Crown.

---

* O. C. 119.
† O. C. 142, 286.
‡ O. C. 284, 287, 294.

The Ceylon Records of this Office comprise reports on the three missions above referred to; proceedings of a committee of investigation into the affairs of Ceylon in 1797–98; proceedings and correspondence of the Governor between the 12th October 1798 and the 18th September 1802, and other miscellaneous documents between 1798 and January 1806.

China and Japan.—The eighth voyage set out by the East India Company in 1611, under the command of Captain Saris, included a visit to Japan, for which purpose a small vessel named the "Clove" was specially assigned. This vessel, with Captain Saris on board, reached Firando on the 12th June 1613, where he established a factory with Mr. Cocks as Chief. From Firando factors were sent to the neighbouring islands and ports, including Nangasaki, Edo, Osaca, Shrongo, Miaco, and Tushma. The Japan factories were, however, closed in 1623, as they afforded neither profit nor expectation of profit.

Trade with China was attempted from both Firando and Tywan, but considerable obstructions were thrown in the way of its successful accomplishment by the Dutch.

In June 1672 Mr. William Gyfford was sent from Bantam to open up a trade with Tonquin. In this he succeeded, and established a factory there, which, however, did not prove very successful, and it was accordingly dissolved on the 30th November 1697.

Up to about the year 1680 the Company had carried on a China trade in country vessels, freighted by the Council at Bantam, but they then determined to employ ships freighted from England direct, as well for the China as for the India trade. Several unsuccessful attempts were made at various dates to establish a factory at Chusan, but the Company had to be content with carrying on trade at Canton through the instrumentality of an official called the Emperor's merchant. By 1715 the intercourse with Canton had assumed somewhat of a regular trade. Ships were despatched to China at stated seasons, and supercargoes were appointed to each ship, who were to live, when at Canton, in one house, to keep but one table, and to meet at least twice a week to consult for the general benefit of the Company's affairs. In 1751 the Court suggested the expediency of hiring a factory at Canton for a term of years instead of pursuing the expensive practice of hiring one every season, and from about this time may be dated the establishment of a factory at Canton.

The earliest China and Japan Records will be found in the O. C. Collection and among the Java Records. Those contained in the present Collection comprise thirteen volumes of extracts, entitled "China Materials, &c.," extending from 1596 to 1725; seven volumes of miscellaneous documents dated between 1614 and 1815; China Supercargoes Diaries from 1721 to 1751, and Canton Consultations, &c., from 1751 to 1843; Letters from China 1823 to 1834; Despatches to China 1829 to 1832, and various miscellaneous documents.

Conimere.—This place is on the Coromandel Coast, about 13 miles north of Pondicherry. In 1681 the Madras Government sent to the Subahdar of Porto Novo to treat about a Cowle for settling a factory at Conimere,* the principal export from which place was cloth. Before this, the Company appears to have traded with the place, and Conimere merchants frequented Madras. The necessary permission having been received from the Subahdar, some factors were sent from Madras to settle a factory there,† which was effected at the end of October 1682. In July 1688 the factories of Cuddalore and Porto Novo were transferred to Conimere, and the latter place was abandoned as a factory on the purchase of Fort St. David in 1698.

* Madras Cons., 11th January 1681. † Madras Cons., 9th October 1682.

Particulars relating to this factory will be found principally in the Madras Records, but a few separate Conimere Records exist which comprise Consultations of the Conimere Factory between the 26th October 1682 and the 28th December 1685; copies of Letters despatched between the 2nd January 1684 and the 28th December 1685, and copies of Letters received for the year 1684.

Cuddalore and Porto Novo.—Cuddalore is a town in the South Arcot District, about 116 miles south of Madras. In 1682 the Company opened negotiations with the Khan of Jinjee to settle here and at Porto Novo. The first building was erected at Cuddalore in 1683, and in the following year a formal lease was obtained for the site of the port and the old fortress. During the next ten years trade increased so rapidly that the Company erected Fort St. David for the protection of the place. On the fall of Madras in 1746 the British administration withdrew to Cuddalore, which place remained the headquarters of the Presidency until 1752, when the Government returned to Madras. In 1755 Clive was in command at Cuddalore. In 1758 the French occupied the town, and stormed and destroyed the fort; but in 1760, after the battle of Wandiwash, the British regained possession. In 1782 it again fell into the hands of the French, but was formally restored to the British in 1785, and in 1801 it was included in the cession of the Karnatic.

These factories were subordinate to that of Fort St. George. The separate records comprise the Commission obtained by the Company for settling factories in the Jinjee country, besides some letters and Consultations for the years 1683 to 1687.

Dacca.—Dakha (so called from the dakh, or Butea frondosa, trees in the neighbourhood) is situated on the north bank of the Buriganga river. This place was celebrated for its muslins. Besides the English, the Dutch and French had factories here. The East India Company's factory at Dacca was established about 1666. The Company greatly fostered the manufacture of the Dacca muslins, but their doom was sealed by the introduction, in 1785, of the mule jenny, and the imposition of a heavy protective duty on Indian muslins. In consequence, the exportation of Dacca muslins to this country gradually fell off, until it ceased altogether in 1817, when the Company's Commercial Residency at Dacca was abolished.

Particulars of the Dacca Factory will be found in the O. C. Collection, and in the Balasor and Calcutta Records. The separate Dacca Records consist of copies of Consultations between the 28th October 1678 and the 21st December 1779.

Dinajpur.—One of the districts of Bengal which came into the possession of the East India Company when the rest of Bengal passed under British rule in 1765. The Dinajpur separate records do not properly belong to the Factory series, but they have, for convenience of classification, been included with it; they consist of Proceedings of the Provincial Council of Revenue for the years 1774 to 1778 inclusive.

Egypt and the Red Sea.—In November 1610 Sir Henry Middleton, in command of the sixth voyage, was unsuccessful in an attempt to trade at Mocha. He was at first well received, but was shortly afterwards attacked and taken prisoner, and all the goods landed were confiscated.* In May 1618, however, Captain Andrew Shilling obtained a firman from the Governor for freedom of trade, and for the establishment of factories at Sana, Ties, Mocha, Aden, or any other places in the

* O. C. 72.

Sultan's dominions.* A factory was accordingly established at Mocha the same year, but this appears to have been neutralized by the opposition of the Guzerattis.† The trade, however, subsequently revived, but it does not appear to have been at any time of much importance. In the early days of this trade the exports from Mocha consisted principally of coral, but the place subsequently became the great emporium for coffee. In 1752, the factory was given up,‡ and the trade at Mocha was subsequently managed by Supercargoes. Mocha eventually was made a Residency, and in more recent years an Agency. At various times the East India Company appointed Agents at Mocha, Cairo, Suez, and Alexandria, the correspondence with whom forms the principal part of the Egypt and Red Sea Records. The Mocha Factory Records appear for the most part in the O. C. Collection, and in the first volume of the Egypt and Red Sea Factory Records. Papers relating to the Mocha Agency begin as early as March 1644, after which there is a gap until 1710, and they go down to January 1828, but there are many gaps and the collection is evidently very imperfect. After this come a number of papers containing correspondence regarding overland routes through Syria and Egypt; Mr. Baldwin's attempts to open up communication with India through Egypt; and French negotiations for trade in that country, &c. Another miscellaneous volume contains papers relating to the occupation of Perim in 1799; the mission of Sir Home Popham to Arabia in 1801; the expedition from India to Egypt in 1801; and Letters from Lord Elgin at Constantinople on the overland conveyance of Despatches, Egyptian affairs, &c., 1800–03. The remainder of this series comprises Correspondence between 1819 and 1870 with the various Agents at Constantinople, Cairo, and other places in Egypt.

Fort St. David (Tegnapatam or Devanapatam) is situated on the left bank of the mouth of the Guddelam river. This place which contained a fort was purchased from Rama Rajah, a son of Sivaji, in 1690. On the 18th December in that year, President Yale succeeded in obtaining a firman, confirming to the English all their factories in the Jinjee country. On the capture of Madras by the French in 1746, the Company's Agent at this station assumed the control of all the Company's possessions in Southern India, and successfully resisted an attack made by Dupleix on the settlement. In 1756 Clive was appointed Governor. In 1758 it was invested by sea and land by the French and, after a short siege, surrendered on the 2nd June, when the fortifications were demolished. It was afterwards included in Cuddalore and its dependencies.

The Fort St. David Records consist of copies of Consultations for 11th February and 24th September 1690; 3rd January 1696 to 22nd December 1712; 3rd January 1723 to 31st December 1756; and letters from 27th September 1692 to 31st July 1759.

Fort St. George (Madras).—In March 1639, Mr. Francis Day, chief of the settlement at Armagaon, obtained from the representative of the Hindu power of Vijayanagar, a grant of the site of land on which Madras now stands. A factory, with some slight fortifications, was at once constructed, and the factors at Armagaon were removed to it. It was at first made subordinate to Bantam, but in 1653 it was raised to the rank of a Presidency. This was the first territorial British possession in India. In 1746 Madras was taken by the French, but it was restored to the English by the treaty of Aix-la-Chapelle in 1748.

---

* O. C. 648.

† O. C. 681, 831, 950.

‡ Bombay Cons., 22nd September 1752.

The Fort St. George Factory Records comprise a somewhat defective series of Consultations between the 31st March 1655 and the 27th December 1704; copie of Letters despatched between the 2nd January 1661 and the 22nd December 1704 (imperfect); Correspondence with the Nawab of Golconda, February 1669 to January 1672; copies of Letters received (also imperfect) from January 1672 to December 1704; and some miscellaneous papers dated between 1676 and 1705. Subsequent Fort St. George Records are contained in the Presidency series.

Hugli.—The Factory at Hugli was established in 1650 under the firman obtained from Sultan Shuja by Dr. Boughton (*see* Report on Balasor Records *ante*), but it was abandoned about 1685, when the settlement was removed to Sutanati by the Agent Job Charnock (*see* Report on Calcutta Records *ante*).

The Hugli Records comprise an imperfect set of copies of Consultations, &c., between the 13th October 1663 and the 9th September 1682, which include also certain proceedings at Balasor and Kasimbazar; copies of Letters despatched and received between the 27th December 1672 and 8th December 1684, and between October 1671 and November 1687 respectively, both series being imperfect.

Java.—In 1602 Captain Lancaster concluded a Treaty with the King of Bantam under which permission was given to the East India Company to establish a factory there. This he accordingly effected, and Bantam was, for some time, the Company's principal settlement in the East. In 1619 the English removed their factory from Bantam to Jakatra, and the factors there assumed the titles of President and Council. Owing to the opposition of the Dutch the English factory was removed in 1624 to the Island of Lagundy, but it did not long remain there.

In October 1626 a factory was established at Japara on the north coast of Java, east of Batavia, but on the 16th January 1628 the President and Council returned to Bantam. In 1630 the establishment at Bantam was reduced to an Agency, and made subordinate to the President and Council at Surat; but it was restored to a Presidency in 1634, and the agencies on the coast of India and in Bengal were made subordinate to it. In August 1682, in consequence of a revolution instigated by the Dutch, in which the Company's factory was taken possession of by the rebels, the establishment withdrew to Batavia, whence they retired in the following August to Surat. The English East India Company had, for a short time, a factory at Batavia, but they retired thence to Banjarmasin in 1702. After this date the East India Company, who had established factories in Sumatra, appear to have held but little trade with Java until 1758, when an Agency was again established at Batavia. When Holland was annexed to France, early in the present century, Java was placed under the administration of General Daendels, supported by a strong military force. A military expedition under Lieutenant-General Sir Samuel Auchmuty was, however, sent against the Island in August 1811, by whom it was taken and annexed to the British Crown; but by a Convention of the 13th August 1814, between the British Government and that of the Netherlands, Java and its dependencies were restored to Holland, who formally took possession on the 4th December 1816.

The Java Records are very voluminous, and comprise altogether 72 volumes. The earlier documents date from 1595, and those relating to the expedition of 1811, and the subsequent administration of the Island, go down to the year 1827.

Karwar.—A town and port of North Kanara, 50 miles south-east of Goa. Karwar possesses the only first-rate harbour on the western coast of India between Bombay and Colombo. The town is of comparatively modern date, and rose to be one of the chief ports in the Bijapur dominions early in the 17th century. In 1638 a factory was settled here by Courten's Association, which he offered, in 1646,* to sell to the President of the London Company at Surat, but the offer was declined, and in 1649 the Factory was seized by the Native Governor.† The two bodies were, however, united in 1650, and shortly afterwards Karwar appears as one of the Company's factories.‡ The establishment was withdrawn in 1679 in consequence of exactions from local Chiefs, but it was restored again in 1682; owing, however, to the hostility of the Sonda Chief, the factory was removed in 1720, and was not re-opened until 1750. In 1752 the Portuguese sent a fleet and took possession of Sadashivgarh, and claimed the monopoly of the Karwar trade; as they were in a position to enforce their claim the English Agent was withdrawn.

The proceedings of the Factory at Karwar will be found principally in the O.C. Collection, and in the Surat and Bombay Records. The only separate volume of Karwar Records contains a copy, and translation, of the firman granting certain privileges to the Company at Karwar, and an account of the siege of the factory by the Sonda Raja in 1717.

Kasimbazar.—Now a decayed town in Murshidabad District; it is said to derive it name from a legendary founder, Kasim Khan. After Satgaon had been ruined by the silting up of the Saraswati mouth of the Ganges, and before Calcutta was founded, Kasimbazar was the great emporium for Bengal. In 1658 the Company established a factory here, which was made subordinate to Fort St. George. Kasimbazar was one of the factories assigned by the London Company to the United Company in 1702. Its decay dates from 1813, when the Bhagirathi river suddenly deserted its ancient bed, and took to a new course three miles from the old town. A number of letters from this Factory will be found in the O. C. Records; the separate Factory Records from Kasimbazar comprise the Diary and Consultations from the 12th October 1676 to the 30th November 1685; there is then a gap till April 1701, in consequence of this and other factories in Bengal having been confiscated by order of the Nawab Shaista Khan in 1686. There are then some Consultations for the year 1701, after which there is another gap till March 1733, also between December 1733 and January 1736. Subsequently to the latter date the Consultations are fairly regular up to February 1759, when the separate Records for this Factory cease.

Madapollam.—This was a weaving and dyeing village near Narsapur, in the Godavery District, and gave its name to goods still known in the market as "Madapollams." This factory, which was subordinate to Masulipatam, is first mentioned in 1676. References to it will be found in the O. C. Collection and in the Masulipatam Records. The Madapollam Records comprise Consultations between the 2nd January 1684 and the 31st December 1686; copies of Letters despatched between the 7th September 1676 and the 30th December 1684; and copies of Letters received between September 1676 and December 1685.

Maldah.—A town of Bengal, situated at the confluence of the Kalindri with the Mahanadi river. The town is admirably situated for river traffic, and probably rose to prosperity as the port of Panduah, one of the two great capitals of the early Muhammadan Kings of Bengal, the other capital being Gaur. It was the seat of

---

* O. C. 2012. † O. C. 2158. ‡ O. C. 2726.

thriving cotton and silk manufactures, and both the French and Dutch had settlements here. The East India Company established a factory in the latter part of the seventeenth century, which was in existence at the union of the two Companies in 1702–9. The separate Maldah Records consist of Diaries and Consultations between the 22nd April 1680 and the 31st January 1693; these are not, however, continuous.

Masulipatam (Machli-patnam, or Fish Town; but according to Sir Henry Yule the name is a relic of Moesolia of the Greek geographers) is the principal sea-port of the Kistna District, 215 miles north of Madras City. The first visit to Masulipatam by any of the Company's officers was by Captain Hippon, in the "Globe," who arrived and landed on the 30th August 1611, and obtained a cowle for trading there. A factory appears to have been established here in 1615,* but it was abandoned in 1628 on account of the oppressions of the native Governor.† It was re-established in 1631,‡ when this station became the centre of English trade in those parts, and was managed by a Chief and Council. In 1685 the factory was again temporarily dissolved, but it was subsequently revived, and was in existence at the union of the two East India Companies.

Many documents relating to Masulipatam are contained in the O. C. Collection. The separate Factory Records comprise Consultations between the 5th July 1670 and the 31st December 1685; copies of Letters despatched, from the 15th September 1640 to the 29th December 1686; copies of Letters received, from April 1622 to December 1685; Diary of William Puckle, January 1675 to January 1676; and Proceedings of the new Company's representatives at Masulipatam for 1699 and 1700.

Murshidabad.—The district of Murshidabad, in the Bengal Presidency, came under the financial administration of the East India Company in 1765 by a grant from the Moghul Emperor, Shah Alam. The Murshidabad Records do not properly belong to the Factory period at all, but rather to the Bengal Revenue Series; they have, however, been included in this Collection for greater convenience of reference; they consist of Proceedings of the Provincial Council of Revenue from the 27th September 1770 to the 27th December 1779, and copies of Letters received and sent for September and October 1770.

Patna.—This city, which has been identified with Pataliputra, and Palibothra mentioned by Megasthenes, has long been a place of considerable importance as a commercial depôt. Its central position at the junction of three great rivers—the Son, the Gandak, and the Ganges, where the traffic of the North-Western Provinces meets that of Bengal and another line of trade branches off to Nepal—gives it in this respect great advantages. It is uncertain at what precise date the East India Company first established a factory here, but it was probably in the early part of the second half of the seventeenth century. In 1686§ the factory was seized by the Nabob, and the Company's servants were taken prisoners. In 1692 the Court ordered the factory to be withdrawn, provided sufficient saltpetre could be procured at Hugli;‖ it continued to exist, however, until the union of the two Companies, but was shortly afterwards withdrawn, though it was subsequently re-established. The Factory Records consist of one volume of Diary and Consultations, between the

* O. C. 349.
† O. C. 1273–1280.
‡ O. C. 1313, 1322, 1374.
§ O. C. 5531.
‖ Letter to Bengal, 22nd January 1692.

6th April 1680 and the 30th September 1685. The District of Patna was conveyed to the East India Company by a grant from Shah Alam in 1765, and amongst these Records are certain Consultations extending to April 1782 (which have, however, more especial reference to the revenues of the district) and narratives of the massacre at Patna in 1763.

Persia and the Persian Gulf.—On the 1st October 1611 Mr. Robert Sherley presented to King James his credentials as an Ambassador from the King of Persia, on whose account he offered to the English the free and absolute use of two ports in his dominions.* A few years after this, in 1614, Mr. Richard Steele, who had gone to Aleppo to recover a debt from a merchant of that city, followed him through Persia to India, and, on arrival at Surat, reported the great advantages to be derived from a trade to Persia.† Thereupon the Factors sent him, together with Mr. Crowther, to England, to represent the matter to the Court.‡ In 1616 the Agency at Surat despatched a vessel with goods to Jask, where the expedition was favourably received and a license granted to land; two Factors were left here, and Messrs. Barker and Connock, who had charge of the expedition, proceeded to Ispahan, where a factory was established.§ Three firmans were obtained in favour of the English, and these were followed by a treaty which gave them considerable facilities for trade in Persia. Obstruction was attempted by the Portuguese, but unsuccessfully, and they were eventually (in 1622) driven out of Ormus by the combined English and Persian forces. A renewed Treaty was also obtained from the Shah.

In 1639 a voyage was undertaken to Bussora, where permission to trade was obtained from the Bashaw, and a factory was shortly afterwards established there, which was described, in 1644, as one of the most important centres of exchange which the Company at that time enjoyed.

At the union of the two Companies in 1702–9, the factories in Persia are described as at Gombroon, Shiraz, and Ispahan. By 1727 the trade at Bussora was paralyzed by the oppression to which it was subjected by the Bashaw, and the Agent accordingly withdrew and retired to Gombroon, but the factory at Bussora was shortly afterwards re-established.

In December 1754, by orders from the Court, a factory was established at Bunder Reig, but the building was demolished two years later, and the Agent retired to Gombroon. In October 1759 the English factory at Gombroon was taken by a French fleet and destroyed, but it was re-established in the following year. Owing to a decline in trade at Gombroon, the English factory was removed thence to Bussora in 1763, and in the same year a factory was established at Bushire. In 1783 a Native Agent was appointed at Bagdad, who was succeeded in 1798 by a Resident, whose chief duty was to watch and report on the proceedings of the French emissaries in connection with Napoleon's projected invasion of India by Egypt and the Red Sea. In 1778 Bushire became the head station of the Company's Persian Gulf trade. In 1808 a Resident was appointed at Muscat. In August 1809 the Bagdad and Bussora Residencies were consolidated, and one Resident was appointed for both places. The Commercial Residency of Bushire was abolished in May 1812.

The Records relating to Persia and the Persian Gulf have been arranged and bound up in 130 volumes, extending from 1620 to 1874. The earliest document consists of a list of sundry commodities and their prices. It is docketted, "To be perused at

---

* Calendar of State Papers (East Indies), Vol. I., Nos. 391 and 503.

† O. C. 163.

‡ O. C. 225.

§ O. C. 407, 410, 420, 422.

Surat and sent for England." This is followed by a copy of a letter from King James I. to Shah Abbas, King of Persia, relative to establishing a trade in the Persian dominions, dated the 19th March 1621*; and next come copies of Letters, dated in 1621 and 1622, from Ispahan, Ghilan, Kharistan, Shiraz, Laur, Minaw, Gombroon, Jiyome (Jeroon, the old name for Ormuz), and Kustack. The documents in this series for the early part of the 17th century are not numerous, but others are contained in the "O. C." volumes. Under date the 3rd August 1697 is a paper containing samples of different coloured silks, which was received overland *viá* Aleppo.

The earliest Gombroon Consultations date from the 1st November 1708. There are gaps in these Consultations between the 31st July 1710 and the 23rd November 1726; between the 31st July 1727 and the 20th November 1728; between the 31st July 1752 and the 3rd August 1754, and between the 31st July 1758 and the 16th January 1760. They finally cease on the 7th February 1763, soon after which date the Factory was removed thence to Bussora.

There are seven volumes of Letters from Bussora, Gombroon, and other places dated between the years 1703 and 1811, followed by eleven volumes of miscellaneous documents between 1764 and 1822, including letters from General Malcolm and Sir Harford Jones relative to their respective missions to Persia. These are followed by one volume of Despatches relative to the Expedition to the Gulf of Persia, dated between the years 1815 and 1821.

From 1817 there is a continuous record of documents up to 1874, consisting principally of letters from Persia, Bagdad, Bushire, Bussora, Damascus, &c., to the Secret Committee of the East India Company, to the Secretary of State for Foreign Affairs, and latterly to the Secretary of State for India.

Other documents relative to Persia and the Persian Gulf will be found in the Surat and Bombay Consultations, and in the Proceedings of the Government of India.

Petapoli (Pettipoly, Pettapoli, from the Telugu *pedda*, great, and *palli*, village) the native name of Nizampatam, adopted by the English. A town and port of the Kistna District. Captain Hippon arrived at Petapoli on the 18th August 1611, where he was well received by the Governor, and allowed to land goods for trade.† On the 7th February 1614 Mr. Floris arrived at this port and established a factory,‡ which was, however, dissolved by William Methwold in 1621,§ but a merchant was retained there in order to continue a trade.‖ The factory appears to have been shortly afterwards revived as it was in existence again in 1633,¶ but it was finally dissolved by order of the Court in 1687. The separate Petapoli Records comprise copies of Consultations, between the 4th January 1683 and 24th May 1687, copies of Letters received, January 1685 to June 1687, and copies of Letters sent, 26th September 1682 to 24th May 1687.

Rajapur.—Chief town of the Rajapur Subdivision of the Ratnagiri District of Bombay. It was once an important place of trade for pepper and cardamoms. In a letter to the Court, dated the 28th January 1640, the Council at Surat reported that Rajapur was the fittest place for the Company's occasions, Bombay excepted.** A factory was established here by Captain Weddell in the same year on account of

---

* Amongst the Parchment Records is also the original of another letter from King James to Shah Abbas, dated the 14th February 1622.

† O. C. 78/81. ‡ O. C. 159. § O. C. 983.

‖ O. C. 1448. ¶ O. C. 1494. ** O. C. 1740.

Courten's Association, which Association was united with the East India Company in 1650. In January 1679 the Council at Surat reported that the trade here had been ruined by Sivaji's robberies,* and the Court in consequence authorized the abandonment of the factory,† but this was strongly opposed by Sivaji, and was with difficulty effected.‡ Records relating to Rajapur will be found principally in the O. C. Collection, the only separate Factory Records now existing being copies of Letters despatched between the 4th October 1659 and the 3rd November 1660.

St. Helena.—The first visit of the East India Company's ships to St. Helena was made by Captain Lancaster on his return from India, in 1603, who reached there on the 16th June. In 1645 the Dutch took formal possession of St. Helena and established a colony there, which, however, they abandoned when settling at the Cape of Good Hope in 1652. In the same year, the homeward bound ships of the East India Company, finding the Island deserted, took possession of it, and King Charles the Second confirmed the Company's right thereto by a charter of the 3rd April 1661. In 1665 the Dutch captured St. Helena from the English but were expelled from it the same year. In January 1673 the Dutch again captured the Island, but a British squadron arriving shortly afterwards they were again driven out. The recapture of the Island gave rise to a question as to the respective rights of the Crown and of the Company in the Island, but by a Charter of the 16th December 1673 His Majesty re-granted the Island to the Company in perpetuity. On the 15th October 1815 the "Northumberland" arrived at St. Helena with Napoleon Bonaparte on board, who landed at this place of his exile about 7 p.m. on the evening of the 17th. By Act 3 & 4 William IV. the Island of St. Helena was vested in the Crown, by whom it was administered from the 31st March 1836.

The volumes of St. Helena Consultations extend from 1676 to 1836; many of these, especially in the earlier years, are very imperfect.

In the "O. C." volumes there are a number of letters from St. Helena, extending from the 21st June 1672 to 1st July 1707; but it is very evident that these are only a few representative documents, and that the larger part of the correspondence between those dates has been missing for a great number of years.

The first letter to the East India Company from St. Helena, in the present Collection is dated in October 1698. These letters extend from that date to the 20th April 1836. No separate copies of Despatches from the Court of Directors to St. Helena appear to have been preserved earlier than the 1st January 1820, from whence to the 21st October 1835 they are to be found in nine bound volumes.

There is very little in existence in this Office relating to Napoleon Bonaparte in St. Helena, as most of the correspondence was carried on, not with, or even through, the Court of Directors, but with the Secretary of State direct. We have, however, one volume of copies of Letters on the subject, extending from the 21st July 1815 to the 6th September 1817, which relate principally to the arrangements to be made for his custody and accommodation. Other miscellaneous volumes include Paymaster's Accounts, Committee Reports on the Island (1818 to 1835), defences of St. Helena, Southern Whale Fishery, &c.

Siam.—In 1613 the King of Siam offered to Captain Best, through his Ambassadors, safe trade in his Kingdom for the English,§ and later in that year a junk was fitted out from Firando for a trade to that port, where a factory was established,‖ but it

---

* O. C. 4563. † Letter to Surat, 15th March 1681. ‡ O. C. 4675/4691.
§ O. C. 107. ‖ O. C. 125 and Court Minutes 5th July 1614.

was dissolved in 1623.* In 1626 the Court decided that the trade at Siam, having been of little or no use, was not to be continued.† A factory was, however, re-established here in 1666,‡ but it was again given up in 1680.§

The separate Siam records are very few, comprising copies of diaries and letters only, from September 1678 to the 28th November 1683. The factory is, however, referred to in several of the O. C. Records, and also in the Java Records.

Straits Settlements.—In 1772 Mr. Francis Light, the master of a merchantman, who had traded a great deal with the native States of the Malay peninsula, and more especially with that of Quedah, wrote to Mr. Hastings, then Governor of Bengal, particularly concerning the country of Quedah, and the utility of Pulo Penang as a commercial port, recommending it as a convenient magazine for Eastern trade. It appears that about this time the Supreme Government of Bengal were seeking to establish a commercial port in the Straits of Malacca, and selected Achin as the most suitable place for that purpose, but the King of Achin refused to comply with their proposals to that effect; they then turned towards Pulo Penang, the King of Quedah having offered to bestow the Island in perpetuity on the East India Company, on condition of their paying him six thousand dollars annually as an indemnification of the loss he might sustain in his revenues from the trade of Quedah being diverted into another channel. This offer was accepted, and the Island was taken possession of with the usual forms on the 12th August 1786, in honour of which day, the birthday of George, Prince of Wales (George IV.), it was called "Prince of Wales Island."

With the rise of Prince of Wales Island, the commercial importance of Malacca decreased, and it became now a place of only secondary rank in that respect, but possessing great agricultural resources. In 1795, in the midst of their reverses in other parts of India, the Dutch surrendered Malacca and its dependencies to the British forces under the command of Captain Newcome, of the "Orpheus," and Major Brown, of the East India Company's Service.

Prince of Wales Island was used as a place of rendezvous for an expedition fitted out in 1797 against Manila, and a considerable body of troops from Bengal and Madras, amounting to 5,000 Europeans, besides a large number of Native troops, met there in August of that year and remained in harbour for a month, after which the expedition was recalled without fulfilling its contemplated object.

In June 1800 the cession of a tract of land on the mainland was obtained from the King of Quedah, comprising a district 18 miles in length and three miles in breadth, now called Province Wellesley.

In 1805 it was resolved to constitute Penang into a regular Presidency with a Governor and Council.

Under the terms of the Treaty of Vienna, Malacca was restored to the Dutch in 1818. In order to protect the British trade, and to secure one of the two passages to the Eastern Archipelago, the Marquis of Hastings, unaware of the fact that Rhio had been occupied by the Dutch, determined to attempt the improvement of our relations with Achin, at the northern entrance, and to form a settlement on Rhio, on account of its being advantageously situated near the southern extremity. For these purposes Sir Stamford Raffles was sent from Bengal in December 1818, with orders to associate himself with Major Farquhar, the Resident at Malacca. On arriving at the Straits it was found that Rhio was already in the hands of the Dutch. The Carimon Isles and Singapore were almost the only eligible spots now left. The latter,

* O. C. 1130.

† Court Minutes, 15th November 1626.

‡ O. C. 3197.

§ Letter to Bantam, 14th April 1680.

with the concurrence of Major Farquhar, was selected by Sir Stamford, who, on the 30th January 1819, concluded a preliminary treaty with a Chief called Datoo Tamanggung, Sre' Maharajah Abdul Rahman, Rajah of Singapore and of the islands adjacent thereto, for himself and for His Highness Sre' Sultan Hussein Mahummud Shah, sovereign of Johore, according to which the Tamanggung, in consideration of being allowed 3,000 dollars annually and taken under British protection, agreed to permit the British Government to establish a factory or factories at Singapore, or in other places subject to his immediate authority.

In 1825 Malacca was restored to the English under a Treaty with Holland, and in 1826 Penang, Singapore, and Malacca were incorporated as one Government, with Penang as the seat of Government.

On the 1st April 1867, the Straits Settlements were transferred from the control of the Indian Government to that of the Secretary of State for the Colonies by an Order in Council, issued under the authority of Act 29 and 30 Vict., c. 115.

The earliest British possessions in these Straits date from 1786, and the earliest records in a separate form relating to those possessions begin from that year. The Prince of Wales Island Consultations commence in 1786 and extend to 1830. The Letters from, and Despatches to, Prince of Wales Island extend from 1805, the date on which Penang was formed into a Presidency, to 1830, after which the correspondence of the Court of Directors relative to the Straits Settlements was conducted through the Government of India, and the documents relating to them will, from that date, be found with the Correspondence and Proceedings of the Supreme Government.

Sumatra.—Captain Lancaster, on his first voyage for the East India Company, arrived off Achin on the 5th June 1602, and obtained from the King a treaty of commerce.* Trade was thereupon commenced here, but a factory was not established until May 1615, and about the same time other factories were settled at Tiku and Priaman.† About six months later another factory was established at Jambi.‡ Subsequently, a factory was started at Indraghiri, but it was dissolved in 1622.§ The Achin factory was dissolved in 1631.‖ In 1649, on an invitation from the Governor of Padang, the President at Bantam sent one of the Company's ships to that port, and to Indrapore, on a voyage of experiment; and this circumstance marks the first trade and settlement of the English at those stations. The English trade with Sumatra had, from the first, been strongly opposed by the Dutch, who so far succeeded in monopolising the trade of the island that in the course of a few years Jambi was the only factory retained by the English. In 1681 the factory at Jambi was dissolved, and in 1684 a factory was established at Bencoolen, where a fort was erected, which was named York Fort. About the same time the factory at Priaman was revived and made subordinate to Fort St. George, and York Fort was subsequently also made a subordinate factory to Fort St. George. Other stations were also occupied, and at the union of the two East India Companies the settlements on the Island of Sumatra were York Fort (afterwards called Fort Marlborough), Bencoolen, Indrapore, Tryamong, and Sillibar. In 1785 Fort Marlborough and its dependencies were placed immediately in subordination to the Government of Bengal. According to the stipulations of a Treaty, signed at London on the 17th March 1824, between the

* Lancaster's Voyages, Hakluyt Society's Publication No. LVI.
† O. C. 308–324.
‡ O. C. 338.
§ O. C. 1076.
‖ O. C. 1229–1341.

King of Great Britain and the King of the Netherlands, all the British possessions on the Island of Sumatra were ceded to the latter in exchange for Malacca and its dependencies, and the Dutch accordingly took possession of the island on the 5th July 1825.

Many of the earliest references to Sumatra are contained in the O. C. Records, but there are a few early fragments, of 1615–16, in the separate Sumatra Collection Copies of York Fort Letters and Consultations extend from 1685 to 1714; Fort Marlborough letters, from 1714 to 1825, Public Consultations from 1705 to 1818, Military Consultations from 1782 to 1796, and Despatches to Fort Marlborough from November 1754 to February 1825; Fort St. George Diary and Proceedings between the 7th January 1772 and the 16th January 1773 relative to a Settlement at Achin; and Bengal Consultations relative to Fort Marlborough from the 21st February 1786 to the 31st August 1795.

Surat.—During the 17th and 18th centuries Surat ranked as the chief export and import centre of India. The first visit to Surat was made in November 1607, when Captain Hawkins was landed and proceeded to Agra on a mission to the Great Moghul. In 1609 Captain Sharpeigh sailed for that port, but, having no pilot on board, he ran his vessel on a shoal at the mouth of the Amlicka river, when she was lost, but he and the crew found their way overland to Surat.* This place was again visited by Sir Henry Middleton, who commanded the sixth voyage; he arrived off Surat on the 26th September 1611, but was for a long time prevented from communicating with the shore by the Portuguese, who put every possible obstruction in his way, but, ultimately, he succeeded in obtaining permission to trade there, as well as at Ahmedabad, Cambay and Gogo. A little later on (11th January 1618) a firman was obtained from the Great Moghul for establishing factories at those places.

Surat soon became the principal seat of the East India Company's trade in India, and continued so until the chief control of all the possessions in India was transferred to Bombay in 1687.

The English East India Company also established a factory at Surat and at its union with the London Company both factories were still in existence.

There are numerous references to Surat in the O. C. Records. The separate Surat Records comprise an incomplete set of Consultations of the London Company's factory, from the 20th July 1622 to the 19th November 1708; Consultations of the English Company's factory, from the 3rd October 1700 to the 21st December 1704. There is a gap in the Consultations between November 1708 and the 1st August 1718, after which they continue, with a few gaps in the earlier years, to the 30th April 1804. There is a Judicial Diary from the 15th March 1796 to the 31st December 1799; copies of Letters despatched (somewhat imperfect) between the 13th May 1631 and the 3rd May 1708; and copies of Letters received (also imperfect) between January 1623 and May 1708.

Tellicherri.—The Presidency at Surat established a factory at Tellicherri in 1683 to secure the pepper and cardamom trade of that district, and on several occasions, between 1708 and 1761, the Company obtained from the Chirakkal Raja, and other local chiefs, not only grants of land in and near Tellicherri, but other important privileges.

The separate Tellicherri Records are but few, and comprise copies of Letters received by the Company from that Factory between February 1716 and April 1756;

---

* O. C. 12.

and Diaries and Consultations (imperfect) from the 1st January 1777 to the 31st December 1793.

Thana.—Chief town of the Thana District of Bombay. Under a Treaty of December 1533, Thana was made over to the Portuguese, but when, in 1739, they lost Bassein, their power in Thana came to an end. In 1771 the English, urged by the news that a fleet had left Portugal to recover Salsette and Bassein, determined to gain possession of Thana. Negotiations for its cession failing, a force was sent to take it, and on the 28th December 1774, the fort was stormed and the greater part of the garrison put to the sword.

The separate Thana Records comprise only Diaries and Consultations between the 8th January 1775 and the 30th November 1799.

Vizagapatam.—Chief town of a district of the same name in the Madras Presidency. About the middle of the 17th century the East India Company established a factory here, which, in 1689, was seized by the Moghuls and the factors murdered. In the following year it was restored, and was in existence at the union of the two Companies. References to this factory will be found principally in the O. C. Collection, and amongst the Madras Records. The only separate Vizagapatam Records consist of one volume of Diary and Consultations between the 16th July 1692 and the 30th March 1695.

F. C. D.

FACTORY RECORDS.

ANJENGO.

Index Number.	Date.	Previous Classification.	Nature of Documents.
1	1775—77	Range 430, No. 75	Diary and Consultations, 4 Jan. 1775 to 31 Dec. 1777.
2	1778—80	„ „ 76	Ditto, 2 Jan. 1778 to 29 Dec. 1780.
3	1781	„ „ 77	Ditto, 1 Jan. to 30 Dec. 1781.
4	1782—84	„ „ 78	Ditto, 2 Jan. 1782 to 31 Dec. 1784.
5	1785—87	„ „ 79	Ditto, 1 Jan. 1785 to 30 Dec. 1787.
6	1788—89	„ „ 80	Ditto, 1 Jan. 1788 to 30 Dec. 1789.
7	1790—91	„ „ 81	Ditto, 1 Jan. 1790 to 30 Dec. 1791.
8	1792—93	„ „ 82	Ditto, 2 Jan. 1792 to 31 Dec. 1793.
9	1794	„ „ 83	Diary, 1 Jan. to 31 Dec. 1794.
10	1795	„ „ 84	Ditto, 1 Jan. to 31 Dec. 1795.
11	1796	„ „ 85	Ditto, 1 Jan. to 24 Dec. 1796.
12	1797	„ „ 86	Ditto, 1 Jan. to 31 Dec. 1797.
13	1798	„ „ 87	Ditto, 1 Jan. to 31 Dec. 1798.
14	1801	„ „ 88	Ditto, 1 Jan. to 31 Dec. 1801.
15	1802	„ „ 89	Ditto, 1 Jan. to 31 Dec. 1802
16	1803	„ „ 90	Ditto, 1 Jan. to 28 Dec. 1803.
17	1804	„ „ 91	Ditto, 1 Jan. to 31 July 1804.
18	1804	„ „ 92	Ditto, 31 July to 31 Dec. 1804.
19	1796	„ „ 93	Political Diary, 21 Aug. to 15 Dec. 1796.
20	1797	„ „ 94	Ditto, 6 Jan. to 27 Dec. 1797.
21	1704—69	Loose papers	Letters, &c., 9 Sept. 1704 to 31 Dec. 1749; 17 Dec. 1769.

BALASOR.

Index Number.	Date.	Previous Classification.	Nature of Documents.
1	1679—87	B. R., XX, 1	Diary and Consultations, 1 Dec. 1679 to 25 Nov. 1680.
		2	Ditto, 3 Dec. 1680 to 30 Nov. 1681.
		DD, 13	Ditto, 1 Jan. to 31 Dec. 1684.
		14	Ditto, 24 April 1685 to 3 May 1686.
		XX, 3	Ditto, 11 May 1686 to 19 March 1687.

BOMBAY.

Index Number.	Date.	Previous Classification.	Nature of Documents.
1	1669—74	B. R., HH, a, 1	Papers relating to disagreements between Deputy Governor Henry Young and his subordinates: 12 Feb. to 12 Nov. 1669.
		DD, a, 6	Consultations: 18 March to 14 Sept. 1670.
		HH, a, 3	Ditto, 6 Dec. 1672 to 1 Dec. 1673.
		4	Ditto, 6 Dec. 1673 to 2 Dec. 1674.
2	1674—81	B. R., HH, a, 5	Consultations: 7 Dec. 1674 to 6 Sept. 1675.
		6	Ditto, 1 Oct. 1675 to 7 Jan. 1677.
		7	Ditto, 2 Jan. to 27 Oct. 1677; 10 Jan. to 2 Nov. 1678.
		DD, 10	Ditto, 3 Jan. to 28 Oct. 1679.
		HH, a, 8	Ditto, 8 Jan. to 3 Dec. 1680.
		DD, 10	Ditto, 27 Jan. to 22 Nov. 1681.
3	1684—90	B. R., DD, 14	Consultations: 12 Dec. 1684 to 6 May 1685.
		HH, a, 9	Ditto (with copies of letters received and sent), 10 May 1685 to 22 June 1686.
		DD, 15	Diary of events during the siege of Bombay by the Sidi, 15 Feb. 1689 to 22 June 1690.
4	1694—96	B. R., HH, a, 10	Consultations: 20 May 1694 to 24 May 1695.
		11 & 12	Ditto, 10 June 1695 to 28 Jan. 1696 (two copies, both in bad condition).
5	1696—1704	B. R., HH, a, 14	Consultations: 13 Nov. 1696 to 30 Nov. 1698.
		15	Ditto, 5 Jan. to 13 March 1699.
		16	Ditto, 14 May to 23 Sept. 1700.
		17	Ditto, 17 Dec. 1702 to 2 July 1703.
		DD, 27	Ditto, 6 July 1703 to 15 May 1704. For subsequent consultations (commencing 18 Nov. 1704) *see* separate list.
6	1670—74	B. R., DD —	Copies of letters despatched: 8 March to 5 Sept. 1670.
		HH, b1, 1	Ditto, 1 Dec. 1672 to 26 Nov. 1673.
		2	Ditto, 15 Dec. 1673 to 12 Dec. 1674.
		DD, a, 7	Extracts relating to the "passes" of Tanna and Karinja.
7	1674—76	B. R., HH, b1, 3	Copies of letters despatched: 2 Nov. 1674 to 20 Dec. 1675
		GG, c1, 15	Ditto, 6 Jan. to 31 Dec. 1676.
8	1677—79	B. R., HH, b1, 4	Copies of letters despatched: 16 Jan. to 30 Dec. 1677.
		5	Ditto, 4 Jan. to 18 Dec. 1678.
			Ditto, 30 Dec. 1678 to 15 Dec. 1679.

Index Number.	Date.	Previous Classification.	Nature of Documents.
9	1679—82	B. R., HH, b1, 7	Copies of letters despatched: 22 Dec. 1679 to 27 Nov. 1680.
		GG, c1, 18	Ditto, 20 Dec. 1680 to 27 Oct. 1681.
		HH, b1, 8	Ditto, 7 Dec. 1681 to 24 Dec. 1682.
10	1694—95	B. R., HH, b1, 10	Copies of letters despatched: 22 May to 30 Aug. 1694.
		9	Ditto, 5 Sept. to 29 Nov. 1694.
		11	Ditto, 5 Dec. 1694 to 11 Feb. 1695.
11	1695—96	B. R., HH, b1, 12	Copies of letters despatched: 11 Feb. to 12 April 1695.
		13	Ditto, 13 April to 29 May 1695.
		14	Ditto, 21 Sept. to 20 Nov. 1695.
		15	Ditto, 27 Nov. 1695 to 15 March 1696.
12	1696	B. R., HH, b1, 17	Copies of letters despatched: 17 March to 29 Oct. 1696.
		16	Ditto, 8 Jan. to 30 Dec. 1696.*
		20	Ditto, 27 Aug. to 7 Nov. 1696.*
13	1696—97	B. R., HH, b1, 21	Copies of letters despatched: 1 June 1696 to 15 Dec. 1697.†
		HH, b2, 1	Ditto, 19 Feb. to 10 May 1697.
		2	Ditto, 28 April to 24 July 1697.
14	1697—98	B. R., HH, b2, 4	Copies of letters despatched: 24 July to 27 Sept. 1697.
		5	Ditto, 30 Sept. to 16 Dec. 1697.
		7	Ditto, 30 Nov. 1697, to 28 Jan. 1698.
		9	Ditto, 25 Jan. to 17 Feb. 1698.
15	1698	B. R., HH, b2, 11	Copies of letters despatched: 22 May to 6 Dec. 1698.
		12	Ditto, 25 May to 6 Dec. 1698.*
16	1698—99	B. R., HH, b2, 14	Copies of letters despatched: 12 Dec. 1698 to 5 April 1699.
		15 (part)	Ditto, 12 April to 12 May 1699.
		17	Ditto, 11 Jan. to 14 May 1699.‡
		DD —	Ditto, 16 May to 20 Aug. 1699.
17	1699—1703	B. R., DD —	Copies of letters despatched: 21 Aug. 1699 to 30 Dec. 1700.
		EE —	Ditto, 4 Feb. to 8 Feb. 1701.
		HH, b2, 18	Ditto, 2 Jan. to 31 Dec. 1700. (To Surat only.)
			Ditto, 9 July 1702 to 30 Jan. 1703.
18	1703—10	B. R., HH, b2, 21	Copies of letters despatched: 2 Feb. to 20 Dec. 1703.
		22	Ditto, 27 Dec. 1703 to 25 April 1704.
		23	Ditto, 19 Nov. 1708 to 4 Jan. 1710.
19	1670—82	B. R., DD —	Copies of letters received: March to Sept. 1670.
		HH, c1, 2	Ditto, Dec. 1678 to Dec. 1679.
		3	Ditto, Dec. 1679 to Nov. 1680.
		4	Ditto, Dec. 1680 to Nov. 1681.
		5	Ditto, Oct. 1681 to Dec. 1682.

* Contains a few letters not in previous sections.
† Letters to the Company only.
‡ Consists of letters written by the General (Sir John Gayer), &c., while at Swally.

Index Number.	Date.	Previous Classification.	Number of Documents.
20	1694	B. R., HH, c1, 6	Copies of letters received: June to Aug. 1694.
		7	Ditto, Aug. to Oct. 1694.
		8	Ditto, Oct. to Dec. 1694.
21	1694—95	B. R., HH, c1, 10	Copies of letters received: Dec. 1694 to Feb. 1695.
		11	Ditto, Feb. to April 1695.
		12	Ditto, April to June 1695.
22	1695	B. R., HH, c1, 13	Copies of letters received: June to Aug. 1695.
		14	Ditto, Aug. to Nov. 1695.
		15	Ditto, Nov. and Dec. 1695.
23	1695—96	B. R., HH, c1, 16	Copies of letters received: Dec. 1695 to Feb. 1696.
		19	Ditto, Feb. to Aug. 1696.
24	1696	B. R., HH, c1, 20	Copies of letters received: Aug. to Oct. 1696.
		21	Ditto, Aug. to Oct. 1696.*
		22	Ditto, Oct. to Dec. 1696.
25	1696—97	B. R., HH, c2, 1	Copies of letters received: Dec. 1696 to Feb. 1697.
		2	Ditto, Dec. 1696 to Feb. 1697.*
		3	Ditto, March and April 1697.
26	1697	B. R., HH, c2, 5	Copies of letters received: April and May 1697.
		6	Ditto, Aug. to Oct. 1697.
		8	Ditto, Oct. and Nov. 1697.
27	1697—98	B. R., HH, c2, 10	Copies of letters received: Nov. and Dec. 1697.
		11	Ditto, Jan. and Feb. 1698.
		12	Ditto, Feb. 1698.
28	1698—99	B. R., HH, c2, 13	Copies of letters received: Feb. to May 1698.
		14	Ditto, March to May 1698.*
		15	Ditto, May to Dec. 1698.
		17	Ditto, Dec. 1698 to March 1699.
29	1699—1700	B.R., DD —	Copies of letters received: March to Aug. 1699; Jan. and Feb. 1700.
30	1702—04	B. R., HH, c2, 18	Copies of letters received: Aug. 1702 to Jan. 1703.
		19	Ditto, Jan. to Dec. 1703.
		20	Ditto, Dec. 1703 to April 1704.

* Partly duplicates the preceding section.

BORNEO.

Index Number.	Date.	Previous Classification.	Nature of Documents.
1	1648—1814	Loose papers, Packet 9. B. R., Ub, Vol. 2. B. R., Uc, 2. Fisher's Papers, Nos. 65, 66, 67. Room 338, No. 766. Range H, 39, Nos. 167, 173.	Letters and Consultations.

BROACH.

Index Number.	Date.	Previous Classification.	Nature of Documents.
1	1775—76	Range 431, No. 11	Diary and Consultations, 1 Jan. 1775 to 30 Dec. 1776.
2	1777—78	" " 13	Ditto, 1 Jan. 1777 to 30 Dec. 1778.
3	1777	" " 12	Proceedings of Special Committee, 4 Feb. to 25 April 1777.
4	1779—81	" " 15	Diary and Consultations, 4 Jan. 1779 to 30 Dec. 1781.
5	1779—80	" " 14	Ditto, Revenue, 1 Jan. 1779 to 30 Dec. 1780.

BURDWAN.

Index Number.	Date.	Previous Classification.	Nature of Documents.
1	1774	Range 70, No. 5	Proceedings of Provincial Council of Revenue, 16 May to 28 July 1774.
2	1774	Range 69, No. 34	Ditto, 1 Aug. to 29 Dec. 1774.
3	1775	„ „ 35	Ditto, 2 Jan. to 25 April 1775.
4	1775	„ „ 36	Ditto, 1 May to 30 June 1775.
5	1775	„ „ 37	Ditto, 1 July to 26 Sept. 1775.
6	1775	„ „ 38	Ditto, 26 Sept. to 29 Dec. 1775.
7	1776	„ „ 39	Ditto, 2 Jan. to 22 April 1776.
8	1776	„ „ 40	Ditto, 25 April to 28 Aug. 1776.
9	1776	„ „ 41	Ditto, 30 Aug. to 31 Dec. 1776.
10	1777	„ „ 42	Ditto, 6 Jan to 22 May 1777.
11	1777	„ „ 43	Ditto, 26 May to 30 Dec. 1777.
12	1778	„ „ 44	Ditto, 3 Jan. to 9 May 1778.
13	1778	„ „ 45	Ditto, 12 May to 28 Dec. 1778.
14	1779	„ „ 46	Ditto, 4 Jan. to 30 Dec. 1779.

CALCUTTA, including Sutanati.

Index Number.	Date.	Previous Classification.	Nature of Documents.
1	1690—91	B. R., RR, a, 1	Diary and Consultations: 16 July to 30 Nov. 1690.
		2	Ditto, 1 Dec. 1690 to 30 Nov. 1691.
2	1694—97	B. R., RR, a, 3	Diary and Consultations: 1 Dec. 1694 to 30 Nov. 1695.
		4	Ditto, 1 Dec. 1696 to 30 Nov. 1697.
3	1697—99	Fisher's Papers, 33.	Diary and Consultations: 1 Dec. 1697 to 30 Nov. 1698.
		B.R., RR, a, 5	Ditto, 1 Dec. 1698 to 30 Nov. 1699.
4	1702—08	B. R., RR, a, 6	Diary and Consultations: 2 Dec. 1702 to 29 Nov. 1703.
		7	Ditto, 5 Dec. 1704 to 9 Nov. 1705.
		DD, —	Ditto, 1 Dec. 1705 to 16 Dec. 1706.
		RR, a, 8	Ditto, 15 Jan. to 22 Dec. 1708 (with Charges General for same period).
		DD 27	Diary for the separate affairs of the London Company, kept by George Petty and Trevor Games, 9 Aug. to 28 Dec. 1705. (For subsequent Consultations, commencing 29 Jan. 1704 *see* separate list.)
5	1690—93	B. R., RR, b, 1	Copies of letters despatched: 17 July to 30 Nov. 1690.
		2	Ditto, [?] Dec. 1690 to 25 Nov. 1691.
		DD, —	Ditto, 1 to 30 Dec. 1692.
		17	Ditto, 18 April to 22 June 1693.
		EE —	Ditto, 22 to 28 Nov. 1693.
6	1695—97	B. R., JJ, c, 15	Copies of letters despatched: 21 Dec. 1695 to 2 Nov. 1696.*
		RR, b, 3	Ditto, 1 Dec. 1696 to 25 Nov. 1697.*
		4	Ditto, 1 Dec. 1696 to 30 Nov. 1697.
7	1697—1700	B. R., RR, b, 5	Copies of letters despatched: 3 Dec. 1697 to 30 Nov. 1698.
		6	Ditto, 6 Dec. 1699 to 30 Nov. 1700.
		7	Ditto, 12 Dec. 1699 to 28 Nov. 1700.†
8	1700—05	B. R., RR, b, 8	Copies of letters despatched: 2 Dec. 1700 to 28 Nov. 1701.
		9	Ditto, 1 Dec. 1701 to 28 Nov. 1702.
		10	Ditto, 8 Dec. 1704 to 21 Aug. 1705.
9	1690—95	B. R., RR, c, 2	Copies of letters received. June to Nov. 1690.
		3	Ditto, Dec. 1694 to Nov. 1695.
10	1695—1701	B. R., RR, c, 4	Copies of letters received: Dec. 1695 to Nov. 1696.
		5	Ditto, Dec. 1699 to Nov. 1700.
		6	Ditto, Dec. 1700 to Nov. 1701.
11	1702—04	B. R., RR, c, 7	Copies of letters received: Dec. 1702 to Nov. 1703.
		8	Ditto, Jan. to Nov. 1704.

* To Sir John Gayer, Commissary-General (Bombay), and Mr. Higginson, Lieutenant-General (Fort St. George), only.
† To Madras, Surat, and Bombay only.

CAMBAY.

Index Number.	Date.	Previous Classification.	Nature of Documents.
1	1804—07	Range 343, No. 18	Proceedings of Resident, 1 Jan. 1804 to 29 June 1807.

CAPE OF GOOD HOPE.

Index Number.	Date.	Previous Classification.	Nature of Documents.
1	1773—1809	Loose papers, Packets 23 and 33. Unrecorded Papers, No. 2928.	Correspondence, &c., 22 Dec. 1773 to 29 Dec. 1809.
2	1810—11	Loose papers, Packets 23 and 33.	Ditto, 2 Jan. 1810 to 19 Dec. 1811.
3	1812—13	" "	Ditto, 29 Jan. 1812 to 31 Dec. 1813.
4	1814—20	" "	Ditto, 11 Feb. 1814 to 4 Dec. 1820.
5	1821—23	" "	Ditto, 17 Feb. 1821 to 2 Aug. 1823.
6	1795—1803	Room 338	Letters from the Cape of Good Hope to the Court of Directors, 4 April 1795 to 17 June 1803.
7	1808—14	"	Ditto, 29 June 1808 to 30 Nov. 1814.
8	1815—19	"	Ditto, 14 Jan. 1815 to 1 Dec. 1819.
9	1820—28	"	Ditto, 8 Jan. 1820 to 22 Dec. 1828.
9A	1808—31	Unnumbered	Extracts from Letters from the Cape of Good Hope to the Court of Directors, 29 June 1808 to 16 March 1831.
10	1808—10	Room 338	Letters received at the Cape from various parts, 31 May 1808 to 27 March 1810.
11	1810—11	"	Ditto, 21 March 1810 to 30 Sept. 1811.
12	1811—13	"	Ditto, 1 Oct. 1811 to 31 Dec. 1813.
13	1813—15	"	Ditto, 31 Dec. 1813 to 22 Dec. 1815.
14	1816—18	"	Ditto, 1 Jan. 1816 to 30 Jan. 1818.
15	1818—21	"	Ditto, 1 Feb. 1818 to 31 Jan. 1821.
16	1821—26	"	Ditto, 1 Feb. 1821 to 31 Jan. 1826.
17	1826—36	"	Ditto, 1 Feb. 1826 to 30 April 1836.
18	1808—11	"	Letters sent from the Cape to various parts, 3 June 1808 to 14 June 1811.
19	1811—13	"	Ditto, 14 June 1811 to 31 Dec. 1813.
20	1814—15	"	Ditto, 1 Jan. 1814 to 23 Dec. 1815.
21	1816—18	"	Letters sent from the Cape to various parts, 1 Jan. 1816 to 30 Jan. 1818.
22	1818—21	"	Ditto, 1 Feb. 1818 to 31 Jan. 1821.
23	1821—26	"	Ditto, 1 Feb. 1821 to 31 Jan. 1826.
24	1826—36	"	Ditto, 1 Feb. 1826 to 30 April 1836.

CELEBES.

Index Number.	Date.	Previous Classification.	Nature of Documents.
1	1613—74	B. R., YY 5, 1.	Materials for a history of the Macassar factory.

CEYLON.

Index Number.	Date.	Previous Classification.	Nature of Documents.
1	1762—95	Miscellaneous Records, Vol. 10. Fisher's Papers, No. 322.	Accounts of the embassies of John Pybus (1762), Hugh Boyd (1781), and R. Andrews (1795).
2	1797—98	Range 430, No. 23	Proceedings of a committee of investigation into the affairs of Ceylon, 4 Aug. 1797 to 12 Nov. 1798.
3	1798—99	" " 31	Proceedings of the Governor in the Public Department, 12 Oct. 1798 to 30 April 1799.
4	1799—1800	" " 32	Ditto, 4 May 1799 to 30 April 1800.
5	1800	" " 33	Ditto, 2 May to 30 Nov. 1800.
6	1800—01	" " 34	Ditto, 1 Dec. 1800 to 28 April 1801.
7	1801	" " 35	Ditto, 1 May to 31 Dec. 1801.
8	1802	" " 37	Ditto, 2 Jan. to 31 March 1802.
9	1802	" " 38	Ditto, 31 March to 30 June 1802.
10	1798—99	" " 68	Proceedings of the Governor in the Commercial Department, 12 Oct. 1798 to 30 April 1799.
11	1799—1800	" " 69	Ditto, 1 May 1799 to 12 April 1800.
12	1798—99	" " 49	Proceedings of the Governor in the Revenue Department, 12 Oct. 1798 to 30 April 1799.
13	1799—1800	" " 50	Ditto, 4 May 1799 to 30 April 1800.
14	1800—01	" " 51	Ditto, 2 May 1800 to 30 April 1801.
15	1801	" " 52	Proceedings of the Governor in the Revenue and Commercial Departments, 2 May to 31 Dec. 1801.
16	1802	" " 55	Ditto, 4 Jan. to 30 June 1802.

Index Number.	Date.	Previous Classification.	Nature of Documents.
17	1801	Range 430, No. 53	Proceedings of the Revenue and Commercial Board, 5 May to 3 Sept. 1801.
18	1801	„ „ 54	Ditto, 4 Sept. to 30 Dec. 1801.
19	1801	„ 36	Index to ditto, 5 May to 30 Dec. 1801.
20	1798	„ „ 63	Proceedings of the Governor in the Political Department, 12 Oct. to 26 Dec. 1798.
21	1799—1800	„ „ 64	Ditto, 1 May 1799 to 5 April 1800.
22	1800—01	„ „ 65	Ditto, 14 May 1800 to 24 April 1801.
23	1801	„ „ 66	Ditto, 28 June to 24 Dec. 1801.
24	1802	„ „ 67	Ditto, 1 Feb. to 18 Sept. 1802.
25	1798—99	Political Department	Proceedings of the Governor in the Secret Department, 12 Oct. 1798 to 25 Feb. 1799.
26	1799—1800	„ „	Ditto, 27 June 1799 to 24 March 1800.
27	1800—01	„ „	Ditto, 19 May 1800 to 21 Dec. 1801.
28	1798—99	Range 430, No. 39	Proceedings of the Governor in the Military Department, 12 Oct. 1798 to 29 April 1799.
29	1799—1800	„ „ 40	Ditto, 3 May 1799 to 30 April 1800.
30	1800—01	„ „ 41	Ditto, 2 May 1800 to 29 April 1801.
31	1801	„ „ 42	Ditto, 2 May to 31 Dec. 1801.
32	1802	„ „ 27	Ditto, 2 Jan. to 30 Aug. 1802.
33	1799—1800	„ „ 43	Proceedings of the Military Board, 15 March 1799 to 29 April 1800.
34	1800—01	„ „ 44	Ditto, 6 May 1800 to 28 April 1801.
35	1801—02	„ „ 45	Ditto, 5 May 1801 to 27 April 1802.
36	1798—1800	„ „ 46	General Orders, 7 Nov. 1798 to 30 April 1800.
37	1800—01	„ „ 47	Ditto, 1 May 1800 to 29 April 1801.
38	1801—02	„ „ 48	Ditto, 5 May 1801 to 26 April 1802.
39	1800—01	„ „ 70	Proceedings of the Committee for Charitable Establishments, 12 May 1800 to 15 Feb. 1801.

Index Number.	Date.	Previous Classification.	Nature of Documents.
40	1800	Range 430, No. 71	Proceedings of the Committee for Charitable Establishments (on circuit), 12 July to 8 Dec. 1800.
41	1801	" " 72	Ditto, 9 May to 6 Dec. 1801.
42	1799—1800	" " 56	Charges and Calendars, Court of Criminal Jurisdiction, 6 Dec. 1799 to 27 Nov. 1800.
43	1799—1800	" " 58	Proceedings of the Court, 2 Dec. 1799 to 27 Jan. 1800.
44	1800	" " 57	Ditto, 27 Jan. to 19 May 1800.
45	1800	" " 59	Ditto, 21 May to 9 July 1800.
46	1800	" " 60	Ditto, 9 July to 14 Aug. 1800.
47	1800	" " 61	Ditto, 14 Aug. to 6 Nov. 1800.
48	1800	" " 62	Ditto, 7 Nov. to 2 Dec. 1800.
49	1799—1800	" " 73	Copies of letters written by the Military Board, 17 March 1799 to 30 April 1800.
50	1800—01	" " 74	Ditto, 3 May 1800 to 30 April 1801.
51	1801—02	" " 75	Ditto, 6 May 1801 to 27 April 1802.
52	1798—1801	Unrecorded Papers, Vol. 211	Correspondence between the Court of Directors and the Governor of Ceylon, 25 May 1798 to 31 Dec. 1801.
53	1797—1802	Unrecorded Papers, Vols. 179, 188, and 211. Loose papers, Packet 17.	Correspondence between the Board of Control and the Court of Directors, 1798—1801; documents connected with the Pearl Fishery, and charges against the Superintendent, 1797—1802; &c.
54	1799—1800	Unrecorded Papers, Vols. 166 and 188.	Notes on various subjects connected with Ceylon, by the Right Hon. Sylvester Douglas, 1799-1800; memoranda on commercial products, &c., of the island, by Major D. Robertson, 1799; and notes on the Manaar Pearl Fishery, by Lieut. the Hon. G. Turnour.
55	1804—05	Range 316, No. 107	Proceedings of the Committee appointed at Fort St. George for the audit and adjustment of accounts of the captured Dutch settlements in Ceylon, Malacca, and the Moluccas, 3 April 1804 to 11 Feb. 1805.
56	1805—06	" " 109	Ditto, 28 Feb. 1805 to 25 Jan. 1806.
57	1804—06	Range 316, Nos. 105, 111, and 112.	Appendix to Proceedings of the Committee, Journal and Ledger.

CHINA AND JAPAN.

Index Number.	Date.	Previous Classification.	Nature of Documents.
1	1596—1675	B.R., T a, 1	China Materials, 1596 to 13 Feb. 1675.
2	1673—83	„ „ 2	Ditto, 2 Aug. 1673 to 21 Aug. 1683.
3	1682—86	„ „ 3	Ditto, 2 Oct. 1682 to 22 Oct. 1686.
4	1684—99	„ „ 4	Ditto, 9 Oct. 1684 to 21 Nov. 1699.
5	1694—1701	„ „ 5	Ditto, 6 June 1694 to 1 July 1701.
6	1699—1702	„ „ 6	Ditto, 11 April 1699 to 24 Oct. 1702.
7	1702—04	„ „ 7	Ditto, 6 Aug. 1702 to 8 Jan. 1704.
8	1712—25	„ „ 8	Ditto, 19 Dec. 1712 to 24 Dec. 1725.
9	1600—1702	„ T b, 1	Supplement to the China Materials, Book I. (Japan), 1600 to 28 Aug. 1702.
10	1606—99	„ T b, 2	Ditto, Book II., 9 March 1606 to 10 June 1699.
11		Range I., No. 25	Memoir. Intercourse with China, 1518—1832. Part I.
12		„ „ 26 and 27	Ditto. Part II., with Index.
13	1623—99	Dundas Papers, Vol. 19	Intercourse with China, Japan, &c., 24 Feb. 1623 to 1699.
14	1699—1759	B.R., T d, 3	Attempts to trade at Chusan.
15	1614—16	„ T c.	Japan and Java. Letters from R. Wickham, 26 April 1614 to 1 Oct. 1616.
16	1614—1703	„ T d, Vol. 2 B.R., D D, 7, 8, 9, 10, 13, 14, 15, and 26. B. R., F F, b 2, III., 58, 88 B. R., E E, 265, 275	Attempt to form a settlement at Amoy. Early Consultations, Letters, &c., at Canton, Macao, Tywan, Amoy, and Japan. Captain Weddall's China Voyage, 1637. Portion of a diary kept in the attempt to form a settlement at Chusan for the New Company, 1701-02.
17	1672—97	B. R., T d, Vol. 1. D D, 8, 9, 10, 12, 20, and 21.	Tonquin* and Cochin China.
18	1753—78	Dundas Papers, Vols. 4, 5, and 17.	Miscellaneous Papers relating to China and Cochin China.
19	1768—97	East Indies, Vols. 1, 2, 3, 6, and 7. Miscellaneous, Vols. 28 and 29.	Miscellaneous Correspondence.
20	1782—1815	Unrecorded Papers, Vols. 106, 179, 181, 187, 192, 195, 199, 209, 212, 213, 218, and 221. Reports, Memoranda, &c., 435.	Miscellaneous Documents.

* See also Java, 7.

Index Number.	Date.	Previous Classification.	Nature of Documents.
21	1721—23	B. R., T d. 4 Range 426, No. 57.	China Supra Cargoes (Ship) Diary, 7 Dec. 1721 to 12 Sept. 1723.
22	1720—22	Range 427, No. 118	Ditto, 31 Dec. 1720 to 25 May 1722.
23	1722—23	„ „ 115	Ditto, 2 Jan. 1722 to 10 April 1723.
24	1722—24	„ „ 116	Ditto, 7 Dec. 1722 to 10 Feb. 1724.
25	1724—25	„ „ 117	Ditto, 4 Jan. 1724 to 7 Aug. 1725.
26	1726—28	„ „ 119	Ditto, 30 Nov. 1726 to 12 July 1728.
27	1727—29	„ „ 120	Ditto, 13 Dec. 1727 to 15 May 1729.
28	1728—29	„ „ 121	Ditto, 6 Dec. 1728 to 17 May 1729.
29	1729—31	„ „ 122	Ditto, 21 Nov. 1729 to 31 May 1731.
30	1730—31	„ „ 123	Ditto, 1 Jan. 1730 to 8 Jan. 1731.
31	1730—32	„ „ 127	Ditto, 7 Dec. 1730 to 11 July 1732.
32	1731	„ „ 125	Ditto, 13 Jan. to 24 June 1731.
33	1731—33	Range 426, No. 58	Ditto, 20 Dec. 1731 to 6 Jan. 1733.
34	1732—33	„ „ 59	Ditto, 16 Oct. 1732 to 22 July 1733.
35	1733—34	„ „ 60	Ditto, 25 May 1733 to 28 May 1734.
36	1733—35	„ „ 61	Ditto, 6 Dec. 1733 to 4 April 1735.
37	1734—35	„ „ 62	Ditto, 5 Jan. 1734 to 26 June 1735.
38	1734—36	„ „ 63	Ditto, 24 Dec. 1734 to 2 Aug. 1736.
39	1735—36	„ „ 64	Ditto, 28 May 1735 to 5 Feb. 1736.
40	1735—37	„ „ 65	Ditto, 4 Nov. 1735 to 8 Jan. 1737.
41	1736—37	Range 427, No. 1	Ditto, 16 Sept. 1736 to 25 July 1737.
42	1737	„ „ 2	Ditto, 3 Jan. to 14 Dec. 1737.
43	1737—38	„ „ 3	Ditto, 3 Jan. 1737 to 4 Jan. 1738.

Index Number.	Date.	Previous Classification.	Nature of Documents.
44	1737—39	Range 427, No. 4	China Supra Cargoes (Ship) Diary, 30 Dec. 1737 to 14 Feb. 1739.
45	1738—39	" " 5	Ditto, 14 Jan. 1738 to 16 May 1739.
46	1738—39	" " 6	Ditto, 3 Nov. 1738 to 27 Dec. 1739.
47	1739—40	" " 7	Ditto, 24 Jan. 1739 to 26 April 1740.
48	1740	" " 8	Ditto, 3 Jan. to 22 Dec. 1740.
49	1741	" " 9	Ditto, 4 March to 30 Dec. 1741.
50	1741—42	" " 10	Ditto, 5 July 1741 to 13 July 1742.
51	1742	" " 11	Ditto, 20 Jan. to 4 Dec. 1742.
52	1745—47	" " 12	Ditto, 7 July 1745 to 18 June 1747.
53	1749—51	" " 13	Ditto, 20 Dec. 1749 to 23 Jan. 1751.
54	1749—51	" " 14	Ditto, 15 Dec. 1749 to 21 Jan. 1751.
55	1750—51	" " 15	Ditto, 7 Dec. 1750 to 18 Dec. 1751.
56	1751	" " 16	Canton Consultations, 26 July to 21 Dec. 1751.
57	1753	" " 17	Ditto, 3 Jan. to 20 Dec. 1753.
58	1775—76	" " 18	Ditto, 12 Jan. 1775 to 29 Jan. 1776.
59	1776—77	" " 19	Ditto, 29 Jan. 1776 to 9 Feb. 1777.
60	1776—78	" " 20	Canton Letter Book, 1 Aug. 1776 to 5 March 1778.
61	1777	" " 21	Canton Consultations, 12 Feb. to 3 March 1777.
62	1777—78	" " 22	Ditto, 25 Feb. 1777 to 19 Feb. 1778.
63	1778	" " 23	Ditto, 19 Feb. to 5 March 1778.
64	1778—79	" " 24	Ditto, 5 March 1778 to 9 March 1779.
65	1779	" " 25	Ditto, 9 March to 26 Oct. 1779; and Letter Book, 24 March to 2 Aug. 1779.
66	1779—80	" " 26	Ditto, 3 Oct. 1779 to 18 Jan. 1780.

Index Number.	Date.	Previous Classification.	Nature of Documents.
67	1779—80	Range 427, No. 144	Canton Diary, 3 Oct. 1779 to 18 Jan. 1780.
68	1779—80	Range 428, No. 48	Canton Diary of the Chinese Debts, 16 Sept. 1779 to 29 Oct. 1780.
69	1780—81	„ „ 49	Ditto, 30 Oct. 1780 to 17 Jan. 1781.
70	1780	Range 427, No. 27	Canton Consultations, 19 Jan. to 27 Dec. 1780.
71	1780—81	„ „ 145	Canton Diary, 18 Jan. 1780 to 25 Jan. 1781.
72	1781	„ „ 28	Canton Consultations, 1 Feb. to 9 Nov. 1781.
73	1781—82	Unnumbered	Ditto, 7 Nov. 1781 to 21 March 1782.
74	1781—82	Range 427, No. 146	Canton Diary, 26 Jan. 1781 to 17 March 1782.
75	1782	„ „ 147	Ditto, 18 March to 28 Dec. 1782.
76	1782—83	„ „ 29	Canton Consultations, 22 March 1782 to 2 Jan. 1783.
77	1783	„ 30	Ditto, 1 Jan. to 29 Dec. 1783.
78	1783—84	„ „ 148	Canton Diary, 1 Jan. 1783 to 24 Feb. 1784.
79	1784—85	„ „ 31	Canton Consultations, 1 Jan. 1784 to 20 Nov. 1785.
80	1784—85	„ „ 149	Canton Diary, 21 Feb. 1784 to 8 Feb. 1785.
81	1785	„ „ 150	Ditto, 8 Feb. to 20 Nov. 1785.
82	1785—86	„ „ 32	Canton Consultations, 20 Nov. 1785 to 7 Dec. 1786.
83	1785—86	„ „ 151	Canton Diary, 20 Nov. 1785 to 28 Feb. 1786.
84	1786—87	„ „ 33	Canton Consultations, 7 Dec. 1786 to 4 April 1787.
85	1786—87	„ „ 152	Canton Diary, 28 Feb. 1786 to 4 April 1787.
86	1787	„ „ 34	Canton Consultations, 4 April to 17 Dec. 1787.
87	1787—88	„ „ 153	Canton Diary, 3 April 1787 to 5 April 1788.
88	1787—88	„ „ 35	Canton Consultations, 16 Dec. 1787 to 7 April 1788.
89	1788	„ „ 36	Ditto, 8 April to 10 Dec. 1788.

Index Number.	Date.	Previous Classification.	Nature of Documents.
90	1787—89	Miscellaneous Records, Vol. 32. Range I, No. 12.	Colonel Cathcart's Embassy to China, 20 June 1787 to 15 Oct. 1788.
91	1787—92	Unrecorded Papers, Vols. 148 and 209.	Lord Macartney's Embassy to China. Miscellaneous Letters, 29 Aug. 1787 to 8 Sept. 1792.
92	1792—95	Unnumbered	Ditto. Letters from Lord Macartney, 18 Sept. 1792 to 13 Feb. 1795.
93	1793—1810	Unrecorded Papers, Vols. 149 and 150.	Ditto. Miscellaneous Letters, 20 April 1793 to 21 April 1810.
94	1788—89	Range 427, No. 37	Canton Consultations, 11 Dec. 1788 to 25 March 1789.
95	1788—89	" " 154	Canton Diary, 5 April 1788 to 27 March 1789.
96	1789—90	" " 38	Canton Consultations, 28 March 1789 to 19 Feb. 1790.
97	1789—90	" " 155	Canton Diary, 28 March 1789 to 19 Feb. 1790.
98	1790—91	" " 39	Canton Consultations, 21 Feb. 1790 to 12 March 1791.
99	1790—91	" " 156	Canton Diary, 21 Feb. 1790 to 12 March 1791.
100	1791	" " 157	Ditto, 13 March to 10 Nov. 1791.
101	1791—92	" " 40	Canton Consultations, 13 March 1791 to 11 Jan. 1792.
102	1791—92	" " 158	Canton Diary, 29 Nov. 1791 to 11 Jan. 1792.
103	1792—93	" " 41	Canton Consultations, 15 Jan. 1792 to 15 March 1793.
104	1792—93	" " 159	Canton Diary, 11 Jan. 1792 to 15 March 1793.
105	1793	" " 42	Canton Consultations, 15 March to 24 Dec. 1793.
106	1793—94	" " 43	Ditto, 25 Dec. 1793 to 8 March 1794.
107	1793—94	" " 160	Canton Diary, 11 March 1793 to 8 March 1794.
108	1794—95	" " 44	Canton Consultations, 11 March 1794 to 10 May 1795.
109	1794—95	" " 161	Canton Diary, 10 March 1794 to 1 May 1795.
110	1795—96	" " 45	Canton Consultations, 14 May 1795 to 28 May 1796.
111	1795—96	" " 162	Canton Diary, 7 May 1795 to 20 March 1796.
112	1796	" " 46	Canton Consultations, 23 May to 19 June 1796.

Index Number.	Date.	Previous Classification.	Nature of Documents.
113	1796	Range 427, No. 47	Canton Consultations, 26 Nov. to 27 Dec. 1796.
114	1796	" " 48	Ditto, 24 June to 25 Nov. 1796.
115	1796	" " 163	Canton Diary, 20 March to 19 June 1796.
116	1796—97	" " 49	Canton Consultations 29 Dec. 1796 to 5 June 1797.
117	1796—97	" " 164	Canton Diary, 20 June 1796 to 27 May 1797.
118	1797	" " 50	Canton Consultations, 9 June to 12 Dec. 1797.
119	1797—98	" " 51	Ditto, 14 Dec. 1797 to 21 March 1798.
120	1797—98	" " 165	Canton Diary, 31 May 1797 to 30 April 1798.
121	1798	" " 52	Canton Consultations, 21 March to 1 May 1798.
122	1798	" " 53	Ditto, 4 May to 31 Dec. 1798.
123	1798—99	" " 166	Canton Diary, 1 May 1798 to 28 Jan. 1799.
124	1799	Range 428, No. 1	Ditto, 2 Feb. to 26 Dec. 1799.
125	1799	Range 427, No. 54	Canton Consultations, 1 Jan. to 2 Feb. 1799.
126	1799—1800	" " 55	Ditto, 4 Feb. 1799 to 9 Jan. 1800.
127	1799—1800	Range 428, No. 2	Canton Diary, 27 Dec. 1799 to 24 March 1800.
128	1800	Range 427, No. 56	Canton Consultations, 13 Jan. to 23 May 1800.
129	1800	" " 57	Ditto, 25 May to 4 Aug. 1800.
130	1800	Range 428, No. 3	Canton Diary, 26 March to 13 May 1800.
131	1800—01	Range 427, No. 58	Canton Consultations, 6 Aug. 1800 to 9 Jan. 1801.
132	1800—01	Range 428, No. 4	Canton Diary, 14 May 1800 to 10 Jan. 1801.
133	1801	Range 427, No. 59	Canton Consultations, 14 Jan. to 5 May 1801.
134	1801	" " 60	Ditto, 6 May to 14 Oct. 1801.
135	1801	Range 428, No. 5	Canton Diary, 10 Jan. to 6 May 1801.

Index Number.	Date.	Previous Classification.	Nature of Documents.
136	1801—02	Range 427, No. 61	Canton Consultations, 14 Oct. 1801 to 16 Jan. 1802.
137	1801—02	Range 428, No. 6	Canton Diary, 6 May 1801 to 11 Jan. 1802.
138	1802	Range 427, No. 62	Canton Consultations, 18 Jan. to 19 May 1802.
139	1802	" " 63	Ditto, 22 May to 30 Oct. 1802.
140	1802	Range 428, No. 7	Canton Diary, 18 Jan. to 13 May 1802.
141	1802	" " 8	Ditto, 21 May to 24 Nov. 1802.
142	1802—03	Range 427, No. 64	Canton Consultations, 31 Oct. 1802 to 31 Jan. 1803.
143	1802—03	Range 428, No. 9	Canton Diary, 10 Nov. 1802 to 31 Jan. 1803.
144	1803	Range 427, No. 65	Canton Consultations, 3 Feb. to 12 Oct. 1803.
145	1803—04	" " 66	Ditto, 19 Oct. 1803 to 3 March 1804.
146	1803—04	Range 428, No. 10	Canton Diary, 10 Feb. 1803 to 25 Jan. 1804.
147	1804	Range 427, No. 67	Canton Consultations, 6 March to 29 Dec. 1804.
148	1804—05	" " 68	Ditto, 29 Dec. 1804 to 2 March 1805.
149	1804—05	Range 428, No. 11	Canton Diary, 29 Jan. 1804 to 28 Feb. 1805.
150	1805—06	Range 427, No. 69	Canton Consultations, 3 March 1805 to 18 Jan. 1806.
151	1805—06	Range 428, No. 12	Canton Diary, 1 March 1805 to 30 March 1806.
152	1806	Range 427, No. 70	Canton Consultations, 18 Jan. to 23 Feb. 1806.
153	1806	" " 71	Ditto, 25 March to 21 Nov. 1806.
154	1806—07	" " 72	Ditto, 22 Oct. 1806 to 4 March 1807.
155	1806—07	Range 428, No. 13	Canton Diary, 29 March 1806 to 4 Jan. 1807.
156	1807	Range 427, No. 73	Canton Consultations, 4 March to 28 April 1807.
157	1807	" " 74	Ditto, 29 April to 16 Nov. 1807.
158	1807	Range 428, No. 14	Canton Diary, 8 Jan. to 27 April 1807.

Index Number.	Date.	Previous Classification.	Nature of Documents.
159	1807	Range 428, No. 15	Canton Diary, 24 April to 28 Dec. 1807.
160	1807—08	Range 427, No. 75	Canton Consultations, 17 Nov. 1807 to 9 Jan. 1808.
161	1807—08	Range 428, No. 16	Canton Diary, 29 Dec. 1807 to 3 March 1808.
162	1808	Range 427, No. 76	Canton Consultations, 7 Jan. to 8 March 1808.
163	1808	" " 77	Ditto, 9 March to 23 Oct. 1808.
164	1808—09	" " 78	Ditto, 28 Oct. 1808 to 26 Jan. 1809.
165	1808—09	Range 428, No. 17	Canton Diary, 8 March 1808 to 1 March 1809.
166	1809	Range 427, No. 79	Canton Consultations, 27 Jan. to 27 Feb. 1809.
167	1809	" " 80	Ditto, 3 March to 7 Oct. 1809.
168	1809—10	" " 81	Ditto, 8 Oct. 1809 to 29 Jan. 1810.
169	1809—10	Range 428, No. 18	Canton Diary, 3 March 1809 to 24 Feb. 1810.
170	1810	Range 427, No. 82	Canton Consultations, 30 Jan. to 25 Feb. 1810.
171	1810	" " 83	Ditto, 26 Feb. to 25 July 1810.
172	1810	" " 84	Ditto, 26 July to 22 Oct. 1810.
173	1810—11	Range 428, No. 19	Canton Diary, 24 Feb. 1810 to 21 March 1811.
174	1810—11	Range 427, No. 85	Canton Consultations, 23 Oct. 1810 to 31 Jan. 1811.
175	1811	" " 86	Ditto, 31 Jan. to 23 March 1811.
176	1811	" " 87	Ditto, 27 March to 27 Sept. 1811.
177	1811—12	Range 428, No. 20	Canton Diary, 21 March 1811 to 10 Jan. 1812.
178	1811—12	Range 427, No. 88	Canton Consultations, 28 Sept. 1811 to 9 Jan. 1812.
179	1812	" " 89	Ditto, 11 Jan. to 1 April 1812.
180	1812	" " 90	Ditto, 6 April to 2 Nov. 1812.
181	1812	" " 91	Ditto, 7 Nov. to 31 Dec. 1812.

Index Number.	Date.	Previous Classification.	Nature of Documents.
182	1812	Range 428, No. 21	Canton Diary, 12 Jan. to 1 April 1812.
183	1812	„ „ 22	Ditto, 4 April to 30 Dec. 1812.
184	1813	Range 427, No. 92	Canton Consultations, 1 Jan. to 28 Feb. 1813.
185	1813	„ „ 93	Ditto, 2 March to 21 Sept. 1813.
186	1813	„ „ 94	Ditto, 21 Sept. to 5 Dec. 1813.
187	1813	Range 428, No. 23	Canton Diary, 1 Jan. to 28 Feb. 1813.
188	1813—14	„ „ 24	Ditto, 3 March 1813 to 15 Feb. 1814.
189	1813—14	Range 427, No. 95	Canton Consultations, 5 Dec. 1813 to 21 Feb. 1814.
190	1814	„ „ 96	Ditto, 24 Feb. to 15 Nov. 1814.
191	1814—15	„ „ 97	Ditto, 20 Nov. 1814 to 15 Jan. 1815.
192	1814—15	Range 428, No. 25	Canton Diary, 1 March 1814 to 5 April 1815.
193	1815	Range 427, No. 98	Canton Consultations, 16 Jan. to 4 April 1815.
194	1815	„ „ 99	Ditto, 9 April to 15 Nov. 1815.
195	1710—1814	Unnumbered Range 1, No. 83	China and Japan: Miscellaneous Documents, 4 Jan. 1710 to 10 Feb. 1814.
196	1815—17	Unnumbered	Lord Amherst's Embassy to China: Copies of Correspondence, 14 Feb. 1815 to 24 Nov. 1817.
197	1815—17	Range I, No. 11	Ditto, ditto: Correspondence, 14 Feb. 1815 to 21 April 1817.
198	1816—17	Unnumbered	Ditto, ditto: Letters from Lord Amherst, 30 Jan. 1816 to 21 April 1817.
199	1815—16	Range 428, No. 26	Canton Diary, 4 April 1815 to 22 Jan. 1816.
200	1815—16	Range 427, No. 100	Canton Consultations, 15 Nov. 1815 to 8 Jan. 1816.
201	1816	„ „ 101	Ditto, 8 Jan. to 20 Feb. 1816.
202	1816	„ „ 102	Ditto, 23 Feb. to 9 Sept. 1816.
203	1816	„ „ 103	Ditto, 9 Sept. to 21 Nov. 1816.
204	1816—17	Range 428, No. 27	Canton Diary, 22 Feb. 1816 to 7 Jan. 1817.

Index Number.	Date.	Previous Classification.	Nature of Documents.
205	1816—17	Range 427, No. 104	Canton Consultations, 22 Nov. 1816 to 28 Feb. 1817.
206	1817	„ „ 105	Ditto, 1 to 25 March 1817.
207	1817	„ „ 106	Ditto, 29 March to 10 Oct. 1817.
208	1817	„ „ 107	Ditto, 10 Oct. to 31 Dec. 1817.
209	1817	Range 428, No. 28	Canton Diary, 5 Jan. to 25 March 1817.
210	1817—18	„ „ 29	Ditto, 24 March 1817 to 17 March 1818.
211	1818	Range 427, No. 108	Canton Consultations, 1 Jan. to 20 March 1818.
212	1818	„ „ 109	Ditto, 20 March to 24 Nov. 1818.
213	1818	Range 428, No. 30	Canton Diary, 21 March to 24 Nov. 1818.
214	1818—19	Range 427, No. 110	Canton Consultations, 25 Nov. 1818 to 26 March 1819.
215	1818—19	Range 428, No. 31	Canton Diary, 25 Nov. 1818 to 27 March 1819.
216	1819	Range 427, No. 111	Canton Consultations, 27 March to 20 Oct. 1819.
217	1819—20	„ „ 112	Ditto, 20 Oct. 1819 to 11 Feb. 1820.
218	1819—20	Range 428, No. 32	Canton Diary, 20 March 1819 to 29 March 1820.
219	1820	Range 427, No. 113	Canton Consultations, 12 Feb. to 25 March 1820.
220	1820	„ „ 114	Ditto, 26 March to 17 Nov. 1820.
221	1820—21	„ „ 128	Ditto, 17 Nov. 1820 to 20 March 1821.
222	1820—21	Range 428, No. 33	Canton Diary, 25 March 1820 to 21 March 1821.
223	1821	Range 427, No. 129	Canton Consultations, 23 March to 4 Oct. 1821.
224	1821—22	„ „ 130	Ditto, 5 Oct. 1821 to 15 Feb. 1822.
225	1821—22	Range 428, No. 34	Canton Diary, 20 March 1821 to 18 April 1822.
226	1822	Range 427, No. 131	Canton Consultations, 15 Feb. to 18 April 1822.
227	1822—23	„ „ 132	Ditto, 18 April 1822 to 4 Feb. 1823.

Index Number.	Date.	Previous Classification.	Nature of Documents.
228	1822—23	Range 428, No. 35	Canton Diary, 15 April 1822 to 4 Feb. 1823.
229	1823—24	Range 427, No. 134	Canton Consultations, 6 Feb. 1823 to 6 Feb. 1824.
230	1823—24	Range 428, No. 36	Canton Diary, 4 Feb. 1823 to 1 Feb. 1824.
231	1824—25	Range 427, No. 135	Canton Consultations, 7 Feb. 1824 to 15 March 1825.
232	1824—25	Range 428, No. 37	Canton Diary, 1 Feb. 1824 to 21 March 1825.
233	1825	Range 427, No. 136	Canton Consultations, 20 March to 16 Nov. 1825.
234	1825—26	Range 427, No. 137	Ditto, 18 Nov. 1825 to 6 March 1826.
235	1825—26	Range 428, No. 38	Canton Diary, 18 March 1825 to 10 March 1826.
236	1826—27	Range 419, No. 60	Canton Consultations, 13 March 1826 to 6 March 1827.
237	1826—27	Range 428, No. 39	Canton Diary, 6 March 1826 to 6 March 1827.
238	1827—28	Range 427, No. 139	Canton Consultations, 6 March 1827 to 8 Feb. 1828.
239	1827—28	Range 428, No. 40	Canton Diary, 3 March 1827 to 8 Feb. 1828.
240	1828—29	Range 427, No. 140	Canton Consultations, 10 Feb. 1828 to 23 Feb. 1829.
241	1828—29	Range 428, No. 41	Canton Diary, 11 Feb. 1828 to 25 Feb. 1829.
242	1829—30	Range 427, No. 141	Canton Consultations, 25 Feb. 1829 to 5 April 1830.
243	1829—30	Range 428, No. 42	Canton Diary, 23 Feb. 1829 to 3 April 1830.
244	1830—31	Range 427, No. 142	Canton Consultations, 5 April 1830 to 28 Jan. 1831.
245	1830—31	Range 428, No. 43	Canton Diary, 3 April 1830 to 25 Jan. 1831.
246	1831—32	Range H, No. 23	Canton Consultations, 28 Jan. 1831 to 28 Feb. 1832.
247	1831—32	Range 428, No. 44	Canton Diary, 11 Jan. 1831 to 29 Feb. 1832.
248	1832	Range H, No. 24	Canton Consultations, 1 March to 18 Aug. 1832.
249	1832—33	„ „ 25	Canton Factory Consultations, 18 Aug. 1832 to 21 Feb. 1833.
250	1832—33	Range 428, No. 54	Canton Commercial Consultations, 17 Aug. 1832 to 31 Jan. 1833.

Index Number.	Date.	Previous Classification.	Nature of Documents.
251	1832—33	Range 428, No. 45	Canton Diary, 1 March 1832 to 25 Feb. 1833.
252	1833—34	,, ,, 52	Canton Factory Consultations, 27 Feb. 1833 to 29 Jan. 1834.
253	1833—34	,, ,, 56	Canton Commercial Consultations, 28 Feb. 1833 to 8 July 1834.
254	1833—34	,, ,, 46	Canton Diary, 25 Feb. 1833 to 28 Jan. 1834.
255	1834	,, ,, 55	Canton Financial Consultations, 29 Jan. to 16 July 1834.
256	1834	,, ,, 47	Canton Diary, 28 Jan. to 8 July 1834.
257	1834	,, ,, 53	Canton Factory Consultations, 30 Jan. to 14 July 1834.
258	1834—35	,, ,, 57	Canton Agency Consultations, 17 July 1834 to 30 April 1835.
259	1835—36	,, ,, 58	Ditto, 1 May 1835 to 30 April 1836.
260	1836—37	,, ,, 59	Ditto, 1 May 1836 to 30 April 1837.
261	1837—38	,, ,, 60	Ditto, 1 May 1837 to 30 April 1838.
262	1838—39	,, ,, 61	Ditto, 1 May 1838 to 30 April 1839.
263	1839—40	,, ,, 62	Ditto, 1 May 1839 to 30 April 1840.
264	1792—94	Political Department	Superintending Committee's Consultations, 24 Sept. 1792 to 10 March 1794.
265	1793	,, ,,	China Secret Committee's Consultations, 17 March to 28 Dec. 1793.
266	1796—98	,, ,,	Ditto, 8 July 1796 to 27 April 1798.
267	1798—1802	,, ,,	Ditto, 4 May 1798 to 25 March 1802.
268	1802—05	,, ,,	Ditto, 22 May 1802 to 20 Jan. 1805.
269	1805—12	,, ,,	Ditto, 3 March 1805 to 1 April 1812.
270	1812—15	,, ,,	Ditto, 6 April 1812 to 9 April 1815.
271	1815—17	,, ,,	Ditto, 9 April 1815 to 18 March 1817.
272	1817—20	,, ,,	Ditto, 27 March 1817 to 28 March 1820.
273	1820—22	,, ,,	Ditto, 30 March 1820 to 18 April 1822.

Index Number.	Date.	Previous Classification.	Nature of Documents.
274	1822—25	Political Department	China Secret Committee's Consultations, 18 April 1822 to 19 March 1825.
275	1825—29	" "	Ditto, 22 March 1825 to 23 Nov. 1829.
276	1829—30	" "	Ditto, 16 Nov. 1829 to 7 April 1830.
277	1830—32	" "	Ditto, 12 April 1830 to 30 Oct. 1832.
278	1823—25	Room 338, Vol. 1377	Letters received from China, 18 March 1823 to 21 March 1825.
279	1825—27	" " 1378	Ditto, 4 May 1825 to 18 March 1827.
280	1827—29	" Vols. 1379 and 1380.	Ditto, 17 April 1827 to 25 Feb. 1829.
281	1829—31	" Vols. 1381 and 1382.	Ditto, 9 March 1829 to 28 Jan. 1831.
282	1832—33	" Vol. 1384	Ditto, 14 May 1832 to 26 Feb. 1833.
283	1833—34	" Vols. 1385 and 1386.	Ditto, 14 March 1833 to 25 July 1834.
284	1821—23	" Vol. 1391	Secret Letters received from China, 27 June 1821 to 6 Feb. 1823.
285	1823—25	" Vol. 1392	Ditto, 26 July 1823 to 20 March 1825.
286	1825—27	" Vol. 1393	Ditto, 16 Nov. 1825 to 18 March 1827.
287	1830—32	" Vols. 1383 and 1394.	Ditto, 28 Jan. 1830 to 12 June 1832.
288	1829—30	" Vol. 1387	Despatches to China, 30 Sept. 1829 to 2 June 1830.
289	1830—31	" " 1388	Ditto, 18 Aug. 1830 to 9 Dec. 1831.
290	1832	" " 1389	Ditto, 11 Jan. to 14 Nov. 1832.
291	1813—32	Political Department	Secret Commercial Drafts to China, 26 Nov. 1813 to 9 March 1832.

CONIMERE.

Index Number.	Date.	Previous Classification.	Nature of Documents.
1	1682—85	B. R., MM, 1	Consultations: 26 Oct. 1682 to 31 Dec. 1683.
		3	Ditto, 2 Jan. to 30 Dec. 1684.*
		4	Ditto, 1 Jan. to 28 Dec. 1685.
2	1684—85	B. R., MM, 5	Copies of letters despatched: 2 Jan. to 20 Dec. 1684.
		DD, 14	Ditto, 14 Jan. to 28 Dec. 1685.
3	1684	B. R., MM, 6	Copies of letters received: Jan. to Dec. 1684.

* With an account of a journey to visit the Subadar of "Chingie."

CUDDALORE and PORTO NOVO.*

Index Number.	Date.	Previous Classification.	Nature of Documents.
1	1681—83	B. R., DD, 139	Commission, &c., for settling factories in the Chengie Country, 1681.
		MM, 2	Diary and Consultations: 5 May to 31 Dec. 1683.
2	1685—87	B. R., OO, 1	Diary and Consultations: 1 Jan. to 31 Dec. 1685.
		2	Ditto, 1 Jan. to 31 Dec. 1686.
		DD, 14	Ditto, 1 Jan. to 31 Dec. 1687.
3	1684—86	B. R., OO, 3	Copies of letters despatched: 2 Jan. 1684 to 31 Dec. 1685.
		5	Ditto, 3 Jan. to 9 Nov. 1686.
		4	Copies of letters received: Jan. to Oct. 1684.
		5	Ditto, Jan. 1685 to Nov. 1686.

* *See also* Fort St. David.

DACCA.

Index Number.	Date.	Previous Classification.	Nature of Documents.
1	1678—91	B. R., FF, II., 16, 15	Diary and Consultations, 4 to 28 Oct. 1678.
		EE —	Ditto, 11 April to 11 Aug. 1681.
		DD, 12	Ditto, 1 Dec. 1681 to 30 Nov. 1682.
		WW	Ditto, 18 Aug. 1690 to 30 April 1691 (with accounts from Nov. 1688).
2	1736—48	Range 68, No. 47	Consultations, 29 Nov. 1736 to 23 Dec. 1748.
3	1749—57	„ „ 48	Ditto, 8 Jan. 1749 to 19 Dec. 1757.
4	1762	„ „ 4	Ditto, 25 Jan. to 31 Dec. 1762.
5	1763	„ „ 50	Ditto, 31 Jan. to 31 Dec. 1763.
6	1773—74	Range 69, No. 1	Separate Proceedings relative to inquiry into Mahomed Reza Khan's accounts, 29 Dec. 1773 to 6 Jan. 1774.
7	1773—74	„ „ 2	Consultations of Provincial Council of Revenue, 9 Dec. 1773 to 29 April 1774.
8	1774	„ „ 3	Ditto, 3 May to 29 Dec. 1774.
9	1775	„ „ 4	Ditto, 4 Jan. to 29 June 1775.
10	1775	„ „ 5	Ditto, 3 July to 21 Dec. 1775.
11	1775	„ „ 6	Ditto (Salt), 12 April to 20 Nov. 1775.
12	1776	„ „ 7	Ditto (General), 8 Jan. to 27 May 1776.
13	1776	„ „ 8	Ditto (Salt), 15 April to 1 Aug. 1776.
14	1776	„ „ 9	Ditto (General), 3 June to 20 Dec. 1776.
15	1777	„ „ 10	Ditto (General), 8 Jan. to 30 May 1777.
16	1777	„ „ 11	Ditto (Settlement), 11 Aug. to 13 Oct. 1777.
17	1777	„ „ 12	Ditto (General), 2 June to 22 Dec. 1777.
18	1777—78	„ „ 16	Ditto (Separate), 26 Sept. 1777 to 16 Jan. 1778.
19	1778	„ „ 13	Ditto (General), 3 Jan. to 29 May 1778.

Index Number.	Date.	Previous Classification.	Nature of Documents.
20	1778	Range 69, No. 14	Consultations (General), 2 June to 16 Dec. 1778.
21	1779	„ „ 15	Ditto (General), 6 Jan. to 21 Dec. 1779.

DINAJPUR.

Index Number.	Date.	Previous Classification.	Nature of Documents.
1	1774	Range 68, No. 56	Proceedings of Provincial Council of Revenue, 22 March to 29 Dec. 1774.
2	1775	„ „ 57	Ditto, 2 Jan. to 22 Dec. 1775.
3	1776	„ „ 58	Ditto, 16 Jan. to 31 Dec. 1776.
4	1777	„ „ 59	Ditto, 7 Jan. to 30 Dec. 1777.
5	1778	„ „ 60	Ditto, 6 Jan. to 30 Dec. 1778.

EGYPT AND RED SEA.

Index Number.	Date.	Previous Classification.	Nature of Documents.
1	1644—1726	B. R., F F, a, II, 13, 8, and b, 2. Loose papers, Packet 19	Letters and accounts from Mocha, 25 March 1644;——1710 to 6 Sept. 1726.
2	1728—40	Loose papers, Packet 19	Ditto, 20 Aug. 1728 to 13 Aug. 1740.
3	1741—1815	" "	Ditto, 20 March 1741 to 4 Feb. 1815.
4	1821—28	Range 431, Nos. 25 and 26	Mocha Journal and Ledger, 30 April 1821 to 31 Jan. 1828.
5	1773—99	Dundas Papers, Vols. 10, 11, and 16. Fisher's Papers, Nos. 165, 197, 198, and 250. Loose papers, Packets 25 and 31. Unrecorded Papers, Vols. 190, 200, 205, 208, 212, 215, and 218.	Correspondence regarding overland routes through Syria and Egypt; Mr. Baldwin's attempts to open up communication with India through Egypt; French negotiations for trade in that country, &c.
6	1787—1807	Fisher's Papers, Nos. 160, 200, 203, and 234. Loose papers, Packets 11 and 25. Range H, No. 1. Unrecorded Papers, Vols. 193, 208, 209, 212, 218, and 220.	Miscellaneous. Occupation of Perim, 1799; mission of Sir Home Popham to Arabia, 1801; expedition from India to Egypt, 1801 letters from Lord Elgin at Constantinople, on the overland conveyance of despatches, Egyptian affairs, &c., 1800–03.
7	1819—25	Range I, No. 4	Copies of letters from Constantinople, Cairo, &c., to the East India Company, 13 May 1819 to 6 Aug. 1825.
8	1837—46	Marine Records	Draft letters from the Company to their Agents in Egypt, the Red Sea, &c., 2 Jan. 1837 to 12 Nov. 1846.
9	1847—57	"	Ditto, 25 Jan. 1847 to 5 Nov. 1857.
10	1834—38	"	Letters to the Company from their Agent in Egypt, 14 March 1834 to 21 May 1838.
11	1838—40	"	Ditto, 1 June 1838 to 14 July 1840.
12	1840—42	"	Ditto, 15 July 1840 to 9 April 1842.
13	1842—44	"	Ditto, 12 April 1842 to 26 Dec. 1844.
14	1845—48	"	Ditto, 11 Jan. 1845 to 20 Dec. 1848.
15	1849—53	"	Ditto, 1 Jan. 1849 to 1 Dec. 1853.
16	1854—58	"	Ditto, 1 Jan. 1854 to 26 Aug. 1858
17	1837—58	"	Rough Abstracts of the foregoing letters from Egypt.
18	1832—37	"	Letters received by the Agent in Egypt, with in some cases drafts of his replies, 27 April 1832 to 27 Dec. 1837.
19	1838	"	Ditto, 5 Jan. to 31 Dec. 1838.

Index Number.	Date.	Previous Classification.	Nature of Documents.
20	1839—40	Marine Records	Letters received by the Agent in Egypt, with in some cases drafts of his replies, 1 Jan. 1839 to 28 Dec. 1840.
21	1841—46	„	Ditto, 6 March 1841 to 31 Dec. 1846.
22	1847—51	„	Ditto, 2 Jan. 1847 to 31 Dec. 1851.
23	1852—57	„	Ditto, 13 Jan. 1852 to 30 Dec. 1857.
24	1858—70	„	Ditto, 2 Jan. 1858 to 11 April 1870.
25	1838—45	„	Letters received by the Packet Agent at Suez, 24 Feb. 1838 to 11 Dec. 1845.
26	1846—53	„	Ditto, 3 Jan. 1846 to 17 Dec. 1853.
27	1837—39	„	Letters received by the Packet Agent at Cairo, 7 July 1837 to 31 Dec. 1839.
28	1840—43	„	Ditto, 5 Jan. 1840 to 28 Dec. 1843.
29	1844—47	„	Ditto, 2 Jan. 1844 to 29 Dec. 1847.
30	1848—53	„	Ditto, 2 Jan. 1848 to 30 Dec. 1853.
31	1854—59	„	Ditto, 27 Jan. 1854 to 13 Oct. 1859.
32	1838—59	„	Letter books of Mr. Walne, Packet Agent at Cairo, 22 Jan. 1838 to 8 Nov. 1859.
33	1839—69	„	Letter books of Captain Henry Johnson, Packet Agent at Alexandria, and afterwards Agent in Egypt, 3 Sept. 1839 to 17 Dec. 1869.
34	1838—41	„	Letter book of Captain John Lyons, Deputy Agent, and afterwards Agent, in Egypt, 11 Feb. 1838 to 12 Aug. 1841.
35	1838—69	„	Accounts of the Agent in Egypt.
36	1838—69	„	Accounts of the Packet Agent at Alexandria.
37	1838—69	„	Accounts of the Packet Agent at Suez.
38	1838—59	„	Accounts of the Packet Agent at Cairo.
39	—	„	Miscellaneous, Arabic commercial receipts, &c.

FORT ST. DAVID.*

Index Number.	Date.	Previous Classification.	Nature of Documents.
1	1690—1704	B. R., K K, 1 to 4	Consultations, 11 Feb. and 24 Sept. 1690; 8 Jan. 1696 to 30 Dec. 1704.
2	1703—12	Range 239, No. 76	Ditto, 28 Dec. 1703 to 22 Dec. 1712.
3	1723—31	" " 77	Ditto, 8 Jan. 1723 to 27 Dec. 1731.
4	1732—39	" " 78	Ditto, 1 Jan. 1732 to 31 Dec. 1739.
5	1740—46	" " 79	Ditto, 7 Jan. 1740 to 29 Dec. 1746.
6	1747—49	" " 80	Ditto, 4 Jan. 1747 to 30 Dec. 1749.
7	1750—51	" " 81	Ditto, 3 Jan. 1750 to 30 Dec. 1751.
8	1752—56	" " 82	Ditto, 4 April 1752 to 31 Dec. 1756.
9	1692—1745	B. R., K K, 5. Loose papers	Letters, 27 Sept. 1692 to 31 Dec. 1745.
10	1746—50	Loose papers	Ditto, 28 Jan. 1746 to 31 Dec. 1750.
11	1751—59	"	Ditto, 24 Jan. 1751 to 31 July 1759.

* For earlier records, *see* Cuddalore.

FORT ST. GEORGE.

Index Number.	Date.	Previous Classification.	Nature of Documents.
1	1655—78	B. R., DD, a, 3	Consultations : 31 March to 4 Dec. 1655.
		JJ, a1, 1	Ditto, 1 Aug. to — Nov. 1662.
		2	Ditto, 19 Jan. 1672 to 10 Jan. 1673.
		DD, a, 8	Ditto, 21 Jan. 1675 to 25 Jan. 1676.
		9	Ditto, 3 Feb. 1677 to 26 Jan. 1678.
2	1680—81	B. R., JJ, a1, 3	Consultations : 26 Jan. 1680 to 10 Jan. 1681.
		EE —	Ditto, 17 March to 3 July 1681.
		JJ, a1, 4	Ditto, 3 July to 29 Dec. 1681.
3	1683—85	B. R., JJ, a1, 5	Consultations : 1 Jan. 1683 to 17 Jan. 1684.
		6	Ditto, 18 Jan. 1684 to 26 Jan. 1685.
4	1686—87	B. R., JJ, a1, 7	Consultations : 2 Feb. 1686 to 3 Feb. 1687.
		8	Ditto, 4 Feb. to 25 July 1687.
5	1688	B. R., JJ, a1, 9	Consultations : 18 Feb. to 24 Sept. 1688.
		10	Ditto, 29 Sept. to [30 or 31] Dec. 1688.
6	1689—90	B. R., JJ, a1, 11	Consultations : 3 Jan. to 4 July 1689.
		12	Ditto, 4 July 1689 to 6 March 1690.
		JJ, a2, 1	Ditto, 6 March to 14 Oct. 1690.
7	1693—94	B. R., EE —	Consultations : 1 to 26 June 1693.
		JJ, a2, 2	Ditto, 1 Feb. to 31 Dec. 1694.
8	1695—97	B. R., JJ, a2, 3	Consultations : 1 Jan. to 30 Dec. 1695.
		4	Ditto, 1 Oct. 1696 to 31 Jan. 1697.
9	1697—98	B. R., JJ, a2, 5	Consultations : 1 Feb. to 13 Sept. 1697.
		6	Ditto, 15 Sept. 1697 to 10 Jan. 1698.
10	1698—99	B. R., JJ, a2, 7	Consultations : 12 Jan. to 29 Dec. 1698.
		EE —	Ditto, 2 Jan. to 29 Dec. 1699.
11	1701	B. R., JJ, a2, 8	Consultations : 1 Jan. to 5 Nov. 1701.
		9 (part)	Ditto, 1 Nov. to 28 Dec. 1701.
12	1702	Range 239. No. 83	Consultations : 1 Jan. to 30 Dec. 1702.
13	1703—04	„ „ 83	Consultations : 1 Jan. 1703 to 27 Dec. 1704. [For subsequent consultations (commencing 1 Jan. 1705), *see* separate list.]

Index Number.	Date.	Previous Classification.	Nature of Documents.
14	1661—63	B. R., JJ, b1, 1	Copies of letters despatched . 2 Jan. 1661 to 15 Jan. 1662.
		2	Ditto, 15 Jan. 1662 to — Jan. 1663.
15	1664—65	B. R., JJ, b1, 3	Copies of letters despatched : 2 Feb. 1664 to 10 Jan. 1665.
16	1668—71	B. R., JJ, b1, 4	Copies of letters despatched : 26 Aug. 1668 to 23 Oct. 1669.
		5	Ditto, 27 Dec. 1670 to 23 Dec. 1671.
17	1673—75	B. R., JJ, b1, 6	Copies of letters despatched : 31 Jan. to 7 Sept. 1673.
		7	Ditto, 13 Sept. 1673 to 3 Jan. 1675.
		8	Ditto, 26 Feb. to 20 Dec. 1675.
18	1676—79	B. R., JJ, b1, 9	Copies of letters despatched : 7 Feb. 1676 to — Jan. 1677.
		10	Ditto, 24 Jan. to 17 Dec. 1677.
		11	Ditto, 6 Jan. to 18 Dec. 1679.
19	1681	B. R., JJ, b1, 12	Copies of letters despatched : 7 July to 28 Dec. 1681.
20	1687	B. R., JJ, b2, 2	Copies of letters despatched : 3 Jan. to 19 July 1687.
21	1687—88	B. R., JJ, b2, 3	Copies of letters despatched : 24 July 1687 to 13 Feb. 1688.
		4	Ditto, 21 Feb. to 12 Dec. 1688.
22	1692—94	B. R., JJ, b2, 5	Copies of letters despatched : 4 Oct. 1692 to 19 May 1693.
		DD, 18	Ditto, 13 May 1693 to 30 Jan. 1694.
		JJ, b2, 6	Ditto, 5 Feb. to 31 Dec. 1694.
23	1696—97	B. R., JJ, b2, 7	Copies of letters despatched : — Jan. to 30 Sept. 1696.
		8	Ditto, — Oct. 1696 to 25 Jan. 1697.
24	1697—98	B. R., DD —	Copies of letters despatched : 9 Sept. to 28 Dec. 1697.
		JJ, b2, 10	Ditto, — Jan. to — Dec. 1698.
25	1699—1704	B. R., JJ, b2, 11	Copies of letters despatched : 3 Jan. to 21 Dec. 1699.
		13	Ditto, 3 Jan. to 8 Oct. 1700.
		DD, 25	Ditto, 22 Oct. to 30 Dec. 1700.
		JJ, b2, 14	Ditto, 10 Jan. to 22 Dec. 1704.
26	1669—74	B. R., DD, a, 5 & 6	Correspondence with the Nawab of Golconda, &c.: Feb. 1669 to Jan. 1672.
		JJ, c, 2	Copies of letters received : Jan. 1672 to Jan. 1673.*
		3	Ditto, March to Sept. 1673.*
		4	Ditto, Sept. 1673 to Nov. 1674.*
27	1674—77	B. R., JJ, c, 5	Copies of letters received : Nov.[?] 1674 to Dec.[?] 1675.*
		7	Ditto, Jan. to Dec. 1676.*
		9	Ditto, Jan. to Dec. 1677.*

* Almost entirely from Golconda and St. Thomé.

Index Number.	Date.	Previous Classification.	Nature of Documents.
28	1676—80	B. R., JJ, c, 6	Copies of letters received : Feb. 1676 to Jan. 1677.
		10	Ditto, Jan. to Dec. 1680.
29	1681	B. R., JJ, c, 11	Copies of letters received : Jan. to June 1681.
		12	Ditto, July to Dec. 1681.
30	1687—88	B. R., JJ, c, 13	Copies of letters received : July 1687 to Feb. 1688.
31	1692—94	B. R., DD, 17	Copies of letters received : Jan. to Sept. 1692.
		19	Ditto, May 1693 to Jan. 1694.
32	1694—97	B. R., JJ, c, 14	Copies of letters received : Feb. to Dec. 1694.
		16	Ditto, Oct. 1696 to Jan. 1697.
33	1697	B. R., JJ, c, 17	Copies of letters received : Jan. to Sept. 1697.
		DD --	Ditto, Sept. to Dec. 1697.
34	1700	B. R., DD 21	Copies of letters received : Jan. to Oct. 1700.
		JJ, c, 19	Ditto, Oct. to Dec. 1700.
35	1703—04	B. R., JJ, c, 20	Copies of letters received : Jan. to Dec. 1703.
		21	Ditto, Dec. 1703 to Dec. 1704.
36	1676—79	B. R., JJ, c, 8	Diary and Letter Book of Richard Mohun, 1676–77.
		CC 4	Account of Gold coined at Fort St. George by Richard Mohun and Vincent Sayon, 1679.
37	1683	B. R., JJ, b2, 1	Letter Book of Thomas Lucas while on a mission to Conjevaram, &c., 1683.
38	1678—94	B. R., CC, 3	Proceedings in the Court of Judicature, 1678.
		DD, 18	Ditto, 1693—94.
39	1703—05	B. R., CC, 5	Correspondence with Native Princes and their Officials, 1703–04.
		7	Ditto, 1704–05.

HUGLI.

Index Number.	Date.	Previous Classification.	Nature of Documents.
1	1663—78	B. R., EE —	Consultations, letters, &c., at Balasor and Hugli: 13 Oct. 1663 to 25 Oct. 1664.
		DD, a, 6	Ditto, 26 April 1669 to 19 Sept. 1670.
		DD, 9	Proceedings of Streynsham Master and Council, at Kasimbazar, Hugli and Balasor: Oct. to Dec. 1676.
		SS, 1	Diary kept at Hugli by Edward Reade: 1 Dec. 1676 to 30 Nov. 1677.
		EE —	Consultations, Balasor and Hugli: 28 July to 20 Dec. 1677.
		SS, 2	Hugli Diary and Consultations: 10 Sept. 1677 to 30 Nov. 1678 (including a diary kept by Mr. Edward Reade during the absence of the Chief).
2	1678—80	B. R., SS, 3	Diary and Consultations: 2 Dec. 1678 to 29 Nov. 1679.
		4	Ditto, 1 Dec. 1679 to 30 Nov. 1680.
3	1680—82	B. R., DD, 10	Diary and Consultations: 3 Dec. 1680 to 30 Nov. 1681.
		EE —	Ditto, 2 Dec. 1681 to 12 June 1682.
		EE —	Ditto, 28 July to 9 Sept. 1682.
4	1672—77	B. R., DD, a, 7	Copies of letters despatched, Balasor and Hugli: 27 Dec. 1672 to 2 Sept. 1674.
		"	Ditto, 28 Sept. 1674 to 30 Nov. 1675.
		EE —	Ditto, Kasimbazar and Hugli: 15 Aug. to 30 Nov. 1677.
5	1678—80	B. R., SS, 5	Copies of letters despatched: 2 Dec. 1678 to 27 Nov. 1679.
		6	Ditto: 3 Dec. 1679 to 30 Nov. 1680.
6	1680—84	B. R., SS, 7	Copies of letters despatched: 23 Oct. 1680 to 2 Sept. 1682.
		DD, 11	Ditto, 20 Feb. to 30 Dec. 1682 (imperfect).
		SS, 8	Ditto, 1 Jan. to 8 Dec. 1684.
7	1671—79	B. R., EE —	Copies of letters received: Oct. 1671 to Oct. 1672.
		RR, c, 1	Ditto, Aug. 1677 to Nov. 1678.
		SS, 9	Ditto, Nov. 1678 to Nov. 1679.
8	1679—82	B. R., SS, 10	Copies of letters received: Nov. 1679 to Nov. 1680.
		EE —	Ditto, Jan. to March 1682.
		EE —	Ditto, Sept. to Nov. 1682.
9	1683	B. R., SS, 11	Copies of letters received: Jan. to Dec. 1683.
10	1684	B. R., SS, 12	Copies of letters received: Jan. to Dec. 1684.
11	1686—87	B. R., DD, 15	Copies of letters received: Dec. 1686 to Nov. 1687.

JAVA.

Index Number.	Date.	Previous Classification.	Nature of Documents.
1	1595—1795	B. R., U, b, 1	Relations between the Dutch and various states in the Eastern seas: compiled principally from the Dutch records at Batavia (1818).
2	1622—25	B. R., U, a, 1, 2	These all relate to the controversies between the English and Dutch Companies, 12 Aug. 1622 to 19 Jan. 1654.
	1624—29	Wilks' Collection, Vol. 13	
	1650—54	B. R., U, a, 3	
3	1613—60	B. R., DD, 1–4; YY 3, 1–3; FF.	Consultations and correspondence, Bantam, &c., 23 Dec. 1613 to 12 Dec. 1660.
4	1664—76	B. R., AA, 8	Extracts from Letters from Bantam to the East India Company, 26 Jan. 1664 to 8 April 1676.
5	1664—70	B. R., DD, 5 and 6.	Consultations, &c., at Bantam, 4 Jan. 1664 to 5 Oct. 1670.
6	1670—1702	B. R., DD, 6, 7, 8, 10, 12, and 26.	Bantam Consultations, &c., 3 April 1670 to 17 Dec. 1702.
7	1677—1707	B. R., AA, 9	Abstracts of Letters from Bantam, 6 July 1677 to 23 Sept. 1682. Tonquin, 26 Dec. 1682 to 10 Jan. 1689. Sumatra, 10 March 1686 to 3 Feb. 1707. *Also* some transcripts from the Dutch archives at the Hague, 1681–82.
8	1684—86	B. R., U, a, 4 and 5	Transactions between the English and Dutch Commissioners, 1 Oct 1684 to 22 June 1686.
9	1707—1818	Loose papers, Packet 6	Letters, &c., from Bantam, 30 Jan. 1707 to 13 April 1818.
10	1796—1812	Fisher's Papers, No. 238, &c.	Miscellaneous, including an account of Amboyna, Banda, and Tidore (1796), and a journal kept during Lord Minto's expedition to Java (1811–12).
11	1811	Range J, No. 32	Expedition to Java. Naval and military arrangements connected with the expedition.
12	1809—11	Range K, No. 40	Expedition to Java. Letters from the Governor-General, 21 Dec. 1809 to 28 Feb. 1811, with enclosures.
13	1811	" 41 and 39	Ditto, ditto, 27 April, and June to Oct. 1811, with enclosures.
14	1811—12	" 42	Ditto, 9 Dec. 1811 to 20 Jan. 1812, with enclosures.
15	1811	Range G, No. 6	Java Public Consultations, 21 Oct. to 20 Dec. 1811.
16	1812	" " 7	Ditto, 4 Jan. to 22 April 1812.
17	1812	" " 8	Ditto, 18 May to 4 Oct. 1812.
18	1812	" " 9	Ditto, 10 Oct. to 23 Dec. 1812.
19	1813	" " 10	Ditto, 5 Jan. to 31 March 1813.

Index Number.	Date.	Previous Classification.	Nature of Documents.
20	1813	Range G, No. 11	Java Public Consultations, 9 April to 28 May 1813.
21	1813	" " 12	Ditto, 7 June to 24 Aug. 1813.
22	1813	" " 13	Ditto, 17 Sept. to 19 Nov. 1813.
23	1813	" " 14	Ditto, 24 Nov. to 31 Dec. 1813.
24	1814	" " 15	Ditto, 17 Jan. to 8 March 1814.
25	1814	" " 16	Ditto, 18 July to 14 Sept. 1814.
26	1814	" " 17	Ditto, 6 Oct. to 22 Dec. 1814.
27	1815	" " 18	Ditto, 6 Jan. to 29 March 1815.
28	1815	" " 19	Ditto, 14 April to 21 June 1815.
29	1815	" " 20	Ditto, 6 July to 28 Sept. 1815.
30	1812	" " 21	Java Military Consultations, 1 Jan. to 29 Sept. 1812.
31	1812	" " 22	Ditto, 1 Sept. to 31 Dec. 1812.
32	1813	" " 23	Ditto, 5 Jan. to 28 May 1813.
33	1813	" " 24	Ditto, 7 June to 24 Aug. 1813.
34	1813	" " 25	Ditto, 17 Sept. to 31 Dec. 1813.
35	1814	" " 26	Ditto, 18 July to 22 Dec. 1814.
36	1815	" " 27	Ditto, 6 Jan. to 21 June 1815.
37	1813	" " 28	Java Separate Consultations, 3 Aug. to 31 Oct. 1813.
38	1813	" " 29	Ditto, 1 Nov. to 22 Nov. 1813.
39	1814	" " 30	Ditto, 29 Jan. to 25 March 1814.
40	1814	" " 31	Java Separate Dependencies Consultations, 29 Jan. to 1 June 1814.
41	1814	" " 32	Ditto, 27 July to 28 Dec. 1814.
42	1815	" " 33	Java Separate and Political Consultations, 6 Jan. to 21 June 1815.

Index Number.	Date.	Previous Classification.	Nature of Documents.
43	1811—12	Range G, No. 34	Java Journal, 2 Sept. 1811 to 30 April 1812.
44	1811—12	" " 35	Java Ledger, 1811–12.
45	1812—13	" " 36	Java Journal, 1 May 1812 to 30 April 1813, Vol. I.
46	1812—13	" " 37	Ditto, ditto, Vol. II.
47	1812—13	" " 38	Java Ledger, 1812–13.
48	1813—14	" " 39	Java Journal, 1813–14, Vol. I.
49	1813—14	" " 40	Ditto, ditto, Vol. II.
50	1813—14	" " 41	Java Ledger, 1813–14.
51	1814—15	" " 42	Java Journal, 1814–15, Vol. I.
52	1814—15	" " 43	Ditto, ditto, Vol. II.
53	1814—15	" " 44	Java Ledger, 1814–15.
54	1815—16	" " 45	Java Journal, 1815–16, Vol. I.
55	1815—16	Range H, No. 1	Ditto, ditto, Vol. II.
56	1815—16	" " 2	Java Ledger, 1815–16.
57	1816—17	" " 3	Java Journal, 1816–17.
58	1816—17	" " 4	Java Ledger, 1816–17.
59	1812—16	" " 5	Java Receipts and Disbursements, 1812–13 to 1815–16.
60	1812—13	Range I, Nos. 40, 41 and 42	Letters from Java, 24 Oct. 1812 to 21 Sept. 1813.
61	1814—16	" " 43, 44 and 45	Ditto, 11 Feb. 1814 to 13 Dec. 1816.
62	1817	" " 39 and 47	Ditto, 20 Feb. and 23 Feb. 1817.
63	1815	Range K, Nos. 75 and 76	Enclosure to Bengal Despatch, 8 Dec. 1815.
64	1813—20	Range J, No. 40, *also* B. R., U, b, 5.	Miscellaneous Memoranda on Java and the Eastern Islands.
65	1800—16	Range H, Nos. 35, 37, 39, 40, 44. Unrecorded Papers, Nos. 2438—44, 3130—32, 3164, 3318 and 3320.	Miscellaneous documents.

Index Number.	Date.	Previous Classification.	Nature of Documents.
66	1816—17	Range J, No. 41	Surrender of Java to the Dutch.
67	1812—17	Unclassified	Original letters from Java, 19 March 1812 to 20 July 1817.
68	1812—13	,,	Original enclosures to ditto, 1812–13.
69	1814	,,	Ditto, ditto, Feb. and March 1814.
70	1814	,,	Ditto, ditto, June to Dec. 1814.
71	1812—27	,,	Papers relating chiefly to Sir T. Stamford Raffles.
72	1812—15	,,	Copies of letters from the Secretary at the India House to Batavia, 2 May 1812 to 4 July 1815.

KARWAR.

Index Number.	Date.	Previous Classification.	Nature of Documents.
1	1666—1717	Loose papers, Packet 21	Letters, &c., giving an account of the siege of the factory by the Sonda Raja, 1717. Also copy and translation of the firman for the settlement, 1666.

KASIMBAZAR.

Index Number.	Date.	Previous Classification.	Nature of Documents.
1	1676—80	B. R., DD, a, 8	Diary and Consultations: 12 to 30 Oct. 1676.
		TT, 1	Ditto, 8 Nov. 1676 to 30 Nov. 1677.
		DD, 9	Ditto, 1 Dec. 1677 to 30 Nov. 1678.
		TT, 2	Ditto, 2 Dec. 1678 to 30 Nov. 1679.
		3	Ditto, 1 Dec. 1679 to 30 Nov. 1680.
2	1681—82	B. R., DD, 11	Diary and Consultations: 27 April to 12 May 1681.
		TT, 4	Ditto, [12 ?] Sept. to 30 Nov. 1681.
		5	Ditto, 1 Dec. 1681 to 30 Nov. 1682.
3	1682—84	B. R., TT, 6	Diary and Consultations: 1 Dec. 1682 to 30 Sept. 1683.
		7	Ditto, 1 Dec. 1683 to 10 July 1684.
4	1684—1701	B. R., TT, 8	Diary and Consultations: 1 Dec. 1684 to 30 Nov. 1685.
			Ditto, 11 April to 27 Nov. 1701.
5	1733—40	Range 70, No. 6	Consultations: 7 March to 27 Dec. 1733; 1 Jan. to 30 Nov. 1736; 5 Feb. 1737 to 20 Oct. 1740.
6	1740—44	" " 7	Ditto, 4 Dec. 1740 to 1 Sept. 1744.
7	1744—48	" " 8	Ditto, 5 Sept. 1744 to 4 Nov. 1745; 18 Feb. to 4 Dec. 1746; 4 Jan. to 27 Dec. 1748.
8	1749	" " 9	Ditto, 7 Jan. to 30 Dec. 1749.
9	1750	" " 10	Ditto, 2 Jan. to 31 Dec. 1750.
10	1751	" " 11	Ditto, 8 Jan. to 29 Dec. 1751.
11	1752	" " 12	Ditto, 11 Jan. to 31 Dec. 1752.
12	1753—57	" " 13	Ditto, 4 Jan. 1753 to 31 Jan. 1756; 24 Aug. to 29 Nov. 1757.
13	1757—59	" " 14	Ditto, 5 Dec. 1757 to 28 Feb. 1759.

MADAPOLLAM.

Index Number.	Date.	Previous Classification.	Nature of Documents.
1	1684—86	B. R., LL, a, 10	Consultations: 2 Jan. to 30 Dec. 1684.*
		12	Ditto, 4 Jan. to 31 Dec. 1685.
		DD, 14	Ditto, 2 Jan. to 31 Dec. 1686.
2	1676—84	B. R., LL, b, 6	Copies of letters despatched: 7th Sept. 1676 to 28 Nov. 1677.
		7	Ditto, 8 July 1681 to 21 Dec. 1682.
		10	Ditto, 11 Jan. to 29 Dec. 1683.
		11	Ditto, 18 Jan. to 30 Dec. 1684.
3	1676—85	B. R., LL, C, 5	Copies of letters received: Sept. 1676 to Nov. 1677.
		8	Ditto, Aug. [?] 1681 to Dec. 1682.
		10	Ditto, Jan. to Dec. 1684.
		11	Ditto, Jan. to Dec. 1685.

* For Consultations in 1678–79, *see* Masulipatam Records, Vol. 2.

MALDAH.

Index Number.	Date.	Previous Classification.	Nature of Documents.
1	1680—82	B. R., UU, 1	Diary and Consultations: 22 April to 29 Nov. 1680.
		2	Ditto, 1 Dec. 1680 to 29 Nov. 1681.
		DD, 11	Ditto, 1 Dec. 1681 to 30 Nov. 1682.
2	1684—93	B. R., UU, 3	Diary and Consultations: 1 Dec. 1684 to 30 Nov. 1685.
		5	Ditto, 27 Sept. 1690 to 31 Jan. 1693.

MASULIPATAM.

Index Number.	Date.	Previous Classification.	Nature of Documents.
1	1670—78	B. R., DD, a, 6	Consultations: 5 July 1670 to March [?] 1671.
		LL, a, 1	Ditto, 23 July to 9 Dec. 1675.
		2	Ditto, 9 Dec. 1675 to 17 Jan. 1677.
		3	Ditto, 25 Jan. 1677 to 3 Jan. 1678.
2	1678—79	B. R., LL, a 5	Consultations, 2 Jan. to 30 Dec. 1678.
		6	Ditto, 1 Jan. to 31 Dec. 1679.
3	1680—81	B. R., LL, a, 7	Consultations, 5 Jan. to 31 Dec. 1680.
		8	Ditto, 3 Jan. to 29 Dec. 1681.
4	1682—85	B. R., LL, a, 9	Consultations, 2 Jan. to 28 Dec. 1682.
		11	Ditto, 1 Jan. to 31 Dec. 1684.
		13	Ditto, 1 Jan. to 31 Dec. 1685.
5	1640—72	B. R., LL, b, 1	Copies of letters despatched: 15 Sept. to 20 Oct. 1640.
		DD —	Ditto, 3 Jan. to Oct. [?] 1666.
		LL, b, 2	Ditto, 9 July 1670 to 1 July 1671.
		3	Ditto, 9 Aug. 1671 to 30 Nov. 1672.
6	1672—77	B. R., DD —	Copies of letters despatched: 8 Dec. 1672 to 14 Aug. 1673.
		LL, b, 4	Ditto, 25 June to 29 Dec. 1675.
		5	Ditto, 28 Dec. 1675 to 6 Jan. 1677.
7	1682—83	B. R., LL, b, 8	Copies of letters despatched: 10 Jan. to 15 Dec. 1682.
		9	Ditto, 1 Jan. to 29 Dec. 1683.
8	1684—86	B. R., LL, b, 12	Copies of letters received: 11 Jan. to 31 Dec. 1684.
		DD, 13	Ditto, 3 Jan. to 31 Dec. 1685.
		LL, b, 13	Ditto, 13 Jan. to 29 Dec. 1686.
9	1622—73	B. R., EE —	Copies of letters received: April [?] 1622 to June 1623.
		DD —	Ditto, Jan. [?] to Oct. 1666.
		LL, c, 1	Ditto, July 1670 to April 1671.
		2	Ditto, Aug. 1671 to June 1672.
		DD, a, 7	Ditto, Dec. 1672 to Aug. 1673.
10	1675—78	B. R., LL, c, 4	Copies of letters received: June to Dec. 1675.
		5	Ditto, Dec. 1675 to Dec. 1676.
		6	Ditto, Oct. 1677 to Dec. 1678.
11	1682—85	B. R., LL, c, 7	Copies of letters received: Jan. to Dec. 1682.
		9	Ditto, Jan. to Dec. 1683.
		DD, 14	Ditto, Jan. to Dec. 1685.

Index Number.	Date.	Previous Classification.	Nature of Documents.
12	1675—76	B. R., CC, 1	Diary of William Puckle, while at Masulipatam and Fort St. George, June 1675 to Jan. 1676.
13	1699—1700		Proceedings of the New Company's representatives at Masulipatam :—
		B. R., DD, 24	Consultations by the Lord Ambassador and Council, 1699—1700.
		EE, 277	Copies of letters despatched, Sept. and Oct. 1699.
		DD, 25	Correspondence with Native Officials, 1699–1700.

MURSHIDABAD.

Index Number.	Date.	Previous Classification.	Nature of Documents.
1	1770	Range 69, No. 47	Proceedings of Provincial Council of Revenue, 27 Sept. to 31 Dec. 1770.
2	1771	„ „ 48	Ditto, 3 Jan. to 18 April 1771.
3	1771	„ „ 49	Ditto, 22 April to 2 Sept. 1771.
4	1771	„ „ 50	Ditto, 2 Sept. to 30 Dec. 1771.
5	1771—72	„ „ 51	Ditto (Separate, relative to Capt. Mackenzie), 2 Sept. 1771 to 22 June 1772.
6	1772	„ „ 52	Ditto, 4 Jan. to 30 April 1772.
7	1772	„ „ 53	Ditto, 4 May to 8 Sept. 1772.
8	1773—74	„ „ 54	Ditto, 14 Dec. 1773 to 26 Dec. 1774.
9	1775	„ „ 55	Ditto, 2 Jan. to 6 July 1775.
10	1775	„ „ 56	Ditto, 6 July to 28 Dec. 1775.
11	1776	„ „ 57	Ditto, 2 Jan. to 27 June 1776.
12	1776	„ „ 58	Ditto, 4 July to 23 Dec. 1776.
13	1777	„ „ 59	Ditto, 2 Jan. to 30 June 1777.
14	1777	Range 70, No. 1	Ditto, 7 July to 29 Dec. 1777.
15	1778	„ „ 2	Ditto, 5 Jan. to 21 Dec. 1778.
16	1779	„ „ 3	Ditto, 4 Jan. to 27 Dec. 1779.
17	1770	„ „ 4	Letters received and sent, Sept. and Oct. 1770.

PATNA.

Index Number.	Date.	Previous Classification.	Nature of Documents.
1	1680—85	B. R., VV, 1	Diary and Consultations, 6 April 1680 to 30 April 1681.
		2	Ditto, 2 May to 30 Nov. 1681.
		3	Ditto, 3 Jan. to 30 Nov. 1683.
		4	Ditto, 1 Dec. 1683 to 29 Nov. 1684.
		DD, 13	Ditto, 2 Dec. 1684 to 30 Sept. 1685.
2	1744—47	Range 69, Vol. 18	Consultations, 28 Feb. 1744 to 11 Nov. 1747.
3	1772—73	„ „ 19	Ditto, of Provincial Council of Revenue, 2 April 1772 to 28 Jan. 1773.
4	1773	„ „ 20	Ditto, 1 Feb. to 23 Dec. 1773.
5	1774	„ „ 21	Ditto, 3 Jan. to 29 Dec. 1774.
6	1775	„ „ 22	Ditto, 2 Jan. to 28 Dec. 1775.
7	1776	„ „ 23	Ditto, 3 Jan. to 26 Dec. 1776.
8	1777	„ „ 24	Ditto, 2 Jan. to 31 July 1777.
9	1777	„ „ 25	Ditto, 4 Aug. to 31 Dec. 1777.
10	1778	„ „ 26	Ditto, 1 Jan. to 11 June 1778.
11	1778	„ „ 27	Ditto, 17 June to 31 Dec. 1778.
12	1779	„ „ 28	Ditto, 4 Jan. to 28 June 1779.
13	1779	„ „ 29	Ditto, 1 July to 30 Dec. 1779.
14	1780	„ „ 30	Ditto, 3 Jan. to 29 June 1780.
15	1779	„ „ 31	Proceedings of Courts of Appeal (Revenue) : 6 Jan. to 15 Dec. 1779.
16	1780	„ „ 32	Ditto, 5 Jan. to 28 Dec. 1780.
17	1781—82	„ „ 33	Accounts and Invoices, Patna, Chapra, &c : May 1781 to April 1782.
18	1763	Fisher's Papers, Nos. 173, 174, 175.	Narratives by Messrs. Campbell, Fullarton, and Anderson, of the massacre at Patna, 1763.

PERSIA AND PERSIAN GULF.

Index Number.	Date.	Previous Classification.	Nature of Documents.
1	1620—97	B. R., D D, 2; S, Vols. 1 and 2; F F.	Early documents relating to Persia.
	1708—10	Range 239, No. 63	Gombroon Diary from 1 Nov. 1708 to 31 July 1710.
2	1726—27	„ „ 64	Gombroon Diary, from 23 Nov. 1726 to 14 March 1727.
3	1727	„ „ 65	Ditto, — March to 31 July 1727.
4	1728—37	„ „ 66	Ditto, 20 Nov. 1728 to 31 July 1739.
5	1737—46	„ „ 67	Ditto, 1 Aug. 1737 to 31 July 1746.
6	1746—52	„ „ 68	Ditto, 1 Aug. 1746 to 31 July 1752.
7	1754—55	„ „ 69	Ditto, 3 Aug. 1754 to 31 July 1755.
8	1755—56	„ „ 70	Ditto, 2 Aug. 1755 to 30 July 1756.
9	1756—57	„ „ 71	Ditto, 4 Aug. 1756 to 31 July 1757.
10	1757—58	„ „ 72	Ditto, 1 Aug. 1757 to 31 July 1758.
11	1760	„ „ 73	Ditto, 16 Jan. to 31 July 1760.
12	1760—61	„ „ 74	Ditto, 2 Oct. 1760 to 1 Dec. 1761.
13	1761—63	„ „ 75	Ditto, 2 Dec. 1761 to 7 Feb. 1763.
14	1703—27	Loose papers, Packet 19	Letters, &c., from Bussora, Gombroon, &c., 12 Feb. 1703 to 17 June 1727.
15	1729—52	„ „	Ditto, 31 July 1729 to 6 Nov. 1752.
16	1758—73	„ „	Ditto, 20 Jan. 1758 to 17 Aug. 1773.
17	1774—83	„ „	Ditto, 10 Jan. 1774 to 14 Dec. 1783.
18	1784—92	„ „	Ditto, 8 Feb. 1784 to 22 Nov. 1792.
19	1792—99	„ „	Ditto, 22 Nov. 1792 to 11 Jan. 1799.
20	1799—1811	„ „	Ditto, 13 Jan. 1799 to 18 Dec. 1811.

Index Number.	Date.	Previous Classification.	Nature of Documents.
21	1764—99	E. Indies Papers. Range I, No. 86. Fisher's Papers, Nos. 168, 204, 233, 260.	Miscellaneous. Home Correspondence on Persian Affairs, 1764—69. Letters from Sir John Lindsay, 1770. Letters from the Resident at Bagdad, 1781 and 1784-85. Report on British Trade with Persia and Arabia, 1791. Deputation of Mehedi Ali Khan to Persian Court, 1798-99. Account of the Wahabee Arabs. General Morrison's proposed treaty with Persia, 1796.
22	1799—1801	Fisher's Papers, No. 229	Letters from General Malcolm, Envoy to Persia, 15 Oct. 1799 to 31 July 1801.
23	1798—1802	Range I, No. 89. " H, Nos. 16, 17, 18, 20, 21. Fisher's Papers, No. 188.	Letters from Mr. Harford Jones, Resident at Bagdad, &c., 1 July 1798 to 8 Nov. 1802.
24	1803—05	Range K, No. 25 " H, No. 439.	Letters from Mr. Samuel Manisty, Resident at Bussora, relating to his political proceedings in Persia, 29 Dec. 1803 to 7 July 1805.
25	1807—08	Range I, Nos. 6 and 7	Letters from Sir Harford Jones, Envoy to Persia, to the President of the Board of Control, — 1807 to 25 Nov. 1808.
26	1809—10	" No. 8	Ditto, ditto, 11 Jan. 1809 to 22 July 1810.
27	1791—1811	" Nos. 33 and 46. Fisher's Papers, 375. Range H, 71, 82, 85, 87, 89. Unrecorded Papers, 1435, 1454, 1923, 2562, 2691, 2711, 2712, 2919, 2947, 3068-70, 3071A.	Ditto to the Secret Committee, 1808—11, with miscellaneous papers connected with his Residency at Bussora and Mission to Persia, 1791—1809.
28	1808	Range K, No. 29	Enclosures to Bengal Secret Letters, February to June 1808.
29	1808	" " 28	Ditto, 17 Sept. 1808.
30	1809	" " 34	Ditto, 31 Aug. 1809.
31	1806—22	Fisher's Papers, No. 231. Range H, Nos. 59, 72, 75, 79, 117, 226, 322, 373, 375, 376, 390, 407, 408. Range J, No. 22.	Miscellaneous. French intrigues in Persia; report on the Missions of Sir Harford Jones and General Malcolm; letters from Sir Gore Ouseley to the Secret Committee, 1811—13, &c.
32	1815—21	- - -	Despatches relative to the Expedition to the Gulf of Persia, 19 May 1815 to 25 May 1821.
33	1817—19	-	Letters from Persia to the Secret Committee, 10 June 1817 to 31 Dec. 1819
34	1820	- -	*Ditto, 10 Jan. to 26 Dec. 1820.
35	1821—23	- -	*Ditto, 8 Feb. 1821 to 12 Nov. 1823.
36	1824	-	*Ditto, 8 Jan. to 20 April 1824.
37	1824	- -	*Ditto, 14 July to 15 Dec. 1824.
38	1825	- -	*Ditto, 8 Feb. to 31 Dec. 1825.
39	1826		*Ditto, 17 Feb. to 23 Dec. 1826.
40	1827	- - -	*Ditto, 6 Jan. to 22 Sept. 1827.
41	1827	- -	*Ditto, — Oct. to 28 Dec. 1827.

* These volumes contain also letters from Bagdad, Bussora, Egypt, Damascus, &c.

Index Number.	Date.	Previous Classification.	Nature of Documents.
42	1828	- - -	*Letters from Persia to the Secret Committee, 15 Jan. to 15 March 1828.
43	1828	- - -	*Ditto, 16 March to 27 Dec. 1828.
44	1829	- - -	*Ditto, 10 Feb. to 10 Dec. 1829.
45	1830	- - -	*Ditto, 5 Jan. to 29 Dec. 1830.
46	1831	- - -	*Ditto, 20 Jan. to 26 Dec. 1831.
47	1832	- -	*Ditto, 9 Jan. to 28 Dec. 1832.
48	1832—33	- - -	Memoranda on various subjects by Sir H. Willock, Sir Gore Ouseley, Mr. Ellis, &c.
49	1833	- - -	†Letters from Persia to the Secret Committee, 3 Jan. to 17 Dec. 1833.
50	1834	-	†Ditto, 1 Jan. to 11 Aug. 1834.
51	1834	- - -	†Ditto, 5 Sept. to 31 Dec. 1834.
52	1835	- -	†Ditto, 1 Jan. to 14 Dec. 1835.
53	1836	- -	†Letters from Persia, &c., to the Secret Committee and to the Secretary of State for Foreign Affairs, — Jan. to 23 July 1836.
54	1836	-	†Ditto, 31 July to 30 Dec. 1836.
55	1837	- -	†Ditto, 5 Jan. to 6 April 1837.
56	1837		†Ditto, 2 May to 29 July 1837.
57	1837	- -	†Ditto, 1 Aug. to 30 Oct. 1837.
58	1837	- - -	†Ditto, 2 Oct. to 31 Dec. 1837.
59	1838	- -	†1 Jan. to 30 March 1838.
60	1838	- -	†Ditto, 1 April to 28 June 1838.
61	1838	-	†Ditto, 7 July to 20 Sept. 1838.
62	1838	- -	†Ditto, 3 Oct. to 19 Nov. 1838.
63	1838		†Ditto, 23 Nov. to 31 Dec. 1838.

* These volumes contain also letters from Bagdad, Bussora, Egypt, Damascus, &c.

† These volumes contain also letters from Bagdad, Bushire, Aden, Egypt, Damascus, Erzeroum, Constantinople, Cabul, Herat, &c.

Index Number.	Date.	Previous Classification.	Nature of Documents.
64	1839	- -	*11 Jan. to 30 April 1839.
65	1839	- - -	*Letters from Persia, &c., to the Secret Committee and to the Secretary of State for Foreign Affairs, 1 May to 29 July 1839.
66	1839	- - -	*Ditto, 1 Aug. to 30 Sept. 1839.
67	1839	- - -	*Ditto, 3 Oct. to 31 Dec. 1839.
68	1840	- - -	*Ditto, 1 Jan. to 28 April 1840.
69	1840	- - -	*Ditto, 1 May to 31 July 1840.
70	1840	- - -	*Ditto, 2 Aug. to 3 Oct. 1840.
71	1840	- - -	*Ditto, 3 Oct. to 28 Dec. 1840.
72	1841	- - -	*Ditto, 4 Jan. to 29 April 1841.
73	1841	-	*Ditto, 6 May to 28 Aug. 1841.
74	1841	- - -	*Ditto, 1 Sept. to 31 Dec. 1841.
75	1842	- - -	Ditto, 4 Jan. to 2 June 1842.
76	1842	- - -	Ditto, 12 May to 12 Dec. 1842.
77	1843	- - -	Ditto, 5 Jan. to 18 June 1843.
78	1843	- - -	Ditto, 22 June to 27 Dec. 1843.
79	1844	- - -	Ditto, 7 Jan. to 30 June 1844.
80	1844	- - -	Ditto, 1 July to 31 Dec. 1844.
81	1845	- - -	Ditto, 3 Jan. to 30 June 1845.
82	1845	- - -	Ditto, 12 July to 31 Dec. 1845.
83	1846	- - -	Ditto, 1 Jan. to 24 April 1846.
84	1846	- - -	Ditto, 26 April to 18 Aug. 1846.
85	1846	- - -	Ditto, 20 Aug. to 31 Dec. 1846.

* These volumes contain also letters from Bagdad, Bushire, Aden, Egypt, Damascus, Erzeroum, Constantinople, Cabul, Herat, &c.

Index Number.	Date.	Previous Classification.	Nature of Documents.
86	1847		Letters from Persia, &c., to the Secret Committee and to the Secretary of State for Foreign Affairs, 1 Jan. to 26 May 1847.
87	1847		Ditto, 28 May to 4 Sept. 1847.
88	1847		Ditto, 22 Sept. to 31 Dec. 1847.
89	1848		Ditto, 18 Jan. to 1 July 1848.
90	1848		Ditto, 10 July to 31 Dec. 1848.
91	1849		Ditto, 1 Jan to 1 July 1849.
92	1849		Ditto, 18 July to 28 Dec. 1849.
93	1850		Ditto, 2 Jan. to 24 April 1850.
94	1850		Ditto, 15 May to 26 Aug. 1850.
95	1850		Ditto, 3 Sept. to 26 Dec. 1850.
96	1851		Ditto, 2 Jan. to 25 March 1851.
97	1851		Ditto, 28 March to 22 July 1851.
98	1851		Ditto, 24 July to 22 Oct. 1851.
99	1851		Ditto, 27 Oct. to 31 Dec. 1851.
100	1852		Ditto, 1 Jan. to 22 April 1852.
101	1852		Ditto, 1 May to 31 Aug. 1852.
102	1852		Ditto, 1 Sept. to 22 Dec. 1852.
103	1853		Ditto, 5 Jan. to 18 March 1853.
104	1853		Ditto, 2 April to 13 July 1853.
105	1853		Ditto, 14 July to 29 Oct. 1853.
106	1853		Ditto, 2 Nov. to 26 Dec. 1853.
107	1854		Ditto, 4 Jan. to 20 March 1854.
108	1854		Ditto, 10 April to 25 Aug. 1854.

Index Number.	Date.	Previous Classification.	Nature of Documents.
109	1854	- -	Letters from Persia, &c., to the Secret Committee and to the Secretary of State for Foreign Affairs, 5 Sept. to 28 Dec. 1854.
110	1855	- - -	Ditto, 1 Jan. to 22 Dec. 1855.
111	1856	- - -	Ditto, 4 Jan. to 22 Dec. 1856.
112	1857	- - -	Ditto, 28 Jan. to 31 Dec. 1857.
113	1858	- - -	Ditto, 14 Jan. to 6 Oct. 1858.
114	1859—60	- - -	Letters from Persia, &c., to the Secretary of State for India and to the Secretary of State for Foreign Affairs, 12 Dec. 1859 to 31 March 1860.
115	1860	- - -	Ditto, 23 April to 19 Dec. 1860.
116	1861	- - -	Ditto, 31 Jan. to 5 Dec. 1861.
117	1862	- - -	Ditto, 5 Jan. to 6 Aug. 1862.
118	1862	- - -	Ditto, 20 Aug. to 18 Dec. 1862.
119*	1863	- - -	Ditto, 6 Jan. to 5 Dec. 1863.
120	1864	- - -	Ditto, 5 Jan. to 19 Dec. 1864.
121	1865	- -	Ditto, 3 Jan. to 30 Dec. 1865.
122	1866	- - -	Ditto, 12 Jan. to 26 Dec. 1866.
123	1867	- - -	Ditto, 15 Jan. to 18 Dec. 1867.
124	1868	- - -	Ditto, 15 Jan. to 31 Dec. 1868.
125	1869	- - -	Ditto, 11 Jan. to 31 Dec. 1869.
126	1870	- - -	Ditto, 7 Jan. to 7 Dec. 1870.
127	1871	- - -	Ditto, 5 Jan. to 6 Dec. 1871.
128	1872	- - -	Ditto, 6 Jan. to 31 Dec. 1872.
129	1873	- - -	Ditto, 6 Jan. to 5 Dec. 1873.
130	1874	- - -	Ditto, 5 Jan. to 2 Dec. 1874.

PETAPOLI.

Index Number.	Date.	Previous Classification.	Nature of Documents.
1	1683—87	B. R., NN, 1	Consultations: 4 Jan. to 30 Nov. 1683.
		2	Ditto, 3 Jan. to 29 Dec. 1684.
		3	Ditto, 1 Jan. to 30 Dec. 1685.
		4	Ditto, 4 Jan. 1686 to 24 May 1687.
2	1682—87	B. R., NN, 5	Copies of letters despatched: 26 Sept. 1682 to 28 Dec. 1684.
		6	Ditto, 2 Jan. to 15 Dec. 1685.
		4	Dito, 12 Jan. 1686 to 24 May 1687.
3	1685—87	B. R., NN, 7	Copies of letters received: Jan. to Dec. 1685.
		4	Ditto, Jan. 1686 to June 1687.

RAJAPUR.

Index Number.	Date.	Previous Classification.	Nature of Documents.
1	1659-60	B. R., GG, cl, 4	Copies of letters despatched. 4 Oct. to 30 Nov. 1659.
		5	Ditto, 19 Nov. 1659 to 3 Nov. 1660.

ST. HELENA.

Index Number.	Date.	Previous Classification.	Nature of Documents.
1	1677—1714	B. R., Z Z, Vol. 1	The Laws and Ordinances of St. Helena.
2	1676—96	B. R., Z Z, Vols. 2–4; D D, Vols. 12, 13	St. Helena Consultations, 29 Jan. to 15 July 1676; 10 April 1682 to 9 April 1683; 13 Oct. 1684 to 5 Jan. 1685; 12 April 1694 to 19 July 1696.
3	1699—1709	Loose papers, Packet 24. Range 424, Nos. 83, 84	Consultations, 18 Feb. 1699 to 20 June 1709.
4	1709—11	Range 424, Nos. 85, 86, 87, 88. Loose papers, Packet 24.	Ditto, 5 July 1709 to 18 Oct. 1711.
5	1711—17	Range 424, No. 89	Ditto, 20 Dec. 1711 to 3 Jan. 1717.
6	1717—20	" " 90	Ditto, 5 Jan. 1717 to 22 Dec. 1720.
7	1720—24	" " 91	Ditto, 28 Dec. 1720 to 24 Nov. 1724.
8	1724—31	" " 92 Loose papers, Packet 24.	Ditto, 24 Nov. 1724 to 20 Dec. 1731.
9	1732—36	Range 424, No. 93. Loose papers, Packet 24. B. R., E E, Vol. 3.	Ditto, 6 Feb. 1732 to 2 July 1736.
10	1737—42	Range 424, No. 94. Loose papers, Packet 24.	Ditto, 28 June 1737 to 22 June 1742.
11	1742—45	Range 425, No. 1. Loose papers, Packet 24.	Ditto, 23 July 1742 to 22 July 1745.
12	1745—48	Range 425, No. 2	Ditto, 9 Aug. 1745 to 26 Jan. 1748.
13	1748—50	" " 3	Ditto, 2 Feb. 1748 to 9 April 1750.
14	1750—52	" " 4	Ditto, 15 April 1750 to 6 Jan. 1752.
15	1752	" " 5	Ditto, 13 Jan. to 18 Dec. 1752.
16	1753—54	" " 6	Ditto, 2 Jan. 1753 to 6 May 1754.
17	1754—56	" " 7	Ditto, 13 May 1754 to 14 June 1756.
18	1756—58	" " 8	Ditto, 29 June 1756 to 10 July 1758.
19	1758—59	" " 9	Ditto, 21 Aug. 1758 to 24 Dec. 1759.
20	1759—60	" " 10	Ditto, 31 Dec. 1759 to 15 Dec. 1760.

Index Number.	Date.	Previous Classification.	Nature of Documents.
21	1760—62	Range 425, No. 11	Consultations, 22 Dec. 1760 to 25 Jan. 1762.
22	1762—63	,, ,, 12	Ditto, 1 Feb. 1762 to 28 Feb. 1763.
23	1763—64	,, ,, 13	Ditto, 7 March 1763 to 28 May 1764.
24	1764—65	,, ,, 14	Ditto, 4 June 1764 to 14 Jan. 1765.
25	1765	,, ,, 15	Ditto, 21 Jan. to 18 Nov. 1765.
26	1765—66	,, ,, 16	Ditto, 25 Nov. 1765 to 3 Nov. 1766.
27	1766—67	,, ,, 17	Ditto, 10 Nov. 1766 to 14 Sept. 1767.
28	1767—68	,, ,, 18	Ditto, 17 Sept. 1767 to 5 Sept. 1768.
29	1768—69	,, ,, 19	Ditto, 12 Sept. 1768 to 27 Oct. 1769.
30	1769—70	,, ,, 20	Ditto, 30 Oct. 1769 to 6 Aug. 1770.
31	1770—71	,, ,, 21	Ditto, 13 Aug. 1770 to 8 July 1771.
32	1771	,, ,, 22	Ditto, 15 July to 4 Nov. 1771.
33	1771—72	,, ,, 23	Ditto, 11 Nov. 1771 to 30 Sept. 1772.
34	1772—73	,, ,, 24	Ditto, 7 Sept. 1772 to 27 Aug. 1773.
35	1773—75	,, ,, 25	Ditto, 1 Nov. 1773 to 11 Feb. 1775.
36	1775—76	,, ,, 26	Ditto, 13 Feb. 1775 to 28 March 1776.
37	1776	,, ,, 27	Ditto, 1 April to 9 Dec. 1776.
38	1776—78	,, ,, 28	Ditto, 16 Dec. 1776 to 7 March 1778.
39	1778	,, ,, 29	Ditto, 9 March to 21 Dec. 1778.
40	1779—80	,, ,, 30	Ditto, 4 Jan. 1779 to 29 May 1780.
41	1780—81	,, ,, 31	Ditto, 5 June 1780 to 28 July 1781.
42	1781—82	,, ,, 32	Ditto, 30 July 1781 to 3 Aug. 1782.
43	1782—83	,, ,, 33	Ditto, 5 Aug. 1782 to 5 June 1783.

Index Number.	Date.	Previous Classification.	Nature of Documents.
44	1783—84	Range 425, No. 34	Consultations, 9 June 1783 to 3 Jan. 1784.
45	1784	„ „ 35	Ditto, 5 Jan. to 21 Aug. 1784.
46	1784—85	„ „ 36	Ditto, 23 Aug. 1784 to 11 July 1785.
47	1785—86	„ „ 37	Ditto, 18 July 1785 to 19 June 1786.
48	1786—87	„ „ 38	Ditto, 26 June 1786 to 12 May 1787.
49	1787—88	„ „ 39	Ditto, 14 May 1787 to 22 March 1788.
50	1788—89	„ „ 40	Ditto, 24 March 1788 to 16 Feb. 1789.
51	1789—90	„ „ 41	Ditto, 23 Feb. 1789 to 6 March 1790.
52	1790	„ „ 42	Ditto, 8 March to 1 Dec. 1790.
53	1790—91	„ „ 43	Ditto, 6 Dec. 1790 to 8 Aug. 1791.
54	1791—92	„ „ 44	Ditto, 15 Aug. 1791 to 8 June 1792.
55	1792—93	„ „ 45	Ditto, 11 June 1792 to 8 May 1793.
56	1793—94	„ „ 46	Ditto, 13 May 1793 to 30 June 1794.
57	1794—95	„ „ 47	Ditto, 4 July 1794 to 14 May 1795.
58	1795—96	„ „ 48	Ditto, 18 May 1795 to 29 Feb. 1796.
59	1796—97	„ „ 49	Ditto, 2 March 1796 to 22 May 1797.
60	1797—98	Range 426, No. 1	Ditto, 29 May 1797 to 30 April 1798.
61	1798	„ „ 2	Ditto, 2 May to 5 Dec. 1798.
62	1798—99	„ „ 3	Ditto, 10 Dec. 1798 to 14 Nov. 1799.
63	1799—1801	„ „ 4	Ditto, 18 Nov. 1799 to 2 Feb. 1801.
64	1801	„ „ 5	Ditto, 9 Feb. to 21 Nov. 1801.
65	1801—02	„ „ 6	Ditto, 23 Nov. 1801 to 29 July 1802.
66	1802—03	„ „ 7 & 8 Loose papers, Packet 24.	Ditto, 2 Aug. 1802 to 29 July 1803.

Index Number.	Date.	Previous Classification.	Nature of Documents.
67	1803—04	Range 426, No. 9	Consultations, 1 Aug. 1803 to 31 March 1804.
68	1804	,, ,, 10	Ditto, 2 April to 10 Sept. 1804.
69	1804—05	,, 11	Ditto, 14 Sept. 1804 to 10 July 1805.
70	1805—06	,, ,, 12	Ditto, 12 July 1805 to 6 Sept. 1806.
71	1806—07	,, ,, 12A	Ditto, 8 Sept. 1806 to 26 Oct. 1807.
72	1807—08	,, ,, 13	Ditto, 2 Nov. 1807 to 16 July 1808.
73	1808—09	,, ,, 14	Ditto, 18 July 1808 to 8 May 1809.
74	1809—10	,, ,, 15	Ditto, 12 May 1809 to 8 Feb. 1810.
75	1810—11	,, ,, 16	Ditto, 12 Feb. 1810 to 2 Feb. 1811.
76	1811	,, ,, 17	Ditto, 4 Feb. to 20 Sept. 1811.
77	1811—12	,, ,, 18	Ditto, 23 Sept. 1811 to 28 Aug. 1812.
78	1812—13	,, ,, 19	Ditto, 7 Sept. 1812 to 18 June 1813.
79	1813—14	,, ,, 20	Ditto, 22 June 1813 to 21 March 1814.
80	1814—15	,, ,, 21	Ditto, 28 March 1814 to 12 June 1815.
81	1815—16	,, ,, 22	From 19 June 1815 to 4 March 1816.
82	1816—17	,, ,, 23	Ditto, 28 March 1816 to 24 Feb. 1817.
83	1817—18	,, ,, 25	Public Consultations, 3rd March 1817 to 18 May 1818.
84	1818—20	,, ,, 26	Ditto, 21 May 1818 to 7 Feb. 1820.
85	1820—21	,, ,, 27	Ditto, 14 Feb. 1820 to 21 July 1821.
86	1821—22	,, ,, 28	Ditto, 25 July 1821 to 17 June 1822.
87	1822—23	,, ,, 29	Ditto, 24 June 1822 to 1 May 1823.
88	1823	,, ,, 30	Ditto, 5 May 1823 to 17 Nov. 1823.
89	1823—24	,, ,, 31	Ditto, 20 Nov. 1823 to 30 Dec. 1824.

Index Number.	Date.	Previous Classification.	Nature of Documents.
90	1825	Range 426, No. 32	Public Consultations, 10 Jan. to 8 Dec. 1825, with Index.
91	1826	„ „ 33	Ditto, 2 Jan. to 14 Dec. 1826, with Index.
92	1827—28	„ „ 34	Ditto, 18 Jan. 1827 to 29 Dec. 1828, with Index.
93	1829	„ „ 35	Ditto, 8 Jan. to 28 Dec. 1829, with Index.
94	1830	„ „ 36	Ditto, 7 Jan. to 20 Dec. 1830, with Index.
95	1831—32	„ „ 37	Ditto, 3 Jan. 1831 to 20 Dec. 1832, with Index.
96	1833—36	„ „ 38 & 39	Ditto, 3 Jan. 1833 to 4 Feb. 1836, with Index for 1834 only.
97	1791—93	„ „ 70	Law Consultations, 20 Dec. 1791 to 2 March 1793.
98	1793—1801	„ „ 68 & 71	Quarter Sessions Proceedings, 16 Jan. 1793 to 7 Oct. 1801.
99	1798	„ „ 72	Proceedings of Courts of Inquiry, 1798.
100	1804—14	„ „ 69	Judicial Consultations, 11 July 1804 to 5 Oct. 1814.
101	1815—20	„ „ 24 & 67	Ditto, 2 Jan. 1815 to 24 Jan. 1820.
102	1820—26	„ „ 44	Ditto, 7 Feb. 1820 to 28 Dec. 1826, with Index for 1823-24.
103	1827—35	„ „ 45	Ditto, 18 Jan. 1827 to 19 March 1835, with Indexes for 1827-28-29-30-31-32 and 34.
104	1824—25	„ „ 49	Land Revenue Consultations, 15 March 1824 to 14 March 1825, with Index.
105	1824—28	„ „ 40	Military Consultations, 15 March 1824 to 22 Dec. 1828, with Index.
106	1829—32	„ „ 41	Ditto, 5 Jan. 1829 to 31 Dec. 1832, with Index.
107	1833—35	„ „ 42 & 43	Ditto, 21 Jan. 1833 to 29 June 1835, with Index for 1834.
108	1824—28	„ „ 46	Commercial Consultations, 1 March 1824 to 24 Dec. 1828, with Index.
109	1829—32	„ „ 47	Ditto, 8 Jan. 1829 to 31 Dec. 1832, with Index.
110	1833—36	„ „ 48 & 50	Ditto, 7 Jan. 1833 to 28 Dec. 1836, with Index for 1834.
111	1805—06	„ „ 66	Paymaster's Accounts, Civil and Military Servants, 30 Sept. 1805 to 30 June 1806.
112	1806—08	„ „ 51	Ditto, 1 July 1806 to 31 March 1808.

Index Number.	Date.	Previous Classification.	Nature of Documents.
113	1808—09	Range 426, No. 52	Paymaster's Accounts, Civil and Military Servants, 1 April 1808 to 30 Sept. 1809.
114	1810—12	" " 53	Ditto, 1 Jan. 1810 to 31 Dec. 1812.
115	1812—14	" " 54	Ditto, 1 June 1812 to 31 Dec. 1814.
116	1815—16	" " 55	Ditto, 1 Jan. 1815 to 31 Dec. 1816.
117	1817—19	" " 56	Ditto, 1 Jan. 1817 to 31 Dec. 1819.
118	1698—1724	Loose papers, Packet 24 and part of 33.	Original Letters, &c., from St. Helena to the Court, Oct. 1698 to Dec. 1724.
119	1725—30	" "	Ditto, Jan. 1725 to Dec. 1730.
120	1731—40	" "	Ditto, Jan. 1731 to Dec. 1740.
121	1741—47	" "	Ditto, Jan. 1741 to Dec. 1747.
122	1748—50	" "	Ditto, Jan. 1748 to Dec. 1750.
123	1751—54	" "	Ditto, Jan. 1751 to Dec. 1754.
124	1755—57	" "	Ditto, Jan. 1755 to Dec. 1757.
125	1758—60	" "	Ditto, Jan. 1758 to Dec. 1760.
126	1761—63	" "	Ditto, Jan. 1761 to Dec. 1763.
127	1764—67	" "	Ditto, Jan. 1764 to Dec. 1767.
128	1768—71	" "	Ditto, Jan. 1768 to Dec. 1771.
129	1772—73	" "	Ditto, Jan. 1772 to Dec. 1773.
130	1774—76	" "	Ditto, Jan. 1774 to Dec. 1776.
131	1777—86	" "	Ditto, Jan. 1777 to Dec. 1786.
132	1787—89	" "	Ditto, Jan. 1787 to Dec. 1789.
133	1790—91	" "	Ditto, Jan. 1790 to Dec. 1791.
134	1792—1801	" "	Ditto, April 1792 to Dec. 1801.
135	1802—03	" "	Ditto, Jan. 1802 to March 1803.

Index Number.	Date.	Previous Classification.	Nature of Documents.
136	1803—06	Loose papers, Packet 24 and part of 33.	Original Letters, &c., from St. Helena to the Court, April 1803 to Dec. 1806.
137	1807—09	" "	Ditto, Jan. 1807 to Dec. 1809.
138	1810—12	" "	Ditto, Jan. 1810 to Dec. 1812.
139	1814—18	Political Department.	Copies of Letters from St. Helena to the Court, 7 Sept. 1814 to 23 Jan. 1818.
140	1818—19		Ditto, with Index, 27 Jan. 1818 to 2 Oct. 1819.
141	1819—20	" "	Ditto, ditto, 3 Oct. 1819 to 30 Sept. 1820.
142	1820—22	" "	Ditto, ditto, 11 Nov. 1820 to 16 Dec. 1822.
143	1823—24	" "	Ditto, ditto, 11 Jan. 1823 to 30 Sept. 1824.
144	1824—27	" "	Ditto, ditto, 30 Dec. 1824 to 3 Nov. 1827.
145	1828—29	" "	Ditto, ditto, 1 Jan. 1828 to 24 Dec. 1829.
146	1828—29	Room 338	Original Letters, &c., from St. Helena to the Court, April 1828 to Aug. 1829.
147	1829—31	"	Ditto, Oct. 1829 to May 1831.
148	1831—32	Political Department.	Ditto, 4 June 1831 to 14 July 1832.
149	1834—36	Room 338	Ditto, Aug. 1834 to April 1836.
150	1820	"	Despatches from the Court to St. Helena, 7 Jan. to 16 Dec. 1820.
151	1820—21	"	Ditto, 21 Dec. 1820 to 11 July 1821.
152	1822	"	Ditto, 9 Jan. to 12 June 1822.
153	1822—23	"	Ditto, 18 Dec. 1822 to 20 Aug. 1823.
154	1823—24	"	Ditto, 5 Nov. 1823 to 29th Sept. 1824.
155	1824—25	"	Ditto, 10 Nov. 1824 to 3 Aug. 1825.
156	1825—27	"	Ditto, 26 Aug. 1825 to 11 Oct. 1827.
157	1827—29	"	Ditto, 31 Oct. 1827 to 2 Sept. 1829.
158	1829—35	"	Ditto, 4 Nov. 1829 to 21 Oct. 1835.

26464. I[1]

Index Number.	Date.	Previous Classification.	Nature of Documents.
159	1818—35	Political Department.	Committee Reports relative to St. Helena, 20 May 1818 to 11 March 1835.
160	1723—1802	Loose papers, Packet 24 and part of 33.	List of Packets, 1728 to 1802.
161	1722—1812	" "	Receipts for Packets, 1722 to 1812. Receipts for money, 1760 to 1811. Bills of Exchange, 1734 to 1808. Receipts for Lists of Packets, 1732 to 1811.
162	1815—17	Room 338	Correspondence relative to Bonaparte's removal to St. Helena, 21 July 1815 to 6 Sept. 1817.
163	1777—1813	Reports, &c., Range H. 30, No. 19. Unsorted papers, 224, 3030 B, 3163 B.	Miscellaneous Papers. Defences of St. Helena.
		Unsorted papers, 884—88, 1631—33, 1634, 1636—43.	Southern Whale Fishery.

Note.—For St. Helena Muster Rolls and Casualty Returns, 1789—1832, *see* List of Publications in Record Branch, p. 140.

SIAM.

Index Number.	Date.	Previous Classification.	Nature of Documents.
1	1679—83	B. R., DD, 10—13; YY 4.	Diary and Letters, 17 Nov. 1679 to 2 Nov. 1680; 1 Sept. 1681 to 18 Jan. 1682; 1 Sept. to 28 Nov. 1683. Copies of Letters despatched, 24 Oct. 1681 to 12 Feb. 1683. Copies of Letters received, Sept. 1678 to Aug. 1679.

STRAITS SETTLEMENTS.

Index Number.	Date.	Previous Classification.	Nature of Documents.
1	1769—95	Fisher's Papers, Nos. 162, 213, 382. Range H, 31, No. 39. Unrecorded Papers, Nos. 114, 716—19, 726—28, 917, 2942—46. Miscellaneous, 1769, 1780, 1784.	Miscellaneous Documents and Reports.
2	1786—87	Range 428, No. 63	Bengal Consultations relative to Prince of Wales Island, 2 March 1786 to 28 Dec. 1787.
3	1788—89	„ „ 64	Ditto, 25 Jan. 1788 to 23 Dec. 1789.
4	1790—91	„ „ 65	Ditto, 14 Jan. 1790 to 28 Dec. 1791.
5	1792—93	„ „ 66	Ditto, 11 Jan. 1792 to 20 Dec. 1793.
6	1794	„ „ 67	Ditto, 6 Jan. to 22 Dec. 1794.
7	1795	„ „ 68	Ditto, 19 Jan. to 9 Oct. 1795.
8	1805—12	Unrecorded Papers, No. 2707 Fisher's Papers, No. 331.	Establishment of a Court of Justice on Prince of Wales Island.
9	1805—10	Fisher's Papers, Nos. 248, 326, 336, 348. Unrecorded Papers, Nos. 2688–89, 2786–87, 2798, 3009.	Miscellaneous Documents and Reports.
10	1808—23	Loose papers, Packet 7. Range H, 47, Nos. 404, 405.	Letters, &c., from 10 June 1808 to 15 Jan. 1823.
11	1805	Range 428, No. 69	Prince of Wales Island Public Consultations, 20 Sept. to 8 Nov. 1805.
12	1805	„ „ 70	Ditto, 12 Nov. to 27 Dec. 1805.
13	1806	„ „ 71	Ditto, 2 Jan. to 31 July 1806.
14	1806	„ „ 72	Ditto, 1 Aug. to 7 Oct. 1806.
15	1806	„ „ 73	Ditto, 10 Oct. to 30 Dec. 1806.
16	1806	„ „ 74	Ditto, Appendix, 1806.
17	1807	„ „ 75	Ditto, 9 Jan. to 6 Aug. 1807.
18	1807	„ „ 76	Ditto, 13 Aug. to 29 Dec. 1807.
19	1808	„ „ 77	Ditto, 2 Jan. to 30 June 1808.
20	1808	„ „ 78	Ditto, 7 July to 29 Dec. 1808.

Index Number.	Date.	Previous Classification.	Nature of Documents.
21	1808	Range 428, No. 79	Prince of Wales Island Public Consultations, Index, 1808.
22	1809	" " 80	Ditto, 5 Jan. to 29 June 1809.
23	1809	" " 81	Ditto, 6 July to 28 Dec. 1809.
24	1809	" " 84	Ditto, Appendix, 1809.
25	1809	" " 85	Ditto, Index, 1809.
26	1810	" " 82	Ditto, 4 Jan. to 14 June 1810.
27	1810	" " 83	Ditto, 22 June to 29 Dec. 1810.
28	1810	" " 86	Ditto, Index, 1810.
29	1810	" " 87	Ditto, Appendix, 1810.
30	1811	" " 88	Ditto, 3 Jan. to 27 June 1811.
31	1811	" " 89	Ditto, 4 July to 26 Dec. 1811.
32	1811	" " 90	Ditto, Index, 1811.
33	1811	" " 91	Ditto, Appendix, 1811.
34	1812	" " 92	Ditto, 2 Jan. to 27 June 1812.
35	1812	" " 93	Ditto, 2 July to 31 Dec. 1812.
36	1812	" " 94	Ditto, Index, 1812.
37	1812	" " 95	Ditto, Appendix, 1812.
38	1813	" " 96	Ditto, 7 Jan. to 27 March 1813.
39	1813	" " 97	Ditto, 1 April to 24 June 1813.
40	1813	" " 98	Ditto, 1 July to 28 Sept. 1813.
41	1813	" " 99	Ditto, 30 Sept. to 30 Dec. 1813.
42	1813	" " 100	Ditto, Appendix, 1813.
43	1814	" " 101	Ditto, 6 Jan. to 30 April 1814.

Index Number.	Date.	Previous Classification.	Nature of Documents.
44	1814	Range 428, No. 102	Prince of Wales Island Public Consultations, 7 May to 25 Aug. 1814.
45	1814	„ „ 103	Ditto, 1 Sept. to 27 Dec. 1814.
46	1814	„ „ 104	Ditto, Appendix, 1814.
47	1814	„ „ 105	Ditto, Index, 1814.
48	1815	„ „ 106	Ditto, 11 Jan. to 30 March 1815.
49	1815	„ „ 107	Ditto, 6 April to 12 July 1815.
50	1815	„ , 108	Ditto, 21 July to 24 Aug. 1815.
51	1815	„ „ 109	Ditto, 31 Aug. to 28 Dec. 1815.
52	1815	„ „ 110	Ditto, Appendix, 1815.
53	815	„ „ 111	Ditto, Index, 1815.
54	1816	„ „ 112	Ditto, 6 Jan. to 23 March 1816.
55	1816	„ „ 113	Ditto, 3 April to 29 June 1816.
56	1816	„ „ 114	Ditto, 6 July to 28 Sept. 1816.
57	1816	„ „ 115	Ditto, 5 Oct. to 26 Dec. 1816.
58	1816	„ „ 116	Ditto, Index, 1816.
59	1816	„ „ 117	Ditto, Appendix, 1816.
60	1817	„ „ 118	Ditto, 2 Jan. to 19 April 1817.
61	1817	„ „ 119	Ditto, 3 May to 4 Sept. 1817.
62	1817	„ „ 120	Ditto, 11 Sept. to 30 Oct. 1817.
63	1817	Range 429, No. 1	Ditto, Index, 1817.
64	1817	„ „ 2	Ditto, Appendix, 1817.
65	1818	„ „ 3	Ditto, 3 Jan. to 3 April 1818.
66	1818	„ „ 4	Ditto, 11 April to 29 Aug. 1818.

Index Number.	Date.	Previous Classification.	Nature of Documents.
67	1818	Range 429, No. 5	Prince of Wales Island Public Consultations, 5 Sept. to 29 Oct. 1818.
68	1818	" " 6	Ditto, 9 Nov. to 31 Dec. 1818.
69	1818	" " 7	Ditto, Index and Appendix, 1818.
70	1819	" " 8	Ditto, 6 Jan. to 27 May 1819.
71	1819	" " 9	Ditto, 18 June to 26 Aug. 1819.
72	1819	" " 10	Ditto, 26 Aug. to 23 Dec. 1819.
73	1819	" " 11	Ditto, Index, 1819.
74	1820	" " 12	Ditto, 6 Jan. to 22 April 1820.
75	1820	" " 13	Ditto, 4 May to 27 July 1820.
76	1820	" " 14	Ditto, 10 Aug. to 19 Oct. 1820.
77	1820	" " 15	Ditto, 19 Oct. to 28 Dec. 1820.
78	1820	" " 16	Ditto, Index, 1820.
79	1821	" " 17	Ditto, 11 Jan. to 28 June 1821.
80	1821	" " 18	Ditto, 6 July to 29 Nov. 1821.
81	1821	" " 19	Ditto, 13 to 27 Dec. 1821.
82	1821	" " 20	Ditto, Index, 1821.
83	1821	" " 21	Ditto, Appendix, 1821.
84	1822	" " 22	Ditto, 10 Jan. to 21 March 1822.
85	1822	" " 23	Ditto, 4 April to 27 June 1822.
86	1822	" " 24	Ditto, 8 July to 31 Oct. 1822.
87	1822	" " 25	Ditto, 14 Nov. to 26 Dec. 1822.
88	1822	" " 26	Ditto, Index, 1822.
89	1823	" " 27	Ditto, 9 Jan. to 17 April 1823.

Index Number.	Date.	Previous Classification.	Nature of Documents.
90	1823	Range 439, No. 28	Prince of Wales Island Public Consultations, 1 May to 21 Aug. 1823.
91	1823	" " 29	Ditto, 1 Sept. to 26 Dec. 1823.
92	1823	" " 30	Ditto, Index, 1823.
93	1823	" " 72–74, 76, 77	Ditto, Appendices, 1823.
94	1824	" " 31	Ditto, 8 Jan. to 27 May 1824.
95	1824	" " 32	Ditto, 10 June to 2 Sept. 1824.
96	1824	" " 33	Ditto, 14 Sept. to 16 Dec. 1824.
97	1824	" " 34	Ditto, Index, 1824.
98	1824	" " 78–79	Ditto, Appendices, 1824.
99	1825	" " 35	Ditto, 4 Jan. to 10 March 1825.
100	1825	" " 36	Ditto, 11 March to 26 April 1825.
101	1825	" " 37	Ditto, 3 May to 10 June 1825.
102	1825	" " 38	Ditto, 10 June to 4 Aug. 1825.
103	1825	" " 39	Ditto, 13 Aug. to 29 Sept. 1825.
104	1825	" " 40	Ditto, 7 Oct. to 24 Nov. 1825.
105	1825	" " 41	Ditto, 1 to 29 Dec. 1825.
106	1825	" " 42	Ditto, Index, 1825.
107	1825	" " 80	Ditto, Appendix, 1825.
108	1826	" " 43	Ditto, 5 Jan. to 16 March 1826.
109	1826	" " 44	Ditto, 23 March to 4 May 1826.
110	1826	" " 45	Ditto, 11 May to 14 Aug. 1826.
111	1826	" " 46	Ditto, 21 Aug. to 26 Oct. 1826.
112	1826	" " 47	Ditto, 2 Nov. to 22 Dec. 1826.

Index Number.	Date.	Previous Classification.	Nature of Documents.
113	1826	Range 429, No. 48	Prince of Wales Island Public Consultations, Index, 1826.
114	1826	„ „ 49	Ditto, Appendix, 1826.
115	1827	„ „ 50	Ditto, 2 Jan. to 15 Feb. 1827.
116	1827	„ „ 51	Ditto, 26 Feb. to 9 April 1827.
117	1827	„ „ 52	Ditto, 12 April to 16 Aug. 1827.
118	1827	„ „ 53	Ditto, 23 Aug. to 6 Nov. 1827.
119	1827	„ „ 54	Ditto, 14 Nov. to 27 Dec. 1827.
120	1827	„ „ 55	Ditto, Index, 1827.
121	1827	„ „ 56	Ditto, Appendix, 1827.
122	1828	„ „ 57	Ditto, 3 Jan. to 21 April 1828.
123	1828	„ „ 58	Ditto, 25 April to 5 Aug. 1828.
124	1828	„ „ 59	Ditto, 14 Aug. to 7 Oct. 1828.
125	1828	„ „ 60	Ditto, 20 Oct. to 30 Dec. 1828.
126	1828	„ „ 61	Ditto, Index, 1828.
127	1829	„ „ 62	Ditto, 3 Jan. to 24 March 1829.
128	1829	„ „ 63	Ditto, 7 April to 25 May 1829.
129	1829	„ „ 64	Ditto, 8 June to 17 Aug. 1829.
130	1829	„ „ 65	Ditto, 18 Aug. to 26 Dec. 1829.
131	1829	„ „ 66	Ditto, Index, 1829.
132	1830	„ „ 67	Ditto, 2 Jan. to 21 April 1830.
133	1830	„ „ 68	Ditto, 29 April to 30 June 1830.
134	1830	„ „ 69	Ditto, Index, 1830.
135	1806	„ „ 70	Prince of Wales Island Secret and Political Consultations, 9 Jan. to 30 Dec. 1806.

Index Number.	Date.	Previous Classification.	Nature of Documents.
136	1807	Range 429, No. 71	Prince of Wales Island Secret and Political Consultations, 9 Jan. to 29 Dec. 1807, with Index.
137	1808—18	Political Department and unnumbered.	Ditto, 2 Jan. 1808 to 22 March 1811; 17 May to 4 Nov. 1813; 26 Feb. 1818.
138	1826	Range 429, No. 81	Ditto, 1 June to 5 Oct. 1826.
139	1826	„ „ 82	Ditto, 19 Oct. to 18 Dec. 1826.
140	1826	„ „ 83	Ditto, Index, 1826.
141	1827	„ „ 84	Ditto, 31 Jan. to 29 Aug. 1827.
142	1827	„ „ 85	Ditto, 30 Aug. to 27 Dec. 1827.
143	1827	„ „ 86	Ditto, Index, 1827.
144	1828	„ „ 87	Ditto, 3 Jan. to 26 Nov. 1828, with Index.
145	1829	„ „ 88	Ditto, 8 Jan. to 7 July 1829, with Index.
146	1806	„ „ 90	Prince of Wales Island Marine Consultations, 9 Jan. to 30 Dec. 1806 with Index.
147	1806	„ „ 91	Ditto, Appendix, 1806.
148	1807	„ „ 96	Ditto, 9 Jan. to 26 Dec. 1807, with Index.
149	1808	„ „ 97	Ditto, 2 Jan. to 29 Dec. 1808, with Index.
150	1809	„ „ 98	Ditto, 5 Jan. to 14 Dec. 1809.
151	1806	„ „ 92	Prince of Wales Island Military Consultations, 9 Jan. to 26 Dec. 1806.
152	1807	„ „ 95	Ditto, 9 Jan. to 16 Dec. 1807, with Index.
153	1827	„ „ 99	Singapore Diary, 4 Jan. to 3 May 1827.
154	1827	„ „ 100	Ditto, 8 May to 22 June 1827.
155	1827	„ „ 101	Ditto, 23 June to 31 Dec. 1827.
156	1828	„ „ 102	Ditto, 2 Jan. to 5 June 1828.
157	1828	Range 430, No. 1	Ditto, 7 June to 29 Dec. 1828.
158	1828	„ „ 2	Ditto, Index, 1828.

26464. R

Index Number.	Date.	Previous Classification.	Nature of Documents.
159	1829	Range 430, No. 3	Singapore Diary, 2 Jan. to 29 June 1829.
160	1829	" " 4	Ditto, 1 July to 31 Dec. 1829.
161	1829	" " 5	Ditto. Index, 1829.
162	1830	" " 6	Ditto, 1 Jan. to 30 June 1830.
163	1827	" " 7	Singapore Political and Secret Consultations, 26 May to 19 June 1827, with Index.
164	1828	" " 8	Ditto, 8 to 18 Feb. 1828, with Index.
165	1826—27	" " 9	Malacca Diary, 15 Aug. 1826 to 25 June 1827.
166	1826—27	" " 10	Ditto, Index, 15 Aug. 1826 to 25 June 1827.
167	1827	" " 12	Ditto, 6 July to 28 Dec. 1827, with Index.
168	1828	" " 13	Ditto, 2 Jan. to 26 Dec. 1828, with Index.
169	1829	" " 14	Ditto, 2 Jan. to 31 Dec. 1829.
170	1829	" " 15	Ditto, Index, 1829.
171	1830	" " 16	Ditto, 2 Jan. to 12 July 1830, with Index.
172	1827	" " 11	Malacca Public Consultations, 26 June to 5 July 1827, with Index.
173	1828	" " 17	Malacca Political Consultations, 21 Jan to 20 June 1828.
174	1826—27	" " 18	Malacca Journal and Ledger, 1 Aug. 1826 to 30 April 1827.
175	1827—28	" " 19	Ditto, 1 May 1827 to 30 April 1828.
176	1828—29	" " 20	Ditto, 1 May 1828 to 30 April 1829.
177	1829—30	" " 21	Ditto, 1 May 1829 to 30 April 1830.
178	1830	" " 22	Ditto, 1 May to 31 July 1830.
179	1805—09	Room 338, No. 1360	Letters received from Prince of Wales Island, 12 Nov. 1805 to 4 April 1809.
180	1809—14	" " 1361	Ditto, 2 Aug. 1809 to 4 Feb. 1814.
181	1814—18	" " 1362	Ditto, 21 Sept. 1814 to 3 April 1818.

Index Number.	Date.	Previous Classification.	Nature of Documents.
182	1818—20	Room 338, No. 1363	Letters received from Prince of Wales Island, 6 May 1818 to 6 Dec. 1820.
183	1821—25	„ „ 1364	Ditto, 28 June 1821 to 14 Oct. 1825.
184	1826—30	„ „ 1365	Ditto, 1 Feb. 1826 to 19 Nov. 1830.
185	1805—30	Room 337	Ditto, Abstracts, 12 Nov. 1805 to 30 June 1830.
186	1805—08	Room 338, No. 1366	Despatches to Prince of Wales Island, 18 April 1805 to 7 Sept. 1808.
187	1809—11	„ „ 1367	Ditto, 11 Jan. 1809 to 10 July 1811.
188	1811—13	„ „ 1368	Ditto, 19 Sept. 1811 to 6 Sept. 1813.
189	1813—15	„ „ 1369	Ditto, 12 Nov. 1813 to 18 Feb. 1815.
190	1815—16	„ „ 1370	Ditto, 6 March 1815 to 24 Dec. 1816.
191	1817—18	„ „ 1371	Ditto, 3 Jan. 1817 to 16 Dec. 1818.
192	1819—22	„ „ 1372	Ditto, 15 Jan. 1819 to 31 May 1822.
193	1822—24	„ „ 1373	Ditto, 17 July 1822 to 31 Dec. 1824.
194	1825—28	„ „ 1374	Ditto, 2 Feb. 1825 to 29 Feb. 1828.
195	1828—30	„ „ 1375	Ditto, 18 March 1828 to 12 May 1830.
196	1805—30	Room 337	Ditto, Abstracts, 18 April 1805 to 12 May 1830.

SUMATRA.

Index Number.	Date.	Previous Classification.	Nature of Documents.
1	1615—16 1685—86	B. R., FF, 11., 4—11, 5—11 B. R., Y Y 1, 5.	Early fragments. Copies of Letters sent from York Fort (partly in duplicate in Borneo, 1), 29 Sept. 1685 to 18 Sept. 1686.
2	1685—92	B. R., D D b, 5, 6, 8	Copies of Letters and Consultations, York Fort, Indrapora, &c., 1 Nov. 1685 to 31 Dec. 1692.
3	1695—96	B. R., Y Y, 3	Diary and Consultations, York Fort and Tryamong, 19 June 1695 to — Feb. 1696.
4	1699—1703	B. R., Y Y, 4, 5 B. R., D D c, 6, 7 B. R., E E, 2	York Fort Diary and Consultations, 4 June 1699 to Jan. 1703.
5	1701—04	B. R., Y Y, 6, 7, 8	Letters from York Fort, 14 April 1701 to 20 Dec. 1703. Letters to York Fort, 6 June 1701 to 28 Jan. 1703. Bencoolen Diary, 1703–04.
6	1703—10	B. R., U, c, 1	York Fort Letters and Consultations, 1 Feb. 1703 to 14 Nov. 1710.
7	1704—18	Unclassified	Abstracts of Letters from Sumatra, 21 March 1704 to 19 June 1718.*
8	1711—37	Loose papers, Packet 5; and B. R., U, c, 1.	York Fort† Letters and Consultations, 7 Feb. 1711 to 24 Dec. 1737.
9	1740—53	Loose papers, Packet 5; B. R., U, c, 1, and Y Y, 2.,	Letters, &c., from Fort Marlborough, 6 Jan. 1740 to 31 Dec. 1753.
10	1754—56	Loose papers, Packet 5; and B. R., U, c, 1.	Letters, &c., from Fort Marlborough, 11 Feb. 1754 to 17 July 1756.
11	1757—58	Ditto, ditto	Ditto, 28 Jan. 1757 to 31 Dec. 1758.
12	1759—62	Loose papers, Packet 5. Unrecorded Papers, No. 1518.	Ditto, Jan. 1759 to 4 Nov. 1762. Charter of Justice for Bencoolen, and Counsel's opinion.
13	1763—65	Loose papers, Packet 5 B. R., U, c, 1.	Ditto, 3 Jan. 1763 to 24 Dec. 1765.
14	1766—72	Ditto, ditto	Ditto, 18 April 1766 to 23 Dec. 1772.
15	1772—73	Range C, No. 60	Fort St. George Diary and Proceedings, 7 Jan. 1772 to 16 Jan. 1773, relative to Settlement at Achin.
16	1773—76	Loose papers, Packet 5	Letters, &c., from Fort Marlborough, 25 Jan. 1773 to 28 Aug. 1776.
17	1777—81	Ditto, ditto	Ditto, 15 Jan. 1777 to 12 Oct. 1781.
18	1778—80	Range E, Nos. 12, 15, 17	Fort Marlborough Committee's Proceedings, 23 Nov. 1778 to Oct. 1780.
19	1778—80	Range E, Nos. 24, 25	Fort Marlborough Select Committee's Letters, 16 Dec. 1778 to 8 Sept. 1780.
20	1779—81	Range E, Nos. 13, 18	Fort Marlborough Select Committee's Consultations, 4 June 1779 to 7 Oct. 1781.

* *See also* Java, 7.

† York Fort was superseded by "Fort Marlborough" in 1714.

Index Number.	Date.	Previous Classification.	Nature of Documents.
21	1765—1801	Unclassified	Paragraphs, &c., for Fort Marlborough, 25 Jan. 1765 to 2 Jan. 1801.
22	1783—91	Range I, No. 20; also B. R., U, b, 3.	Bencoolen Letters received, 5 Sept. 1783 to 13 Sept. 1791.
23	1781—98	Loose papers, Packet 5 B.R., U, c, 1. Unrecorded Papers, No. 714	Letters, &c., from Fort Marlborough, 14 April 1781 to 8 Sept. 1798. Also appointment of Mr. Kinlock to be Resident at Achin.
24	1799—1808	Ditto, ditto	Ditto, 10 Jan. 1799 to 30 Dec. 1808.
25	1792—1804	Range I, No. 21; also B. R., U, b, 4.	Bencoolen Letters received, 18 March 1792 to 6 June 1804.
26	1790—1811	Unclassified	Abstracts of Letters to Bencoolen, 19 May 1790 to 18 Sept. 1811.
27 in duplicate.	1814	B. R., U, c, 2 and Range K, No. 72.	Captain Canning's Mission to Achin.
28	1809—19	Loose papers, Packet 5 B. R., U, c, 1.	Fort Marlborough Letters and Consultations, 30 April 1809 to 1 Sept. 1819.
29	1820—25	Ditto, ditto	Ditto, 7 Jan. 1820 to 4 July 1825.
30	1801—21	Unrecorded Papers, Nos. 2406 and 2764. Range H, Nos. 44—46, 47.	Miscellaneous Papers.
31	1754—65	Room No. 338	Rough drafts of Despatches from the Court to Fort Marlborough, 27 Nov. 1754 to 25 Jan. 1765.
32	1766—70	Ditto	Ditto, 15 Jan. 1766 to 23 Nov. 1770.
33	1771—77	Ditto	Ditto, 11 Jan. 1771 to 5 Feb. 1777.
34	1778—83	Ditto	Ditto, 6 Nov. 1778 to 11 April 1783.
35	1783—87	Ditto	Ditto, 10 Sept. 1783 to 31 July 1787.
36	1787—94	Ditto	Ditto, 28 Dec. 1787 to 2 July 1794.
37	1795—97	Ditto	Ditto, 15 April 1795 to 1 July 1797.
38	1798—1803	Ditto	Ditto, 20 April 1798 to 24 Jan. 1803.
39	1804—12	Ditto	Ditto, 23 Jan. 1804 to 22 July 1812.
40	1812—16	Ditto	Ditto, 19 Dec. 1812 to 13 Dec. 1816.
41	1817—20	Ditto	Ditto, 6 Jan. 1817 to 29 Dec. 1820.
42	1821—25	Ditto	Ditto, 4 Jan. 1821 to 8 Feb. 1825.
43	1784—1801	Ditto	Fair copies of General Despatches from the Court to Fort Marlborough, 10 Dec. 1784 to 8 April 1801.

Index Number.	Date.	Previous Classification.	Nature of Documents.
43A	1784—1801	Unclassified	Draft paragraphs to Fort Marlborough submitted by the Court to the Board of Control, 10 Dec. 1784 to 7 May 1801.
44	1760—98	Room No. 338	Abstracts of Letters from Fort Marlborough to the Court, 11 Aug. 1760 to 3 Jan. 1798.
45	1793—1805	Ditto	Original Letters from Fort Marlborough to the Court, 11 Nov. 1793 to 1 July 1805.
46	1805—18	Ditto	Ditto, 15 Nov. 1805 to 20 March 1818.
47	1818—19	Ditto	Ditto, 22 March 1818 to 2 Oct. 1819.
48	1818—21	Ditto	Ditto, 22 March 1818 to 25 Oct. 1821.
49	1822—25	Ditto	Ditto, 1 Jan. 1822 to 4 July 1825.
50	1819—21	Ditto	Original Letters from Sir Stamford Raffles to the Secretary, East India Company, 8 Oct. 1819 to 12 Dec. 1821.
51	1821—24	Ditto	Copies of ditto, 30 Nov. 1821 to 27 Dec. 1824.
52	1785—1800	Ditto	Abstracts of Bengal Correspondence respecting Fort Marlborough, 11 April 1785 to 10 Jan. 1800.
53	1792—98	Ditto	Letters from Bengal to Fort Marlborough, 8 Feb. 1792 to 1 Jan. 1798.
54	1792—1800	Ditto	Letters from Fort Marlborough to Bengal, 24 March 1792 to 10 Jan. 1800.
55	1818—21	Ditto	Letters to Fort Marlborough from various places, Feb. 1818 to Jan. 1821.
56	1705—10	Range 16, No. 74	Fort Marlborough Public Consultations, 6 Feb. 1705 to 31 Dec. 1710.
57	1711—16	" " 75	Ditto, 1 Jan. 1711 to 4 Aug. 1716.
58	1716—23	" " 76	Ditto, 29 Sept. 1716 to 12 Jan. 1723.
59	1723—27	" " 77	Ditto, 4 Sept. 1723 to 10 April 1727.
60	1727—31	Range 17, No. 1	Ditto, 26 April 1727 to 7 Jan. 1731.
61	1731—35	" " 2	Ditto, 13 Jan. 1731 to 20 Dec. 1735.
62	1735—39	" " 3	Ditto, 24 Dec. 1735 to 19 Dec. 1739.
63	1739—45	" " 4	Ditto, 26 Dec. 1739 to 21 Jan. 1745.
64	1744—48	" " 5	Ditto, 28 Dec. 1744 to 13 Jan. 1748.
65	1748—51	" " 6	Ditto, 26 Jan. 1748 to 24 Dec. 1751.

Index Number.	Date.	Previous Classification.	Nature of Documents.
66	1751—53	Range 17, No. 7	Fort Marlborough Public Consultations, 11 Dec. 1751 to 31 Dec. 1753.
67	1754—55	„ „ 8	Ditto, 3 Jan. 1754 to 6 Jan. 1755.
68	1755	„ „ 9	Ditto, 10 Jan. to 31 Dec. 1755.
69	1756	„ „ 10	Ditto, 1 Jan. to 31 Dec. 1756.
70	1758—69	„ „ 11	Ditto, 3 Jan. 1758 to 5 Feb. 1760.
71	1762—63	„ „ 12	Ditto, 4 Feb. 1762 to 30 Dec. 1763.
72	1764	„ „ 13	Ditto, pro Anno 1764.
73	1765	„ „ 14	Ditto, ditto, 1765.
74	1766	„ „ 15	Ditto, ditto, 1766.
75	1767	„ „ 16	Ditto, ditto, 1767.
76	1768—69	„ „ 17	Ditto, 4 Jan. 1768 to 3 Jan. 1769.
77	1769—70	„ „ 18	Ditto, 7 Jan. 1769 to 12 Jan. 1770.
78	1770—71	„ „ 19	Ditto, 12 Jan. 1770 to 6 March 1771.
79	1771—72	„ „ 20	Ditto, 18 May 1771 to 25 Dec. 1772.
80	1773—74	„ „ 21	Ditto, 6 Jan. 1773 to 31 Dec. 1774.
81	1774—76	„ „ 22	Ditto, 13 Aug. 1774 to 5 Feb. 1776.
82	1776	„ „ 23	Ditto, 5 Jan. to 30 Dec. 1776, with Index.
83	1777—78	„ „ 24	Ditto, 28 July 1777 to 28 Aug. 1778.
84	1778—79	„ „ 25	Ditto, 30 Aug. 1778 to 6 June 1779.
85	1780—81	„ „ 26	Ditto, 20 Oct. 1780 to 7 Oct. 1781.
86	1781—83	„ „ 27	Ditto, 16 Oct. 1781 to 8 March 1783, with Index.
87	1783	„ „ 28	Ditto, 22 March to 4 Oct. 1783.
88	1783—85	„ „ 29	Ditto, 13 Oct. 1783 to 28 Feb. 1785.

Index Number.	Date.	Previous Classification.	Nature of Documents.
89	1785—87	Range 17, No. 30	Fort Marlborough Public Consultations, 10 March 1785 to 3 Jan. 1787.
90	1787—88	„ „ 31	Ditto, 15 Jan. 1787 to 3 March 1788.
91	1788—89	„ „ 32	Ditto, 22 March 1788 to 14 April 1789.
92	1789—90	„ „ 33	Ditto, 18 April 1789 to 23 March 1790.
93	1790—92	„ „ 34	Ditto, 30 March 1790 to 31 May 1792.
94	1792—93	„ „ 35	Ditto, 8 June 1792 to 9 Nov. 1793.
95	1793—95	„ „ 36	Ditto, 12 Nov. 1793 to 12 March 1795.
96	1795—96	„ „ 37	Ditto, 31 March 1795 to 13 Aug. 1796.
97	1796—97	„ „ 38	Ditto, 19 Aug. 1796 to 6 Sept. 1797.
98	1797—99	„ „ 39	Ditto, 8 Sept. 1797 to 20 Jan. 1799.
99	1799—1800	„ „ 40	Ditto, 18 Jan. 1799 to 29 Jan. 1800.
100	1800	„ „ 41	Ditto, 29 Jan. to 25 Dec. 1800.
101	1801	„ „ 42	Ditto, 1 Jan. to 31 Aug. 1801.
102	1801—02	„ „ 43	Ditto, 31 Aug. 1801 to 27 Feb. 1802.
103	1802	„ „ 44	Ditto, 28 Feb. to 3 Dec. 1802, with Index.
104	1802—03	„ „ 45	Ditto, Dec. 1802 to Dec. 1803.
105	1804	„ „ 46	Ditto, pro Anno 1804.
106	1805	„ „ 47	Ditto, Jan. to Sept. 1805.
107	1805	„ „ 48	Ditto, Oct. to Dec. 1805.
108	1806	„ „ 49	Ditto, 1 Jan. to 31 July 1806.
109	1806	„ „ 50	Ditto, 1 Aug. to 31 Dec. 1806.
110	1807	„ „ 51	Ditto, 1 Jan. to 29 April 1807.
111	1807	„ „ 52	Ditto, 1 May to 30 Aug. 1807.

Index Number.	Date.	Previous Classification.	Nature of Documents.
112	1807—08	Range 17, No. 53	Fort Marlborough Public Consultations, 1 Sept. 1807 to 25 March 1808.
113	1808	" " 54	Ditto, 1 April to 30 June 1808.
114	1808	" " 55	Ditto, 1 July to 30 Sept. 1808.
115	1808	" " 56	Ditto, 1 Oct. to 31 Dec. 1808.
116	1809	" " 57	Ditto, 1 Jan. to 31 March 1809.
117	1809	" " 58	Ditto, 1 April to 30 June 1809.
118	1809	" " 59	Ditto, 1 July to 30 Sept. 1809.
119	1809	" " 60	Ditto, 1 Oct. to 26 Dec. 1809.
120	1810	" " 61	Ditto, 1 Jan. to 28 Feb. 1810.
121	1810	" " 62	Ditto, 1 March to 31 May 1810.
122	1810	" " 63	Ditto, 1 June to 31 Aug. 1810.
123	1810	Range 18, No. 1	Ditto, 1 Sept. to 29 Dec. 1810.
124	1811	" " 2	Ditto, 1 Jan. to 30 June 1811.
125	1811	" " 3	Ditto, 1 July to 31 Dec. 1811.
126	1812	" " 4	Ditto, 2 Jan. to 30 June 1812.
127	1812	" " 5	Ditto, 1 July to 31 Dec. 1812.
128	1813	" " 6	Ditto, 1 Jan. to 1 March 1813.
129	1813	" " 7	Ditto, 2 March to 31 July 1813.
130	1813	" " 8	Ditto, 4 Aug. to 31 Dec. 1813.
131	1814	" " 9	Ditto, 1 Jan. to 30 March 1814, with Index.
132	1814	" " 10	Ditto, 2 April to 30 June 1814, with Index.
133	1814	" " 11	Ditto, 1 July to 30 Sept. 1814, with Index.
134	1814	" " 12	Ditto, 1 Oct. to 31 Dec. 1814, with Index.

26464. T

Index Number.	Date.	Previous Classification.	Nature of Documents.
135	1815	Range 18, No. 13	Fort Marlborough Public Consultations, 2 Jan. to 31 March 1815, with Index.
136	1815	" " 14	Ditto, 1 April to 30 June 1815.
137	1815	" " 15	Ditto, 1 July to 30 Sept. 1815.
138	1815	" " 16	Ditto, 2 Oct. to 31 Dec. 1815.
139	1816	" " 17	Ditto, 1 Jan. to 28 Feb. 1816.
140	1816	" " 18	Ditto, 1 March to 30 April 1816.
141	1816	" " 19	Ditto, 1 May to 29 June 1816.
142	1816	" " 20	Ditto, 1 July to 30 Aug. 1816.
143	1816	" " 21	Ditto, 2 Sept. to 30 Oct. 1816.
144	1816	" " 22	Ditto, 1 Nov. to 31 Dec. 1816.
145	1817	" " 23	Ditto, 1 Jan. to 31 March 1817.
146	1817	" " 24	Ditto, 1 April to 30 June 1817.
147	1817	" " 25	Ditto, 1 July to 30 Sept. 1817.
148	1817	" " 26	Ditto, 1 Oct. to 31 Dec. 1817.
149	1818	" " 27	Ditto, 1 Jan. to 28 Feb. 1818.
150	1782—88	" " 28	Fort Marlborough Military Consultations, 6 July 1782 to 31 Oct. 1788.
151	1794—96	" " 29	Ditto, 3 June 1794 to 13 Aug. 1796.
152	1766—79	" " 30	Fort Marlborough Wills, Commissions, Courts-martial, &c.: Register, 10 Jan. 1766 to 27 March 1779.
153	1779—91	" " 31	Ditto, 7 April 1779 to 23 June 1791.
154	1791—1803	" " 32	Ditto, 22 July 1791 to 10 Nov. 1803.
155	1803—10	" " 33	Ditto, 19 Nov. 1803 to 10 April 1810.
156	1786—87	" " 34	Bengal Consultations relative to Fort Marlborough, 21 Feb. 1786 to 28 Dec. 1787.
157	1788	" " 35	Ditto, 6 Feb. to 29 Dec. 1788.

Index Number.	Date.	Previous Classification.	Nature of Documents.
158	1789	Range 18, No. 36	Bengal Consultations relative to Fort Marlborough, 5 Jan. to 31 Dec. 1789.
159	1790—91	" " 37	Ditto, 14 Jan. 1790 to 30 Dec. 1791.
160	1792—93	" " 38	Ditto, 4 Jan. 1792 to 23 Dec. 1793.
161	1794	" " 39	Ditto, 5 Jan. to 29 Dec. 1794.
162	1795	" " 40	Ditto, 2 Jan. to 31 Aug. 1795.

SURAT.

Index Number.	Date.	Previous Classification.	Nature of Documents.
1	1622—36	B. R., DD —	Consultations (with copies of Commissions): 20 July 1622; 30 Dec. 1622 to 9 Jan. 1624; 16 March 1625 to 20 Feb. 1626; 14 April 1628 (Commission only); 10 Oct. to 18 Dec. 1628.
		GG, a, 1	Ditto, 29 Dec. 1631 to 10 April 1632.
		2	Ditto, 3 Dec. 1632 to 25 Sept. 1633.
		3	Ditto, 12 Nov. 1633 to 8 Dec. 1634.
		DD, a, 3	Ditto, 23 Dec. 1634 to 2 Oct. 1635; 20 Nov. 1635 to 3 Sept. 1636.
2	1660—66	B. R., GG, a, 4	Consultations (with copies of Commissions): 12 Jan. 1660 to 17 Jan. 1661.
		5	Ditto, 3 Jan. to 26 Aug. 1662.
		6	Ditto, 6 Dec. 1662 to 6th Nov. 1663.
		7	Ditto, 10 Dec. 1663 to 22 Feb. 1665.
		8	Ditto, 14 March 1665 to 14 July 1666 (and correspondence with Captain James Baker, commencing 15 Dec. 1664).
3	1669 75	B. R., GG, a, 9	Consultations (with copies of Commissions): 25 Nov. 1669 to 21 Dec. 1670.
		10	Ditto, 30 May to 30 Dec. 1672.
		12	Ditto, 6 Jan. 1673 to 2 Jan., 1674.
		13	Ditto, 12 Jan. 1674 to 4 Jan. 1675.
4	1677—82	B. R., GG, a, 14	Consultations (with copies of Commissions): 1 Jan. to 27 Dec. 1677.
		15	Ditto, 6 Jan. to 29 Dec. 1679.
		16	Ditto, 12 Jan. to 30 Dec. 1682.
5	1683—1708	B. R., GG, a, 17	Consultations (with copies of Commissions): 1 Jan. to 26 Dec. 1683.
		18	Ditto, 1 Jan. to 31 Dec. 1696.
		19	Ditto, 1 Jan. to 22 Nov. 1697.
		DD, 27	Ditto, 31 July 1706 to 19 Nov. 1708.
6	1700—02	Range 424, No. 6	Consultations of English Company's President and Council: 3 Oct. 1700 to 3 Mar. 1702.
7	1701—03	" " 7	Consultations of English Company's President and Council: 2 Oct. 1701 to 30 Sept. 1703 (duplicating in part the previous volume).
8	1702—04	B. R., GG, a, 20	Consultations of English Company's President and Council: 1 Oct. 1702 to 21 Dec. 1704.
9	1718	Range 424, No. 9	Transactions of Special Committee for examination of the old brokers' accounts, 22 Feb. to 7 March 1718.
10	1718—19	" " 10	Diary and Consultations: 1 Aug. 1718 to 31 July 1719.

Index Number.	Date.	Previous Classification.	Nature of Documents.
11	1724—25	Range 424, No. 11	Diary and Consultations: 1 Aug. 1724 to 31 July 1725.
12	1726—27	" " 12	Ditto, 4 Aug. 1726 to 31 July 1727.
13	1727—28	" " 13	Ditto, 1 Aug. 1727 to 31 July 1728.
14	1729—30	" " 14	Ditto, 1 Aug. 1729 to 31 July 1730.
15	1730—31	" " 15	Ditto, 1 Aug. 1730 to 31 July 1731.
16	1731—32	" " 16	Ditto, 2 Aug. 1731 to 31 July 1732. (Also duplicate of Diary, Sept.—Dec. 1732.)
17	1732—33	" " 17	Ditto, 1 Aug. 1732 to 31 July 1733.
18	1733—34	" " 18	Ditto, 7 Aug. 1733 to 31 July 1734.
19	1734—35	" " 19	Ditto, 3 Aug. 1734 to 31 July 1735.
20	1735—36	" " 20	Ditto, 1 Aug. 1735 to 19 July 1736.
21	1737	" " 21	Ditto, 1 Jan. to 30 July 1737.
22	1737—38	" " 22	Ditto, 1 Aug. 1737 to 31 July 1738.
23	1738—39	" " 23	Ditto, 2 Aug. 1738 to 31 July 1739.
24	1739—40	" " 24	Ditto, 1 Aug. 1739 to 31 July 1740.
25	1740—41	" " 25	Ditto, 2 Aug. 1740 to 30 July 1741.
26	1741—42	" " 26	Ditto, 1 Aug. 1741 to 31 July 1742.
27	1742—43	" " 27	Ditto, 2 Aug. 1742 to 31 July 1743.
28	1743—44	" " 28	Ditto, 4 Aug. 1743 to 31 July 1744.
29	1744	" 29	Ditto, 2 Aug. to 31 Dec. 1744.
30	1745—46	" " 30	Ditto, 30 Sept. 1745 to 31 July 1746
31	1746—47	" " 31	Ditto, 1 Aug. 1746 to 31 July 1747.
32	1747—48	" " 32	Ditto, 4 Aug. 1747 to 29 July 1748.
33	1748—49	" " 33	Ditto, 3 Aug. 1748 to 31 July 1749.

Index Number.	Date.	Previous Classification.	Nature of Documents.
34	1749—50	Range 424, No. 34	Diary and Consultations: 2 Aug. 1749 to 31 July 1750.
35	1750—51	" " 35	Ditto, 1 Aug. 1750 to 31 July 1751.
36	1751	" " 36	Ditto, 7 Aug. to 30 Oct. 1751.
37	1751—52	" " 37	Diary of transactions at Bombay regarding the troubles at Surat: 20 Dec. 1751 to 27 March 1752.
38	1752	" " 38	Diary and Consultations; 23 March to 31 July 1752.
39	1753—54	" " 39	Ditto, 1 Aug. 1753 to 31 July 1754.
40	1754—55	" " 40	Ditto, 5 Aug. 1754 to 31 July 1755.
41	1755—56	" " 41	Ditto, 4 Aug. 1755 to 31 July 1756.
42	1756—57	" " 42	Ditto, 6 Aug. 1756 to 30 July 1757.
43	1757—58	" " 43	Ditto, 7 Aug. 1757 to 31 July 1758.
44	1758—59	" " 44	Ditto, 12 Aug. 1758 to 31 July 1759.
45	1759—60	" " 45	Ditto, 1 Aug. 1759 to 31 July 1760.
46	1760—61	" " 46	Ditto, 2 Aug. 1760 to 31 July 1761.
47	1762—64	" " 47	Ditto, 30 Oct. 1762 to 27 Feb. 1764.
48	1764—66	" " 48	Ditto, 14 Nov. 1764 to 21 Jan. 1766.
49	1768—69	" " 49	Ditto, 11 Nov. 1768 to 10 Nov. 1769.
50	1771	" " 50	Ditto, 1 Jan. to 30 Dec. 1771.
51	1772	" " 51	Ditto, 1 Jan. to 31 Dec. 1772.
52	1774	" " 52	Ditto, 1 Jan. to 31 Dec. 1774.
53	1775	" " 53	Ditto, 2 Jan. to 31 Dec. 1775.*
54	1776	" " 54	Ditto, 20 May to 31 Dec. 1776.
55	1777	" " 55	Ditto, 1 Jan. to 30 Dec. 1777.

* Also (at end) copies of treaty with Ragunath Rao, 30 March 1775, and of grants to the Ostend Company from Shah Jahan, Aurangzib, Jahander Shah, and Muhammad Shah, 1643, 1662, 1712 and 1729.

Index Number.	Date.	Previous Classification.	Nature of Documents.
56	1778	Range 424, No. 56	Diary and Consultations: 1 Jan. to 31 Dec. 1778.
57	1779	" " 57	Ditto, 1 Jan. to 31 Dec. 1779.
58	1780	" " 58	Ditto, 1 Jan. to 26 Dec. 1780.
59	1781	" " 59	Ditto, 1 Jan. to 31 Dec. 1781.
60	1782	" " 60	Ditto, 1 Jan. to 31 Dec. 1782.
61	1783	" " 61	Ditto, 1 Jan. to 29 Dec. 1783.
62	1784	" " 62	Ditto, 3 Jan. to 31 Dec. 1784.
63	1785	" " 63	Ditto, 1 Jan. to 31 Dec. 1785.
64	1786	" " 64	Ditto, 1 Jan. to 31 Dec. 1786.
65	1787	" " 65	Ditto, 1 Jan. to 31 Dec. 1787.
66	1788	" " 66	Ditto, 1 Jan. to 30 Dec. 1788.
67	1789	" " 67	Ditto, 1 Jan. to 31 Dec. 1789.
68	1790	" " 68	Ditto, 1 Jan. to 31 Dec. 1790.
69	1791	" " 69	Ditto, 1 Jan. to 31 Dec. 1791.
70	1792	" " 70	Ditto, 1 Jan. to 31 Dec. 1792.
71	1793	" " 71	Ditto, 1 Jan. to 30 Dec. 1793.
72	1794	" " 72	Ditto, 1 Jan. to 31 Dec. 1794.
73	1795	" " 73	Ditto, 1 Jan. to 31 Dec. 1795.
74	1796	" " 74	Ditto, 1 Jan. to 27 June 1796.
75	1796	" " 74	Ditto, 27 June to 31 Dec. 1796.
76	1797	Range 426, No. 75	Ditto, 1 Jan. to 31 Dec. 1797.
77	1798	" " 76	Ditto, 1 Jan. to 31 Dec. 1798.
78	1799	" " 77	Ditto, 1 Jan. to 31 Dec. 1799.

Index Number.	Date.	Previous Classification.	Nature of Documents.
79	1800	Range 426, No. 78	Diary and Consultations: 1 Jan. to 10 July 1800.
80	1800—04	„ „ 79	Commercial Diary and Consultations, 1 Jan. 1800 to 30 April 1804.
81	1796	„ „ 80	Judicial Diary, 15 March to 31 Dec. 1796.
82	1797	„ „ 81	Ditto, 1 Jan. to 31 Dec. 1797.
83	1799	„ „ 82	Ditto, 1 Jan. to 31 Dec. 1799.
84	1631—59	B. R., DD —	Copies of letters despatched: 13 May and 10 June 1631; 14 Dec. 1633 to 14 Nov. 1634.
		GG, bl, 1	Ditto, 2 Feb. to 9 Aug. 1636 (imperfect).
		2	Ditto, 16 Sept. 1658 to 15 Dec. 1659.
85	1659—62	B. R., GG, bl, 3	Copies of letters despatched: 16 Dec. 1659 to 27 Dec. 1660.
		4	Ditto, 7 Dec. 1661 to 10 Sept. 1662.
		5	Ditto, 22 Sept. to 8 Dec. 1662.
86	1663—66	B. R., GG, bl, 6	Copies of letters despatched: 19 Dec. 1663 to 2 Jan. 1665.
		7	Ditto, 13 Jan. 1665 to 27 Aug. 1666.
87	1671—74	B. R., GG, bl, 8	Copies of letters despatched: 30 Sept. 1671 to 13 Dec. 1672.
		9	Ditto, 1 Nov. 1672 to 29 Oct. 1674.
88	1673—75	B. R., HH, cl, 1	Copies of letters despatched: 8 Nov. 1673 to 14 Dec. 1674.*
		GG, cl, 14	Ditto, 22 Sept. 1674 to 12 Dec. 1675.
89	1675—78	B. R., GG, bl, 10	Copies of letters despatched: 13 Dec. 1675 to 21 Dec. 1676.
		11	Ditto, 1 Jan. to 18 Dec. 1677.
		12	Ditto, 3 Dec. 1677 to 30 Nov. 1678.
90	1678—82	B. R., GG, bl, 13	Copies of letters despatched: 12 Jan. to 11 Dec. 1678 (duplicating in part the preceding volume).
		14	Ditto, 4 Dec. 1680 to 28 Nov. 1681.
		15	Ditto, 1 Dec. 1681 to 30 Nov. 1682.
91	1682—84	B. R., GG, bl, 16	Copies of letters despatched: 1 Dec. 1682 to 30 Nov. 1683.
		17	Ditto, 2 Dec. 1683 to 29 Nov. 1684.
92	1684—90	B. R., GG, bl, 18	Copies of letters despatched: 1 Dec. 1684 to 23 Nov. 1685.
		19	Ditto, 6 April to 31 Dec. 1690.
93	1691—93	B. R., DD, 16	Copies of letters despatched: 1 Jan. to 30 Dec. 1691.
		„	Ditto, 1 Jan. to 31 Dec. 1692.
		GG, bl, 20	Ditto, 5 Jan. to 27 Dec. 1693.

* Letters to Bombay only. From 1672 to 1675 the President was at Bombay; consequently the letters sent from Surat during that period include a number received from subordinate factories and forwarded to Bombay.

Index Number.	Date.	Previous Classification.	Nature of Documents.
94	1694—96	B. R., DD, 18	Copies of letters despatched: 30 May to 6 Nov. 1694.
		GG, b1, 21	Ditto, 8 Jan. 1695 to 1 Jan. 1696 (*see also* Volume 111).
95	1696—97	B. R., GG, c2, 6	Copies of letters despatched: 3 Jan. to 29 Dec. 1696.
		b2, 1	Ditto, 18 Aug. 1696; 2 Jan. to 30 Dec. 1697.
96	1697—98	B. R., GG, b2, 2	Copies of letters despatched: 18 Nov. 1697 to 30 Dec. 1698.
		3	Ditto, 3 Jan. to 29 Dec. 1698.*
97	1698—99	B. R., GG, b2, 4	Copies of letters despatched: 27 Dec. 1698 to 28 Feb. 1699.*
		6	Ditto, 2 Jan. to 20 Feb. 1699* (including duplicates of some in the preceding volume).
		5	Ditto, 20 Feb. to 13 Nov. 1699.*
98	1699—1700	B. R., GG, b2, 10	Copies of letters despatched: 16 Nov. to 29 Dec. 1699.*
		9	Ditto, 1 Jan. to 3 Oct. 1699.
		12	Ditto, 1 Jan. to 18 Nov. 1700.*
99	1700	B. R., GG, b2, 13	Copies of letters despatched: 14 Aug. to 31 Dec. 1700* (including duplicates of some in the previous volume).
		15	Ditto, 1 Jan. to 31 Dec. 1700.
100	1702—04	B. R., GG, b2, 16	Copies of letters despatched: 3 Jan. to 17 Dec. 1702.
		17	Ditto, 20 Jan. to 22 Dec. 1703.
		18	Ditto, 7 Jan. to 31 Dec. 1703.*
		19	Ditto, 8 Jan. to 21 Dec. 1704.*
101	1704—08	B. R., GG, b2, 20	Copies of letters despatched: 1 Jan. to 14 Dec. 1704.
		21	Ditto, 4 Jan. to 1 Oct. 1705.
		22	Ditto, 2 Jan. to 6 Dec. 1706.†
		23	Ditto, 7 Feb. 1707 to 3 May 1708.†
102	1623—28	B. R., DD —	Copies of letters received: Jan. to Dec. 1623.
		GG, c1, 1	Ditto, Jan. to April 1628.
103	1655—63	B. R., GG, c1, 3	Copies of letters received: Dec. 1655 to Nov. 1656.
		6	Ditto, Dec. 1662 to Dec. 1663.
104	1663—66	B. R., GG, c1, 7	Copies of letters received: Nov. 1663 to Dec. 1664.
		8	Ditto, Jan. 1665 to Aug. 1666.
105	1668—71	B. R., GG, c1, 9	Copies of letters received: Sept. 1668 to Nov. 1669.
		10	Ditto, Aug. 1670 to Aug. 1671.
106	1671—73	B. R., GG, c1, 11	Copies of letters received: Sept. 1671 to Oct. 1672.
		12	Ditto, Oct. [?] 1672 to Oct. 1673.

* To Bombay only.
† Contains also letters received for same period.

Index Number.	Date.	Previous Classification.	Nature of Documents.
107	1674—78	B. R., GG, c1, 13	Copies of letters received: Oct. 1674 to Nov. 1675.
		16	Ditto, Nov. 1677 to Nov. 1678.
108	1679—82	B. R., GG, c1, 17	Copies of letters received: Nov.[?] 1679 to Nov. 1680.
		19	Ditto, Nov. 1681 to Nov. 1682.
109	1683—85	B. R., GG, c1, 20	Copies of letters received: Oct. 1683 to Nov. 1684.
		21	Ditto, Dec. 1684 to Dec. 1685.
110	1691—93	B. R., DD, 16	Copies of letters received: Jan. to Dec. 1691.
		DD, 17	Ditto, Dec. 1691 to Oct. 1692.
		GG, c2, 1	Ditto, Nov. 1692 to Dec. 1693.
111	1695	B. R., GG, c2, 2	Copies of letters received: May to Dec. 1695.*†
112	1695—96	B. R., GG, c2, 4	Copies of letters received: Jan. to Sept. 1695.
		5	Ditto, Jan. to Dec. 1696.
113	1697—98	B. R., HH, b1, 22	Copies of letters received: Jan. to Dec. 1697.*
		HH, b2, 10	Ditto, Jan. to Dec. 1698.*
		GG, c2, 7	Ditto, Aug. 1697 to Dec. 1698.‡
114	1697—99	B. R., HH, b2, 16	Copies of letters received: Jan. to Mar. 1699.*
		GG, c2, 9	Ditto, Jan. to April 1699.§
		10	Ditto, Nov. and Dec. 1699.*
115	1700	B. R., JJ, b2, 12	Copies of letters received. Jan. to Dec. 1700.
		GG, c2, 12	Ditto, Jan. to Sept. 1700.*
116	1701—03	B. R., GG, c2, 13	Copies of letters received: Jan. to Dec. 1701.
		14	Ditto, Jan. 1702 to Jan. 1703.‡
117	1703—04	B. R., GG, c2, 15	Copies of letters received: Jan. to Dec. 1703.‡
		HH, b2, 20	Ditto, Jan. to Dec. 1703.*
		GG, c2, 17	Ditto, Jan. to Dec. 1704.*
118	1704—05	B. R., GG, c2, 16	Copies of letters received: Jan. to Dec. 1704.‡
		18	Ditto, Jan. to Dec. 1704‡ (mostly duplicating preceding section).
		20	Ditto, Jan. to Dec. 1705.
			(For letters received, 1706–08, see Volume 101).
119	1759—1800	Unnumbered. Fisher's Papers, Nos. 191 & 345.	Miscellaneous. Mr. Erskine's report on the revenues of Surat Castle and Tanka, 5 Nov. 1759; Information regarding Surat, 1775; Governor Duncan's report on his proceedings at Surat, 25 July 1800.

* From Bombay only. † Contains also letters *to* Bombay for same period. ‡ Bombay excepted.
§ From Broach only.

26464. X

TELLICHERRI.

Index Number.	Date.	Previous Classification.	Nature of Documents.
1	1716—56	Loose papers	Letters, &c., received by the Company from Tellicherri, 19 Feb. 1716 to 23 April 1756.
2	1777	Range 430, No. 106	Diary and Consultations, 1 Jan. to 30 Dec. 1777.
3	1779—80	„ „ 107	Ditto, 1 Jan. 1779 to 31 Dec. 1780.
4	1781—82	„ „ 108	Ditto, 1 Jan. 1781 to 31 Dec. 1782.
5	1783—84	Range 431, No. 1	Ditto, 1 Jan. 1783 to 31 Dec. 1784.
6	1785—86	„ „ 2	Ditto, 1 Jan. 1785 to 31 Dec. 1786.
7	1787—88	„ „ 3	Ditto, 1 Jan. 1787 to 31 Dec. 1788.
8	1789—90	„ „ 4	Ditto, 1 Jan. 1789 to 31 Dec. 1790.
9	1791—92	„ „ 5	Ditto, 1 Jan. 1791 to 31 Dec. 1792.
10	1793	„ „ 6	Ditto, 1 Jan. to 31 Dec. 1793.
11	1792—93	„ „ 7 and 8	Ditto (Political), 2 Jan. 1792 to 18 Sept. 1793.
12	1781—84	„ „ 9	Correspondence between the Select Committee at Bombay and the Chief, &c., at Tellicherri, 1 Jan. 1781 to 27 Dec. 1784.

THANA.

Index Number.	Date.	Previous Classification.	Nature of Documents.
1	1775—76	Range 430, No. 96	Diary and Consultations, 8 Jan. 1775 to 18 Dec. 1776.
2	1777—78	„ „ 97	Ditto, 6 Jan. 1777 to 26 Dec. 1778.
3	1779—80	„ „ 98	Ditto, 3 Jan. 1779 to 29 Dec. 1780.
4	1781—82	„ „ 99	Ditto, 1 Jan. 1781 to 3 Dec. 1782.
5	1783—84	„ „ 100	Ditto, 1 Jan. 1783 to 27 Dec. 1784.
6	1785—87	„ „ 101	Ditto, 2 Jan. 1785 to 26 Dec. 1787.
7	1788—89	„ „ 102	Ditto, 14 Jan. 1788 to 29 Dec. 1789.
8	1790—91	„ „ 103	Ditto, 5 Jan. 1790 to 31 Dec. 1791.
9	1792—94	„ „ 104	Ditto, 2 Jan. 1792 to 28 Dec. 1794.
10	1795—99	„ „ 105	Ditto, 1 Jan. 1795 to 30 Nov. 1799.

VIZAGAPATAM.

Index Number.	Date.	Previous Classification.	Nature of Documents.
1	1692—95	B. R., PP, 1	Diary and Consultations: 16 July 1692 to 17 June 1693.
		2	Ditto, 3 July 1693 to 25 Aug. 1694.
		3	Ditto, 26 Aug. 1694 to 30 March 1695.

MISCELLANEOUS.

Index Number.	Date.	Previous Classification.	Nature of Documents.
1	1617—32	B. R., AA, 1	Abstracts of letters received from various factories: 20 Dec. 1617 to 24 April 1632.
2	1663—72	B. R., AA, 5	Extracts from Letters and Consultations received from various factories: 5 March 1663 to 21 Dec. 1672.
3	1664—81	B. R., AA, 2	Extracts from Letters and Consultations received from various factories:—1664, to 12 Oct. 1673, with (at end) three letters of 1680–81.
4	1675—96	B. R., AA, 6	Abstracts of Letters received from Surat, Bombay, and Persia: 10 Oct. 1675 to 10 July 1696.
5	1696—1707	B. R., AA, 7	Abstracts of Letters received from Surat, Bombay, and Persia: 1 April 1696 to 1 March 1707.
6	1699—1707	B. R., AA, 3	Abstracts of Letters received by the New Company from India: 5 Aug. 1699 to 20 Dec. 1707.
7	1716—23	B. R., AA, 4	Extracts from Letters from various factories: 9 Oct. 1716 to 18 Jan. 1723.
8	1608—24	Unnumbered	Copies of Letters, Consultations, &c., regarding various factories from 17 Sept. 1608 to 6 Dec. 1624.
9	1626—81	B. R., QQ	Collections (put together in 1788–89), relating to . (1) The establishment of factories in Tanjore (1624), Armagon (1626), Petapoli (1625–31), Masulipatam (1628–38); an extract from a Letter from Fort St. George (1658); and an account of Triplicane (1681).
		Wilks's Collection, No. 9.	(2.) The origin of Fort St. George, &c.
		" 8	(3.) Revenues of the Company at Calcutta.
10	1616—1759	Wilks's Collections, R.—Y.	Copies of papers relating to Sir Thomas Roe's embassy (1616); the Danish factory at Balasore (1676); the Tanka for a fleet to protect the trade of Surat (1759); Henry Oxinden's journey to the court of Sivaji (1674); the jaghir of the Governor of Surat Castle (1759); and the English annexation of Saldana Bay (1620).
11	1629	Unnumbered	Charges brought by the President and Council of Surat against Richard Boothby, with his answers, and connected papers, 1629.
12	1642—44	B. R., GG, cl, 2	Letter book of Edward Knipe, sent out as supercargo of the *Crispiana* and *Aleppo Merchant* to Surat and Persia, 1642–44.
13	1669	B. R., DD, a, 6	Charges by Thomas Stiles against Shem Bridges and Council at Balasore, 1669.
14	1675—77	B. R., CC, 2	Diary of Streynsham Master in his inspection of the Masulipatam and Bay of Bengal factories, Dec. 1675 to Jan. 1677.
15	1681—88	Unnumbered	Journal of William Hedges, Agent and Governor in Bengal, commencing 25 Nov. 1681 and ending 6 March 1688.
16	1682—83	B. R., DD —	Correspondence regarding the Interlopers Petit, Bowcher, &c., Dec., 1682 and Jan. 1683.
17	1693	B. R., DD —	Copies of letters sent or received by Commissary-General Sir John Goldsborough, June—Nov. 1693.
18	1695—97	B. R., DD, 21	Instructions, Journals, Letters, &c., in Mr. Francis Bowyear's mission from Fort St. George to Pegu and Cochin China, May 1695 to Sept., 1697.

Index Number.	Date.	Previous Classification.	Nature of Documents.
19	1699—1700	B. R., R, a, 1	Letter Book of Sir William Norris, Ambassador to the Great Mogul, 15 Feb. 1699 to 22 Aug. 1700.
20	1701—02	Unnumbered	Letter Book of Sir William Norris, Ambassador to the Great Mogul, March 1701 to 5th May 1702.
21	1717—25	B. R., II, 1	Copies of or extracts from letters relating to Anjengo, Dec. 1717 to Jan. 1725 (compiled for the purposes of the suit East India Co. *versus* Catharine Gyfford).
22	1727	B. R., II, 2	A short treatise on Attinga, the English settlement at Anjengo, &c., by John Wallis, 1727.
23	1618—1725	Received from Estates and Wills Department (R. & L. 1995/93).	Copies of wills, inventories, &c., of persons deceased in various parts of the East Indies.
24	1610—1711	B. R., EE and FF	Miscellaneous documents.

LETTERS FROM INDIA, &c.

The "O. C." Records or Collection of Original Correspondence from India, with Collateral Documents originating at any places between England and Japan.

Index Number.	Date.	Numbers of Documents.	Nature of Documents.
1	1602—14	1—137	Correspondence, &c., — 1602 to 22 March 1614.
2	1614—15	138—272	Ditto, 1 April 1614 to 24 March 1615.
3	1615—16	273—351	Ditto, 25 March 1615 to — March 1616.
4	1616—17	352—461	Ditto, 30 March 1616 to 21 March 1617.
5	1617—18	462—635	Ditto, March [?] 1617 to March [?] 1618.
6	1618—19	639—793	Ditto, 8 April 1618 to April [?] 1619.
7	1619—21	794—947	Ditto, 14 April 1619 to 28 Aug. 1621.
8	1621—22	948—1,042	Ditto, 27 March 1621 to 30 March 1622.
9	1622	1,046—1,113	Ditto, 3 April 1622 to — 1622.
10	1623—24	1,114—1,183	Ditto, 4 May 1623 to — 1624.
11	1625—27	1,184—1,272	Ditto, 31 March 1625 to — 1627.
12	1628—30	1,273—1,352	Ditto, 20 June 1628 to — 1630.
13	1631—32	1,353—1,427	Ditto, 25 March 1631 to — 1632.
14	1632—34	1,425—1,521	Ditto, 24 April 1632 to 26 Feb. 1634.
15	1634—37	1,522—1,595	Ditto, 21 April 1634 to 30 March 1637.
16	1637—39	1,596—1,670	Ditto, 27 March 1637 to 14 March 1639.
17	1639—41	1,671—1,768	Ditto, 1 April 1639 to — 1641.
18	1641—44	1,769—1,863	Ditto, 26 March 1641 to 19 Sept. 1644.
19	1644—46	1,864—1,983	Ditto, 26 March 1644 to — 1646.
20	1646—48	1,984—2,071	Ditto, 30 March 1646 to 8 March 1648; also a paper on Agra accounts to 1651.

Index Number.	Date.	Numbers of Documents.	Nature of Documents.
21	1648—50	2,072—2,158	Correspondence, &c., 5 April 1648 to 29 March 1650.
22	1650—52	2,159—2,263	Ditto, 27 April 1650 to 20 March 1652.
23	1652—54	2,264—2,373	Ditto, 31 March 1652 to 21 March 1654.
24	1654—56	2,374—2,542	Ditto, 27 March 1654 to 15 March 1656.
25	1656—59	2,543—2,726	Ditto, 26 March 1656 to 23 March 1659.
26	1659—61	2,727—2,873	Ditto, 26 March 1659 to 23 March 1661.
27	1661—63	2,874—2,973	Ditto, 26 March 1661 to 2 March 1663.
28	1663—65	2,974—3,056	Ditto, 30 March 1663 to 27 Feb. 1665 (also letters from J. Sambrooke to 28 Oct. 1665).
29	1665—69	3,057—3,256	Ditto, 25 March 1665 to 22 March 1669.
30	1669—70	3,257—3,413	Ditto, — March 1669 to 16 March 1670.
31	1670—71	3,414—3,561	Ditto, 28 March 1670 to 24 March 1671.
32	1671—72	3,562—3,631	Ditto, 29 March 1671 to — March 1672.
33	1672—73	3,632—3,770	Ditto, 28 March 1672 to 21 March 1673.
34	1673—74	3,771—3,954	Ditto, 27 March 1673 to 1 April 1674.
35	1674—75	3,955—4,086	Ditto, 28 March 1674 to 20 March 1675.
36	1675—76	4,087—4,199	Ditto, 25 March 1675 to — March 1676.
37	1676—77	4,200—4,277	Ditto, 5 April 1676 to — March 1677.
38	1677—78	4,278—4,383	Ditto, 2 April 1677 to — March 1678.
39	1678—79	4,384—4,587	Ditto, 25 March 1678 to 24 March 1679.
40	1679—81	4,588—4,725	Ditto, 28 March 1679 to 5 April 1681.
41	1681—82	4,726—4,812	Ditto, 25 March 1681 to 20 March 1682.
42	1682—83	4,813—4,919	Ditto, 25 March 1682 to 24 March 1683.
43	1683—84	4,920—5,121	Ditto, 31 March 1683 to 22 March 1684 (also a Broker's Account to 1692).

Index Number.	Date.	Numbers of Documents.	Nature of Documents.
44	1684—85	5,122—5,350	Correspondence, &c., 26 March 1684 to 24 March 1685.
45	168 —86	5,351—5,483	Ditto, 29 March 1685 to 24 March 1686.
46	1686—87	5,484—5,574	Ditto, 9 April 1686 to — March 1687.
47	1687—89	5,575—5,665	Ditto, 11 April 1687 to 22 March 1689 (also abstract of L. Blackmore's voyages to 1693).
48	1689—91	5,666—5,764	Ditto, 3 April 1689 to 20 March 1691.
49	1691—93	5,765—5,874	Ditto, 27 March 1691 to 16 March 1693.
50	1693—95	5,875—5,997	Ditto, 22 April 1693 to 24 March 1695.
51	1695—96	5,998—6,195	Ditto, 25 March 1695 to 21 March 1696.
52	1696—97	6,196—6,378	Ditto, 25 March 1696 to 20 March 1697.
53	1697—98	6,379—6,539	Ditto, 25 March 1697 to 14 March 1698 (also papers concerning Mr. Burniston at Calicut to 1704).
54	1698—99	6,540—6,624	Ditto, 6 April 1698 to 24 March 1699 (also abstracts of letters relative to seizure of private property at Surat, to 1702).
55, Vol. 1	1699	6,625—6,813	Ditto, 29 March to 31 Dec. 1699.
55, Vol. 2	1700	6,814—6,991	Ditto, 1 Jan. to 23 March 1700.
56, Vol. 1	1700	6,992—7,127	Ditto, 25 March to 26 July 1700.
56, Vol. 2	1700	7,128—7,224	Ditto, 1 Aug. to 30 Nov. 1700.
56, Vol. 3	1700—01	7,225—7,359	Ditto, 1 Dec. 1700 to 14 Jan. 1701.
56, Vol. 4	1701	7,360—7,527	Ditto, 14 Jan. to 24 March 1701.
57, Vol. 1	1701	7,528—7,675	Ditto, 25 March to 1 Aug. 1701.
57, Vol. 2	1701	7,676—7,796	Ditto, 1 Aug. to 11 Dec. 1701.
57, Vol. 3	1702	7,797—7,910	Ditto, 12 Dec. 1701 to 24 March 1702.
58, Vol. 1	1702	7,911—8,053	Ditto, 24 March to 27 Oct. 1702.
58, Vol. 2	1702—03	8,054—8,167	Ditto, 28 Oct. 1702 to 10 March 1703.
59	1703—04	8,168—8,252	Ditto, 25 March 1703 to 14 Feb. 1704.

Index Number.	Date.	Numbers of Documents.	Nature of Documents.
60	1704—05	8,253—8,347	Correspondence, &c., 27 March 1704 to 22 March 1705.
61	1705—06	8,348—8,447	Ditto, 26 March 1705 to 20 Feb. 1706 (also extracts from Surat letters relating to Mr. Colt, to 13 Nov. 1706).
62	1706—09	8,448—8,556	Ditto, 31 March 1706 to 7 Feb. 1709.

Duplicates.

Duplicate copies of certain of the "O. C." documents, in some cases exhibiting slight variations from the originals. The first and the last numbers of the original series in each volume are given; the intervening numbers are very incomplete.

Index Number.	Date.	Numbers of Documents.	Nature of Documents.
1	1602—36	1—1,551	Correspondence, &c., — 1602 to 20 July 1636.
2	1636—49	1,554—2,115	Ditto, — 1636 to 31 Jan. 1649.
3	1649—66	2,121—3,154	Ditto, 5 April 1649 to 1 March 1666.
4	1666—81	3,163—4,716	Ditto, 30 March 1666 to 24 Jan. 1681.
5	1681—85	4,729—5,337	Ditto, 11 April 1681 to 23 Feb. 1685.
6	1685—96	5,379—6,187	Ditto, 9 May 1685 to 19 March 1696.
7	1696—1700	6,199—6,983	Ditto, 10 April 1696 to 20 March 1700.
8	1700—01	6,993—7,485	Ditto, 25 March 1700 to 15 March 1701.
9	1701—09	7,487—8,555	Ditto, 10 March 1701 to 7 Feb. 1709.

Triplicates.

Index Number.	Date.	Numbers of Documents.	Nature of Documents.
1	1614—96	168—6,318	Correspondence, &c., 17 Oct. 1614 to 27 Nov. 1696.
2	1697—1707	6,381—8,499	Ditto, 8 April 1697 to 10 Feb. 1707.

LETTERS TO INDIA, &c.

DESPATCH BOOKS.

Copies of Despatches to Bengal, Madras, Bombay, Bencoolen, Surat, St. Helena, and other places in the East.

Index Number.	Date.	Previous Classification.	Nature of Documents.
1	1626—69	Room 338	Copies of Despatches, 28 April 1626 to 23 Feb. 1660; and two letters of 18 Feb. 1669.
2	1657—61	"	Ditto, 9 Nov. 1657 to 28 Jan. 1661.
3	1661—66	"	Ditto, 6 Feb. 1661 to 12 Jan. 1666.
4	1666—72	"	Ditto, 7 March 1666 to 27 June 1672.
5	1672—78	"	Ditto, 5 July 1672 to 9 Sept. 1678.
6	1678—82	"	Ditto, 8 Nov. 1678 to 28 June 1682.
7	1682—85	"	Ditto, 5 July 1682 to 15 Oct. 1685.
8	1685—88	"	Ditto, 21 Oct. 1685 to 10 Dec. 1688.
9	1689—97	"	Ditto, 11 Jan. 1689 to 7 May 1697.
10	1698—1709	"	Ditto, 26 Jan. 1698 to 28 Jan. 1709 (London East India Co.).
11	1699—1708	"	Ditto, 12 Jan. 1699 to 20 April 1708 (English East India Co.).
12	1702—06	"	Ditto, 31 July 1702 to 4 Oct. 1706.
13	1706—10	"	Ditto, 18 Dec. 1706 to 30 June 1710.
14	1710—13	"	Ditto, 18 Oct. 1710 to 2 Feb. 1713.
15	1713—16	"	Ditto, 20 March 1713 to 31 March 1716.
16	1716—19	"	Ditto, 19 Oct. 1716 to 23 April 1719.
17	1719—21	"	Ditto, 4 Nov. 1719 to 31 May 1721.
18	1721—23	"	Ditto, 10 Nov. 1721 to 10 July 1723.
19	1723—25	"	Ditto, 30 Oct. 1723 to 2 April 1725.
20	1725—27	"	Ditto, 21 Oct. 1725 to 5 April 1727.
21	1727—30	"	Ditto, 10 Nov. 1727 to 27 Feb. 1730.

Index Number.	Date.	Previous Classification.	Nature of Documents.
22	1730—33	Room 338	Copies of Despatches, 4 Nov. 1730 to 7 March 1733.
23	1733—36	„	Ditto, 26 Oct. 1733 to 3 July 1736.
24	1736—39	„	Ditto, 3 Nov. 1736 to 10 Oct. 1739.
25	1739—43	„	Ditto, 19 Dec. 1739 to 2 April 1743.
26	1743—47	„	Ditto, 8 June 1743 to 16 Oct. 1747.
27	1747—50	„	Ditto, 24 Dec. 1747 to 28 Nov. 1750.
28	1750—53	„	Ditto, 28 Nov. 1750 to 4 April 1753.

Drafts of Despatches.

Original Drafts of Despatches to Bengal, Madras, Bombay, Bencoolen, St. Helena, and other places.

Index Number.	Date.	Previous Classification.	Nature of Documents.
1	1703—11	Room 338	Draft Despatches, 18 Jan. 1703 to 19 Jan. 1711.
2	1710—18	„	Ditto, 5 July 1710 to 21 March 1718.
3	1718—25	„	Ditto, 17 Oct. 1718 to 12 Feb. 1725.
4	1725—31	„	Ditto, 2 April 1725 to 12 March 1731.
5	1731—34	„	Ditto, 19 Nov. 1731 to 15 March 1734.
6	1734—38	„	Ditto, 29 Nov. 1734 to 26 April 1738.
7	1738—41	„	Ditto, 21 July 1738 to 24 April 1741.
8	1741—46	„	Ditto, 29 May 1741 to 12 June 1746.
9	1746—51	„	Ditto, 9 July 1746 to 22 May 1751.
10	1751—53	„	Ditto, 23 Aug. 1751 to 4 April 1753.

Zeitfracht Medien GmbH
Ferdinand-Jühlke-Straße 7
99095 Erfurt, Deutschland
produktsicherheit@kolibri360.de